D0122952

THE FEMINIST QUESTION

The Feminist Question

Feminist Theology
in the Light of Christian Tradition

Francis Martin

WILLIAM B. EERDMANS PUBLISHING COMPANY
GRAND RAPIDS, MICHIGAN

© 1994 Wm. B. Eerdmans Publishing Co.
255 Jefferson Ave. S.E., Grand Rapids, Michigan 49503

Printed in the United States of America

00 99 98 97 96 95 94   7 6 5 4 3 2 1

Library of Congress Cataloging-in-Publication Data

Martin, Francis, 1930-
The feminist question: feminist theology in the light of Christian tradition /
Francis Martin.
p.   cm.
Includes bibliographical references and index.
ISBN 8028-0794-1 (pbk.)
1. Feminist theology — Controversial literature. 2. Bible — Hermeneutics.
3. Woman (Christian theology) 4. Women in Christianity.
5. Catholic Church — Doctrines. I. Title.
BT83.55.M27   1994
230'.082 — dc20   94-32318
                                                           CIP

Contents

Preface

In the last few centuries something has been stirring within humanity. There has been an increased sensitivity to the rights of every human person and a move to insure that everyone has the means to live in a way that is worthy of a human being. *The Declaration of Human Rights,* set forth by the United Nations in 1948, marked a culminating point in this regard. Its very title evokes memories of the *Declaration of the Rights of Man* produced in 1789 by the French revolutionaries, expressing the best humanism of the Enlightenment philosophes. The difference is that now it was being enunciated in a world forum, and for the first time in history the world seemed to agree upon the inalienable dignity and inviolability of the human person.

Fifteen years later, in his famous encyclical *Pacem in Terris,* Pope John XXIII dwelt upon some of the consequences of this universal recognition of human dignity. He listed three characteristics of the present day: the improvement in the conditions of workers and their right to participate in the decision-making process, the increased political and social role of women, and the growing autonomy of former colonial nations. Regarding the role of women, the Pope spoke explicitly of an increase in an awareness of their dignity and their legitimate demands for recognition of their rights and duties.[1]

---

1. "Secondly, the part that women are now playing in political life is very evident. This is a development that is perhaps of swifter growth among Christian nations, but it is also happening extensively, if more slowly, among nations that are heirs to different traditions and imbued with a different culture. Women are gaining an increasing awareness of their natural dignity. Far from being content with a merely passive role of allowing themselves to be regarded as a kind of instrument, they are demanding both in domestic and public life the rights and duties which belong to them as human persons." *Pacem in Terris* #41, in *The Encyclicals and Other Messages of John XXIII,* arranged and edited by the staff of *The Pope Speaks* Magazine (Washington, D.C: TPS Press, 1964), 337.

John XXIII was not alone in pointing out the particular manner in which this deepened respect for human dignity applied to women. The United Nations in its report on the *Convention on the Elimination of All Forms of Discrimination Against Women* (December 18, 1979)[2] explicitly applied to women the more general norms of the 1948 Declaration.

Literature of an official nature touching upon the rights of women continues to appear. For example, within the Catholic Church there is the Apostolic Letter *On the Dignity and Vocation of Women (Mulieris Dignitatem)* by Pope John Paul II,[3] while between governments there is the international agreement on *The Protection of Human Rights,* January 16, 1989,[4] and the statement of the United Nations World Conference on Human Rights (Vienna, 1993) and its proposal to appoint a special rapporteur in regard to violence against women.[5]

The inalienable dignity of every person and the right to a way of life that fosters, protects, and expresses that dignity in the exercise of freedom is a fundamental and unique tenet of modern Western society. The roots of this notion lie in the Judeo-Christian teaching about humankind. Thus, it may be said that the political and social liberties that characterize modern Western life and that are being expanded in an ever-widening circle derive from the philosophical extension of a concept of the human person first found in the biblical tradition. This can be asserted despite the fact that many adherents of that tradition have opposed some practical applications of the inherent dignity of the human person in the political, economic, and ecclesiastical spheres.[6] The modern desire to secure rights for all human beings faces the dilemma of finding an ultimate basis for these rights that all can agree upon.[7] I will

2. The many statements of the Commission on the Status of Women paved the way for this document. Background to the 1979 convention can be found in various issues of the *Department of State Bulletin* (for example, vol. 31 [1954]: 23-36; vol. 28 [April 6, 1953]: 516-17).

3. Boston, Mass.: St. Paul Books and Media, 1988. Several other ecclesiastical documents that treat the same theme are referred to in the opening lines of this letter.

4. Excerpts from the agreement on *The Protection of Human Rights* were published in the *New York Times,* January 17, 1989, A12.

5. Press Release HR/3872, June 28, 1993, 2.

6. "However, there have been periods in the Church's history when in thought and action the rights of the human person have not been promoted or defended with sufficient clarity or energy. . . . As we are well aware, the Church's attitude towards human rights during the last two centuries too frequently has been characterized by hesitations, objections, reservations, and on occasion, even vehement reaction on the Catholic side to any declaration of human rights made from the standpoint of liberalism and laicism." *The Church and Human Rights,* Pontifical Commission "Justitia et Pax," Working Paper no. 1 (Vatican City, 1975) nos. 17-18.

7. I address this dilemma in chapter 10.

suggest that this will require a deepening of the notion of person, one that sees relation as constitutive, if we are to arrive at an adequate basis for human rights and dignity. With this new stirring within humanity as a stimulus, I wish to consider the way it has given rise to the feminist question.

Introduction

The origins of this book go back to 1988 when I was preparing the annual address in observance of St. Thomas Aquinas day at the Dominican House of Studies in Washington, D.C. The organizers of the day requested that I speak on the topic "Feminist Hermeneutics." As I read feminist literature, I consistently came to the same twofold conclusion, namely, that feminism contained a profound and valid critique of our culture, and yet suffered from many of the deficiencies it sought to criticize. I continued to work on this topic and later published a developed form of the address.[1] I received encouragement from people who represented both sides of the feminist debate, and this led me to undertake a broader study into feminist theology. In preparing this book, I have become even more convinced of the importance of the issues raised by Christian feminist thought and also more aware of the shortcomings of feminism.[2]

I was challenged frequently as I studied — feminist issues engage one at every theoretical and practical level. Sometimes it was difficult to distinguish between immoderate rhetoric and valid insight. I learned as I listened, my views changed on several issues, and I came to appreciate the sincerity and earnestness of some of those whom I criticize most sharply in this book.

In this book I am concerned with one aspect of the modern understanding of human rights — the movement toward a more adequate expression of the dignity and rights of women within the Christian community. I apply the phrase "the feminist question" to this movement, wishing thereby to call attention to two of its dimensions. It is a question in the

1. "Feminist Hermeneutics," *Communio* 18 (1991): 144-63; 398-424.
2. I published a brief form of my work as "Feminist Theology: A Proposal," *Communio* 20 (1993): 334-76.

sense that it is an "issue," something being discussed and debated, promoted and opposed. It is also a question because it confronts the Christian tradition by asking how this modern sensitivity to rights and dignity relates to the light of revelation

An ancient adage attributed to Ambrose of Milan states: "Anything true, by no matter whom said, is from the Holy Spirit." Such optimism must animate any attempt of ours to listen in faith to what is stirring in the heart of humanity. The Second Vatican Council's Constitution on *The Church in the Modern World* lays down for us two important principles governing an undertaking such as this one. The familiar opening statement calls attention to the role of human experience:

> The joy and hope, the grief and anguish of the men and women of our time, especially those who are poor or afflicted in any way, are the joy and hope, the grief and anguish of the followers of Christ as well. Nothing that is genuinely human fails to find an echo in their hearts.

The second principle highlights the necessity for divine revelation and is found later in the document when speaking about "Christ, the New Man":

> In reality it is only in the mystery of the Word made flesh that the mystery of man truly becomes clear. For Adam, the first man, was a type of him who was to come. Christ the Lord, Christ the new Adam, in the very revelation of the mystery of the Father and of his love, fully reveals man to himself and brings to light his most high calling.[3]

Applied practically to the theological enterprise, these principles imply a sort of correlative method by which what is learned in and through the joy, hope, grief, and anguish of human experience is brought into contact with what has been already acquired, but imperfectly understood, through divine revelation. From this interactive process, new knowledge is gained, making possible a genuine development of doctrine. It is often a lengthy process, painstaking and even tumultuous, but amid human weakness, the Holy Spirit leads the church more deeply into all truth.[4]

Practically, participation in this correlative procedure meant, for me,

---

3. *Gaudium et Spes,* nos. 1 and 22. Translation is basically that of *Vatican Council II: The Conciliar and Post Conciliar Documents,* ed. Austin Flannery (Northport, N.Y.: Costello Publishing Company, 1975).

4. For an account of this process see Aidan Nichols, *From Newman to Congar: The Idea of Doctrinal Development from the Victorians to the Second Vatican Council* (Edinburgh: T. & T. Clark, 1990). For an application to the field of morality see John T. Noonan Jr., "Development in Moral Doctrine," *Theological Studies* (1993): 662-77.

coming to grips with the fact that sometimes in the past the teaching authority in the church has attempted to close an issue prematurely without allowing the full truth of the question to be heard. I had to avoid, however, the dilemma of those who mediate between new insights and the tradition without according the light of revelation its rightful role as the integrating source of our Christian knowledge. The danger here is that the theologian becomes the ultimate norm of God's Word. There is a delicate balance to be achieved through an activity most aptly called "thinking with assent." It is "thinking" because it reflects on truth personally acquired and learned from others "no matter whom." It is "assent" insofar as it is illumined by and obedient to faith. This faith, moreover, is a manifold reality, mediated to us by the past, lived in the whole community around us, and appropriated by an interior gesture that allows it to change us.

Thomas Aquinas, when faced with the objection that allowing human insights into theology would water down faith's intensity, responded: "Those who use the work of the philosophers in sacred doctrine by bringing that work of the human mind into the service of faith, do not mix water with wine, but rather change water into wine."[5] The optimism of Aquinas's response is based on a vision of God and the unity of his work among us that needs to be recovered. Our modern theological effort is often deeply influenced by a fear that yielding to the revealing action of God will somehow corrupt the integrity or autonomy of our thought. Because feminism is such an intense form of theological effort with wide-ranging practical consequences, it forced me to look more deeply at how we actually proceed in our theological thinking. I realized that, precisely because these issues are so important, any form of undue haste or uncritical acceptance of a distorted understanding of God or of humanity could have enormous consequences for the church's ability to live and proclaim the gospel.

The rhythm of the process I am describing consists in a hermeneutical spiral that oscillates between the original feminist question, i.e., feminism, and the revelation being expressed in the church's life and Scriptures. The question may challenge our present understanding of the tradition, while an openness to God's revealing activity within our own lives and within the whole believing community enables revelation to question the question. This first step in the process liberates the truth in the question from what is limited and erroneous, and results in a new, rephrased question. The new

---

5. *Commentary on the De Trinitate of Boethius* 2,4,ad5, in St. Thomas Aquinas, *Faith, Reason and Theology: Questions I-IV of his Commentary on the De Trinitate of Boethius,* Medieval Sources in Translation, 32, trans. A. Maurer (Toronto: Pontifical Institute of Medieval Studies, 1987), 50.

question must incorporate both the truth of the original question and the truth of revelation by holding these two aspects of truth together in tension. The tension is resolved through a communal and individual fidelity to the truth until we are able to see how the light of revelation illumines and answers the truth of the question by enlarging our minds, with the result that something new has been gained.

The divided condition of the body of Christ constitutes a serious obstacle to realizing this dialogical process between question and revelation. In matters of development of doctrine, growth in one communion may contribute to growth in another, but integral growth is impeded by the fact that the light of revelation is only partially refracted through our division. I was made aware of this while studying the question of feminism. I believe, however, that the very effort to understand how women and men should live together as the body of Christ will contribute to an understanding of other dimensions of unity as well.

I write as a Roman Catholic theologian, but when I use the term *church,* I am most often thinking of the one, though divided, body of Christ made up of all those who are baptized and believe in the tenets of the ancient creeds. Of course, I approach the question from within my tradition, but, I hope, in a way that is broad enough to be acceptable to the commonly held tradition, which I often describe by using the term *biblical.* The most salient area where my position represents that held principally by the Orthodox and Roman Catholic Churches in contradistinction to many other churches is that of church office. I distinguish "ecclesial office" from the charisms and ministries that all God's people, men and women, are meant to exercise and whose authority must be recognized.

What do I wish to accomplish by publishing this book? I want to contribute to church unity, beginning with that unity between men and women intended by God. On the authority of John 17:21-23, we know that only insofar as we Christians are made one by sharing in the glory bestowed on us by Christ, will the world have a living icon of God's intention for all humanity and believe that the Father sent the Son. Practically, then, I want to facilitate dialogue between those who are interested in listening to each other on this important matter. My contribution is an attempt to distinguish, in the light of God's word, what is true from what is false in the feminist question. I will have accomplished my objective if, in fact, the dialogue matures.

There are two parts to this book. The first part (chapters 1–5) seeks to establish the view of theology operative in the study and to set the correct historical framework for understanding the significance of feminism. The second part (chapters 6–12) considers the underlying presuppositions of much feminist thought and critiques them in light of the biblical tradition. After five years of daily acquaintance with feminist thought, I am aware of how difficult it is to place its various proponents in neat categories. Nevertheless, I believe that there are some general tendencies and presuppositions that can be held up for comparison with a biblical interpretation of reality.

The first chapter is dedicated to listening to the witness of the New Testament and the early Christian theologians regarding the dynamic and noetic quality of faith as they seek to respond to the questions of their own day and set the pattern for how to "think with assent." In order to realize the first step in the process I am describing, namely that of rephrasing the feminist question, it was necessary first and foremost to establish the fact that faith is *a way of knowing,* and not merely an inherited plausibility structure.

The second chapter continues the reflection on theology by tracing its gradual alienation from the life of the community, and the steps taken by some of the great theologians of our century to recover and advance a more genuine understanding of theology.

At this point, the study takes a new direction that will be sustained through chapters 3–5. These chapters are largely historical. The more I studied feminism and the issues raised by the discussions to which it gives rise, the more I became aware of the need for greater historical perspective on the part of all concerned.

Chapter 3 begins with a rather extended discussion of methodological questions having to do with the role of historical investigation in theology. My purpose is to raise the question of the larger or second order heuristic structure that presides over the specifically historical hermeneutic and to suggest an alternate model for understanding the vicissitudes in the church's life. From that point the chapter enters into a discussion of the roles of women in the early life of the church. It is here that I first introduce the distinction between charism, ministry, and office.

The fourth chapter surveys what historians say regarding the roles of women throughout the history of the Western Church. This may come as a surprise to many, since it tends to disprove the myth of "total oppression" and indicates that many feminist aspirations were already partially realized, only to be lost in subsequent centuries. I propose that this loss, which gave rise to a pagan view of human existence and of our relation to God that culminated in the Enlightenment, has skewed our understanding of God, of his manner of causing, and of the role of power in human life. As a consequence, our manner of viewing what is feminine about creation, history, and men and women has been distorted.

Chapter 5 is a very brief history of feminism. For those familiar with the topic, there will be little that is new. For those less familiar, the chapter will help provide a framework for what follows. The history of feminist theology indicates that it began by using the theological tools available to it, and this has made it dependent upon a set of post-Enlightenment principles that cannot be accepted uncritically. In the last part of the chapter, I set forth what I consider to be the three errors of modernity that have deeply affected feminist theology and that must be corrected if feminism is to have a dialogue with revelation. These errors are foundationalism and representationalism in epistemology, and individualism in anthropology.

The second half of the book deals with these three errors. Chapter 6 concerns itself with epistemological foundationalism. Feminism places experience as the matrix and norm of knowledge in an often unconscious fidelity to the isolation and anxiety introduced into Western thought by William of Ockham, developed by Descartes, and systematized by Kant. I propose that the root of this view lies in the failure to understand God's power as an expression of his generosity rather than a form of domination. *Being* itself, as participating in God, is generous — it shares in the act of knowing. This enables us to understand how receptivity is a perfection and why the notion of "Word" as applied within God uncovers for us a dimension of our own existence that gives rise to trust. From this viewpoint I reconsider the role of experience in knowing.

In Chapter 7 the foundationalist epistemology described in the previous chapter is portrayed as underlying feminist hermeneutics. By placing the subject at the center, the text becomes an occasion for self-realization rather than an instance of communication. This reduces the text to a record of representationalist reporting on human experiences of the Transcendent. After discussing the decentering of the Bible, I give examples of how this is effected by considering three different feminist approaches to Scripture.

Chapter 8 considers another effect of feminist foundationalism, the mistaken notion of the significance of our words about God. My purpose here is to set forth an understanding of analogy as a judgment of similarity based on something objectively shared rather than a comparison of concepts. Then, taking as a starting point the work of Gilbert Durand, I classify images according to their degree of interiority and then apply this to the work of Phyllis Trible, whose pioneering studies in this regard are still considered basic by feminist thinkers. By way of experiment in understanding the role of image, I consider the image of Jesus as Mother as this was present in the early centuries and reached a mature theological expression in Julian of Norwich. The last third of the chapter deals with Sallie McFague's understanding of metaphorical theology. At this point, I wished to give an illustration of how a nonfoundationalist mode of thought would proceed. I call the method "indwelling the tradition," following Michael Polanyi, and characterize its two movements as "familiarity" and "connaturality." The method is then applied to the New Testament expression, "the God and Father of Our Lord Jesus Christ."

The last three chapters consider the question of individualism; the third of the three discusses influences of modernity upon feminist theology. My purpose in Chapter 10 is to set forth two views of the human person. I define individualism as considering the human being to be constituted and endowed with rights *prior* to any relationship. This is then contrasted with relationalism, which understands the human person to be constituted by relation, first to God as Creator, and then to all human beings who make up the network (past, present, and future) within which the person exists. The place where personhood is fully realized is the church, since it joins heaven and earth and portrays the immortality that gives a person his or her ultimate meaning.

Chapters 11 and 12 concentrate on the physical dimension of human personhood since the body, as a symbol, expresses the person as male and female. In Chapter 11 I establish the link between body and historicality and thus between the body and salvation. The body of Jesus Christ is the cause of our salvation, while the locus of our salvation is the church, Christ's historical presence in and through our body persons. This vision contrasts sharply with our adversative individualism, accent on sexuality, and Cartesian dichotomy between body and mind.

Chapter 12 continues the presentation of the history of Christian thought about the human body begun in the prior chapter and considers some instances of modern thinking that, sometimes unknowingly and sometimes quite consciously, are returning to a more biblical understanding of the body person. Utilizing the distinction between person and persona, I apply the results of the historical survey and the anthropological insights to the question of woman-man relations in church life and order. By considering this question under the aspect of relationality rather than physicality in the abstract, I intend to contribute to the discussion on the ordination of women.[6]

Finally, in the epilogue I sum up the result of the interaction between the feminist question and the questioning of this question that I have attempted throughout the book. As a last step, I offer a rephrasing of that

---

6. This book was already in the press when Pope John Paul II issued his apostolic letter *Ordinatio Sacerdotalis* on May 22, 1994. What I say is in accord with the apostolic constitution, but I could not treat of it more substantially.

question and propose a direction for an answer based on the notion of "recapitulation" as it is developed in Ephesians 1:10 and Irenaeus.

ACKNOWLEDGMENTS

I have covered a number of topics where I felt the need for consultation and correction. Many friends and colleagues have taken the trouble to read parts of this book and to engage in conversation about it. Their suggestions have been invaluable, and I am grateful to all of them, particularly to Michael Duggan; Peter Hocken; Kenneth Schmitz; Prudence Allen, RSM; Robert Sokolowski; David Schindler; Robin Darling Young; Alvin Kimel; Mary Malone; and John Grabowski.

Mary Healy's help as research assistant, particularly in some of the historical sections, has been indispensable, as has been her correcting of the manuscript along with Gertrude Gillette, OSB, and Maria Herald. I am grateful as well to Lisa Lickona and especially to Raymond Vandegrift, OP, and Matthew Rzeczkowski, OP, and the library staff at the Dominican House of Studies, whose cooperation and generosity were equal to my incessant requests.

Finally, I would like to express my thanks to the staff at Wm. B. Eerdmans for their cheerful efficiency in seeing this book through to publication.

Some of the material in this book was published previously in another form in *Communio* as I already mentioned, and an earlier version of chapter 9 was published in *Anthropotes*. I am grateful to both publishers for allowing me to use the material here.

I

Theology and the Light of Faith

The goal of chapters 1 and 2 is to locate our modern theological efforts, particularly in this instance our efforts to understand the meaning and role of women in the Christian community, within the faith activity of that community and its history. These two chapters will set forth the methodological principles that will be operative in the whole study. In order for this consideration of feminism to be a theological effort, it is important to be clear about what theology is.

In this chapter I wish to accomplish three things. I wish first to discuss the relationship between theology and revelation. Then, in order to understand the various levels and manifestations of what we call theology, I will introduce the notion of a "potential whole." Third, I will trace a continuity within the biblical tradition concerning the nature of theology, finding the common thread to be a divinely conferred knowledge of God and of God's plan, that is, revelation.

Theology is ordered faith discourse about God and all things in relation to God. It is faith discourse not because it treats of those things that Christians believe and practice — religious science also does this — but because faith is the light that presides over the process by which theological thinking and discourse is carried on.[1] It is ordered discourse in that it proceeds according to the norms of human communication. By this last statement I wish to distance myself from the notion that only the type of faith discourse that conforms to the procedural modes of modern Western scientific thinking should be called "theology." After nearly a century of careful study of the modes of the faith discourse of John, Luke, Paul,

---

1. I will restrict my considerations here to the notion of Christian theology, leaving to others the discussion as to whether and how Judaism, Islam, and other non-Christian religions desire or possess a theology.

I

Jeremiah, the Yahwist, the Priestly author, Origen, Gregory, Ephrem, and others, all of whom were writing theology, we have become more circumspect in our instinctive post-Enlightenment judgment that discourse is genuinely intellectual to the degree that it conforms to our manner of ordering thought and speech.

In saying this, of course, I do not deny the legitimacy and importance of that process of transposition by which a reality expressed in one mode of discourse achieves expression in another. In the New Testament itself Jesus' death and resurrection are expressed in the interpretive narratives of the Gospels, in the discursive thought of Paul and others, in creedal summary formulations, and in hymns.[2] The process of transmitting this faith interpretation of reality has continued in the church throughout the centuries, with the Scriptures acting as the privileged means of transmission and the norm against which other expressions are judged.

THEOLOGY AND REVELATION

The distinctive nature of theology consists in the fact that it is derived *from* revelation as well as being *about* revelation. Revelation may be described as an act of God by which he communicates himself and the mystery of his will to human beings.[3] This act reaches us in two ways. There is first God's activity in history that is accomplished through intimately connected words and deeds, culminating in Jesus Christ, who is both the mediator and the fullness of revelation. Second, there is the activity, also historical and also mediated by Jesus Christ, by which God moves and assists someone to believe, that is, to commit himself or herself to God, yielding to and accepting the divine self-communication. While the first activity was brought to completion by the resurrection of Jesus Christ, the second is still continuing. This second dimension is always present as the Holy Spirit brings each person into living contact with the Father's self-revelation in Jesus Christ risen from the dead. In a mysterious interaction of divine initiative and human freedom, the Holy Spirit leads those who assent to his action from the first act of yielding in faith to its consummation in a transforming vision of God. Only then does God completely manifest and

2. For examples of creedal formulae see 1 Thess 4:14; 1 Cor 15:1-3. For examples of hymnic and similar expressions often connected with baptism see Phil 2:6-11; 1 Tim 3:16; Rev 5:9-10, 12-13.

3. This definition is based on the Vatican II Constitution *Dei Verbum,* particularly §§2-6.

communicate himself, which allows us to obtain a clear knowledge of the eternal mystery of his will.

Revelation actually exists only when both dimensions of the divine activity are present: the words and deeds culminating in Christ and the personal appropriation of these realities. As an unknown preacher of the fourth or fifth century put it: "As far as we are concerned, Christ's immolation on our behalf takes place when we become aware of this grace and we understand the life conferred on us by this sacrifice."[4] In this sense, revelation only exists on a personal level. We must not, however, confuse personal with individualistic. In the whole of the biblical tradition the personal dimension of revelation reaches its perfection only in community. What is revealed and appropriated belongs to the whole people of God, and from this it follows that the first dimension of revelation, that of revelatory words and deeds, is committed to the community to be accepted, commemorated, lived, and transmitted. Thus, what is appropriated personally is possessed communally. The initial divine act, the process of its transmission, and its interiorization on an individual level are all part of the one activity we call revelation. It is in this light that Thomas Aquinas can consider these phases as all participating in the same grace.

> After the level of those who receive revelation directly from God, another level of grace is necessary. Because men receive revelation from God not only for their own time but also for the instruction of all who come after them, it was necessary that the things revealed to them be passed on not only in speech to their contemporaries but also as written down for the instruction of those to come after them. And thus it was also necessary that there be those who could interpret what was written down. This also must be done by divine grace. And so we read in Gen 40:8, "Does not interpretation come from God?"[5]

What then, is the place of theology? As discourse from and about revelation it is a function of the community in its life of worship and preaching, whereby the words and deeds that transmit the divine activity are made accessible. Faith is always a response to revelation, and since faith grows deeper to the degree that the revelation is personally appropriated, we may say that theology also admits of degrees. In its highest form theology is a living and personal knowledge of God as he communicates himself in and through what he has done in history. In its derivative forms, such as historical theology, theology serves this primary participa-

---

4. Pseudo-Chrysostom, *Homily on Easter* 1,7 (*Sources Chrétiennes* 36,61).
5. *Summa Contra Gentiles* 3,154.

tion in revelation by explaining, defending, and transmitting the symbols by which God's acts are made known. Since these derivative functions are part of tradition, that is, the act of the Holy Spirit making revelation present in both its dimensions, they can never be carried on without faith. At the very least there must be an acceptance of the teaching of the community entrusted with the revelation. When this is not present there can be discourse *about* revelation but not *from* revelation. I would call such discourse religious science or the philosophy of religion.

Because this point is so important, I wish to show from a rapid look at the testimony of past theologians that theology is discourse founded on and drawing from the living experience of faith. Before I do so, however, I wish to offer a model that may help us understand how this traditional witness relates to the more conceptual idea of theology prevalent today.

THEOLOGY AS A POTENTIAL WHOLE

We are often faced with the problem of trying to determine what is a genuinely theological consideration of a topic and what is not. One reason for this is that we do not find ready at hand a model that can render our intuitions more intelligible as we instinctively search for a way to account for various types of theology and various degrees of success in theologizing. I propose looking upon theology as a "potential whole."[6] In the writings of Thomas Aquinas, we find a distinction regarding three types of wholes: a universal whole, equally present in all of its parts; an integral whole, not completely present in any of its parts; and a potential whole, present in all of its parts, but not in equal power.[7] The example of a potential whole

---

6. I am indebted to an article by Francisco Muniz for the basic thesis that the notion of potential whole can be used to analyze theology: "De Diversis Muneribus S. Theologiae Secundum Doctrinam D. Thomae," *Angelicum* 24 (1947) 93-123. This appeared in English as *The Work of Theology,* trans. John Reid (Washington, D.C.: The Thomist Press, 1953). Muniz has in common with many others that most of his discussion concerns the operations of theology. I wish to suggest that there be a greater emphasis on the formal light of theology in using this model.

7. One of the most complete descriptions given by Aquinas is to be found in his treatise *On Spiritual Creatures* (2,ad2):

It must be observed that there are three types of whole. One is universal, which is present to each part in its complete essence and power; hence it is properly predicated of its parts, as when we say: man is an animal. A second type is an integral whole, which is found in any one of its parts neither in its full essence nor by virtue of its total power; in no way, then, is it predicated of a part, for

given consistently by Aquinas is that of the human soul. The "parts" of the soul are vegetative, animal, and intellectual. There is only one soul, all of the essence of the soul is present in all its parts, and yet the full power of the soul is only present in that intellectual or spiritual activity that subsumes all the parts of the soul.[8]

Theology is similarly a unified, potential whole. In its essence it is a body of knowledge that considers all things "in so far as they are knowable by divine light."[9] Therefore, an activity is theological if (and only if) it proceeds by the light of God, imparted to us as faith. This is the essence of theology. Yet, even when the whole essence is present, the whole power may not be present — as with the human soul. The full power of theology is present when God himself, in his Triune Mystery, is known and worshiped in an experiential faith. This is the gift of Wisdom, an act by which the Word visits the soul; he is not just any word "but a word breathing forth love." "Thus, not according to any perfection of the mind whatever is the Son sent, but according to that teaching action *(institutio)* or instruction of the mind by which it bursts forth in an affection of love as it is said in John 6:45, 'All who hear from the Father and learn, come to me'. . . ."[10]

Two things must be considered in determining whether or not theology is operating in accord with its full power: object and intensity. The object of theology is God as he reveals himself in his activity, in creation, in the whole history of redemption culminating in Jesus Christ, and in the imparting of that revelation to each believer. The object of theology is secondarily all things insofar as they can be known by faith in the way that God knows them. Thus, the power of the activity can be judged according to what it considers: God or creatures. Next, we must consider the intensity

---

example: a wall is not a house. A third type of whole is a potential whole, which is a mean between the other two; for it is present to each of its parts in its complete essence, but not in all its power. Consequently, it is predicated in a manner which is midway between that of the other two types: for it is sometimes predicated of its parts, but not properly.

8. *Summa Theologiae* 1,76,8; 77,1,ad1. For a complete list of the places where Aquinas discusses the potential whole see Muniz, *The Work of Theology,* 1.

9. The two quoted phrases are found in *Summa Theologiae* 1,1,3,ad2; 4c, respectively. The term *light* used by Aquinas in company with most ancient theologians refers to the power to know conferred upon all intelligent creatures as a participation in the divine knowledge. I will use the metaphor of light in this study in this general sense, acknowledging that its specific content differs depending upon theories of knowledge that need not concern us here.

10. *Summa Theologiae* 1,43,5,ad2.

of the act. Faith in all its forms is a manner of knowing.[11] The full power of theology is present to the degree that the believer has that intensity of faith that I have described above as "Wisdom" and that is denoted by the New Testament and the early tradition as *gnosis* (knowledge).[12]

We may say, then, that discourse about God or about things in relation to God is theological when faith as "thinking with assent" is the operating principle.[13] When that assent is not present at all, the activity is not theology. When faith is an intensely living activity by which one is conscious of learning from God, then, from the point of view of intensity, the full power of theology is present. When this activity reaches God himself, the full power of theology is present in both object and intensity.[14] When the object is something else, such as the sacraments or Christian anthropology, even though it may be regarded in the light of faith and thus be a theological act, the full power of theology is not realized.

The highest realization of theology this side of beatitude is knowledge of the Trinity, in and through an action of the Holy Spirit by which a resemblance to the Word is actualized in the interior of a person and expressed in communal worship. From this point down to the most humble historical and philological research undertaken as part of the effort toward faith understanding, there is a continuum that is called theology because all that it considers is "brought into the same focus and pictured in the field of divine revelation."[15] In dividing this continuum into discrete parts, "mysticism" and "theology," we have done both parts a disservice and have been false to the nature of theology.

The two aspects of intensity and object may also be considered from

---

11. "The act of faith essentially consists in an act of knowing; that is its formal or specific perfection; this is clear from what its object is." *De Veritate* 14,2,ad10. Translation is that of T. C. O'Brien in *Summa Theologiae,* Blackfriars Edition, vol. 31, *Faith,* 208, n. 14. See also 1-2,110,4.

12. See the study by Louis Bouyer, *Gnosis: La connaissance de Dieu dans l'Écriture* (Paris: Cerf, 1988).

13. The expression *cum assensione cogitare* is from Augustine's *De Praedestinatione Sanctorum Liber ad Prosperum et Hilarium Primus,* 2 (*Patrologia Latina* 44,963). Aquinas frequently refers to this phrase; see, for example, *Summa Theologiae* 2-2,2,1.

14. "When we believe God by faith, we reach God himself. . . . This is why I have said [in 2-2,1,1] that God is the object of faith not simply in the sense that we believe in God *(credimus Deum)* but also that we believe God *(credimus Deo)." Summa Theologiae* 2-2,81,5, Blackfriars Edition, vol. 31, 190.

15. *Summa Theologiae* 1,1,3,ad2. Translation is that of Gilby. Aquinas is making the point that what is considered in diverse *scientiae philosophicae* are considered by *sacra doctrina,* "sub una ratione inquantum sunt divinitus revelabilia."

the point of view of the "two lights" that make up faith knowledge. The medievals delighted in alluding to these by invoking Psalm 36:10, "In your light we see (the) light." This formula expresses in one phrase what I referred to earlier as the two dimensions of the act of God in revelation: the words and deeds of Jesus Christ and those others that participate in them by way of preparation or continuance, and the work of faith by which this first dimension is assimilated. I would like to conclude this section by citing a text from Aquinas that considers theology from the point of view of these two lights. Note how for him the light that gives access to the light functions *consciously,* in bringing the believer to an assent.

> So also in the faith by which we believe in God there is not only the accepting of the object of assent, but something moving us to the assent. This is a kind of light — the habit of faith — divinely imparted to the human mind. It is more capable of causing assent than any demonstration. . . . Thus this light is an adequate means of making judgments. The habit of faith, however, does not move us by way of the intellect but rather by way of the will. As a consequence it does not make us see what we believe, nor does it force our assent, but it causes us to assent to it voluntarily. It is clear, then, that faith comes from God in two ways: by way of an interior light that leads to assent and by way of the realities that are proposed from without and that had as their source divine revelation.[16]

THEOLOGY IN THE PRECRITICAL AGE

It is common today when tracing the history of some aspect of Christian thought to divide the investigation into three parts, usually called premodern, modern, and postmodern. The point of reference, obviously, is *modern.* Avery Dulles has recently divided the three stages of theology as precritical, critical, and postcritical.[17] This has the advantage of steering

16. *In Boet. De Trin.* 3,1,ad4, in St. Thomas Aquinas, *Faith, Reason and Theology: Questions I-IV of his Commentary on the De Trinitate of Boethius,* Medieval Sources in Translation, 32, trans. A. Maurer (Toronto: Pontifical Institute of Medieval Studies, 1987), 69. The Latin text of the last words in the citation runs as follows: *quae ex divina revelatione initium sumpserunt.* See as well *Summa Theologiae* 2-2,6,1. In commenting on the words of Rom 1:19, "God made it [what can be known about him] manifest to them," Aquinas speaks of God's activity in creating as that of a teacher "proposing exterior signs of his wisdom" (Sir 1:10) but also uniquely "conferring an interior light by which a person actually knows" (*Super Epistulas S. Pauli Lectura* [Rome: Marietti, 1953], *Ad Romanos* §116.).

17. *The Craft of Theology* (New York: Crossroad, 1992).

clear of the debate concerning what constitutes "modern"; however, I will
return to include some aspects of modernity in my discussion of what
constitutes "critical theology."

If we are to classify theology as precritical, critical, and postcritical,
then we should attempt to define *critical.* Broad definitions of the term
such as "the subjecting of things to a norm," are not satisfactory since
such a mental function has characterized all thought, including theological
thought, throughout the centuries. If such a definition is adopted, then the
term *precritical* would be the same as *gullible* or at least *prerational.* The
very fact that the word *canon* (norm) was used to establish the list of
normative writings is evidence enough that the ancients knew how to think
critically in this sense.[18] What characterizes the age of criticism is not
reflective thinking according to norms, but the insistence that the only norm
is human reason. This has been discussed frequently enough.

My point in adducing the evidence to follow is to show that there is
a continuity in the precritical period regarding the nature of theology. The
whole process I have just described above as revelation contains as an
essential element that ordered faith discourse by which it is made available
to successive generations of believers, particularly in their common worship. Although the roots of the Christian view of theology are to be found,
of course, in the Old Testament, I will begin the investigation with a
consideration of how the New Testament speaks of faith as a God-given
access to the knowledge of the mystery of Christ. The writings of the New
Testament itself are a privileged instance of that ordered faith discourse by
which the mystery is transmitted. The written text is one dimension of that
faith activity by which the community makes present to itself throughout
its history the revelation of God that took place in Jesus Christ. Because
this revelation is appropriated in varying degrees through the light by which
the light of revelation is received, it will be helpful to view this rapid survey
in terms of the two aspects of God's revelatory act, or the two lights
mentioned above. These varying degrees of personalization account for the
fact that we can also apply the notion of potential whole to the theology
of the New Testament and the succeeding centuries.

---

18. "Ancient critics, like their modern counterparts, questioned received opinions
about the authorship and integrity of canonical writings and tried to write a history of
how they came to be composed and about the relationships in which they stood to each
other." J. C. O'Neil, "Biblical Criticism," in *The Anchor Dictionary of the Bible,* ed.
David Noel Freedman (New York: Doubleday, 1992), 1,725-30; quotation is from
p. 726.

The New Testament

The basic principle of what one might call New Testament theology is found in the prologue to the fourth Gospel: "God, no one has ever seen, the Only Begotten God, who is in the bosom of the Father, he has made him known" (Jn 1:18). In this one text we have a statement of the incomprehensibility of God and the fact that he is known in the revelation effected by Jesus Christ, most especially in his death on the cross and in his risen life, which he bestows on those who believe him.

The Early Articulations of Faith

If we consider the two lights that constitute revelation, we have in 2 Corinthians 4:6 one of the most dramatic expressions of the fact that they are two aspects of one act on the part of God: "The God who said, 'Out of darkness light shall shine,' is the one who has caused his light to shine in our hearts, for the enlightenment which consists in the knowledge of the glory of God on the face of Jesus Christ." The light of God moves our hearts to assent to the true and objective reality of Jesus Christ. In and through this assent comes a genuine knowledge. It is by the light that comes from God that one is able to grasp the light of God in the face of Jesus Christ. The activity by which a person yields to the reality of Christ brings with it a certain elevation and certitude. As this yielding intensifies, it is able to preside over the verbal and textual articulation of divine reality by providing a kind of intuition not unlike the one that presides over the composition of a poem. As Paul says a few lines later, quoting the Septuagint version of Psalm 115:1, "I believed, therefore I spoke out" (2 Cor 4:13).

This same rhythm of believing and speaking out, of being enlightened and communicating this in ordered discourse, underlies all of the multifaceted activity by which the New Testament was composed. We have very little idea of the early stages of the process by which the gospel was transmitted and interpreted, though most of this must have been accomplished in oral presentations. Writing served to fix the oral performance, and thus prepared for the activity of composing a text in the full sense of the term.[19] In a particular way, this can be seen in the way the gospel

19. For a discussion of oral transmission see the article by Paul Achtemeier, "*Omne verbum sonat:* The New Testament and the Oral Environment of Late Western Antiquity," *Journal of Biblical Literature* 109 (1990): 3-27. For an excellent study on the nature of a text one may consult Werner Jeanrond, *Text and Interpretation as Categories of Theological Thinking,* trans. Thomas Wilson (New York: Crossroad, 1988).

writers transpose and order the material that preexisted their composi-
tions.[20] We see the same phenomenon in the way the hymns and creedal
formulations now imbedded in the Letters and other New Testament material were first composed and then incorporated.

This intimate interaction between the large number of Christians who
expressed their faith in narrative or hymns and those who composed the
canonical texts is important to bear in mind when we read Paul's clear claim
that what he knows has been conferred upon him by God: "For I declare to
you brothers, that the Gospel that was preached by me is not of human origin,
I neither received it from someone else nor was I taught it; rather [I possess it]
through the revelation of Jesus Christ" (Gal. 1:11-12). We should not imagine
that this kind of knowledge was restricted to the great prophets and mystics of
the early community, though they possessed it to an extraordinary degree. Paul
challenges his whole Galatian audience by appealing to their common experience of the Holy Spirit: "I want to learn only this from you, was it from works
of the law that you received the Spirit or from the message of faith?" (Gal.
3:2). If reception of the Spirit were not a commonly shared experience Paul's
whole argument would be senseless. The same can be said of another remark
of Paul's in the letter to the Galatians, in which he says: "I have been crucified
with Christ. I am living, but not really I: Christ lives in me. The life I now live
in the flesh, I live in faith, faith in the Son of God who loved me and gave
himself up for me" (Gal 2:20). Paul is undoubtedly witnessing here to
something he knows is true about himself. It is important to note how far this
experience is from a vague "contact with the Transcendent." It is a living
awareness of a living person who interacts with Paul, who has transformed his
life and his person, and who loves Paul to the point of giving his life for him.[21]
It is equally important to realize that the *ego* of this text, while it refers to the
author of the statement who is conscious of himself, refers to him as part of a
believing community, "in Christ." What Paul says of himself he says as a
believer who is aware that what he says is true, to some degree, of everyone
who has accepted God's witness in the person and activity of Jesus Christ.[22]

---

20. I have discussed this transposing activity in the introduction to *Narrative
Parallels to the New Testament*, SBL Resources for Biblical Study 22 (Atlanta: Scholars
Press, 1988).

21. The term translated "gave himself up" *(paradidonai)* is a technical term in
the New Testament writings, deriving from the Septuagint version of Is 53:6, 12, and
alluding to the whole process of the Passion.

22. For a study of the text one may consult Edmond Farahian, *Le "Je" Paulinien:
Etude pour mieux comprendre Gal. 2,19-21*, Analecta Gregoriana, 253 (Rome: Editrice
Pontificia Università Gregoriana, 1988).

The Johannine Teaching on Faith and Its Articulation

Much of the teaching of the Johannine school on the topic of coming to the knowledge of God in Christ and transmitting it centers around the notion of truth. Truth in this tradition is the gift of revelation of the Father communicated by the life, death, and resurrection of Jesus Christ, and interiorized by each believer under the action of the Holy Spirit.[23] The rhythm of revelation is expressed variously. In 1 John 5:6 the author uses two aorist participles to characterize the activity of Christ and the Spirit: the first is "the one who came" *(ho elthōn);* that is, became historically present and effected the redemption, while the second is "the one bearing witness" *(ho martyroun),* that is, making the historical work of God in Christ available in a personal way to the believing community. This same notion is expressed by saying that the Son of God appeared, or that the love of God appeared: "In this God's love has appeared among us. God has sent his Son, his Only Begotten into the world, that we might live through him" (1 Jn 4:9). This appearance is still present in the church — our knowledge is founded on what God has done to make himself known, both in the historical act of Jesus and the witnessing act of the Holy Spirit.[24] It is for this reason that the author of 1 John can tell his community that there is no need for anyone to teach them because they have the "oil of anointing" that they "have received from the Holy One," which abides in them and because of which they know the *truth* (2:27). The oil of anointing is the word by which the historical, revelatory act of Christ continues through the church's preaching, worship, and sacramental gestures, precisely as this word is rendered effective by the action of the Holy Spirit in the interior of each believer who accepts his activity.

Once again we see verified the two dimensions of God's act in revealing himself — the *words* and *deeds* as these culminate in Christ, and the light to penetrate into the reality they mediate. If we concentrate on this latter, we can appreciate the directness and experiential quality that the

23. The most complete study of the notion of truth in the Johannine tradition is that by Ignace de la Potterie, *La Vérité dans Saint Jean,* Analecta Biblica, 73/74 (Rome: Pontifical Biblical Institute, 1977).

24. Rudolf Schnackenburg, commenting on this statement, says that the *ephanerothē* of the text means that God's love "has become experienceable *(erfahrbar)." Die Johannesbriefe,* Herders theologischer Kommentar zum Neuen Testament, XIII/3, 7ed. (Freiburg: Herder, 1984), 229. This same notion of the ongoing availability of God's act of self-revelation is also mediated by the Johannine use of the vocabulary of "seeing." One may consult C. Traets, *Voir Jésus et le Père en Lui selon l'Évangile de Saint Jean,* Analecta Gregoriana, 159 (Rome: Editrice Pontificia Università Gregoriana, 1967).

notion of *knowing God* takes on in the Johannine tradition. In an article that has become a classic, M.-E. Boismard has analyzed the concept of knowing God in 1 John:

Now we can define the "knowledge of God," comparing it with our divine birth and the presence of God [in us]. The expression "to be born of God" indicates that we have received in us a principle of life causing us to act like God because this principle emanates from God. The phrase "we abide in God and God in us" describes the presence of God in our soul, a presence implied by his activity in us. Finally, then, the expression "to know God" *denotes the subjective coming to awareness of this divine presence brought about by his action in our soul.* But we should note carefully: the presence of God is not "known" except in so far as it is the principle of activity, and this activity of God is above all his love. God is love and God loves in us, and God gives us the capacity to love with his love. To know God is, therefore, to know love; it is to become aware of God-Love radiating love in our soul. This conclusion becomes clearer and more precise if we place this knowledge of God within the perspectives of the Old Testament which it extends and brings to perfection.[25]

So far in the discussion, I have placed the accent on the witness of the New Testament that faith is a way of knowing. What is known is not vague or abstract; it is the activity of God in an historical dimension. God's true reality is only available in the light of faith, what Jean Lacroix calls the "interior dimension" of history.[26] Two aspects of the manner in which the New Testament speaks of this penetration to the interior dimension of history are closer to what we today generally consider theology to be. I am referring to the use of the term *mystery* and the elaboration of creedal formulas.

The Notion of Mystery

All told, the Greek word *mystērion* (mystery) is found twenty-eight times in the New Testament.[27] It occurs in the Synoptic accounts of Jesus' reply

---

25. "La connaissance dans l'Alliance Nouvelle d'après la Première Lettre de Saint Jean," *Revue Biblique* 56 (1949): 366-91; citation is from p. 388. Emphasis is in original.
26. *Histoire et Mystère* (Tournai: Castermann, 1962).
27. By accepting the variant reading *martyrion* at 1 Cor 2:1, some authors count 27 instances. A fundamental study of the notion of mystery in the New Testament is that by Raymond Brown, "The Semitic Background of the New Testament *Mysterion*," *Biblica* 39 (1958): 426-48; 40 (1959): 70-87.

to the disciples' question concerning his teaching in parables (Mt 13:11; Mk 4:11; Lk 8:10) and four times in the book of Revelation. All the other occurrences are found in the Pauline corpus. *Mystērion* can be defined broadly as some aspect of the hidden counsel of God now being made manifest. Thus, the term can refer to the secret meaning of a text or a symbol, as in Revelation 1:20 and 17:5 and Ephesians 5:32,[28] or the hidden designs of Providence, as in Revelation 10:7. Mostly, however, it refers to some aspect of God's plan of salvation in Christ that is being made known in and through the preaching and faith of the church. The mysteries of the kingdom of God have been confided to the disciples (Mt 13:11; Mk 4:11; Lk 8:10). *Mystery* can designate the wisdom Paul shares with the Corinthians (1 Cor 2:7; 15:51), though such revelation is useless without *agapē* (1 Cor 13:2). In a profound sense the Lordship of Jesus in his life, death, and resurrection is the mystery (Rom 16:25), and this notion is orchestrated variously in Colossians (1:26-27; 4:3) and Ephesians (1:9; 3:2-13), where it is extended to include the working out of this plan in the ongoing ages of the church. In the two occurrences of the term in 1 Timothy (3:9, 16), the term *mystery* describes the content of belief.[29]

Although the text in 1 Timothy accents the intellectual content of the mystery, it is obvious as well from the passages in the Corinthian, Roman, and captivity correspondences[30] that the mystery was something known and articulated; there is a right way and a wrong way of enunciating God's revealed plan for the salvation of the human race. In another context, Paul can speak of "another Gospel" (Gal 1:6), contrasting it with the right proclamation of the truth. Once again we see that theological statements derive from both aspects of the divine act of revelation: an event and the light to understand it. The word *mystery* in the New Testament refers to the event of Jesus Christ perceived as the ongoing historical existence and manifestation of God's eternal plan. Basically, what is at stake here is the correct understanding of what took place historically in the career of Jesus Christ, who he is, what his state is at this moment, and what significance that has for believers. Although the language in which this is expressed is inadequate, it is not arbitrary. There is, first of all, the confession that "Jesus Christ came in the flesh" (1 Jn 4:2), an understanding that his death was

28. This text is a special instance of *mystērion* referring to a deeper christological significance of an Old Testament passage. For an initial discussion see Markus Barth, *Ephesians 4–6*, Anchor Bible 34A (New York: Doubleday, 1974), 641-47.

29. "We might say that the mystery of faith is what is believed, as the mystery of the gospel is what is preached." Brown, "The Semitic Background," 85.

30. The question of Pauline authorship of the captivity and pastoral letters does not affect the use I am making of the material here.

"for us" or "for our sins,"[31] that he was resurrected,[32] that he is and will
be our Savior,[33] that he is now recognized as "Lord,"[34] and that he will
"come" again.[35]

Creedal Statements

In the list of assertions given just above, we can see evidence of the process
by which the interpretive narratives concerning Jesus were transposed to
the level of discursive statements. The significance of the process lies in
the fact that these statements articulate a judgment. Historical narrative has
the unique power to transpose an event to the level of word and to re-present
it in the form of a text, that is, in an interconnected set of symbols that, by
creating a world, interprets the original event. In the case of the Gospels,
this interpretation partakes of the revelatory activity by which God
manifests and communicates himself in the life, death, and resurrection of

31. Among the significant occurrences of "for us" we may list: Rom 5:8; 8:32,
34; 2 Cor 5:21; Gal 2:20; 3:13; Eph 5:2; Tit 2:14; Heb 6:20; 1 Jn 3:16. Twice Paul
speaks of Christ's death as being "for our sins" (1 Cor 15:3; Gal 1:4).

32. The attempt to distinguish two chronologically and intellectually differing
views of the resurrection based on the expressions *exalt (hyperypsoun)* and *raise/rise
(egeirein/anastēnai)* is misguided. All these expressions are found in texts that were
composed before the New Testament (see, for example, Phil 2:9; 1 Cor 15:4; 1 Thess
4:14), and thus it is impossible to attribute priority to one or the other. In addition, it
is clear that none of them is necessary in order to speak of the risen reality of Jesus,
as is witnessed by the fact that though the letter to the Hebrews is one long treatise on
the heavenly state of Jesus Christ it never uses any of the above terms.

33. Jesus is spoken of as the one who "will rescue us from the wrath to come"
(1 Thess 1:10); who "snatched us from this present evil age" (Gal 1:4); and who "will
appear a second time not to take away sin but to bring salvation to those who eagerly
await him" (Heb 9:28). He is given the title *Savior,* sometimes because of his past
activity (Acts 5:31; Tit 3:6; 1 Jn 4:14), sometimes for what he will do in the future
(Phil 3:20; 2 Tim 1:10), and sometimes as a general eponym denoting his relation to
the human race (Jn 4:42; Eph 5:23; Tit 1:4).

34. There are times when this title clearly applies to Jesus the Septuagint designation for Yhwh, as in Phil 2:11 (see Is 45:22-25); Rom 10:9; 10:13; 1 Thess 5:2;
2 Thess 2:2; 1 Cor 1:2. For an excellent study of the Aramaic origins of this way of
speaking see Joseph Fitzmyer, "The Semitic Background of the New Testament *Kyrios*-Title," in *A Wandering Aramean,* SBL Monograph Series 25 (Missoula: Scholars
Press, 1979), 115-42.

35. Besides the texts that speak of Jesus' future role as Savior, there are those
such as 1 Cor 11:26 that state that the Eucharistic celebration declares "the death of
the Lord until he comes." A convenient gathering of the relevant texts can be found in
John A. T. Robinson, *Jesus and His Coming: The Emergence of a Doctrine* (New
York/Nashville: Abingdon, 1957).

Jesus. In this sense, narrative shares the priority of the event that it mediates symbolically. Discursive statements have another priority, however, since, by articulating a judgment, they enunciate and distinguish true from false. This is the function of the creedal statements. Assertions such as "Jesus Christ is Lord" (Phil 2:11), "Jesus is the Christ" (1 Jn 2:22), or "Jesus died and rose" (1 Thess 4:14) are creedal statements *in nucleo*. They are not making a "meaning claim," they are making a "truth claim," and their opposite is false. They are setting the boundaries, as it were, for the interpretation of the narrated events.

The longer pieces of tradition found in the New Testament exhibit the same characteristics. As in the case of the shorter statements, these are often introduced by a declarative, "that" (Greek, *hoti*). A clear example of this is found in 1 Corinthians 15:3-5:

> I passed on to you as of first importance what I received: *that* Christ died for our sins according to the Scriptures; and *that* he was buried; and *that* he has been raised on the third day according to the Scriptures; and *that* he appeared to Cephas and then to the twelve.

The assertions in this formulation transpose the narrated events to the level of a judgment: in this case, the truth of certain happenings. In 1 Corinthians 11:23 we have the events of the Last Supper introduced by the same formulation: "I received," "I passed on," "that." In this instance what follows is a narrative-type liturgical account of the institution of the Eucharist.

Some of this material can best be described as confessions of faith, either taken from the life of the community ("Jesus is Lord") or used by the writers of the New Testament as models to be imitated by their audience: "You are the Messiah, the Son of God, who has come into the world" (Jn 11:27); "We have believed and have come to know that you are the Holy One of God" (Jn 6:69); "Truly this man was the Son of God" (Mk 15:39). Some of the other assertions are found in rhythmical formulae that are catechetical or hymnic summaries: "Who was manifested in the flesh, vindicated in the Spirit, seen by angels, proclaimed to the Gentiles, believed in throughout the world, taken up in glory" (1 Tim 3:16).[36] The importance of this type of linguistic utterance is that it makes up a certain "second order" level of predication, the level, as I have said, that is expressive of judgment and thus states something whose opposite is not true.

---

36. Other examples would be 1 Cor 8:6; 1 Tim 2:5; 2 Tim 2:8; Phil 2:6-11; 1 Pet 3:18-22; Rom 1:3-4; 4:25; 8:34. For a discussion of these formulae see J. N. D. Kelly, *Early Christian Creeds,* 3rd ed. (London: Longman, 1972), 13-29.

It is characteristic of these assertions that they all use ordinary words, and that their touchstone is an event or series of events that they directly or implicitly comment upon and interpret. Hans Frei has already pointed out the ordinariness of the narratives that mediate events completely out of the ordinary.[37] The same ordinariness characterizes the terms in which these second-order statements are couched. Whatever may be the cultural factors that entered into this type of vocabulary, there is as well the conviction that ordinary people, enlightened by the action of God that we call faith, could know the truth of these realities and experience their life-changing power. I make this point to accentuate the fact that the normative expressions of the Christian tradition did not need to have recourse to a specialized vocabulary to mediate the reality to which they bear witness. The meaning of the statements we have considered is generally obvious, though their full significance can be grasped only in the vision of God. Thus, even now, an appreciation of all that a New Testament text is *saying* requires a careful historical and literary analysis, while a grasp of the reality it is *talking about* can take place only through the light of faith. The depth of this understanding may vary considerably in the "potential whole" of Christian knowing.

The other characteristic of the statements we are considering is that their focal point is a reality of history — Jesus Christ. Jesus is the "unsubstitutable" subject of the predicates. No one else is Savior, is risen from the dead, is Lord, is coming again to complete all of history. This fact about early Christian predication is deceptively simple, yet it forms a touchstone with which to test all subsequent Christian utterances. The presupposition of New Testament speech about God is that the definitive moment of revelation is always available in the risen Jesus Christ. In one sense, what was accomplished belongs to a very particular moment in time and space, but in another sense it continues to exist, not only in its effective history, but in the person who accomplished it and who is now, in his transformed state, "the source of an eternal salvation for all who obey him" (Heb 5:9). Since it is possible to obey him and to receive salvation from him, he must be in contact with those who seek him. He is present in the body that is formed by all who are joined to him and in whom he dwells, and he is present as well in the symbolic expression (in bread and wine) of his act of self-donation by which this body is formed. This twofold abiding presence, effected by the Holy Spirit, of the act in history by which God definitively manifests and communicates himself, is the concrete measure

37. *The Identity of Jesus Christ: The Hermeneutical Basis of Dogmatic Theology* (Philadelphia: Fortress, 1975).

of the truth of what is said about God and about his revelatory act in any subsequent statements that across the span of the centuries seek to express and draw out the full significance and power of that act. It is in this sense, as I hope to show, that there can be a genuine correlation in the theological effort to exploit the full potential of God's act of revelation precisely in and through the questions brought to it by succeeding generations.

The Power of the Word

There is one final aspect of the act of God received in faith that is important to consider when we speak of theology: that this knowledge, or rather that which is known, is effective; it brings about a change. The truth of Jesus Christ conveyed through the preaching is the Word of God. This is manifest not only in the manner in which the New Testament uses the terms *logos* (word) and *logos tou Theou* (Word of God),[38] but in the fact that this word is active in the believers. In writing his first letter to the Thessalonians, Paul is expressing his gratitude to God "because, having received the word of God preached by us, you accepted it not as a human word but as it truly is, the word of God which is at work in you the believers" (2:13). From among many such expressions, we may note: "the word of the cross . . . is the power of God" (1 Cor 1:18); "the word of truth, the gospel . . . is bearing fruit and growing" (Col 1:5-6); "you have been born anew not from a perishable seed but from an imperishable one, the living and abiding word of God . . . . This is the word that has been proclaimed to you" (1 Pet 1:23-25; see also Js 1:18). This notion is found as well in the synoptic explanation of the parable of the seed sown and producing various quantities of fruit: "the seed is the word of God" (Lk 8:11; see also Mt 13:18-23; Mk 4:13-20).

We have already seen the manner in which 1 John considers the message heard at baptism to be an oil of anointing when it is interiorized and allowed to produce its effect in the believer. The same can be said of the "seed of God" that abides in the believer: "All who are born of God do not commit sin, because his seed abides in them and they cannot sin because they are born of God" (1 Jn 3:9).

Ignace de la Potterie offers the Greek patristic interpretation of these words: "The seed of God is an interior force through whose action the soul ceases to be in harmony with sin; in letting itself be led by the dynamism

---

38. See, among other studies, the article on *legō* in the *Theological Dictionary of the New Testament*, vol. IV, ed. G. Kittel, trans. G. W. Bromiley (Grand Rapids: Eerdmans, 1967), 114-36.

that is in it, the soul becomes in truth incapable of choosing what is evil."
He goes on to understand the "seed" in this text to be, as it is often
elsewhere, the Word of God, specifically the baptismal catechesis. He then
concludes: "From the side of human beings, the only condition laid down
to obtain victory over sin is entire docility and submission to the teaching
and the direction of the Holy Spirit."[39]

The conviction that the word of truth makes Christ present in the
believer, and that Christian moral effort is the attempt to yield more and
more completely to this effective revelation, is at the root of the hortatory
passages in the New Testament. As Rudolf Schnackenburg expresses it:
"Christian preaching is not merely moral exhortation with a religious
aspect; it proceeds, rather, from God's effective saving activity in regard
to human beings."[40] Sometimes the Christians are reminded of the work
of God in them through baptism, as in Romans 6:1-14, though even in this
context Paul says that his audience was freed from slavery to sin because
they obeyed from the heart the "pattern of teaching to which you were
entrusted." Sometimes, as we have seen, appeal is made directly to the
good news they have heard: "through it you are being saved if you hold
fast to the word I preached to you; otherwise you believed in vain" (1 Cor
15:2). It is because of the dynamic and effective power of what is believed
and appropriated, the event itself of Christ in and through the word, that a
criterion of correct belief is a life in keeping with the full implications of
the good news. As a person allows the power of the death and resurrection
of Christ to have sway in all of his or her life, the word planted there
through the twofold act of God, presenting the event-revelation as well as
enlightening and moving the person to welcome it, will produce a changed
life. When the essence of "thinking with assent" reaches its full power we
have the experience and evidence of the fact that "you have put on the
new self, which is being renewed, for knowledge, in the image of its
creator" (Col 3:10).

The Early Patristic Era as Setting the Form for Theology

I have tried to show that the New Testament witnesses to a certain state of
awareness of God in Christ. We can catch a glimpse of this in the narrative

---

39. "L'impeccabilité du Chrétien d'après I Joh. 3,6-9," in *L'Évangile de Jean:
Études et Problèmes,* Recherches Bibliques, 3 (Desclée de Brouwer, 1958), 161-78.
The two citations are from pp. 162 and 167, respectively.
40. *Die Johannesbriefe,* 163.

worlds created by the gospel writers. It is more clearly perceived in the discursive texts, and it is obvious in the manner in which the New Testament speaks about the mystery and formulates creedal and catechetical material. The reality known and accepted by faith becomes a dynamic and life-changing force for those who assent to it. This state of awareness is rightly called knowledge and can be expressed in judgments.[41] It is the type of knowledge that can only be investigated by what Paul Ricoeur felicitously calls "the hermeneutics of testimony."[42]

My purpose in this brief section is to show that there is a continuity between the New Testament writers and those who came immediately after them. While these latter progressively conferred upon the New Testament writings a special authority, they did not consider them to be the only works that were "inspired." It was because these writings expressed the widespread "rule of faith," were consistently read at the liturgy throughout the church, and were in continuity with the apostolic faith and authority that they were recognized to be canonical, a particular instance of the Spirit's teaching action.[43] In this section I will consider some examples of the continuity between the characteristics of the New Testament understanding of faith and its communication and the period that immediately followed.

The *Didache*

One of the earliest examples of Christian prayer, found in connection with the Eucharist in the *Didache,* speaks three times of God's action in making something known *(gnōrizein):*

> We give thanks to you, our Father, for the holy vine of David your servant which you made known to us through Jesus Christ your servant. . . . We

41. I insist on the fact that these statements clearly indicate that there is a judgment being made, because in the judgment truth or falsity can be found. For a discussion of this point see J. R. Price, "The Objectivity of Mystical Truth Claims," *The Thomist* 49 (1985): 81-98.

42. See the essay by the same name in *Essays on Biblical Interpretation,* ed. Lewis S. Mudge (Philadelphia: Fortress, 1980), 119-54. Ricoeur is reflecting on the question posed by Jean Nabert, "Does one have the right to invest with an absolute character a moment of history?"

43. For a more ample discussion of this point one may consult: T. Hoffman, "Inspiration, Normativeness, Canonicity, and the Unique Sacred Character of the Bible," *Catholic Biblical Quarterly* 44 (1982): 447-69; Francis Martin, "The Biblical Canon and Church Life," in *Recovering the Sacred: Catholic Faith, Worship and Practice,* Proceedings of the Twelfth Convention of the Fellowship of Catholic Scholars, ed. Paul Williams (Pittston, Pa.: Northeast Books, 1990), 117-36.

give thanks to you, our Father, for the life and knowledge which you
made known to us through Jesus Christ your servant. . . . We give thanks
to you, holy Father, for your holy name which you have caused to dwell
in our hearts, and for the knowledge, faith, and immortality which you
made known to us through Jesus Christ your servant.[44]

The repeated use of a term that in the New Testament often has overtones
of revelation (Lk 2:15; Jn 15:15; 17:26; Rom 16:26; Eph 1:9; 3:3; Col
1:27) is not without its significance here. By thanking the Father for his
revelatory action through Jesus Christ, the believers are acknowledging
that God has acted in such a way that their awareness of reality is different
— they know something they did not know before.

First Clement, Ignatius, Barnabas, and Epistle to Diognetus

The same awareness that faith is a response to revelation and thus has a
specific noetic content can be found in all of the early literature. Thus, in
1 Clement (ca. A.D. 96) the Corinthians are reminded of their former "mature
and stable knowledge" (1,2). Later their coming to salvation is described as
coming about through Christ: "Through him the eyes of our heart were
opened, through him our ignorant and darkened mind blossoms *(anathallei)*
into the light; through him the Master willed to have us taste immortal
knowledge" (36,2; see also 40,1; 48,5). In the letters of Ignatius (ca. A.D. 110)
we find as a constant theme Ignatius's own awareness of the action of the
Lord in his life. In addition, we have two texts that may be summaries of
creedal statements[45] and the notion that the Philadelphians are "children of
the light of truth" (*To the Philadelphians* 2,1). The *Epistle to Diognetus* (ca.
A.D. 125), besides speaking of the mysteries revealed to Christians by God
(4,6; 7,1-2; 10,7; 11,2.5; and especially 8,10) concludes (12,1-9) with an
exhortation to acquire true knowledge and a description of what that is. In the
Epistle of Barnabas, written about the same time, we read of the virtues such
as fear, patience, and self-control, which protect "wisdom, understanding,
insight and knowledge" (2,3). Again, Christians are described as possessing
"the perfection of our knowledge" (13,7) some of whose attributes are later
described as "the way of light" (19,1-12).[46]

44. *Didache* 9,2–10,2. The date of this document is not agreed upon, but most
commentators date it before the end of the first century.
45. *To the Trallians* 9,1-2; *To the Smyrnaeans* 1,1-2; *Sources Chrétiennes* 10,
100-02; 132.
46. This investigation into early Christian literature could be extended to include
not only such works as *The Letter* of Polycarp, the account of his martyrdom, *The*

The Apologists

The bridge between this early literature and the intellectuals of the late second century and beyond is formed by the so-called apologists. The activity of these writers is significant since they were the first to bring the knowledge they possessed through faith into relation with the world of thought and political existence that surrounded them. The characteristic all these men had in common was the conviction that what they had received was a view of reality that could commend itself to anyone and was available to anyone who accepted the gospel. While the light of faith is necessary in order to perceive the world, human life, and history as they really are, this light is denied to no one who asks for it and who is ready to accept what God has revealed of himself in Jesus Christ. Among the earliest extant examples of such writing are the *Apology* of Aristides of Athens and the *First Apology* of Justin, both of which were probably addressed to the Emperor Antoninus Pius (died 161);[47] the *Second Apology* of Justin (probably addressed to the Roman Senate under Marcus Aurelius); and Justin's *Dialogue with Trypho,* the oldest existing apology that treats the relationship between Christianity and Judaism. There are as well the *Epistle to Diognetus* already mentioned;[48] the work of Athenagoras of Athens, who addressed his *Supplication (Presbeia) for the Christians* to Marcus Aurelius and to his son Commodus (ca. 177); the writings of Justin's disciple Tatian; and those of Theophilus of Antioch and Melito of Sardis.[49]

Generally, the apologies addressed to the emperors treat three points: (1) Christians are being persecuted without due process of law; (2) accusations made by popular public opinion are calumnious; and (3) the Christian understanding of divine things and of human history is obviously superior to that of the pagans. It is in discussing this third point that we see the

---

Shepherd of Hermas (not very helpful in this regard), *The Odes of Solomon* (quite useful; see especially Ode 12), the Christian redactionary activity in the *Sibylline Oracles,* the early Acts of the martyrs, Christian tomb inscriptions and poetry, etc. In nearly all of these one can find evidence that faith was looked upon as a divinely conferred and very specific way of looking upon reality, that is, could be expressed in specific terms whose fundamental point of reference was the life, death, and resurrection of Jesus Christ and the continuance of this mystery in the church.

47. There are still scholars who, in accord with Eusebius (*Ecclesiastical History* 4,3,2), presume that the Emperor addressed by Aristides was Hadrian (117-38).

48. The name Diognetus may be an allusion to Hadrian, though the date of the letter may also be quite a bit later.

49. Melito is famous for his *Homily on the Passion,* but he also wrote an *Apology* addressed to Marcus Aurelius that is lost but for a fragment preserved by Eusebius in his *Ecclesiastical History* (4,26,7-8).

apologists' particular development of a line of thought whose origins are to be found in the Jewish confrontation with the same milieus. The apologists' position on the uniqueness of God the Creator, the folly of idolatry, and the moral superiority of the way of life outlined in the Scriptures is sometimes elaborated in a manner much like that of the Jewish apologists and philosophers, and depends at times upon their arguments.[50] What is, of course, peculiarly their own is their insistence on the fact that God has revealed himself in a unique and definitive way in Jesus Christ, whose teaching and life are a light to the world, whose death has brought liberation for the whole world, who has been raised from the dead, and who will come again to confer upon those who believe in him an eternal life with God.

The interesting point for our consideration here is that the apologists often referred to their vision of reality and the way of life that flows from it as a "philosophy," and some of them, including Aristides, Justin, and Tatian, wore the *pallium,* a cloak characteristic of the Greek philosophers. They never thought that their Christian faith was something that they had achieved by their own efforts or investigations, yet they saw it as the complete understanding of reality that was capable of producing in those who submitted to it a life free from the confusion and error they saw in the best of their contemporaries, and that, moreover, lifted from human beings the fear of death.

> The Christians more than any other nation on the earth have found the truth. They know God, the Creator and Fashioner of the Universe, in his Son Jesus Christ and the Holy Spirit, and they do not worship any other God besides this. They guard the commandments of this same Lord, Jesus Christ, engraved on their hearts, and these they keep, looking forward to the resurrection of the dead and the life of the age to come. They do not commit adultery or fornication. . . . Those who wrong them they exhort and try to make them friends. They are eager to do good to their enemies, they are meek and forbearing. . . . If they see a stranger they take him under their roof and rejoice over him as really a brother. . . . They are ready to lay down their lives for Christ. They keep his commandments without wavering, living holy and righteous lives as the Lord

---

50. The necessity of defending the teaching of the Jewish position was clearly perceived by Origen, who does not hesitate to refer to works that antedate his own, including Josephus's *Against Apion.* See Nicholas de Lange, *Origen and the Jews: Studies in Jewish-Christian Relations in Third Century Palestine,* University of Cambridge Oriental Publications 25 (Cambridge: Cambridge University Press, 1976), esp. chapter 6.

their God ordered them. . . . Certainly, this is the way of truth which leads those who travel on it to the eternal kingdom promised by Christ in the life to come.[51]

These remarks, while rhetorical in the sense that they are attempting to persuade, are nevertheless meant sincerely to portray the way of life of committed Christians. Similar descriptions can be found in other authors; Justin places a particular accent on the fact that at baptism the believer receives an empowering enlightenment that makes what has been already received become effective and able to change one's life. Describing baptism in his *First Apology* (par. 61), Justin recounts how those who have been "made new" *(kainopoiēthentes)* through Christ first acknowledge that "they are persuaded and believe that the things taught and said by us are true and they promise that they are able to live them." Then, after fasting and prayer on the part of all concerned, the one to be baptized is brought to a place where there is water in order to be born anew *(anagennēsis)* "in the name of the Father of the Universe, the Master and God, and of our Savior Jesus Christ, and the Holy Spirit." He goes on to say: "This bath is called 'enlightenment' *(phōtismos)* as enlightening the minds of those who have learned these things."[52] A few paragraphs later, describing the Eucharist that follows the baptism, the newly baptized is called "the one enlightened," while in the *Dialogue with Trypho* the whole process of faith seems to be designated by the term.[53]

Justin's use of the notion of enlightenment reflects the New Testament, where words related to the root *phōs* are also used of the activity of God in the believer, presenting the act of revelation in history and conferring the light that allows one to participate in that act consciously and with understanding. As we have seen, Paul attributes "the enlightenment" *(phōtismos)*, which is the knowledge of the glory of God on the face of Jesus Christ, to an act of God that resembles the creation of light at the beginning (2 Cor 4:6). This contrasts with the action of the god of this world, who blinds the minds of those who do not believe in order to prevent the enlightenment, which is the gospel of the glory of Christ, the image of God, from shining forth (2 Cor 4:4). Other significant New Testament uses of the concept that Christian faith is an enlightenment are Ephesians 1:18 ("with the eyes of your heart having

51. From the Greek fragments of the *Apology* of Aristides 15,3-9, published by Daniel Ruiz Bueno in *Padres Apologetas Griegos,* Biblioteca de Autores Cristianos, 116 (Madrid: BAC, 1954), 130-31.

52. Ruiz Bueno, *Padres Apologetas Griegos,* 250-51.

53. The first reference is in the *First Apology* 65,1 (Ruiz Bueno, 256), and the second is in *Dialogue with Trypho* 122,5 (Ruiz Bueno, 515).

been opened to *know* . . .*"*); 3:9 ("to enlighten everyone as to what is the mystery hidden in God from ages past . . ."); 5:14 ("Awake sleeper, rise from the dead, and Christ will shine upon you"); 2 Timothy 1:10 (". . . bringing life and immortality to light through the gospel"); and Hebrews 6:4 and 10:32, both of which seem to refer specifically to the baptismal catechesis and rite. The use of "enlightenment" terms to refer to faith and baptism was to have an important history in the early church.[54]

In the apologists, and particularly in Justin, we encounter a functioning of the mind that is able to see all reality focused in the light of faith. All these writers witness to the fact that faith is a way of knowing; they speak of knowledge and of enlightenment, and they presume that their vision of the universe and of history is capable of being mediated to others in such a way that they too would be willing to believe in God and thus receive from him the same enlightenment. Instructive in this regard is Justin's account of his conversion in the *Dialogue with Trypho* (2,3–8,2). After praising philosophy, he recounts his journey through various systems of thought until, as a Platonist, he meets an old man who by means of Socratic questioning leads him to see the contradictions in his thought, then speaks to him of the prophets who were friends of God and who, inspired by the divine Spirit, announced things that have since come to pass. The elder says of them that they were "witnesses of the truth" *(martyres tēs alētheias)* worthy of credence, who composed their works without recourse to proof *(apodeixeis),* though not without a righteous life and miracles.

In this stylized account of what was most probably a real dialogue, Justin is endeavoring not only to recount his own conversion but to lead others to the same commitment. As he tells it, the elder leads him through a dialectical use of his mind to a point where Justin must exercise the "hermeneutics of testimony" in regard to what he calls the "witnesses of the truth." That is, he must think with assent — he must yield to something that is attractive and satisfying to his desire for truth but that will neither subject itself to his need for mental control nor impose itself as compelling evidence. He must believe. In fact, he did believe. The old man left him and, as he tells us:

> All of a sudden a fire was kindled in my soul and a love for the prophets and those men who are friends of Christ took hold of me. Pondering the old man's words within myself, I found that this philosophy alone was solid and profitable. Thus, and for these reasons, I am a philosopher.[55]

54. See A. Segovia, *La iluminación bautismal en el antiguo cristianismo* (Granada: Camacho, 1958).
55. *Dialogue* 8,1-2 (Ruiz Bueno, 314-15).

For Justin, then — and here he is merely articulating the conviction of his Christian contemporaries — faith completes the mind's capacity for truth. It is a prophetic interpretation of reality.[56] It is for this reason that he can maintain that whatever anyone has uttered rightly is part of the Christian heritage, since we know, adore and love the Word whose seed and imitation is found in all true things and who has entered human history in Jesus Christ.[57]

I have spent a great deal of time on Justin in order to pinpoint the way faith functioned in the minds of the early Christians, particularly those who confronted the vision of reality embraced by their contemporaries, which still formed part of their own outlook. Before trying to sum up this activity in terms such as "mystical," "theological," or "popular," I would like to take a brief look at the three men generally recognized as the founders of what we call theology: Irenaeus, Clement, and Origen.

Irenaeus, Clement, and Origen

Irenaeus

Irenaeus was thirty-five years old when Justin was beheaded in Rome along with several companions in the year A.D. 165. Hans Urs von Balthasar, upon whose study I am largely relying, notes that Irenaeus needed Justin in order to attain the heights he reached in much the same way that Mozart drew on Christian Bach.[58] In addition to possessing a greater intellectual and spiritual vitality, Irenaeus was faced with a system of thought that confronted Christianity with a competing vision of reality but used some of the same elements as Christianity itself. "Gnosis was the opponent Christian thought needed in order fully to find itself."[59] The poetic philosophy of Gnosticism comprises

---

56. I owe this phrase to Walter Kasper in *The God of Jesus Christ*, trans. Matthew J. O'Connell (New York: Crossroad, 1984), 67: "In the background of this unreflective yet extensively practiced natural theology there is a conviction that is basic to both the Old and New Testament: the conviction that the order of creation and the order of salvation fit together. The Bible understands the revelation given in the course of salvation history as being a prophetic interpretation of reality."

57. *Second Apology* 13,1-4 (Ruiz Bueno, 276-77). This whole part of the *Apology* is a development of Justin's notion of the *logos spermatikos*.

58. *The Glory of the Lord: A Theological Aesthetics*, vol. II: *Studies in Theological Style: Clerical Styles*, trans. A. Louth, Fr. McDonagh, B. McNeil; ed. J. Riches (San Francisco, New York: Ignatius, Crossroad, 1984), 31-94.

59. Ibid., 32.

mental constructs endowed with reality only by the imagination of the master and disciple, who seek peace and assurance in an elaborate discipline of thought. The complexity of the system and the intricacy of its demands often serve to hide the fact that beneath a surface of self-surrender lies a categorical refusal to trust anything but one's own mind. Irenaeus studied these systems with a thoroughness that is still exemplary, and his response was based on one simple principle: in the light of the Creator shining with unique brilliance in Jesus Christ we can understand the meaning and direction of all that is. Irenaeus counters thought with existence, anxious theories with the revealed Love that is the source of being.

> Truth helps us to faith, for faith's object is the things which really are, and so we believe in things as they are and by believing in things as they are, we retain ever after our firm conviction of them. And since our faith is the basis of our salvation, we must take trouble over it to see that it gives us a true understanding of the things which exist.[60]

Faith is the light that gives a true understanding of that which exists. God who has revealed himself in the material universe, in the history of humankind, and especially in the human history of Jesus Christ, confers the ability to understand these things as they are. Once again we see that revelation is, to adapt the words of Jean Nabert's question, the manifestation of the Absolute within the confines of the contingent. To ignore this manifestation is to die of sloth; to flee its material confines in a self-willed search for the Transcendent is to become lost in Gnosticism. The core of Irenaeus's thought is that revelation, the manifestation of the Absolute in history, *is still going on*. We can see it in the power of the cross and resurrection of Jesus Christ, who, in and through the church, is still in the process of summing up and recapitulating all things in himself. Irenaeus's insight is particularly relevant to the question with which this book is concerned, and we will return at the end of our study to consider it more at length.

Clement

Just fifteen years before Justin died, Clement was born in Athens. After a search not unlike that of Justin, he became a Christian and the disciple of the famous Pantaenus at Alexandria. There is no need to belabor Clement's intellectual faith or his enthusiasm for philosophy. I wish only to cite a few

---

60. *The Demonstration of the Apostolic Teaching,* 3. Translation is from von Balthasar, *The Glory of the Lord,* vol. II, 45.

of his texts that illustrate the two points I am making here: (1) faith is the light that changes the mind of the one who believes and provides an understanding of reality, and (2) this faith is basically the same in all believers although it does not exist in the same intensity in everyone. That faith is what makes someone a true gnostic is a constantly recurring theme in Clement. After discussing the fact that no one can name God or rightly express him, and thus no one can grasp the rest of reality adequately, Clement then speaks of the Word who has made God known. He concludes: "It remains that we understand the Unknown by divine grace and by the Word alone that proceeds from him."[61] He says again: "We define wisdom as certain knowledge, a sure and unbreakable gnosis of divine and human realities, comprehending the present, past and future, which the Lord taught us both through his presence and through the prophets."[62] The possession of this wisdom marks someone as a gnostic, yet it is but the full development of what was conferred at baptism. Indeed, for Clement, it is the same Logos, the *philanthropos,* "eager to bring us to perfection," who has laid out a splendid program by which he first is the one who converts us and then becomes our teacher.[63] What is brought about in the Christian gnostic is thus an intensification of what is begun at conversion: "The life of the Gnostic is, in my view, no other than the works and words which correspond to the tradition of the Lord."[64] When we add to this Clement's teaching on the role of the church, his exhortation to the practice of humility, and his esteem for the sacraments, we see that, as McGinn expresses it, "Belief, not gnosis, is the key to salvation."[65]

Origen

Origen was some thirty-five years younger than Clement and shared in the same Alexandrian milieu, though he probably was never Clement's dis-

---

61. *Stromata* 5,12,82,4 (*Sources Chrétiennes* 278,161). Clement is explicitly basing himself on the text in Jn 1:18 ("No one has ever seen God, the Only Begotten God . . . has made him known") and concludes this section by quoting Paul's words to the Athenians: "What you worship but do not know — this is what I now proclaim" (Acts 17:22-23). In *The Pedagogue* 1,7,57,1-2 Clement says it was the Word who wrestled with Jacob and refused to give his name. Nevertheless Jacob declared that he had seen the face of God: "The face of God is the Logos through whom God is revealed and made known" (*Sources Chrétiennes* 70,212).

62. *Stromata* 6,7,54. Translation is that of Bernard McGinn, *The Presence of God: A History of Western Christian Mysticism,* vol. 1, *The Foundations of Mysticism* (New York: Crossroad, 1992), 104.

63. *The Pedagogue* 1,3,3 (*Sources Chrétiennes* 70,112).

64. *Stromata* 7,16,104. *The Foundations of Mysticism,* 104.

65. *The Foundations of Mysticism,* 104.

ciple.[66] The themes we saw in Clement occur in Origen with greater clarity and intensity, though with a vocabulary that is at once broader and more circumspect. The notion that revelation is a free work of grace enabling the believer to understand and correctly interpret reality is a constant in Origen. In keeping with nearly all his predecessors, he insisted that, though God remains incomprehensible both before and after the revelation brought by the Word, this revelation, brought to completion in the Incarnation, has given us genuine knowledge of God and a capacity to share in his light. Origen is at once the towering intellectual ascetic who insists on the glorious light brought to humankind by the Word and the humble believer who loves Jesus with an affection only equally expressed later by Bernard and Francis.

This is the man who spent a large part of his life preaching to ordinary people in the church and often repeating to them that his only desire was to share with them the treasures the Lord had entrusted to the church.

I want to be a man of the Church. I do not want to be called by the name of some founder of a heresy, but by the name of Christ, and to bear that name which is blessed on earth. It is my desire, in deed as in spirit, both to be and to be called a Christian.[67]

It is not a difficult task to establish that for Origen true knowledge of God comes through the revealing action of the Word and is received by faith, which is itself a gift from God. It is also plain from many passages in his writings that this faith is shared by all who belong to the church, though it is found in degrees that correspond to the intensity with which each believer has yielded to the life-changing light that is granted them.

The Word enlightens all men: "But the Savior, who shines on beings with intellect and sovereign reason, that their mind might look upon their proper object of vision, is the light of the world."[68] Although some correct

---

66. In addition to the splendid pages on Origen in the work by McGinn (*The Foundations of Mysticism*), the reader is referred to the study by Henri Crouzel, *Origen: The Life and Thought of the First Great Theologian*, trans. A. S. Worall (San Francisco: Harper and Row, 1989). Of particular importance in this latter work is chapter 6, "The Doctrine of Knowledge."

67. *Homilies on Luke* 16,6 (*Sources Chrétiennes* 87,244). For a good discussion of the importance of the title "man of the Church" in Origen and his successors, see the same volume of *Sources Chrétiennes*, 111, n. 2. The above translation is taken from *Origen: Spirit and Fire; A Thematic Anthology of His Writings*, ed. Hans Urs von Balthasar, trans. Robert J. Daly (Washington: The Catholic University of America Press, 1984), Frontispiece. Von Balthasar's introduction to this volume is probably still the best short treatment of Origen's thought.

68. *Commentary on John* 1,24 (*Spirit and Fire*, #132).

things can be known about the divine, true knowledge of God comes about through the initiative of the Word: "When the Word of God says: 'No one knows the Father except the Son and anyone to whom the Son chooses to reveal him' (Mt 11:27), he is affirming that it is only by divine grace, and not without God coming to the soul by way of a certain divine inspiration, that one comes to know God."[69]

All believers hold in common the life and faith that come to us through the church in its preaching and sacraments, particularly baptism. "You have to leave Egypt, and having left Egypt, pass through the Red Sea in order to be able to sing the first song, 'Let us sing to the Lord, he has been gloriously magnified' " (Ex 15:1).[70] Thus does Origen begin his analysis of the six sacred songs that lead to the seventh, the Song of Songs. The allusion to baptism in his discussion of the first song is unmistakable, though he would be far from thinking that this would apply to someone who was not taking baptism seriously. Starting from this point, Origen, who is addressing an ordinary gathering of the faithful, goes on to encourage his audience to listen to this song, so that even if they are not able to say to the Lord what the bride says and hear what she hears, they may perhaps join the Bridegroom's companions or at least the maidens in the bride's retinue who share in her joy. It is clear that for Origen the initial grace of faith and baptism is the foundation of all the rest: anyone who turns to the Lord will be able at least to share in the joy of the Church as she hears the voice of the Bridegroom. And if, whoever they are, they obey that voice and lay aside all else, yielding to and enabled by its invitation, they will come to an intimate and transforming union with the Word of God.

The Golden Age of Christian Thought

In the period from the fourth to the seventh centuries, the initiatives begun in the first three centuries flowered into a "Golden Age" associated with the names of Augustine, the Cappadocians,[71] Chrysostom, Gregory, Leo,

---

69. *Against Celsus* 7,44 (*Spirit and Fire*, #147).

70. *Homilies on the Song of Songs* 1,1 (*Sources Chrétiennes* 37, 2nd. ed., 67).

71. Among the Cappadocians, we should include Gorgonia, the sister of Gregory Nazianzen; and Macrina the Elder and the Younger, the grandmother and older sister of Basil and Gregory (of Nyssa). It is hard at this date to obtain an adequate idea of the influence of the latter on her brothers, though there is no reason to doubt Gregory of Nyssa's witness that the treatise *On the Soul and the Resurrection* is really the work of his sister. In general, with the exception of Monica's relation to Augustine, the present

Evagrius, Denys, and others. Studies devoted to these thinkers could substantiate what has been established so far in regard to faith being a consciously held prophetic interpretation of reality, where intensity of experience and expression varies but where essence remains an assent to divine
truth on the basis of divine light.[72] I wish merely to point to the intimate
connection between what would later develop into "speculative," "pastoral," and "monastic" theology. To illustrate my point, I will select two
men of this period, both bishops, both devoted to the monastic life, and
both capable of refined speculative thought: Diadochus of Photike and
Augustine of Hippo.

Diadochus

Little is known of Diadochus's life (400–468).[73] His extant works include
One Hundred Chapters on Gnosis, Homily on the Ascension, The Vision,
and *The Catechesis.*[74] Typical of the thought of Diadochus is the very first
of the ten definitions that precedes the *Hundred Chapters:* "Faith is dispassionate understanding *(ennoia apathēs)* of God." First, faith is a mental
activity: *ennoia* implies an insight or an understanding. Second, this is
without disordered emotional accompaniment: *apathēs* and *apatheia* express a notion dear to early monastic thinking. They describe not a state
of unfeeling — Diadochus insists on this — but a lack of what we would
call compulsive thinking, being dominated by one's emotional complexes.
The desire for a tranquil interior in order to commune with the Beloved

---

state of research does not allow us to give an adequate estimate of the contribution of
women to the golden age of patristic thought. It must have consisted principally in their
influence upon and instruction of the authors we do possess, since no direct literary
evidence is available.

72. In addition to the individual monographs existing on each one of these
figures, one may consult the studies of McGinn and von Balthasar already mentioned,
and the bibliographical material given in each.

73. For what follows I am indebted to the introduction and comments on the
text of Diadochus's work edited and translated by Édouard des Places in *Sources
Chrétiennes* 5, and the treatment by Johannes Quasten in *Patrology,* vol. III, *The Golden
Age of Greek Patristic Literature, From the Council of Nicea to the Council of Chalcedon* (Westminster, Md.: Newman, 1960), 509-13. See also McGinn, *The Foundations
of Mysticism,* 144-57; and Irenée Hausherr, *Leçons d'un contemplatif. La Traité de
l'Oraison d'Evagre le Pontique* (Paris: Beauchesne, 1960).

74. All of these are found in the volume edited by des Places mentioned previously. The authenticity of *The Catechesis* is controverted. For the English translation
of the *Hundred Chapters* I usually follow that found in *The Philokalia,* trans. and ed.
G. E. H. Palmer, Philip Sherrard, and Kallistos Ware, vol. 1 (London: Faber and Faber,
1979), 252-96.

led many fervent Christians to an authority over their "thoughts," that is, those basic imaginative patterns deriving from sinful disorders in the personality that in turn give rise to angers, fears, and lusts and their expression. Although the ideal was first articulated by pagan philosophers, the Christians saw in *apatheia* the power of the Cross to put habit patterns of sin to death. It is in this sense that Evagrius could enunciate the famous dictum: "If you are a theologian *(theologos)*, you truly pray; and if you truly pray, you are a theologian."[75] If you speak of God in a way that comes from personal knowledge, then your prayer is pure and your interior is dispassionate — you truly pray. Diadochus expresses it this way:

> Spiritual discourse *(logos pneumatikos)* fully satisfies our intellectual perception, because it comes from God through the energy of love. It is on account of this that the intellect continues undisturbed in its concentration on theology. It does not suffer then from the emptiness which produces a state of anxiety, since in its contemplation it is filled to the degree that the energy of love desires. So it is right always to wait, with a faith energized by love [Galatians 5:6], for the illumination *(phōtismon)* which will enable us to speak. For nothing is so destitute as a mind philosophizing about God when it is without him.[76]

Diadochus was a contemplative and a mystic, a father to the monks in his care, and a theologian with great intellectual acumen. He was also a zealous bishop who had a real love for those entrusted to him. Although his talents were more than ordinary, no one saw any contradiction in these multiple aspects of his life and their center in this theology: "Gnosis comes through prayer, deep stillness and complete detachment, while wisdom *(sophia)* comes through humble meditation on the words of God and first of all through the grace given by God."[77]

Augustine

If there are illusions that every church leader in the patristic era was a mystic, a pastor, and a competent theologian, Peter Brown's *Augustine of Hippo* will dispel them.[78] Many of those involved in the controversies of that time were not theologians in any sense of the term; however, using

---

75. *On Prayer,* chapter 60, *Patrologia Graeca* 79, 1179. (This work of Evagrius is under the name of Nilus.)
76. Chapter 6, *Sources Chrétiennes* 5,87; *Philokalia,* 254.
77. Chapter 9, *Sources Chrétiennes* 5,88-89; *Philokalia,* 255.
78. Berkeley and Los Angeles: University of California Press, 1967.

the concept of potential whole as a starting point, we may say that those who still maintained a minimum faith possessed the essence of theology if not the fullness of its power.

It is clear that for Augustine, whose influence on the West and its theology is incalculable, faith is a way of knowing: through the light that it confers on the mind it gives a knowledge, based on love, of God who remains incomprehensible. At the same time faith is a divinely conferred capacity empowering the mind to interpret reality correctly and the common possession of all those who accept the witness of God in the preaching of the church, particularly as expressed in the Scriptures.

In the overwhelming task of trying to fit Augustine's life work into the three categories of mystical, speculative, and pastoral theology, I have been greatly helped by Bernard McGinn's study, in which he considers Augustine's mysticism under these three aspects: (1) the soul's ascension to the experience of the divine presence; (2) the ground for the possibility of this experience in human nature as an image of the Trinity; and (3) the necessary role of Christ and the church in attaining this experience.[79] It is significant that the treatise *On the Psalms,* an important source of Augustine's mystical teaching, was delivered as sermons to his congregation at Hippo.[80]

While we must theorize the monastic connections of Diadochus, we are well informed regarding Augustine's way of life and prayer. The monastic dimension of his theology is evident in the manner he looks into his own life for verification of the truths of faith, and describes how the knowledge of God is deepened. His own life was, as it were, a laboratory where he tested out his understanding of the divine realities and discovered how and in what way they are true. At the same time, Augustine is clear that what he is describing is open to all believers. This is evident from his account of the experience of God both he and his mother shared at Ostia.[81] Although she was neither a monk nor a scholar, she obviously was more advanced in her Christian life than he, as he is careful to note in the paragraphs just preceding the account of the vision. We should also note that the experience was communal not solitary, that the other party was a woman, and that Augustine's allusive language referring to an "enclosed garden" is probably referring to the church.[82]

79. McGinn, *The Foundations of Mysticism,* 228-64.

80. See McGinn, *The Foundations of Mysticism,* and Agostino Trapè in *Patrology,* ed. Angelo de Berardino, trans. Placid Solari (Westminster: Christian Classics, 1986), 342-462, esp. 396-98. This work is considered as volume IV of the *Patrology* written by Quasten.

81. *Confessions* 9,23-25.

82. McGinn, *The Foundations of Mysticism,* 234.

Many of these same themes are present in the famous commentary or *Ennarratio* on Psalm 41 (42). The Psalmist speaks of thirsting for God as a deer thirsts for the fountains of water. Augustine asks, "Who is it that says this?" and replies that the words are ours if we wish it *(si volumus, nos sumus)*. He then goes on to apply the words to the catechumens thirsting for baptism, but points out that even after baptism there is still more for which to thirst, namely, for him with whom is the fount of life and in whose light we see light (Ps 35/36:9). We thirst to see the face of God. Augustine tells his people that there are two qualities of the deer that they should imitate in order to arrive at this vision. First, as it is a characteristic of the deer to kill serpents, so we must kill our vices. Second, it is said that when deer set out on a long journey, they walk in single file so that the head of each may be supported by resting upon the one just in front. When the leader grows tired, it changes place with another and is able thus to receive the same support. Is this not what we are urged to do when the Apostle tells us, "Bear one another's burdens and thus you will fulfill the law of Christ"? Someone, however, even after imitating these qualities, viz. mutual love and support and the elimination of sin, still exists in a state of faith and not yet that of sight. He still hears the taunt, "Where is your God?"

> I too, hearing every day, "Where is your God?" and being fed daily by my tears, have meditated on what I have heard, "Where is your God?" I too, have sought my God so that, if I might be able, I would not only believe but also see him.

Augustine then traces the search for God in the things he has made and within the soul itself, only to conclude that he cannot be seen in any of these things. Like the psalmist he must pour out his soul above itself *(effudi super me animam meam)* and attain to the "house of God." This is not directly possible, but he who has a house very high in secret places, also has a tent on earth — namely the church — which is still a pilgrim.

> I enter into the tent, this wonderful tent, up as far as the house of God. . . . God's tent on earth is the faithful. . . . I admire the obedience of its members, because sin does not reign in them so that they obey its desires, nor do they present the members of their bodies to sin as weapons of unrighteousness. . . . I pass through this and, as admirable as the members of the tent may be, I am awed when I arrive at the house of God. . . . Here is the fount of understanding, in the sanctuary of God, in the house of God. . . . Ascending the tent, the soul comes to the house of God. While it admires the members of the tent it thus is led to the house of God by following a certain sweetness, an indescribable interior hidden pleasure. It is as if a musical

instrument sweetly sounded from the house of God, and while walking in the tent he heard the interior sound and, led by its sweetness, he followed what had sounded, separating himself from every clamor of flesh and blood until he arrived at the house of God.[83]

Although there are many things that can be commented upon in these lines, I wish only to note how it sounds some of the themes we frequently have met with: faith is a way of knowing and it can mature into understanding and a deep, personal knowledge of God, who always remains hidden and attractive. This growth in faith is open to all the baptized, if they will let the power of Christ's death put sin to death in them and will earnestly love each other. Faith binds all the faithful together who thus make up the church, God's tent and the antechamber of his house. Christian discourse about God derives its authenticity from its consonance with the Mystery dwelling in the church.

Given the countless studies dedicated to the relation between Augustine's faith life and his speculative theology, I will omit any discussion of this and pass immediately on to some remarks by way of a summary of this chapter.[84]

Conclusion

In this section we have been considering a period of about 400 to 450 years when the general physiognomy of the church was achieved. I have tried to show that there was general agreement among the patristic theologians regarding faith as an act of consent to the light of revelation and that this light actually affects the believer and brings about a change in the way reality is perceived and life is lived.

Theology articulates what the light of faith makes known in a personal and appropriated manner. It is best done, therefore, by those whose lives have been transformed by the dynamics of the Word at work in them so that they know by personal experience the realities transmitted by the tradition of the church in its life of worship, its leadership and its writings. Let Clement say it for them all:

---

83. *Treatise on the Psalms,* 41,2-10; *Patrologia Latina* 36,461-71. The last lines of the translation are taken substantially from McGinn, *Foundations of Mysticism,* 239-40. For a study of the commentary on Psalm 41 (42) see Cuthbert Butler, *Western Mysticism: The Teaching of SS Augustine, Gregory and Bernard on Contemplation and the Contemplative Life* (New York: Dutton, 1923), 26-36.

84. The best treatment of this aspect is that by Agostino Trapè, *San Agostino — L'uomo, il pastore, il mistico* (Fossano: Esperienze, 1976).

Faith is, so to speak, a summary *(syntomos)* gnosis of the necessary truths; and gnosis is the solid and sure demonstration of the truths received through faith, built upon faith by the Lord's teaching, leading to an unshakable certitude and a scientific comprehension.[85]

The kind of "certitude" and "science" envisaged here are the result of "an inseparable combination of both theological demonstration and mystical contemplation."[86] It requires intellectual vigor, solid training in and understanding of philosophical insights, and a deep familiarity with the Scriptures. But it also requires a love for Jesus Christ, a personal knowledge of him, and an obedience to his active teaching within one's life, willingness to learn from the community tradition, acceptance of death to self, and the ensuing gift of humility. It is when these characterize the theologian that the full essence and the full power of theology are present. When a similar mental function is undertaken on the basis of a "summary knowledge" of what faith conveys and the church proclaims, it can be called theology in so far as the essence is present, namely a thinking with assent, but this is not what theology is meant to be any more than the lower functions of the soul can define the human soul.

It goes without saying that the people we have been considering were imperfect and capable of mistakes, sometimes serious ones. At times their philosophical knowledge was too powerful a filter for their faith intuitions; at times their cultural presuppositions allowed attitudes to perdure that were contrary to the gospel. Their work, however, was genuinely theological — it proceeded from a commonly held faith and sought understanding that was submissive to the effective power of the light they received from God. They did not despise what their predecessors and contemporaries had achieved philosophically, though they knew that these achievements only reached maturity in the light of Christ. Generally speaking, they tended to contrast their *theologia* with that of the pagan authors by insisting that theirs was a *true* knowledge of God. Theology, therefore, is knowledge, a knowledge gained in and through an action of God in the world and in the community of believers corporately and individually.[87] This notion distin-

---

85. *Stromata* 7,10,57, *Patrologia Graeca* 9,481. It should be pointed out that in Clement's mind "scientific" *(met' epistēmēs* or *epistēmonikē)* relates to what is solid, rather than to what can be established by purely human resources. The finest study of Clement's thinking in this regard is that by Th. Camelot, *Foi et Gnose. Introduction à l'Étude de la Connaissance Mystique chez Clément d'Alexandrie.* Études de Théologie et d'Histoire de la Spiritualité, 3 (Paris: Vrin, 1945).

86. McGinn, *The Foundations of Mysticism,* 104. He is summing up the thought of Camelot.

87. "What the Lord really taught us is this: no one can know God unless God

guishes the early thinkers from our modern view that considers theology as a systematically organized body of articulations about God.[88]

It is not that the theoreticians among the early thinkers were unaware of the need to articulate the knowledge of God and the universe in terms that were intelligible to non-Christian thinkers. It is simply that they saw this as part of the twofold manner that allowed the one theology to proceed. Thus Origen could say that the "sixty queens, eighty concubines and maidens without number" in the Song of Solomon 6:8 apply to the philosophies of this world, while of the knowledge of Christ it is said: "One alone is my dove, my perfect one, her mother's chosen, the favorite of the one who bore her" (Song 6:9).[89] Nevertheless, his treatise *On First Principles* implements his own teaching that the destroyed city of Heshbon, "the city of [philosophical] thoughts" must not be allowed to remain in ruins but rather its materials must be reutilized in building a Christian philosophy, that is a theology.[90] About 150 years later, Gregory of Nyssa made a similar use of biblical imagery to say the same thing: the sterile daughter of Pharaoh — philosophy — can bring us up only if we continue to be nourished at the same time by the milk of our mother, the church.[91] A similar line of thought can be found in Denys, Gregory Nazianzen, Augustine, Diadochus of Photike, and indeed all of the early Christian theologians who treated the nature of the Christian knowledge of God and its expression.[92] An important exception to this integration of

---

teaches him; in other words, without God, God cannot be known. What is more it is the Father's will that God be known." Irenaeus, *Against the Heresies* 4,6,4. Translation taken from *The Scandal of the Incarnation. Selected and Introduced by Hans Urs von Balthasar,* trans. John Saward (San Francisco: Ignatius, 1990), 45.

88. This point is made in other terms by Yves Congar in his *A History of Theology,* trans. and ed. Hunter Guthrie (New York: Doubleday, 1968), esp. 28-49. One may also consult with profit two studies by Andrew Louth: *The Origins of the Christian Mystical Tradition: From Plato to Denys* (Oxford: University Press, 1981), and *Discerning the Mystery: An Essay on the Nature of Theology* (Oxford: University Press, 1983).

89. *Homilies on Numbers* 20,3, *Patrologia Graeca* 12,731-32.

90. *Homilies on Numbers* 13,2, *Patrologia Graeca* 12,668-69. For a balanced discussion of Origen's view of philosophy see Henri Crouzel, *Origen,* 153-56.

91. *The Life of Moses* 2,12, *Sources Chrétiennes* 1 (3rd ed.), 112. The milk consists of the "usages" *(nomima)* and "customs" *(ethē)* of the church.

92. For Denys see especially his *Letter 9, To Titus, Patrologia Graeca* 3,1103, and the commentary on his work by Hans Urs von Balthasar in *The Glory of the Lord,* vol. 2, 144-210. For Gregory Nazianzen see *The Theological Discourses (Sources Chrétiennes,* 250), esp. 27,4-5; 28,6; 29,21; 31,28. Augustine's teaching on the activity of the *magister interior* is well known. One may also consult von Balthasar, 95-143. In regard to Diadochus of Photike and his teaching on enlightenment, *gnōsis,* and *sophia,* one may consult the introduction to his collected works by Édouard des Places in *Sources Chrétiennes* 5 (2nd ed.).

pagan philosophical thought can be found in the writings of Ephrem, whose hymns have set the tone for the Syrian tradition of both East and West.[93]

In regard to their sense of obligation to the church at large, we have already seen how many of these men were committed pastors and preachers. In this function their language was calculated to convey the objective act of God revealing himself in such a way that it was capable of being assimilated by their audience. Cyril of Jerusalem around the year 350 told his audience preparing for baptism, "Therefore let us seek the testimonies to Christ's Passion. For we have come together now not to make a speculative exposition of the Scriptures, but rather to be convinced of what we already believe."[94] He had already instructed them in his opening address that they should not talk about the mysteries of faith contained in the creed, since the uninitiated will make no sense of what they are saying and only be harmed in the process: "When you grasp by experience the sublimity of the doctrines, then you will understand that the catechumens are not worthy to hear them."[95] Cyril's preaching was "theology" in the sense defined by Evagrius.

In the next chapter, I wish to offer a brief analysis of the movement toward critical theology and beyond. This will provide us with the principles needed to consider feminist theology.

93. For a good presentation of Ephrem's thought see Sebastian Brock, *The Luminous Eye: The Spiritual World Vision of St. Ephrem* (Rome: C.I.I.S., 1985). As is well known, Tertullian also objected to the intrusion of "Athens" into "Jerusalem." However, Tertullian still brings a good deal of the legal oratory of the Aeropagus into the temple.

94. *Catecheses* 13,9. Translation is taken from *The Works of Saint Cyril of Jerusalem,* The Fathers of the Church 64, vol. 2, 10, trans. Leo P. McCauley and Anthony Stephenson (Washington: Catholic University of America Press, 1970).

95. *Protocatechesis* 12, *The Works of Saint Cyril,* vol. 1, Fathers of the Church, 61,80. For my treatment of St. Cyril I am indebted to the fine article by Pamela Jackson, "Cyril of Jerusalem's Use of Scripture in Catechesis," *Theological Studies* 52 (1991), 431-50.

2

The Isolation of Theology

In the attempt to understand the background for what is called "theology" today, and the influence that both the positive and negative aspects of this have upon feminist theology, I have been considering theology from two perspectives: its light and its intensity. Without the light of faith by which we can grasp what is revealed precisely as revelation, there is no theology. In this sense, everyone who believes is a theologian, and is so to the degree that he or she has actual experiential faith knowledge, conferred by God, concerning what has been handed on to be believed by the church. In actual practice, however, we bestow the term "theologian" on someone who combines this faith knowledge with a capacity to mediate it in ordered discourse. By a certain discernment of spirits the believing community has also recognized degrees of intensity in the depth and vitality of the theology thus communicated.

There are many excellent studies of the history of theology in the period from the seventh to the fourteenth centuries.[1] From these and from contact with the medieval texts themselves it is possible to isolate certain factors as significant, both positively and negatively, in the move toward a more critical form of thought. The devastation finally wrought by the Enlightenment was due to the fact that what it achieved positively was understood, by proponents and foes alike, to be at the expense of the Christian understanding of reality. That need not have been.

---

1. In addition to Yves Congar's *A History of Theology,* trans. and ed. Hunter Guthrie (New York: Doubleday, 1968), there is the work by Jaroslav Pelikan, *The Christian Tradition: A History of the Development of Doctrine,* vol. 3, *The Growth of Medieval Theology (600-1300)* (Chicago: University of Chicago Press, 1978), and specialized studies such as that of Étienne Gilson, *Reason and Revelation in the Middle Ages* (New York: Scribners, 1938), and M.-D. Chenu, *La Théologie comme Science au XIIIe Siècle,* 3rd ed. (Paris: Vrin, 1957).

In this chapter, I hope to achieve four things. First, to look at the move toward criticism in order to understand where it marks an advance in human thought and where it is deficient. Second, to look at the characteristics of the critical or modern period. Third, to note some of the directions indicated by the major theologians of our time in their effort to do for our age what the early theologians did for theirs. Finally, in this context, to consider the procedure known as correlation and its role in the theological framing of what I am calling the feminist question.

THE MOVE TOWARD CRITICISM

This section considers some of the factors that led to the initial stages of the critical age. In order to do this I will present a brief summary of three characteristics of the theology that this period inherited from the preceding centuries and that it perpetuated though modifying these characterisitics in such that they became separated from each other. The resulting separation was important in providing a transition to the period when reason, now understood as a separate and superior source of knowledge, gained its ascendancy. Thus, in addition to the enormous positive contribution of this period, we should note the negative developments. Among these are lack of popular participation in the liturgy, the separation of the monastic life from the ordinary life of the faithful, excessive clericalization, the development of the dialectical method in theology, and the rise of the universities. I will consider these in inverse order.

Three Characteristics of Theology in the Period from the Early Middle Ages until Modernity

We can sum up the characteristics of this theology as noetic, biblical, and popular. I will briefly treat each in turn. It is not my intent to present these in order to idealize an age in the church's history, but rather to try to relocate the essence of theology for our own time. In the next section I will consider how these three characteristics became less a common possession of believers and more the patrimony of different and restricted groups in the church. It should be noted that since I am tracing the trajectory that led to the isolation and diminution of the theological function in the church, I am overlooking the contribution of many great thinkers who possessed both the essence and the full power of theology. Their contribution, like that of Anselm of Bec whom we will presently consider, contained the elements that could have served to modify the trajectory, but the cultural division between theology and rest of church life was eventually too powerful a factor.

Theology and Knowledge

The fundamental conviction, based on experience, that belief in Jesus Christ confers upon the believer a new and prophetic interpretation of reality continued to be operative in this period. Yves Congar, for one, has noted that faith and reason for Anselm of Bec are not two *domains* but two *types of knowledge.*

> Rather there are two types of unequal capacities in one and the same domain, namely that of truth. . . . For him [Anselm], reason could function in two ways. First as the faculty of a man without wisdom either outside the faith or before its arrival. In this case the faculty does not attain its *rectitude* or fullness. Secondly, as the faculty of a believing and religious man on his way to celestial beatitude. The intellect in such a man is an organ of perception beyond pure faith but this side of vision. . . . Anselm's approach utilizes the power of reason such as is exercised in faith, rather in a life of loving faith, of prayer, of conversion of the entire man to the *Rectitudo* of God whereby he realizes his own *rectitudo* or truth.[2]

This view of the relation between faith and the mind became the unbroken heritage of Christian thinking until the fourteenth century. Of course it did not go unchallenged, nor was everyone equally conscious of the influence of faith upon his or her mind. It was rather that the division of knowledge into reason and faith in this period was a division between the incomplete and what completes it, not between two incommensurable disciplines.[3]

One of the characteristics of theological knowledge is that it tests all truth on the touchstone of God's revelation in the concrete reality of history, most specifically in Jesus Christ. This touchstone provided the means by which Irenaeus established that Gnosticism was false. It was applied by his successors such as Clement and Origen, who might have appeared at times to be advocating a knowledge of God in his eternal Word that

2. Congar, *A History of Theology,* 67.
3. It is sufficient to read the discussion in the *Summa Contra Gentiles* 2,4 to appreciate the sense in which the term *philosopher* continued to be understood up to the thirteenth century. Basically, Aquinas says that *philosophy* ignores the fact that the universe is created by God, who is revealing himself through it.

prescinds from the Word's appearance in history. Actually, although they appreciated and penetrated deeply into the beauty contained and conveyed in Christ, they never tried the impossible task of separating the beauty from its living manifestation.[4] For these thinkers, knowledge of Christ, even in its most mature forms, always has some link to the sacraments. The same centrality of Christ was maintained by the great scholastics: Bonaventure said that "Christ is the source-principle and the origin of every human science. As the one sun sends out many rays, so the numerous and varied sciences proceed from the one spiritual sun, the one teacher."[5] When all of Aquinas's statements are considered, this is not far from his position.[6]

Another aspect of this knowledge is its freshness and creativity. Such qualities would be expected in the newness of beginnings, yet they continue side by side with a more pedestrian kind of language throughout the history of Christianity. While no speech arises from a complete linguistic vacuum, and while the philosophical type of theology tends toward an isotopic ideal, this literature often evinces a creative use of the imagination redolent with the enthusiasm of discovery. This can be seen not only in the treatises composed during this millennium and more but also in the liturgical development, the mystery plays, and in a particular manner in the monastic literature.[7]

Theology and the Bible

Theology in this period was also biblical. I mean this in two senses. First, since the source of the knowledge is revelation, theology looks to Scripture as the instrument and authoritative literary expression of *sacra doctrina*, God's teaching action. Second, not only did biblical texts serve as authorities, but the expressions of Scripture tended to be used allusively in order to link present realities to an entire complex of themes found in the Bible.

4. There is a helpful list of patristic texts on Christ the Revealer of God in the appendix to an article by Yves Congar, "Dum Visibiliter Deum Cognoscimus: A Theological Meditation," in *The Revelation of God*, trans. A. Manson, L. C. Sheppard (New York: Herder and Herder, 1968), 67-96.

5. *Sermon 1, Twenty-second Sunday after Pentecost*. Both the citation and the translation are from von Balthasar, *The Glory of the Lord*, II, 326, n. 319.

6. For a discussion of this point see Emile Mersch, *The Theology of the Mystical Body*, trans. Cyril Vollert (St. Louis: Herder, 1952), chapters 2 and 3.

7. See Jean Leclercq, *The Love of Learning and the Desire for God: A Study of Monastic Culture*, trans. Catharine Misrahi (New York: Fordham University Press, 1974). For a sampling of the wider literature one may consult Erich Auerbach, *Mimesis: The Representation of Reality in Western Literature*, trans. Willard Trask (New York: Doubleday Anchor, 1953); Ernst Robert Curtius, *European Literature and the Latin Middle Ages*, trans. Willard Trask (New York: Harper and Row, 1953).

This practice later developed into what may be called a sacred language to be used in speaking of sacred themes.

I have already explained how revelation brings about an interpretation of reality. This view, centered in Jesus Christ, which is summed up in the creeds, may be spoken of as a biblical understanding of the universe and of history. The most primary elements of this understanding can be summed up in the notions of creation, salvation, the church and ongoing transformation, and final consummation. While these notions are often expressed within the framework of the insights and deficiencies of a particular culture, their essential truth is guaranteed when they pass the test of the touchstone mentioned above. When this fundamental outlook on the relation between God and creation is subjected to and modified by a contrary viewpoint, that is, one that is in opposition to the teaching of Scripture, then the thought is no longer biblical and therefore not theological.

The second sense in which this faith view was biblical can be exemplified in the way the Scriptures provided a way for people to understand themselves in the light of God's revelatory activity. An article by Eric Auerbach is perhaps the most adequate study of the mentality that intuitively grasped the open quality of biblical events.[8] Because these events are related to God, they can be a way of understanding one's own history. The former events are thus understood to be a *figura* of what is transpiring in the present.[9]

Figural interpretation differs from symbolic interpretation in that figural interpretation establishes a connection between two events or persons, while a symbolic interpretation, popular from the time of the Reformation, connects the historical reality with an idea, or a mystical or ethical system.[10] Figure sees events as related to one another because of their relationship to God. Symbol sees events as significant because they are expressions of a meaning. The Christ event has made God's promises to Israel present and available, though still in a manner compatible with the perduring presence of this age. Augustine described the relation between the presence of the promised realities and our position in the new dispensation by saying, "The Old Testament is the promise in figure *[promissio*

---

8. "Figura," in *Scenes from the Drama of European Literature* (Gloucester, Mass.: Peter Smith, 1973), 11-76.

9. *Figura* is preferred in the West to *typus*. The former grew and exploited its roots in both popular and rhetorical language, while the latter, though it continued to be understood and used, "remained an imported lifeless sign." Ibid., 48-49.

10. Ibid., 54-55. This same point was made in regard to the Old Testament by G. von Rad in his treatment of "Typology" in *Old Testament Theology*, trans. D. M. G. Stalker, vol. 2, *The Theology of Israel's Prophetic Traditions* (New York: Harper and Row, 1965).

figurata], the New is the promise understood in the Spirit *[spiritualiter intellecta]*."[11]

Theology and the People

The final quality of the theology I am discussing can be summed up under the notion of "popular" — it was connected to and drew from the faith life of the community that it in turn was destined to serve. It is hard for us in our individualistic mode of thought to understand how in antiquity, and particularly in Christian antiquity, the artist, the saint, the theologian, the military hero, were all considered community property. Although there were class distinctions, and these could be rigid, there was an underlying justice that exerted itself in a freedom of communication that we hardly possess today.

As we will see in subsequent chapters, the understanding that underlies this outlook is that the church is a *koinōnia* or *communio:* all are equally the object of God's free and spontaneous gift of mercy in Jesus Christ. Origen wanted only to be a priest of the church and devoted much time and energy in sharing his mystical insights with groups of very ordinary people. Augustine did the same. Ephrem was famous among other things for his innovation in composing hymns for the women to sing. "Ephrem, who proved a second Moses to women folk, taught them to sing praise with the sweetest of songs."[12] In the later period, as we shall see, when monasticism and university life had separated themselves from the life of the ordinary believer, some of the negative effects of this separation were overcome by the preaching of the friars. What characterized this thirteen-hundred-year period, however, was something that cannot be measured but only gleaned from the literature and customs of the day. It was a common intuition that the bond holding people together was deeper than a common faith practice; it was the conviction that what all Christians have is neither virtue nor wisdom but the Spirit of mercy.

Adverse Developments

As the centuries progressed, certain factors that were present from the first began to exercise an influence that set the stage for the dramatic changes

---

11. *Sermon* 4,8 (*Patrologia Latina* 38,37). It hardly needs pointing out that this view of history underlies the ancient notion of the four senses of Scripture, a teaching that is hard for modern theologians to understand or adapt. The standard work on this topic is that by Henri de Lubac, *Exégèse Médiévale. Les Quatre Sens de l'Écriture,* vols. I and II, Théologie, 41-42 (Paris: Aubier, 1959-60).

12. Poem of Jacob of Serugh on Ephrem, cited by Brock, *The Luminous Eye,* 140-41.

that took place from the fourteenth to the eighteenth century in Western thought. The story has been told often and well, and I do not wish to repeat it at any length here. My purpose is rather to look briefly at the three characteristics of theological thinking just outlined and see the problems with their development. We will see fissures that were in the structure from the beginning become cracks, and finally identifiable flaws. Once again, my perspective will be that of looking at theology from the point of view of the *fides qua,* the light by which revealed reality is appropriated, and of seeing this realized in a series of gradated actualizations that share the same essence but not the same power; that is, as a potential whole.

The Age of Faith

The most significant shift in this period is that from faith knowledge to faith culture. By this I mean the transition in the manner of conceiving Christianity itself. In the first six centuries, at least, Christianity was an alternate interpretation of the universe, of history, and of the meaning of humanity. Gradually, Christianity itself became the prevailing interpretation; it became the accepted culture. In the early period, faith provided what I have been calling a prophetic interpretation of reality. To become a Christian meant a change of mind as well as a change of behavior. Coming to faith meant understanding oneself and all of reality in a different way. The exhortations to Christians, already abundantly present in the New Testament itself and repeated in all the sermons we possess, give ample proof that there was a great deal of unevenness in the way the light of faith was accepted and allowed its full sway in one's life. Nevertheless, Christians were conscious of being different from others in their culture even if among themselves they differed greatly in insight and moral rectitude.

A Plausibility Structure   At a certain point, beginning with the official adoption of Christianity as the religion of the Empire, the understanding that came through faith and the faith community now became mediated through the forms of speech and institutions of the society at large. There was thus created, to use Peter Berger's expression, a "plausibility structure," a socially constructed world that gave meaning, as both objective expression and subjective appreciation, to individual and social existence.[13]

13. See *The Sacred Canopy: Elements of a Sociological Theory of Religion* (New York: Doubleday Anchor, 1969); also, written with Thomas Luckman, *The Social Construction of Reality: A Treatise on the Sociology of Knowledge* (New York: Doubleday Anchor, 1967).

Obviously, it requires much less individual effort and decision to live within a prefabricated social world than it does to commit to an alternative view. Thus, as Christianity became a socially established plausibility structure it could be a cultural inheritance rather than a life-changing discovery. This made for ambiguity. Constantine's reform of the Empire was greeted with an enthusiasm and a theological vision that would appall a modern Westerner.[14] The clergy became civil servants, and this was to set a pattern that existed in other forms during the Merovingian and Carolingian periods.[15]

It seemed then as though the revelation brought by the Logos would succeed in touching upon every aspect of human life, bringing it into conformity with the mind of God. At the same time, a rift was created between those who were satisfied with the socially constructed reality and those who looked for reform on a deeper and more personally appropriated level. At this point "conversion" no longer meant abandoning a pagan way of life and interpretation of reality but rather a search for a way of life that more adequately realized the commonly accepted Christian interpretation. This interpretation of conversion was adopted not only by monks but by many Christians who sought to live the gospel fully.

The commonly held plausibility structure provided the framework for the "age of faith," as the medieval period is often called. The designation is correct if we mean by it a common and objective interpretation of reality that is grounded on the Christian revelation. Thus, the term *theologize* could even refer to the evangelization of the heathen — it brought them the *fides quae creditur,* the objective content of the faith.[16] The very fact of possessing such a common vision meant that even those who divorced themselves from ordinary pursuits or whose way of life marked them as deeply committed to Christ were still understood within a common heritage. The intensity and vitality of the vision of society as a

---

*14. I am indebted in this section to the fine study by Gerhart Ladner, *The Idea of Reform: Its Impact on Christian Thought and Action in the Age of the Fathers* (Cambridge, Mass.: Harvard University Press, 1959). Augustine's *Civitas Dei* was often interpreted in the Middle Ages as a manifesto of the Constantinian arrangement. For a more nuanced view of his position see R. A. Markus, *Saeculum: History and Society in the Theology of St. Augustine* (New York: Cambridge University Press, 1988), especially chapter 3.

15. For an account of this process see studies of the history of the priesthood such as Patrick J. Dunn, *Priesthood: A Re-examination of the Roman Catholic Theology of the Presbyterate* (New York: Alba House, 1990); Kenan B. Osborne, *Priesthood: A History of the Ordained Ministry in the Roman Catholic Church* (New York: Paulist, 1988).

16. For a consideration of faith in medieval times as being primarily an objective body of knowledge see Pelikan, *The Christian Tradition,* esp. 1-8.

whole was due to those people seriously dedicated to Christ, precisely because their witness was understood, if not always comfortably accepted.

As faith knowledge became faith culture, with all the positive dimensions of such a thing in the predisposition of the mind and imagination for a total life of faith, there also occurred a specialization that ultimately became a separation. At this point fissures grew into large cracks and the vitality of faith became splintered into segments unable to sustain themselves within the integrity of a unified vision and way of life. Most significant in terms of the shift from faith as knowledge to faith as culture was the rise of the universities. I am going to reserve for the next section a discussion of the role of the universities in promoting the dialectical method. Here I wish only to accent two effects that derived from their increased importance in Europe: the divorce between contemplation and intellectual vigor, and the exclusion of women from the new centers of learning.

Contemplation Versus Science The story of how universities grew up from the initiative of the guilds of professors and students, congealing factors already present in some of the monastic and cathedral schools, is a significant one.[17] In the late twelfth and early thirteenth centuries, Paris, Oxford, and Bologna saw the rise of schools protected by the ecclesiastical and civil authorities, though not without conflicts, where eventually the faculty of arts played a foundational role, preparing students for theology, law, or medicine. The arts faculties also enjoyed an increased freedom in the consideration of philosophical issues, and this in turn impacted the manner in which theology was done. As Aristotelian thought entered the stage this philosophical mode of thought became both decisive and necessary.[18] The new world opened up by the crusades, the incursion of the new learning, and the important shift of interest and power to the cities, all brought about a change in the perception of reality, even if this still presumed the plausibility structure of former times.

Monastic humanism was unequal to the challenge of this new outlook. The very success of the golden age of Christian thought had provided such a

17. For a presentation of this phenomonon within the context of European history one may consult *History of the Church,* ed. Hubert Jedin, vol. 3, *The Church in the Age of Feudalism,* trans. Anselm Biggs, and vol. 4, *From the High Middle Ages to the Eve of the Reformation,* trans. Anselm Biggs (New York: Seabury, 1980). For its impact on theology, see Congar, *A History of Theology.*

18. For an analysis of the more profound intellectual shift this represents see Hans Urs von Balthasar, "Patristik, Scholastik und wir," *Theologie der Zeit* 3 (1939): 65-109.

firm plausibility structure that it was never questioned. The dialectical methods introduced to render the divergent opinions of the witnesses of tradition intelligible proved generally to be too much of a challenge. The optimism of an Irenaeus, a Clement, or an Augustine, based on their own appropriation of the light of the Word and their confidence in the life of the Christian community to incorporate whatever was true, gave place to a timidity and an over-reliance on what had been already established. This new movement of thought, however, was embraced by many thinkers who were "cultural Christians" rather than men affected by the kind of living faith that had characterized the leaders of an earlier age. The result was the institutionalization of a division between contemplative reflection and intellectual inquiry. Some of the early scholastics were great contemplatives, the equal of the great thinkers of the patristic age, and some of the monks and nuns were persons of intense intellectual endowments, quite capable of integrating what was being discovered. The temper of the times, however, and the simple geographical and cultural separation between cloister and city served to create a distinction between an experienced faith and an intellectual discipline. Thus, what earlier ages had looked upon as two facets of one faith activity now became two different activities; prayer was divorced from theological accountability and theology became the application of philosophy, still interpreted within a Christian plausibility structure, to venerable texts.

The Failure to Incorporate Women   The decision of the University of Paris, which was in effect by 1231, to restrict all students and masters to the clergy, a decision emulated by nearly every university in Europe (Bologna being an exception), automatically excluded women from participating in the furtherance of the intellectual life. The following remarks of Prudence Allen are informative:

> Interestingly, this shift in the access of women to higher learning may not have been as much the result of the church structure attempting to rid women of any opportunity they once enjoyed within the monastic setting as of the fact that the university was modeled upon a military conception of knighthood. Masters were sworn into their positions as knights had been into a brotherhood of arms. . . . Blanche of Castille (1182–1252), the Queen-Regent of France also played a role. . . . It is an unfortunate missed opportunity in history that Blanche of Castille did not attempt to introduce the means for women's orders to establish parallel bases in Paris in order to further their educational opportunities.[19]

19. *The Concept of Woman: The Aristotelian Revolution 750 BC–AD 1250* (Montréal: Eden Press, 1985), 416-17.

Allen's use of the term *shift* is correct. In the Merovingian period, women, particularly religious women, had already formed monasteries that were centers of learning. These were strengthened by the coming of Anglo-Saxon women called over in the eighth century by St. Boniface, "so that his clerics and the children of the nobles might be educated by them and imbued with the ministry of heavenly preaching."[20] In this period, lives of women saints were written by women who also worked side by side with men in the *scriptoria*, who recounted their religious experiences and sometimes served as peacemakers and intermediaries in civil conflict.

The Carolingian attempt to restrict women to the cloister (there had been "active religious" and "consecrated lay women") and to separate men's and women's monasteries contributed somewhat to the weakening of the general level of womens' scholarship, but it did not prevent some monasteries of women from maintaining a high standard of learning and from producing scholars of exceptional attainments. "The nunnery was a refuge for female intellectuals, as the monastery was for the male. Although the majority of nuns were at best literate, most of the learned women of the Middle Ages — the literary, artistic, scientific and philosophical stars — were nuns."[21]

Just about the time that the University of Paris was making its decision there were in Europe a whole group of scholars, philosophical theologians, and spiritual writers whose influence was exceptional. The most outstanding of these was Hildegard of Bingen, a Benedictine abbess whose attainments in many fields were exceptional, and who was the only woman of her day to be officially commissioned to preach. In addition there was Hadewijch, a Flemish Beguine and one of the most attractive of the medieval mystical authors.[22] A complete list of women scholars and reformers would be impressively long and would still overlook the many women who had begun to attend the schools in Paris and elsewhere in the period immediately preceding this.[23]

---

20. *Life of St. Boniface.* I owe this quote (though I have translated it in a slightly different manner) and much of the material on women's scholarship in the early middle ages to the excellent study by Suzanne Fonay Wemple, *Women in Frankish Society: Marriage and the Cloister 500 to 900* (Philadelphia: University of Pennsylvania Press, 1981); the quote is found on p. 177.

21. Frances and Joseph Gies, *Women in the Middle Ages* (New York: Thomas Crowell, 1978), 64. Cited by Allen, *The Concept of Woman*, 415.

22. For information and bibliographies on both Hildegard and Hadewijch, the reader is directed to the volumes dedicated to these women in the series The Classics of Western Spirituality: Hildegard of Bingen, *Scivias*, trans. Mother Columba Hart and Jane Bishop (New York: Paulist, 1990); Hadewijch, *The Complete Works*, trans. Mother Columba Hart (New York: Paulist, 1980).

23. It was in just such a context that Héloise was Abelard's disciple at the cathedral school in Paris 1108-18.

The universities, whose achievements are vital to our present civilization and whose subsequent influence on Western thought is incalculable, began by cutting themselves off from two of the most important sources of faith life in their day. And yet there was a further division created at the universities themselves. At the University of Paris, by the end of the thirteenth century, a law had been enacted forbidding the discussion of theological topics by those who taught philosophy, that is, in the faculty of arts.[24] This served to institutionalize a disjunction rather than a distinction between reason and faith, and paved the way for many similar disjunctions that are with us still, such as that between "nature" and "grace."

In the rise of the universities we see another instance in the history of Christianity in which a necessary and important advance is accompanied by a certain ambiguity, not clearly perceived at the time, but momentous in its later consequences. In this case, a common plausibility structure masked the divisions set up in theology by the tendency to limit it to the rational articulation of the faith. With the continuum between this function and the living experience of the truths of faith interrupted, there was no vital flow of energy in either direction, and both have suffered. The potential whole was divided into compartments that run the risk of dying without each other. With the elimination of the direct contribution of women to the theological process, not only was their monastic experience excluded but also a tendency to divorce the public and the private realms of life and to restrict men and women to each respective realm became enforced more and more. In terms of theology, this meant that women were not allowed to participate in the elaboration of the theological syntheses to which they could have brought important contributions. Their own faith experience suffered in turn because their lack of training inhibited them in expressing adequately what they were learning from the Holy Spirit. These tendencies were offset at the time by many other factors, but they were present to be crystallized out of the solution of their culture and to become a permanent feature of theology until very recently.

---

24. See Frederick Copleston, *A History of Philosophy,* vol. 2, *Medieval Philosophy* (New York: Doubleday Image, 1962), part II, 162; Michael Haren, *Medieval Thought* (New York: St. Martin's Press, 1985), 204. It seems as though the initiative for this injunction may have come from the Faculty of Arts itself in which the majority were opposed to Siger of Brabant and Boethius of Dacia. For a good overall view of the functioning of the University of Paris at this time see Hastings Rashdall, *The Universities of Europe in the Middle Ages,* vol. 1, ed. F. M. Powicke and A. B. Emden (Oxford: Clarendon, 1936), chapter 5.

Dialectics and the Bible

Basically, what is at stake here is the whole hermeneutical question. My objective is merely to trace, in the briefest terms, how theology moved from being the attempt to articulate what was being learned in faith to being a commentary on texts. We have seen the power and legitimacy of the figural reading of the text; it is basically an *analogia entis historici*. Very early, however, the plethora of written witnesses to the revealed truth, biblical and nonbiblical, posed a problem of interpretation. The task of the master was to interpret the texts. This he did with the aid of grammar and what logic was available, mostly through Boethius's mediation of Aristotle's *Categories* and *Perihermenias*. In time the commentaries themselves took on the nature of a genre with a life of their own.[25] Throughout this period, the works of the earlier theologians, usually designated as *sancti patres*, were collected and studied.

The first critical move consisted in applying to discordant patristic texts the methods employed in resolving conflicts in the legal tradition that had been handed down. It was most probably at Laon, under the leadership of Anselm (d. 1117), who was himself a disciple of Anselm of Bec, that the *sententiae* of the fathers were first collected and compared.[26] Peter Abelard, who was among the illustrious disciples of Anselm of Laon, is the most famous of the dialecticians who attempted by a method of *sic et non* to establish agreement among statements that did not agree *(concordantia discordantium)*. The excesses in Abelard's method drew the attention of Bernard of Clairvaux, who saw to it that Abelard was condemned and separated from Héloise. Some modern historians are less inclined to make of this incident the lurid tale of manipulation and intolerance it was once made out to be.[27]

The issue was fundamentally not that of method but of stance. When confronted with an antinomy, where does one stand, and how does one resolve it? There are three possible positions: under, above, and within. To stand under the appearance of contradiction in authoritative texts is to allow

---

25. For an example of this, see the work by E. Ann Matter, *The Voice of My Beloved: The Song of Songs in Western Medieval Christianity* (Philadelphia: University of Pennsylvania Press, 1990).

26. See Jedin, *History of the Church,* IV, 45.

27. "In this matter, culminating in the Sens condemnation of 1141, there was involved an objective and not a personal confrontation and . . . one must not speak of bad blood between the two great theologians." Jedin, *History of the Church,* IV, 47. See also Rashdall, *Medieval Universities,* vol. 1, 49-58, who perpetuates much of the older view.

that they are only contradictory to me and to accept what they say even though I cannot resolve their discordance. This is an attitude of respect and modesty, and can often be appropriate especially if the statements emanate from those who are considered to have the authority that comes from God's work of enlightenment in their lives and who are recognized by the community. This position can also be due to sloth or fear, and derive from a lack of "faith that seeks understanding."

The second stance is above the texts. It is an attempt to resolve the conflict in the light of a higher principle. Such a reaction is instinctive to the human mind that searches for a more elevated viewpoint, a higher truth, in order to put together things that are opposed at another level. It is here, of course, that a useful heuristic tool runs the risk of becoming an all-embracing epistemological position, a *general* hermeneutics that governs, if not the functioning, then at least the results of the *specific* hermeneutics of faith. This is the risk incurred by the critical stance of Abelard, who sought resolution in the laws of logic and dialectic, or that of the philosophers who submitted the expressions of faith to an ontotheology, or that of modern historical investigators who submit them to the heuristic models they construct, or of the modern philosophy of consciousness that subsumes these expressions under the horizon of the thinking subject. Despite his own lack of skill or interest in Abelard's method, Bernard saw the problem of having criteria foreign to faith judge the adequacy of faith. Abelard, however, despite his overt exhortation to the reader to "read the sacred Scriptures carefully and relate your other reading to them,"[28] did not avoid this pitfall entirely.

The third stance is within the texts. This is a faith movement that dwells in the realities talked about in the text rather than restricts itself to a consideration of what the text is saying. In this operation, faith is a light moving the believer to yield to the truth of what is revealed and providing a place to stand that "makes sense" out of what seems to be contradictory or is, to use Luther's phrase, *adversarius noster.* Of course, given the weakness of our mind and the greatness of what is to be understood, there are always failures in this function. Our own prejudices and ignorance restrict what we can understand and distort what we do understand. Yet, there is a vast difference between this operation and the preceding two. For these latter, faith is an objective norm outside of the individual by which we judge the correctness of our articulations by measuring them against what has been accepted as authoritative expressions. For the former, faith is, to repeat Aquinas's phrase, a "certain imprint of the divine knowl-

---

28. *Patrologia Latina*, 188,1760. Cited in Congar, *A History of Theology*, 51.

edge" leading us to know what is always beyond knowledge. The true dialectic of theology is between these two aspects of faith.

In the period under discussion, the advent of critical thought proved to be for some a rejuvenating principle that opened the faith in Europe to a deepening and development urgently needed by the times. For others, it was more like bacteria, undetected, yet able to affect the functioning of the theological enterprise and in some cases take it over. If we apply once again the notion of potential whole to this theology, we may say that for those who accepted faith as a norm there was a minimum theological functioning. For those in whose lives there was a conscious awareness of and submission to the power of the revealing word, theology operated to a greater fullness of its power. In a vigorous faith environment, the influence of the bacteria contributed to its health and strengthened the immune system. The problem, however, was that the very factors that could most effectively have kept the system healthy were gradually impeded from the interchange of life that both sides required.

We have seen how the universities became distanced from the more contemplative dimension of theology that the monastic life of both men and women could have brought to them. In addition, the new intellectual life was not open to the contribution of women. Thus, added to the shift from faith knowledge to a plausibility structure was the divorce between individual and community ways of approaching faith, which should have been complementary. I would like now to consider another way that theology became isolated.

The Loss of Popularity

At the outset of this chapter, I listed three aspects of this period that contributed to the decreasing effect that theology had on the general faithful. The people at large were less involved in the liturgy, in the life of serious prayer and *lectio divina,* and in the actual life of the church.

A Liturgy for Experts Basically the story of popular participation in the liturgical life of the community can be summed up in the following trajectory: from actors, to listeners, to spectators. One of the principal reasons for this movement was language. The people had difficulty spontaneously participating when the language of the liturgy was not their own. The difficulty was further increased by the growing formality of the ceremonies, the lack of catechesis after infant baptism, the weakness of the preaching, the architecture of the church buildings, with altars placed way back, the introduction of roods, and the tendency to allegorize the gestures at the

Eucharistic liturgy rather than explain them. The following lines by Erwin Iserloh describe the situation in the latter part of the high Middle Ages and give a good idea of the outcome of the trajectory just described:

> The community nature of the celebration of the Eucharist became constantly less clear, and the "private" Mass more and more preempted the field. It gradually determined the very form of the solemn Mass. . . . The liturgy was no longer understood as the service of the whole Church, whose membership was expressed in the distribution of functions among priest, choir, and community, but was a clerical or even a priestly liturgy. . . . The Mass ceased to be a proclamation of the word. The unintelligible language barred any approach by the people to an understanding. All the more importance was attached to the ritual — the external ceremonies and sacramental signs — but without the word this threatened to become a splendid but empty covering. . . . Popular piety invented substitutes for this liturgy, and then succumbed all the more easily to the danger of superficiality to the extent that they were no longer connected to the center of the mystery. . . . If there was nothing to listen to, even greater prominence was given to seeing.[29]

Growing Distance between Laity and Priests and Monks With the specialization that took place in the liturgy, the Christian community lost a place where all the baptized met and shared. This gave rise to popular piety that leaned toward individualism and lacked an instinctive biblical sense of reality. The Carolingian reforms tended to blur in the popular mind (and in the mind of many clerics) the difference between prince and important cleric, while the move toward the cities created a gap between the monks and the people, a gap partially filled by the friars. It should also be noted that the intellectual and moral condition of the country clergy was, at this time, lamentable. The division was not only between clergy and laity, but also between university or urban clergy and their rural counterparts.

The result was a general neglect of the people, who no longer had an active role in the Church, whose lives of faith had little to do with the public liturgy or even with the Scriptures in a direct manner, and who often did not receive adequate instruction.

The final effect of this on theology was that it became an intellectual discipline, taught in the universities, no longer considered dependent upon a personally appropriated faith, making little contribution to the communal life of worship and thus lacking a doxological dimension of its own, and too remote from the people to gain from their faith experience or contribute

29. Jedin, *History of the Church*, IV, 570-71.

to it. The fissures had become cracks. Theology, when practiced well, was still a splendid and important intellectual contribution to the Christian life, but it had become too narrow a pursuit to be equal to the challenges which the next four hundred years were to offer it.

THE DEVELOPMENT OF RATIONAL CRITICISM

The Nominalists

By common consent the story begins with William of Ockham. Yves Congar maintains that the medieval ideal of "faith seeking understanding" is completely absent from Ockham: "For him, there is, of course, faith on the one side and scientific knowledges or dialectics on the other. There is a certain give and take between the two, which is precisely theology. But in this give and take the extremes remain juxtaposed, heterogene, and exterior to each other."[30]

For Ockham, the intelligible content of faith is simply unknowable. Faith is opaque. The faith dealt with by theology is rather what we would call today a cultural construct, a plausibility structure. The result was to be expected: people were forced to choose between a spirituality that looked to internal experience and a logic and dialectic that dealt with the propositions concerning faith. This was the final step in the dismantling of the vision of faith as a light that provided a prophetic interpretation of all reality because it gave us a share in the very knowledge God has of himself. Once the heritage common to all believers was considered accessible only by an interior, inarticulatable experience, the cracks in the believing community that began to appear in the previous epoch began to harden into divisions. The most significant of these, for our consideration, was the division between theology and ordinary belief, particularly the maturing of that belief into a life transformed by the power of the Word.

Older theologians had maintained that the proper object of theological effort was the faith as presented in the articulations (articles) of the creed. In more modern terminology we might say that it is a consideration of the divine acts of revelation as they have been transposed from existing in narrative to being stated in proposition. It is in this sense that Aquinas cites the definition of an "article of faith" as "a taking hold [perceptio] of divine truth that leads us to the truth itself [tendens in ipsam]."[31] The movement

---

30. Congar, A History of Theology, 133-34.
31. Summa Theologiae 2-2, 1,6, sed contra: In III Sententiae 25,1,1. For a

of the mind toward intelligibility, including the expression of conclusions, is performed in virtue of the light of the *divine reality itself,* which becomes a principle of knowledge: *sacra doctrina,* for Aquinas, is, as we have seen, an imprint of the divine knowledge.[32] For Ockham, the conclusions of theology come about by the application of the light of logic to the proposition in which the article of faith is expressed. A greater difference in viewpoint could not be imagined. It was, unfortunately, this latter view that began to prevail.

The *via moderna* initiated by Ockham gained ground throughout all of Europe, so that by the end of the fourteenth century most universities had abandoned the *via antiqua* associated with Augustinianism and a decadent scholasticism and had embraced the teaching of the nominalists. The effects of this were far-reaching.

> This formidable Franciscan [Ockham] creates space even more radically for the sole sovereignty of God when, sweeping away the entire Platonic and Aristotelian tradition, he directly opposes to the yawning abyss of freedom a world which is fragmented into irrational points of reality. With this rupture within the tradition of a mediating or natural (philosophical) theology, every contemplative dimension of the *fides quaerens intellectum* is in principle removed. Theology, which now closes in upon itself, must become fideistic and can ultimately only be practical. And the Franciscan image of God — love beyond the limits of knowledge — must therefore degenerate into an image of fear (which is no longer even that of the Old Testament), since this God of pure freedom might always posit what is contrary.[33]

Because reality does not reflect God's mind, but only the decrees of his will, he could command what is now sinful, he could destroy the world as though it had never been, he can predestine to damnation, he can create

---

discussion of the origin of this definition see T. C. O'Brien, *Summa Theologiae,* Blackfriars Edition, vol. 31, *Faith,* 28.

32. "When Aquinas speaks of the effect of 'holy teaching' (which is first to last *God's* teaching and only by his free grace our human participation in such pedagogy) as being to set a kind of 'imprint' on our minds of God's own knowledge, he is speaking in a different figure of putting on the mind of Christ." Nicholas Lash, "When Did the Theologians Lose Interest in Theology?" *Theology and Dialogue,* ed. Bruce Marshall (Notre Dame, Ind.: University of Notre Dame Press, 1990), 131-47; citation is from p. 139.

33. Hans Urs von Balthasar, *The Glory of the Lord,* vol. V, *The Realm of Metaphysics in the Modern Age,* trans. Oliver Davies, et al., ed. Brian McNeil and John Riches (San Francisco: Ignatius, 1991), 20.

appearances of things that are not. From here there is a short step to the anti-reason of some of the Reformers, the ultimate reliance upon it by others, such as the Socinians, and the despair of any certitude outside of consciousness that gripped Descartes.

The two centuries that followed Ockham saw, alongside of the widespread acceptance of nominalism, the growth of a strong pietistic movement (Eckhart, Suso, Gerson), the beginning of the philological and historical criticism of texts (Pico della Mirandola, Ficino, Colet, Erasmus), the origins of modern science (Buridan, Copernicus),[34] the initial political disintegration of Europe and attempts to restore unity on every level (Nicholas of Cusa). It may even be argued that the liberation of philosophical and other thought from the hegemony of what passed for theology was a good thing, in that it allowed for a more untrammeled development.[35] The problem was not the growth in understanding of the universe and history, much less the progress in epistemological sophistication; the problem lay in the fact that all of these advances of the mind were considered to have a mutually exterior relationship to faith. The "blindness" of faith no longer lay in the fact that what it considered far exceeded the powers of the mind; it was found rather in the fact that faith had no intelligible content — it could shed no light on what was being learned and could provide no integrating and healing power to the mind. The rising human sciences and theology began, painfully, to agree on this one point: reason and faith were extrinsic to each other in the elaboration of a vision of reality.

The Reformation and Its Sequel

It was in this period that the Reformation erupted onto the scene. The integration of the light of faith and the understanding of created reality that characterized the great theologians of the first fourteen centuries had long since given way to a disgust with scholasticism, the prevalent nominalism, and the nonintellectual piety that set the tone for the age. Martin Luther's

---

34. Herbert Butterfield says of the scientific revolution that it "outshines everything since the rise of Christianity and reduces the Renaissance and Reformation to the rank of mere episodes, mere internal displacements, within the system of medieval Christendom." *The Origins of Modern Science,* rev. ed. (New York: The Free Press, 1957), 7. The truth in this statement is to be found in the fact that the viewpoint on reality that finally emerged completed the destruction of the medieval plausibility structure and remained extrinsic to the light of faith until some efforts in our own day.

35. This position is ably set forth by Frederick Copleston, *A History of Medieval Philosophy* (first published in 1972, republished by the University of Notre Dame Press, 1990). See for instance p. 314.

place in setting the direction for Reformation thought is decisive. There are passages in Luther's writings that seem to make the distinction, common in his day, between the "knowable" (the subject matter of philosophy), and the credible but not really knowable (the subject matter of theology). Although his position is actually more subtle, the ultimate result is to maintain a hermetically sealed wall between the two types of knowledge and to reduce theology to an application of grammar to the statements of faith, particularly those in the Scriptures.

> The basic distinction for Luther, therefore, is not between analogical and non-analogical discourse within theology but between theological and non-theological (or philosophical) discourse. This involves a transformation of the problem of analogy from a doctrine of analogical predication to a hermeneutical theory about the functioning of words of the same language (e.g. Latin or English) in two different universes of discourse, viz. philosophy and theology. . . . Grammatical analysis, therefore, not philosophical speculation, is the key to theological insight.[36]

It is simply impossible that the light of faith and the light of the mind without faith remain extrinsic to each other without, sooner or later, one absorbing or canceling out the other. This, according to Klaus Scholder, is exactly what happened in the wake of the division of Europe into competing camps, each claiming to be the authentic interpreter of Christianity and its traditional writings.[37] The word that most often occurs in the polemic writings of the age is *certitudo* precisely because people no longer knew how to establish it. Theology had long since, for all practical purposes, cut itself off from the contemplative and experiential dimension of faith either as *lectio divina*, liturgy, doxology, or popular piety. Having agreed that its business was with *names* not things, and that God's incomprehensibility meant his complete unknowability, it was unconsciously relying for its certainty upon a plausibility structure that, after centuries of weakening, had just fallen apart. The story of the centuries that followed down to our own has been that of a search for or a despair of certainty.

---

36. Ingolf U. Dalferth, *Theology and Philosophy*, Signposts in Theology (Oxford, New York: Blackwell, 1988), 82.

37. *The Birth of Modern Critical Theology. Origins and Problems of Biblical Criticism in the Seventeenth Century*, trans. John Bowden (London: SCM, 1990). Scholder fixes on Socinianism as the point at which previous movements in this direction finally achieved a coherent expression and furtherance.

The Socinians

Before the end of the sixteenth century a movement arose that, despite the small number of its adherents and their lack of ecclesiastical or civil power, managed to unite Catholics, Lutherans, and Reformed.[38] In 1570, Faustus Sozzini went to Rakow in Poland to join some of his fellow Italian anti-Trinitarian exiles who had begun to gather people from Poland and elsewhere into a coherent group. By the year 1605, Sozzini, with help from others, managed to produce a catechism that was translated into German and Latin within the next four years. Thus was born the Socinian problem.

Briefly put, the Socinian position was this: God and the way to salvation are radically unknowable except for the revelation that has come to us in the Scriptures. These Scriptures have been distorted both by the Papist insistence on an authority external to them and the Protestant appeal to an inner experience of the Holy Spirit. In order to defend the unique authority of the Scriptures and to protect them from the imposition of dogmas invented by theologians, which have become fixed in creeds, certain rules must be established for their interpretation. Among the imposed dogmas that must be eliminated because they are not taught by the Scriptures are: the Trinity, the Incarnation, and the Atonement.

The Socinian movement began as a biblical positivism, but was forced to elaborate hermeneutical principles for three reasons: First, there was the unrelenting polemic of its opponents; second, there was the near anarchy of opinion concerning the nature of Christianity; and third, since Scripture had come unmoored from any connection to tradition, faith experience, or community, it had to be proven self-sufficient. The first three of the four principles elaborated dealt with reading a text in its context, comparing it with other and clearer expressions, and interpreting obscure passages in the light of clear passages — still sound principles. The fourth read: "Nothing may be asserted which contradicts sound reason or contains a contradiction in itself."[39] This principle too, can be unexceptional. In practice, however, this meant that the text had to be clear on the basis of principles other than its own. In the centuries to follow, with the growth of cosmological knowledge and critical acumen, this meant that the meaning of the text was judged in the light of the horizon of the investigator who had no other light but that of his present view of reality. The divorce of theology

38. In what follows, I am particularly indebted to the work of Scholder just cited. Also helpful is Jaroslav Pelikan, *The Christian Tradition*, vol. 4, *The Reformation of Church and Dogma (1300-1700)*, 322-31.

39. As cited by Scholder, *The Birth of Modern Critical Theology*, 37.

from other activities of the mind was now complete, though this was not yet totally apparent. Two worlds existed side by side, but only one was intelligible. This one, of course, became the judge. As Klaus Scholder expresses it: "They looked for a new, clear and generally understandable way of clarifying the word and will of God, and in so doing came upon that authority which was a rising star on the horizon of the century: reason."[40]

"Reason Must Judge"

It is important to consider the growing divergence between reason and theology, and the ultimate hegemony of reason during the two centuries that followed the Reformation and Counter-Reformation since, it is precisely this heritage that stamps modern, and thus feminist, theology. An understanding of this heritage involves a grasp on modernity, and I will return to this after having traced the history of feminism. I wish here to outline how the hegemony of reason prepared for the subservience of what is termed today *religious thought*.

The Socinian controversy was still in its beginnings when a Flemish Jesuit, Leonard Lessius, published his refutation of atheism with the title *On the Providence of the Deity and the Immortality of the Soul* (Latin in 1613, English in 1631).[41] Two aspects of this study make it particularly significant. First, Lessius, a Christian and considered to be a man of prayer, was able to maintain a completely philosophical stance throughout: he shows not the slightest memory of the approach to this question as it characterized Clement of Alexandria, Irenaeus, or Augustine, for whom the Word is the radiant Light who integrates our knowledge and brings us to know the Father. Second, this philosophical work is considered to be not only practically independent of theology but a necessary prolegomenon to it. Thus, while the Socinians absorb the Scriptural witness into the judgment of reason, Lessius and his followers make it dependent upon a preliminary and separate work of reason. In either case faith is not a light that raises and intensifies the functioning of the mind, it is rather an inert body of doctrine that enables human beings to order their lives correctly.

40. Ibid., 38.
41. For a very helpful treatment of the failure of theology in this period see Michael Buckley, "The Newtonian Settlement and the Origins of Atheism," in *Physics, Philosophy, and Theology: A Common Quest for Understanding*, ed. R. Russell, W. Stoeger and G. Coyne (Vatican City State: Vatican Observatory, 1988), 81-102. This is a summary of his larger work, *At the Origins of Modern Atheism* (New Haven: Yale University Press, 1988).

Just twenty-eight years after the first edition of the Rakow catechism, René Descartes published his *Discourse on the Method of Properly Conducting One's Reason and of Seeking the Truth in the Sciences,* to be followed four years later by his *Meditations* and then in 1644 by *The Principles of Philosophy.* The "Cartesian anxiety" was made up of several components. Fundamentally, there were the extreme effects of nominalism. A material universe that depends upon what might be an arbitrary will of God can yield no reliable intelligibility — the senses cannot be trusted, and thought must begin with the thinking subject. In a Socinian manner, the utter confusion concerning ultimate truths meant that traditions cannot be relied upon, and that the isolated subject must make the final decision. Finally, the success of mathematics showed that this mode of thinking is most apt to produce certainty and must be transposed into philosophy.

Mathematics proved to be the approach that combined features of both Lessius and Descartes. Sir Isaac Newton's *Philosophia naturalis principia mathematica* (1687) provided the same certainty about the physical universe, by being able to reduce the movements of both celestial and earthly bodies to one law, which Descartes's reduction of the principles of thought to consciousness had done for the mind. Christian apologists, with Newton's approval, quickly seized the opportunity, but their results only confirmed the divorce between philosophy and Christian faith begun by Lessius.[42]

A common outlook can be discerned in the work of Newton and the apologists and philosophers who relied on him. Newton's friend and admirer John Locke not only established a representationalist epistemology that was concerned with the truth of propositions, he also applied this to the biblical text itself. Thus, Locke states that when God speaks to men, "I do not think, he speaks differently from them in crossing the Rules of language in use among them."[43] Of course, Locke understands these "Rules" to be in keeping with his own epistemological theory.[44] In the same vein, and with accents that, consciously or not, echo the Socinians, Locke stated: "No Proposition can be received for Divine Revelation or obtain the Assent due

---

42. For a good study of this period see Henning Graf Reventlow, *The Authority of the Bible and the Rise of the Modern World,* trans. J. Bowden (Philadelphia: Fortress, 1985), esp. part III, chapter 2, "Forms of Apologetic."

43. *Treatise on Civil Government,* I,46. *The Works of John Locke,* vol. 5 (London: Robinson, 1801), 245-46.

44. For a discussion of Locke's notions in this regard, one may consult F. Copleston, *A History of Philosophy,* vol. 5, *Modern Philosophy: The British Philosophers* (New York: Doubleday Image, 1964), chapter 6, "Locke (3)"; also C. Gunton, *Enlightenment and Alienation* (Grand Rapids: Eerdmans, 1985), 17-20.

to all such if it be contradictory to our clear intuitive Knowledge. . . . Whether it be a divine Revelation or no, Reason must judge. . . ."[45]

Unfortunately, the Christian minds who first confronted the new mentality were unequal to the challenge of integrating a perfectly legitimate search for an intrinsic or autonomous intelligibility of the universe based on horizontal causality with a correlative understanding based on vertical causality.

There were reasons for this. The atmosphere was stridently opposed to tradition in any form and in particular to the authority of a Christian vision of reality.[46] Then, too, the universal extent of the Newtonian explanation of the universe persuaded Christian apologists to adopt Newton's optimism that the existence of the Creator could be established by the consideration of the laws of that universe. They failed to see that by abandoning any faith view of creation, they had changed it from being a word from God to being a vestige of the Prime Mover. Thus, they tacitly accepted the position that the Christian faith neither established nor defended its own first principle, namely, the existence of God, but rather relied on natural philosophy to do that.

Modern atheism arose when it became evident that while religion needed physics to establish its fundamental principle, physics did not need religion. Thus, the Newtonian world was set on its head by men like Denis Diderot and Baron Paul d'Holbach, who correctly saw that a rather coherent explanation of the universe could be supplied by the use of Newtonian physics without any recourse to a Supreme Being. In the words of Michael Buckley, "Atheism came out of a turn in the road in the development and autonomy of physics."[47]

Most of the influences that marked the age from the Socinians to the Encyclopedists found their culminating expression in the genius of Immanuel Kant. Kant was not an atheist, though there are some remarks in the *Opus Postumum* that lead one to ask exactly what kind of a deist he might have been.[48] Some of the consequences of Kantian thought will be treated

---

45. *An Essay Concerning Human Understanding,* IV,18,5 (London: Routledge, nd), 586. I am not aware of any study that links Socinian thinking with Newton, Locke, and the Apologists, yet their thinking on the Incarnation and the Atonement is similar. Basically, they are all Deists who see the Scriptures as an important expression of the proper way of approaching and thinking about the Deity. See Reventlow, *The Authority of the Bible,* 41.

46. In addition to the works cited above, one should consult Paul Hazard's vivid description of the thought climate of the day in his *European Thought in the Eighteenth Century: From Montesquieu to Lessing,* trans. L. May (Gloucester, Mass.: Peter Smith, 1973, repr.).

47. "The Newtonian Settlement," 96. I am indebted in this portion of my paper to both of Buckley's studies mentioned previously.

48. See Italo Mancini, *Kant e la teologia* (Assisi: Cittadella, nd), esp. chapter 1,

in the following chapters. Here I would like to observe simply that the theme that "reason must judge" that characterizes this period finds a magnificent articulation in *Religion Within the Limits of Reason Alone*. This work, in its earnest respect for the idea of God and the primacy of morality, expresses once again, though in a manner profoundly affected by Christian notions, the ideal of the Greek philosophers in the age before the gospel. This time, however, the memory of Christian thought affected the manner in which this was conceived. Not only the successes but also the failures of the preceding four hundred years profoundly marked the thought of Kant and of the whole critical age that he sums up and perpetuates. Some of those failures also affect feminist theology. I would now like to consider some postcritical efforts to reestablish theology on a basis that takes into account both the successes and the failures of the critical age.

POSTCRITICAL REACTIONS

In this brief concluding section, I wish first to look at some theologians in terms of their efforts to retrieve in a *post*critical manner the precritical dimensions of theology in regard to faith as knowledge, its return to Scripture, and its opening up to the experience of the whole people of God.[49] This effort had the further consequence of reintegrating theological thought within an academic milieu. Prior to this, though there had been much theological reflection and transmission of revelation, this was effected more by the poets and playwrights than by those who called themselves theologians.[50] After that, I will look at correlation as a mode of procedure that characterizes much modern theology, including feminism, and try to assess its importance and deficiencies.

"Pensar Dio." Also Frederick Copleston, *A History of Philosophy,* vol. 6, *Modern Philosophy* (New York: Doubleday Image, 1964), part 2, 177: "Now, some statements in the *Opus Postumum,* if they are taken in isolation, that is to say, naturally tend to suggest that Kant has abandoned any notion of there being a God independently of the Idea of God."

49. Although the orientation is different, one can find close attention paid to these same three elements in the study by Avery Dulles already referred to: *The Craft of Theology,* esp. chapter 1, "Toward a Postcritical Theology."

50. Much work remains to be done in clarifying the theological contribution of Dante, Blake, the Mystery Plays, the *Chansons de geste,* etc. For a beginning one may consult Hans Urs von Balthasar, *The Glory of the Lord: A Theological Aesthetics,* vol. III, *Studies in Theological Style: Lay Styles,* ed. J. Riches, trans. A. Louth, J. Saward, M. Simon, R. Williams (San Francisco: Ignatius, 1986).

Postcritical Retrieval

Men and women whose faith and prayer marked and sustained the life of the faithful were never lacking throughout the whole period that saw the rise of the critical age. If we consider only the time since the eighteenth century, we find many living examples of the praxis of the gospel, especially in the care shown for those whose lives were impoverished by the industrial and economic upheavals. There were many contemplatives who came into living contact with the divine realities through the action of God in their lives, and many ordinary believers were being nourished on popular piety. Finally, there were some theologians who tried to understand and preach the faith within a world vastly different from the one that saw the beginnings of theology. The efforts of these latter have been recorded in several studies, and we can see there people of great faith and honesty who were for the most part still under the "sky" of the Enlightenment, accepting or opposing the consequences of the new understanding of humanity and the universe, but largely unable to question the total horizon they had inherited.[51]

After two hundred years of searching, the efforts of these theologians seemed to reach a critical mass that gave rise in Germany to dialectical theology and in France to the *ressourcement* with its *nouvelle théologie*. From this point there came as well, particularly from the Catholic theologians, an attempt to stop speaking "medieval-ese" and enter into dialogue with the critical and existential theologies of their contemporaries. I wish to look at four theologians of our century, from among a much larger group of important thinkers.[52] The four I have chosen are Karl Barth, Henri de Lubac, Karl Rahner, and Hans Urs von Balthasar. Although they differ considerably among themselves, they seem to be in accord in their understanding of the three qualities of theology I listed at the beginning of this chapter.

51. For a good account of these efforts see: Gerald A. McCool, *Catholic Theology in the Nineteenth Century: The Quest for a Unitary Method* (New York: Seabury, 1977); Hendrikus Berkof, *Two Hundred Years of Theology: Report of a Personal Journey* (Grand Rapids: Eerdmans, 1989); and Mark Shoof, *A Survey of Catholic Theology 1800-1970,* trans. N. D. Smith (Paramus, N.J.: Paulist, 1970).

52. I am sure no one will take exception to those whom I have included. There will be questions, I presume, about those not mentioned, especially thinkers such as Marie Joseph Lagrange and Yves Congar. Because his statement is so apposite, I cite here a remark of Congar that is characteristic of his viewpoint. After citing Aquinas's definition of an article of faith ("a perception of the divine truth, tending toward that truth itself"), Congar adds: "I do not underestimate the efforts made by theologians. After all, I have devoted my whole life to theology! But I still consider the highest mode of theology to be doxology." *The Word and the Spirit,* trans. David Smith (San Francisco: Harper and Row, 1986), 5.

Theology and Faith: Knowledge Conferred by God

All of the theologians we are going to consider agree that theology is only mature when it is founded on a personal experience of the truth of the gospel. Although they may differ on the appropriateness of applying the term "mysticism" to this experience, they all concur in maintaining that faith affects one's consciousness. This is certainly true of Karl Barth, who clearly states that faith is a way of knowing. Though the early Barth may have been excessive in his rejection of human pretensions to know anything about God without a faith acceptance of revelation, even the Barth of the *Church Dogmatics* never divorces faith and knowledge.

> In the Gospels, faith and knowledge are not neatly separated from each other but are called the common way by which we come to a decision for Jesus. The reason for this rests on the fact that Jesus' own participation in the divine and his own human nature are not counterbalancing realities. It is his very participation in the divine that grounds his human being. . . . To hear God's Word means to know God.[53]

Barth's insistence on the experiential and individual dimensions of faith led him to adopt some aspects of Schleiermacher's thinking. As von Balthasar sums up Barth's thinking: "Faith is the experience of God, the immediate awareness of a life force lying beyond this world, to which the individual is raised and which gives to the individual a transindividual life."[54]

Henri de Lubac wrote in his *Mémoir* that his projected book on mysticism was the directing energy of all that he did, yet he never wrote the book.[55] As a disciple of Rousselot and Blondel, and as one of the most learned and sympathetic patristic scholars of the age, de Lubac was convinced that only the recovery of an experiential faith lived within the community of the church could once again make Christian intellectual life a means of offering the world the riches of the gospel. His own life of faith gave him a sure instinct in understanding the theology of the people he wrote about, most especially Origen. Thus, there are times when, speaking of Origen, he speaks "from the inside" as it were.

53. *Kirkliche Dogmatik,* vol. VI, 76 and 210. All citations from Barth are taken from Hans Urs von Balthasar, *The Theology of Karl Barth,* trans. Edward Oates (San Francisco: Ignatius, 1992), a work to which I am particularly indebted. The above quotation is from pp. 141-42.

54. *The Theology of Karl Barth,* 211. Von Balthasar also goes on to point out the ways in which Barth distances himself from Schleiermacher.

55. *Mémoire sur l'occasion de mes écrits* (Namur: Culture et Vérité, 1989), 113.

In his [Origen's] devotion to the person of the Savior there is a note of tenderness that is quite special to him. He greets with deep feeling the first appearance of the name of Jesus in the Bible and observes that this name is never borne by a sinner. A remote precursor of St. Bernard, he knows that Jesus cannot be "found" except in solitude and silence of heart; Jesus wants to be sought with enthusiasm and with perseverance, when necessary in the anguish of suffering; he wants to be asked questions and have his answers listened to: that is for Origen what it means to seek out the meaning of the Scriptures.[56]

The closest de Lubac ever came to writing his book on mysticism was the introduction to a collection of essays edited by A. Ravier on mysticism and mystics. This essay is important because it allows us to see how de Lubac combined an open approach to the mysticism found in many religions with the assertion that Christian mysticism is unique and uniquely true since it is a maturation of faith in the mystery of Christ, the Incarnate Word of God and mediator of salvation and knowledge of the Father:

Unless the mystery is received by the believer, mysticism vanishes, or it is degraded. On the other hand, without mysticism — a mysticism that is at least incipient — the mystery is exteriorized and risks getting lost in mere formulas and empty abstractions that can become rigid. . . . The spiritual adhesion to the mystery will be replaced by conformity, and the person who, in this spirit — or rather in this absence of spirit — makes himself a specialist of mystery will be, to use an expression of Gregory IX, "a theoretician of God" but not a true "theologian." . . . The mystical experience of the Christian, rather than being a deepening of self, is — in its most intimate being — a deepening of faith.[57]

The two authors we are going to consider now leave so little doubt about the relationship they see between faith and theology or the role they attribute to experiential faith in the doing of theology that I need hardly do more than cite some well known aspects of their work. Harvey Egan, writing about Karl Rahner says: "Rahner's theology . . . begins from his own religious experience by which he critically evaluates the community's faith consciousness and by which he allows the community's faith experience to be a critique of his own."[58] Of particular importance in assessing

---

56. "Introduction" to Origen's *Homilies on Genesis* (*Sources Chrétiennes* 7, 27).
57. "Mysticism and Mystery," an expanded form of the introduction to A. Ravier's *La mystique et les mystiques,* in *Theological Fragments,* trans. Rebecca Howell Balinski (San Francisco: Ignatius, 1989), 53-55.
58. " 'The Devout Christian of the Future Will . . . be a "Mystic.' " Mysticism

Rahner's own mind is his essay, "The Logic of Concrete Individual Knowledge in Ignatius Loyola," particularly the section, "The existence of divine influences and the problem of their recognition."[59] The significance of this essay for an understanding of what "faith experience" might mean in regard to theology lies in the fact that, though he has to wrestle with Ignatius' teaching in terms of his own notions of "categorical" and "transcendental," Rahner never parts from the clear Ignatian position that God acts in a special and concretely discernible manner in the life of the believer.

> The first thing that may be found striking about these Rules is that Ignatius reckons on psychological experiences, arising in consciousness, which originate from God. This happens, too, in such a way that these divine promptings are distinct and can be distinguished from others which also occur and which have a different origin.[60]

After remarking on the embarrassing fact that since the great period of scholasticism, few theologians, that is, those whose vocation is to expound revelation in its fullness, have been canonized saints, Hans Urs von Balthasar goes on to develop the relationship between theology and holiness.[61] He attributes our modern difficulties to the separation of theology from spirituality and proposes as the remedy a living Christocentric faith. He often sounds this theme particularly when speaking of the light of faith that "alone makes it possible for the believer to submit to an external authority."

> For, correctly understood, the infused *lumen fidei* in him, to whose illumination he submits, is not any more "heteronomous" than the light of rational nature, which is innate in him: for even this light (as *lumen intellectus agentis*) is not properly speaking man's own light, but rather

---

and Karl Rahner's Theology," in *Theology and Discovery: Essays in Honor of Karl Rahner*, ed. William Kelly (Milwaukee: Marquette University Press, 1980), 139-58; citation is from p. 144.

59. The essay is found in *The Dynamic Element in the Church*, Quaestiones Disputatae, 12, trans. W. J. O'Hara (New York: Herder and Herder, 1964), 84-170.

60. Ibid., 117. A complete treatment of Rahner's teaching on mysticism and theology would have to cover the same ground as that covered by Harvey Egan. In line with the passage I have already quoted, one should consult Rahner's studies on the consciousness of grace, among which are "Reflections on the Experience of Grace," in *Theological Investigations* 3, trans. Karl-H. and Boniface Kruger (Baltimore: Helicon, 1967), 86-90; "Religious Enthusiasm and the Experience of Grace," in *Theological Investigations* 16, trans. David Morland (New York: Seabury, 1979), 35-47.

61. "Theology and Sanctity," in *Explorations in Theology*, vol. 1, *The Word Made Flesh*, trans. A. V. Littledale, 2nd ed. (San Francisco: Ignatius, 1989), 181-210.

his openness to the light of Being itself which illumines him. . . . It follows for the internal development of *theology* that this light [of faith], and no other must control and give evidence of itself in every branch of theological speculation no matter how detailed. This is possible only so long as the Christian thinker continually renews, in a living way, his own primal act of *a priori* faith — that obedient surrender to the radiant light in which alone by faith and not by vision he partakes in the wisdom of the self-revealing God. The more obediently he thinks, the more accurately will he see.[62]

The Scriptures — the Soul of Theology

In trying to assess the role of Scripture in the theology of the four men we are considering and comparing with the role of Scripture in the life of the early theologians, we meet with a problem. The earlier thinkers shared an outlook, a worldview, with the Scriptures at the level of cosmology, history, and anthropology impossible for us today. This does not mean that the divine realities are any less accessible to us through the mediation of the Sacred Text, but it does mean that we must understand and speak of these in a thought context very different from that of the Bible. This is an extremely delicate procedure, since we may often impose upon the biblical witness a viewpoint of our own culture that itself needs to be refocused. A good example of this can be seen in the manner in which biblical narrative was considered until recently. It was either treated as a product of humankind in its infancy, giving expression to truths that are now directly grasped by reason (Kant),[63] or it was evaluated in terms of its ostensive reference or "historicity" (Locke and much historical criticism). Yet we see things much differently now. The most important driving force in the general reconsideration of narrative was the effort to understand the kind of truth being mediated by the biblical narratives.

It would be an easy matter to multiply citations by or about these theologians to show their esteem for and obedience to the Scriptures. My point here is slightly different. A real assessment of how "biblical" they are would involve comparing their teaching with the fundamental prophetic interpretation of reality that is contained in and mediated by the Scriptures. Their stance was one of faith; they understood a good deal of what revelation is saying about God, human existence, sin, redemption and history, the reality and majesty of Jesus Christ risen from the dead, and the way we are to live in accord with the will of God. Their instinctive recourse

---

62. Von Balthasar, *The Glory of the Lord,* I, 164-65.
63. See, for instance, *Religion Within the Limits of Reason Alone,* Book Two.

was to the teaching of Scripture, and it was authoritative for them. It established the authenticity of the knowledge they derived from their faith. The question, much too vast for treatment here, is the degree to which this teaching actually provided a principle of unity in their efforts to interact with the rest of human thought. That they succeeded much better than most of us ever will is clear. Yet, it must be acknowledged that they were not well served by the historical studies of the biblical text — the divergence and positivism of much of this work made it difficult for them to assimilate the genuine retrievals and advances that have been realized.[64]

Theology and Community

In maintaining that the theological approach of Barth, de Lubac, Rahner, and von Balthasar is in continuity with the popular dimension of the early theologians, I am stating four things: 1) that it is open to receive from the faith experience of those who are not professional theologians, 2) that it is conscious of being indebted to the whole tradition, 3) that it attempts to expound the divine realities in a service to the community, and 4) that it is pastorally accountable not only to the faith instinct of God's people but also to the authority of its leaders.

Perhaps the two who stand out most in regard to the first point, openness to nontheologians, are Rahner and von Balthasar. Rahner, as we have seen, was one of the pioneers in trying to exploit the theological riches of the *Exercises*. In addition, he studied the lives and writings of the saints and considered these a *locus theologicus*.[65] As is well known, von Balthasar attributed many of his basic insights to Adrienne von Speyr, a laywoman and physician, whose theological work (much of which he personally transcribed at her dictation) he put ahead of his own.[66] Volume III of his *Glory of the Lord* is dedicated to lay styles of theology and includes studies of Dante, Pascal, Hamann, and Péguy.[67] Evidence for the same attitude can

---

64. This difficulty is well appreciated by Pheme Perkins in her presidential address to the Catholic Biblical Association: "Theological Implications of New Testament Pluralism," *Catholic Biblical Quarterly* 50 (1988): 5-23.

65. This is developed in the essay by Egan already mentioned ("The Devout Christian of the Future Will . . . be a 'Mystic' ").

66. See Peter Henrici, "Hans Urs von Balthasar: A Sketch of His Life," in *Hans Urs von Balthasar: His Life and Work,* ed. David Schindler (San Francisco: Ignatius, 1991), 7-44. Several other essays in this volume also mention the influence of von Speyr on von Balthasar.

67. *Studies in Theological Style: Lay Styles,* trans. A. Louth, J. Saward, M. Simon, and R. Williams; ed. J. Riches (San Francisco: Ignatius, 1986).

be found in the writings of de Lubac and Barth, but the point is sufficiently clear so as not to need belaboring.

There is one aspect, however, of the popular or more inclusive nature of a renewed theology that should be remarked upon — the presence of the feminine and the presence of women in theology. The theologian among the four being considered who most explicitly treats of the first of these issues is von Balthasar, whose language may appear at times to be somewhat remote or romantic, but who is profoundly sensitive to what is lacking in modern and postmodern thought.[68] In regard to the presence and role of women in theology and in the church, the clearest voice is that of Karl Rahner, whose 1964 essay is probably the source for the phrase the "*ekklesia* of women."[69]

It would be hard to say which of the four theologians evinces the greatest respect for tradition. Rahner edited several printings of Denziger's *Enchiridion Symbolorum, Definitionum, Declarationum* and published articles on the teaching of the Fathers of the church.[70] De Lubac's whole life was spent in studying the Fathers and making them known. Barth considered his study on Anselm to be one of the most important of his works.[71] Von Balthasar's immense output is a conscious effort to dialogue with modern thought from out of the tradition. Another dimension of this respect for tradition is their understanding of the church's liturgical life. Although Karl Barth would have a different orientation and accent than the other three, all would recognize in the community's life of worship an authentic expression of the faith that has been committed to the church by God. In all these men we can see a sensitivity to that work of the Holy Spirit throughout the ages that finds expression in the concrete life of the church.

An extension of this attitude can be discerned in their sense of accountability to God's people. All of them invested much time and energy in communicating with nontheologians because they knew that this was

68. See for instance *Theodramatik,* vol. 4, *Das Endspiel* (Einseideln: Johannes Verlag, 1983), 74-80. I will return to consider von Balthasar's contribution to this theme in chapter 5.

69. See "The Position of Woman in the New Situation in Which the Church Finds Herself," in *Theological Investigations* 8, trans. David Bourke (New York: Herder and Herder, 1971), 75-93.

70. See, for instance, "The 'Spiritual Senses' According to Origen," and "The Doctrine of the 'Spiritual Senses' in the Middle Ages," both in *Theological Investigations* 16.

71. See von Balthasar, *The Theology of Karl Barth,* 137, 164-65 et passim. For the importance of tradition up to the time of Barth see as well the remarks by Jaroslav Pelikan in *The Christian Tradition: A History of the Development of Doctrine,* vol. 5, *Christian Doctrine and Modern Culture since 1700* (University of Chicago Press, 1989), 299-301.

part of their service in and to the church. Barth was an effective preacher and founded the series *Theologische Existenz heute* precisely to address the layperson. Herbert Vorgimler wrote of Rahner:

[B]y every means and as well as he possibly can, he seeks to help the priest and the educated layman to preach afresh and to seize in its original spirit the old Gospel so that it really reaches man in his present situation. To Rahner it does not really matter at all whether or not such an enterprise appears scholarly.[72]

Many of de Lubac's writings were directed to the same type of audience for the same reasons, and the same can be said for von Balthasar, who after long deliberation made the painful decision to leave the Jesuits in order to continue to care for the lay community he had helped to found.[73]

Barth's position in regard to accountability to the pastoral leaders of the church is, obviously, different from that of the other three. His struggles with this point, between an obedient church and a commanding church, are sensitively dealt with in von Balthasar's study of his theology.[74] In the lives as well as in the writings of the three Catholics we see both the practice and the theory of how a theologian is to maintain his own vocation in freedom and still respect the pastoral decisions of those who are entrusted with caring for God's people and guiding them.[75] All three, in varying degrees with the extreme case being that of de Lubac, suffered unjustly from misunderstanding and a misguided use of authority. In each case, however, they preferred to respect the decisions of their superiors and bishops rather than disrupt the unity of the Body. Their theological faith

72. *Karl Rahner: His Life, Thought and Work,* trans. Edward Quinn (Montreal: Palm, 1965), 63-64.

73. See Maximilian Greiner, "The Community of St. John: A Conversation with Cornelia and Martha Gisi," in *Hans Urs von Balthasar: His Life and Work,* 87-102.

74. *The Theology of Karl Barth,* 103-07.

75. For von Balthasar's thinking see among other places, *The Office of Peter and the Structure of the Church,* trans. Andrée Emery (San Francisco: Ignatius, 1986). Rahner often considers this topic. See, for instance, "Courage for an Ecclesial Christianity," in *Theological Investigations* 20, trans. Edward Quinn (New York: Crossroad, 1981), 3-12, and for an example of his practical attitude in the same volume, see pp. 35-50, "Women and the Priesthood," which is a critical reflection on the 1976 Declaration of Congregation for the Doctrine of the Faith on "The Question of the Admission of Women to the Ministerial Priesthood." Much of de Lubac's thinking is manifest in *The Splendor of the Church,* trans. Michael Mason (San Francisco: Ignatius, 1986 repr.), chapter 8, "Our Temptations Concerning the Church." For a discussion of the concrete issue of theologians and church authority, see Avery Dulles, *The Craft of Theology,* chapters 7 and 11.

allowed them to see that even in its sinfulness and shortsightedness the office dimension of church life is part of the way Christ exercises his authority on earth.[76] The prophetic word of the gospel can only be protected from the weakness of human misunderstanding by a prophetic ministry of leadership whose minimum functioning at least is guaranteed by Christ himself. Although their reaction to both correction and encouragement on the part of the Magisterium was different, de Lubac, Rahner, and von Balthasar showed themselves to be, in the ancient sense of the term, *viri ecclesiastici.*

The Rhythm of Correlation and Theological Method

In order to situate feminist theology correctly, I would like to conclude this chapter by reflecting upon an approach that characterizes most modern theology. Generally speaking, this approach consists in the attempt to bring into organic relation the authentic teaching of the gospel and the legitimate insights and questions of our day. The activity by which a mutually influencing confrontation is effected without sacrificing the autonomy of either partner to the conversation and yet results in a development of dogma is what I mean by correlation. Described in this way, correlation has been the characteristic of most genuine theological effort since the early sages of Israel respectfully took up the philosophical efforts of their predecessors in order to discuss the question of origins (as in Genesis and elsewhere), or to incorporate the wisdom of Egypt (as in Pr 22:17–24:22).

In modern theological discussion, however, the term *correlation* has been associated with the efforts of a "mediating theology" to bring together Schleiermacher's starting point in a certain form of religious experience and the symbolic expressions of the Christian tradition.[77] These efforts are most often linked with the name of Paul Tillich.[78] According to Francis Schüssler Fiorenza, the four Catholics who have most consistently employed the method of correlation are Edward Schillebeeckx, Hans Küng,

76. I will discuss office as distinguished from charism and ministry in the next chapter.
77. A good general survey of this type of thought can be found in part II of *The Modern Theologians: An Introduction to Christian Theology in the Twentieth Century,* vol. I, ed. David Ford (London: Blackwell, 1989), 107-80.
78. The most complete study of Tillich's use of correlation is that of John P. Clayton, *The Concept of Correlation: Paul Tillich and the Possibility of a Mediating Theology* (Berlin, New York: De Gruyter, 1980).

Rosemary Radford Ruether, and David Tracy.[79] While Tillich and the four Catholics differ considerably from each other in their approaches, they have in common a desire to undertake the absolutely necessary task of relating modern experience and the Christian witness. I think that they also have a common failing to which I will return later, namely, that they do not take seriously the fact that faith is a light, an activity of God within the believer by which the testimony of the Christian tradition is made intelligible. Without this action of God the human mind must mediate between two cultural expressions of a generically similar experience of the divine. Thus, in such a viewpoint, when it comes to distinguishing the original experience from what is no longer valid in its expression, "reason must judge."[80]

The process of correlation to which I am referring also follows a rhythm, what may be called a hermeneutical spiral, but it resembles more the activity we have seen in the early theologians, very notably in Clement and Origen. At that time a ruling culture, foreign to the gospel, provided a plausibility structure very different from that of the Christian message. With an extraordinary optimism these thinkers, who were mystics and philosophers, listened to the questions their culture posed to them and in the conscious light of faith sought to understand what was being asked and to respond to it. Because they were affected by the same pagan culture, they did not need to try to "sympathize" with what surrounded them; rather, they had to see how the living Christ, in whom and for whom all things have been created (cf. Col 1:16), actually sustained and guided their world. The light revealed on the face of Jesus Christ was a healing grace that took up what was true in all creation and in all human aspirations, healed them, and brought them to their final goal.

I suggest that this is the method we must follow today. The theologian must make of her or his life a laboratory where the divine truths are experimented with and experienced. There is an activity that we use to test the realities to which we have basic access because we have consented to the witness of church in its life and in its Scriptures. If faith is a way of knowing, then we are not merely in contact with "the divine" or experiencing "the transcendent." Someone else is acting and coming to meet us and his identity is unmistakable — he is the icon of the invisible God (cf. Col 1:15). The surest sign of the work of the Holy Spirit in our lives is a

79. In *Systematic Theology: Roman Catholic Perspectives,* vol. I, ed. Francis Schüssler Fiorenza and John P. Galvin (Philadelphia: Fortress, 1991), 55-61.

80. See the essay by Louis Dupré, "Experience and Interpretation: A Philosophical Reflection on Schillebeeckx' *Jesus* and *Christ,*" *Theological Studies* 43 (1982): 30-51.

deep repentance for our sin and for the sin of the world, in which we knowingly and half-knowingly connive. We must, through this repentance, come to know experientially what it means to say that we are saved from darkness. It is possible to experience the actualization of the fact that the body of sin has been rendered powerless (cf. Rom 6:6). This fundamental and irreplaceably personal experience by which we come to know the power of the cross to put sin to death provides the touchstone to measure the authenticity of our other experiences.

The first modern mind to which we must bring the light of the gospel is our own. The "turn toward the subject" means that I must be conscious of the life that Christ died to bring to us. Revelation is not primarily a noetic transaction. It is an act where God manifests himself and gives a knowledge of his plan of salvation. Reflection on that act as it touches me gives rise to a deeper awareness of God and a deeper grasp of the mystery whose center is Jesus Christ, who once died but now lives for ever (Rev 1:18). It is indeed useful to study the success and the darkness of our culture, but regardless, that culture is *ours,* and it is in our own lives that we must experience the reality of the new life given us through the death and resurrection of Jesus Christ. We must experience for ourselves the healing grace of revelation and come to know the truth of testimony made to us by the believing community and by God himself (cf. 1 Jn 5:9-10). At this personal level correlation is a struggle — it is the confrontation between our obscure grasp of the truth, colored by our cherished pretensions, and the purity of the light of Christ that separates the wheat from the weeds. Only if the theologian lives with other sisters and brothers and learns the true demands of *agapē* is there a well founded hope that this sifting can be effected and authenticated. Within the community's life of praise there is to be found life. No one can live without a living knowledge of God and a personal consciousness of what he has done for us. This praise is not routine, it is life. Its opposite is death, for in the biblical view, "the whole life of man passes into death at the precise moment when the praise of God falls silent."[81]

In this process the particular power of the Scriptures to witness to and to describe the realities that we come to know, but which always exceed us, is borne in on us in a new manner. Their truth is appropriated and personalized, and their words and symbols reveal more of the realities they talk about. We begin to grasp why this sacred tradition speaks the way it does. Our mind begins to understand the Mystery, the divine plan for the

81. Hans Walter Wolff, *Anthropology of the Old Testament,* trans. Margaret Kohl (Philadelphia: Fortress, 1974), 111.

human race. This is not an exalted mysticism, but a simple, if sometimes painful, consent to the truth we have already professed to believe.

From this confrontation within us between culture and faith comes a capacity to say something to others. Whatever we say will be debilitated by our own ignorance and unhealed darkness, but it will also commend itself to a conscience that is open to catch the sound of truth. The objective reality and majesty of Jesus Christ can be mediated in such a way. We can share with each other as we cast up against the larger canvas of the totality of revelation and the full expanse of what our contemporaries recognize as true the truth we have come to know in an undeniable but still to be contextualized manner.

It is in this sense, it seems to me, that feminism is asking a question. We have been made aware of something deeply wrong with us. Something true about every human being has been denied, and women have been deprived in some important ways of the esteem and the exercise of rights that are theirs as persons made in the image of God. How do we answer that question if not by listening to each other and trying to dialogue? In the pages that follow, I am going to criticize the multifaceted reality that goes by the name of feminist theology. My criticisms are based on what I see as the uncorrected aberrations of the critical, modern approach to reality that forms the basis of much of that theology. I am concerned that the question, poorly asked, can only promote confusion in an area of our life that needs to be called out of anguish and alienation. If we are theologians we truly pray. In this prayer Someone else is acting and meeting us. We learn to praise him because we come to understand who he is and what he has done for us.

3
Christian Origins and the Roles of Women

Most recent discussion centering around feminist theology necessarily has had recourse to historical research in order to try to achieve some perspective on the question of women's dignity and roles within the Christian community. The purpose of this chapter is to present a brief overview of that history during the first two centuries. There are two opposing tendencies in feminist reconstructions of Christian history. The first is a study of the oppression of women, the second a record of the roles they once enjoyed but have since been deprived of. There is a danger of exaggeration in both directions, though there is no doubt that any account of the past will show it to have been ambiguous in its attitudes toward women and the roles it accorded to them.[1] The chapter will have two principal sections. There will first be a discussion of how history is used in modern theological research. I will pay special attention to the manner in which feminism approaches historical reconstruction from an "advocacy stance." This will be followed by a brief consideration of the place of women in early Christianity, with special attention to method and heuristic structures.

SOME METHODOLOGICAL CONSIDERATIONS

Historians and philosophers have long recognized that it is a peculiarity of the discipline of history that it must create a special kind of framework to

---

1. I will propose in chapter 4 that this ambiguity has been poorly interpreted because of a process, initiated by the Enlightenment return to a pre-Christian understanding of humanity, which has given us a false lens through which to view the past.

75

interpret data. I will call this a "first order heuristic structure." This framework or heuristic structure differs from the paradigms found in the positive
sciences in that it is always some form of narrative, what may be called a
"narrative substance."[2] That is, as Paul Ricoeur has pointed out, historical
knowledge proceeds by way of "grasping together" within a narrative
structure, and thus rendering intelligible the traces left of the past.[3] Thus,
the activity proper to history is that of making the past intelligible by
providing the right "fit" between the data and a heuristic narrative structure.

The process of reciprocally fitting heuristic structure and data to each
other is, as Kant correctly saw, a mediating function. I leave to others a
more nuanced critique of Kant's position.[4] Here, I wish only to show that
the heuristic narrative structure employed by the historian is similar to the
inchoate series of implicit judgments that are activated by a concrete
situation in an act of common sense. This is Bernard Lonergan's description
of such a commonsense judgment:

> Common sense, unlike the sciences, is a specialization of intelligence in
> the particular and the concrete. It is common knowledge without being

2. This term comes from F. R. Ankersmit, *Narrative Logic: A Semantic Analysis
of the Historian's Language,* Martinus Nijhoff Philosophy Library, 7 (The Hague,
Boston, London: Nijhoff, 1983), who says that he is developing and refining the notion
of "colligation" proposed by W. H. Walsh, *Philosophy of History: An Introduction*
(New York: Harper Torchbooks, 1960), 59ff.

3. *Time and Narrative,* trans. Kathleen McLaughlin Blamey and David Pellauer,
3 volumes (Chicago: University of Chicago Press, 1984-88). For this notion, Ricoeur
acknowledges his debt to an article by L. O. Mink entitled "The Autonomy of Historical
Understanding," *History and Theory* 5 (1965): 24-47. Ricoeur's valuable insight is
somewhat weakened by the overly Kantian bias in his understanding of the role of the
"productive imagination," which, as Ricoeur describes it, constructs rather than dis-
covers the narrative structure of the past. It may be that, as Stephen Carr points out,
Ricoeur is slightly deflected from a more adequate understanding of an epistemology
of historical knowledge by the fact that he considers such knowledge to be a function
of self-understanding. See his review in *History and Theory* 23 (1984): 357-70. Some
of Ricoeur's own statements would tend to corroborate this: "By overcoming this
distance, by making himself contemporary with the text, the exegete can appropriate
its meaning to himself: foreign, he makes it familiar, that is, he makes it his own. It is
thus the growth of his own understanding of himself that he pursues through his
understanding of the other. Every hermeneutic is thus, explicitly or implicitly, self-understanding by means of understanding others." *Conflict of Interpretations,* Northwestern University Studies in Phenomenology and Existential Philosophy (Evanston,
Ill.: Northwestern University Press, 1974), 17.

4. See for instance, Rudolf A. Makkreel, *Imagination and Interpretation in Kant:
The Hermeneutical Import of the Critique of Judgment* (Chicago: University of Chicago
Press, 1990).

general, for it consists in a set of insights that remains incomplete, until there is added at least one further insight into the situation at hand; and once the situation has passed, the added insight is no longer relevant, so that common sense at once reverts to its normal state of incompleteness.[5]

A heuristic structure is presumed to be "common knowledge without being general." This means that the critique of an historical judgment can proceed on two levels. It can criticize the fit between a commonly held "set of insights" and the data to be considered. That is, it can allege that the set of insights is inadequate to the task, or that it is not allowing itself to be sufficiently modified by the data. On a second level, the whole set of insights itself can be criticized, but this must take place on a higher level, on the basis of a correlation between this set of insights and a larger view of reality. I call this second and more general set of insights the "second order heuristic structure." It is not often attended to, but it is crucial in the elaboration and critique of what governs the operation of the first order heuristic structure.

An Example: The Meier-Crossan Debate

In order to illustrate my point concerning the two orders of heuristic structures, I will consider the debate between John Meier and John Dominic Crossan, both of whom are engaged in writing about the historical Jesus.

In a recent review of Crossan's study on the historical Jesus,[6] Meier challenges his method on two counts. First, Crossan takes for granted that certain apocryphal works contain independent versions of Jesus' authentic words, and second, he ignores "the most natural view of the development of a particular Gospel tradition in favor of some convoluted theory."

These objections are based on another reading of the data. They are, in my opinion, basically sound. They open up, however, a methodological question that is deeper still, one that touches on the very epistemology of historical knowledge. The question is this: on what basis do we judge one reconstruction of history to be better than another? That we do so, and that there is some objectivity to the enterprise is admitted by nearly all scholars. Sometimes one interpretive reconstruction is better simply because more

5. *Insight: A Study of Human Understanding* (London, New York: Longmans, Green, 1958), 175.
6. *The Historical Jesus: The Life of a Mediterranean Jewish Peasant* (New York: Harper, 1991). The review is in *America* 166, no. 8 (4150) (March 7, 1992): 198-99.

data have been taken into account; that is simple enough. But what of the case when the data are shared by two authors who disagree as to the degree of importance to attach to various aspects of it, and who thus arrive at very different presentations of the composite picture made up by the data?

There are, as I have said, two levels at which this question can be considered. The first is within the discipline of history itself, and the second is beyond history. In regard to the first or intra-historical level, different interpretations as to how the data should be made to relate derive from different heuristic structures, differing narratives, within which the data is organized.

Let us continue the example from Crossan and Meier. Both authors know the basic data concerning certain of the apocryphal Gospels — their language, where and when they were found, their contents. They disagree as to the date of their composition and their relation to the canonical Gospels. For Crossan, some of the material in four documents from the second or early third centuries antedates the canonical Gospels. These four texts are: the *Gospel of Peter,* the coptic *Gospel of Thomas, Papyrus Egerton 2,* and *The Secret Gospel of Mark.*[7] Meier holds that all of these works postdate the canonical Gospels and are typical of the imaginative or gnostic reworking of gospel material characteristic of some circles in the second century.[8]

Judgments of dependence when comparing two texts involve painstaking literary and philological investigation. The search is for the most plausible explanation of phenomena found in both texts. Although the argument is somewhat technical, I would like to consider the example of *Papyrus Egerton 2,* which consists of four small papyrus fragments dating from about AD 150 that contain fragments of four pericopes. The first fragment seems to be an account of a trial in which Jesus answers in vocabulary similar to John 5:39, 45; 9:29; 12:31. The second, after employing vocabulary which is like John 7:30, 32, 34, 44; 8:20, 59; 10:31, 33, 39, goes on to give a variant of the leper story found in Mark 1:40-44;

---

7. Crossan's position is developed in his previous books: *Four Other Gospels: Shadows on the Contours of Canon* (Minneapolis: Winston, 1985); *The Cross that Spoke: The Origins of the Passion Narrative* (San Francisco: Harper and Row, 1988). Meier's discussion on the position of Crossan and the Jesus Seminar in general can be found in Meier's own book, *A Marginal Jew: Rethinking the Historical Jesus* (New York: Doubleday, 1991), 116-41.

8. Meier, of course, is not alone in this position, and in the pages I have cited in the preceding note, lists many of those who agree with him. For a judgment on the *Gospel of Peter* and some criteria of assessment, see R. Brown, "The *Gospel of Peter* and Canonical Gospel Priority," *New Testament Studies* 33 (1987): 321-43; and *The Death of the Messiah* (New York: Doubleday, 1994), vol. 2, 1317-49.

Matthew 8:2-4; and Luke 5:12-14. The third fragment contains a mixture of the pericope concerned with paying taxes to Caesar (Mk 12:13-15 and par.), introduced by words resembling those of Nicodemus (Jn 3:2) and concluding with the quotation from Isaiah 29:13 (LXX) quoted in Matthew 15:7-9 and Mark 7:6-7. The final fragment contains a phrase reminiscent of John 12:24 but is otherwise not recognizable or very intelligible.

A careful study of these fragments shows that it is much more likely that they are mosaics drawn from gospel texts known by memory and dependent as well upon oral sources than that they are precanonical texts utilized by the gospel writers. This does not preclude that they may include material that predates the canonical Gospels, but the very mosaic form of their present state makes it impossible to imagine these texts as being a source for the canonical material.[9] By such a statement I do not mean that lines from a narrative cannot be found isolated in another context (compare Mk 14:36, 42 and Jn 18:11; 14:31), but that the composition of a narrative from disparate material already existing in a narrative text is much more likely than the incorporation of that material into a narrative where, incidentally, it makes more sense than in its supposed original location.

This first judgment, then, is based primarily on literary considerations and is buttressed by what is known of the composition of texts from preexisting texts at that time, particularly in Christian circles. It is an example of the first-order heuristic spiral that oscillates between the data and a successively modified explanatory hypothesis. For example, someone working under a car may look at a nut on a bolt and conclude that it is ¾. After trying the wrench, he or she modifies the first hypothesis in favor of 13/16. This will continue until he or she gets a "fit." Unfortunately, the *data* of history are not as available as the nut on a bolt and this allows for many more hypotheses that must account for the ordering of an event and are thus narrative by nature — more in the nature of a detective trying out various scenarios as explanations of a crime.

The second judgment regards what I have called the second-order heuristic structure, the overall view of reality that can govern the relative importance attached to various elements of the data. In the article already referred to, Raymond Brown points to a constellation of convictions on the part of those who, along with Crossan, view the canonical Gospels as

9. For a more detailed study, see, C. H. Dodd, "A New Gospel," *New Testament Studies* (Manchester: Manchester University, repr. with correction, 1967), 12-52, and David F. Wright, "Apocryphal Gospels: The 'Unknown Gospel' (Pap. Egerton 2) and the *Gospel of Peter*," in *Gospel Perspectives: The Jesus Tradition Outside the Gospels*, ed. David Wenham (Sheffield: JSOT, 1984), 207-32.

reworkings of earlier still extant material, or who use the canonical material to reconstruct a precanonical situation of the early communities.[10] The factors in this constellation make up a heuristic structure. They are not derived from the texts as such, but govern their interpretation and the value judgment made regarding the data. One such conviction is that "the New Testament writings distort what preceded," whether this be the orientation of texts or the practices of the communities. This notion is supported by the uncritical acceptance of Walter Bauer's notion that "orthodoxy" only appeared in the second century as the imposition of the views of the politically predominant group.[11] Such a view ignores the greater appreciation we have of the complexities of that situation. Again, as Meier sums up Brown's argument:

> Unlike the picture painted by those who want to make some form of gnostic Christianity an equally valid manifestation of first-generation Christian experience, the mainstream picture of Christianity presented by documents and traditions that definitely do come from the first and second generations are different from some of the wilder developments among certain Christians in the second century.[12]

Another element in the heuristic structure of those who tend to have some of the apocryphal material pre-date the canonical Gospels is the notion that the earliest followers of Jesus were not interested in biographical data about him, but only in his reality as Lord and teacher. The imposition of a biographical grid upon the material by the earliest canonical text (presumed to be Mark) represents a capitulation to the Pauline gospel with its accent on the death and resurrection of Jesus. Earlier believers did not share this need to connect the events of the life of Jesus with his message, and material such as that in *Papyrus Egerton 2* illustrates this different preoccupation. Such a position, arguing as it does from fragmentary material whose dating on other grounds is questionable and from an hypothesis concerning the existence of Q and the intentions of its author(s), presumes what it sets out to prove.

The criticism made by Brown, Meier, and others of the work of those who approach the New Testament with a hermeneutics of suspicion, presuming a more pluralistic expression, both in text and in practice, of the original religious experience, is explicitly a criticism of the first-order heuristic model or "narrative substance." Such a criticism is intra-histori-

10. "The *Gospel of Peter*," 321-25.

11. For a critique of Bauer's position see John Behr, "Shifting Sands: Foucault, Brown and the Framework of Christian Asceticism," *Heythrop Journal* 34 (1993): 1-21.

12. Meier, *A Marginal Jew*, 118.

cal, critiquing the lack of "fit" between a view of Christian origins and a dating of precanonical material on two counts. First, the correlation is not adequate, and secondly, both the heuristic structure and the proposed data stand in need of serious modification.

A better correlation or fit is provided by matching a view of Christian origins that is more unified, but by no means homogeneous, with a location of the adduced apocryphal material within the scattered and heterodox exuberance of the second and early third centuries.

From a methodological point of view, what is being considered in the above critique of the position of Crossan and others is a flaw in the hermeneutical spiral (since its successive realizations are on different planes). What I am doing here is instituting an epistemological analysis of how such a spiral is brought to criticism. So far I have used the notion of correlation or fit. That is, there must be a correspondence between data and heuristic structure that respects the true nature of each and provides a more intelligible narrative of the traces by which the past is represented.[13]

If we move the discussion to the plane of the more overarching, second order heuristic structures, we see that they involve a philosophy of religious experience. I will consider this philosophy more at length in some of the chapters to follow. Here I wish to observe merely that one aspect of the flaw in the larger hermeneutical spiral is the notion that religious language is "instrumental" not realistic. That is, language about God is useful for orienting the subject and enhancing self-knowledge, but it can have no verifiable referent.[14] Further, since experience can only be filtered through culturally determined media of conception and expression, it is to be expected that, at the origins of the movement, there would be competing Christianities, all equally "orthodox," and that some would be later suppressed by high Christologies, patriarchies, and the rest.[15] But as Brown points out, in such a view the recognizable coherence of outlook which constituted what Ignatius called the universal Church and Celsus designated as the "great Church" would have been without foundation.[16]

---

13. I am using here the notions developed by P. Ricoeur in *Time and Narrative* 3, particularly chapter 6, "The Reality of the Past."

14. I will consider this at more length in the chapter on metaphor.

15. In Dupré's critique of Schillebeeckx, the crucial question asked of this approach, but not as yet answered as far as I know, is, Why of all the culturally limited modes of expression available to the authors of the New Testament did they pick just these modes of expression and dismiss others not as less meaningful but as false? See Louis Dupré, "Experience and Interpretation: A Philosophical Reflection on Schillebeeckx' *Jesus* and *Christ*," *Theological Studies* 43 (1982): 30-51.

16. "The *Gospel of Peter*," 324.

In trying to understand the epistemology latent in historical reconstructions of early Christianity, we have seen that such reconstructions take place within the same epistemological rhythms that characterize any historical investigation. There are two hermeneutical spirals. The first is between the data confronted and the narrative heuristic structure elaborated in order to organize the data and make an intelligible "story" of the past. This first order activity can be critiqued on intra-historical grounds on the basis of its capacity to achieve a fit between the data and the structure. Truth is approached through the succession of better narrative structures that have greater probability and provide a better fit for the data.

The second hermeneutical spiral is extra-historical. It is between the first spiral, taken as a dynamic whole, and a broader heuristic structure concerned with ultimate meaning. There is constant oscillation between this heuristic structure and the first order operation, but it is not always attended to. Some historians tend to reject the existence of this second spiral, but their very intellectual effort to dispel it proves its existence, since their arguments must be meta- or extra-historical. History as a discipline is a first order mental function that is carried out on the basis of larger presuppositions, convictions, or principles. In short, history transpires within a horizon. This forms the basis for Hayden White's understanding of the historical enterprise, and in this he is correct.

In the example I have been using, the Jesus Seminar view (to use a convenient summary label) of Christian origins is judged adequate by Crossan and others not because of the superiority of its fit between data and heuristic structure, but because of its fit between this first-order spiral and a larger, more embracing view of religious knowledge which denies the possibility of revelation in the usual Christian sense and either does not know or rejects the Christian understanding of how God and the created universe relate. The Jesus Seminar position can be shown to be inadequate on an intra-historical basis, and has been shown to be so by Brown, Meier, and many others. A complete critique, however, must also address itself to the larger horizon within which the inadequacy of the original spiral tends to be minimized because it "fits" with a larger world view or heuristic structure. There is, moreover, one further aspect of this larger issue that touches directly upon historical reconstruction.

In a recent letter to George Coyne, the director of the Vatican Observatory, Pope John Paul II described what can be called the mutual service that science and religion can offer one another: "Science can purify religion from error and superstition; religion can purify science from idolatry and false absolutes. Each can draw the other into a wider world, a world in which both can flourish."[17] "Science" in this statement, as the context makes clear, refers to physical science. The second order heuristic spiral in the physical sciences can and must retain its autonomy, but it must also relate to religion and to the teaching about God. The meeting ground for this interaction is philosophy.

History, however, is not a science in the same sense as physics, biology, and the other empirical sciences. This has been made abundantly clear often enough by philosophers of history. While it can aspire to a certain level of second order understanding whose relation to religion can correspond to that outlined by John Paul II, history tends by its very nature to make judgments about the same reality as the Christian faith. Religion, at least as a generic concept, makes no claims about the specific meaning of contingent and individual events. Biblical faith, however, is precisely a prophetic interpretation of those events in the light of God known as Creator and as agent in the world, however difficult this latter concept is to understand.[18]

Thus, the meeting ground for history and faith is not the same as that for science and religion. Science and religion interact on the level of second order discourse concerning general principles. History and faith must interact precisely on the basis of their understanding of concrete events. History as a discipline of knowledge has its own autonomy and methods: these are the intra-historical judgments made on the basis of data and heuristic structure. Faith also makes judgments about events, particularly those that are intimately related to the event of Jesus Christ. Ideally, the two approaches are complementary. Actually, there is a good deal of conflict. This is often caused by the fact that the biblical manner of interpreting events is not appreciated in our time. There has been an "eclipse of biblical narrative"[19] in the shadow of the second order judgments that govern modern historiography.

As deeper understandings of the interpretive narratives of the Scrip-

17. This letter is published as the prefatory document to the collection of essays *Physics, Philosophy and Theology,* mentioned previously. It is also published in *Origins* 18, no. 23 (Nov. 17, 1988). My citation comes from Michael J. Buckley, "Religion and Science: Paul Davies and John Paul II," *Theological Studies* 51 (1990): 310-24; citation is from p. 324.

18. See the study by Frans Jozef van Beeck, "Divine Revelation: Intervention or Self-Communication?" *Theological Studies* 52 (1991): 199-226.

19. See the study *The Eclipse of Biblical Narrative: A Study in Eighteenth and Nineteenth Century Hermeneutics* (New Haven, London: Yale University Press, 1974) by Hans Frei, and my development of this theme in "Critique historique et enseignement du Nouveau Testament sur l'imitation du Christ," *Revue Thomiste* 103 (1993): 234-62.

tures are allowed their own prophetic truth and method of expounding it, the conflict with an historiography that sheds the Lockean epistemology that colors it will be considerably lessened. It is precisely here that the understanding of theology discussed earlier comes into play and challenges our post-Enlightenment compartmentalization of the role of the mind in investigating "nature." It is John Meier's failure to think this issue through that has created his own dichotomy between reason and faith in the investigation of history. It is to be hoped that he will address this issue in the future.[20]

When we seek to establish the ultimate meeting ground for history and faith we discover that, as for science and religion, this is to be found at the level of second order judgments. Faith and the discipline of history both make judgments about the nature of events and the overall meaning of history that in turn influence the plausibility they are willing to allow to certain intra-historical heuristic structures. There can be dialogue between these two to the degree that faith is willing to allow itself to be questioned by what history wants to ask and history is willing to allow a dimension of mystery to surround every human act and every collective history. If history cannot allow for a certain transcendent dimension to the human person, then dialogue must shift from this terrain to a philosophical discussion between science and religion.[21]

Recovery and Reconstruction

I wish now to discuss another aspect of the historical method, this time restricting myself to the actual practice of history. There are two complementary methods characteristic of modern historical critical investigation: recovery and reconstruction. The first of these deals primarily with texts, the second has to do more explicitly with events and situations of the past. The first of these approaches may be called "recovery" because

20. This lack of methological cogency has been pointed out by several reviewers: Rino Fisichella, Biblica 74 (1993): 123-29; Avery Dulles, First Things 28 (December, 1992): 20-25; Roch Kereszty, Communio 19 (1992): 576-600; Augustine DiNoia, Pro Ecclesia 2 (1993): 122-25.

21. For a nuanced discussion of this point see J. Lacroix, Histoire et Mystère, Cahiers de l'Actualité Religieuse 18 (Paris: Castermann, 1962). For a philosophical, more precisely, phenomenological, approach to the question of religious truth see, Daniel Guerrière, ed., Phenomenology of the Truth Proper to Religion (State University of New York Press, 1990), especially the studies by Louis Dupré, "Truth in Religion and Truth of Religion," 19-42, and Philip Clayton, "Religious Truth and Scientific Truth," 43-59.

it recovers for us a dimension of the texts that has been distorted or forgotten because successive generations have imposed upon the past their own cultural and theological limitations. Thus, a careful reading of the New Testament, particularly the Pauline letters, serves to nuance our understanding of the term *apostolos* by recovering for us the milieu in which it was used and to whom it was applied.[22] A very fruitful application of the method of recovery can be seen in the volume published as the fruit of the Lutheran-Catholic dialogue concerning Peter in the New Testament.[23] Although the method is not exclusively that of recovery, the studies of various New Testament texts do contribute to a much more nuanced presentation of Peter. We will return to some fruits of this study shortly. The recovery method was employed very early in the search for a better understanding of the biblical teaching on the role of women.[24]

If "recovery" may be used to designate the dimension of the activity that uses the text to change the horizon of its recipients, "reconstruction" describes the historical work done in order to understand the original context in and for which the text was produced. This activity serves to alert us to dimensions of an historical situation and to maintain the distance that exists between the text and ourselves, thus impeding us from reading our context into the original situation. The method of reconstruction has characterized

22. For a study of this point see Rudolf Schnackenburg, "Apostles Before and During Paul's Time," in *Apostolic History and the Gospel: Biblical and Historical Essays Presented to F. F. Bruce,* ed. W. Gasque and R. Martin (Grand Rapids: Eerdmans, 1970), 287-303.

23. *Peter in the New Testament,* A Collaborative Assessment by Protestant and Roman Catholic Scholars, ed. R. Brown, K. Donfried, J. Reumann (Minneapolis: Augsburg, New York: Paulist, 1973). Particularly apposite for our consideration are the remarks in chapter 2, section, C, "Theological Methodology in Evaluating the New Testament Evidence," and chapter 10, section B, "The Images of Peter in New Testament Thought."

24. Some early examples of this work would be: Krister Stendahl, *The Bible and the Role of Women,* trans. E. Sanders Facet Books, Biblical Ser., 15 (Philadelphia: Fortress Press, 1966); Irene Brennan, "Women in the Gospels," *New Blackfriars* 52 (1971): 291-99; Samuel Terrien, "Toward a Biblical Theology of Womanhood," *Religion in Life* 42 (1973): 322-33; Raymond Brown, "Roles of Women in the Fourth Gospel," *Theological Studies* 36 (1975): 688-99. A more recent example of such an approach is found in the work of Alice L. Laffey, *An Introduction to the Old Testament: A Feminist Perspective* (Philadelphia: Fortress Press, 1988). A reading of New Testament and other material in a useful but "maximalist" manner can be found in Elisabeth Schüssler Fiorenza, *In Memory of Her: A Feminist Theological Reconstruction of Christian Origins* (New York: Crossroad, 1987). Another more recent work which concentrates on details to the falsification of the whole is that by Karen Jo Torjesen, *When Women Were Priests* (San Francisco: Harper's, 1993).

biblical studies for more than a century, and it has helped to clarify many
aspects of the biblical text. Another volume published as a result of the same
Lutheran-Catholic dialogue may illustrate the fruitfulness of a reconstructive
method. The seventh dialogue was devoted to the topic of justification by
faith.[25] Although the method of reconstruction was not employed exclusively,
it is apparent both in the "Common Statement" produced by the scholars
participating in the dialogue and in the contribution by John Reumann (with
responses by Joseph Fitzmyer and Jerome Quinn, published as a separate
volume[26]) that careful historical research into the context of the Pauline
expressions sheds real light on the meaning which the terms of the discussion
had for Paul and the rest of the New Testament writers.

Reconstruction has proved valuable in the effort to render the Christian community sensitive to the implications contained in many texts referring to women in the Scriptures. Thus, an awareness of the prevailing
view of women in the world in which Genesis 1 was written enables us to
appreciate the prophetic force of the assertion that both man and woman
are made in the image of God.[27] In the same way, knowledge of the Roman
practice of identifying and sometimes killing those who showed too much
sympathy for a crucified man adds another dimension to the notice that
"There were also women looking on from a distance . . . who had followed
him and ministered to him . . . [who later] bought spices so that they might
go and anoint him . . . and [they] came to the tomb" (Mk 15:40-41; 16:1-2).

It is important, then, to observe at the outset that these two methods
which are characteristic of the critical reading of the biblical text as it is
done in our time are a valuable contribution to its understanding. It is also
important to bear in mind, however, that a method, by its very nature, is
at the service of a wider and more pervasive view of the text itself. This
affects judgments both in regard to its originating context and to the
parameters of its possible meanings. In terms of the earlier discussion,
attention must be paid to both hermeneutical spirals and the poles within
which they oscillate. Otherwise, particularly in regard to an approach which
includes a rhetorical dimension, information is gathered and interpreted

25. *Justification by Faith,* Lutherans and Catholics in Dialogue, VII, ed. H. G.
Anderson, T. A. Murphy, J. A. Burgess (Minneapolis: Augsburg, 1985).
26. *Righteousness in the New Testament* (Philadelphia, New York: Fortress,
Paulist, 1982).
27. This has been long appreciated. See the remarks of Gerhard von Rad and
the other authors he quotes: *Genesis,* trans. John H. Marks, Old Testament Library
(Philadelphia: Westminster Press, 1961), 58. Similar remarks regarding Gen 2:23a can
be found in Walter Brueggemann, "Of the Same Flesh and Bone (Gen 2,23a)," *Catholic
Biblical Quarterly* 32 (1970): 532-42.

within a hermeneutical construct that does not adapt to the data but rather selects and organizes the data in virtue of its predetermined goals.

In what follows, I will consider the evidence provided by the New Testament and the history of Christianity for an understanding of how the light of Christ affected, both theoretically and practically, the understanding of humanity as male and female. Since only a small minority of those who have lived have been able to make a sufficient mark on their time to still be accessible to our historical study, whatever is said must be approximate. Feminists often point this out, but it is true of the vast majority of men as well as of women. Nevertheless, the present state of research allows us to be prudently confident in our understanding of what John Meier called "the mainstream picture of Christianity."

An Application to Feminist Research

The task of offering a critique of feminist reconstructions of history must face the same problems that I have just discussed, with the added consideration that most such reconstructions function within a position that is sometimes avowedly and more often unexpressedly rhetorical. That is, it is employing "the faculty of observing in any given case the available means of persuasion."[28] It is literature designed to persuade.[29] Feminism is openly an "advocacy stance" inasmuch as it marshals its evidence with a goal of persuading others to change their attitudes and activities. In this connection, Elisabeth Schüssler Fiorenza wrote:

> As the intersection of a multiplicity of public emancipatory discourses and as a site of contested sociopolitical contradictions, feminist alternatives, and unrealized possibilities, the *ekklesia* of women requires a rhetorical rather than a scientific conceptualization of theology.[30]

28. Aristotle, *Rhetoric* 2,1 (1355b), trans. W. Rhys Roberts, in *The Basic Works of Aristotle,* ed. Richard McKeon (New York: Random House, 1941), 1329. Aristotle distinguishes rhetoric from dialectic, which is the art of logical discussion.

29. See Cicero, *Orator,* 69.

30. *Discipleship of Equals: A Critical Feminist Ekklēsia-logy of Liberation* (New York: Crossroad, 1993), 369-70. The rhetorical agenda of most feminist theology is becoming more evident. Robin Darling Young, in a review of Elizabeth Johnson's *She Who Is,* makes the following observation: "[T]he real mission of theology is neither revolutionary nor utopian, but pedagogical: instead of using a feminist hermeneutic to select remnants of acceptable Christian teaching, theologians might consider learning and communicating the entire body of Christian tradition in order that doctrine rightly develop and believers know it for their benefit." *The Thomist,* forthcoming.

It is often alleged that since everyone approaches reality from a particular point of view, feminism should not be singled out as being distinctive in that regard. A distinction, however, should be made here. There is a difference between a *perspective* and a *stance*. A *perspective* is a consciously assumed relation to history or a biblical text that is aware of its own preoccupations and takes into account the contextual and cultural biases of a given object of study while not eliminating any text or ignoring any historical data because of such biases. A *stance* also assumes a relation to history or to the text but it goes further and submits both text and tradition to a judgment, explicitly eliminating as "unusable" those parts of either that cannot be fitted into the norms determined for it.[31] Thus, a perspective is *investigative*, a stance is *regulative*. The further allegation that since all records of the past are biased, another bias is called for, presumes the very thing that is to be proved and derives, explicitly or implicitly, from the *Ideologiekritik* of Habermas and the Frankfurt School. Such a position cannot be presumed; it must be established. Yet, this is only possible if one accepts the materialistic premises upon which it is based.

The danger of approaching data from the past, be it in the canonical text or elsewhere, with a rhetorical stance, is that one often yields to the temptation to take details from the larger picture and imaginatively tease out possible reconstructions that are then imposed upon the evidence with the presupposition that the former view was "prejudiced." It is a bit like someone taking some bones from a substantially integral skeleton of a dinosaur and then, by dint of hard work and imagination, reconstructing a pterodactyl.[32]

---

31. Another name for "stance" would be "bias," as this is discussed by Bernard Lonergan, *Insight: A Study of Human Understanding* (London: Longmans, Green, 1958), especially 191-203, 218-22. Elisabeth Schüssler Fiorenza considers the question of heuristic models and history writing in her article, "Remembering the Past in Creating the Future: Historical-Critical Scholarship and Feminist Biblical Interpretation" in *Feminist Perspectives on Biblical Scholarship*, ed. Adela Y. Collins, SBL Centennial Pub. 10 (Chico, Calif.: Scholars Press, 1985), 43-64. Her dependence upon Hayden White for a notion of the relationship between ideology and the rhetoric of history writing would profit from a study of the critique offered by Paul Ricoeur, *Time and Narrative*, vol. I, 161-68.

32. This danger is aptly signaled in regard to Peter Brown's *The Body and Society: Men, Women and Sexual Renunciation in Early Christianity* (New York: Columbia University Press, 1988) by John Behr, "Shifting Sands: Foucault, Brown and the Framework of Christian Asceticism," *Heythrop Journal* 34 (1993): 1-21.

THE POSITION AND ROLES
OF WOMEN IN EARLY CHRISTIANITY

The first step in any study of the impact of a Christian view of reality on the position and roles of women is to consider the teaching of Jesus both in what he said and in how he acted. This is followed by a consideration of the life of the earliest communities, particularly as this can be reconstructed from the Pauline correspondence and, usually, Acts, as well as the redactionary level of the Gospels. A trajectory is then established, extending from Jesus through the Gospels, the Pauline and Deutero-Pauline letters (usually dated in the order: Colossians, Ephesians, Pastorals) and 1 Peter up to the period of the Apostolic Fathers, the Apologists and the authors that follow.

Although the dating of the material is not as secure as some scholars like to suppose, the practice of stringing the New Testament writings along a time line has proved to be an effective means of understanding them. Two things, however, should be noted about the way this particular aspect of the material is dealt with. First, some scholars make no distinction between those writings the church came to recognize as canonical and those that are not canonical. For them, the only authority any document of the past can have is as a witness in a reconstruction of early practice. All the writings available to us are equally brought before the judgment of contemporary preoccupations and interests and evaluated in that light. This ultimately leads to what I will call "foundational hermeneutics," with the foundation being the experience and rhetorical goal of the interpreter.[33]

The second thing to observe in reconstructions of this type is that they all use the same heuristic structure or "narrative substance," which is basically that which we identified with the Jesus Seminar view.[34] It might be described as the paradigm that frames what may be called "ordinary science" in regard to the study of Christian origins.[35] The narrative line is established somewhat like this: Jesus established a community of equals, thus obliterating the social and sexual distinctions common to the Judaism of his day. After the resurrection, the early Christian communities, particularly those founded

---

33. See chapter seven. For a more extended treatment of how feminist hermeneutics establishes its own version of canonicity, see as well Francis Martin, "Feminist Hermeneutics: An Overview," *Communio* 18 (1991): 144-63; 398-424.

34. For a presentation of the feminist adaptation of this heuristic structure see, in addition to the article already mentioned, Elisabeth Schüssler Fiorenza, *In Memory of Her,* chapter 3.

35. I am, of course, taking the notion and the terminology from Thomas S. Kuhn, *The Structure of Scientific Revolutions,* 2nd ed., International Encyclopedia of Unified Science, II, 2 (Chicago: University of Chicago Press, 1970).

by Paul, continued this egalitarianism, at once profiting from the liberty accorded to women in some parts of the Roman empire and disrupting the caste system still in place. At this point, leadership and responsibility were exercised by men and women indifferently, with each community feeling itself free to organize itself according to its needs. Then there occurred a "loss of nerve." Under the pressure and persecution exerted by the surrounding society, the Christian communities began to capitulate and allow patriarchal modes of life to creep back in, particularly in regard to leadership. This is witnessed to by the "household order texts" in the New Testament and elsewhere,[36] as well as by injunctions that women refrain from certain activities at the community gatherings.[37] This return of patriarchal domination has marked the life of the church ever since.

Charism, Ministry, and Office

I would like to propose another heuristic structure, a "narrative substance" that respects on the one hand the paucity and indeterminate nature of the data and on the other the self-description that the church, in faith, gives of itself. In order to do this I wish to distinguish between a charism of service, a ministry, and an office. By *charism of service* I refer to a particular endowment, conferred by the Holy Spirit, enabling a believer to perform certain activities that contribute to the life of the community. Some of these are found enumerated in New Testament lists of various special endowments conferred upon members of the Church (e.g., Rom. 12:6-18; 1 Cor 12:4-11, 27-31; 13:1-3; 14 passim; 1 Pet 4:10-11). Some are referred to in passing in other contexts (e.g., 1 Cor 7:7) while at other times activities listed as charisms are mentioned without ever using the term (e.g., Mk 16:17-20; Acts 2:4; 10:44-47; 19:1-7). I am obliged to qualify the charisms I am speaking of with the term *service,* since, while all "manifestations of the Spirit" are given for "some useful purpose" (1 Cor 12:7), this need not imply service. Consider, for example, Paul's description of the gift of tongues (1 Cor 14:6-19) as primarily building up the individual or his referring to his single state as a *charism* (1 Cor 7:7). In fact, as Albert Vanhoye notes, "The only unvarying feature of the use of *charisma* in the New Testament is that it always refers

36. The texts usually grouped under this heading are: Col 3:18–4:1; Eph 5:21–6:9; 1 Pet 2:17–3:9; 1 Tim 2:8-15; 6:1-10; *Didache* 4:9-11; Epistle of Barnabas 19:5-7; 1 Clement 21:6-9; The Epistle of Polycarp to the Philippians 4:2–6:3.

37. See especially 1 Cor 11:2-16; 14:33b-36; 1 Tim 2:9-15. Some authors, correctly as I will try to show in chapter 10, deny that *all* women are being addressed in these texts.

to divine gifts, and is never used for a gift given by one human person to another."[38] Thus, as Norbert Baumert observes, the multiple uses of the term can only be covered by speaking generally of a "free gift" from God whose exact nature is determined by the qualifying terms in the context.[39] Examples of charisms of service are prophecy, teaching, words of wisdom or knowledge, speaking (*lalei,* 1 Pet 4:11, probably to be translated "preaching"), healing,[40] the interpretation of tongues, *antilēmpsis* (helping others, particularly in regard to physical needs; 1 Cor 12:28; see also 1 Cor 13:3; Rom 12:8, *eleōn*). I classify these as charisms because they can be conferred and exercised sporadically for the good of the community.

By *ministry* I refer to divinely conferred activities that also build up the community but are exercised on a more permanent basis. Most of the terms by which the charisms of service are referred to can also indicate stable functions within the community. This is particularly true of terms such as *prophet, teacher, exhortation* (Rom 12:8), *antilēmpsis,* and perhaps the very term *diakonia* itself (Rom 12:7) as indicating a form of word-gift.[41] Other gifts mentioned in the New Testament seem rather to imply a more permanent type of exercise. These would include ministerial gifts such as *kubernēsis* (guidance, administration, or leadership — 1 Cor 12:28),[42] some forms of *diakonia,* and some functions included under the term as *apostolos,* as an itinerant preacher whose role was the building up of the local communities.[43]

38. "The Biblical Question of 'Charisms' After Vatican II," in *Vatican II: Assessment and Perspectives,* vol. I, ed. René Latourelle, trans. Leslie Wearne (New York: Paulist, 1988), 439-68; citation is from pp. 456-57.

39. "Charisma und Amt bei Paulus," in *L'Apôtre Paul. Personalité, style et conception du ministère,* ed. Albert Vanhoye, Bibliotheca Ephemeridum Theologicarum Lovaniensium 73 (Leuven, 1986), 203-28.

40. Paul speaks of *charismata iamatōn* in 1 Cor 12:9, 28, 30, which can refer to a gift of healing someone else or to a gift of being healed by the Holy Spirit. Vanhoye, in "The Biblical Question of 'Charisms,' " opts for the second intepretation, while I have argued for the first in "Healing, Gift of," in *Dictionary of Pentecostal and Charismatic Movements,* ed. Stanley M. Burgess and Gary B. McGee (Grand Rapids: Zondervan, 1988), 350-53.

41. For this understanding see the solid work by John N. Collins, *Diakonia: Re-interpreting the Ancient Sources* (New York: Oxford University Press, 1990), 233.

42. For various opinions on the reality referred to in this word see Hans Conzelmann, *1 Corinthians,* Hermeneia, trans. James W. Leitch (Philadelphia: Fortress, 1975), 215; Gordon D. Fee, *The First Epistle to the Corinthians,* The New International Commentary on the New Testament (Grand Rapids: Eerdmans, 1987), 622; H. W. Beyer, *Theological Dictionary of the New Testament* III, 1035-37. Obviously, the classification of *kubernēsis* as primarily a permanent or transitory activity depends upon whether it is considered to be a form of administration, guidance, or leadership.

43. That the term *apostolos* could signify such a role is established by Rudolf

Finally, by *office* I refer to a stable ministry whose function is to secure the permanence of the apostolic teaching, the *regula fidei,* by giving it a genuinely historical dimension, a consistent existence extending over both space and time. While charisms and ministries are expressions of the aspect of "otherness" inherent in the source of the church's life, office adds to this the expression of an aspect of otherness that works within the corporeal and thus historical nature of the church. In the same way, while both charisms and ministries are endowed with authority in that they can affect the life and the direction of the church, the authority of office adds to this the dimension of objectivity — office is transmitted through some form of human historical activity. It is quite likely that the function I have described here was exercised by some who were outstanding for their teaching and prophetic ministry. The gift by which the apostolic heritage is kept intact and developed in accord with divine truth is itself prophetic since it must function to protect the truth and efficacy of prophecy and teaching that in turn influence how office is exercised. In our own day this is expressed in the Lima Document's statement on Ministry (No. 36) in the following terms:

> Under the particular historical circumstances of the growing Church in the early centuries, the succession of bishops became one of the ways, together with the transmission of the Gospel and the life of the community, in which the apostolic tradition of the Church was expressed. This succession was understood as serving, symbolizing and guarding the continuity of the apostolic faith and communion.[44]

In using the term *bishops* of those who exercised the function just described, the Faith and Order Commission is quite consciously simplifying nomenclature that it knows was much more complex in New Testament times. The function of office is intimately bound up with what one may call the activity of "remembering" the apostolic message.[45] It is in this way that the continuity of apostolic faith is "served, symbolized and

---

Schnackenburg, "Apostles Before and During Paul's Time," in *Apostolic History and the Gospel: Biblical and Historical Essays Presented to F. F. Bruce,* ed. W. Gasque and R. Martin (Grand Rapids: Eerdmans, 1970) 287-303.

44. Faith and Order Commission, "Baptism, Eucharist and Ministry," in *Lima Paper,* Faith and Order Paper No. 111 (Geneva: World Council of Churches, 1982), 29.

45. For the notion of "remembering," I am indebted to the study of Karl Kertlege, "Der Ort des Amtes in der Ekklesiologie des Paulus," in *L'Apôtre Paul: Personalité, style et conception du ministère,* ed. Albert Vanhoye, Bibliotheca Ephemeridum Theologicarum Lovaniensium 73 (Leuven: Leuven University Press, 1986), 184-202.

guarded." The reality of the life, death, and resurrection of Jesus Christ is *remembered,* in the biblical sense of the term, when it is correctly understood, communally experienced, sacramentally celebrated, and personally assimilated. For this to take place there must be a divinely conferred function that, historical and stable in itself, ensures the temporal and geographical unity of expression given to the Mystery. Later theological language will describe this function as being at once *within* the church and *over against* the church. It is this very specific realization of Christ's authority over the church that I am calling "office."[46]

For over a hundred years now there has been a view of the early Church that saw it as a voluntary association made up of charismatic preachers and teachers and humanly instituted presbyters/bishops. In 1892 Rudolf Sohm challenged this view by maintaining that only the charismatic element belonged to the church, and this sufficed to direct it — the notion of a permanent office was a worldly intrusion. Sohm's thesis has had a checkered career in theology, and it has contributed significantly to forming the heuristic structure mentioned previously.[47] It figures in the proposals made by Hans Küng and criticized by Yves Congar, Pierre Grelot, and more recently Albert Vanhoye.[48] The fundamental lines of this view were revived in a modified form by Edward Schillebeeckx in his studies on ministry,[49] in which he maintains that the early communities were egalitarian democracies that organized themselves more or less after the model

46. Thus, we read in the "Malta Report" of the Joint Lutheran-Roman Catholic Study Commission on "The Gospel and the Church" (1972) that both Lutherans and Catholics agree that "the office of the ministry stands over against the community as well as within the community. Further they agree that the ministerial office represents Christ and his over-againstness to the community only insofar as it gives expression to the gospel." *Growth in Agreement. Reports and Agreed Statements of Ecumenical Conversations on a World Level,* ed. Harding Meyer and Lukas Vischer, Ecumenical Documents, II, Faith and Order Paper, No. 108 (New York, Geneva: Paulist, World Council of Churches, 1984), 180.

47. Throughout this section I am heavily indebted to the judicious article by Enrique Nardoni, "Charism in the Early Church since Sohm: An Ecumenical Challenge," *Theological Studies* 53 (1992): 646-62.

48. Hans Küng, *The Church,* trans. Ray and Rosaleen Ockenden (New York: Sheed and Ward, 1967). For a list of Küng's critics see the article by Nardoni. The article by Vanhoye is "The Biblical Question of 'Charisms' After Vatican II," in *Vatican II: Assessment and Perspectives,* vol. I, ed. René Latourelle, trans. Leslie Wearne (New York: Paulist, 1988), 439-68.

49. *Ministry: Leadership in the Community of Jesus Christ,* trans. John Bowden (New York: Crossroad, 1981). This was expanded in a further study, *The Church with a Human Face: A New and Expanded Theology of Ministry,* trans. John Bowden (New York: Crossroad, 1985).

of the civil and religious "free associations" of the time. This position is maintained by systematically minimizing the New Testament evidence for the role played by the apostles and maximizing the notion of the spontaneous creation of ministries "from below." This distortion has been pointed out frequently enough.[50]

Having minimized that aspect of the church's minsterial life that I have defined here as office, Schillebeeckx can only see the presence of that function as a capitulation to pagan norms, this time not the pagan norms of the free associations, but those of the "non-Christian, pagan, patriarchal household code of the Graeco-Roman family."[51] This remark clearly places Schillebeeckx in the company of those who have embraced the narrative substance that I discussed previously and that characterizes most feminist reading of early church history. In his case the second-order heuristic structure, the general view of church life, has presided over the ordering of the data in a subtle but consistent manner that never allows itself to be questioned. Schillebeeckx correctly poses the critical problem as being "whether one simply looks to history to confirm one's own already established views, or whether one allows them to be put to the test by history."[52] In keeping with this principle Schillebeeckx should respond more adequately to the substantial historical objections his peers have made in regard to his work.[53]

In place of a progressive paganization of the church's life, brought about by a loss of nerve and capitulation to the world surrounding it, I would like to propose another heuristic structure, that of the organic growth and differentiation of God-given endowments necessary to the church's existence and vitality. Such a view provides a better framework for the

50. For examples of critiques of *Ministry,* see Pierre Grelot, *Église et ministères. Pour un dialogue critique avec Edward Schillebeeckx* (Paris: Cerf, 1983); Albert Vanhoye and Henri Crouzel, "The Ministry in the Church. Reflections on a Recent Publication," *The Clergy Review* 5 (1983). Objections to Schillebeeckx' position in both books are summarized in Patrick J. Dunn, *Priesthood: A Re-examination of the Roman Catholic Theology of the Presbyterate* (New York: Alba House, 1990), 31-44.

51. *The Church with a Human Face,* 68.

52. Schillebeeckx, *Ministry,* 100.

53. Joyce Little in her review of *The Church with a Human Face* remarks: "There is one sense in which his book does not, and indeed cannot, fail, given how the facts which he presents for the reader's judgment arise out of the theory with which he begins and necessarily point to the conclusion which his theory already presupposes. This is a fail-safe method for getting where one wants to go" (*The Thomist* 52 [1988]: 165). In this book Schillebeeckx complains of being misunderstood, particularly by Grelot, but he does not deal in any extensive manner with the objections raised by Grelot, Crouzel, and Vanhoye.

data available to us and is in keeping with the second order heuristic faith principle — the church is the work of the Holy Spirit. It is God who "has placed in the Church first apostles, second prophets, third teachers, then mighty deeds, then gifts of healings" (1 Cor 12:28). The model for such a growth is provided by the single-cell zygote that already contains within itself the chromosomes and vital code that will produce a full human being, fully differentiated in all its parts. In the earliest stages of development, the various parts of the body are scarcely distinguishable, but an electronic microscope can make out the progressive cellular differentiation that eventually will result in a developed human being.

The church's growth was similar. There was a period when the charisms, ministries, and offices just mentioned were not differentiated, though they clearly existed and achieved differentiation and identifiability as the church grew. One indication of this situation can be found in the fluidity of terminology used to designate the various gifts. I will consider some examples of this.

Paul can treat prophecy as a charism of service, telling the Corinthians that they should all strive to prophesy (1 Cor 14:5-19), and presuming that when they come together some will have a "teaching" or a "revelation" (1 Cor 14:26). Nevertheless, in the same Corinthian passage Paul addresses some who are resident in the community, who apparently exercise the gift of prophecy on a more stable basis and who can be considered to be endowed with a prophetic ministry (1 Cor 11:4-5;[54] 14:32-37; Rom 12:8; see also Rev 11:18; 16:6; 18:20-24; 22:9). This latter usage is found in several passages in Acts. Thus, prophets are described as coming from Jersualem to Antioch and the prophecy of one of them, Agabus, is recalled (Acts 11:27-28). Agabus is further mentioned as a prophet in Acts 21:10, a context that also describes the four virgin daughters of Philip, who seem to have had a stable prophetic ministry since they are described as "prophesying" (present participle), though no examples are given in the context (see Acts 21:9). In addition to a peripatetic ministry such as that of Agabus and others who are mentioned in the early literature,[55] there are others who are sent by one group to another. The only clear New Testament example is that of Judas and Silas in Acts 15:27-33. The "apostles and presbyters" (Acts 15:22-23) sent (*pempein, apostellein;* 15:25-27) these two men who "being themselves prophets, exhorted the brothers with many words." As

---

54. The passage refers to men and women who pray or prophesy. It probably includes both charism and ministry.

55. These are presupposed for instance in *Didache* 1,7; 11,1-12; 13,1; Justin, *Dialogue with Trypho* 82,1.

emissaries Judas and Silas could have been called *apostoloi,* as prophets they were able to exhort the community at Antioch.[56] There is, finally, the use of the term *prophētēs* to designate someone who held some office, that is, who had some directing and supervisory role in and over the community. This seems to be the case in the triad expressly enumerated by Paul in 1 Corinthians 12:28, in the instance of the "prophets and teachers" of Acts 13:1, and in the particular way that Ephesians uses the terms *apostle* and *prophet* (Eph 2:20; 3:5; 4-11).[57]

The elusive nature of the term *prophet* can be illustrated from the statement in the *Didache* (10,1): "Allow the prophets to give thanks as much as they desire." Is this saying that an itinerant prophet is to be allowed to preside at the Eucharistic celebration (presuming that *eucharistein* refers to Eucharistic worship), or does "prophet" here refer to someone with a stable function, an office, in the community? The latter understanding may be indicated by another text in the *Didache* (15:1-2) that seems to indicate a shift in terminology from "prophet" as applied to an institutional leader to other terms that appear later as designations for office.

> Choose for yourselves supervisors *[episkopous]* and servants *[diakonous],* worthy of the Lord, of gentle disposition, not attached to money, honest and well tried. For they too perform the service of the prophets and the teachers. Do not despise them for they too are in honor among you along with the prophets and teachers.[58]

The term *teacher (didaskalos)* is not easily applied to a transient charismatic activity, though, as we just saw, Paul envisages that someone may come to the community meeting with a "teaching" (*didachē,* 1 Cor 14:26), and it may be that the expressions "word of wisdom" and "word of knowledge"

---

56. They are in fact called "leading men" *(andres ēgoumenoi),* but whether this makes them institutionalized "leaders" (as for instance in Heb 13:7.17-18) is impossible to tell. For the notion of *paraklēsis* as a prophetic function, and for a discussion of other prophetic functions see the article *prophētēs* in *The New International Dictionary of New Testament Theology,* vol. 3, ed. Colin Brown (Grand Rapids: Zondervan, 1986), 74-92.

57. See the article by Kertlege, "Der Ort des Amtes," 199-200. A clear example of fluid vocabulary can be seen in the third gift mentioned in Eph 4:11, namely *evangelist.* This term occurs only twice more in the New Testament, applied to Philip in Acts 21:8 and to Timothy in 2 Tim 4:5, though these two seem to have nothing else in common.

58. For a discussion of ministries in the *Didache* see Jean Colson, *Ministre de Jésus-Christ ou le Sacerdoce de l'Évangile,* Théologique Historique 4 (Paris: Beauchesne, 1966), 258-63.

(1 Cor 12:8) apply to some dimension of teaching. Usually, however, teaching is a stable gift, giving rise to a ministry. This probably is the sense in Romans 12:7 and Colossians 3:16 and perhaps James 3:1. In the vast majority of cases in the New Testament, however, words related to the stem *didask* are used to describe a specific function, namely that of an authoritative transmission of the gospel. While Luke's constant use of the verb in relation to the apostles need not always convey a sense of what we would mean by "office," the number of times he uses *didaskein* to describe their activity in a formal sense is, however, impressive.[59] In the Pastorals the terms *kērux, apostolos,* and *didaskalos* are all applied to Paul (1 Tim 2:7; 2 Tim 1:11). In other contexts, as we have seen, *didaskalos* is used to describe a function in conjunction with *prophet,* and once (Eph 4:11) *shepherds* and *teachers* are so described that the two terms seem to apply to the same function.[60] Teaching, by its very nature, is an authoritative function. Although there is no reason theoretically why the term *didaskalos* could not be applied to the authoritative exercise of the ministry of teaching, and indeed this seems to have been done on occasion, the tendency in the New Testament is to relate the function to those other apostolic and pastoral functions that imply what I am calling office. That is, the teachers were part of a body of leaders who possessed a permanent and directive authority and who were responsible for ensuring that the same gospel be preached in their community as was preached generally.[61]

The last term to be considered here is *apostle.*[62] In New Testament times *apostolos* carried with it different connotations that often overlapped but did not necessarily include each other. The basic meaning was that of "emissary" or "authorized representative," reflecting the semitic practice, not yet a legal category, of the *šalîăḥ,* and the Greek notion of an emissary. The term was easily adapted to the various nuances given to it in the Christian community. It is possible to abstract five notes or qualities of an

59. The verb occurs 16 times in Acts; 11 of these describe what may be called *apostolic* activity. The exceptions are 1:1 (of Jesus); 15:1 (false teachers); 18:25 (Apollos); 21:21.28 (accusation against Paul).

60. "And he gave some as apostles, some as prophets, some as evangelists and some as pastors and teachers. . . ."

61. This point is brought out well by Bernard Cooke, *Ministry to Word and Sacraments* (Philadelphia: Fortress, 1976), see especially 236-237. See also the article by H. Greeven, "Propheten, Lehrer, Vorstehr bei Paulus," *Zeitschrift für die neutestamentliche Wissenschaft* 44 (1952-53): 1-43, who describes the teaching function as "presentation, transmission, and enrichment of the tradition" (p. 28).

62. In addition to the article by Schnackenburg mentioned earlier, one may consult the article by J.-A. Bühner, *"Apostolos,"* in *Exegetical Dictionary of the New Testament,* vol. 1, ed. Horst Balz and Gerhard Schneider (Grand Rapids: Eerdmans, 1990), 142-46, and the literature given there.

apostle without implying that they were all present every time the term was used, or that everyone would accept the term being applied to someone who lacked a specific note.

(1) *A vision of the risen Christ.* This was the fundamental note of those who were called apostles in the Palestinian community, most particularly in and around Jerusalem. Paul is careful to claim this experience for himself in 1 Corinthians 9:1 and 15:8. That more than this was required is obvious from the fact that "five hundred brethren" are also mentioned as having seen the risen Lord (1 Cor 15:6). In fact, with the exception of the difficult 1 Corinthians 15:5-7, the term *apostle* is reserved in this tradition for the group called the Twelve, as can be seen from the (anachronistic?) designation in the synoptic tradition and Luke's hesitation in Acts to apply the term *apostle* to Paul.[63]

(2) *A commission from Christ.* There are two possible sources of this commission from Christ: *(a)* this commission may be part of the vision of the risen Christ (Mt 28:16-20; Mk 16:15-18; Lk 24:46-49; Acts 1:6-8; Jn 20:21-23; Gal 1:15-16), or *(b)* the commission may be in the gift of apostleship itself that is at least sometimes established by the community that sends the apostle out, as is the case with Paul and Barnabas in Acts 13:1-3. Paul recognizes an unspecified number of people as "apostles" when speaking of the lot of "us apostles" (1 Cor 4:9), or the right of the "other apostles" to travel with a "sister woman" (1 Cor 9:5), and he seems to include Silvanus and Timothy as apostles in 1 Thessalonians 2:7.[64] It is interesting to observe that the "false apostles" mentioned by Paul in 2 Corinthians 11:13 have arrogated to themselves other titles that are intimately bound with the gift of apostleship, such as "servant" or "slave" (see Rom 1:1; Tit 1:1), "workman" (2 Tim 2:15), and even "apostle of Christ," which at least on some occasions refers to a direct commission from Christ.[65] The presence of these false or "super" apostles (2 Cor 11:5; 12:11) who were able to point to charismatic activity attested to by other communities they had visited (2 Cor 3:1-3) allows us to see that there were a certain number of itinerant preachers, genuine or false, who, sent by other communities or considering themselves sent directly by Christ, traveled about and, according to the case, strengthened or confused local communities. Those whose office

---

63. In the synoptic tradition, we find *apostolos* used in the calling of the twelve (Mt 10:2; Mk 3:14; Lk 6:13), in an enigmatic application at Mark 6:30 and in 5 places in Luke (9:10; 11:49; 17:3; 22:14; 24:10). Although Luke uses *apostolos* 28 times in Acts, he applies the term to Paul only in Acts 14:4,14, perhaps in dependence upon a source. He lists the qualities of an apostle in Acts 1:21-22.

64. Consult also the language in 2 Cor 8:23.

65. Eleven New Testament letters begin by designating their sender in this way: Rom, 1 Cor, 2 Cor, Gal, Eph, Col, 1 Tim, 2 Tim, Tit, 1 Pet, 2 Pet.

of apostleship was a genuine gift from the Lord had, as one of their most important duties, the establishment of criteria by which true and false apostles and prophets could be recognized. This resulted early in that coherence of outlook mentioned by Raymond Brown.[66]

(3) *Possession of apostolic gifts.* We can glean from Paul the basic criteria of genuine apostleship in the strict definition of the term — the ability to preach the truth of the gospel in the power of the Holy Spirit and to care for those who responded to it in such a way that a community is founded. It is for this reason that Paul tells the Corinthians that they are his "letter of recommendation" (2 Cor 3:1-6), and he addresses both the Philippian and Thessalonian communities as his "crown" (Phil 4:1; 1 Thes 2:19; 2 Thes 4:8).[67] In this outlook, much more important than having seen the risen Christ is the existence of these communities attesting to the reality of a commission from Christ.[68]

Another criterion of true apostleship is the ability to imitate Christ, particularly in his suffering in love through which the power of God is made manifest (2 Cor 13:4). This enables the apostle to admonish those for whom he is responsible to imitate him (1 Cor 4:16; 11:1; 1 Thess 1:6).[69] It is this criterion that Paul holds up in comparing himself with the false apostles. Not only does he list his accomplishments by speaking of his sufferings (1 Cor 4:9-13; 2 Cor 11:21-22), but he is careful to qualify the "signs and wonders and deeds of power" that mark an apostle by saying that, in this case, they are performed in "great endurance" (2 Cor 12:12). Colossians 1:24 characterized the apostolic service as including "suffering for your sake," so that "in my flesh I complete what is lacking in Christ's afflictions for the sake of his body, that is, the Church." This spells out in more detail that essential dimension of apostolic activity that consists in "carrying about in the body the dying of Jesus so that the life of Jesus may also be manifested in our body" (2 Cor 4:10).

Apostolic activity is accomplished "in power, in the Holy Spirit and

66. "The *Gospel of Peter.*" Interesting evidence is provided by the *Didache* that criteria were being established for distinguishing true and false apostles/prophets. As part of the advice on how to discern these (*Didache* 11:1-12), the community is told that if an "apostle" comes and stays until the third day he is a false *prophet.* Obviously the itinerant nature of a genuine apostle/prophet was part of the asceticsm of his calling, but it also precluded such a one from exercizing a stable office.

67. Paul also speaks of these communities as his "joy" and his "boast" both now and on "the day of Christ" (Phil 2:16). For a more extended treatment of this point see Schnackenburg, "Apostles."

68. It is quite likely for instance that the "apostles" referred to in Jude 17 refers to the founders of the churches to whom the author is writing.

69. See the study by David Stanley, "Become Imitators of Me: The Pauline Conception of Apostolic Tradition," *Biblica* 40 (1959): 859-77.

in much conviction" (1 Thess 1:5), and this undoubtedly includes "signs and wonders and deeds of power." The difference between mere charismatic or even ministerial manifestations of the Spirit and the same activity as being apostolic in the strong sense of the term lies precisely in those qualities mentioned above. In addition to the more dramatic gifts, seemingly cultivated by the false apostles, there are also the gifts of discernment, exhortation, teaching, and the like.

I would conclude, then, that there are strict and loose senses of the term *apostle*. In the strict sense, one must have seen the resurrected Lord or at least been commissioned by a community of believers. The absolute minimum for the existence of the apostolic gift in the loose sense, which often differs little from the prophetic gift, would be the commissioning by a faith community and a demonstration of the Spirit's power. The exercise of this gift probably included the notion of travel undertaken for the good of the communities, and this served to distinguish the apostles from the local prophets. Paul often overlaps these definitions. He also uses *apostolos* in both a strict and a loose sense.[70] Thus, the expression *the apostles* in Galatians 1:17-19 refers to a different set of criteria than the same expression in 1 Corinthians 4:9 and 9:5. Again, calling Andronicus and Junia "apostles" in Romans 16:7 may approximate the use in 2 Corinthians 8:23, but it is far from the strong sense implied in Paul's self-designation or in lists such as 1 Corinthians 12:28 and Ephesians 4:11.[71]

It has not been my intention here to discuss all the terms that could refer variously to a service charism, a ministry, or an office, or at least two of the three. Such a study would have to include such overlapping terms as *elder (presbyteros), overseer (episkopos), servant* or *messenger (diakonos)*, as well as *witness (martys)*. I have wanted to call attention to the fact that the designation of someone as an apostle or prophet or servant need not imply more than a charism or a ministry. This is true of the "apostles" mentioned in 1 Corinthians 4:9; 9:5; 2 Corinthians 8:23; and Romans 16:7. It is true of the prophets and teachers and servants.[72] Thus, the fact that

---

70. It is sometimes asserted that Paul does not have a "strict" and a "loose" meaning for *apostolos*. This is said on the presumption that what is listed under (1) above is the "strict" sense and what is under (2) is the "loose" sense. From what I have said, it should be clear that I agree that for Paul the second possibility listed under (2) includes a strong meaning.

71. It is rather generally agreed that the *Iounian* of this verse refers to a woman. It is likely that Andronicus is her husband and that they were prominent among the "itinerant missionaries" (Schnackenburg, "The Apostles," 294) known personally to Paul.

72. For a discussion of words related to the root *diakon* see the work already mentioned by John N. Collins, *Diakonia*.

Phoebe is called a *diakonos* (common gender) "of the Church which is in Cenchreae" (Rom 16:1), probably means that she is traveling as a representative of her community. She is also described as a "patroness" *(prostatis)*, probably indicating that she put her wealth and perhaps her house at the service of the community. Although her influence was great and beneficial, there is no indication that she fulfilled what would later be recognized as an office.

Both Phoebe and Junia are examples of people with important positions in a local church or in an itinerant ministry whose significance was minimized throughout most of church history. There are others mentioned in the New Testament, both men and women, whose contribution to the life of the early church has not been sufficiently appreciated. Perhaps they were eclipsed by the figures of Paul, Peter, and others, or, more probably, their charisms and ministries disappeared from church life and with this disappearance went an understanding of what these gifts meant and should mean in the Body. In an attempt to rectify some of that eclipse, at least in regard to the roles of women in the early church, I will present a brief summary of the results of some present efforts at reconstruction.[73]

Women in the New Testament

The Gospels

In considering the Gospels, we must bear in mind that we are dealing with three different historical levels: the activity of Jesus, the interpretive transmission of his words and deeds in the post-Resurrection tradition, both written and oral, and the actual composition of the Gospels.[74] We may say briefly that Jesus' way of relating to women was part of his symbolic way of acting intended by him to be a revelation of both the presence and the nature of the kingdom. It was in order to demonstrate the Father's love in a particular way to those who were marginalized that Jesus went out of his

---

73. For bibliographical information on these efforts see the works by Witherington and Heine in the bibliography and also Elisabeth Schüssler Fiorenza, *In Memory of Her.*

74. These three stages seem to be implied in the opening verses of Luke's Gospel (Lk 1:1-4), which speak of "eyewitnesses," "ministers of the word," and the author himself who is going to "write an orderly account." These same stages are explicitly taught in the *Instruction on the Historical Truth of the Gospels* by the Pontifical Biblical Commission (*Acta Apostolicae Sedis* 56 [1964]: 712-18), which is referred to in the Constitution *Dei Verbum,* §19.

way to associate with them. Luke, by placing the event at Nazareth early in his Gospel and by associating it with Isaiah 61:1-2, intends to place all of Jesus' activity in the light of this prophecy of the kingdom of God being preached to "the poor, the prisoners, and the downtrodden" (Lk 4:16-21). In addition, there were many aspects of the Jewish society of his day that did not correspond to the Father's will for the kingdom, and this included some ways in which women were treated.[75] Jesus' comportment and his words are at the origin of a tradition that developed in the second and third stages of the gospel tradition and provided a reference point in the Spirit-led life of the early communities. I wish to give here only some examples of the origin and development of that tradition.

The number of references to women in Jesus' parables is striking, though it is an exaggeration to say that it is unique.[76] It is interesting to observe how often in the gospel (and pre-gospel?) tradition these are presented as part of a male-female pair of stories. Some examples are the oppressed widow and the despised tax collector as models of prayer (Lk 18:1-14); the farmer sowing mustard seed and the woman using leaven (Mt 13:31-33; Lk 13:18-21); the lost sheep and the lost coin (Lk 15:3-10).

The tendency to form male-female pairs is evident also in stories of healing. The only two healings at a distance recorded in the Gospels involve accounts of Jesus' care for a pagan officer of the occupation forces and a pagan woman in Matthew 8:5-13 (par. Lk 7:1-10) and Matthew 15:21-28 (par. Mk 7:24-30). Besides illustrating Jesus' care for those outside the pale of usual Jewish concern, Matthew's pairing is meant to teach us something about his abiding and equal concern for both women and men. Luke's regular practice of pairing stories about men and women[77] finds expression in the stories of the centurion's boy and the raising of the son of the widow of Nain (Lk 7:1-17); the sabbath healings of the woman bowed over and the man with dropsy (Lk 13:10-17; 14:1-5).

75. For a brief overview with bibliography see Witherington, *Women in the Ministry of Jesus,* chapter 1. For an historical reconstruction that maximizes the evidence for the importance of women particularly in diaspora Judaism see Bernadette J. Brooten, *Women Leaders in the Ancient Synagogue: Inscriptional Evidence and Background Issues,* Brown Judaic Studies 36 (Chico, Calif.: Scholars Press, 1982).

76. The later talmudic material contains many, sometimes ancient, stories in which women figure in a favorable light. For some examples see Francis Martin, *Narrative Parallels to the New Testament,* SBL Resources for Biblical Study 22 (Atlanta: Scholars Press, 1988), R 70, R 82, etc. There are also stories in which a gentile woman is portrayed favorably: ibid., R 116, R 123, R 136, etc.

77. A convenient chart can be found in Witherington, *Women in the Earliest Churches,* 129.

There are also stories that contrast men and women, to the advantage of the figure of the woman. There is the contrast between the penitent woman and the Pharisee, Simon (Lk 7:36-50), and the famous story of the woman who broke her jar of precious ointment and emptied it over Jesus while the disciples complained (Mt 26:6-13; Mk 14:3-9; Jn 12:1-8). This woman is portrayed as an ideal disciple who pours out what is precious to her as she anoints Jesus' head in recognition of his messianic reality. In this she is not only contrasted with all the disciples in the story itself, but, particularly in the Markan redaction, she is ostensibly placed at the head of the passion narrative between the mention of the Jewish leaders who want to kill Jesus (Mk 14:1-2) and Judas who betrays him (14:10-11). In addition, Mark places this nameless woman and the nameless centurion at the cross (15:39) as a female-male pair of models whose faith and open confession frame the account of the passion.[78]

The gospel tradition's use of vocabulary in describing aspects of Jesus' public life is also significant. Thus, Mark describes the women at the cross in terms redolent of discipleship when he says that they "had *followed* him and *ministered* to him" (Mk 15:41). The use of the term *minister (diēkonoun)* in Luke 8:3 probably conveys the same nuance, and this is also true of the story of the healing of Peter's mother-in-law (Mt 8:14-15; Mk 1:29-31; Lk 4:38-39), whose concluding notice that she "ministered to them/him (Mt)" adds the notion of discipleship to a healing story.

All of the Gospels record the part played by women as the first witnesses to the resurrection. Again, the events of level one are described at the third level, that of gospel composition, in ways that attribute an important role to women. All four Gospels recount that women were first to go to the

78. It is for this reason that Elisabeth Schüssler Fiorenza's remarks in this regard are puzzling. She first states (*In Memory of Her,* xiii), in obvious contradiction to the fact that the story is firmly embedded in the gospel tradition and frequently commented upon, that "the woman's prophetic sign-action did not become a part of the gospel knowledge of Christians." She goes on to say, "The name of the betrayer is remembered, but the name of the faithful disciple is forgotten because she is a woman." If the omission of a name is a sign of gender prejudice, what shall we say of the omission of the centurion's name? It is more likely that they are both nameless in order to accent their typological function. Again, how can we explain the anonymity of another significant figure in the same passion account, the young man who fled away naked? Furthermore, in the story of the raising of the synagogue ruler's daughter (Mk 5:21-43, Mt 9:18-28, Lk 8:40-56), we must conclude, at least on the hypothesis of Markan priority, that Matthew left out the father's name, Jairus. Was this gynocentric fanaticism? On the basis of the same hypothesis, what shall we say of the fact that Luke fails to name Bartimaeus, the blind man near Jericho, and Matthew dissolves him into an anonymous duo? See Mk 10:46-52, Mt 20:29-34, Lk 18:35-43 and Mt 9:27-30. Fiorenza's example is an unconvincing use of rhetoric.

tomb and find it empty,[79] though their subsequent witness was not accepted by the male disciples (e.g., Lk 24:22-24). John is careful to portray Mary Magdalene as the first to bear the apostolic witness, "I have seen the Lord."[80] The fact that the Gospels were redacted after the Pauline letters were written indicates that the role played by the women continued to be important in the tradition, though it is not mentioned by Paul, for instance in 1 Corinthians 15:5-8. This aspect was very significant to the church in Jerusalem, whose viewpoint seems to underlie this whole passage.

We may say in summary, then, that Jesus' attitudes, words, and gestures, had an "effective history" in the subsequent passing on of the gospel tradition.[81] This can be seen in the vocabulary and structure of the canonical Gospels, which interpret and transmit his life to the church. In this interpretation women are considered to be disciples in a way equal to men; however, it is worthy of note that with all the development of the role of women in the gospel redactions there is never any description of them, either directly or by allusive vocabulary, which would pair them with the apostolic group explicitly called and commissioned by Jesus. Time does not permit an application of the principle of the three levels of the Gospel tradition to Mary, the mother of Jesus, whose historical role has its own effective history now reflected in the various gospel traditions. This is an important dimension of New Testament teaching on the role of women in the new dispensation.[82]

The Tradition Outside the Gospels

Only in the book of Acts do we have a canonical and prophetic interpretation of the historical existence of the church that corresponds in some way to the

79. This convergence is one of the reasons arguing for a basic factuality in the discovery of the empty tomb, though apologetic motifs have influenced the manner in which this has been transmitted, particularly by Matthew (see Mt 27:51-53; 28:2-4).

80. See the study by Raymond Brown, "The Roles of Women in the Fourth Gospel," *Theological Studies* 36 (1975): 688-99.

81. A powerful example of the effective history of Jesus' words can be seen in the present gospel tradition regarding his teaching on divorce (Mt 19:3-9; Mk 10:2-12; and Mt 5:31-32; Lk 16:18; 1 Cor 7:10-11). In each of these instances Jesus' concern to set right an unjust situation which treated women in a way that contradicted the Father's mind as revealed in Gen 1 and 2 is preserved and applied to different situations. For a study which respects the complexity of this issue see Raymond Collins, *Divorce in the New Testament* (Collegeville, Minn.: The Liturgical Press, 1992), though I do not accept Collins's conclusions.

82. There is, at least as far as I am aware of, no thorough study of this question which applies the three stages of the gospel tradition to Mary and is alert to what these have to say about the role of woman in the Christian dispensation.

interpretation of Jesus' historical existence transmitted in the Gospels. We see there many of the traits of the third Gospel. Thus, there is the healing of the man Aeneas and the woman Tabitha (9:32-43); the conversion of Lydia and the Philippian jailer (16:13:14-15, 25-34); the frequent mention of the couple Priscilla and Aquila (Ananias and Sapphira are a negative example, 5:1-11), and the fact that in accounts of both conversion and persecution Luke mentions "men as well as women" (5:14; 8:3-12; 9:2; 22:4).

The Lydia just mentioned was from Thyatira and a business woman, not an unusual thing for a woman of Macedonia. She lived in Philippi and participated in Jewish worship along with some other women at a "place for prayer" *(proseuchē)*. The Lord "opened her heart" and she and her household were baptized, upon which she prevailed upon Paul and his companions to accept her hospitality (16:14-15, 40). This brief account contains many features mentioned elsewhere in Acts and in the Pauline correspondence. First, there is the fact that Lydia is prominent. Luke mentions prominent women as well in Acts 17:4-12, and probably means to imply that Damaris, who was converted along with Dionysius, a member of the Areopagus Court, and several others (note a man and woman are named) was of some social standing. Second, Lydia was the head of a household. This can be seen in the fact that her conversion and that of her household are described in a manner typical of one in such a position (cf. Jn 4:53; Acts 10:2; 11:14; 16:31; 18:8; 1 Cor 1:16). It is clear as well that her house became a meeting place for the "brothers."[83] This places her in the company of such women as Mary the mother of John Mark, at whose house at least some of the community at Jerusalem met (Acts 12:12-17), Nympha who is greeted along with "the Church at her house" (Col 4:15),[84] probably also Phoebe as we have seen, perhaps Chloe (1 Cor 1:11), and Priscilla, who along with her husband Aquila provided a meeting place in both Ephesus and Rome when they lived in these cities (1 Cor 16:19; Rom 16:5). Providing a meeting place for the house church that met there obviously made the host an important component of the group, but not necessarily its leader. Among the men, Aristobolus and Narcissus, for example (Rom 16:10-11), seem not to have been Christians themselves,[85]

---

83. After Paul and Silas had been released from prison, "they went to Lydia's house where they saw and encouraged the brothers and then they left" (Acts 16:40).

84. The manuscript evidence is far from clear at this point, but the balance of the evidence points in favor of reading *Nymphan* as a feminine name and reading *autēs* (her) as the possessive pronoun. For a judicious discussion see Peter T. O'Brien, *Colossians, Philemon,* Word Biblical Commentary 44 (Waco: Word Books, 1982), 245-46.

85. In both these instances Paul is careful to send greetings to "those of (the

while others such as Gaius (Rom 16:23) and Philemon (Phlm 2) clearly
are Christian (see also Rom 16:14.15; 1 Cor 1:16; 16:15).

Priscilla and Aquila (named in this order four of the six times they
are mentioned) are a useful starting point for a consideration of Paul's
feminine collaborators as well as women teachers in general. In his note
of recommendation and greeting that now forms chapter 16 of Romans,
we read:

> Greet Prisca and Aquila, my coworkers in Christ Jesus; they risked their
> own necks for the sake of my life. To them not only I give thanks but
> also all the Churches of the Gentiles as well; and (greet) the Church at
> their house. (16:3-5a)

The couple are called "co-workers" *(synergoi),* a term Paul applies to
people some nine times in his letters. It seems to be a title he reserves for
those who have generously extended themselves for the sake of the gospel,
but nothing more precise can be garnered from it. In the same note Paul
gives the title to an otherwise unknown Urbanus (16:9) and to Timothy
(16:21). Elsewhere he applies it to Titus (2 Cor 8:23), Epaphroditus (Phil
2:25; also called "my fellow soldier and your apostle [emissary] and
minister *[leitourgos]* of my need"), and Clement (as one of the "my
co-workers," Phil 4:3). Aristarchus, Barnabas, and Jesus called Justus are
given the appelation in Colossians 4:11, as are Philemon (Phlm 1), Mark,
Aristarchus, and Demas (Phlm 24). Paul may be referring to all the
Corinthians in 2 Corinthians 1:24 and 6:1, and he calls Apollos and himself
"God's co-workers" in 1 Corinthians 3:9, saying the same of Timothy in
1 Thessalonians 3:2. Given this usage of the term and the fluidity of
vocabulary we have already seen, it is possible to say of Prisca (Priscilla)
that she, along with her husband, was an outstanding proponent of the
gospel, whose authority came from the grace of ministry she received, but
not that she held some "official" position in the church at large.

I think this is confirmed by observing the manner in which Luke
describes this same couple in Acts (18:1-3, 18-19, 26-27). He first recounts
the meeting between them and Paul in Corinth and the fact that since they
were all tentmakers, Paul lodged with them. Then, we are told that Paul
took them with him to Ephesus, where he left them. Finally, we are told
how Priscilla and Aquila took Apollos aside and "explained the Way to

---

house of) Aristobolus/Narcissus," but not to these men themselves, probably implying
that many in their household were Christian, and perhaps that they permitted meetings
in their houses, but that they themselves were not Christian.

him more accurately." From the fact that Paul lodged with them, and even more, took them with him to Ephesus, we can gather the esteem he had for them.[86] In the description of their instruction of Apollos, the positing of Priscilla's name first is probably a subtle indication of her leading role in this, though it was not unknown in that milieu for the name of the wife to be given first.[87] Again, we see the prominence and influence of a ministry divinely conferred upon both a woman and a man. They are not, however, presented in a way that would lead one to classify either of them along with the "teachers" mentioned in 1 Corinthians 12:28 and Ephesians 4:11, where the term implies office.

There are two other passages in Paul's letters that allow us to reconstruct the role of women in the early communities. In Philippians 4:2-3 we read:

> I beg Euodia and I beg Synteche to come to agreement in the Lord. Yes, and I ask you, loyal yoke-fellow, go to their help; for these women strove along with me for the Gospel along with Clement and the rest of my co-workers; their names are in the book of life.

Obviously these two women are important enough to be causing a community problem by their disagreement. Paul appeals to someone who has the respect of both of them to help them "have the same thoughts and sentiments," an ideal presented earlier in the letter to the whole community (2:2).[88] Euodia and Synteche are described as those who strove along with Paul in the work of the gospel, and they are classed with Clement and Paul's other co-workers. We may imagine them as people who helped Paul and who own homes where a church meets, or they may be teachers of some sort, or both. It would be easier to undertand their position at Philippi if we could understand what function Paul's "yoke-fellow" fulfilled there. Is he one of the "overseers" *(episkopoi)* addressed in Philippians 1:1? Somehow his position is different from that of the two women — he is *Paul's* yoke-fellow, not theirs. It is probably impossible to reconstruct the institutional reality at Philippi at this time, but what we do see enables us to appreciate how different forms of authority are meant to support each other.

The other Pauline passage is found in Romans 16:1-23, some aspects

---

86. Chrysostom does not hesitate to say that Priscilla as well as Aquila was brought along to teach: *Homilies on Acts,* 40 (*Patrologia Graeca* 60,281-82).

87. See the remarks in Witherington, *Women in the Earliest Churches,* 153.

88. The question regarding the composition of the present letter, probably made up of several letters, does not affect what is said here.

of which we have already considered. At least twenty-seven persons in Rome and eight in Corinth are named or referred to explicitly ("his mother," "his sister") in this "greeting card." Of the thirty-five people named, ten are women: three of these are probably married to the men mentioned with them. Paul uses a variety of terms to express something about many of those named: *beloved* (4 times); *relative* or *country-man/woman (syngenēs,* 3 times), *brother, sister* (1 time each), "the elect one in the Lord" (1 time), "approved in Christ" (1 time). He also describes some of them with expressions that denote a particular role in the work of the gospel: *co-worker* (3 times), one who *labored* (3 times); in addition Andronicus and Junia are described as having "shared imprisonment" and being "outstanding among the apostles," and Phoebe, as we have seen, is described as a *diakonos* and a *patroness (prostatēs).* Eight of those so singled out are women. Some commentators wish to draw from the fact that Junia is called a "co-worker" and that the verb *kopian* (labor) is applied to Mary, Tryphaena, Tryphosa, and Persis, that these should be equated with other co-workers such as Timothy and the leaders mentioned in 1 Thessalonians 5:12 and 1 Corinthians 16:16 to whom *kopian* is also applied. Such a way of reasoning imposes a rigidity of terminology foreign to the New Testament in general and Paul in particular. Certainly these women, sometimes along with their husbands, were endowed with significant ministerial gifts and great courage. There is, however, no address to a woman or quality attributed to a woman that would suggest that their leadership was of the type I have described as *office.*

In order to complete this discussion two more aspects of the question must be considered. There are first, those texts in the Pauline corpus that explicitly treat women. I am referring to Galatians 3:28, which asserts that for baptized Christians "there is not male and female," and 1 Corinthians 11:2-16 and 14:33-36, which are concerned with women's conduct at community gatherings and which provide a basis for later New Testament texts concerned with the same topic (1 Tim 2:9-15) or with marriage (Eph 5:21-33). I postpone a discussion of these until chapter 10. The other question has to do with the emergence of that particular ministry I have spoken of as *office.* I will treat that briefly now.

Office in the New Testament and the Apostolic Church

Certain ministerial gifts enable a person to exercise a very particular function, namely that of presiding over the faithful transmission of the gospel reality as this is done in word, worship, and sacrament. Such a function, which is what I mean by *office,* was never meant to be exercised in isolation from other persons who possess other gifts. In fact there must be other prophets and teachers if this important gift is to produce its full fruit. I have already stated that office is required by the historical nature of the church itself. Unity in the church must be as historical as human beings are. It must be embodied; it must find expression in a unified community life that provides a space for the truth. For such a thing to exist, there must be a stable, historically identifiable prophetic gift of guidance that partakes in the otherness of Christ as he is "over against" the community in the sense in which this expression is used in the ecumenical documents I quoted above.

It is obvious that we are not going to find the reality of office existing in a clearly distinct form in the New Testament. This is due to the fluidity of language of which I have spoken, and also to the fact that the charisms and other ministries were vigorously operative at that period and were performing functions that have since been absorbed by office, a thing not always to the benefit of the church.

Rather than the heuristic narrative of a progressive takeover by an "orthodox" movement that, through the manipulation of imported power structures, managed to impose itself on a vague and extremely diversified collection of groups, I have proposed the model of a living organism that in its origins contains in an undifferentiated mode all that it needs to achieve its identity. In such an organism there are two things that contribute to the realization of ultimate identity: a complex interactive genetic network and nongenetic (epigenetic) factors such as the place of origin of the cells and the dynamic patterns of cell divisions. In music the basic genetic network is the *score;* the actually existing and developing individual is the *performance* by a specific set of musicians who are *epigenetic* factors.[89] Thus, the function of office belongs to the intrinsic genetic code of the church, it is part of the score to be played. The actual mode of its existence, however, even in the developing stages was due to cultural or epigenetic factors. As time went on, some of the factors were responsible for performances that obscured rather than manifested the original score.[90]

89. For the basic scientific information about genetic development and for the analogy to music in the model I am applying, I am indebted to the study by Rudolf B. Brun, "Principles of Morphogenesis in Embryonic Development, Music, and Evolution," *Communio* 20 (1993): 528-43.

90. What I have just said about church order can be applied to the canon of Scriptures as well, with this difference: the written expression of the rule of faith, once established, is not intrinsically affected in its movement through time, while the human dimension of office is an historically labile reality. For a discussion of the canon of Scripture see Francis Martin, "The Biblical Canon and Church Life," in *Recovering*

Where can we find indications of the basic genetic network that governs the development of office? We find it first in the prophetic assurance with which some of the figures in the New Testament teach. This is, of course, true of Jesus, but it is also true of Paul, who says in 2 Corinthians 10:8, "And even if I should boast a little too much of our authority *(exousia)* which the Lord gave for building up and not for tearing down, I will not be put to shame." We also come upon lines like the following: "If anyone thinks he is a prophet or a spiritual person, he should recognize that what I am writing to you is a commandment of the Lord" (1 Cor 14:37), and "We belong to God, and anyone who does not belong to God refuses to hear us. This is how we know the Spirit of truth and the spirit of deceit" (1 Jn 4:6). These texts reflect the gospel tradition of Jesus' words: "Whoever listens to you, listens to me; whoever rejects you rejects me, whoever rejects me rejects the one who sent me" (Lk 10:16).[91] Authority in the church is only possible where there is a desire to make a faith response to a divine word. Without the willingness to respect and listen to the guidance of Christ, no exercise of any authority in the church, be it of office or any other ministry, is possible. Without this faith the Lord's direction will not be discerned or accepted where the weakness of the person or the challenge of the message make it unpalatable.[92]

A second indication that the reality of office pertains to the "genetic code" of the church is found in the way the church is described in Acts, and by the manner in which the function of certain leaders is described in other parts of the New Testament. In regard to Acts, it has often been objected that Luke's picture of the church represents his idealizing retrojection of what he considers normative for the Christian community. Actually, however, Luke is doing in Acts what he did in his Gospel — using allusive terminology to point to the significance and typological value of an event on the first level of the tradition. It is a prophetic way of writing history. Thus, when he uses the verb *diakonein* of the women who accompanied Jesus (Lk 8:2-3) or of Peter's mother-in-law (Lk 4:39) or even of Martha (Lk 10:40), he expects the reader to catch the overtones of disciple

---

the Sacred: Catholic Faith, Worship and Practice, Proceedings of the Twelfth Convention of the Fellowship of Catholic Scholars, ed. Paul Williams (Pittston, Pa.: Northeast Books, 1990), 117-36, and the literature given there.

91. See also Mt 10:40; 18:5; Mk 9:35; Lk 9:48; Jn 5:23; 7:28; 12:44-45; 13:20.

92. The problem of unworthy people in office is perennial and was treated with remarkable clarity by many Fathers of the church. For a good theological account of this, see Hans Urs von Balthasar, *The Office of Peter and the Structure of the Church,* trans. Andrée Emery (San Francisco: Ignatius, 1986). The matter of failure to discern through hardness of heart is a constant biblical theme: Jer 8:7; Ps 95:7-8, etc.

in his choice of word. What transpired in the life of Jesus is best understood in its effective history in the community. For this reason a discipleship term (Lk 22:26-27) is used to describe what these women did.[93] Or again, Luke's use of the image of Mary as an ideal disciple is largely effected by the vocabulary he uses in her regard.[94]

Luke's prophetic history writing in Acts is effected not only by means of vocabulary but also in his manner of portraying various roles.[95] We have already seen his basic fidelity to the Palestinian notion of apostle as including an experience of the risen Christ and membership in the Twelve. His unique use of the term *episkopos* in Acts 20:28 and his extensive use of *presbyteros* (ten times of Christian *elders*) probably also reflect the institutions and vocabulary of the Palestinian church, though both terms are also at home in hellenistic culture.[96] Not only does Luke apply the term *elder* to those who are with the *apostles* (Acts 15:2, 4, 22-23; 16:4 [11:30]) or with James (Acts 21:18), but also to those appointed to positions of leadership in the towns visited in the first journey (Acts 14:23) and at Miletus (Acts 20:17). These latter are also called "overseers" as we have seen; their role is described in Paul's words to them, and it also serves as a brief description of the duties of the apostles and elders he has already mentioned: "Keep watch over yourselves and over the whole flock of which the Holy Spirit has appointed you overseers, in which you tend the Church of God which he acquired with his own blood" (Acts 20:28).

Paul probably has in mind a similar function when he addresses the "overseers" at Philippi along with the *diakonoi* (Phil 1:1), and the same can be said for *episkopos* as it occurs in the Pastorals (1 Tim 3:2; Tit 1:7).[97]

---

93. I cannot agree with Katherine E. Corley when she restricts this term to its first-level referent, that of the supplying the wants of Jesus and the disciples: *Private Women Public Meals: Social Conflict in the Synoptic Tradition* (Peabody: Hendrickson, 1993), 119-21. Such a reading of the Gospels fails to appreciate their capacity to mediate between the life of Jesus and the life of the community in the way they speak of the former in terms which better apply to the latter. I have discussed some of this in "Critique historique et enseignement du Nouveau Testament sur l'imitation du Christ," *Revue Thomiste* 93 (1993): 234-62; especially 238-40, 254-56.

94. For a discussion of this see Raymond E. Brown, *The Birth of the Messiah* (New York: Doubleday, 1977), 318 and elsewhere.

95. We have, for instance, in Acts 6:1-7 the clearest presentation in the New Testament of the designation of new leaders.

96. For a brief discussion of these terms consult the articles in *Exegetical Dictionary of the New Testament*.

97. These four instances of the word *episkopos*, along with one application of the word to Christ in 1 Pet 2:25, are the only places in the New Testament where the word occurs.

In this latter material the contours of the position are more clearly defined, and the same can be said for at least some of the occurrences of *presbyteros* (1 Tim 5:1, 2, 17, 19; Tit 1:5).[98]

In 1 Thessalonians 5:12 Paul's exhorts the community there to "acknowledge *(eidenai)* those who are laboring among you, and who care for you [or 'are over you']"[99] in the Lord and who instruct you." The same type of reference to local leaders is found in Hebrews, which makes a link between the "leaders" *(ēgoumenoi)* who first preached the word to the group and the *ēgoumenoi* who are now to be obeyed and who deserve deference because "they keep watch over your souls as those who have to give an account" (Heb 13:7, 17). Either these same leaders or others are greeted at the end of the letter.[100]

The function I have described as office is found connected with those who are called apostles in the strict sense mentioned above, in some who are sent by the apostles,[101] and by some local leaders. The terminology applied to these people was not fixed. Thus, in addition to the terms *apostle, overseer, elder, leader,* and *servant (diakonos),* we must count as well certain uses of *prophet, teacher, those who care for,* and *those who labor.* The difficulty experienced in isolating the reality of office in the information available to us is caused not only by the vagueness of terminology but also by the fact that it was clearly but one function among others. This does not obscure the fact, however, that a close look at the *score* played by the early communities included the note of function, or to change the model, office is part of the genetic code that presided over the development of the church. Many who were endowed with charismatic and ministerial gifts served to deepen and solidify the understanding and practice of the gospel reality, but it would be anachronistic to attribute to them all the

98. Although this is not the case with Jas 5:14 and 1 Pet 5:1, the only other two places where the term designates Christian leaders.

99. The verb *proïstasthai,* translated here as "care for," means to lead, protect, or care for, often with some nuance of an authoritative role: looking after a household (1 Tim 3:3, 5, 12), promoting good works (Tit 3:8, 14; perhaps also Rom 12:8), and fulfilling the role of elder (1 Tim 5:17). It is another example of fluid nomenclature.

100. A decision in this regard depends upon deciding whether the earlier part of chapter 13 belongs to the original discourse or is part of what is added when it is sent to other communities. There is little difference made either way for our concerns. For a discussion see William L. Lane, *Hebrews 9–13,* Word Biblical Commentary 47B (Waco: Word Books, 1991), 521-58.

101. This would apply to Judas and Silas, sent by the leaders of the Jerusalem community, and to Timothy, co-author of some of Paul's letters (1 Thess 1:1; 2 Cor 1:1; Phil 1:1) and sent by him to Thessalonica (1 Thess 3:2), Philippi (Phil 2:19), and Corinth (1 Cor 4:17).

reality of office. The fact that even at the earliest level, when women were rightfully prominent and influential because of their gifts and services, there is no clear evidence that a woman was ever an office holder, is not an accident in the data, nor a patriarchal reading of it.[102] It pertains, rather, to an intuitive understanding of the mode of relating properly to the body person, and the symbolic nature of the human body. To grasp this intuition it will be necessary to rectify much of what we have received from the Enlightenment in regard to our thinking about human nature, its mode of knowing, and its causality. After treating of these last issues, I will return in chapter 11 to discuss body person and relations in the church.

The Increasing Importance of Office

There is plenty of evidence within the New Testament itself that it was necessary from the outset to accomplish two things: defend the truth of Jesus Christ from misunderstanding and error,[103] and defend Christians from the fear and discouragement that resulted from persecution.[104] While this is always a duty of the whole community (see, for example, Rev 2:2-6; 14-16; 18-25), it is particularly the domain of those who hold office. This can be seen in the advice given to Timothy and Titus. But perhaps the most striking illustration of the faith instinct of the church in appreciating the function of office can be found in the manner in which the figure of Peter developed.[105] Peter is the great Christian fisherman (missionary), and the rock upon which Jesus builds his church. As the life of the church developed in the latter part of the first century, other aspects of his character and role were accentuated in the prophetic redescriptions of him: he is also the shepherd and martyr, the confessor of the true faith, the guardian against false teaching, and always the weak and sinful man, outrun by some, corrected by others, perplexed at first by the resurrection of the Lord despite the witness of the women, but the one for whom Christ prayed in a special way so that he could strengthen his brethren (Lk 22:32), and who ultimately glorified God by his death (Jn 21:19).

---

102. Evidence to the contrary is sometimes adduced, most recently by Torjesen, *When Women Were Priests*. Torjesen's study relies on a combination of a rigid reading of terminology that is still fluid and a revisionist reinterpretation of the data.

103. This not only can be seen in Paul's teaching in Gal 1:6-10, most of 1 Corinthians, and the two concluding chapters of 1 Thessalonians, but is also implied in Luke's description of his motive for composing his Gospel (Lk 1:4, see as well Jn 20:31), and clearly asserted in the first letter of John.

104. See, among other places, Heb 10:32-39.

105. I am indebted here to the excellent work done by the members of the Lutheran-Roman Catholic dialogue, *Peter in the New Testament*, especially 164-68.

Peter is very much a part of a community of believers, each of whom possesses his or her own charisms and ministries. Within this he bears a particular witness to the "otherness" of the authority and truth of Christ. At the end of the first century and the beginning of the second, however, the pressure of error and persecution and the fact of larger communities began to force a certain separation between office and the other gifts. The two factors I just mentioned can be considered environmental influences in the process of development. They affected the development but they did not make the result inevitable. This was also due to the interaction between the environment and epigenetic factors more intrinsic to the system.

In the subapostolic period this tendency, already evident in the later writings of the New Testament, becomes more pronounced. There was error, mostly various forms of proto-gnosticism; there was persecution, not only government initiated but also spontaneous and local; and there was the growth of the communities. All this forced those who were charged in a special way with guarding the life of the communities to assume a more prominent role. The need for safety meant a closer control over the exercise of the other gifts, both charismatic and ministerial. In this situation office absorbed many functions that belong more properly to other gifts, with the result that many Christians, men as well as women, no longer have the causality within the life of the community that belongs to them.[106] Although there may have been some anti-feminine sentiment, it is quite wrong to see this loss of active participation in the life of the community as necessarily misogynist. The developing organism, while still faithful to its basic orientation, grew disproportionately in some areas and suffered a severe weakening in others. I have already given examples of this and will point out others in the next chapter.

This process of centralization is reflected in the progressive standardizing of terminology. It is generally agreed that by the end of the second century the triad *"episcopos, presbyteros,* and *diakonos"* was firmly in place,[107] though their interrelation was not always clear, nor was the relation

106. It is important to notice the difference in what I am proposing here and that proposed by the adherents of the prevailing heuristic structure in regard to Christian origins. For the organic developmental model I propose, office was always a part of the church, although it later assumed an undue importance. The other view is well described by Elisabeth Schüssler Fiorenza, who also speaks of an absorption but describes it in terms of "a shift from alternating leadership available to all the baptized to patriarchal leadership restricted to male heads of households . . ." (*In Memory of Her,* 286-87). There was not "alternating leadership" but different forms of leadership, with that of charism and ministry being exercised by women as well as by men.

107. See for instance Schillebeeckx, *The Church with a Human Face,* 91; Dunn, *The Priesthood,* 63-65; Osborne, *Priesthood,* 89-129.

between office and the other gifts articulated satisfactorily. We do see, however, in the Pastorals and elsewhere the beginning of certain groupings in the church such as "widow" or "deaconess."[108] At this early stage neither could be considered as an order, and in any event order is not office.

There were many elements in the church's life during the latter part of the second century that are more clearly understood in the light of the full development in the third century. For that reason a discussion of them has been postponed until the next chapter.

108. For a discussion of these see Witherington, *Women in the Earliest Churches*, 199-205.

4

The Move toward Crystallization

At the end of the last chapter I pointed to several indications within the New Testament itself that office was beginning to assume a greater importance at the expense of charisms and other ministries. I wish to take up that question again to the degree that it touches upon the place of women in the early church. The first part of this chapter will thus be devoted to a consideration of how the church interacted with the environment created by heresy, persecution, and ultimately approval. All three had both positive and negative effects. The second part of the chapter is a brief overview of the roles of women in the culture created by the church of the West. The purpose of this section is to confer some perspective on the problems raised by the feminists in regard to both Western culture and the Christian church. In the third part of the chapter I offer an analysis of the "crystallizing" effect of the Enlightenment thinking, which managed to eliminate the ambiguity of the preceding eras by creating a greater ambiguity of its own made up of a reinforced pagan notion of power and an originally Christian notion of the dignity of the human person. Feminism, particularly in its theoretical presuppositions, is heir to this ambiguity.

OFFICE, CHARISMA, MINISTRIES, AND WOMEN'S ROLES IN THE EARLY CENTURIES

The Pressure from Without

Throughout the second century the score or genetic code that gives the church its specificity was played out amid some very particular pressures that left their stamp on its growth. We can catch glimpses of some of these influences already in the New Testament. Paul in the Letter to the Galatians confronts a particular kind of Judaizing influence that may have included a sort of cosmic mysticism (4:8-11; 5:2-12). Again, at Corinth the influence of the "super apostles" and perhaps others seems to have produced various currents of thought loosely connected with what may be called "proto-gnosticism."[1] It is difficult to determine the drift of a certain cosmic mysticism combated by Colossians (esp. 2:8-23). But the atmosphere inferred from the letters to Timothy, including the remark concerning Hymenaeus and Philetus, who say that "the resurrection has already taken place" (2 Tim 2:18), implies a certain gnosticizing tendency at Ephesus.[2]

The important theoreticians of early Gnosticism elaborated a cosmic-religious theory that purported to bring its adherents to an understanding of themselves and their existence that would enable them to achieve liberation from the enslaving powers of the material world. Their precise views are known to us almost entirely from the writings of those who opposed them,[3] yet it seems clear that their approach was immensely attractive in an "age of anxiety."[4] Although the raw material for Gnosticism was found in many different places, the gnostic synthesis was effected by means of a distortion of Christian insights. For this reason the leaders of the church opposed it from the outset. In general their arguments were based on the incarnational reality of Jesus, in his death and present resurrected state, and on his presence in the church. The foremost representative of the first approach was Irenaeus, who saw clearly that the Gnostics in effect denied the true nature of human historicality and thus could not accept bodily existence for themselves or their savior. Echoes of this can be found in the polemics of Ignatius of Antioch and Tertullian. I will return to consider the patristic teaching on the human body in chapter 11.

The second mode of argument was based on the incarnational nature of the church and thus appealed to the human transmission, in example,

---

1. See the article by Hans Dieter Betz and Margaret M. Mitchell, "Corinthians, First Epistle to the," in the *Anchor Bible Dictionary* 1, 1139-48, and also Simone Pétrement, *A Separate God: The Christian Origins of Gnosticism,* trans. Carol Harrison (San Francisco: Harper, 1990), especially part 2, chapter II, "The 'Gnostics' at Corinth," which provides a good account of the various opinions of those who have attempted to identify Paul's opponents at Corinth.

2. Pétrement, *A Separate God,* part 2, chapter IV, "The Signs of Gnosticizing Heresies at Ephesus."

3. In addition to Pétrement, see the article by Kurt Rudolf, "Gnosticism," in the *Anchor Bible Dictionary* 2, 1033-40.

4. I take the expression from the work of E. R. Dodds, *Pagan and Christian in an Age of Anxiety* (Cambridge: Cambridge University Press, 1965). Dodds's work contains many good insights into the climate of the period, but his understanding of Christianity is reductionist.

word, and writing, of the apostolic teaching by those who had received the office to do so. This is clearly one of the motives for the consistent message of Ignatius regarding obedience to the bishop, and it forms the basis of Irenaeus's tracing of the teaching through Polycarp back to the apostolic era and his attention to the canon of the Scriptures. It was, in fact, during this same period of the second century that the canon emerged in a recognizable, if not totally complete, form.[5]

The same type of pressure on the leaders of the various communities was created by movements such as Montanism and Marcionism. Marcion (d. 160) possessed great organizational skills that necessarily forced the church to close ranks in regard to determining both who had the right to teach authoritatively and what was to be included in the canon. Montanism, a charismatic sect that arose in Phrygia during this period, featured two women, Priscilla and Maxima, as prophetesses and leaders. An oracle of the time claims that Priscilla had a dream in which she received wisdom from Christ, who appeared as a woman.[6] The aggressive apocalyptic and ascetic fervor of the movement made it suspect and was another element in making both prophecy and feminine leadership suspect.

Within the literature of the Gnostic sects women were often the recipients of secret revelations. For example, in the *Gospel of Mary* Mary Magdalene proclaims, "Jesus prepared us and made us men."[7] There is abundant patristic evidence that in Gnosticism and Marcionism as well as in Montanism, women were prominent and may have been especially sought after. Hence Tertullian's pre-Montanist exclamation: "These heretical women — how bold they are! They have no modesty, they are audacious

---

5. "By the close of the second century, however, we can see the outlines of what may be described as the nucleus of the New Testament. Although the fringes of the emerging canon remained unsettled for generations, a high degree of unaminity concerning the greater part of the New Testament was attained among the very diverse and scattered congregations of believers not only throughout the Mediterranean world but also over an area extending from Britain to Mesopotamia." Bruce Metzger, *The Canon of the New Testament: Its Origin, Development and Significance* (Oxford: Clarendon Press, 1988 repr.), 74. The same basic judgment is made by H. Y. Gamble, "The Canon of the New Testament," in *The New Testament and its Modern Interpreters,* ed. Eldon Jay Epp and George W. McCrae (Atlanta: Scholars Press, 1989), 201-43.

6. See Monique Alexandre, "Early Christian Women," in *A History of Women in the West,* vol. 1, *From Ancient Goddesses to Christian Saints,* ed. Pauline Schmitt Pantel (Cambridge, Mass.: The Belknap Press of Harvard University Press, 1992), 428.

7. Quoted in Alexandre, 426. For corroboration of the statements made in this paragraph, one may conveniently consult this portion of Alexandre's study.

enough to teach, to engage in argument, to perform exorcisms, to undertake cures, and maybe even to baptize."[8]

Nevertheless, the presence of women in Gnosticism and elsewhere does not necessarily indicate that women sought and found in these movements a freedom denied them in the church. In fact, despite their claims, the Montanists did not begin ordaining women until the fourth century.[9] For their part, the Gnostics were capable of polemic against women that went beyond that of the harshest Christian attacks.[10] Thus, the connection between Gnostic doctrine and female leadership comes into question: the roles of women in Gnosticism may have reflected the many legal rights afforded women in Egypt or the fact that the membership of Gnostic sects was overwhelmingly aristocratic.[11] It is also possible that the same aspects of asceticism that attracted women to Christianity drew them to Gnosticism.[12]

The result of the various movements just discussed was a tightening of leadership, not uncontested, on the part of those who held office. Office, as I have defined it, belongs to the essential nature of the church, and its contours necessarily become more evident as the church grows. The pressures placed upon the church resulted in a suspicion of charismatic and prophetic claims to enlightenment, whether these were made by men or by women, and a reluctance to allow women positions of influence in the community. The prominent place given to women by heretical groups actually contributed to restricting the roles of women in the church. This last-named tendency could also be accompanied by a particular interpretation of New Testament tradition.[13] It

8. Tertullian, *On the Prescription of Heretics,* 41.

9. See Manfred Hauke, *Women in the Priesthood? A Systematic Analysis in the Light of the Order of Creation and Redemption,* trans. David Kipp (San Francisco: Ignatius, 1988), 408.

10. Susanne Heine, *Women and Early Christianity: A Reappraisal* (Minneapolis: Augsburg Publishing House, 1987) offers a telling critique of much feminist reading of gnostic texts, especially those dependent upon Elaine Pagels, *The Gnostic Gospels* (Penguin Books, 1980).

11. See the references in Elizabeth A. Clark, "Devil's Gateway and Bride of Christ: Women in the Early Christian World," and in her *Ascetic Piety and Women's Faith: Essays on Late Ancient Christianity* (Lewiston: The Edwin Mellen Press, 1986), 36.

12. Anne Ewing Hickey, *Women of the Roman Aristocracy as Christian Monastics* (Ann Arbor, Mich.: University Microfilms, 1983), 7.

13. Witness the fourth century Syrian, perhaps Arianizing, document, the *Apostolic Constitutions* (III, 6, 1-2,): "We do not allow women to teach in the Church. We allow them only to pray and to listen to the masters. Indeed, our Master himself, Jesus Christ, when he sent us Twelve to teach peoples and nations, did not send women to preach, although there was no lack of them, for with us were the mother of the Lord and her sisters, as well as Mary Magdalene and Mary, mother of James, and Martha and Mary, the sisters of Lazarus, and Salome, and others. If it were necessary for women

would be a mistake, however, to portray this period and those that followed it as one long tale of the oppression of women (and of non-office-holding men). Although the divorce between office and other ministries and charisms eventually led to the practical absence of these latter, this was due more to the fact that the Christian vision of reality became less a living faith on the part of many and more a plausibility structure, as I argued in chapter 2. As Christianity was domesticated and ecclesial office became a civil status as well, there was a diminution of general awareness of the otherness of the church's source of life. That this was not complete and that there were charisms and ministries raised up by the Holy Spirit and recognized by the church's office holders is obvious from the history of the period. I wish now to give some examples in order to locate more correctly the position of women in the early centuries.

The Presence of Charisms and Ministries

The most striking charism of the early period of the Church, and of any period, is that of witness *(martyr)*. The literature containing accounts of women martyrs is quite extensive.[14] In *The Martyrdom of Perpetua and Felicity,* Vibia Perpetua, a noblewoman martyred in 203, represents the "self-discipline by which the follower in the footsteps of the crucified One was to train himself unto virtue."[15] Perpetua's *imitatio Christi* is reflected in the "sacramental motifs" that abound in her story. In one vision Perpetua ascends Jacob's ladder, a baptismal motif, and meets a grey-haired man who gives her milk to drink — recalling both the Eucharist and North African baptismal ceremonies. Another vision has Perpetua being prepared for an encounter in the amphitheater with the Devil, who is in the guise of an Egyptian, by being rubbed down with oil, again recalling the baptismal rite.[16]

A particularly interesting example of early hagiography is the story of Thecla represented in the apocryphal *Acts of Paul.* The fact that the story reveals Montanist leanings did not prevent the Christians of the second to fifth centuries from reading and retelling it. Tertullian identifies the hereti-

---

to teach, he himself would have been the first to order them to instruct the people. If 'the head of the woman is the man,' it is not right for the rest of the body to command the head."

14. For some examples see Elizabeth Clark, *Women in the Early Church,* Message of the Fathers of the Church 13 (Wilmington, Del.: Glazier, 1983).

15. Alvyn Petersen, "Perpetua — Prisoner of Conscience," *Vigiliae Christianae* 41 (1987): 139-53; citation is from p. 139.

16. Ibid., 147-48.

cal elements in his attack on Gnostic literature: Thecla herself preaches and baptizes. And yet, Thecla's feats recall the missionary activities of women in the early church, and her heroic stand before the lions earned her a valiant reputation. Gregory of Nyssa claims that Thecla was the secret name of his sister Macrina, recalling a woman "of much fame among the virgins."[17] Jerome writes approvingly of "Saint Thecla" but also denies that the story is of apostolic origin.[18] Thus early Christians affirmed the heroic virtue of a woman while at the same time rejecting the heretical elements that were injected by the storyteller.[19]

Another charism prominent among women was that of perpetual chastity and consecrated celibacy. The earliest organized role for women in the early church was that of the widows. Three kinds of widows are mentioned in the New Testament. Widows, poor women who have lost their husbands, are described in Acts 6:1-2 and 9:39 as deserving care from the Christian community. In Titus 2:3-4 a group of older "widows" are exhorted to care for the younger women and to set a standard of perfection within the community. Finally, by the time of the first letter to Timothy (5:3-10), the "widows" are set apart as a distinct class. They must be at least sixty years of age and married only once. The widow is expected to be exemplary in Christian charity and hospitality. It is of this latter group that Polycarp speaks when he calls the widows the "altar of God" (Phil 4:3). Widows are appointed for prayer for the entire community.[20]

At about the time that the widows were being organized into an order in the third century, the ideal of widowhood was giving way to that of perpetual virginity. The first virgins were often martyrs. At a certain period

17. Gregory of Nyssa, *Life of St. Macrina* in *Saint Gregory of Nyssa: Ascetical Works*, The Fathers of the Church (Washington: Catholic University of America Press, 1967), 164.

18. Lynne C. Boughton, "From Pious Legend to Feminist Fantasy: Distinguishing Hagiographical License from Apostolic Practice in the *Acts of Paul/Acts of Thecla*," *Journal of Religion* 71 (1991): 376.

19. In asserting that "the *Acts of Thecla* were long considered canonical, even by the mainstream Church" ("Word, Spirit and Power: Women in Early Christian Communities," in Rosemary Radford Reuther and Eleanor McLaughlin, eds., *Women of Spirit: Female Leadership in the Jewish and Christian Traditions* [New York: Simon and Schuster, 1979], 51), Elisabeth Schüssler Fiorenza uses the terms *canonical* and *Church* "in a manner differently from the way those terms were used in the first three Christian centuries." Boughton, ibid., 370. Boughton's essay is a compelling critique of the whole manner of proceeding characteristic of the heuristic structure I criticized in chapter 3.

20. Jean Danielou, *The Ministry of Women in the Early Church*, trans. Glyn Simon (Leighton Buzzard: The Faith Press, 1974), 13-14.

in the Roman Empire, virginity carried with it a penalty of death.[21] Yet, by the fourth century there were Christian women consecrated as virgins in infancy by their parents. Newly converted Christians may have viewed the consecration of their daughters as an alternative to infanticide.[22] Certainly as an ascetic ideal consecration was almost uniformly rejected by the Roman aristocracy; noble women were expected to perpetuate family names and fortunes.[23] Thus those Roman noblewomen who did dedicate themselves to virginity belie the claim that asceticism merely served societal functions — for them, sexual renunciation was truly counter-cultural.[24] Furthermore, since most noblewomen who embraced asceticism surrounded themselves with a retinue of other women, "women from the poorest classes may thus have benefited from the generosity of wealthy ascetics, finding shelter and a livelihood from the consecrated rich."[25]

Whereas the *Life of Anthony* heralded the founding of the Desert Fathers, "female asceticism grew out of the Christian household."[26] From their household fourth-century ascetics engaged in a variety of charitable works, a "particularly feminine activity."[27] But asceticism also allowed women to engage in activities previously considered unfeminine. Consecrated women were permitted to travel. "Proper Christian wives did not wander about the world unaccompanied by husbands or fathers, yet such 'wandering' was acceptable for these ascetics when it was blessed with the name of pilgrimage or when undertaken as a religious duty."[28] Female ascetics were also encouraged to become well educated; some, like Marcella, mastered Hebrew and Greek.[29] Such instruction equipped women to

21. Jo Ann McNamara, "Muffled Voices: The Lives of Consecrated Women in the Fourth Century," in *Medieval Religious Women*, vol. 1, *Distant Echoes*, ed. John A. Nichols and Lillian Thomas Shank (Kalamazoo, Mich.: Cistercian Publications, 1984), 14.

22. Ibid.; cf. Peter Brown, *The Body and Society: Men, Women and Sexual Renunciation in Early Christianity* (New York: Columbia University Press, 1988), 261.

23. Elizabeth A. Clark, "Ascetic Renunciation and Feminine Advancement: A Paradox of Late Christianity," in *Ascetic Piety and Women's Faith*, 177.

24. See Anne Yarbrough, "Christianization in the Fourth Century: The Example of Roman Women," *Church History* (1976): 149-65. For a clear critique of an excessively social understanding of Christian asceticism that ignores the clear faith and Christological statements of the women and men who practiced it, see Robin Darling Young, "Recent Interpretations of Early Christian Asceticism," *The Thomist* 54 (1990): 123-40.

25. McNamara, "Muffled Voices," 20.

26. Brown, *The Body and Society,* 263.

27. McNamara, "Muffled Voices," 25.

28. Clark, "Ascetic Renunciation and Feminine Advancement," 186.

29. J. N. D. Kelly, *Jerome: His Life, Writings, and Controversies* (London: Gerald Duckworth & Co, 1975), 95.

withstand heresy as when Melania the Younger defended the faith against Nestorianism.[30]

The leisure that made such intellectual accomplishments possible was, however, short-lived. The fifth century saw the advancing decay of the Roman Empire, and the institutionalization of female asceticism became a way of protecting women. Nevertheless, even in the barbarian invasions women had important roles. The communities of consecrated women in Gaul, for instance, acted as partners of bishops by evangelizing their neighbors.[31] Baudonivia, the female biographer of Saint Radegund, emphasized the feminine values of the holy woman who acted as a peacemaker not only in her monastery but also between the church and the reigning families amid the tumult of Gallic politics.[32] We will treat this period shortly.

The ministry of teaching was widely exercised by women, many of whom were ascetics. We saw some examples of these teachers in chapters 1 and 2. It is easier to appreciate the importance and authority of this ministry and those who exercised it, whether men or women, when it is seen to be distinct, but not separate, from office. Because of the pressure already described, which, in other forms, continued in the subsequent centuries, and because of the isolation of theology, the ministry of teacher was not and has not been adequately incorporated into the faith life of the church, though exceptional teachers have demonstrated how this incorporation should take place.

Closely linked, though not identical to widows and ascetics, is the ministry of deaconnesses. The origin of this ministry is difficult to determine;[33] however, it may generally be said that the rise of the order of deaconesses was a response to the needs of the early communities, and of the male-female segregation that took place in the early church.[34] Deaconesses prepared women for baptism and the catechumenate, and ministered to sick women. Although there is debate over the significance of the

30. Clark, "Ascetic Renunciation and Feminine Advancement," 187.

31. Jo Ann McNamara, "Living Sermons: Consecrated Women and the Conversion of Gaul," in *Medieval Religious Women*, vol. 2, *Peacemakers*, ed. Lillian Thomas Shank and John A. Nichols (Kalamazoo, Mich.: Cistercian Publications, 1987), 22.

32. Suzanne Fonay Wemple, "Female Spirituality and Mysticism in Frankish Monasteries: Radegund, Bathild and Aldegund" in *Peaceweavers*, 44.

33. For convenient sources for information and bibliography one may consult two recent articles on "Deaconess." The first is by Everett Ferguson, in *Encyclopedia of Early Christianity*, ed. Everett Ferguson (New York: Garland Publishing Company, 1990), 258-59. The second is by M. G. Biancho in *Encyclopedia of the Early Church*, vol. 1, ed. Angelo de Berardino, trans. Adrian Walford (Cambridge: James Clark and Co., 1992), 221.

34. Alexandre, 433; Danielou, 14.

ceremony of the laying on of hands associated with the ordination of deaconesses, there is general agreement that their ministry was never considered to be an office.

If we combine what has been said thus far with the historical survey in chapter 2, we see that there is an authentic organic growth of the church that is faithful to and manifests its essential notes. This judgment is contrary to the prevailing paradigm of successive compromise with and capitulation to influences outside the church. It is certainly true, however, that the players who executed the musical score (to return to this comparison) left their cultural mark on the church. This is evident, for instance, in the manner in which the clergy of the Constantinian, Merovingian, and Carolingian periods were assimilated in some ways to the civil service. This intertwining of the religious and the secular must be borne in mind in the following brief survey of the ages that followed upon the fall of Rome.

THE ROLES OF WOMEN IN THE HISTORY OF EUROPE

Even a cursory look at the history of preindustrial Europe easily refutes the "myth of total subjection,"[35] whose most effective proponents were John Stuart Mill and Simone de Beauvoir.[36] Rather, what is immediately conspicuous among the medieval sources is their disconcerting ambiguity toward women. The harshest misogynist writings are found alongside records of actual women possessing immense power and influence. Apparently, rigid sex roles were consistently ignored at all levels of society. Strict gender-based laws were belied by actual practice. The inconsistencies are such that an historian can collect innumerable historical facts and examples to build the case either for or against the pervasive oppression of women, depending on his or her intent.[37] This inability to give an

---

35. The phrase is used by Berenice A. Carroll in "Mary Beard's *Women As a Force in History: A Critique,*" in Berenice A. Carroll, ed., *Liberating Women's History: Theoretical and Critical Essays* (Chicago: University of Illinois Press, 1976), 26-41.

36. See Mill, *On the Subjection of Women* (Greenwich, Conn.: Fawcett Publications, 1970); de Beauvoir, *Le deuxième sexe* (Paris: Gallimard, 1949). For an interesting insight into the influence exercised over Mill by his friend and ultimately wife, Harriet Taylor, and the resulting "platonic" philosophy he produced, see Phyllis Rose, *Parallel Lives: Five Victorian Marriages* (New York: Alfred A. Knopf Inc., 1983), chapter 3.

37. See for instance the studies by Mary Beard, Eileen Power, and Régine Pernaud, who posit a practical equality between men and women, versus those of Brenda Bolton, Sharon Elkins, Joan Kelly-Gadol, and Janet Nelson, who seem to see women as unremittingly oppressed.

adequate account of the record reveals a handicap in our reading of history. The past remains obscure because it tends to be viewed in the postfeminist terms that presuppose a conscious power struggle between the sexes and a sharp public-private distinction.

In assessing the status of women in a given society, a variety of social indicators can be used, such as women's relative control over property, their economic contribution, work outside the home, participation in political life, authority over children, and the conditions of marriage.[38] These factors must be evaluated with care, however, since they fluctuate widely among different societies and are not equally indicative of the status of women. A society with liberal inheritance laws may at the same time accord women a very limited political role.[39] The factors also vary in their relative significance — the right to vote, considered fundamental in modern Western society, had comparably little importance to medieval Europeans. To interpret one society according to the hierarchy of values of another is to risk the distortions of cultural myopia. But contemporary analyses of "patriarchy" tend to do just that, when they read other cultures through the lens of what our own culture most esteems — personal autonomy and power.

That historians are not immune to this danger is evident from their occasional comments. One author, citing a medieval noblewoman whose seal depicted herself kneeling at the Virgin Mary's feet, refers to the image as "this religious and somewhat mutilating symbol,"[40] a description that would have been absolutely inconceivable to the seal's owner. A study on women in religious life asserts that women "began to demand recognition of their real and separate identity" in the face of male orders determined to exclude them.[41] This presumption of unilateral exclusion and resistance is more a modern reading than one based on historical sensitivity. Again, other scholars base their interpretation of events on the unquestioned assumption that any historical development truly threatening to male supremacy would have been suppressed, as these statements witness: "As

38. See Martin King Whyte, *The Status of Women in Preindustrial Societies* (Princeton, N.J.: Princeton University Press, 1978).

39. See Olivia Vlahos, "The Goddess That Failed," *First Things* 28 (1992): 12-19, esp. p. 16.

40. Brigitte Bedos Rezak, "Women, Seals and Power in Medieval France, 1150-1350," in *Women and Power in the Middle Ages,* ed. Mary Erler and Maryanne Kowaleski (Athens, Ga.: University of Georgia Press, 1988), 61-82; citation is from p. 76.

41. Brenda Bolton, "Mulieres Sanctae," in *Women in Medieval Society,* ed. Susan Mosher Stuard (Philadelphia: University of Pennsylvania Press, 1976), 141-58; citation is from p. 143.

society became better organized and ecclesiastically more right-minded, the necessity for male dominance began to assert itself";[42] "[The twelfth-century experience] highlights the forms of early medieval female activity that, yes, were permitted because in the interests of male-dominated institutions."[43] Quite a few studies portray the changing status and roles of medieval women in terms of a power struggle.

In all of this there is the presumption that human beings have always placed the same value on the various dimensions of life that we, living in a liberal democracy, see fit to place. This results in a twofold myopia: the uncritical assumption that our values are always the best, and the certitude that people of the past who held other values were really oppressed but did not know it. This latter presumption forms the basis for what we call in our day the "raising of consciousness," whose theoretical legitimacy but sometimes coercive practice I will discuss further on.

When the modern lens is cast off, the apparent contradictions in the sources begin to take on some coherence. The general trajectory that emerges, despite historical and geographical fluctuations, is that women occupied an increasingly prominent and respected place in the early Middle Ages, which in later centuries gave way to a gradual decline, and finally downright oppression. At no time did women (or any members of society) have the independence and variety of options they have today, but neither were they ever completely silenced as a class. Not infrequently they had as individuals political and economic weight comparable to the twentieth century's most powerful women.

Women's Legal and Economic Status

David Herlihy and others have documented the significant advances for women that characterized the early Middle Ages.[44] Using such sources as

42. R. W. Southern, *Western Society and the Church in the Middle Ages,* Pelican History of the Church, vol. 2 (Baltimore: Penguin Books, 1970), 310.

43. Janet L. Nelson, "Women and the Word in the Earlier Middle Ages," in *Women in the Church,* Papers Read at the 1989 Summer Meeting and the 1990 Winter Meeting of the Ecclesiastical History Society, ed. W. J. Sheils and Diana Wood (Oxford: Basil Blackwell, 1990), 53-78.

44. See David Herlihy, "Land, Family and Women in Continental Europe, 701-1200" *Traditio* 18 (1962): 89-119; Suzanne Wemple, *Women in Frankish Society: Marriage and the Cloister 500 to 900* (Philadelphia: University of Pennsylvania Press, 1981); Jo Ann McNamara and Suzanne Wemple, "The Power of Woman through the Family in Medieval Europe, 500-1100," in *Women and Power in the Middle Ages,* 83-101.

property charters, field perambulations, and wills, Herlihy shows that women's legal and economic status rose steadily, reaching an apex around the eleventh century. In the late Roman Empire the custom of manus, in which women were perpetual minors under the guardianship of their husbands, gradually became extinct, while Germanic laws granted women increasing property and inheritance rights.[45] The practice of bride purchase disappeared in favor of the bride gift, a settlement usually of landed property providing for the woman's economic security. Visigothic and Burgundian laws were particularly progressive in allowing girls to inherit equally with boys and in considering acquisitions gained after marriage as community property, of which the wife or her heirs could claim a share upon death or dissolution of the family. A widow retained administrative control over family property and even over the total patrimony of her minor children. Gallic and Anglo-Saxon laws made similar gains in later centuries.[46] As managers and disposers of property, women played significant roles in the flow of wealth and wielded impressive political clout. It was a matter of course that women who inherited an estate exercised its concomitant managerial responsibilities, often including the administration of justice, legislation, coining money, and raising armies. A concurrent phenomenon, occurring most frequently among the nobility, was the increasingly common use of a matronymic for the surname rather than a patronymic.[47] This usage was often simply due to the fact that one's mother happened to be more socially prominent, or that one's inheritance came through her. Herlihy posits a correlation between this practice and women's rising economic importance as land owners and managers.

Throughout all classes of society, women exercised essential economic functions in regard to family property. Among the working classes, where the economic contribution of all family members was imperative, women's essential functions gave them important status in the household. There was no place for the Victorian ideal of the economically useless "angel in the house."[48] "The wife characteristically supervised the household's 'inner economy' . . . those activities carried on in or near the house, cooking, brewing, spinning and weaving, usually too the garden and the raising and care of yard animals. Conversely, the 'outer economy' . . . principally the work in outlying fields and the tending of herds, was the

45. Herlihy, "Land," 91.

46. See Frances and Joseph Gies, *Women in the Middle Ages* (New York: Barnes and Noble, 1978), 18-20.

47. Herlihy, "Land," 92.

48. See Judith M. Bennett, "Public Power and Authority in Medieval English Countryside," in *Women and Power in the Middle Ages,* 18-36.

man's domain."[49] Manors retained not only male but female villeins and
cotters, both widowed and single, who rendered the same services as men
to the manorial lord. Such functions as sheepshearing, care of the dairy,
and keeping of small poultry were usually committed to women.[50] For the
noble and royal classes, women's domain of responsibility typically included the distribution of salaries and management of financial and domestic affairs. This was in large part due to the practical requirements of
household management during the extended absences of men at war. Christine de Pisan wrote of the responsibilities of wives: "because that knights,
esquires and gentlemen go upon journeys and follow the wars, it beseemeth
their wives to be wise and of great governance, and to see clearly in all
that they do, for that most often they dwell at home without their husbands,
who are at court or in divers lands."[51] Herlihy concludes that although
there were variations according to class, region, and time period, in general
"the woman comes to play an extraordinary role in the management of
family property in the early Middle Ages, and social customs as well as
economic life were influenced by her prominence."[52]

In her study of women in Frankish society, Suzanne Wemple also
traces the legal and social progress of early medieval women as compared
to their predecessors of antiquity. Women of Roman descent could now
manage their own property, act as guardians of their children, and inherit
land, sometimes equally with their brothers. Queens and noblewomen could
exercise considerable power as regents for their children or as patrons of
churchmen and secular officials. "The wives of magnates issued donations
jointly with their husbands, founded monasteries, endowed churches, cultivated interfamilial ties, transmitted clan ideology to their children, supervised the household, and administered the family's estates when their
husbands were away."[53] Women's economic importance was underscored
by the fact that barbarian laws often imposed a higher penalty, or wergild,
for killing a woman than a man. Women could sue and be sued, make wills
and contracts, plead their own cases in court, execute their deceased
spouses' wills, and even act as their husbands' attorneys.[54]

There were wide variations in the relative positions of women of the

49. Herlihy, "Land," 102.
50. See Eileen Power, *Medieval Women* (Cambridge: Cambridge University
Press, 1975), 411.
51. Quoted in Power, 418.
52. Herlihy, "Land," 89.
53. *Women in Frankish Society,* 190.
54. See Joseph and Frances Gies, *Life in a Medieval City* (New York: Harper
Colophon Books, 1969), 52.

upper and lower classes. Herlihy finds that "the importance of women seems to advance as we ascend the social scale, becoming most pronounced among the warriors and the married clergy, the two chief propertied classes of early medieval Europe."[55] Michael Kaufman, speaking of a later time period after the emergence of feudalism, argues that among the lower classes, the simple necessities of survival and the near-equal economic contribution of both marriage partners resulted in a practical equality of men and women.[56] Lower-class inheritance customs favored daughters over a strictly male line. Women actively protected their rights to property ownership in court and frequently won disputes with their husbands. Aristocratic women, in contrast, "were considered minors at best, chattel at worst."[57] They were often sold as a means of upward social mobility, could not marry without the consent of their lord, and were legally subject to their husband's will. Undoubtedly, the rise of feudal law in the ninth and tenth centuries, with its linkage of military obligation to property ownership, was particularly detrimental to aristocratic women, who eventually resumed their status as minors under the guardianship of men.

Women's Economic Role Outside the Home

Women's economic weight was felt not only in the domestic realm. In a volume of guild records collected by the English Parliament in 1389, during England's Catholic period, only five of five hundred guilds were exclusively male.[58] Most of the eighty-five craft guilds gave women equal opportunities and penalties, including election of officers, participation in feast days, and punishment for misdeeds. Women were even admitted as lay members to religious guilds managed by priests. Married women could carry on separate businesses as femmes soles, a status recognized in many town regulations. Many craft regulations, however, barred women except for the craftsman's wives and daughters, mostly because of competition for labor.[59] Similarly, of five hundred crafts listed in the Parisian *Livre des Metiers,* five were the monopoly of women, and many others employed both sexes, though usually

55. "Land," 110.
56. "Spare Ribs: The Conception of Woman in the Middle Ages and the Renaissance," *Soundings* 16 (1973): 139-63.
57. Ibid., 147.
58. Ibid.
59. See Eileen Power, "The Position of Women," in *The Legacy of the Middle Ages,* ed. C. G. Crump and E. F. Jacob (Oxford: Clarendon, 1926), 401-33; citation is from p. 412.

at unequal wages. Women were particularly important in the textile, ale-brewing, and food-producing industries, but were also known to work as master craftswomen, teachers, doctors, merchants, even blacksmiths and carpenters, often continuing their husband's trade as widows. This is true, for instance, of the colorful mystic Margery Kempe, who took over her husband's wood-producing mill upon his death and managed it more successfully than he had. Clerical denunciations of women for usury, pawnbroking, and price manipulations testify to their financial powers.[60]

Women's Cultural Influence

The early church's lenient approach to the biblical injunctions on women is illustrated by the fact that Paul's prohibition of women teaching was virtually ignored through the eighth century.[61] One of the earliest extant educational handbooks, the *Liber Manualis*, was written by a woman, Dhuoda, for the instruction of her son. Convents and monasteries educated children of both sexes until Carolingian laws began to mandate segregation. But even this was not necessarily to the advantage of men — since nuns and canonesses, the chief pedagogues, were increasingly cloistered and could no longer teach boys, noble laywomen often received a better education than their brothers.[62] Frequently, men's education was considered primarily training for war. A not unusual case was that of the illiterate Henry I, founder of the Saxon dynasty of German emperors, whose wife Matilda was not only well educated but a patron of learning and founder of one of the chief literary and scholastic centers of the West, Quedlinburg. The romance *Galeran* portrayed a noble boy and girl receiving typically different educations — the girl learned to embroider, read, write, speak Latin, play the harp, and sing; the boy to hawk, hunt, shoot, ride, and play chess.[63]

Medieval art belies the stereotype of a rigid division of sex roles. Many paintings of the Annunciation portray Mary as an avid reader, and

---

60. Gies, *Women,* 56.

61. Jo Ann McNamara and Suzanne F. Wemple, "Sanctity and Power: The Dual Pursuit of Medieval Women," in *Becoming Visible: Women in European History,* ed. Renate Bridenthal and Claudia Koonz (Boston: Houghton Mifflin, 1977), 90-118; see p. 100. For some examples of women in teaching roles from an earlier period in Cappadocia see the literature referred to in chapter 1.

62. See the quotations from various authorities in Manfred Hauke, *Women in the Priesthood? A Systematic Analysis in the Light of the Order of Creation and Redemption,* trans. David Kipp (San Francisco: Ignatius, 1988), 465-66.

63. Gies, *Women,* 53.

portraits of the Holy Family often show Joseph rocking or carrying the infant Jesus while she reads. Often a book owner would have a portrait of herself reading painted in a margin. Susan Groag Bell has shown the importance of women as transmitters of culture through passing down books to daughters and bringing literature to other lands at marriage.[64] Even after the rise of universities, which contributed to the exclusion of women from higher education, women substantially contributed to the development of lay piety and vernacular literature because of their role in the education of the young and their ignorance of Latin. When the Bolognese jurist Giovanni Andrea was busy, his daughter Novella gave his lectures for him, obliged to speak from behind a curtain so the students would not be distracted by her beauty.[65]

Women's Political Power

It would be hard to overestimate the political sway exercised by queens and noblewomen in the Middle Ages, especially during the volatile age of the Crusades, when the family became all-important as the primary source of stability.[66] In tenth-century England, Aethelflaed, a daughter of King Alfred, led warriors against the Vikings, built fortresses along the Mercian frontier, and conquered much of eastern England. Matilda, an abbess of Quedlinburg and sister of Emperor Otto II of Germany, ruled in her brother's name when he was occupied, and even presided over church councils. Matilda of Tuscany sometimes donned armor to lead her troops in support of the popes against the German emperors. Abbesses sent their knights to war, noblewomen sat in judgment with their husbands and held the castle while they went to war. In Byzantium, too, empresses accompanied their husbands on campaigns, engaged in political intrigues, and even reigned in their own right. "Wherever one looks during this period there seem to be no effective barriers to the exercise of power by women. They appear as military leaders, judges, chatelaines, and controllers of property."[67] At the other end of the scale, women voted along with men in some town and rural assemblies.[68]

---

64. "Medieval Women Book Owners: Arbiters of Lay Piety and Ambassadors of Culture," in *Women and Power in the Middle Ages*, 149-187.

65. Marina Warner, Foreword to Christine de Pizan, *The Book of the City of Ladies*, trans. Earl Jeffrey Richards (New York: Persea Books, 1982), xxxvii.

66. The following accounts are given in Gies, *Women*, 23-25.

67. McNamara and Wemple, "Sanctity and Power," 109.

68. Régine Pernaud, *Pour en finir avec le Moyen Age* (Paris: Éditions du Seuil, 1977), 98.

Women's Religious Influence

Religious women of the early Middle Ages were remarkably free of the restrictions to which they were later subjected. Convents and abbeys often enjoyed formidable influence. The Saxon abbey of Gandersheim, an important religious and intellectual center of its day, was freed from royal rule by Otto Leven in 947 and granted autonomy such that the abbess could keep her own army and court of law, coin money, and have a seat in the imperial diet.[69] Gandersheim's most famous canoness, Hrotsvit, can boast of being the first dramatist of Christianity, the first Saxon poet, and the author of the first performable plays of the Middle Ages and the only extant Latin epics written by a woman. In Italy, comparable authority was exercised by the abbess of the monastery of S. Salvatore or S. Giulia in Brescia.[70] She routinely engaged in major land transactions, managed and developed large territorial holdings, received property gifts from emperors and popes, and oversaw thousands of dependent workers. In 1370 the Abbess Mabilia II "had such power that she was able to issue an order to the brothers of San Daniello that began as follows: 'Mabilia by God's grace abbess of the monastery of Santa Giulia,'" a form of title permitted only to popes and emperors.[71]

The abbesses of Notre-Dame-aux-Nonnains enjoyed rights over the bishop of Troyes: when a new bishop was installed, he would lead a procession to the abbey, mounted on a palfrey, then kneel and receive cross, miter, and prayer book from the abbess's hands.[72] In Spain the Cistercian abbesses held their own chapters, undertook the benediction of their own nuns, preached, and had their own dependent houses.[73] In England, too, "by the end of the thirteenth century . . . prioresses and abbesses were becoming increasingly visible in the church hierarchy and influential in ecclesiastical affairs."[74]

Double monasteries, in which women often had a dominant posi-

69. Katharina M. Wilson, "The Saxon Canoness: Hrotsvit of Gandersheim," in *Medieval Women Writers,* ed. Katharina M. Wilson (Athens, Ga.: University of Georgia Press, 1984), 30-63.

70. See Suzanne Wemple, "S. Salvatore/S. Giulia: A Case Study in the Endowment and Patronage of a Major Female Monastery in Northern Italy," in *Women of the Medieval World: Essays in Honor of John H. Mundy,* ed. Julius Kirschner and Suzanne F. Wemple (Oxford: Basil Blackwell, 1985), 85-102.

71. Ibid., 100-101.

72. Gies, *Life,* 54.

73. Bolton, 155 n. 10.

74. Kaufman, 143.

tion,[75] were a common phenomenon up to the tenth and eleventh centuries.[76] These had varying origins. Some were originally founded for the benefit of women and had communities of men attached for spiritual and material support. Others, like the Premonstratensians, began as male communities and took on the care of women who came to them for protection. In England, St. Gilbert founded double monasteries composed primarily of women but directed by resident male clerics. The order of Fontevrault, founded by Robert of Arbrissel after double monasteries had nearly disappeared, was unaccountably nonsexist by modern standards. Its communities were made up of women living the contemplative life and clerics and laymen who supported them by active labor. According to the rule of the order, the men were under obedience to the nuns and the community was governed by the abbess. Writings by early medieval nuns reveal that female ideals and modes of conduct were upheld as the way to salvation and as models of sanctity in the monasteries led by women.[77]

Women were also frequently at the forefront of heretical movements, one of the reasons for the severe restrictions later imposed. Some of the great medieval church reforms indirectly diminished the influence of women by restricting clerical marriage, eliminating lay influence in bestowing church offices, and removing the centers of church leadership from convents and monasteries to the bishoprics and Rome.[78]

Christianity as a Liberating Force

The facts mentioned above are evidence of the moderating influence of Christianity. Imperfect though its witness was, the church broke with the mindset of the ancient world by affirming the spiritual equality of men and women. "Although Christianity did not obviate sexual discrimination in the late Roman Empire, it did offer women the opportunity to regard themselves as independent personalities rather than as someone else's daughter, wife, or mother. It enabled women to develop self-esteem as spiritual beings who possessed the same potential for moral perfection as men."[79] The affirmation

75. Southern, 310.
76. Penny Schine Gold, "Male/Female Cooperation: The Example of Fontevrault," in *Medieval Religious Women*, ed. John A. Nichols and Lillian Thomas Shank, vol. I, *Distant Echoes* (Kalamazoo, Mich.: Cistercian Publications, 1984), 151-68; citation is from p. 156.
77. Wemple, *Women*, 191.
78. McNamara and Wemple, "Sanctity and Power," 110.
79. Wemple, *Women*, 19.

of spiritual equality had inevitable ramifications in the secular realm. By its high regard for such "feminine" values as prayer, social charity, and care for the poor, the church moderated the over-masculinized ideals of both Romans and barbarians.

> In unequivocally asserting that men and women shared a common spiritual destiny and dignity, the Christian Church undoubtedly helped prevent the woman from anywhere becoming a chattel of her husband; in seeking to establish the sanctity and permanence of marriage, the Church helped confirm her importance as established mistress of her household. At the same time, Christian teaching was hardly such as to allow a real social matriarchy to develop anywhere in Europe.[80]

Writings About Women

Of all the indicators of women's status, literature is the most unreliable and potentially misleading. Michael Kaufman critiques the "literary fallacy . . . the error of assuming that imaginative literature affords a complete and authentic interpretation of an age."[81] Nowhere would this mistake be more glaring than in medieval history. Comparing medieval literature (almost all of which is aristocratic) with records describing actual life reveals "a startling discrepancy between the viciously abusive or patronizingly idealized literary images and woman's actual role as the greater part of the medieval world understood and accepted her."[82]

The literature of church and aristocracy, as Eileen Power observed, was marked by an extreme inconsistency toward women, regarding her now as the supreme temptress and instrument of Satan, now as the idol of courtly love. "Women found themselves perpetually oscillating between a pit and a pedestal."[83] Tirades against women and demonstrations of their inferiority are not hard to find, like this one of Conrad of Marchtal: "recognizing that the wickedness of women is greater than all the other wickedness of the world, and that there is no anger like that of women, and that the poison of asps and dragons is more curable and less dangerous to men than the familiarity of women . . . [we] will avoid them like poisonous animals."[84] Or Bernard of Parma: "A woman, on the other hand, should not have [juris-

80. Herlihy, "Land," 91.
81. Kaufman, 140.
82. Ibid., 141.
83. Power, 401.
84. Quoted in Southern, 314.

dictional] power . . . because she is not made in the image of God; rather man is the image and glory of God and woman ought to be subject to man and, as it were, like his servant. . . ."[85] The anonymous author of *Proverbia quae dicuntur super natura feminarum* contended that "no man should trust a woman, after she deceived Adam, for which reason she should be made to cover her head and forehead, in order to show her shame. Woman's love is no love, but only bitterness; it should rather be called a school for fools."[86] Such outbursts, while deplorable, give indirect evidence of the power women were in fact exercising. "The frequency and violence of these attacks attest to the importance of women in the ecclesiastical hierarchy."[87]

On the other hand, less frequent but still significant were eulogies of the virtues of women. "Woman is to be preferred to man, to wit: in material, because Adam was made from clay and Eve from the side of Adam; in place, because Adam was made outside paradise and Eve within; in conception, because a woman conceived God, which a man could not do; in apparition, because Christ appeared to a woman after the Resurrection, to wit, the Magdalen; in exaltation, because a woman is exalted above the choirs of angels, to wit, the Blessed Mary."[88] St. Bernardino of Siena declared that "it is a great grace to be a woman, because more women are saved than men."[89] Peter Lombard, echoing a rabbinic tradition, reasoned that God did not create woman from Adam's head, because she was not to be his master, nor from his foot, because she was not to be his slave, but from his side, because she was to be his companion and friend. Chivalric literature went further in its accolades, with knights avowing their devotion in motifs that became clichés: a lover is "the servant and friend and slave to his lady."[90] But these did not necessarily contribute to a greater esteem for women in practice. Even "the growth of a romantic and erotic literature only strengthened belief in the moral and social dangers of feminine wantonness; and the devotional literature of the twelfth century, with its intense interest in virginity, helped to create in many minds a strong and sometimes hysterical aversion to the state of matrimony."[91]

85. Quoted in James A. Brundage, "Sexual Equality in Medieval Canon Law," in *Women and the Sources of Medieval History,* ed. Joel T. Rosenthal (Athens, London: University of Georgia Press, 1990), 66-79; see p. 66.

86. Quoted in Erika Uitz, *The Legend of Good Women: Medieval Women in Towns and Cities,* trans. Sheila Marnie (Mt. Kisco, N.Y.: Moyer Bell, 1988), 156.

87. Kaufman, 143.

88. Quoted in Power, 402.

89. Ibid., 432.

90. Kaufman, 146.

91. Southern, 311-12.

The *"Querrelle des femmes,"* a four-hundred-year-long literary controversy about the merits or deficiencies of women, brought to the fore some of the most strident claims on either side. Christine de Pisan in France, Mary Astell and Jane Anger in England, and others rebutted the stereotype of the sexually insatiable temptress luring men to their damnation with the counterstereotype of the pure, chaste woman and the seductive man. The anonymous female author of the 1620 English pamphlet *Haec Vir* claimed equality with men and demanded the freedom to live as she chose.[92] She was not an anomaly, since in the same year King James ordered preachers to condemn the "insolence" of women who were wearing male dress.

The Decline in Women's Status

For a variety of reasons, the steady progress of women in medieval society did not sustain its momentum, and the position they had gained began to be undermined by other forces. "By most social indicators, women, especially elite women, were losing status, power and visibility as the Middle Ages progressed."[93] The introduction of feudalism, beginning in ninth-century France, was one of the leading factors in this shift.

> A system by which a lord granted land to a vassal in return for services that were primarily military, [feudalism] produced a society organized for war, an essentially masculine world. . . . Feudal estates usually passed intact, with their military obligations, to a single male heir. Only in the absence of male heirs could a woman inherit. Even if not an heiress, a woman spent most of her life under the guardianship of a man — of her father until she married, of her father's lord if her father died, and of her husband until she was widowed.[94]

An English law in the reign of Henry II decreed that "Even if a female heir is of age, she shall remain in the wardship of her lord until she

92. See Katherine Usher Henderson and Barbara F. McManus, *Half Humankind. Contexts and Texts of the Controversy about Women in England, 1540-1640* (Chicago: University of Illinois Press, 1985).

93. David Herlihy, "Did Women Have a Renaissance?: A Reconsideration," in *Medievalia et Humanistica: Studies in Medieval and Renaissance Culture,* New Series, no. 13, ed. Paul Maurice Clogan (Totowa, N.J.: Rowman and Allanheld, 1985), 1-22; citation is from p. 15. Herlihy's article is a reponse to Joan Kelly-Gadol, "Did Women Have a Renaissance?" in *Becoming Visible: Women in European History,* ed. Renate Bridenthal and Claudia Koonz (Boston: Houghton Mifflin, 1977), 138-64.

94. Gies, *Women,* 27.

is married according to the desire and with the consent of her lord. . . .
And if a girl . . . marries without the consent of her lord, by the just law
and custom of the realm she shall lose her inheritance."[95] Wardships were
bought and sold like any investment, although widows and single women
could buy the right to remain single or choose their own husbands — a
lucrative source of income for King John II. The loss of rights was never
as complete as the laws implied, however. A man could not sell his wife's
inheritance without her consent; women could still sell or give away land,
make wills and contracts, and defend their titles in court. Loopholes were
found by families who preferred to keep their estate in the bloodline rather
than pass it to a distant male relative.

Patrilineal lineage, a new type of kinship system which excluded
daughters and their descendants from the family line, began to evolve in
the eleventh century. That is, a family would form its identity by tracing
the male line back to a particular ancestor and by adoption of a family
name, coat of arms, mottoes, and sometimes a mythology. The nuclear
family replaced the extended kinship unit, fostering individualism, privacy,
and economic self-sufficiency. Women's economic and social responsibilities, which had helped sustain the entire medieval community, became
confined to the home. "Women further lost their functions as principal
conduits in the flow of wealth down the generations. The patrilineal family
now managed its resources primarily for the benefit of sons. Daughters
lost their traditional claim to an equal share with their brothers in their
parents' property."[96] Marriage arrangements reverted to the true dowry,
making daughters an economic burden rather than an asset to the family.
At the same time, the growth in population made it more difficult to keep
landed patrimonies intact. Preserving the integrity of a family's estate meant
severely limiting or suspending altogether the inheritance claims of
daughters and younger sons.

The most pronounced setback for women in religious life occurred,
ironically, during the great period of monastic foundation, from the early
tenth to the early twelfth centuries.[97] This was due to the movement to
regularize various forms of organized religious life. Privileges and responsibilities previously assumed by abbesses began to be removed to the authority of the bishop or abbot.[98] Orders to which women had flocked in

95. Quoted in ibid., 28.
96. Herlihy, "Did Women," 13.
97. Southern, 310.
98. See Jane Tibbetts Schulenburg, "Strict Active Enclosure and Its Effects on
the Female Monastic Experience (500-1100)," in *Medieval Religious Women,* vol. I,
51-86.

large numbers began to suppress double monasteries, distance themselves from their female members, and restrict the admission of women, despite the exhortations of successive popes to the contrary. At the end of the twelfth century the Premonstratensians, who had some ten thousand female members, decreed that women would no longer be accepted. Cistercian nunneries, which had sprung up throughout Europe despite having no formal place in the structure of the order, began to be strictly regulated and finally refused acceptance by the order.[99] The Franciscans and Dominicans resisted the incorporation of convents but were deterred by papal policies. In 1215 the Fourth Lateran Council prohibited the foundation of new orders, further limiting religious options for women. The policy of strict claustration decreed by Boniface VIII in 1298 contributed to the increasing economic dependence of convents.[100] At the same time, as we have seen, the shift of intellectual life from the monastery to the university, where women were excluded, limited the intellectual possibilities for women. The imposition of clerical celibacy and reforms prohibiting lay investiture restricted the power of the family and thus of women; with monastic reforms and the decline of double monasteries, the status of abbesses and nuns diminished as well.[101]

The rise of mercantile capitalism was yet another development adversely affecting the position of women. Kaufman holds that "the change from an agrarian community to an urban marketplace helped to accelerate and extend woman's subjugation."[102] As home industries were replaced by more centralized manufacturing, a labor surplus was created and women came to be seen as both economically expendable and a competitive threat to men. The haute bourgeoisie imitated the gentry in regarding women as "social ornaments." "Without a functional role in the labor force, the upperclass woman no longer counted, and an early consequence of this new attitude was that she became merely a domestic slave and a reproductive agent."[103] The view of women as mere procreative agents was reinforced by primitive biology — Leeuwenhoek's discoveries under the microscope only confirmed the ancient theory that men alone could reproduce, passing on their offspring to women to nurture. Henrie Smith aptly ex-

99. Southern, 317.

100. Pernaud, 96.

101. Yet it should be observed that certain abbesses retained almost episcopal authority until the Council of Trent and even to the nineteenth century. See Kathleen O'Neill, "Seminar on Women's Spirituality in the Cisterican Tradition. New Melleray/12-20 May 1987," *Cistercian Studies* 23 (1988): 86-94.

102. Kaufman, 150.

103. Ibid.

pressed the opinion of his day regarding the respective roles of marriage partners: "The husband is the cocke and the wife is the dam: the cocke flieth abroad to bring in, the dam sitteth upon the nest to keep all at home. For the man's pleasure is most abroad and the woman's within."[104]

The growing ranks of professional administrators, clerks, and officials encroached on noblewomen's traditional role in administration — although not supplanting it entirely. The fifteenth-century Paston letters testify to the breadth of capabilities still expected of a wife: during her husband's extended absences, Margaret of Paston managed her household and several large landholdings, engaged in shrewd legal maneuvering to keep them, monitored the condition of the crops and market fluctuations, procured supplies, including weapons for defense of the castle, informed her husband of local political trends with accompanying advice, and even on one occasion withstood a siege by one thousand armed men.[105]

Women and the Enlightenment

But it was not until the seventeenth and eighteenth centuries, when the public and private spheres were becoming increasingly separate, that the "ideology of domesticity" became entrenched. Increasingly, men took on the role of provider outside the household or estate and women remained at home, even when maintaining the household came to be a more limited task. It was among the philosophes, particularly Rousseau and d'Holbach, that the ideal of an exclusively domestic role for women was most forcefully articulated.[106] The Enlightenment was perhaps more subtle in its depreciation of women than any previous development. "The Enlightenment, like the Renaissance, was a cultural event that aimed to liberate the human spirit. However, like the French Revolution it helped to shape, the Enlightenment not only failed to improve women's lot but worsened it in some ways."[107] No less than medieval courtly literature, the writings of the philosophes were divided between praise and contempt. On the one

104. Ibid., 152. Herlihy takes a more qualified view of the effect of the medieval economic development: "Where the work involved high levels of family participation, the contribution of women remained substantial. Where guilds dominated the productive processes, women played a diminished role" ("Did Women," 106).

105. H. S. Bennett, *The Pastons and Their England: Studies in an Age of Transition* (Cambridge: At the University Press, 1932).

106. See Kelly-Gadol, "Did Women Have a Renaissance?"

107. Preface to Abby R. Kleinbaum, "Women in the Age of Light," in *Becoming Visible*, 217.

hand were arguments for the natural equality of women (at least in some
aspects, not necessarily including intellectual ability) advanced by the
Chevalier de Jaucourt, Voltaire, Montesquieu, and Antoine Thomas; on the
other hand was "a second, even stronger trend in Enlightenment thought,
which stressed the sexual differences and the appropriateness of an exclusively domestic role for women."[108] It was the latter, an undisguised return
to classical Greek values, which shaped the Enlightenment view of women,
according to Kleinbaum.[109] Rousseau endorsed the Athenian practices of
cloistering women, excluding them from public life, and refusing to even
dine with them, since he deemed women to be naturally vain, narcissistic,
childish, and weak. "In the Age of Reason, woman was a being of passion."[110] Rousseau presents the ideal female education in his educational
work *Emile:* Emile's future wife learns that "women are made for the
delight of men, and that the bearing of children is their proper business."
Her natural vanity is encouraged and she is taught to dress dolls as a practice
for self-adornment, since "in due time she will be her own doll."[111] Her
mind is cultivated for practical studies rather than abstract science. In *Julie,
ou la nouvelle Heloise,* Rousseau describes the gynaeceum, or women's
apartment, where women sing, dance, and eat sweet cakes and other foods
"such as suit the taste of women and children."[112] Clearly, women are
little more than charming and mindless creatures devoted to the comforts
of home and family. "Ironically, this idealization of the family and of
motherhood seemed to contemporaries more modern and forward looking
than the apparent independence of the upper-class woman. In fact, it was
more modern since it reflected the coming of age of the bourgeoisie and
the triumph of its values."[113]

Almost the identical values were expressed at the same time by the
English lawyer Blackstone, who certified the legal nonexistence of women
under common law: "By marriage, the husband and wife are one person
in law; that is, the very being or legal existence of the woman is suspended
during the marriage, or at least is incorporated and consolidated into that
of the husband; under whose wing, protection, and cover she performs

108. Kleinbaum, 223.

109. Ibid.

110. Frédéric Deloffre, Preface to Terry Smiley Dock, *Women in the Encyclopédie: A Compendium* (Potomac, Md.: Studia Humanitatis, 1983), xii.

111. Quoted in ibid., 228.

112. Quoted in ibid., 229. For a good analysis of Rousseau's thinking in this
book, see Vincent A. McCarthy, *Quest for a Philosophical Jesus: Christianity and
Philosophy in Rousseau, Kant, Hegel, and Schelling* (Macon, Ga.: Mercer, 1986).

113. Ibid., 223.

every thing. . . . A man cannot grant anything to his wife, or enter into covenant with her: for the grant would be to suppose her separate existence. . . ."[114] Mary Beard has shown that Blackstone's assertions were true only in a highly restricted and technical sense; in practice the rise of equity jurisprudence did much to mitigate common-law restrictions on women. Yet Blackstone's theory formed the basis for Mill's later claim, in *The Subjection of Women,* that "the principle which regulates social relations between the sexes is the legal subjection of one to the other."[115] Similarly, Mary Wollstonecraft's *Vindication of the Rights of Women* presumed as a given to be combated Rousseau's ideas and the genteel theory that women assert themselves by deluding and gratifying men with their charms.

THE ENLIGHTENMENT CRYSTALLIZATION

The early history of Europe was, as we have seen, composed of Christian values and inherited prejudices. The Enlightenment was a rebellion against the piety of an anemic Christianity, a return to a pagan view of women, in which they were deeply mistrusted.

> The philosophes were at home with intelligent women — one thinks of Diderot's Sophie Volland, Voltaire's Madame du Châtelet, and the cultivated Parisian ladies who played hostess to philosophes from all over the world — and they made attempts to treat them as equals, as well as an item on the agenda of reform. But while the philosophes were feminists in their way, they were feminists with misgivings: the age-old fear of women, the antique superstition that women were vessels of wrath and sources of corruption, was too deeply rooted to be easily discarded.[116]

Absent from this passage is the observation of how thoroughly in keeping with the outlook of pre-Christian Greece this attitude really was — women generally are for man's pleasure, some may contribute as well to his intellectual pleasure, and for the good of the state, he should have a wife to bear and raise his children.[117] Although Christians may have believed

---

114. Quoted in Gies, *Women,* 30.
115. Mill, 1.
116. Peter Gay, *The Enlightenment: An Interpretation,* vol. 2, *The Science of Freedom* (Norton: New York, 1969), 33.
117. "Mistresses (*etairas,* well educated companions) we keep for the sake of

like this, there is nothing in the New Testament that can justify it. The eighteenth century's recapturing of the Greek ideal was but the definitive act in the crystallization of the negative elements already present in the society that had been gaining ground as the developments in the structure proved stronger than the gospel ideals.[118]

The Enlightenment, with its explicit return to a pagan view of reality and its cultivation of power,[119] definitively set its stamp upon a return to a pre-Christian view of women and also upon subsequent attempts to assert human rights, and specifically for our concerns, the rights of women.

Perhaps an image will help. A common experiment for beginners in chemistry consists in taking a beaker containing something held in solution and then inserting into it a string that has been saturated with another chemical. Immediately, the elements held in solution crystallize around the string, their shape and content being determined by both what was held in solution and what was inserted. In a similar way the attitudes and practices now identified as anti-feminine were present in the generations preceding the Enlightenment, but they were "held in solution" and existed side by side with other elements deriving from the gospel. With the advent of Enlightenment thought, the anti-feminine elements crystallized around it to form a coherent and effective force.

It should be pointed out that the Enlightenment was not designedly misogynist.[120] It resulted, however, in a view of human life that exalted

---

pleasure, concubines [*pallakas,* what we would call "mistress" today] for the daily care of our person, wives to bear us legitimate children and to be faithful guardians of our households." Pseudo-Demosthenes (340 B.C.), *Against Neaera,* 122; *Private Orations* (Loeb Classical Library 6, 444-47).

118. One of the significant elements in this development was the Cartesian split between mind and body that made the mind "sexless." While at first this was a help in promoting woman in society, it eventually turned against them as in the French Revolution when a disembodied reason could no longer appreciate anything but its own rigid dictates. See Prudence Allen, "Descartes, The Concept of Woman and the French Revolution," in *Revolution, Violence, and Equality,* ed. Yeager Hudson and Creighton Peden (New York: Edwin Mellen Press, 1990), 61-78.

119. "I see the philosophes' rebellion succeeding in both of its aims: theirs was a paganism directed against their Christian inheritance and dependent upon the paganism of classical antiquity, but it was also a *modern* paganism, emancipated from classical thought as much as from Christian dogma. The ancients taught the philosophes the uses of criticism, but it was modern philosophers who taught them the possibilities of power." Peter Gay, *The Enlightenment,* xi.

120. See however the study by Susan Bordo, "The Cartesian Masculinization of Thought," *Signs* 11 (1986): 439-57. Bordo, following the lead of Karl Stern (*The Flight From Woman* [New York: Noonday Press, 1966]), brings to light the almost total lack of genuine feminine influence in Descartes's life.

power and the use of the practical reason. That, combined with the con-comitant and sometimes derivative forces of the Industrial Revolution, finally resulted in a "masculine" world in which the public dimension of life, associated with struggle, achievement, and conflict, was privileged over the private or "feminine" dimension of life that was characterized by domestic virtues. It is not easy to describe the manner in which these two forces, Enlightenment thinking about human nature and the centripetal force of the Industrial Revolution, strengthened each other and resulted not only in many injustices to women but in the resurgence of slavery either in its explicit form or in the form of the oppression of the new poor who were forced to become a work force for the new society.

The clearest expression of the epistemology that lay beneath this crystallization is finally expressed in the anti-feminist rejection of that deeper function of the human mind that is characterized as receptivity. W. Norris Clarke, in discussing the unrestricted drive of the mind toward being, makes the following observation that encapsulates that aspect of Kant's thinking which itself embodies, as we have seen, the epistemological orientation of Europe since Ockham: the need of the mind to create, not receive, intelligibility. Although the text is somewhat long, its viewpoint is important for what is to follow.

This absolutely fundamental mutual correlation of mind and being, mind for being and being for mind, has been beautifully termed by Maritain a "nuptial relation". . . . To know truly a reality that it has not itself made, the mind must be open to receive this reality, to be actively informed by it. The mind, fecundated, informed, by reality, then actively responds, pours its own spiritual life into what it receives, gestates, then gives birth to the mental "word" or concept, which in turn flows over into the verbal word expressed to others. . . . Thus *theoretical* intelligence (knowing the world as it already is) is more like a *she;* practical intelligence, on the other hand is more like a *he,* since it actively changes or re-creates the world though creative initiative and action. . . . For despite the many partial insights of Kant, Kantian epistemology seems to me at root what can be called an *anti-feminist* epistemology. Rather than allowing reality to reveal itself to the human mind by actively informing it, the Kantian mind is more like an aggressive all-male activist, actively imposing its own pre-fabricated *a priori* forms on the disordered raw material of the sense manifold coming into it.[121]

121. *The Universe as Journey: Conversations with W. Norris Clarke, S.J.,* ed. Gerald McCool (New York: Fordham University Press, 1988), 60-61. Emphasis in the original.

Nurtured by anxiety and the need for a certitude determined according to norms derived from the human mind, Western thought suffered a loss of nerve. It moved from a loss of confidence in the information supplied by the senses to a rejection of any information deriving from tradition, sacred or secular, that cannot be verified according to the norms established as reason. According to this view, any acceptance of what cannot be so verified deprives the subject of its rightful autonomy. The story has been told often enough, and the illusions generated by this approach have been dealt with by philosophers such as Michael Polanyi and Hans Georg Gadamer.[122] After a brief look at the history of feminism itself, we will return to consider three presuppositions that characterize this approach to reality, and the effect they have had on feminist thinking.[123]

122. The relevance of Polanyi's critiques to theology is illustrated by Dulles in *The Craft of Theology,* and by Colin Gunton, *Enlightenment and Alienation: An Essay towards a Trinitarian Theology* (Grand Rapids, Mich.: Eerdmans, 1985), who also points out the relevance of Gadamer's critiques.

123. For an overview of the movement of thought that has brought us to "post-modernity," see Richard Tarnas, *The Passion of the Western Mind* (New York: Ballantine Books, 1991).

5

An Historical Overview of Feminism and Feminist Theology

After having established some principles by which to judge the theological quality of feminist theology, and after having traced the history of the position of women in the church and in the society largely influenced by the church, we arrived at the point in the history of the West when the negative aspects of the thinking and practice in regard to women were crystallized out during the Enlightenment. This chapter is dedicated to two further dimensions of that history which are necessary for an understanding of the present form of feminist theology. There will be two parts in the presentation. First, a brief historical overview of the origins and development of what is now called feminism. This is undertaken as a help to the reader who is not familiar with such background, and will refer to other more complete studies in the course of the presentation. Second, a look at the origins and direction of feminist theology itself. This last part of the chapter will conclude with a look at the three aspects of feminist modernity that must be modified if there is to be effective dialogue in the church. The seven chapters to follow are concerned with these three aspects.

A History of Modern Feminism

While the women's movements of the last two centuries are basically modern phenomena, some feminist scholars have attempted to make feminism far older, tracing it as far back as the fifteenth century.[1] It is undoubtedly true that

---

1. The difficulty experienced in defining feminism and locating the proper chronological point at which to begin speaking about it is discussed successfully by

one can find criticisms of the declining status of women in the later Middle Ages articulated by women.[2] Such criticism, however, often reflects not a protofeminist consciousness but prophetic judgments or condemnations of specific injustices made from the standpoint of conscious Christian faith.[3]

Most scholars see these movements as, at least in large part, an out-growth of the Enlightenment and the impetus that it gave to thinking about human rights. Such a judgment is made in the light of the individualist and rights-oriented feminism of the United States and Britain. Karen Offen has pointed to the relational orientation of much early French and German femi-nism, and advocates an incorporation of some of this approach in the modern American effort.[4] In terms of the dominant rights-oriented approach, Mary Wollstonecraft's *Vindication of the Rights of Women* is a more apt example of an early feminist work. Paralleling the Declaration of the Rights of Man produced by the French Revolution, this 1792 tract applied the emerging language of political rights to the particular domestic and social situation of women.[5] In similar fashion, the American women meeting at Seneca Falls, New York, in 1848 based their "Declaration of Sentiments" upon the earlier American Declaration of Independence. The early movements for women's rights and contemporary feminism both reflect the egalitarian impulse of this period and its resulting legitimation of rebellion on the basis of rights. This aspect of the movement was concerned with the achievement of equality for women through property reform, child custody in cases of divorce, access to education, and ultimately the right to vote.[6]

Karen Offen, "Defining Feminism: A Comparative Historical Approach," *Signs* 14 (1988): 119-57. I will call on this article at certain points in my own discussion.

2. Joan Kelly cites Christine de Pisan's *Book of the City Ladies* and its subsequent development by seventeenth and eighteenth century writers as an example of a develop-ing feminist tradition; see "Early Feminist Theory and the *Querelle des Femmes, 1400-1789*" in *Women, History, and Theory: The Essays of Joan Kelly* (Chicago: University of Chicago Press, 1984), 65-109.

3. Even Christine de Pisan, for all of the Renaissance education and obvious literary skill which she brings to bear on the *Querelle des femmes,* writes from the standpoint of a deeply committed Christian, eager to use stories of female saints and martyrs to demonstrate women's equality in virtue and holiness. See *The Book of the City Ladies,* trans. Earl Jeffrey Richards (New York: Persea Books, 1982), esp. 217-57.

4. Offen, "Defining Feminism."

5. See Elizabeth Fox-Genovese, *Feminism without Illusions: A Critique of Individu-alism* (Chapel Hill: The University of North Carolina Press, 1991), 131. Fox-Genovese also regards Wollstonecraft's work as illustrative of the feminist propensity toward individual-ism. Mention is also occasionally made of Olympe de Georges' 1791 work *Declaration of the Rights of Women* which was written in a similar vein; see Patricia Branca, *Women in Europe since 1750* (New York: St. Martin's Press, 1987), 152.

6. See Olive Banks, *Faces of Feminism: A Study of Feminism as a Social*

Another key influence that lead to the rise of these movements in both Britain and the United States was that provided by evangelical Christianity. The participation of women in the revivalist movements of the eighteenth century has been shown to be linked to growing participation of women in reform movements such as abolition, temperance, and various public purity campaigns.[7] This evangelical impulse remained active throughout the quest for women's suffrage (the vote was often seen as a key to enabling women to undertake the moral reform of society) and beyond in women's continuing involvement in social issues. With the emergence of feminism in the 1960s, the influence of this stream within the women's movements has declined.

Another and very different source of inspiration was provided by socialism. The socialism that grew up after the French revolution as developed by Saint-Simon, Owens, and later Marx and Engels gave an ideological basis for the thinking of some of the more radical feminists of both centuries.[8] It also furnished a broader agenda of social issues as objects of women's concern. Among these were the reform of property laws (a concern shared with the "rights" element of the movement), the improvement of the lot of working women, the liberalization of divorce laws, and in some cases the restructuring or elimination of the traditional family. A constant tension in the varying forms of socialist feminism is that between the attempt to make women's concerns central and the view that saw them as subordinate to the larger socialist or Marxist agenda.[9]

Studies by Banks and others have demonstrated that all of these impulses have been a part of the women's movements from their beginning until the present.[10] This explains the diversity of what is often called feminism and why its proponents often demonstrate disagreement on fun-

---

Movement (Oxford: Basil Blackwell, 1981), 35-46. In regard to the specific situation of European women, see Branca, 152-53; 161-88.

7. One might also note the impetus provided by the Quakers, who gave women leadership positions and allowed them access to education earlier than society did as a whole. See the excellent discussion of these matters provided by Banks, 13-27. Cf. Janet Saltzman Chafetz and Anthony Gary Dworkin, *Female Revolt: Women's Movements in World and Historical Perspective* (Totowa, N.J.: Rowman & Allanheld, 1986), 15-16.

8. On the socialist stream within feminism see Banks, *Faces of Feminism*, 48-59; Chafetz and Dworkin, *Female Revolt*, 38-42. In regard to the close connection between socialism and the women's movements of Germany and France, see Branca, 154.

9. See Chafetz and Dworkin, *Female Revolt*, 39-40; Banks, *Faces of Feminism*, 53-54, 59.

10. Although it should be noted that their respective influence has waxed and waned over the years. The evangelical current was particularly strong in the 19th and early 20th centuries, while the socialist stream was fairly marginal in the 19th century but emerged with great intensity in the radical feminism of the 1960s.

damental issues (e.g., the emphasis on women's differences versus that of sexual sameness, protection of women and their unique role versus equality of rights and identity of opportunity). Only issues of great importance (such as women's suffrage) could unite all of these streams in a short-lived working unity.[11]

Other factors are often cited as contributing to the emergence of these movements as well. One such factor is industrialization and the resulting displacement of the family as the primary means of economic production — a development that gradually forced more women into the work force, especially in times of war.[12] Another is clearly the growing educational opportunities available to middle- and upper-class women over the past two centuries, especially following the Second World War.[13] In the current century, mention is also made of demographic factors such as the increase in longevity and the decline in birthrates due to improved medical and contraceptive technologies.[14]

The coalescence of these intellectual and social factors does much to explain the rise of the various women's movements, or "waves" of feminism as they are often called. They do not, however, tell the whole of their history. I will continue to speak of "waves" because it serves to identify both the difference and the continuity in the different historical periods. The account that follows will focus primarily on the rise of the women's movement in America.

The First Wave

The women's movement that began in the latter half of the nineteenth century is identified as the "first wave" of feminism.[15] In many cases,

11. Cf. Banks, *Faces of Feminism,* 149.

12. See Jo Freeman, "Women's Movements," in *Colliers Encyclopedia,* vol. 23 (1986), 562.

13. See Chafetz and Dworkin, *Female Revolt,* 54. At times, however, it was precisely the lack of such opportunities or the difficulty involved in pursuing them that led to activism in regard to women's issues on the part of the 19th century "pioneers" of the women's movement.

14. See Chafetz and Dworkin, *Female Revolt,* 51. Here too, however, the relationship is a complex one since some of the more radical feminists were actively involved in promoting birth control and later abortion; see Banks, *Faces of Feminism,* 182-94, 198-203.

15. A helpful overview of the terminology associated with this history — *women's movement, women's emancipation, women's liberation,* and the identification of these last two with the first and second waves of feminism — is provided by Sandra Schneiders, *Beyond Patching* (Mahwah, N.J.: Paulist, 1989), 6-9.

however, the women involved in this movement had very different concerns than those now identified as demonstrating "feminist consciousness." Many women whose lives had been touched by the great revivals of the century remained active outside of their homes in working for evangelism or moral reform of various kinds. Among the most important of these moral issues were those of abolition, temperance, and purity campaigns (which included efforts to eliminate prostitution and help the women engaged in it as well as the attempt to eliminate the double standard of sexual morality).[16]

It was in the course of such work that many of these women were confronted with the limitations placed upon them because of their sex. The male members of the abolition and temperance movements often proved hostile to the idea of working alongside women or allowing them to speak or serve in leadership roles. The result was that many women withdrew from these groups to form organizations of their own. Some took with them the desire to confront the disabilities placed on them as women and began to work for the rights of women as well as for these other causes.

Such was the case of Susan Anthony, who campaigned unsuccessfully for a woman's right to address temperance meetings. She was also thwarted in getting the Women's State Temperance Society, for which she served as secretary, to accept her friend and mentor Elizabeth Cady Stanton and to deal with issues of women's rights.[17] Olivia Coolidge notes that Anthony's attempt to have Stanton elected president of the group was doomed because of the irreconcilable differences between Stanton, who viewed the Bible as oppressive to women, and the clergy who were prominent in the temperance movement.[18] In 1853 Anthony resigned and the organization foundered. Anthony then heeded Stanton's urging to work full time on issues of women's rights; the two remained close friends and collaborators throughout the remainder of their lives.

It was Stanton who was largely responsible for the *Woman's Bible,* a mixture of deism, rationalist Protestantism, devout Christianity, and current culture, published in two parts in 1895 and 1898. This seems to have been part of her political strategy, as she recognized that the Bible was invoked by many and had great cultural power.[19] She herself said that the *Woman's Bible*

16. See Banks, *Faces of Feminism,* 63-84. Cf. William O' Neill, "The Origins of American Feminism," in *The Other Half: Roads to Women's Equality,* ed. Cynthia Fuchs Epstein and William J. Goode (Englewood Cliffs, N.J.: Prentice-Hall, 1971), 159-64.

17. Banks, *Faces of Feminism,* 18-19.

18. See Olivia Coolidge, *Women's Rights: The Suffrage Movement in America 1848-1920* (New York: E. P. Dutton, 1966), 35-37.

19. See Mary D. Pellauer, *Towards a Tradition of Feminist Theology: The Reli-*

was needed because so many people appealed to the Bible as a source of arguments against her causes. This need to reinterpret the Bible because it was a cultural monument, not because it was the word of God, set the tone for much of later feminist hermeneutics. It should also be pointed out here that part of her argument was well taken: many ministers of the gospel were more in tune with the post-Enlightenment thinking about human rights than they were with the Scriptural basis for these rights. Thus, they easily adopted the "masculinized" views regarding the roles of men and women that characterized the neo-pagan political thinking of the day.

Women in the abolition movement encountered obstacles similar to Stanton's. Lucretia Mott, a Quaker minister, was one of the first women active in the American Anti-Slavery Society and helped to found a women's counterpart, the Philadelphia Female Anti-Slavery Society. Also outspoken in the abolitionist cause were the Grimké sisters, Sarah and Angelina. Born to wealthy southern Episcopalians, they witnessed the horrors of slavery firsthand. They later became Quakers, moved north, and were soon noted for their fiery antislavery rhetoric, both as authors of various tracts and articles and as public speakers. They, too, encountered a good deal of hostility, especially when speaking to mixed audiences, and from this opposition seem to have developed increasingly outspoken views on the equality of the sexes.[20] In one letter published by a newspaper in 1837, Sarah went so far as to assert that "whatsoever it is morally right for a man to do, it is morally right for a woman to do."[21] In the same year Angelina penned *An Appeal to the Women of the Nominally Free States,* which linked the struggles of both blacks and women to a larger struggle for human rights.[22]

The most significant turning point came in 1840 when a number of women, including Mott and Stanton, were sent to London as delegates to the International Anti-Slavery Convention. To their dismay and over their vociferous objections they were not allowed to participate.[23] This rebuff resulted in the 1848 Women's Rights Convention at Seneca Falls, which Mott and Stanton organized. The convention adopted ten resolutions drawn up by Stanton that included the right of women to own property, the right

---

gious Social Thought of Elizabeth Cady Stanton, Susan B. Anthony, and Anna Howard Shaw, Chicago Studies in the History of American Religion (Brooklyn: Carlson, 1991).

20. See Banks, *Faces of Feminism,* 21.

21. Gerda Lerner, *The Grimké Sisters from South Carolina: Rebels against Slavery* (Boston: Houghton Mifflin, 1967), 193; cited in Banks, 21.

22. Chafetz and Dworkin, *Female Revolt,* 22.

23. See Coolidge, *Women's Rights,* 25-26.

to their own earnings, the right to share legal custody of their children, the right to have access to education and the professions, and the right to vote. This last provision was so radical that Stanton's husband (generally supportive of women's rights) and even Lucretia Mott objected, but Stanton perceived that it was the linchpin of all the legal and social reforms she sought. With the support of Frederick Douglass, the provision was passed by the convention.[24] This event, along with a second convention two years later in Worcester (which included other prominent suffragette abolitionists such as Lucy Stone) launched the women's movement as a national phenomenon.

The women's movement did not wholly separate itself from abolition, however, until slavery was outlawed with the passage of the Thirteenth Amendment in 1865.[25] In return for the women ceasing their agitation for women's rights during the war, abolitionist leaders had promised that they would support not only black but also women's suffrage. After discovering in the aftermath of the war that both causes were more unpopular than anticipated, they jettisoned their support for the women's issue. While some women activists (e.g., Stone) were prepared to accept such a development on pragmatic grounds, Anthony and Stanton were not.[26] In spite of their efforts the Fourteenth Amendment, which granted the vote to the former slaves, explicitly limited the right to men.

The period that followed this defeat was a difficult one for the women's movement. Rocked by scandals and disagreements, it split into two groups, the National Woman Suffrage Association, headed by Stanton and Anthony, and the American Woman's Suffrage Organization, headed by Lucy Stone.[27] Each had its own journal: the National's *Revolution* was devoted not only to women's suffrage but to other controversial issues such as divorce law and the organization of female workers, while the American's *Woman's Journal* appealed to conservative women not yet committed to suffrage.[28] In addition to internal division, the movement was damaged

---

24. See Coolidge, *Women's Rights,* 27-29. It should be noted that some recent scholarship has suggested that legal reforms such as the Married Women's Property Act (passed in the state of New York in 1848) served as the catalyst for the drive toward women's suffrage (not vice versa). This position, however, also sees suffrage as the key to maintaining changed property rights for women. See Peggy A. Rabkin, *Fathers to Daughters: The Legal Foundations of Female Emancipation* (Westport, Conn.: Greenwood Press, 1980).

25. Chafetz and Dworkin, *Female Revolt,* 23.

26. See Coolidge, *Women's Rights,* 48-50.

27. Ibid., 50-55.

28. See Banks, *Faces of Feminism,* 135.

by public backlash following Victoria Woodhull's public advocacy of "free love" in her lectures and her spiritualist newspaper *Woodhull and Clafin's Weekly.*[29] Woodhull's 1871 report of an affair between Henry Ward Beecher and Elizabeth Tilton (both of whom were involved in the women's cause)[30] again confirmed public perception of the women's movement as a fringe phenomenon dangerous to public life and morality.

Perception gradually began to change in the ensuing decades, particularly after the large Women's Christian Temperance Union was persuaded to include women's suffrage as one of its goals in 1883. The effect was an immediate increase in numbers and respectability, and an increasingly conservative tone that broadened its appeal.[31] Women's suffrage became closely allied with a defense of the family and traditional morality.[32] Ironically, the move toward the mainstream through its growing association with temperance also had the negative effect of making the women's movement "dull and respectable."[33] The union of the two suffrage associations in 1890 under the title of the National American Woman Suffrage Association (NAWSA) with Elizabeth Cady Stanton as president did little to invigorate the movement.

It was only with the arrival of a new generation of leaders and new styles of political action that the cause regained some of its earlier force. The needed transfusion came from England. There, too, the movement had lapsed into an anemic condition, but around 1905 it discovered militant activism as a means to spark public interest in the suffrage question.[34] While some of these activities produced negative publicity, circumstances such as the forced feeding of arrested women who had gone on hunger strikes provoked public sympathy and helped push the suffrage issue to the forefront of national interest. In 1912, two American women involved

29. Some, such as Banks, believe that by this term Woodhull meant the liberalization of divorce laws. This is, however, not likely the case since the paper also won notoriety for its views on abortion, birth control, venereal disease, and female sexuality; see Banks, *Faces of Feminism,* 57.

30. See Coolidge, *Women's Rights,* 59-60; Banks, *Faces of Feminism,* 57-58.

31. In England temperance and women's suffrage remained for the most part distinct movements; see Banks, 79-80. On the vast disparity in numbers between the two American movements, Chafetz and Dworkin report that "at the turn-of-the-century, temperance women outnumbered suffragist women by 10 to 1," *Female Revolt,* 111-12.

32. See Chafetz and Dworkin, *Female Revolt,* 26. Banks observes that this period also saw a growing ideology of female moral superiority in the United States and, to a lesser degree, in Britain, *Faces of Feminism,* 87-96.

33. See Coolidge, *Women's Rights,* 84-96.

34. For a description of the WSPU's tactics and their origin see Coolidge, *Women's Rights,* 98-100.

in the British movement, Lucy Burns and Alice Paul, returned to the United States determined to emulate the tactics of the British. They introduced large outdoor demonstrations, picketing, and direct pressure upon Congress and the President. Disowned by NAWSA, Burns and Paul maintained their militancy and their place in the public eye even through the First World War and in spite of arrests and imprisonments.[35] It should be pointed out that in both Britain and the United States the absence of men on the home front during World War I profoundly changed the perception and role of women in civil life.

With the election of Carrie Chapman Catt as president in 1915, the NAWSA found an organizer capable of harnessing the swelling tide of interest and energy in the suffrage issue, while maintaining a discreet distance from the more radical forms of activism. Catt had played a key role in the NAWSA's decision in 1896 to pass a resolution distancing itself from Stanton's *Women's Bible*. As Banks observes, "she represented the younger women in the movement who saw the issue of suffrage as paramount and were deeply resentful of any expression that might alienate its acceptance."[36] She designed and implemented the ultimately victorious strategy of national organization and intensive lobbying that helped push the Nineteenth Amendment through Congress and secure its ratification on August 26, 1920.[37]

The United States actually lagged behind some other countries in granting women the right to vote. British women over the age of 30 were enfranchised by Parliament in 1918 (the age was finally lowered to 21 in 1928). Germany, Poland, and Sweden all granted female suffrage in 1919. Other European countries followed more slowly, with France in 1944, Italy in 1945, Yugoslavia in 1946, and Greece in 1952.[38] In other parts of the world the results vary widely, with Australia being among the first to enfranchise women (1902) and Kenya and Iran among the last (1963).[39] Communist countries granted women voting rights upon the communist

35. Ibid., 113-33.
36. Banks, *Faces of Feminism*, 140.
37. See Freeman, "Women's Movements," 565. Cf. Coolidge, *Women's Rights*, 149-66.
38. Branca observes that there is some irony in the fact that France, which was in many respects the ideological birthplace of the women's movement, was among the last European countries to grant suffrage to women. See 180-81.
39. For a helpful table that compiles data on women's suffrage throughout the world see *Encyclopedia Britannica*, s.v. "Woman Suffrage." For a worldwide overview of the first wave of the women's movements see Chafetz and Dworkin, *Female Revolt*, 103-62.

assumption of power (e.g., the former U.S.S.R. in 1917 and China in 1947), but even many feminists will admit that the real status of women and the women's movements in such societies is deplorable.[40]

Intermission

Having won the right to vote, the women's movements in many countries dissipated their energies and organization rather quickly. Scholars attribute this to a number of factors. Some point to the failure of the suffrage organizations themselves to provide any long-term goals or objectives for the newly enfranchised women.[41] Others, such as Banks, observe that the disparate strands and diverse positions that made up the women's movement could not have maintained any extended unity with the issue of suffrage no longer there to unite them.[42]

This is not to say that no activity or organization remained from the first wave. The NAWSA led by Carrie Catt became the League of Women Voters, which was designed to educate and encourage women in the use of their newly won right. The League has also remained a forum for women's political action over the years, espousing a variety of civic (though not always feminist) causes.[43] The Women's Party founded by Alice Paul devoted itself to continuing the work of ending discrimination against women and to that end sought the passage of the Equal Rights Amendment, but the measure was to remain locked in congressional committees until its passage in 1972.[44]

Here, however, the divisions between the differing strands of the women's movement become apparent. Some of the most staunch opponents of the emphasis on equal rights were women who had themselves been active in the movement and who saw protective legislation as the best way to protect women in the workplace. These women became in the New Deal atmosphere of the 1930s what Banks describes as proponents of "welfare feminism." Emphasizing the distinctive maternal role of women, they sought to protect this role through legislation designed to protect women

---

40. See Chafetz and Dworkin, *Female Revolt,* 131, 140.
41. See, for example, Freeman, "Women's Movements," 565.
42. See Banks, *Faces of Feminism,* 149-50.
43. See Coolidge, "Women's Rights," 174-80.
44. After its passage the attempt to ratify the ERA failed to garner the requisite number of states for ratification in spite of a three-year extension by Congress. See Freeman, "Women's Movements," 566. On the work of the Women's Party, see Coolidge, *Women's Rights,* 171-74.

and children both at work (through protective legislation) and at home (through social welfare programs).[45] They were opposed by those who sought equal rights in the form of equal pay and opportunity. This latter group, whose nucleus was the Women's Party, was, however, far smaller and had less influence.[46] Hence, the years between 1920 and 1960 "were dominated by a tradition of feminism which had little to do with the Enlightenment. Instead its origins lie in the evangelical tradition of moral reform and female superiority that gave women a commitment to a new moral order."[47]

An equally divisive issue during this period was that of birth control. The earlier generation of suffrage leaders had themselves generally opposed such measures and advocated greater emphasis on chastity, but birth control had always been viewed more favorably by some of the radical members of the movement. As the birth control movement gained public acceptance, and especially after the approval given to artificial means of contraception by the Lambeth Conference of Anglican Bishops in 1930, the burgeoning birth control and eugenics movements became more closely aligned with the aspirations of welfare feminism.[48] The connection remained somewhat tenuous, however, and did not have a fully developed ideological legitimation until the feminism of the 1960s asserted that contraception (and abortion) are aspects of the right of women to control their bodies.[49]

The Second Wave

While the first wave, or women's rights movement, was characterized by action in the realm of politics, the second wave, which often used the expression "women's liberation," was directed more to securing a greater place for women in society's life as a whole. It was and is an effort to get women and men — the whole society — to look upon women in a new

45. See Banks, *Faces of Feminism*, 154-62.
46. Ibid., 156-57.
47. Ibid., 162.
48. See Banks, *Faces of Feminism*, 182-91. Banks erroneously, however, dates the Anglican Church's reversal of its position on contraception to 1958 (see p. 184).
49. Cf. Banks, *Faces of Feminism*, 191. It should be noted, however, that Banks views the advocacy of abortion as distinct from the birth control movement — an idea that the career of Margaret Sanger and Planned Parenthood, which she founded, would seem to call into question. See George Grant, *Grand Illusions: The Legacy of Planned Parenthood* (Brentwood, Tenn.: Wolgemuth and Hyatt, 1988).

way and to adjust society correspondingly. In this sense it began to articulate the goals of feminism, which seeks to raise or modify consciousness.

Given the continuance of the various strands that made up the earlier women's movements, the sudden emergence of the "women's lib" movement in the 1960s is not wholly surprising. Critics of feminism tend to dismiss any claim of continuity between the two waves, identifying the earlier women's movements with the evangelical impulse and the rise of feminism solely with radicalism.[50] But this would seem to overlook the coexistence of real differences of policy and position in both waves.

The advent of what has become the predominant mode of feminism may be traced to a variety of social, intellectual, and political factors. On the political front the women who continued to work for equal rights received an unexpected opportunity when a Southern congressman in a last-minute attempt to kill the Civil Rights Act of 1964 added the word "sex" to a bill originally targeted at ending racial discrimination.[51] While many in government regarded this addition as a fluke, many activist women did not. These women came together to form the National Organization for Women (NOW) and a host of other organizations in order to pressure the Equal Employment Opportunity Commission to begin to enforce this provision.[52] Within a few years of this development, large numbers of groups of younger women began to form around the country for the purpose of feminist "consciousness raising." These groups were primarily an outgrowth of the student and civil rights movements of the 1960s and the New Left.[53] They had little organization within themselves or with one another. In time these two distinct movements grew together, as NOW gradually embraced much of the radical agenda of the younger groups (such as abortion and lesbian rights) and the activism of the smaller groups gradually dissipated for want of organization or agenda.[54]

50. Thus William Oddie views feminism primarily as an outgrowth of the student radicalism of the 1960s. See *What Will Happen to God? Feminism and the Reconstruction of Christian Belief* (San Francisco: Ignatius Press, 1988), 8-9. Cf. Jutta Burgraff, "The Mother of the Church and the Women in the Church: A Correction of Feminist Theology Gone Astray," trans. Maria Shrady, in *The Church and Women: A Compendium* (San Francisco: Ignatius, 1988), 238.

51. See Banks, *Faces of Feminism,* 212.

52. See Freeman, "Women's Movements," 566.

53. See Chafetz and Dworkin, *Female Revolt,* 166. Here there is an interesting parallel with the rise of the first wave since it was disillusionment with the male leadership of these radical groups which caused many women to branch out on their own. Cf. Odie, 8-9.

54. There is some disagreement as to whether this growing together should be

The author whose work succeeded in setting the direction for most feminist consciousness raising and social critique is undoubtedly the French existentialist Simone de Beauvoir.[55] Her basic thesis is that women have themselves to be defined exclusively in relation to men and not on their own terms. De Beauvoir's thought has rightly been criticized for promoting the same kind of assimilation to the male norm against which she inveighed by her invidious comparisons between women and men, especially on the bodily level.

As the price of admission to the realm of Transcendence de Beauvoir's female subjects must shuck off their female identities. Civilization de Beauvoir declares to be male and men its essential parts; women, the flip side of the coin, lie outside civilization and are unessential.[56]

In the United States, a successor to de Beauvoir, but one whose interest in integrating women in the social sphere was more accented, was Betty Friedan.[57] Friedan announced a revolt against the "feminine mystique" crystallized by the strong emphasis on women's roles and on motherhood during the 1940s and '50s and the concomitant "baby boom."[58] The "mystique" would better be described as an "ideology." What Friedan's work did on the popular level other works were already outlining in more academic and theoretical fashion.

Kate Millet is another writer who has had a marked influence on the history and future of feminism.[59] Millet may be classified as a radical feminist in that (1) she tends to classify all men as oppressors, (2) she accepts a post-Kantian position regarding the "reality-making" function of symbolization, and (3) she therefore reduces all gender differences to culture. In this latter effort she uses the notion of patriarchy as a critical tool. The American radical Shulamith Firestone took these ideas even further, seeing the complete liberation of women coming only with the elimination of the biological aspects of maternity, that is, when all human reproduction would be carried out in laboratories.[60]

---

regarded as the radicalization of NOW or the de-radicalization of the feminist left: see Banks, *Faces of Feminism,* 234-37.

55. *Le deuxième sexe* (Paris: Gallimard, 1949).

56. Elshtain, *Public Man, Private Woman,* 307. For a list of the type of statements de Beauvoir makes when comparing men and women, particularly on the physical level, see 307-10.

57. *The Feminine Mystique* (New York: Norton, 1963).

58. See Banks, *Faces of Feminism,* 203.

59. See her *Sexual Politics* (New York: Doubleday, 1970).

60. See *The Dialectic of Sex: The Case for a Feminist Revolution* (London: Jonathan Cape, 1971).

On a more intellectual level, there began an effort at consciousness raising that aimed at critiquing and changing society's view of women and their roles. This included the growing insistence that women should express their own self-perception and not merely adopt that of men. This is a positive step. One difficulty, however, consistently faced by those who wish to raise consciousness is defining the norms by which one consciousness is considered better than another and by whom. Either this is done on the basis of rational discourse concerning the true moral end of human existence, or it runs the risk of being another instance of social engineering on the part of an enlightened elite who have access to the means of communication. Feminism does not always avoid this alternative because, as I will maintain, it shares the modernity's tendency to equate authority with dominative power.

As far as I know, there has never been a balanced epistemological analysis of that function by which the consciousness or horizon of the thinking subject is modified, particularly in regard to one's own social or political situation. In terms of its role in social change, the first person to make the notion popular outside strictly Marxist circles was Paulo Freire in his *Pedagogy of the Oppressed.*[61] On the philosophical level, the notion can be found in the works of writers as diverse as Gadamer and Lonergan. Within feminism, the force of the consciousness-raising (conscientization) effort has been directed toward an appreciation of the oppression of women. The primary goal was to get women to see that they looked upon the world and upon themselves within a horizon set by men. The symbols used, the values desired, the basic mode of interpreting reality were considered masculine. There could be no change in the position of women until they perceived themselves differently. This is the type of application of a Marxist insight already utilized by Freire.

It is noteworthy that most of the early writers considered that the fundamental awareness that had to be achieved was that of the manner in which women were deprived of an equal access to the goods of life, especially the public goods of power, status, the opportunity for public discourse, and important public responsibilities. With the exception of the Marxist feminists, very few people ever seem to have questioned that these goods, as modern society views them, may not be unequivocal goods. Often, the advocates of women's liberation were themselves still viewing reality with the eyes of the practical reason inherited from the Enlightenment and with the individualism begun by Descartes and perpetuated in American society by a constellation of forces.

Few among the founders of this second wave ever stopped to think that there might be something wrong with the *perception itself.* Thus, they

61. Trans. Myra Bergman Ramos (New York: Herder and Herder, 1970).

did not think of restructuring society but rather sought to give women a more equitable portion of what the culture esteemed as goods. To put this another way, consciousness was raised only in regard to the way women were excluded from a world defined by the masculinization effected by the Enlightenment. The oppression worked on all of humankind by this outlook was not rendered conscious. One of the discouraging dimensions of this period is the fact that there were not many theoretical or practical alternatives being offered by traditional Christians.

In spite of clear differences in both presuppositions and conclusions, this sampling of some feminist theorists reveals many of the key tenets uniting much contemporary feminism: the right of women to define or create themselves (autonomy), the identification of equality and identity (true especially of equal rights feminism), and the ascription of the status of oppressors to men by virtue of their sex (patriarchy). Thus, Karen Offen describes those who ought to be considered feminist:

(1) they recognize the validity of women's own interpretation of their lived experience and needs and acknowledge the values women claim publicly as their own (as distinct from the aesthetic ideal of womanhood invented by men) in assessing their status in society relative to men; (2) they exhibit consciousness of, discomfort at, or even anger over institutionalized injustice (or inequity) toward women as a group by men as a group in a given society; (3) they advocate the elimination of that injustice by challenging, through efforts to alter prevailing ideas and/or social institutions and practices, the coercive power, force, or authority that upholds male prerogatives in that particular culture. Thus, to be a feminist is necessarily to be at odds with male-dominated culture and society.[62]

While the feminism of today draws its ideological inspiration primarily from the equal rights and socialist or radical traditions, there is still a good deal of diversity of thought within it. In spite of the predominance of the emphasis on equality, there is still a sizable segment that insists on the importance of sexual difference.[63] There is likewise considerable debate

62. "Defining Feminism," p. 152.
63. Much French feminism, for example, has continued to insist on the significance of sexual difference. This is reflected, for example, in many of the selections in *New French Feminisms,* ed. Elaine Marks and Isabelle de Courtivron. A similar emphasis on difference is found in the writing of the influential developmental psychologist Carol Gilligan, *In a Different Voice.* On the dilemma faced by feminists in choosing between equality or difference, see Schneiders, 9-11. Cf. Alison M. Jaggar, "Sexual Difference and Sexual Equality" in *Theoretical Perspectives on Sexual Difference* (New Haven: Yale University Press, 1990), 239-54.

about the utility of the Western liberal tradition of equality or fairness itself, out of which the language of rights emerges.[64] Hence the term *feminist movement* can be misleading since there are a variety of influences, ideas, groups, and agendas that make up contemporary feminism.

SOME ASPECTS OF FEMINIST THEOLOGY

Since the rest of this book is a dialogue with feminist theology, there is no need to treat it at length here. It will be useful, however, to dedicate some paragraphs to a consideration of certain aspects of its origins and present situation.

With the outbreak of the second wave, feminist consciousness gradually made its way into both the churches and the various branches of academia, including theology.[65] While this development has precursors in some of the writings of women within the first wave such as Sarah Grimké, Antoinnette Brown, and especially Elizabeth Cady Stanton,[66] it is nevertheless basically coterminous with contemporary feminism and it contains some of the same diversity.[67]

The emergence of feminist theology can be dated to Valerie Saiving Goldstein's 1960 article "The Human Situation: A Feminine View," which appealed for the consideration of distinctively female experience in religious studies that had previously considered only male experience.[68] This

64. Thus Elizabeth Fox-Genovese in her *Feminism without Illusions* critiques the feminist adoption of the individualism inherent in the Liberal tradition which renders it blind to other differences of race or class. Similar observations are made by Jean Bethke Elshtain, *Public Man, Private Woman*, 244-53. For a defense of feminist utilization of the liberal notion of justice see Moller Okin, *Justice, Gender and the Family*.

65. On the spread of feminism in the U.S. church, see Mary Jo Weaver, *New Catholic Women: A Contemporary Challenge to Traditional Religious Authority* (San Francisco: Harper, 1985). See especially the discussion of the emergence of feminism on the parish level (37-70) and within many orders of women religious (71-108).

66. Current surveys of feminist theology tend to emphasize the continuity between the theology of the two waves. See, for example, Rosemary Radford Ruether, "Feminist Theology," in *The New Dictionary of Theology,* ed. J. Komonchak and M. Collins (Wilmington, Del.: Glazier, 1987), 391-96; Ann Loades, "Feminist Theology," in *The Modern Theologians: An Introduction to Christian Theology in the Twentieth Century,* ed. D. F. Ford (New York: Blackwell, 1989), II, 235-52.

67. In addition to literature cited below, there is a very helpful book, complete with graphic dateline charting of events significant to feminism since 1960: Maria Riley, *Transforming Feminism* (Kansas City: Sheed and Ward, 1989). Also useful is the long article in the *Theologische Realenzyklopedie,* vol. 11 (Berlin: de Gruyter, 1983), 422-81.

68. "It is my contention that there are significant differences between masculine

notion was developed at greater length by Judith Plaskow in her 1981 dissertation *Sex, Sin and Grace: Women's Experience in the Theologies of Reinhold Niebuhr and Paul Tillich*, which also described the deformation of uniquely female experience by male theological categories.[69] During the intervening period, Mary Daly developed her critique of Christian belief and theology as inherently patriarchal and oppressive to women.[70] Her subsequent works have argued that it is irredeemably so and have moved into a "post-Christian" radical separatism that views men as inherently evil and calls women to lives of lesbian separatism.[71]

Although the initial stirrings of feminist theology were a call to consider women's perspectives on theological issues, most of the energy in the theological effort derived from liberationist thinking and praxis. This can be seen, for instance, in Rosemary Radford Ruether's personal account of her early involvement in feminist issues,[72] from different classifications of feminist theology, and from an examination of the literature itself. There have been many attempts to identify and categorize feminist thought in the period from 1960 to the present. Among the authors whom I have found most useful are Catherina Halkes,[73] Herlinde Pissarek-Hudelist,[74] and Barbara Brown Zikmund.[75] In addition, there are several scholars who have presented useful typologies of feminist hermeneutics.

Mary Ann Tolbert discusses three different responses to the Bible that she terms (1) searching for a "prophetic-liberating tradition of biblical

---

and feminine experience and that feminine experience reveals in a more emphatic fashion certain aspects of the human situation which are present but less obvious in the experience of men." *Journal of Religion* 40 (1960): 100-112, citation is from p. 101.

69. Washington: University Press.

70. See *Beyond God the Father: Toward a Philosophy of Women's Liberation* (Boston: Beacon, 1973).

71. See *Gyn/Ecology: The Metaethics of Radical Feminism* (Boston: Beacon, 1978), 27-42, 376.

72. Rosemary Radford Ruether, "The Development of My Theology," *Religious Studies Review* 15/1 (1989): 1-11.

73. "Feminist Theology: An Interim Assessment," in *Women in a Men's Church*, ed. V. Elizondo and N. Greinacher, *Concilium* 134 (New York: Seabury, 1980), 110-23.

74. "Feministische Theologie — Eine Herausforderung?" *Zeitschrift für katholische Theologie* 103 (1981): 289-308; 400-425.

75. "Feminist Consciousness in Historical Perspective," in *Feminist Interpretation of the Bible*, ed. Letty M. Russell (Philadelphia: Westminster Press, 1985), 21-29. One may consult as well Dorothy C. Bass, "Women's Studies and Biblical Studies: An Historical Perspective," *Journal for the Study of the Old Testament* 22 (Feb 1982): 6-12. An overview of American Catholic feminism is provided by Rosemary Rader in "Catholic Feminism: Its Impact on U.S. Catholic Women," *American Catholic Women*, ed. K. Kennelly (New York: Macmillan, 1989), 182-219.

faith," (2) a "remnant standpoint," and (3) the "reconstruction of biblical history."[76] Katherine Doob Sakenfeld distinguishes three different emphases with which Christian feminists approach the biblical text: (1) looking to texts about women to counteract texts used against women (reinterpreting "forgotten" texts), (2) looking to the Bible generally for a theological perspective offering a critique of patriarchy (this includes Tolbert's first response), and (3) looking to texts about women to learn from the history and stories of ancient and modern women living in patriarchal cultures (this includes Tolbert's third response).[77] In a further study, these categories are repeated and nuanced in a larger context.[78]

Carolyn Osiek, between the publications of the first and second of Sakenfeld's articles, offered a more inclusive classification of the hermeneutical alternatives employed by feminist theologians: (1) *rejectionist* (rejecting the Bible as authoritative or useful while retaining or rejecting the religious tradition it represents), (2) *loyalist* (accepting, but not uncritically, the biblical tradition as the Word of God), (3) *revisionist* (attempting to separate the content from the patriarchal mold of Scripture by what I would call "recovery" and/or "reconstruction"; this resembles Tolbert's second and third responses), (4) *sublimationist* (searching for the eternal feminine in biblical and extrabiblical symbolism and imagery), and (5) *liberationist* (using a revised understanding of biblical eschatology as the interpretive principle with which to judge the revelatory character of biblical texts).[79] These categories are taken up by Elizabeth Johnson.[80]

In 1991, I suggested a theological assessment of feminist hermeneutics based on its treatment of the canon.[81] There is a difference of approach among feminists in this regard. Some accept the canon that the church gradually established between the end of the second and the middle of the fourth centuries (e.g., Heine, Jewett). Some consider the Scriptures capable of generating a principle of their own by which the patriarchal parts may

---

76. "Defining the Problem: The Bible and Feminist Hermeneutics," in *The Bible and Feminist Hermeneutics,* ed. Mary Anne Tolbert, *Semeia* 28 (Chico, Calif.: Scholars Press, 1983), 113-26.

77. "Feminist Uses of Biblical Materials," in *Feminist Interpretation of the Bible,* 55-64.

78. "Feminist Perspectives on Bible and Theology. An Introduction to Selected Issues and Literature," *Interp* 42 (1988): 5-18.

79. "The Feminist and the Bible: Hermeneutical Alternatives," in *Feminist Perspectives on Biblical Scholarship,* ed. Adela Y. Collins, SBL Centennial Pub. 10 (Chico, Calif.: Scholars Press, 1985), 93-106.

80. "Feminist Hermeneutics," *Chicago Studies* 27 (1988): 123-35.

81. "Feminist Hermeneutics: An Overview," *Communio* 18 (1991): 144-63; 398-424.

be subordinated or eliminated (canon within the canon, e.g., Ruether). Others maintain that only in virtue of an extrabiblical principle, women's experience, can the Scriptures be interpreted and found useful (canon outside the canon, e.g., Fiorenza). Still others consider a hermeneutic that can be applied to a hopelessly patriarchal text in order to render it liberating (Schneiders).[82]

The last thirty years have seen a veritable explosion of feminist publications and conferences. In addition to collected works, books, and many new journals, there have been courses initiated at universities and doctorates undertaken. The academic milieu at large has been clearly influenced by the presence of feminism, as can be seen by consulting any established journal. Besides being a boon to the religion industry, this considerable output has called attention to many theoretical and practical aspects of church life that should be addressed.

Those who first engaged in feminist theology were for the most part white, middle-class academics. Responding to the complaints of women of other races, social classes, states of life, and religions, there has been a conscious attempt to form a sort of "rainbow coalition." This has broadened the base of feminist thought and theology, but it has also made it necessary to establish feminist consciousness as the basic category of thought in which all can meet. The result has been that feminist consciousness or spirituality has become the genus, and Christian, Jewish, Muslim, and other religious thought have become species whose specificity, whatever that may consist in, is governed by the outlook and demands of feminism.

In dependence upon liberationist thought, a great stress is placed on the raising of consciousness mentioned previously. It is in this connection that the term *patriarchy* is applied to the church at large and particularly to the language of the Scriptures and theology in general, which is thus labeled androcentric and patriarchal. The same raising of consciousness is applied to a Christian version of feminist spirituality. Feminist spirituality arises "from feminist consciousness, the result of the process of consciousness-raising, when that consciousness becomes operative in the sphere of one's lived faith experience."[83] Linked to both theological reflection and

---

82. In another context Schneiders classifies feminism in general as *Liberal* (concerned with equal rights), *Cultural* (concerned with women's special contribution), *Socialist* (concerned to change the economic class/sex structure), and *Radical* (concerned to eliminate patriarchy as the predominant system of class oppression): *Beyond Patching*, 18-25.

83. Sandra M. Schneiders, "Feminist Spirituality," in *The New Dictionary of Catholic Spirituality*, ed. Michael Downey (Collegeville, Minn.: Liturgical Press, 1993), 394-406; citation is from p. 401. For a similar account of feminist spirituality see

spirituality is the call for a revised conception of and language about God that more nearly represents women's experience. This involves efforts in several directions. There is first the attempt to minimize the biblical manner of referring to God as "he" by the substitution of other expressions for pronouns of the masculine gender. In this connection biblical expressions that seem noninclusive (e.g., "brother") are changed to be inclusive ("brother and sister"). In regard to the theological language and outlook that has developed from the Bible, there is an attempt to insist on feminine and other nonmasculine imagery for God, and the use of other terminology for "Father," "Son," and "Holy Spirit."

In order to effect this change of outlook, biblical and other texts from the past are read from a consciously feminist perspective. At the same time, a revisionist reading of history is undertaken that recovers a knowledge of the roles of women in the early church, while at the same time challenging what is termed a patriarchal reading of history that has been used to justify claims that are unfounded.

Finally, there is both a call for and theological planning for an effective change in the church's way of life and worship that is adequate to the vision and heightened consciousness claimed to have been brought about by feminist theological speculation and historical research.

The force of the feminist position in the church derives from the many ways in which it shows us how we, as Christians, allow our share in the darkness and sin of humanity to obfuscate the gospel both in theory and in practice. Feminism's potential for harm is found in the uncritical way it has submitted itself to an understanding of God, the world, and humankind that is at odds with the light of faith. It is to separating the feminist contribution from the feminist capitulation to what is foreign to the gospel that the next chapters are dedicated.

Foundationalism, Representationalism, and Individualism

I have already had occasion in chapter 4 to challenge the myth of "total oppression" often spoken of by feminists, and in chapter 3 I proposed a more adequate heuristic structure for the study of Christian origins. The principal difficulties are, however, on a more profound and pervasive level.

Sally B. Purvis, "Christian Feminist Spirituality," in *Christian Spirituality: Post-Reformation and Modern*, ed. Louis Dupré and Don E. Sallers, vol. 18 of *World Spirituality: An Encyclopedic History of the Religious Quest* (New York: Crossroad, 1989), 500-519.

They derive from the fact that feminism relies on precisely that mode of thought that is responsible for the situation it wishes to change. I am referring to what is vaguely called "modernity." As I mentioned in the introduction, there are three aspects of modernity that have profoundly affected all theological thought and thus feminist thought as well.

In what follows, I have been influenced by the study of Nancey Murphy and James Wm. McClendon, Jr., though my understanding and use of these three characteristics are my own.[84] These are the characteristics as they list them:

1. Epistemological foundationalism: "[T]he view that knowledge can be justified only by finding indubitable 'foundational' beliefs upon which it is constructed." (I would say "foundational tenets," though they are in fact beliefs.)

2. A representational-expressivist theory of language: "[T]he view that language must gain its primary meaning by representing the objects or facts to which it refers; otherwise it merely expresses the attitudes of the speaker." This must be extended to include both Kantian and Schleiermachian versions of representationalism in which, in fact, language represents not the attitudes of the speaker but the mental construct produced by the subject.

3. Atomism or reductionism: "[A]n attempt to understand reality by reducing it to its smallest parts. Here we find the modern approach to ethics and political philosophy which sees the individual as prior to the community, and the community as merely a collection of like individuals, a mass." The word *prior* here refers to the notion that the person is totally constituted and is considered the locus of rights before any consideration of relation to another.

Feminist foundationalism is found principally in two areas: the appeal to experience as the foundation of knowledge, and the conviction, influenced by Kantianism, that any act of knowledge in which the subject is receptive is a diminishment of the subject. This latter point derives from the Enlightenment identification of causality with domination. I consider this attitude, which is completely unbiblical, to be the most pervasive and destructive of the presuppositions of feminism, though it is, in fact, the underlying attitude that feminism is trying to combat. With this type of accent placed on the knowing subject, the interpretation of

---

84. "Distinguishing Modern and Postmodern Theologies," *Theology Today* 5 (1989): 191-214. The following descriptions are from p. 192 of their article. I used this threefold classification in a previous study, "Feminist Theology: A Proposal," *Communio* 20 (1993): 334-76.

the biblical text becomes an act by which the subject utilizes the text in an effort at self-realization rather than as an instance of communication on the part of an author to be actively received by the reader. Furthermore, after having accepted the post-Enlightenment concept of *religion* and its consequent placing of Christianity within an overall category that adjudicates its truth claims, feminist theologians are hard put to demonstrate any continuity between their enterprise and the understanding of theology that sees it as coming from faith as a unique and God-given interpretation of reality.[85]

The Kantian and Schleiermachian form of representationalism characteristic of feminism is to be found in the manner in which language for God is treated, either implicitly or explicitly, as expressive of the subject's experience but not of what is experienced. This gives rise to a very specific understanding of metaphor and models that is basically agnostic. With the accent on consciousness and consciousness raising now deprived of any objective referent to measure it against, feminist analysis of the position of women combines a sometimes accurate estimation of the situation with an interpretation that is foreign to the prophetic interpretation of reality provided by revelation.

Feminist individualism derives from its liberationist heritage and its imitation of Marxist analysis. Rights are located in the individual apart from considerations of relationship, and this notion is applied to life in the church. In addition, this form of individualism gives rise to a false understanding of the body person. The body is either ignored in discussing the meaning of person, or it is made the means of entering into contact with the immanent powers of the universe. In the first case "body parts" are considered to be what is meant by physicality, and this leads to a misunderstanding of the sacramentality of the body and its significance in appreciating the ministries of men and women in the church. In the second case, immanentism runs the risk of being substituted for an understanding of the body as a dimension of a transcendentally related person who relates to a personal God.

The influence of these aspects of modernity weakens the theological nature of feminist theology as it has done to much modern theology. Theology's isolation, as was pointed out previously, allows Christianity to be treated as a species under the general genus *religion,* rather than as a unique work of God in Christ. This is false to the nature of the revelation

---

85. See chapter 2 of this book. For a good analysis of Enlightenment thinking about religion see Peter Harrison, *'Religion' and the Religions in the English Enlightenment* (New York: Cambridge University Press, 1990).

itself and to the understanding of theology maintained by earlier theologians and recovered by some of the great theologians of our own century. It is with the desire to bring the light of faith into correlative relation with what is true in the feminist perspective that I take up an analysis of these three operative presuppositions in feminist theology.

6

Do We Need Foundations?

In metaphysics and in epistemology, a foundation is "a place to stand," it is a mental acquisition that can form the basis for further thinking. It is something that is solid enough to provide stability for a system and practice of thought. The need to establish foundations arose with the move in European thought to seek certitude within the confines of the human mind. We have seen that this was codified into a consistent attitude of thought by William of Ockham. The immediate source of the search for an unshakable foundation for all human knowledge, which has been termed *Cartesian anxiety,* is itself but a reflection of the search for *certitudo* in the period immediately following the Catholic-Protestant split. The whole of the critical era has been preoccupied with establishing the foundation for knowledge and has sought to place it, one way or another, within the human mind conceived as an isolated "subject."

This chapter will proceed in five steps. After tracing briefly the search for foundations in recent philosophy, there will be a discussion of experience as a foundation, and then a consideration of the feminist appeal to experience. The next three steps will be: a reflection on being and knowing in the context of the biblical teaching on creation, a reconsideration of experience in that light, and finally an attempt to describe the contribution of women's experience in a nonfoundational context.

The most salient characteristic of foundationalist thinking is isolation — the isolated subject must be responsible for certitude. Nurtured by anxiety and the need for a certitude determined according to norms established by a particular understanding of reason, Western thought suffered a "loss of nerve." There was first of all a loss of confidence in the information supplied by the senses — since the universe did not represent a word from God about himself, but was rather the expression of his will, which is unfathomable at best, arbitrary at worst, "appearances" are untrustworthy. Next, came the need to subject tradition to the critical assessment of the norms of those writing history, with the consequent loss of confidence in antiquity, whether sacred or secular. With this came the need to establish reason as the only reliable source of truth. Finally, then, the last question had to be solved — on what can reason be grounded so that the certitude so ardently sought for will no longer be able to escape human control?

The first thoroughgoing answer to this question was, of course, that of Descartes, who consistently and frequently speaks of his search for a foundation.

> I realized that it was necessary, once in the course of my life, to demolish everything completely and start again right from the foundations if I wanted to establish anything at all in the sciences that was stable and likely to last.[1]

From this moment on it was considered to be the philosopher's task to find a foundation upon which we can base our knowledge. This was the inspiration of the anxious attempt to search for "some fixed, permanent constraints to which we can appeal and which are secure and stable."[2]

Instructive in this regard is the well known paragraph in Kant's *Critique of Pure Reason* in which he compares the thinking subject and its attainments in the realm of knowledge to an island surrounded by many dark and uncontrollable realities that are not part of the small "land of truth" that the mind has managed to civilize.

> We have now not merely explored the territory of pure understanding, and carefully surveyed every part of it, but have also measured its extent, and assigned to everything in it its rightful place. This domain is an island, enclosed by nature itself with unalterable limits. It is the land of truth — enchanting name! — surrounded by a wide and stormy ocean, the native home of illusion, where many a fog bank and many a swiftly melting iceberg give the deceptive appearance of farther shores, deluding the adventurous seafarer ever anew with empty hopes, and engaging him in enterprises which he can never abandon and yet is unable to carry to completion.[3]

---

1. René Descartes, *Meditations on First Philosophy* I, in *The Philosophical Writings of Descartes,* vol. II, trans. John Cottingham, Robert Stoothoff, and Dugald Murdoch (Cambridge: Cambridge University Press, 1985), 12. See also the appeal to mathematics as having "firm and solid foundations," *Discourse on Method* I, Cottingham, vol. I, 114.

2. Richard Bernstein, *Beyond Objectivism and Relativism: Science, Hemeneutics, and Praxis* (Philadelphia: University of Pennsylvania Press, 1985), 19. This search comprises in large measure what Bernstein terms "objectivism."

3. Trans. Norman Kemp Smith (New York: St. Martin's Press, 1929), 257.

I have already remarked upon some aspects of the imagery employed here. Other aspects are equally important to an understanding of the Kantian legacy. There is first the presupposition that what surrounds the tiny island of subjectivity is "nature," a foreboding, recalcitrant, and deceptive environment that refuses to yield to human effort, though it continually invites it. This is Kant's image of human freedom — an area of retreat within a world of necessity. We will have reason to recall this when discussing the search for human rights and the meaning of autonomy. Second, and this is more apposite to our present preoccupation, there is the notion that intelligibility, where everything has its "rightful place," is not something discovered but something imposed by the thinking subject on a domain of chaos.

THE BEGINNINGS OF FOUNDATIONALISM

Descartes and Kant stand as the two pillars that support the arch of modernity. Their search for a foundation has, as we will continue to observe, misdirected much of the recent efforts of philosophy.[4] On the positive side, their work initiated a Copernican revolution in thought that we may designate by the term a *philosophy of consciousness*. This reflexive awareness of the subject must be part of any genuine metaphysics, and is an important component in an understanding of how the act of knowledge is neither with nor without foundations.[5]

This section will consider the manner in which experience itself functions as a foundation in feminist thinking. This is due to two factors: 1) the generally foundationalist orientation of critical thought, and 2) the specific influence of Freidrich Schleiermacher. Enough has been said about the first point; it remains now to discuss the second.

It is not totally clear that Descartes considered his *cogito* to be an exclusive foundation despite the fact that he tells us he is searching for a single foundation and states, "I decided I could accept [I think, therefore I am] without scruple as the first principle of the philosophy I was seeking."[6] The reason for the ambiguity lies in statements such as the following: "I see that the certainty of all other things depends on that [that the supreme

4. In addition to the work of Bernstein mentioned above see the study by Jerry Gill, *Mediated Transcendence: A Postmodern Reflection* (Macon, Ga.: Mercer University Press, 1989).
5. See the article by Kenneth Schmitz, "Neither With Nor Without Foundations," *Review of Metaphysics* 42 (1988): 3-25.
6. *Discourse on Method* IV, Cottingham, vol. I, 127.

being exists], so that without it nothing can ever be perfectly known."[7] Kant's foundationalism is of another order. It is not the subject's immediate awareness of itself through interior activity, but the manner in which reason precipitates itself out onto the "darkness and contradictions" of the noumenal world, conforming it to the structure of the knowing subject and thus rendering it intelligible.

Schleiermacher was correct in his attempt to get below, or beyond, the epistemological impasse established by Descartes's subject-object dichotomy. His mistake, and the mistake of most of those who follow him today, lay in his own dichotomy between a direct apprehension of God and a subsequent articulation of this in terms of a religious tradition.

> So that in this first instance God signifies for us simply that which is the co-determinant in this feeling and to which we trace our being in such a state; and any further content of the idea must be evolved out of this fundamental import assigned to it.[8]

In such a theory each person names that upon which he or she has cast the feeling of utter dependence according to the predispositions and cultural norms that are available. Their speech is representative not of the object of their knowledge but of their experience.

In regard to the first step in the argument, namely Schleiermacher's notion of the universality of the experience of absolute dependence, I leave it to others to decide whether, despite his protestations, Schleiermacher avoids the Kantian idealism he attempts to eschew. What is certain is that, for Schleiermacher, this fundamental feeling or apprehension remains indeterminate. As Ingolf Dalferth expresses it:

> Still, even if we take this apprehension to be a mode of discovery and not of inference, it is not obvious that we are all utterly dependent on the same source of dependence. . . . The problem with his approach is the identity of the Whence of our existence in different cases. . . . That we could not exist without god does not imply that the god without whom we could not exist is God or that it is the same god for all of us.[9]

The Cartesian argument from consciousness, which was given a particularly subjective twist by Kant, and against which Schleiermacher is

7. *Meditations* V, Cottingham, vol. II, 48; see also *Discourse on Method* IV, Cottingham, vol. I, 130.

8. *The Christian Faith* 4,4 (Torchbook edition, p. 17).

9. *Theology and Philosophy,* 109.

rebelling, is not at all that of Augustine. The difference is significant not only in itself but also because it points to what is missing in the feminist dependence upon the popular notion, derived from Schleiermacher, that religious symbols are second-order predications pointing to a particular kind of mediated experience and referring to the state of the experiencing subject, not to what is being experienced. The basic notion that lies behind this epistemology is that since the Transcendent is beyond words, only our experience of the Transcendent can be expressed. To borrow terms from the philosophy of science, predication about the transcendent can only be *instrumentalist* and not *realist*.[10]

FEMINIST THEOLOGICAL DISCOURSE BASED ON EXPERIENCE

Many feminist theologians explicitly structure their thinking on the foundation of experience. It is clear from their studies that the majority of such thinkers treat women's experience as the ultimate norm, or resting place of their discourse. The movement of thought is correlational, yet the normative place of interpretation is present experience, more precisely, the experience of women. This, of course, leads to the question often quite honestly faced: "Whose experience?" A question, as we will see, that has no answer so long as experience is considered foundationally.

In this part of the discussion, some preliminary remarks will be made about correlation, and then some examples will be adduced of feminist theologians and the manner in which they correlate women's experience with other sources of theology.

---

10. These two terms are defined by Janet Soskice: "By theological realists I mean here those who, while aware of the inability of any theological formulation to catch the divine realities, nonetheless accept that there are divine realities that the theologians, however ham-fistedly, are trying to catch. By theological instrumentalists I mean those who believe that religious language provides a useful, even uniquely useful, system of symbols which is action guiding for the believer, but which is not to be taken as making reference to a cosmos-transcending being in the traditional sense." "Knowledge and Experience in Science and Religion: Can We Be Realists?" in *Physics, Philosophy, and Theology: A Common Quest for Understanding*, ed. Robert J. Russel, William R. Stoeger, George V. Coyne (Vatican City State: Vatican Observatory, 1988), 173-84; citation is from p. 175.

Correlation

The process of correlation has been described previously. To repeat somewhat, correlation is the process by which the advances in human understanding of the world and of existence, and the consequent change in perspective that these advances effect, are brought into dialogue with the sacred tradition so that, by a reciprocal process, both the reality and perspectives acquired and the understanding of revelation may be deepened and corrected. The process is a hermeneutical spiral, in which the growth in human understanding is modified by being brought into the light of the prophetic understanding of revelation, and the prophetic understanding is deepened and extended in the light of the advance in human understanding.

In this process there is mutual modification of what is understood by the light of revelation and what is understood in the light of reason. In regard both to philosophy (I use this term to include all the rational endeavors, particularly the historical disciplines) and sacred teaching (God's act of teaching and the instruments of that teaching) "what is understood" is surrounded by a "tacit dimension" of what is yet to be understood.[11] The very possibility of this tacit dimension is due to the light of the human mind and the intensification of that light by faith and revelation. At this level, the two understandings are not equal. The light of faith is an integrating and transforming factor in the dialogue and the light of reason is the integrated and transformed factor. In the words of Aquinas already quoted: "Those who use the work of the philosophers in sacred doctrine by bringing that work of the human mind into the service of faith, do not mix water with wine, but rather change water into wine."[12]

The mistake most often made in bringing contemporary experience into contact with faith is that the correlation is understood to be between experience and text, as in this description by David Tracy: "The two principal sources for theology are Christian texts and common human experience and language. . . ."[13] Such a view completely ignores the fact

11. I owe this notion of tacit dimension to Michael Polanyi, *Personal Knowledge: Towards a Post-Critical Philosophy* (Chicago: University of Chicago Press, 1958).

12. *In Boethius de Trinitate* 2,4,ad5. See Thomas Aquinas, *Faith, Reason and Theology,* trans. Armand Maurer (Toronto: Pontifical Institute of Medieval Studies, 1987), 50.

13. *Blessed Rage for Order* (New York: Seabury, 1975), 9. That this is not an isolated expression of his view can be seen in his description of mediating theology expressed again in his article, "The Uneasy Alliance Reconceived: Catholic Theological Method, Modernity, and Postmodernity," *Theological Studies* 50 (1989): 548-70. Significant in this article is the renaming of von Hügel's "mystical" element as "religious" that is then deemed to be the domain of religious sociology.

that faith is a present activity of God consented to by the believer, enabling him or her to yield to the truth of the divine realities being presented. Thus, faith sheds light on the light of revelation, making it actual and bringing it into contact with the believer's actual milieu. It is imperative that we find a way of articulating the process by which the water of human understanding becomes, in the light and healing power of faith, wine as an integral component of revelation. If theology is to recover its place in the life of the church, it must be "popular" in the sense I have outlined above — it must share in the experienced faith life of God's people and serve God in grateful praise.

Revelation is not only to be studied, it is to be received. This means that the theologian is not an impartial arbiter "mediating" between a past witnessed to only by texts and a present that has an autonomous intelligibility. She or he is rather a believer who is seeking to understand present experience in the light of faith. While the process is rigorous and demanding, the resources are not only human; theology is the work of the Holy Spirit working within and according to the laws and resources of the human spirit.

Growth in human understanding necessarily poses new questions to the Christian tradition. At the point at which these questions actually confront the tradition, the process of correlation begins. The question, as it is posed, comes with an admixture of truth and falsehood, of authentic growth in understanding and a certain amount of misunderstanding. The light of faith is a discerning and healing factor that separates the new or deeper truth from the error that is admixed with it. That is, by respecting what is true in the question and letting itself be modified by it, revelation acquires a healing capacity to distinguish truth from falsehood and thus to liberate the question to play its full and legitimate role in the development of doctrine.

Present experience, in our case women's experience, can be said to act foundationally when it is the ultimate norm against which everything else is judged. This is inevitable when the other partner in the correlation process is considered to be the witness of the past as this is represented in texts, practices, symbols, and the like, of the community. The theologian is then faced with the choice of what is to be the foundation of thought, the past as present in its witness or the present as operative in experience.

The problem is with seeking foundations at all. The knowledge that comes from the light of faith, the knowledge to which the Christian tradition bears constant witness, takes place, as does all knowledge, in the dynamic presence to the knower of what is known. Although few of us may achieve this maturity, we must acknowledge that, as those who have learned this have attested, true faith knowledge not only sees God in all things but sees all things in God. That is because Christian theology is a knowledge of the Son through whom and for whom are all things.

This sort of understanding of theology must be operative if the essence of theology, to be realized in varying degrees of the potential whole, is to be present at all. When it is not present, then the structure of the knowing subject, in one way or another, is the foundational norm of thought. The result is that faith's witness is subjected to an epistemology that claims an unjustified competence to judge all speech in terms of its own presuppositions. As Louis Dupré expresses it:

> Religion has been allotted a specific field of consciousness ruled by methods of its own, but the final judgment on truth has been withdrawn from its jurisdiction and removed to the general domain of epistemic criteriology.[14]

I would like now to give some examples of how feminist theology is foundationalist and how, specifically, it takes some women's experience as its foundation, and in turn seeks to reproduce that experience in others, making it normative.

Foundationalism in Theology: Anne Carr, Rosemary Radford Ruether, and Elizabeth Johnson

Anne Carr

Anne Carr's recent book, *Transforming Grace: Christian Tradition and Women's Experience,*[15] as the subtitle implies, is an attempt to bring together in a correlating process Christian tradition and women's experience. The reception given to this work seems to indicate that it represents a relatively moderate and mainline feminist approach to the Christian tradition. Carr explicitly states that her method is correlational and locates herself in the line of David Tracy, Hans Küng, and Edward Schillebeeckx: "feminist theology seeks to correlate the central and liberating themes of biblical and Christian tradition with the experience of women in the contemporary situation." "Beyond reflection on the past (though it surely includes that), theology is the correlation of faith with other knowledge,

---

14. "Notes on the Idea of Religious Truth in the Christian Tradition," *The Thomist* 52 (1988): 499-512; citation is from p. 509.
15. San Francisco: Harper and Row, 1988.

with the natural, social, and human sciences, and with the common experience of humankind both in the present and with the view to the future."[16]

Statements similar to the above two quotations could be multiplied. They present a general method of correlation that adequately describes the practice of many if not all theologians.[17] The difficulty begins with a more specific description of the method and with its actual practice. Carr cites David Tracy's reformulation of Tillich's method as "the critical correlation of the meaning and the truth of the interpreted Christian fact (. . . the texts, symbols, witnesses, and tradition of the past and present) and the meaning and truth of the interpreted contemporary situation."[18] This, in effect, places the theologian in a mediating position between Christian tradition and modern culture.[19]

This Archimedean place is as unattainable in the realm of revelation as it is in that of physics. Such a concept of mediation implies that the only light available is that of the theologian's unaided resources and that he or she stands somehow outside both faith and culture and is able to meditate between them. The essential note of theology, that it is a knowledge conferred by God in and through the light of faith, is not operative. The result is that correlation can only be a sort of compromise, a retaining of Christian symbolism by emptying it of any content save that of experience — the symbols refer not to any reality but to the state of the experiencing subject. The witness of Christian thinkers, the witness we considered in the first two chapters and the witness of countless believers in every age, is reduced to the articulation of their interior state filtered through the symbols of their culture. The object of their experience is their own selves somehow modified by what they contact. Such a foundationalist view of experience verifies the remark of Louis Dupré cited earlier, namely that epistemic

16. Ibid., 9, 6.

17. For a good description of various theological methods one may consult the introduction to *The Modern Theologians: An Introduction to Christian Theology in the Twentieth Century,* vol. I, ed. David Ford (Cambridge, Mass.: Blackwell, 1989), 1-19. One may also consult David Kelsey, "Method, Theological," in *The Westminster Dictionary of Christian Theology,* ed. Alan Richardson and John Bowden (Philadelphia: Westminster, 1983).

18. The quote is from Tracy's article, "Particular Questions within General Consensus," in *Consensus in Theology?* ed. Leonard Swidler (Philadelphia: Westminster, 1980), 34.

19. For a description of this dilemma in the work of Paul Tillich see John P. Clayton, *The Concept of Correlation: Paul Tillich and the Possibility of a Mediating Theology* (Berlin, New York: de Gruyter, 1980), especially 248-49. Clayton proposes that the only way out of the dilemma is not to renounce an unchangeable "content" in revelation.

criteria are imported from a general philosophy of religion and are called upon to judge the meaning of what the New Testament and other Christian writings are really saying. There is only the thinking subject, judging in the light of contemporary experience, the experience of another thinking subject. The notion of revelation as an act of God revealing an understanding of human existence in the history of Jesus Christ is simply not operative.

The correlation proposed by Carr and those she quotes is revisionist, but no criteria are given by which the truth of the revision can be judged except that of a correspondence or relevance to women's experience: "All the symbols yield to awareness that none of the pictures depict God; none of the symbols grasps the transcendent. They can only be interpreted anew, in succeeding historical situations, 'constantly needing,' in Schleiermacher's phrase, 'to be refashioned for these present times.' "[20] "From these examples in historical and biblical studies, the profoundly ambiguous character of the Christian tradition and its symbolism when read from a contemporary feminist perspective is apparent."

> This Christian feminist theology sees feminism itself — the woman — as the focal symbol, the original "other" in a culture and society that generates a series of oppressive relationships. . . . Transformation of the male/female relational system and the analogous series of exploitative relationships parallels new interpretations of the doctrine of God in relation to the self, human freedom, autonomy, the future, and to collective struggles for justice.

> [After enumerating the sources of theological reflection in Christology.] Each category is important for feminist theology, which maintains the centrality of the experience of women and focuses on feminist interpretations of society, culture, history, religion. . . . In my understanding, feminist theology requires some form of mutually critical correlation procedure in which Scripture and tradition, on one side, and contemporary experience, on the other, have equal voice.[21]

In the second of the above two quotations, women's experience is given a central position and then placed on a par with Scripture and tradition. Once again, we encounter a mediating theologian who is faced

20. Carr, *Transforming Grace,* 110. Among the many problems with this phrase is the false epistemological notion that symbols are attempts to "picture" or "grasp" reality, and that, since they fail to do so, they can only be interpreted anew.

21. Ibid., 111, 116. The examples are drawn mostly from the works of Elisabeth Schüssler Fiorenza. There is no attempt to distinguish a "hierarchy of symbolism" within the tradition.

with two sources of knowledge whose truth is judged by the thinking subject modified by experience and in contact with witnesses from the past. There is no presence of faith as a light, as an action of God in the believer, instructing her or him and providing an integration. There is only the interpretation of reality in the light of a central experience, that of women.[22]

Rosemary Radford Ruether

As illustrative of this point, I would like to cite Rosemary Radford Ruether, who is unsuccessfully attempting to respond to Daphne Hampson's charge that Ruether may not be a theist at all:

> It seems to me questionable that Ruether herself is theistic. . . . In fact, if one reads her work carefully, one notices that she never speaks of God, but rather of people's concept of God, which may lead them on in their striving for justice.[23]

It should be first noted that nowhere in the article does Ruether respond to the remark of Hampson.[24] Ruether first attempts to deny to Hampson, with whom she once co-authored a study,[25] the right to criticize a tradition she has left. Her main point in her own review article is that the historical revelation of Christianity is to be compared to the memory of a living person.

> But, just as a living person continually re-evaluates and even revises what it remembers in response to new demands and new perceptions of meaning, so the church, as a historical community, continually re-evaluates how it reads its past memories and even revises that which it remembers.[26]

22. In the article already referred to, Louis Dupré makes the following remark: "The divine light that informs the mind, or the interior voice that addresses it, enlightens the believer not only in regard to Scripture but to profane learning as well. The very source and condition of truth becomes sacred for Augustine. . . . What for the early Fathers had consisted essentially in a process of explication, now becomes an illumination simultaneously derived from two different sources (objective and subjective)." "Notes on the Idea of Religious Truth in the Christian Tradition," 503.

23. Daphne Hampson, *Theology and Feminism* (Oxford, Cambridge, Mass.: Blackwell, 1990), 29.

24. "Is Feminism the End of Christianity? A Critique of Daphne Hampson's *Theology and Feminism,*" *Scottish Journal of Theology* 43 (1990): 390-400.

25. "Is There a Place for Feminists in a Christian Church?" *New Blackfriars* 68, no. 801 (January, 1987): 7-24.

26. "Is Feminism the End of Christianity?" 396.

The process of reevaluating and revising sees continuity in the symbolic expressions of past experiences as they are now being reinterpreted. Once again, nowhere does Ruether speak of God, or of God's activity, but prefers to speak of "paradigms," a normative future, "the Christian concept of the Trinity," etc.

> I would see scripture as normative, not in the sense of infallible truths disclosed from beyond normal experience, or as unique experiences incomparable with other experiences, but rather as a foundational memory, in much the same way that any community develops its identity through foundational collections of stories, laws and ethical norms.[27]

The revisability of such material, as far as Christians are concerned, ought to be obvious from the fact that the Christianity rejected "the closed canon of the rabbinic authorities of its time, and by declaring that the Spirit was disclosing new truths through contemporary religious experience."[28] In the first place, there was no "closed canon of the rabbinic authorities" of that time.[29] Second, the "new truths" were an understanding of a new event and not "religious experiences" (never defined). In the light of this understanding the sacred writings of Israel were given a new and irreversible meaning.

Daphne Hampson correctly sees that the Christian claim is realist, and she rejects it. Rosemary Radford Ruether wrongly considers all the language of Christianity to be "instrumentalist," and she proposes adapting it to a "redemptive future," which, rather than past events, "is ultimately normative."[30] Once again, it seems to me, we are faced with a neo-Schleiermachian and idealist view of revelation that is based on religious experiences that do not differ in kind from any other experiences. There is, in this view, nothing but a fundamental experience of the Transcendent as the other, an ultimately unknowable pole opposite the feeling of absolute dependence, and the expression of this in terms of a religious symbolism proper to various, and conflicting, historical communities. This experience is then absorbed into the fundamental feminist experience, that of the oppression of women.

27. Ibid., 397.
28. Ibid.
29. I refer the reader to my study, "The Biblical Canon and Church Life," in *Recovering the Sacred: Catholic Faith, Worship and Practice,* ed. Paul L. Williams, Proceedings of the Twelfth Convention of the Fellowship of Catholic Scholars (Pittston, Pa.: Northeast Books, 1990), 117- 36, esp. 118-20, and the literature given there.
30. "Is Feminism the End of Christianity?" 399.

Elizabeth Johnson

In her recent study, Elizabeth Johnson devotes a chapter to "Women's Interpreted Experience."[31] The basic argument of the chapter may be summarized as follows. Women are coming to a new affirmation of their own worth. "This foundational experience can be suitably described in the classic language of conversion." The awakening can be interpreted as a new experience of God. In regard to conversion, this is a twofold dialectic. First, contrast: "an experience of lived oppression, interpreted precisely as oppressive and therefore wrong." Second, confirmation: "Through memory, narrative, and solidarity a positive acknowledgement of women's beauty and power as active subjects of history also begins to come to speech." Johnson seeks to establish that this experience is an experience of God on the basis of principles laid down by Karl Rahner in his article, "Experience of Self and Experience of God."[32]

The notion of "contrast" is depicted in terms that rely on the "myth of total oppression" already discussed. This myth is operative throughout the whole work, though Johnson does acknowledge that "just what precisely comprises women's experience is a matter of intense study and debate." That there are dimensions to our post-Enlightenment culture that are injurious to women and to men, and that these have resulted from the crystallization process mentioned previously, can be taken for granted. That this results in an undifferentiated situation of "lived oppression" is contradicted by the witness of many women, including some who are active in promoting the recognition of women's dignity.[33]

Johnson's appeal to experience overlooks some rather important dimensions of the function of such an appeal in discourse. As George Schner expresses it, an appeal to experience either can be part of the dialectic of an argument or can be based on the presumption that the fact of the assertion is the conclusion of the argument. In regard to this latter he says:

> When the appeal is actually a demand for "my experience" to be dominant, to overcome and displace the other opinions of the conversation,

---

31. In *She who Is: The Mystery of God in Feminist Theological Discourse* (New York: Crossroad, 1992), 62, 63.

32. *Theological Investigations XIII*, trans. David Bourke (London: Darton, Longman and Todd, 1975), 122-32.

33. See for instance, Elizabeth Fox-Genovese, *Feminism Without Illusions. A Critique of Individualism* (Chapel Hill: University of North Carolina Press, 1991); Jean Bethke Elshtain, *Public Man, Private Woman: Women in Social and Political Thought* (Princeton: Princeton University Press, 1981).

then the appeal to experience degenerates to an appeal to authority in the pejorative sense, resulting in an antinomy of opinions at best, and unmoving opposition at worst.[34]

"Confirmation," the other half of the dialectic, does express the experience of some women, and we can only rejoice in that. I question, however, whether it requires the first part of the dialectic to be operative in order for confirmation to transpire, and whether this confirmation must be as oppositional as Johnson describes it. In any case, this is far from the classic notion of conversion, unless we are willing to acknowledge that self-depreciation is a form of pride and that humility is the way to confirmation.

I doubt whether Rahner would acknowledge the conclusions at which Johnson arrives from the principles enunciated in his article, though he must take some responsibility for them. Rahner's transcendentalist foundationalism easily elides from a description of an unthematic experience and its correlate, an experience of being, to a quite thematic experience that also finds its correlate in God and his plan of salvation. The accusation of ontologism has been made frequently enough and has some validity.[35] Rahner, however, is no Descartes, deriving all his conclusions mathematically from a foundation. This explains why so much of what he writes can be understood profitably without recourse to his particular brand of foundationalism. It must be said, however, that his identification of the necessary background of all thought with being, and then this being with God, neglects a fundamental biblical teaching, namely that God, as creator, is not to be identified with the constructs or demands of the structure of the thinking subject.

Johnson has exploited this weakest aspect of Rahner's thought. The more the experience of self becomes capable of articulation, then, even on Rahner's terms, the more it becomes differentiated from an experience of God who cannot be the correlate of my thematic experience of myself. As Schner has pointed out, an articulatable experience implies a level of awareness by which I am able to know that I am appealing to something that I myself have constructed out of all the various elements of my life. These include language, social and psychological location, and values accepted and rejected. The history of this experience is not the history of

34. "The Appeal to Experience," *Theological Studies* 53 (1992): 40-59; citation is from p. 45.

35. See for instance, Paul Molnar, "Can We Know God Directly? Rahner's Solution From Experience," *Theological Studies* 46 (1985): 228-61; Francis Schüssler Fiorenza, *Foundational Theology: Jesus and the Church* (New York: Crossroad, 1984), especially chapter 11, "Foundational Theology as a Reconstructive Hermeneutics."

the experience of God; it is rather the modification of my horizon that enables or inhibits me in interpreting my experience of God correctly.

God is never known immediately in this life, but he is known in his effects, and these include those effects he works in the believer, conforming him or her to Christ, and thus conferring a participated sharing in the divine life. God communicates himself and a knowledge of his plan of salvation. The touchstone of true knowledge of God is thus, as 1 John has elaborated: (1) a confessed faith in Jesus Christ as the Son of God (and therefore a faith knowledge of God as Triune), and (2) a love for God and for all human beings, especially those who believe in Christ. The sense of immediacy within which the Trinity is known is explained theologically as being the result of an action by which an effect is produced in the soul, an impressed image of each of the Persons by which they are made manifest. The Person is known directly, the image only indirectly. "This is the image dynamically considered, not only likening the soul to God, but bearing it by actual or habitual movement towards Him."[36] Such knowledge is the fullness of theology, a knowledge of God as he knows himself, which is effected in the dim light of faith but which nevertheless forms the constant witness of the Scriptures and of countless believers in every age.

I will return to this point in the next chapter while considering the difference between God as incomprehensible and God as indeterminate. I wish now to investigate how the biblical teaching on creation can help us understand nonfoundational knowledge and thus locate the role of experience in the act of knowledge.

BEING AND KNOWING IN THE CONTEXT OF CREATION

Many attempts have been made to overcome the subject-object dichotomy introduced into our thinking by foundationalism. We will consider some of them briefly in the discussion to follow. A biblical response to the problem begins with the understanding of the presence of God as Creator, conferring and sustaining the existence of both knower and known. Speaking of Israel's understanding of creation, Claus Westermann says:

> The object of creation is without exception something outside the divine. The action of God as creator is directed exclusively to the world. God is outside creation; to be created means to be not-god.[37]

36. William Hill, *Proper Relations to the Indwelling Divine Persons* (Washington: The Thomist Press, nd.), 111.
37. *Genesis 1–11*, 26.

There are thus three aspects to the biblical understanding of creation. First, all that is exists by the free will act of God; it is an act of generosity. Second, what is created is not God, nor is it an emanation of God. Third, creation adds nothing to God: God plus the world results in no more "being" than God alone.[38] In just such a perspective the earlier Christian philosopher-theologians understood both the incomprehensibility of God and the fact that he could make himself known. They saw the foundation of all human knowledge as the very capacity to think given to human beings, making them the image of God by giving them a share in the light who is the Word.[39] In the power of this light the harmonics of the universe, as they impinge upon the senses, are transposed to the level of sharing in the intelligibility of the world as it participates in the being of God.

Some neo-scholastic thinking has joined in the search for foundations and has claimed to find it in what is called "the principle of contradiction" ("something cannot simultaneously be and not be"). For the perennial philosophy, however, it is not that the principle of contradiction provides a foundation, it is rather that the light by which such a principle can be enunciated and immediately understood is itself the principle, that is the source, of knowledge.[40] This light was not considered "heteronomous" but intrinsic to the integrity of the created order, establishing a nuptial relation between intelligence and intelligibility. That light, as I hope to show now, is a receptive capacity, an openness to the witness of being itself. Basically, such an understanding is a philosophical elaboration of a biblical teaching, and it may serve to correct the subjective foundationalism characteristic of most feminism.

The Witness of Being

The search for foundations has resulted in a concentration on the human mind and its functioning rather than on what is known. The consequence

---

38. See Robert Sokolowski, *The God of Faith and Reason,* especially chapter 1.

39. See for example this remark of Aquinas: "Because the Word is the true light by his nature, it is necessary that whatever sheds light do so because of him in so far as it participates in him. Therefore it is he who enlightens every man coming into the world." *Super Evangelium S. Joannis Lectura* 5,1, §127. The same teaching can be found when Aquinas is commenting on Rom 1:19; see the Marietti edition, §113ff. One may also consult this remark from *De Veritate* 11,1,ad13: "Et ideo quod aliquid per certitudinem sciatur, est ex lumine rationis divinitus interius indito, quo in nobis loquitur Deus."

40. In a significant statement Aquinas remarks that the *primae conceptiones per se notae* are to be compared to the light of the agent intellect "as tools are to the workman" *(sicut instrumenta ad artificem). De Veritate* 11,3,c.

has been that a foundation may be thought of as either a stable interlocking set of notions that form the bedrock of human knowing and can be conceptualized and expressed in a formula (the "first principles"), as a starting point for the methodical development of later knowledge (self-consciousness), or as the matrix that absorbs and interprets the subject's encounters with reality (experience). This means that we are constantly tempted to consider individual concrete entities more as occasions for knowledge than as objects of knowledge. Knowing becomes the process by which the knower assimilates being to his or her subjective structure.[41]

The reason for this interpretation lies in what I would consider to be the most destructive aspect of neo-pagan Enlightenment thought — that all causality is domination. Being, itself, must be denied any active role in regard to the knowing subject. For if being has an active, causative role in the process by which it becomes known, if it makes an active witness, this would imply that it has a dominating relation to the thinking subject. The "island of truth" so carefully rescued from the anonymity of necessity would once again be invaded by the "stormy ocean, the native home of illusion." This preoccupation underlies most, if not all, of the need to consider knowledge as the exclusive product of the thinking subject.

The anti-feminine nature of such a position has already been pointed out by W. Norris Clarke in the lines quoted in the previous chapter. Feminist thinking shares with most of modernity the presupposed equation between causality and domination. It attacks attitudes and practices that are, usually unconsciously, motivated by this premise while having itself accepted the premise. Because the issue is so important I wish to take some time to consider how profoundly unbiblical is this identification of cause and coercion.

Causality and Domination

In a recent study, Reiner Schürmann attempts to articulate the basic Heideggerian attack on the very notion of principle (archē), which, at least as interpreted by Reiner Schürmann, is the central point of Heidegger's ob-

---

41. In the article alluded to previously, Kenneth Schmitz discusses the search for foundations in terms of what he calls "the individuality of entity." He insists that "entities must not be relegated to a merely secondary, derivative status, as though they rest upon their principles and causes; for that is a perverse sort of foundationalism which places the only real things that *are*, at the mercy of the human formalisms by which we *think* them" ("Neither With Nor Without Foundations," 5).

jection to the Aristotelian notion of causality.[42] Kenneth Schmitz sums up the argument in this way:

> [T]o the older meaning of principle as inception or beginning, Aristotle added the energy of domination, so that a first principle (whether *ousia* among the Greeks, or God among the medievals, or human subjectivity among the moderns) has come to be an amalgam of primacy and power. . . . Metaphysics has become more and more what it has been from its inception: an agent of coercive power.[43]

It seems to me that this objection, as framed by Schürmann and Heidegger, perfectly illustrates the extent to which the legacy of modernity has distorted our thinking. It is so difficult for us to envision any form of causality that is not domination that even Christian thinkers have difficulty with the notion of God's power found in early medieval theology.[44] I do not deny that Aristotle's notion of cause contained an ambiguity that was resolved in one direction by the Enlightenment. I certainly agree as well that modern subjectivity is a form of imposition upon reality. But I do not accept that such a notion applies to the God revealed to us in the biblical tradition, who neither needs nor exercises dominative power in creating. Nor do I accept that creation's share in God's causality is necessarily dominative.

Schmitz's reply to Schürmann's objection does not explicitly appeal to the notion of creation; it is rather a philosophical reflection on the notion of principle. It is an example of a Christian philosophy — a vision of reality made sensitive to what is *there* because of the prophetic interpretation given in the revealed tradition. He replies by observing that an effective principle is neither inceptional nor coercive power. It is the communication of actuality in some form. A painter is the principle of his painting. He further suggests that the metaphor of roots may at times be more apt than that of first principle, given the use to which foundationalism has put the term.

I would like now to look more closely at how Christian tradition understood God's causality, and thus all causality that is a deficient and analogous imitation of God.

---

42. *Heidegger on Being and Acting: From Principles to Anarchy,* trans. Christine-Marie Gros and Reiner Schürmann (Bloomington, Ind.: Indiana University Press, 1987).

43. "Neither With Nor Without Foundations," 11.

44. This seems to be what underlies Colin Gunton's understanding of Aquinas's notion of creation. See *Enlightenment and Alienation* (Grand Rapids: Eerdmans, 1985), 65-70. Schmitz's reply to Schürmann applies to Gunton as well.

Causality and Generosity

Because God's motive in creating is *agapē*, there is what Maritain calls "the basic generosity of existence."[45] Aquinas reflects this intuition when he states that "from the very fact that something exists in act, it is active."[46] In a remarkable passage, obviously indebted to Denys's treatise on *The Divine Names,* Aquinas moves from the observation of the "generosity" of all beings to an understanding of the generosity of their source. Note how this vision of reality follows upon the biblical teaching that God's act of creation is totally free and adds nothing to God:

> For natural things have a natural inclination not only toward their own proper good, to acquire it, if not possessed, and if possessed, to rest therein; but also to diffuse their own goodness among others as far as possible. . . . Hence if natural things, insofar as they are perfect, communicate their goodness to others, much more does it pertain to the divine will to communicate by likeness its own goodness to others as far as possible.[47]

If we apply this notion to the act of knowledge we may say that the very act of existing is a communicable perfection that is bestowed on the knower by what is known. This understanding of the manner in which all entities can imitate God not only eliminates the isolation of foundationalism, which leaves to the knowing subject the sole task of conferring intelligibility, it shows the universe to be a place characterized by relation: "Communication follows upon the very intelligibility *(ratio)* of actuality. Hence every form is of itself communicable."[48]

There is a certain generosity in effective activity; it is sharing, not a coercion. This is especially noticeable in the act of knowing. The mind is not a dominating principle imposing intelligibility from its own resources, nor is

---

45. Jacques Maritain, *Existence and the Existent* (New York: Doubleday, 1957), 90.

46. *Summa Contra Gentiles,* 2,7

47. *Summa Theologiae* 1,19,2. Translation is that of Clarke, ibid., 604, as are all the quotations of St. Thomas in this section.

48. *Summa Contra Gentiles* 3,64. As W. Norris Clarke expresses it: "It turns out, then, that relationality and substantiality go together as two distinct but inseparable modes of reality. Substance is the primary mode, in that all else, including relations, depend on it as their ground. But since 'every substance exists for the sake of its operations,' as St. Thomas has just told us, being as substance, as existing *in itself,* naturally flows over into being as relational, turned *toward others* by its self-communicating action. To be is to be *substance in relation.*" "Person, Being, and St. Thomas," *Communio* 19 (1992): 601-18; citation is from p. 607, the emphasis is in original.

the object known in an act by which it coerces the mind to produce its representation. There is a nuptial relation already described above. Truth is not primarily in the proposition but rather in the "original concord between thing and intellect," in the "resonant symmetry of knower and known."[49] In the terms I used before, knowing takes place in the receptive and creative imitation of reality effected by the mind. Being shares in the generosity of God, it is diffusive of itself. Mind, while it fashions the entity according to its own energy, can only do so as fecundated by the entity itself which, far from passively receiving intelligibility, actively imparts its reality to the mind. There is no foundation either in the subjectivity of the knower, deriving all certitude from a seemingly unassailable experience, or in the known that requires to be known in order to be actually intelligible. Both are principles communicating actuality and both are receivers needing union in order for truth to exist.

The original truth, spoken of previously, the union between the mind and what is known, is only possible because what is known is imitated by the mind. To imitate is to transpose a reality to another plane of existence. If, in response to a request that I imitate the chair in my room, I make another chair, I have not imitated, I have reproduced. To imitate the chair I must transpose it to the level of word, or line and color, or some other mode of being. Thus, in the act of knowledge, the energy by which being is imitated derives both from the dynamism of the substance in relation and that particular way in which I, as a knower, share in the dynamic light of God, a light which, even apart from faith St. Thomas does not hesitate to call "a certain imprint of the divine light."[50]

The mode of discourse proper to this original truth is called "noetic discourse." "It is an original, spontaneous, yet receptive discourse under the influence of the concrete situation . . . it has its own integrity and can find expression in various ways."[51] I would add that such discourse can employ great reflective artistry in order to preserve precisely the originality and spontaneity of the primary act of knowledge. An example of this would be the biblical narratives of both Testaments that are mediating a divinely conferred understanding of an event, imitating it by transposing it to the level of word. It treats the event as an entity in context. The second mode of discourse is called by Schmitz "epistemic."

It is, a secondary modification of the discursive character of language, a modification which arises out of the methodical preoccupation with

49. Schmitz, "Neither With Nor Without Foundations," 15.
50. *Summa Theologiae* 1,12,11,ad3; 1-2,91,2.
51. Schmitz, "Neither With Nor Without Foundations," 18.

the conditions of truth and the systematic possibilities of cognition. . . .
Epistemic discourse is methodically assertive language about some referent, however vague and elusive that referent may be.[52]

On the level of epistemic discourse there are principles that may function
as a foundation. The error arises when foundations are sought for knowledge itself and for the first or noetic level of discourse.

Thus, from the two points established, the dynamic and relational
character of being on the one hand, and the mutually active and receptive
nature of the act of knowing on the other, we are able to appreciate that
knowledge is neither with nor without foundations. The bias to replace
commonality by a systemic totality swallows the irreducible nature of the
individual in context by making it correspond to a prefabricated structure.
Furthermore, the bias to replace being by thought sacrifices a confidence
in creation to the anxiety of isolation. When these biases are surrendered,
logic's need for a starting point is recognized as both valid and limited,
but it is clearly recognized as pertaining to second order discourse. Clarity
in this regard has been achieved not in spite of, but precisely because of
the turn to the subject. It is a metaphysical achievement nurtured by a
biblical sense of the manner in which all that is created shares in the
dynamism and generosity of the Creator. In order to understand, however,
the role that experience plays in the actual functioning of those who are
engaged in the activity of knowing and loving, we must try to take another
step.

So far I have considered the structure of the act of knowledge and
have indicated how foundationalism is mistaken. The quotations from Carr,
Ruether and Johnson given earlier in this chapter should indicate the fact
that mainline feminism treats experience as a foundation, and that in so
doing it embraces the two biases I have just mentioned. Similar statements
are found throughout the feminist literature in such profusion that they are
sometimes criticized by other feminists.[53] But if experience is not a foundation, what is it? Or to put it another way: if experience does not figure

---

52. Ibid., 19.

53. An example of this can be found in a recent article by Lisa Sowle Cahill,
"Accent on the Masculine," *The Tablet* 247, no. 8001 (11 December 1993): 1618-19.
On the first of these pages we read: "Yet one problem that arises as a result of feminist
theology's appeal to "experience" is the danger of replacing oppressive generalisations
with bottomless particularity. If women's experience alone is exalted as the final moral
standard, we run the risk of feminist relativism which is unable to give any real reasons
for preferring equality rather than hierarchy." (Cahill is not clear why these two are
incompatible.)

in the structure of knowledge, how does it relate to the act of knowledge existentially, or if you will, phenomenologically, considered? I will attempt an answer in the following pages.

THE ROLE OF EXPERIENCE IN KNOWING

This section is dedicated to accomplishing two things: sketching out a rudimentary understanding of experience and validating the feminist appeal to experience, this time not as a foundation of knowledge but as a mode of consciousness that leads to knowledge.

Although my approach will not directly institute a reflection of this sort, it may be that the most effective manner of understanding experience is in reflecting on the actual functioning of the light of faith (that light by which we see the light) in the life of the believer. Since a thing is intelligible insofar as it is an act, the more dynamic the act of knowledge, the more it stands the kind of scrutiny that leads to understanding. In that act by which the mind is strengthened and enlightened by God's initiative, we have the conditions necessary for such an understanding — the recipient of such an action must articulate it himself or herself. In this instance, there must be a special quality to the knowledge — it must be born of personal reflection. As valuable as the accounts of others may be in controlling and enlightening what is said about the personal reception of divine revelation, knowledge about that act of knowledge can only be achieved by the person's own analysis as she or he observes introspectively what occurs in the act of knowing. Dialogue can occur because we all share in a commonality, which, as Kenneth Schmitz has just reminded us, is not the same as a systemic totality.

The Notes of Experience

The fact that everyone has experience, and that no one can successfully talk about it, ought to indicate that in experiencing we are brought into some sort of direct contact with being in all its concrete manifold mystery, and that we lack the ability to transpose it satisfactorily into our usual modes of understanding and discourse. Not only that, we are often able to tell whether someone else has really experienced what they are talking about. Thus, it seems that there are four aspects or notes to experience: familiarity, directness or immediacy, receptivity or passivity, and partial incommunicability.[54]

54. I retain these notes because they are able to highlight aspects of experience

When we say of someone that he or she is an experienced sailor, we mean that they have had multiple and cumulative contacts with the actual art of sailing and that these have brought about a certain state within them by which they are able to bring this knowledge to bear in judging individual situations. They are *familiar* with sailing. This note of experience is located by Aristotle in the reproductive memory *(aisthētikē phantasia),* and he allies it with *phronēsis,* which we usually call prudence.[55] This sort of experience derives from multiple contacts with the same dimension of human life or activity and produces the experienced politician, teacher, and the like. The background of familiarity is activated by the presence of a new concrete instance and there is a commonsense judgment, described by Bernard Lonergan in a passage already quoted:

> Common sense, unlike the sciences, is a specialization of intelligence in the particular and the concrete. It is common without being general, for it consists in a series of insights that remains incomplete, until there is added at least one further insight into the situation at hand; and, once that situation has passed, the added insight is no longer relevant, so that common sense at once reverts to its normal state of incompleteness.[56]

The second note of experience is that of directness or immediacy. We only speak of experiencing something when there is some sort of direct apprehension or contact. In popular speech we distinguish between knowing something abstractly or theoretically and knowing it by experience, by direct contact. This is probably the most determinative of the notes of experience; it underlies the notion of familiarity and is closely linked with the fact that experience implies a certain receptivity or passivity, a being acted upon. Again, because of its direct nature, it is always at least partially incommunicable. The two notes of passivity and partial incommunicability will be bracketed for the moment in order to concentrate on immediacy.

Experience is generated by some sort of unmediated contact, but it

---

that facilitate the dialogue with feminist theology. For four general rules in discussing experience, see George Schner, "The Appeal to Experience." For other studies, see the still valuable work by Jean Mouroux, *The Christian Experience: An Introduction to a Theology,* trans. George Lamb (New York: Sheed and Ward, 1954); *Revelation and Experience,* Concilium 113, ed. Edward Schillebeeckx and Bas van Iersel (New York: Seabury, 1979).

55. One of the best treatments of *phronēsis* is still that of Th. Deman, "La Prudence," in *St. Thomas D'Aquin, Somme Théologique,* 2me ed. (Paris: Desclée, 1949), Appendice II.

56. *Insight* (London, New York: Longmans, Green, 1958), 175.

adds to the notion of contact that of awareness. I do not experience something of which I am unaware, even if I am in contact with it. The insistence on the experiential element in modern theological, particularly feminist, thought is due, I think, to a rejection of the model of knowing that isolates the subject from the object and encloses the former in a world of its own making. Our present-day reaction against such an epistemology puts the accent on the notion of immediate contact, but since it has not first liberated the subject from the need for foundations in the act of knowing, it is left with the necessity of making experience itself something that is self-enclosed.

The directness of experience involves, then, contact and awareness, or better, the awareness of contact. Just as the whole person knows through the mind, so too the whole person experiences in an act of subjective awareness that includes interpretation. The very multidimensionality of what is contacted in the particularity of its being means that the most apt manner of expressing this contact is through what was called above "noetic discourse." Poetry, symbol, and narrative mediate the reality as experientially interpreted. By saying that noetic discourse mediates the reality as imitated, I wish to distance myself from those who would maintain that it merely expresses the subjective state of the one experiencing. Unless an utterance appeals to commonality while it expresses subjectivity, the discourse is meaningless.

The third note of experience is the correlate of directness or immediacy: it is receptivity or passivity. If I experience something it is because somehow it acts on me, it impinges on me. This is the reasoning that underlies the Greek commonplace which plays on the two roots *mathein/pathein* ("to learn" and "to suffer" or "to experience"). Thus Aeschylus says of Zeus that he is the one who has "marked out the path of wisdom for mortals, and decreed as a sure law that learning comes by suffering *(pathei mathos).*"[57] As is well known, Denys's use of this distinction in theology had a profound and fruitful influence on subsequent Christian understanding of mystical experience.[58]

---

57. *Agamemnon,* 176ff. For a study of this theme, see J. Coste, "Notion grecque et notion biblique de la 'souffrance educatrice' (A propos d'Hébreux, v,8)," *Recherches de science religieuse* 43 (1955): 481-523; H. Dörrie, *Leid und Erfahrung: Die Wort und Sinn-Verbindung* παθεῖν – μαθεῖν *im griechieschen Denken* (Wiesbaden: Steiner, 1956).

58. See McGinn, *The Foundations of Mysticism,* 172. The passage from the treatise *On the Divine Names* 2,9 speaks of Hierotheus, who was initiated into the divine truths "by some more divine inspiration, not only learning the things of God but experiencing them *(ou monon mathōn alla kai pathōn). . . .*"

Finally, there seems to be a dimension of experience that is incommunicable. I would never think that my personal understanding of a theorem of Euclid is not totally communicable, but I would consider that my experience of love, failure, friendship, a sunset, or God has something personal about it that cannot be totally shared. I stressed above the fact that my experience must also have something of commonality about it, what George Schner calls intentionality and construct, if it is to be intelligible to me and to others. In speaking about the incommunicable dimension of experience I am no longer discussing the structure of the knowledge act that transpires in experience, I am speaking rather of that aspect of my existence in which I am more subject than object. In an initial act of reflection, I can objectify myself and thus discuss what it is that I have experienced and how it affects me. This act is intermediate between the act of cognition and a second, reflexive act by which I experience myself.

The consequence of the reflexive turn of consciousness is that this object — just because it is from the ontological point of view the subject — while having the experience of his own ego also has experience of himself as the subject. . . . We then discern clearly that it is one thing to *be* the subject [of action], another to *be cognized* (that is objectivized) as the subject, and a still different thing to *experience* oneself as the subject of one's own acts and experiences.[59]

The act by which one experiences oneself as the *subject* of an experience is the incommunicable dimension of experience. It is important to bear in mind here that, in contra-distinction to an idealist position, this dimension is not coterminous with the act of knowledge — consciousness does not constitute knowledge, it is rather a dimension of the knowing *person*. Failure to make this distinction leads to a notion of knowledge in which what is presented in discourse is the state of the subject, not the reality encountered.

I would like to add another manner of discussing the incommunicable dimension of experience, namely, to consider with Husserl the manner in which an object presents itself to the person. Let us suppose that we are

59. Karol Wojtyla, *The Acting Person, Analecta Husserliana* 10, trans. Andrej Potocki, ed. Anna-Teresa Tymieniecka (Dodrecht, Boston: Reidel, 1979), 44. For a more complete treatment of reflexivity by the same author, see "The Person: Subject and Community," *Review of Metaphysics* 33 (1979): 273-308. I am indebted in this section to the study by Kenneth Schmitz, *At the Center of the Human Drama: The Anthropology of Karol Wojtyla/Pope John Paul II* (Washington: Catholic University of America Press, 1993).

standing in a field, looking at a very beautiful tree. As you stand there looking at the tree, it presents one aspect of itself to you. You can imagine looking at the tree from several aspects, yet only one side of its many-dimensioned reality is available to you. I, standing a few feet from you, receive a slightly different aspect of the same tree. Now, if I move over and take up exactly your stand, the tree presents exactly the same aspect to me as it did to you, but there is one difference: this same aspect is being perceived by a different subject. Let us call the side of the tree available equally to both of us its *aspect,* and let us call the aspect of the tree in relation to different knowing subjects its *profile. It is the same tree and the same aspect, yet there are two profiles. The commonality is provided by the tree, by its aspect; the uniqueness of its relation to you and to me, its profile, is constituted by the fact that we are different conscious persons.*[60]

The difference in the profile of a tree may not be significant, but if we extend the consideration to other more complex examples, it can be important. Let us first, however, consider the question of aspect. Aspect belongs to the thing being considered — it is the aspect *of* something. If you are standing on the other side of the tree, you can describe its aspect from there and I can share in that aspect of the tree from your description, or I can walk over and let the tree present that aspect to me. It is the same tree; we both experience it with this aspect. It is not merely your experience of the tree and mine; there is something different from that which either of us experiences.

Now instead of a tree, let the thing be an act of revelation, as described in chapter 1, an act by which God manifests and communicates something of himself and his plan of salvation. In this instance, you have a view of God that I can share vicariously, but I cannot simply change my position and have the same aspect. Or let the thing be some suffering you are enduring. Again it is something objective, independent of you and me, that is impinging on you. I can appreciate what you are experiencing to a certain degree, but not totally. But note, the reason for the lack of sharing the experience is not due to the incommunicable nature of your experience, but to the fact that a particular aspect of God, or of suffering loss or whatever, has not impinged upon me. If God reveals himself to me in some similar way, or if I suffer in some similar way, there can be an overlap of aspect in our experiences, even though there can never be an overlap of profile.

This distinction points to two conclusions: First, the need for genuine

60. I am following here the analysis of Robert Sokolowski, *Husserlian Meditations,* Northwestern University Studies in Phenomenology and Existential Philosophy (Evanston: Northwestern University Press, 1974), chapter 4.

community in which what we experience can be shared with others so that they can, at least vicariously, see another aspect. Second, the experience of God is not a totally subjective event — even to this experience there is aspect as well as profile. It is God who is known in the act by which he reveals himself. The self-revealing aspect of God can be known and shared, because it is not merely the modification of the subject that is known, but God who is known. He is incomprehensible but not indeterminate.

I would like now to try to articulate briefly both the importance and the nonfoundational function of women's experience in the church.

WOMEN'S EXPERIENCE AND THEOLOGY

All women have familiarity with being women; it is an immediate and direct kind of knowledge of something that is basically a given in their existence. In addition, every woman knows a certain incommunicable character to this perception. The problem, of course, in searching for a hermeneutical stance is to determine "whose experience counts in theological reflection?"[61] The question, which has to be asked, presupposes some standards by which an answer can be given. These criteria have to appeal beyond or through the experience to truth. You can only judge whether or not my statements about the aspects that the tree presents to me are acceptable as truth by considering the tree. If, for example, you tell me, on the basis of your experience, that I have a false consciousness, your claim that my awareness is deficient is based on *the truth* to which your experience has given you access; it cannot simply be based on your experience. Otherwise, why is your consciousness any better than mine?

The question, then, is: how does familiarity, direct contact, receptivity to an aspect of reality bring about an understanding that can and should be shared? If we return to the notion that in an experience it is the whole person and not merely consciousness that is involved, we may approach an answer to this question. Knowledge is effected when the actuality of something impinges on a person and is transposed to the level of intelligibility. It then follows that the more the reality impinges on the person, the more it can be rendered intelligible and the more the consciousness of the person can objectify the experience of the union of subject and object. As the Greek epigram has it: *ean mē pathēs, ou mē mathēs,* "Unless you suffer/experience,

---

61. I am alluding here to the title of the work by Monika Hellwig, *Whose Experience Counts in Theological Reflection?* The 1982 Père Marquette Theology Lecture (Milwaukee: Marquette University Press, 1982).

you do not learn."[62] At this level, all the physical, psychological, cultural, and linguistic dimensions of the person, as these have already been modified by experience, are activated by the presence of this one reality, enabling the person to be affected by this aspect of what is contacted. Because it is an aspect of a *reality*, it can be witnessed to and others can appreciate it. Because it is an *aspect* of a reality, it must be completed by other aspects even though its profile dimension remains incommunicable.

It seems to me that feminists are correct in insisting that the aspect or aspects of reality that women perceive be not reduced to those aspects of the same reality already familiar in theological discourse. While there is something new in the consciousness of the state of women in our world, the same must be said of the witness of the poor, the suffering, and the marginalized of either sex. This is one manner in which, in a reflexive manner, the popular dimension of theology can be recovered. Those who can articulate this experience, even if that very fact means that they can never fully share the helplessness of the very poor and illiterate, bring a balance to a discipline that has become, as we have seen, alienated from its proper place within the Christian community and from its role as servant of that community.[63]

If this witness is to be part of the understanding of the church at large, however, certain things must be borne in mind. First, what is witnessed to is an aspect of reality and not its totality. It must become part of a family of discourse and make its contribution, but it cannot claim preeminence over all other aspects of revealed reality. It is, as is any appeal to experience, an appeal to authority, but the authority lies not in the experience but in the truth it lays hold of and shares. After speaking of experience as a form of encounter, George Schner describes the possibility of its making an "appeal constructive":

> As such it enters the argument not as foundational but as interruptive. It enters as a moment of discontinuity into a larger already established context. It is interruptive since, if it were simply continuous with what is already operative, it would not need to be adverted to precisely as "experience." It might well be considered disruptive, and as such take its place in an argument (or in life) as a challenge to be learnt from or refused. Thus, the insertion invites consideration, discussion, revision, change.[64]

62. Plato, *The Symposium* 222B. Cited by Coste, "Notion grecque. . . ." 487.

63. In this regard, the work by Arthur McGill is prophetic both as foretelling and forthtelling: *Suffering: A Test of Theological Method* (first published, 1968; republished, Philadelphia: Westminster, 1982).

64. "The Appeal to Experience," 54.

The insertion of women's experience into the church's life and discourse has been both interruptive and disruptive. It is, along with liberation theology, a prophetic call to repentance, to a change of the way we look at reality and a corresponding change in the way we act. In the light of what I have tried to elaborate thus far in regard to the biblical prophetic vision of reality and its obfuscation, particularly since the Enlightenment, I would like to try to articulate the three aspects of reality that women's experience has uncovered and that must be attended to if the church is to return to the gospel.

The first of these aspects is that of femininity itself: the feminine, receptive dimension of every human being. Having been obliterated from an understanding of the act of knowledge itself and ignored in the way we think of our relating to God, receptivity has become the enemy of autonomy. The result is a sense of shame that is all the deeper because it appears to be a diminution of what is authentically human. From this has come that distortion of masculinity which identifies it with coercive power. Recall what was said above about Heidegger's rejection of the notion of principle. When causality is identified with power rather than with generosity, then receptivity can be nothing else but passivity and not creative response. This is a caricature of the Christian view of God, with whom, as the *Epistle to Diognetus* already said, "there is no coercion."[65]

The feminist use of the term *patriarchal* represents an attempt to name this distortion of masculinity, but since coercive power is not a male monopoly, the term is misleading in the profound sense of the term. The exaltation of power, the cultivation of the practical intellect, the manipulation of people in social engineering, the subjectivizing of rights, all these have come from a rejection of what, in the Christian view of creation and redemption and of the God who brought this about, is the most active form of response — creative receptivity. I would like to place here a Christian view of power as it is described by Martin Luther King:

> Power, properly understood, is the ability to achieve purpose. It is the strength required to bring about social, political, or economic changes. In this sense power is not only desirable but necessary to implement the demands of love and justice. One of the greatest problems of history is that the concepts of love and power are usually contrasted as polar opposites. . . . What is needed is a realization that power without love

---

65. "The wish to save, to persuade, and not to coerce, inspired his mission. Coercion *(bia)* is incompatible with God." 7,4. Trans. James A. Kleist, *Ancient Christian Writers* 6 (New York: Paulist 1948), 141.

is reckless and abusive and love without power is sentimental and anemic. Power at its best is love implementing the demands of justice. Justice at its best is love correcting everything that stands against love. . . . It is precisely this collision of immoral power with powerless morality that constitutes the moral crisis of our time.[66]

The second aspect of our culture that is experienced and articulated by women follows from the first. Since women literally embody receptivity, a loss of esteem for this dimension of humanity as a whole led to a loss of esteem for women. This is a much more profound thing than the misogynist outbursts that characterized the era before the crystallization described earlier. Here there is a privileging of the public over the private, of accomplishment over contemplation, of production over appreciation, of power over love (as Martin Luther King just described them) and a corresponding, and false, identification of the second of these in each instance not with femininity but with women. It is difficult to give a proper expression to the atmosphere in which the lack of esteem flourishes, yet its effect is unmistakable. It is not unlike that which occurs as a result of prejudice. Coupled with violence, this attitude of nonrespect can cripple a person, as anyone who has experienced it, in prison, in a family, as a child, or as a woman, can attest. Not to be esteemed has a much greater debilitating effect than not exercising rights because it affects a deeper part of human relationships.

The third aspect of women's experience is precisely the inability to exercise rights. This will be treated more explicitly in chapter 10, where the notion of rights will be considered within the biblical context of *koinōnia* or communion.

What aspect of reality is attested to in these general summations of women's experience? I would say the distortion of masculinity at every level of the human being. This important witness is, as I have said, a call to conversion, not only to men, but also to women who have fallen victim to the very thing they are reacting against. To make the experience I have just described foundational is to suppose that the act of knowledge is effected totally by the thinking subject. It is an act of power in a universe rendered explicable only in terms of power. This is to misunderstand the very nature of being itself as created by a generous God, with whom there is no coercion, and who has given to all created things the possibility of sharing themselves in imitation of him. It is because of this quality that

66. *Where Do We Go From Here: Chaos or Community?* (New York: Harper and Row, 1967), 37.

being witnesses to God: "All cognitive beings also know God in any object of knowledge. Just as nothing has the note of desirability except by a likeness to the first goodness, so nothing is knowable except by a likeness to the first truth."[67]

Experience, therefore, is not a foundation, that to which all knowledge must be submitted as to an ultimate principle. It is a privileged means of coming to understand an aspect of reality. It is a moment in which the actuality of what is known establishes itself without doubt as an effective component in the act of knowledge. It is that commonly held dimension of knowing that is often more active in those outside the comforts of academia than in those within. To accent experience is, therefore, to accent the biblical teaching not only about knowledge but more importantly about what is known and how it is known. It is also to touch upon the mystery of suffering, a mystery that can lead, through experiencing it and in efforts to relieve it, to an understanding not only of creation but also of redemption, which was effected by Jesus who, "Son though he was, learned obedience from what he suffered" (Heb 5:8).

---

67. Thomas Aquinas, *De Veritate* 22,2ad1. It should be noted here, in contrast to Rahner's appeal to an unthematic knowledge of God, that the knowledge of God is only possible because what is knowable has a "likeness to the first truth."

7

Foundational Hermeneutics

By *foundational hermeneutics* I mean to designate those theories and practices of interpretation that locate the foundational norm of interpretation within the subject. Feminism is not the only field to use this hermeneutical procedure, but it has particular force there because it is linked with the specific foundation of feminism, namely, women's experience or feminist consciousness.

This chapter has three parts. A brief initial part treats of hermeneutics and communication. The purpose of this part is to establish some principles by which to critique the foundational hermeneutics of most feminist thought. The second part considers two examples of interpretation theory that rely on what is called "multiple competent readings." The third part looks at the hermeneutical procedures of two leading advocates of a liberationist approach to the text, Elisabeth Schüssler Fiorenza and Rosemary Radford Ruether.

A HERMENEUTICS OF COMMUNICATION

This discussion is restricted to a consideration of communication by means of texts, though the basic contours of the discussion remain the same in regard to other forms of communication. Authors compose texts in order to communicate something: a text is an instance of intersubjective communication. As Werner Jeanrond expresses it:

> Text composition and text reception stand to each other in a correlative relationship of communication. Text composition is the procedure which forms a text as a semantic potential, and reading is the procedure which realizes a written text as a form of sense. Text composition and reading

199

— in other words, text production and text reception — are both guided by communicative intentions, in other words by that which the text has to say.[1]

A text may be defined as an act of communication consisting of a complex and interlocking linguistic sign organized according to the rules of a linguistic system. It is a multilevel reality that sublates more fundamental levels of literary components into a formal dynamic unity.[2] It is important here to note that the text "needs, includes, and preserves" all the lower levels of linguistic utterance while it "carries them forward to a fuller realization within a richer context." An atomistic reading of the biblical text concentrates on the propositional dimension of the text and does not reach an understanding of the sense of the text as an integrated act of communication. Conversely, those who concentrate exclusively on the overall text ignore the fact that at the propositional dimension, the various credal formulae for instance, it still operates on its own level of existence and must be respected as such even while its function in the overall structure is identified.

It is important to understand that a text is an act of communication. The author induces in the reader a certain dynamic of thought that leads to a personal acquisition of what the author is transmitting. The process by which the reader, by means of the text, arrives at some participation in what is being communicated by the writer is a complex one. According to the nonfoundational understanding of knowledge discussed in the last chapter, the active dimension of being itself provides the dynamic unity of the process. The union of knower and known that brings about the truth of the initial understanding is imitated in the poetic (making) process by which this is given a word existence. The audience receives this witness of being as it has passed through the consciousness of the original knower and has been expressed in the "artifact." The one receiving the communication can make a judgment concerning its truth by attending not only to the act of communication (the text) but also to *what* is communicated. This is possible because of the active role of being itself in the original act of knowing, as

---

1. *Text and Interpretation as Categories of Theological Thinking,* trans. Thomas J. Wilson (New York: Crossroad, 1988), 83.

2. I recall here the definition of *sublation* by Bernard Lonergan: "What sublates goes beyond what is sublated, introduces something new and distinct, yet so far from interfering with the sublated or destroying it, on the contrary needs it, includes it, preserves all its proper features and properties, and carries them forward to a fuller realization within a richer context." *Method in Theology* (New York: Herder and Herder, 1972), 241.

well as in the attempt to give it word existence, and in the derivative act of knowing that is induced in the recipient by the text itself. The truth of a Shakespearean play, for example, is neither propositional nor directly metaphysical, but it is true and is judged as true because (1) it mediates a union of knower and that which is found in the author and (2) it creates a derivative union of knower and that which is in the recipient, who acknowledges its truth because he or she can make a judgment concerning the conformity of what is communicated with being itself.

In a foundationalist understanding of text composition and text reception, the original act of knowledge consists in rescuing some dimension of existence from its unintelligibility by reforming it according to the structure of the knowing subject. The original act of knowledge is in turn communicated in a text, but it is known only in and through a similar act on the part of the recipient. The text contributes to the act of knowledge, but only according to the mode of the interpreting subject. Truth is in a conformity by which being submits to the exigencies of the subject.

Sensitivity to the modification of both author and reader effected by their historical, social, and cultural situation must, of course, enter into any critical appropriation of what is communicated by a text. But it is precisely here that the distinction between aspect and profile introduced in the last chapter can bring about a clarification. The situation of the author provides some dimensions of the aspect from which he receives the witness of being, and it brings about a particular modification of his personal appropriation of this witness, the profile of the entity considered (let this "entity" be whatever the author is considering). Despite differences in situation there can be an overlap of aspect, a shared perspective of what is considered. This is due to three factors: (1) the unity of being; (2) the active communicative action on the part of the author; (3) the active communicative receptivity on the part of the reader. Thus, while the profile remains incommunicable, the aspect can be shared.

Applied to the Scriptures, these three factors which can effect an overlap of *aspect* may be restated as follows: (1) the identity of God who manifests and communicates both himself and a knowledge of his plan of salvation; (2) the active communicative action on the part of the one who, after having received revelation, transposes it to a word dimension; (3) the active communicative receptivity, that is the faith, of the reader who, by means of the text, appropriates what is communicated, namely the act through which God manifests and communicates himself.[3] This returns us to the notions of revelation and theology discussed in the first two chapters.

3. In this regard there is an interesting text of Aquinas, who is discussing the need for the grace of prophecy in both text composition and text reception: "After the

God is present to both the author and the receiver of the text, and this fact makes the dynamic continuity joining the acts of composing and receiving the text. In saying this I mean to avoid another post-Enlightenment fallacy, namely that of conceiving causality exclusively in terms of efficient causality. While efficient causality is present in the composing and receiving of texts mediating revelation, there is also the presence of God himself, making himself known. This is a form of friendship that is best viewed in terms of interpersonal communication, for which, perhaps, the notion of formal causality may provide some analogous categories.[4]

It is obvious that the Scriptures do not frequently mediate their truth in propositional terms, but rather principally through narrative. Much fruitful work has been done in this regard, particularly by Paul Ricoeur.[5] There is, however, one aspect of this thinking, one linked to the notion of metaphor that will be considered in the following chapter, that requires some modification. I refer to his notion of *world*. Ricouer distinguishes three worlds: that *behind* the text, namely the milieu impinging on the author; that *within* the text, namely the environment created by the system of interlocking signs that make the text; and that *in front of* the text, by which he means the vision of what is possible opened up for the reader, which enables one to realize one's "ownmost powers."[6] This latter world is for Ricoeur the significance of literature. It is achieved by the effacement of the descriptive referent of the text (the world it is talking about) in order to redescribe reality in terms of its possibilities for the individual. Ricoeur's primary concern throughout his various discussions of literature is with the possibilities of human existence, and not with literature as an act of communica-

---

level of those who receive revelation directly from God, another level of grace is necessary. Because people receive revelation from God not only for their own time but also for the instruction of all who come after them, it was necessary that the things revealed to them be not only passed on in speech to their contemporaries, but also written down for the instruction of those to follow them. And thus it was necessary that there be those who could interpret what was written down. This also must be done by divine grace. So we read in Gen 40:8, 'Does not interpretation come from God?' (*Summa Contra Gentiles* 3, 154).

4. This is not the place for the type of extended discussion required by this insight, which I owe to Franz Jozef van Beeck, "Divine Revelation: Intervention or Self-Communication?" *Theological Studies* 52 (1991): 199-226.

5. See especially his *Time and Narrative* just mentioned.

6. *Time and Narrative*, vol. 1, trans. Kathleen McLaughlin and David Pellauer (Chicago: University of Chicago Press, 1984), 81. Again, we read: "By changing his imagination man alters his existence." *History and Truth*, trans. Charles A. Kelbley, Northwestern University Studies in Phenomenology and Existential Philosophy (Evanston: Northwestern University Press, 1965), 127.

tion. This is a deficiency he owes to aspects of Kantian thought that will be discussed in the next chapter.

Werner Jeanrond has a similar difficulty with the subjectifying tendency in Ricoeur's thought at this point. After asking, "How is it possible in any way whatever to conceive of an ideal sense of a text without reference to reality?" he goes on:

> Would it not be more accurate to say that the sense of a text has two dimensions which are to be distinguished but never separated: namely, an internal texture of references *(Bedeutungsverflechtung)* which, by reason of the nature of the act of reading, build up *simultaneously* a textuality of reference to the world?[7]

This bond between the world created by the text and the world referred to by the text, coupled with the fact that the referential statements within the text continue to function as such, provides the ground for rejecting the split between text and world proposed by Ricoeur and utilized particularly by Sandra Schneiders, as we will see momentarily.

A FEMINIST CONSCIOUSNESS AS THE PLACE OF INTERPRETATION

Decentering the Bible

Although the expression is somewhat differently understood, it is clear that, as feminism has developed in the last two decades, it has moved more and more in the direction of a foundationalism that takes feminist consciousness as its matrix of interpretation.[8] While this is, from an epistemological point of view, the same as taking women's experience as the basic framework, the term *consciousness* is broader and describes a vision of reality that makes women's experience not only a contributing factor in knowledge but the basic horizon within which everything is interpreted. Thus, in a

---

7. *Text and Interpretation,* 59. Jeanrond's discussion at this point concerns Ricoeur's remarks in *Interpretation Theory: Discourse and the Surplus of Meaning* (Fort Worth: Texas Christian University Press, 6th pr., 1967), 87-88. While these views are modified in Ricoeur's *Time and Narrative* (3 volumes, University of Chicago Press, 1984-88), they are substantially the same.

8. It suffices to look at a recent book that purports to offer a feminist perspective on some of the basic issues in theology: *Freeing Theology: The Essentials of Theology in Feminist Perspective,* ed. Catherine Mowry LaCugna (San Francisco: Harper, 1993).

recent book that presents various aspects of feminist consciousness in interaction with different themes, Elisabeth Schüssler Fiorenza writes that her interest in the Bible is one of finding ways to deconstruct "the patriarchal center of biblical traditions and to elaborate the alternative political discourse of the *ekklēsia* within biblical religions."[9] The need for a critical interpretation of the Bible in the interests of liberation is "not to keep women in biblical religions, but because biblical texts affect all women in Western society." Her method applies to all the androcentric texts of the dominant culture: "In this book, I engage in a theoretical exploration of the hermeneutical conditions and epistemological possibilities for a critical practice of reading androcentric texts by elaborating on such readings within the context of interdisciplinary feminist critical theory."[10]

Fiorenza's position moves beyond the vague notion of experience to that of accepting responsibility for the fact that, as we saw in the last chapter, experience capable of being articulated is always interpreted experience, whether this be first-level noetic articulation or, as in this case, second-level theoretical articulation. The problem is, of course, that if this framework of interpretation is to be valid, it must be able to establish itself within a wider world of discourse. But, by definition, such a thing is impossible because it would mean entering into the androcentric and patriarchalized world of Western culture. Feminist consciousness has become, in spite of itself, a very patriarchal reality — an ideology.

Interpreting the Bible in this view, then, means finding ways of using the text to subvert the patriarchal culture that the Bible purportedly established and maintains. This can only be done by refusing to give it any other authority than that which any canon of classical literature enjoys. It must be read and reinterpreted because it "affects all women in Western society." From a faith perspective, I invite anyone to read once again the expressions of the early Christians regarding the Word of God in the Scriptures, ex-

9. *But She Said: Feminist Practices of Biblical Interpretation* (Boston: Beacon Press, 1992), 7. All the quotations from Fiorenza in this paragraph are from pp. 7-9 of *But She Said.* In Fiorenza's writings the term *ekklēsia* is a shorthand formula for the "*ekklēsia* of women," a term first coined by Karl Rahner in "The Position of Woman in the New Situation in Which the Church Finds Herself," in *Theological Investigations,* vol. 8, trans. David Bourke (New York: Herder and Herder, 1971), 75-93. In Fiorenza's later writings it applies to any and all women, of any or no faith, who share a raised feminist consciousness.

10. On an earlier page we can read: "The question of how feminist biblical interpretation can keep our biblical readings from reinforcing the dominant patriarchal system and phallocentric mind-set of Gilead (the patriarchal republic of Margaret Atwood's novel, *The Handmaid's Tale*) has become one of the driving forces behind my work." Ibid., 4.

amples of which can be found in chapter 1, and compare it with this stance. The feminist interpretation is not theology in any sense of the term; there is no thinking with assent, if assent means consenting to the light of revelation. It represents a capitulation to the Enlightenment refusal to accept any interventions of God in this world. There is no revelation, and there is no body of texts that expresses the church's interpretation of the life, death, and resurrection of Jesus Christ.[11]

Two Examples

Examples of feminist readings of biblical texts are easy to find. They are part of the hermeneutical position which presumes that there are multiple competent readings of any text, which is another way of saying that there are as many readings of a text as there are contexts within it and from which it can be read. This position is part of the wider foundationalism mentioned previously that cannot be treated here, except insofar as feminism understands its consciousness as one of the contexts.[12]

The first example of this type of reading can be found in an article by Danna Nolan Fewell and David M. Gunn entitled "Tipping the Balance: Sternberg's Reader and the Rape of Dinah."[13] Fewell and Gunn challenge Meir Sternberg's interpretation of Genesis 34:1-31,[14] based as it is on his principle of "foolproof composition," by which he means that despite the complexity and artistic ambiguities of the narratives in the Prior Testament, "by no great exertion you will be making tolerable sense of the world you are in . . . and the point of it all."[15] Basing themselves on the approach of reader's response, Fewell and Gunn offer an alternative competent reading that concentrates on Dinah rather than on the rights, deceit, and violence of the men. After claiming that such an approach frees the text from Sternberg's tight (implied androcentric) control, they conclude: "We have

11. In a recent study, P. Vallin makes the distinction between the biblical canon as viewed culturally and as viewed in the light of the Church's rule of faith expressed in the Creeds. See his "La Bible, Object Culturel ou Livre Chrétien?" in *Le Canon des Écritures. Études Historiques, Exégétiques et Systématiques,* ed. C. Theobald (Paris: Cerf, 1990), 551-58.

12. For an assessment of such an approach and a tentative return to allowing the text some regulatory function in its own interpretation see *Semeia* 62 (1993), ed. Robert C. Culley, Robert B. Robinson, *Textual Determinacy,* part one.

13. *Journal of Biblical Literature* 110 (1991): 193-211.

14. *The Poetics of Biblical Narrative. Ideological Literature and the Drama of Reading* (Bloomington: Indiana University Press, 1987), 445-75.

15. Ibid., 51.

described Sternberg's reading as one that serves the patriarchy." Then, while admitting that their own interpretation is not without its risks, they insist that justice cannot be served in a society where "men, men's rights, and men's honor control women's lives" and propose that it would have been better for Jacob's sons to have allowed the marriage between Schechem and Dinah as the best solution in those cultural circumstances.[16]

In a subsequent article, Sternberg replied to his critics.[17] He remarks first of all that his principle of foolproof reading requires that an individual text, such as Genesis 34:1-31, be read in the context of the whole of the Bible, with its repertoire of literary means of transmitting a vision of reality and of human conduct: "With all those coordinates of design and signification left unaddressed, the sad apology for a counter argument amounts to tearing the Dinah example out of the poetic system, the part out of the whole." The argument is then pursued further in two directions. The first consists in contrasting his own approach with that of Fewell and Gunn, where Sternberg says that this hinges on the general issue of "the poetic versus the political reading of ideology." This distinction reflects the one I have made between approaching the text as an instance of communication versus approaching it as an occasion for reinforcing feminist consciousness. The second direction is more fundamental still. It hinges on the source of the value judgments one brings to the biblical text. Here Sternberg confronts an approach to the text which presupposes that the text is a neutral object, open to any number of competent readings. He insists once again that the Bible's poetics forms an indissoluble unity with its value systems and moral judgments. He goes on to say: "If anything, a reader unable or unwilling to postulate the articles of faith (from God down) will forfeit competence as a hopeless counter reader, where one unequal to narrative finesse may still belong to the lower limit [of reader competence]."

Sternberg's whole approach, that of poetics, presupposes that the text is a medium of communication operating within a system that it both requires and activates in becoming intelligible. Fewell and Gunn, on the other hand, isolate the text from the matrix of its faith vision of reality, and from its author, and treat it as an object to be transported into a foreign thought system and made to serve a particular agenda. For them, the Bible is made a neutral object lying between two value systems and moral judgments. A reading from either context is equally "competent." In such a situation, "the text comes to figure

16. "Tipping the Balance," 211.
17. "Biblical Poetics and Sexual Politics: From Reading to Counter-Reading," *Journal of Biblical Literature* 111 (1992): 463-88.

as a kind of glorified Rorschach ink blot on which to project one's ideology, among other forms of licensed desire." [18]

The second example is drawn from Sandra Schneiders' several descriptions of a feminist hermeneutical agenda. Basically, this proceeds in three steps: recognition of the problem, elaboration of a hermeneutical theory, and actual text interpretation. I will treat of the first two steps, since in regard to the third, her results are about the same as other feminist interpreters.

In regard to the first step, the problem may be stated as follows: "The major problem facing feminist interpreters is how to engage the biblical text in such a way that the oppressive potential of the Bible is neutralized, while its liberating power is invoked on behalf of the victims of church and society." [19] Or, again, "how can a text which is not just accidentally but intrinsically oppressive function normatively for a faith community?" [20] This problem arises because the text is confronted with feminist consciousness: "[F]eminism is a comprehensive theoretical system for analyzing, criticizing, and evaluating ideas, social structures, procedures and practices, indeed the whole of experienced reality. . . . Feminism, although it is an ideology, i.e., a theoretical system, does not begin in theory but in experience." [21] The experience of oppression, when appropriated is feminist consciousness.

The judgment that the text is "intrinsically oppressive," and not merely manipulated for oppressive goals, derives from comparing it with the "theoretical system" that is adequate to judge "the whole of experienced reality." Is there any such theoretical system in the world? The only vision of reality that makes such a claim is the Christian faith that renounces any pretension to being a "system" and is rather a God-given light that, while adequate in itself, has never made any human being or group of human beings competent to analyze, criticize, and evaluate all of reality. In addition, to seek a way of making an intrinsically oppressive text normative for a faith community is a little like asking, "How can *Das Kapital* be interpreted to

---

18. Ibid., 465, 466, 469, 470. Later, on p. 473, he correctly criticizes the fixation of Fewell and Gunn on the individual text with their consequent interpretation that the author (presumably a patriarchalist) does not condemn the rape itself. This, of course, ignores the whole biblical context shared by both author and audience. In all of this summary of the article, I am necessarily simplifying a complex argument. For the full argument, see Sternberg's reply itself.

19. "The Bible and Feminism: Biblical Theology," in *Freeing Theology: The Essentials of Theology in Feminist Perspective,* ed. Catherine Mowry LaCugna (San Francisco: Harper, 1993), 31-57; quotation is from p. 49.

20. "Feminist Ideology Criticism and Biblical Hermeneutics," *Biblical Theology Bulletin* 19 (1989): 3-10; quotation is from p. 4. A similar question is posed in *Beyond Patching* (New York: Paulist, 1989), 54.

21. *Beyond Patching,* 16.

serve as the charter for the free enterprise system?" What is lacking in this diagnosis is any attempt to critique the feminist analysis in the *light of faith*, and therefore any attempt to enter into a correlative process of allowing the light of revelation to question the question, or to search for what is true in an outlook obviously indebted to a very particular post-Enlightenment understanding of human beings and human destiny.

With the problem posed this way, Schneiders proceeds to elaborate a hermeneutical approach to the text, beginning with the fact that interpretation always involves a process of interaction between the text and the interpreter. This basic principle has three implications:

> First . . . that a text does not have one right meaning, which was put into it by its author and is to be extracted by its reader. Rather, the text is a linguistic structure that is susceptible of a number of valid readings by different readers or the same reader at different times. . . . Second . . . the meaning is not "in" the text but occurs in the interaction between text and reader . . . the reader makes a genuine contribution to the meaning rather than being simply a passive consumer of prefabricated meaning. Third, the meaning is not under the control of the author.[22]

As thus posed, the principle and its implications are the common property of any hermeneutical theory. The problem begins when we seek for any norm by which the success of an interpretation is to be judged. A symphony, for example, is never interpreted in exactly the same way twice even by the same orchestra and conductor, but this does not mean that they are free to do what they want with it. It is possible, by consulting the score and by paying attention to previous interpretations, to establish certain criteria by which a rendering of the piece may be judged good or bad, faithful or unfaithful. The problem Schneiders poses to herself is, how to take a perverse score and make good music. Why bother with the score at all, unless with Fiorenza, one judges the Bible to be possessed of great cultural power that must be offset? Schneiders is not clear in her response, as I see it.

Her attempts to respond can be found in several places, among which are two essays with similar titles: "Scripture: Tool of Patriarchy or Resource for Transformation?"[23] and "Living Word or Dead(ly) Letter? The Encounter Between the New Testament and Contemporary Experience."[24] Schneiders

---

22. "The Bible and Feminism," 47-48.

23. Chapter two of *Beyond Patching*.

24. *Proceedings of the Forty-Seventh Annual Meeting*, ed. Paul Crowley, Catholic Theological Society of America, 1992, 45-60. In this text Schneiders refers to her article "Feminist Ideology Criticism" for a more complete treatment of the issue.

avails herself of two insights. First, the notion of "effective historical consciousness" elaborated by Hans Georg Gadamer. This means, in regard to
interpretation, that the reader of an important text already stands within a
tradition generated by the text. It is not merely the text, but also the effective
history of that text that reaches the interpreter.[25] The second insight derives
from Paul Ricoeur's notion of the world in front of the text already discussed.
By divorcing text from the world and allowing for the effective history of the
liberating dimension of the Christ event, Schneiders maintains we may enable
an "intrinsically oppressive text" to create a "world of Christian discipleship
structured by the paschal mystery of Jesus."[26]

Surely this world structured by the paschal mystery of Jesus is the right
goal. It is arrived at, however, by first condemning the text and then situating
it in another context; her terms for this are "decontextualizing" and "recontextualizing." I have already said enough concerning the pretensions of
feminist consciousness to adjudicate all of reality including God's present act
of revelation. The notion of recontextualizing is a variant of the theory of
"multi-contextual readings" that underlies the approach of Fewell and Gunn.
The new notion is precisely that of Ricoeur's world in front of the text that
requires that the text have no further referential function, but rather provides
the subject with a vision of what is possible in terms of self-understanding
and self-actuation: "Every hermeneutics is thus, explicitly or implicitly,
self-understanding by means of understanding others."[27] We are faced once
again with two views of the hermeneutical project. One sees the text as an
instance of communication, produced in a limited and limiting environment,
affected by and effecting history, received in a limited and limiting environment, but still communicating. The other sees the text as so unmoored from
its author that it can be received into any number of contexts and become the
object of a competent reading. One such context is feminist consciousness
and one such reading is to split text from world and recontextualize this world.
I find it significant that Donald Senior, in responding to Sandra Schneiders'
paper "Living Word or Dead(ly) Letter? The Encounter Between the New
Testament and Contemporary Experience," first points out that if the world
in front of the text can be recontextualized in a series of diverse and equally
competent readings, it is impossible to deny an apartheid or anti-feminine
reading an equal hearing with a feminist reading. In my terms, there must be

25. See Hans George Gadamer, *Truth and Method*, trans. Joel Weinsheimer and
Donald Marshall (New York: Seabury, 1989), 341-79.
26. "Feminist Ideology Criticism," 7.
27. Paul Ricoeur, *Conflict of Interpertations: Essays in Hermeneutics*, Northwestern University Studies in Phenomenology and Existential Philosophy (Evanston:
Northwestern University Press, 1974), 17.

some criteria of judgment, one generated by revelation, witnessed to by the text, indebted to the effective history of the text and able to provide an authoritative context. In Senior's terms:

> [T]he full range of the community's reading of the biblical witness, a reading encoded in the deepest currents of the community's life and thought, provides an important control on what is a legitimate Christian interpretation of Scripture, over and beyond the contours of the text established through literary criticism and historical-critical assessments about the original context.[28]

This appeal to the life and thought of the community may be understood as applying to the environment of text composition as well as text reception. It includes the ever present action of the Holy Spirit as well as the effective historical consciousness that has intervened between composition and present-day reception. It can be understood as an extension of Meir Sternberg's insistence that an individual passage of the Bible can only be interpreted within the context of the faith and value systems of the Bible as a whole.

ANOTHER USE OF EXPERIENCE
AS A HERMENEUTICAL TOOL

I wish now to consider the work of Elisabeth Schüssler Fiorenza and Rosemary Radford Ruether as illustrative of another feminist approach based on experience. In Fiorenza's words, her earlier interpretive effort represents a "different perspective" from that which she is undertaking now, but this does not signify that the earlier work is superseded.[29] I will restrict myself to this earlier work here and join it to that of Ruether because of their similarities.

Both of these theologians express themselves clearly on the methodology they employ. Although they differ from each other in many respects,[30] they share in common the principle that women's experience is the predominant component in a correlative method that seeks some reciprocity between the horizon of the investigator today and the teaching of the textual expression of tradition.[31] Both seek an interpretive norm by which the biblical text can be

28. "A Response to a Paper of Sandra Schneiders," *Proceedings of the Forty-Seventh Annual Meeting,* ed. Paul Crowley, Catholic Theological Society of America, 1992, 61-68; quotation is from p. 66.

29. See *But She Said,* 7.

30. See for instance Fiorenza's response to Ruether's review of *Bread Not Stone: The Challenge of Feminist Biblical Interpretation* (Boston: Beacon Press, 1984), found in Fiorenza's more recent work, *But She Said,* 219, n. 8.

31. "An understanding of authority, and particularly of the place of experience

judged by establishing a canon within or outside of the scriptural canon.[32] In the case of both the predominant factor in establishing this normative principle is women's experience. This is how Rosemary Radford Ruether expresses it:

> By women's experience as a key to hermeneutics or theory of interpretation, we mean precisely that experience which arises when women become critically aware of these falsifying and alienating experiences imposed upon them as women by a male-dominated culture.[33]

Or again:

> The Bible can be appropriated as a source of liberating paradigms only if it can be seen that there is a correlation between the feminist critical principle and that critical principle by which biblical thought critiques itself and renews its vision as the authentic Word of God over against corrupting and sinful deformations. . . . The biblical critical principle is that of the prophetic-messianic tradition.[34]

This establishes a "usable" and "unusable" part of the canon. Fiorenza is opposed to this type of correlation, and indeed rejects the term, yet her own procedure, as I will show, is correlational, between women's experience and ancient practice. Nothing she has said in her more recent work indicates that she has been able to respond to the criticism that she does indeed proceed in this way.[35]

Feminists in these schools of thought tend to maintain that since all interpreters approach the text with a given set of presuppositions, feminism should not be singled out as unique in this regard: "No value neutral position exists or ever has."[36] There is, however, as pointed out in chapter 3, a great difference between a perspective and a stance.

---

in that understanding, thus undergirds every feminist use of the Bible, whatever interpretive option is being employed." Katherine Doob Sakenfeld, "Feminist Perspectives on Bible and Theology: An Introduction to Selected Issues and Literature," *Interpretation* 42 (1988): 5-18; citation is from p. 11.

32. See Francis Martin, "Feminist Hermeneutics: An Overview," *Communio* 18 (1991): 144-63; 398-424.

33. Rosemary Radford Ruether, "Feminist Interpretation: A Method of Correlation," in *Feminist Interpretation of the Bible,* ed. Letty M. Russel (Philadelphia: Westminster, 1985), 111-24; citation is from 114.

34. Ibid., 117.

35. See for instance *But She Said,* 5-6.

36. Mary Ann Tolbert, "Defining the Problem: The Bible and Feminist Hermeneutics," in *The Bible and Feminist Hermeneutics,* ed. Mary Ann Tolbert, *Semeia* 28 (Chico, Calif.: Scholars Press, 1983), 113-23; citation is from p. 118. One could consult with profit the remarks of George W. Stroup on this and other aspects of feminism: "Between Echo and Narcissus," *Interpretation* 42 (1988): 19-32.

The Four Issues

As a basis for the discussion, I will take an article published by Elisabeth Schüssler Fiorenza in 1985.[37] Other materials will be added from both Fiorenza and Rosemary Radford Ruether as it seems appropriate. Although their positions have been nuanced in the ensuing years, they are basically the same on the following four issues.

1. Regarding the biblical text

While a Christian feminist apologetics submits to the "word of God" (quotation marks in text) and applies the hermeneutics of suspicion only to later interpretation, and while a liberation theological interpretation affirms the liberating dynamics of the biblical texts, a feminist critical hermeneutics of suspicion must recognize that the Bible is a male book. Therefore, the first and never-ending task of a hermeneutics of suspicion elaborates the patriarchal, destructive, and oppressive elements in the Bible.[38]

2. Regarding the method to be adopted

Rather than select some texts or traditions as critically normative, feminist hermeneutics must first identify and reject all androcentric texts and those that perpetuate the patriarchal power structure, ancient and modern. The remaining texts, the egalitarian-feminist surplus, may thus speak.[39] Then, there must be a recovery of all biblical texts through a process of feminist reconstruction by which the sufferings of women are commemorated in such a way that they become a subversive power. The feminist critical method thus moves beyond the silence of the androcentric text to the reconstructed history of women and an understanding of their true role, particularly in the early church (131-33).[40]

---

37. "The Will to Choose or Reject: Continuing Our Critical Work," in *Feminist Interpretation of the Bible,* 125-36.

38. I have omitted from this passage, because it is hard to determine how Fiorenza means them, expressions such as avoiding the Bible "like the plague"; labeling the Bible, "Caution! Could be dangerous to your health and survival"; and describing the task of hermeneutics as that of "naming the language of hate."

39. This approach differs from that of Schneiders, who denies that there are any such texts.

40. This method is more fully described, though not as clearly, in Part I of *In Memory of Her,* and is applied in Part II.

3. Regarding the place of revelation

The locus or place of divine revelation and grace is therefore not the Bible or the tradition of a patriarchal church but the *ekklēsia* of women and the lives of women who live the "option for our women selves." A feminist critical hermeneutics of liberation shares the "advocacy stance" of liberation theologies but, at the same time, it elaborates not only women's oppression but also women's power as the locus of revelation.[41]

4. Regarding the goal of feminist interpretation

"A feminist biblical interpretation is thus first of all a political task."[42] This is so not only because the Bible has been used as a political weapon in the oppression of women, but also because by properly interpreting the biblical text and correctly locating the locus of revelation, the Bible can become, not an ancient archetype of what must always be, but a prototype of what can be.[43]

A Response: The Androcentrism and Patriarchalism of the Bible

In describing the Bible as androcentric, such scholars mean to point to the fact that its authors and outlook were predominantly male. This can be granted, just as we must acknowledge that they were predominantly Semitic, that their understanding of the universe was defective, and, at least in regard to the Old Testament, that most of the authors had no knowledge of life after death. To describe the Bible as "androcentric," however, is to impose modern sensitivities, which have their own bias, on a text that makes sense without such labels. This is to return to the question of feminist consciousness.[44]

Elisabeth Schüssler Fiorenza recognizes that there are many women

41. *In Memory of Her,* 35.

42. We also read: "A feminist Christian spirituality, therefore, calls us to gather together the *ekklēsia* of women who, in the angry power of the Spirit, are sent forth to feed, heal, and liberate our own people who are women." *In Memory of Her,* 346.

43. This notion of prototype occurs frequently in Fiorenza's writings. See, for example, "The Function of Scripture in the Liberation Struggle: A Critical Feminist Hermeneutics and Liberation Theology," first published in *The Challenge of Liberation Theology,* ed. L. Dale Richesin and Brian Mahan (Maryknoll: Orbis Books, 1981) under the title, "Toward a Feminist Biblical Hermeneutics: Biblical Interpretation and Liberation Theology," subsequently published under the current title in *Bread Not Stone* (Boston: Beacon, 1984), 43-63.

44. I will discuss androcentricism and its language in chapter 8.

in our own culture who cannot be written off as "unliberated and unfeminist" and who have a "different, inspiring, challenging, and liberating experience with the Bible."[45] This surely weakens her claim to have found the unique stance from which to judge the Bible, label it irremediably androcentric, and look beyond it to a reconstructed history, itself based on the same narrow stance, as the norm for interpreting biblical tradition. Androcentrism, where it genuinely exists, is a cultural phenomenon that can and should be taken into account both in modern church life and in reading the Scriptures. It is not, however, evidence that the Bible should be treated as part of some sinister misogynist plot. Such a view is inaccurate, unjust, and anachronistic. It ignores the crystallization process already described and the individualism of modern Western thought.

While androcentrism is a cultural judgment, the charge of patriarchalism is an historical and social judgment. In practice, of course, the two are not so easily distinguished. Patriarchalism is variously defined. Rosemary Radford Ruether defines it this way: "By patriarchy we mean not only the subordination of females to males, but the whole structure of Father-ruled society: aristocracy over serfs, masters over slaves, king over subjects, racial overlords over colonized people."[46]

Elisabeth Schüssler Fiorenza offers several descriptions. In a recent essay, she refers the reader to a study by Heidi Hartmann[47] and goes on to describe patriarchy as a "male pyramid." In an essay commemorating the twenty-fifth anniversary of *Concilium,* Fiorenza says that she understands patriarchy in the narrow sense of "father-right and father-might," going on to state: "I understand it as a complex systemic interstructuring of sexism, racism, classism and cultural-religious imperialism that has produced the Western 'politics of Otherness.' "[48] The phrase *the politics of*

45. "The Will to Choose or to Reject," 130-31. Her reaction to this is a call for a further use of a hermeneutics of suspicion "to detect the antipatriarchal elements and functions of biblical texts, which are obscured by androcentric language and concepts."

46. *Sexism and God-Talk* (Boston: Beacon Press, 1983), 61.

47. "Capitalism, Patriarchy, and Job Segregation by Sex," in *The Signs Reader: Women, Gender, and the Scholarship,* ed. Elizabeth and Emily K. Abel (Chicago: University of Chicago Press, 1983), 193-225. Fiorenza refers to this study in "The Will to Choose or to Reject," 127.

48. "Justified by all her Children: Struggle, Memory, and Vision," *On the Threshold of the Third Millennium,* ed. The Foundation, *Concilium* Special Issue (Philadelphia: Trinity Press, 1990), 19-38; the citation is from note 6. Further on in the essay, in note 30, Fiorenza proposes a distinction between an androcentric text and a patriarchal system and rhetoric. "While all biblical texts are androcentric, *i.e.* written in grammatically masculine language, they do not all *advocate* patriarchal structures and values." Emphasis is in the original.

Otherness is explained in still another essay in which patriarchy is defined as "a differentiated political system of graduated domination and subordination that found its classic Western legitimation in the philosophy of otherness." Or again, "the governing dominance of elite propertied male heads of households."[49]

Both Ruether and Fiorenza prove too much. In Fiorenza's "male pyramid," there are in fact dyads made up of oppressing males and oppressed females at every level. This must mean that the females at level "A" are oppressing the males at levels "B," "C," "D," and so on. How can this be called "patriarchy"? Having been launched as a woman's liberation movement, feminism is committed to the abolition of patriarchalism. Since black, poor, and third-world women have expressed their displeasure at the narrow white middle-class European and American preoccupation with feminism, the base has broadened. The net result is that feminists such as Elisabeth Schüssler Fiorenza must declare themselves in favor of the liberation of all "nonpersons," whether women or men.[50] This is as it should be, but why, in a totalizing generalization, call the opponent patriarchal unless you are willing to specify whether you mean male or female patriarchalism? At this point, of course, the term has become meaningless.

It is more in keeping with the true state of affairs to point to the oppression of both women and men in this world and to declare such a thing to be clearly contrary to the Word of God both in the Scriptures and in the hearts of genuine prophets of our own time. On the other hand, to describe every oppressive structure as patriarchal is irresponsible, though it often derives from an awareness that there has been a profound distortion of what masculinity really is. It is precisely this failure to understand how profoundly a biblical understanding of existence changes our concept of effective action that vitiates the otherwise insightful critiques of power that are to be found in *But She Said.* Having accepted the thoroughly Enlightenment notions that underlie *Ideologiekritik,* the only possible recourse is to insist on changes, worked through the coercive power of social engineer-

49. "The Politics of Otherness: Biblical Interpretation as a Critical Praxis for Liberation," in *The Future of Liberation Theology: Essays in Honor of Gustavo Gutierrez,* ed. Marc H. Ellis and Otto Maduro (Maryknoll: Orbis Books, 1989), 311-25; citations are from pp. 311 and 315.

50. Ibid., 315, 323 and passim. It is interesting that in this article Fiorenza's attempt to differentiate the reading subject of the biblical text and argue for a multiple set of equally acceptable readings is based on deconstructionist principles. She is unable, however, to indicate how the text and its reading audience will not continue to disintegrate into an easily manipulable mass of monads: without the unifying power of truth we have only the coercive truth of power.

ing, whose justification is "the future." This has been, as Albert Borgmann points out, the liberal justification for its own form of power rule by which the elite force changes upon those who do not form part of the power structure.[51] When effective action, beginning with God's creative action, is understood as generosity not coercion, there is the possibility of discerning true and false exercises of causality.

Correlation: With the Text or with History?

The correlation described by these feminists consists in establishing a reciprocal relationship between present experience and some aspect of Christian tradition. This then becomes normative for interpreting the whole of that tradition. Aspects of the Christian tradition that do not correspond to the norm are either ignored, rejected, or subordinated. In this regard, both Ruether and Fiorenza agree that patriarchal texts should be definitively rejected. (Ruether provides a rite for the exorcism of patriarchal texts in her collection of women-church liturgies.)[52]

Their hermeneutical methods are not, however, the same. The correlative approach of Elisabeth Schüssler Fiorenza seeks to establish a commonalty between women's present experience of oppression and the reconstructed history of the social situations in which the biblical texts originated. This has a distinct disadvantage even over the liberationist model adopted by Ruether. For while liberation theology seeks correlation between experience and text, Fiorenza seeks correlation between experience and a reconstructed history. The first method resorts to "proof texts," the second to "proof facts." In addition, therefore, to the danger of circularity inherent in all correlating procedures, Fiorenza's correlation (the designation, obviously, is mine not hers) runs a double risk. There is first of all the danger of establishing a narrow and not widely shared analysis of women's experience as an adequate correlate, and then using this analysis as a heuristic model to establish the "facts" of history. In regard to reconstructive work in general, Mary Ann Tolbert has already observed: ". . . the crucial question from my standpoint is whether or not *any* historical reconstruction can form the basis of Christian faith and practice."[53]

51. *Crossing the Postmodern Divide* (Chicago, London: University of Chicago Press, 1992).

52. *Women-Church* (San Francisco: Harper and Row, 1985), 137. The ritual provides a list of "suggested texts in need of exorcism:" Lev 12:1-5; Ex 19:1, 7-9, 14-15; Jgs 19; Eph 5:21-23; 1 Tim 2:11-15; 1 Pet 2:18-20.

53. "Defining the Problem," 124. Carolyn Osiek, who includes Elisabeth

We find in these thinkers a similarly one-sided interpretation of oppression. The truth present in this grasp of an aspect of our modern situation
is distorted by a rights-oriented notion of the subject that labels anything
which seems opposed to these rights as oppressive. This notion in turn
becomes the heuristic structure governing the reconstruction of women's
experience of the past:

> Rather than relinquish patriarchal biblical traditions, a hermeneutics of
> remembrance seeks to develop a feminist critical method for moving
> beyond the androcentric text to the history of women in biblical reli-
> gion. . . . In conclusion, what leads us to perceive biblical texts as pro-
> viding resources in the struggle for liberation from patriarchal oppression
> as well as models for the transformation of the patriarchal church, is not
> some special canon of texts that can claim divine authority. Rather it is
> the experience of women themselves in their struggles for liberation.[54]

This is correlation but not of experience with text on the basis of an
abiding content in the Christian tradition. Rather, this correlation is effected
on the basis of a supposed transcendent identity between modern experience
interpreted in a particular way and a past reconstructed in the light of the
same experience. Elisabeth Schüssler Fiorenza's reconstruction of Christian
origins in *In Memory of Her* contains many valid results, though there have
been criticisms of some of her conclusions,[55] and the recent works of Ben
Witherington III have presented many of the same results within the framework of a more adequate historical model.[56] My point here is that once

---

Schüssler Fiorenza among the "liberationists," remarks concerning their historical
approach that it "leads the liberationist method to eulogize [this word would not apply
to Fiorenza] the prophets, Jesus, and sometimes Paul while writing off other, particularly
later New Testament, writers who do not meet the liberation criterion, thus forming a
new 'canon within the canon' on very slim foundations." "The Feminist and the Bible:
Hermeneutical Alternatives," in *Feminist Perspectives on Biblical Scholarship*, 93-106;
citation is from p. 104.

54. "The Will to Choose or to Reject," 133 and 135. Similar expressions are
frequently found in Fiorenza's writings. See, for example, the introduction to *Bread
Not Stone*, xvi.

55. The reader may consult the reviews by Ross S. Kraemer in *Journal of Biblical
Literature* 104 (1985): 722-25; *Religious Studies Review* 11 (Jan. 1985): 6-9; Robert M.
Grant in *Journal of Religion* 65 (1985): 83-88; and William S. Babock in *Second
Century* 4 (1984): 177-84.

56. *Women in the Earliest Churches*, SNTS Monograph Series, 59 (Cambridge:
Cambridge University Press, 1988); and *Women in the Ministry of Jesus: A Study of
Jesus' Attitudes to Women and their Roles as Reflected in his Earthly Life*, SNTS
Monograph Series 51 (Cambridge: Cambridge University Press, 1984). I would call

again a very particular interpretation of women's experience is the foundation, the governing norm of how reality is to be viewed.

The Place of Revelation

It requires a very particular view of revelation, one that to my knowledge Elisabeth Schüssler Fiorenza has not elaborated,[57] to locate it in "the *ekklēsia* of women" and to contrast this with "the Bible or the tradition of a patriarchal church."[58] Revelation, by any account, is a noetic reality and therefore must always take place within persons. In that sense, the "place" of revelation, both communal and individual, is always in an *ekklēsia* that is apostolic and not in a text or a tradition. At the same time, the biblical text, and the tradition to which it witnesses and which sustains its message, is the privileged expression and transmitting instrument of revelation. In that sense, it too has been called a *locus theologicus*.

The Bible, as interpreted in the light of reconstructed history, is deemed revelatory to the degree that it provides a prototypical model for action now. This is basically a praxis model of revelation deriving from liberation theology. The introduction of praxis as a goal of revelation and as a means of changing the receptive horizon of those who consult the Scriptures is a very valuable reminder of the transforming role of the Word of God.[59] It is a misunderstanding of revelation, however, to restrict it, as Fiorenza seems to do, to an experience of God's sustaining presence in the struggle, present and past, of women for liberation. In the New Testament, as we have seen, words having to do with revelation are linked with terms that imply knowledge. It is in fact the understanding of God's action among us in the historical Jesus Christ that is the touchstone of what is a valid understanding of revelation.

---

the reader's attention to the balanced assessment of the second title by Pheme Perkins in *Religious Studies Review* 16 (1990): 152.

57. Very often in contexts which speak of revelation, Fiorenza alludes to the experience of God's sustaining presence. This may be her concept of revelation. See *Bread Not Stone,* xv and xiv. She also discusses revelation in *Bread Not Stone;* see " 'For the Sake of our Salvation . . .': Biblical Interpretation and the Community of Faith," 23-42, esp. 39-41. See also the introduction to *But She Said.*

58. "The Will to Choose or to Reject," in *Feminist Interpretation of the Bible,* 128.

59. Fiorenza makes many valid criticisms of modern biblical exegesis in her article "Toward a Critical-Theological Self-Understanding of Biblical Scholarship," in *Bread Not Stone,* 117-49.

The recipient of revelation is the community of believers who assimilate personally the act by which God wills to "manifest and communicate himself and the eternal decrees of his will concerning humanity's salvation" (*Dei Verbum*, §6). Of its nature, such a communication is life-changing because it affects the whole of a person, especially the mind. To restrict revelation to a prototype for action or to an awareness of divine presence in struggle is to risk trivializing the human person. A human person is *capax Dei,* and that life-giving knowledge of God, by which the mind is changed and shares in the events of salvation, begins in this life. Once again, we can see how placing a primacy on the state of the knowing subject subverts any possibility of dialogue within the church, since this foundationalist and totalizing view of revelation must demand acceptance as the starting point of analysis.

The Goal of Feminist Hermeneutics

Praxis, as an activity by which the person successively appropriates mediated reality and through this appropriates selfhood, is an integral component of interpretation. Such appropriation requires symbolically situated historical activity by which understanding is both embodied and deepened.[60] The position, therefore, of those who, like Elisabeth Schüssler Fiorenza, point to the goal of feminist hermeneutics as political action cannot be faulted on the ground that hermeneutics as such does not include practical activity.

Feminist hermeneutics acts correctly in counteracting those false interpretations of the Bible that have in fact been used to oppress women. The designation of the text as prototypical rather than archetypal, however, suffers from two defects. There is first of all the concentration on one aspect of the life of Jesus and the early church as reconstructed historically. This one aspect of reconstructed praxis provides a model enabling us to work for liberation in our own day. But what of the primordial *typos* of the New

---

60. An elaboration of the relationship between interpretation, understanding, and praxis is beyond the scope of this study, although it should be pointed out that feminism has brought this question to the fore in a particularly acute manner. For some beginnings of a consideration of this issue, one may consult Paul Ricoeur, "Explanation and Understanding: On Some Remarkable Connections Among the Theory of the Text, Theory of Action, and Theory of History," in *The Philosophy of Paul Ricoeur: An Anthology of His Work,* ed. Charles E. Reagan and David Stewart (Boston: Beacon Press, 1978), 149-66. In a very different vein, one may consult with profit the remarks of Walter Brueggemann, *Israel's Praise: Doxology Against Idolatry and Ideology* (Philadelphia: Fortress, 1988), chapter 1, "Praise as a Constitutive Act."

Testament, the cross and resurrection of Jesus Christ? This is surely the center of concentration of the New Testament, the enabling point that gives us understanding of the true meaning of liberation and the true face of oppression, which is humankind's bondage to the evil of alienation from God and consequently the evil of mutual alienation.

The second and more serious defect has to do with the use of the terms *prototype* and *archetype,* which casts the text exclusively as a type or a model and ignores it as a means of communication. The authors of the New Testament, while they were addressing particular audiences and situations, were making truth claims that transcended their immediate context. This is obvious from the fact that readers and hearers of their texts still grow in an understanding of God and his plan of salvation in the act of reading or hearing. The truth mediated by the text both requires and transcends the limitations of its original utterance.

Conclusion

Having established experience as the controlling element in interpretation, feminist hermeneutics shows itself to be another instance of the search for foundations. It seems as though theological feminism began in the 1960s with the intellectual inheritance accepted by most theology. It has never looked back to critique its own presuppositions in a thorough and philosophical manner. The result is that it has committed nearly all its resources in an effort to legitimate its foundation in women's experience or feminist consciousness. This seriously weakens many of its otherwise valuable insights and programs for action, and it may result in its becoming so estranged from the rest of the Christian body that dialogue will be practically impossible. That would be very unfortunate.

The next chapter considers some further consequences of pursuing an agenda inherited from critical theology without criticizing it.

8

Analogy, Images, Metaphors, and Theology

It might be said that the mood of foundationalism is one of isolation and anxiety. It suffices to read the lines from Kant cited in the previous chapter to appreciate this. The isolated subject, in danger of being dominated by some heteronomous factor, be this the universe, the state, tradition, or religion, must establish the norms by which knowledge is truly such. Only such a position, such an escape from tutelage, is worthy of a thinking being.

> Enlightenment is man's release from his self-incurred tutelage. Tutelage is man's inability to make use of his understanding without direction from another. Self-incurred is this tutelage when its cause lies not in lack of reason but in lack of resolution and courage to use it without direction from another. *Sapere audere!* "Have courage to use your own reason!" — that is the motto of enlightenment.[1]

The problem is that this stance obliges the thinking subject to determine beforehand the conditions under which knowledge is to be acquired, since otherwise there is always the risk that one is falling into tutelage and receiving from another. The self must be the ultimate deciding factor.

A foundation is a means of insuring that the thinking subject will be able to determine what will be considered knowledge. It pertains to that level of discourse that, as we have seen, is second order, or epistemic, discourse. It is a characteristic of such thinking and discourse that it must move from general to particular — it must first establish the norms for thinking before it can accept the results of thinking; it must establish a

---

1. Immanuel Kant, *What is Enlightenment?* trans. Lewis White Beck, The Library of Liberal Arts (New York: MacMillan, 1959), 85.

genus, let us say "religion," before it can discuss any particular religion. It cannot deal with the spectacular divergence of individual entities seen in their particular contexts, for this would mean allowing being itself a determinative causality in the act of knowing, and thus subjecting oneself to domination.

The previous two chapters were dedicated to a consideration of how feminist theology continues the foundationalist fallacy by insisting that the experiencing subject is the touchstone and norm of knowledge. This chapter extends the discussion to consider our concepts. The basic question may be framed as follows: do concepts represent reality or do they mediate reality? A representationalist understanding of knowledge can take one of two contrary forms. There is on the one hand the view that concepts represent, what Lonergan calls the "already out there now."[2] Reality impresses itself on the mind and the freer the mind is of any previous information the more objective it is. On the other hand, there is the view that the mind has such an active role in the forming of concepts that the resulting representation is the coalescence of the sensible and the universal in keeping with the structure of the subject. This is basically the Kantian view and it is the one that lies at the origin of the type of representationalism to be discussed here.

A *mediationist* (to coin a term) understanding denies both these extremes by maintaining that what is formed in the mind is literally a conception, the result of the act of being as it is shared by what is known and by which the act of conceiving is done by the mind. Reality is not represented, it is mediated by this activity. The thinking subject is brought into genuine contact with reality through the mediation of the concept that is the result of the union between the mind and what is known. Words, therefore, do not arbitrarily represent what is passively absorbed into the mind, as in the Lockean scheme, nor do they represent what the mind imposes on reality to make it intelligible as in the Kantian theory. They are, rather, the use of a commonly held preexistent medium in order to mediate, through imitation, what the mind has conceived as a result of receiving reality into itself. The fact of language's commonality makes of it a unique medium, able to create in the recipient the original imitation of reality and some of the multitudinous splendor of being that was received and conceived by the one uttering the speech.

This chapter considers speech about God in four stages. First, there is a brief consideration of analogical speech, both as a noetic function and

---

2. Bernard Lonergan, *Insight: A Study of Human Understanding* (London: Longmans, Green, 1958), 440, and passim.

as the object of epistemic reflection. This is followed by a look at how the Bible uses images in a first-order level of predication about God and how the tradition has continued this manner of speaking. As a corollary to this, there is a schematic presentation of how gender-specific language and its opposite are both forms of image predication. Finally, there is reflection on the use of metaphors and models in theology. There is no attempt here to resolve all the problems these issues raise; rather this chapter sets for itself the much more modest objective of demonstrating that the representationalist bias of feminist theology inhibits it from arriving at some quite legitimate goals.

ANALOGY

Our word *analogy* derives from the Greek term that signified *proportion* and *correspondence*. It describes the way in which words are used. A word may apply to different realities in the same sense, and this is called univocity — a Ford and a Cadillac are both called *cars*. A word may be applied in a completely different sense, and this is called equivocity — *bank* as predicated of the side of a river and of a commercial institution. But a word may also be applied to different realities because, even though they are different, there is something similar about them (e.g., *power* said of the mind, the will, a person, a novel, an athlete, and so on). In this latter case, there is a *stretch* quality to the term that allows it to be used in such a way; such words while clearly designating a reality are hard to pin down, they are vague.[3]

Our first order or noetic level of discourse is replete with analogies in this broad sense of the term. Most of the images and metaphors we employ can be so classified, and this is true of the noetic discourse of the Scriptures.[4] In a more restricted sense, however, some of our predication, while it is still in the nature of a comparison, is more precise. "[T]he concept (and term) is

---

3. "There is an indispensable role played in our thought and language by those systematically vague and elastic terms that alone can catch the similarities and affinities running all up and down and across the universe, especially between the realms of matter and spirit, cosmos and psyche. This is the secret life of the mind nourishing all metaphor, poetry, and art: the insight into authentic similarities and affinities across the universe." William Norris Clarke, *The Philosophical Approach to God: A Neo-Thomist Perspective,* The Fourth James Montgomery Hester Seminar (Winston-Salem: Wake Forest University, 1979), 52.

4. For a good account see Luis Alonso Schökel, *A Manual of Hebrew Poetics,* Subsidia Biblica 11 (Rome: Pontifical Biblical Institute, 1988), chapter 8, "Images."

actually used in the living act of judgment when the mind actually applies it to a given subject and knows what it is doing."[5] In actual practice, only this latter form of predication is called analogical. While the distinction must often remain roughhewn and leave a border of overlap between analogy and metaphor, there is a real difference. It lies in the fact that in an analogy a *judgment* is made that somehow or other there is an objective feature about certain diverse realities that they hold in common, even if the nature of the commonality is not always specified. Thus, we may say of Tom, his complexion, and the food he eats, that they are "healthy." There is some perceived relation between these three, and a judgment is made that the word *healthy*, which applies properly to Tom, can also be applied to his complexion as a sign of health and to his diet as a cause of health. Analogy always includes a judgment concerning this objective correspondence. Metaphor, on the other hand, while it expresses a perceived similarity, is directed more to creating the correspondence than to asserting the multiple possession of the reality so imputed.[6] Failure to make this distinction is the source of some of the greatest confusion in the talk about metaphorical theology.

At this point in the discussion we are close to a consideration of second level or epistemic discourse, and it is important to observe that discussion about analogy takes place properly at this level. The traditional, particularly the Thomistic, consideration of analogy is not an effort to establish the a priori conditions for knowledge, what can be known, how it can be known, and so forth, it is rather a systematic reflection on the validity of what is already known.[7] It suffices to read the testimonies

---

5. Clarke, *The Philosophical Approach to God,* 52.

6. Among the theoreticians of metaphor who are also sensitive to the specificity of analogy, there is a general agreement on this point, although they do not often place the accent on the role of judgment. Thus Janet Martin Soskice (*Metaphor and Religious Language* [Oxford: Clarendon Press, 1985], 65) says, "Analogical usage can be distinguished from a metaphorical usage by the fact that from its inception it seems appropriate." That is, I would interpret, it is based on a correct judgment of objective correspondence. Richard Swinburne (*Revelation: From Metaphor to Analogy* [Oxford: Clarendon Press, 1992], 48-49) speaks of the fact that when an analogy first created by metaphor passes into established use, it is no longer metaphorical (relying on context) but still retains its character as "vague." That is, again I interpret, the objective correspondence does not require any specific context for its transposition to be understood.

7. Colman O'Neil says of analogy that it "has to do with the linguistic expression of a knowledge about God that is held, whether rightly or wrongly, to be *already* acquired and to be *true,* even though necessarily imperfect. . . . All that the theory of analogy is meant to do is to account for the oddities of linguistic expression which result from this conviction." "Analogy, Dialectic, and Inter-Confessional Theology," *The Thomist* 47 (1983): 43-65.

collected in chapter 1 to be clear that our predecessors had no doubt at all that they possessed knowledge about God, that they knew God, and that they understood his plan as revealed in Jesus Christ. They were equally clear that God is incomprehensible, that he is the one "who alone has immortality, who dwells in unapproachable light, and whom no human being has seen or can see" (1 Tim 6:16); "No one has ever seen God" (Jn 1:18).[8]

The theory of analogical predication is precisely an attempt to validify the two extreme tenets of faith-knowledge, namely that there is genuine knowledge of God, and that God is radically beyond all knowing. To those who hold that our knowledge of God is univocal, it suffices to point to the witness of the Scriptures and the mystics of both Testaments who assert that no one can see the face of God (Ex 33:18-20). To those who hold that all our knowledge about God is equivocal it suffices to point to the three thousand years' faith experience of God's people, who, on the level of noetic discourse, speak of what they know and what they have learned from God. To approach this witness with an a priori need for an epistemic foundation and thus to reinterpret this witness to mean that these people were speaking not of God, but merely of their subjective experience, is to reveal our present ignorance, not theirs, and it is to deny the common experience of believers who know that they know something of God even if, on the second level of discourse, they lack the means to justify it.

What then is the theory of analogy?[9] It is a theory about actual linguistic expressions of judgments. We have seen that an analogous term is one that is predicated of several different subjects with a meaning that is partly the same and partly different: "Jane is happy," "the song is happy," "that is a happy smile." In the example, the word *happy* is stretched to include Jane, where it is used properly, a song where it is used to indicate a quality expressive of and capable of communicating happiness, and a smile that is a sign of happiness.

Let us take another example. Helen is wise; God is wise. Here the

---

8. See as well Ps 139:6, 17-18; Prv 30:3-4; Sir 42: 21-22; 43: 27-30; Jb 26:14; 36:26; 37:5, 23; Rom 1:20; 11:33; 2 Cor 5:7; 9:15; 12:4.

9. For a fine brief account of the Thomistic theory of analogy, by far the most coherent, see Gregory P. Rocca, "Aquinas on God Talk: Hovering Over the Abyss," *Theological Studies* 54 (1993): 641-61. Other valuable studies include W. Norris Clarke, "Analogy and the Meaningfulness of Language About God: A Reply to Kai Nielsen," *The Thomist* (1976): 61-95; David Burrell, *Analogy and Philosophical Language* (New Haven: Yale University Press, 1973); Hans Urs von Balthasar, *The Theology of Karl Barth*, trans. Edward Oates (San Francisco: Ignatius, 1992), part II, chapters 3 and 4.

term *wise* is stretched beyond sight. We know that there is something true in predicating wisdom of God, and yet we know as well that we take our understanding of wisdom from the limited wisdom of which we have experience and that this is inapplicable to God. What kind of a mental operation is this? First, let it be clearly said that there is here no attempt to abstract the notion *wise* from both Helen and God, and thus obtain a neutral concept, which can then be applied differently to them both. Even if one were to say that in such a case the application of *wise* to God is done supereminently, that is with the acknowledgment that we are not completely sure how the concept applies to God, the result is still disastrous. How is it possible to have a concept of *wise* that is so broad and great as to somehow include God under its limits?[10] The opponents of analogical predication usually misunderstand it precisely because they consider it to be concerned with analogous concepts; but this is to misunderstand the very nature of analogy. It should be acknowledged, however, that until recently they received little help from neo-scholastic proponents of analogy who, under the sway of Kantian a priori thinking, also dealt with analogy as a discussion of the prior conditions for comparing concepts.[11]

We learn from the Bible, from the teaching of mature Christians, from the liturgical life of the church, and from our own experience that certain words such as *wise, merciful, powerful,* or *righteous* are fittingly said of God. In this regard our faith affirmations are the fruit of the light of the action of Holy Spirit strengthening the inner dynamic of our minds that tends always toward greater and greater conscious appropriation of

---

10. In the *Summa Theologiae* 1,44,1, ad 1, Aquinas deals with the objection that, since "being created" can be abstracted from some existing thing, it is possible that there could be beings not created by God. His answer is that it is of the very nature *(ratio)* of any existing thing that it be "through participation" and thus "being created" cannot be abstracted from it any more than the ability to laugh can be abstracted from a human being. The corollary is, of course, that since "being created" cannot be abstracted from our notion of being, there is a Being who is not created, but we can have no concept of him. For a list of authors who set forth the notion that analogy, particularly analogical speech about God, has to do with the judgment of applicability but not the application of concepts, see Rocca, "Aquinas on God Talk," 652, n. 47.

11. One of the important works that recovered the Thomistic understanding of analogy was that by Bernard Montagnes, *La Doctrine de L'Analogie de L'être d'après Saint Thomas d'Aquin,* Philosophes Médiévaux, 6 (Louvain/Paris: Publications Universitaires/Béatrice-Nauwelaerts, 1963). Elizabeth Johnson's study of Wolfhart Pannenberg's objections to analogy is instructive in that it reveals both his inability to understand the non-Kantian epistemological basis for analogy, and Johnson's own misunderstandings: "The Right Way to Speak About God? Pannenberg on Analogy," *Theological Studies* 43 (1982): 673-92.

reality.[12] Aquinas sought an ontological basis for our conviction that the resultant knowledge of God, while radically inadequate, is nonetheless true. He found it in the generosity of God's creative act by which he confers on creatures a share in his ineffable being. This is, perhaps, the clearest concise expression of his thinking.

> Names are predicated according to proportion [recall the Greek *analogia*] in two ways: either because many things bear a proportion to one reality, as medicine and urine are called healthy insofar as both possess an order and proportion to the animal's health, since medicine is the cause of health and urine is one of its signs; or because one thing bears a direct proportion to the other, as medicine and the animal are called healthy insofar as medicine is the cause of the health which exists in the animal. *And in this second way some things are predicated of God and creatures analogically, neither purely equivocally nor univocally. For we are not able to name God except from creatures, and thus whatever is said about God and creatures is predicated inasmuch as the creature is ordered to God as to its causal principle in whom all the perfections of things preexist surpassingly.* Now the analogical type of commonality is a mean between pure equivocity and simple univocity. For in analogical predications there is neither one meaning, as occurs in univocal predications, nor totally diverse meanings, as occurs in equivocal predications, but the name which is predicated analogically in multiple ways signifies different proportions to one single reality: as when *healthy*, said of urine, refers to the sign of an animal's health, but when said of medicine signifies the cause of that same health.[13]

In the earlier part of this same article, Aquinas makes another observation that is important for our purposes. In speaking of the manner in which we apply the term *wise* to God and to a human being, he notes that we must attend to three things. First, *what* is said of God and the human being *(res significata),* namely an endowment they both possess. Second, *the meaning* of what is said *(ratio nominis),* in this case *wisdom.* Third, *the way* in which

---

12. This is how W. Norris Clarke describes it: "The general rule is this: whenever the mind finds it rationally necessary or fruitful, either under the anticipation of a possible new dimension of experience [a projective model in science] or under the pressure of finding necessary conditions of intelligibility outside our experience for what we encounter within our experience, it simply expands its conscious horizon of being as intelligible to open up some new determinate beachhead in the already unlimited, indeterminate horizon of being in which the mind lives implicitly all the time." *The Philosophical Approach to God,* 53.

13. *Summa Theologiae* 1,13,5,c. Trans. by Rocca, "Aquinas on God Talk," 655; first italics mine.

it is said *(modus significandi)*, in this case a predication, a positive statement.[14] In the statement "God is wise," we have no direct knowledge of the
referent of the first word — we do not "see" God. Furthermore, we cannot
conceive of the way *(modus signficandi)* in which the word *is* applies to God
since it refers to an identity between God and his wisdom, and this is literally
inconceivable. Therefore, the full *meaning (ratio nominis)* of the term *wisdom* as applied to God likewise escapes us. We do know this, however: God
is the "causal principle in whom all the perfections of things preexist
surpassingly," and therefore our noetic predication and our reflexive
epistemic judgment which concludes that it is appropriate to say "wise" of
God are grounded in reality. The statement "God is wise" and other similar
statements made in the biblical tradition are literally true. While these realities
are *named* from creatures to God, they actually apply *primarily* to God and
then by extension to creatures: "to the only wise God, through Jesus Christ
be glory for ever and ever. Amen!" (Rom 16:27).

So far, the discussion has been limited to terms that apply to God, as
denoting the divine reality shared by the Persons of the Trinity. Although, as
we will see in the next chapter, this is contrary to the nearly unanimous New
Testament use of *Theos* to refer to the Father, within a Christian milieu that is
strong and aware of itself, it is a valid form of predication. The question now
posed concerns the words that do refer precisely to the divine Persons: are they
metaphorical or analogical? As applied to predication about God, the distinction between metaphor and analogy is this: analogical terms, as we have just
seen, apply primarily to God and secondarily to creatures; metaphorical terms,
on the other hand, apply primarily to creatures and only secondarily to God.
The term *Father,* for instance, as meaning *source* or *creator* is applied
metaphorically to the divine nature as shared by all three Persons — *God* is
the source of all that is. In another way, since the Father in the Trinity is the
source of all within the Trinity itself, it is apt to assign (the theological term is
appropriate) the act of creating to him, though this act is one that is common
to all three Persons. There is, finally, the naming of *Theos* as *Patēr* in a personal
way, and this deserves some particular consideration.

The authority for the names by which we call upon the Persons of
the Trinity derives not from a faith experience of the created world but
from the teaching of the New Testament as this directs and confirms the
faith experience of the church and of individual believers.[15] This will be

14. For an extended treatment of this distinction see Gregory Rocca, "Res
Significata and Modus Significandi in Aquinas," *The Thomist* 55 (1991): 173-98.
15. See J. Coppens, "Dieu le Père dans la théologie paulinienne. Note sur *Theos
patēr,*" in *La Notion Biblique de Dieu. Le Dieu de la Bible et le Dieu des Philosophes,*

considered at length in the following chapter. Here I wish merely to indicate that such predication is not metaphorical but analogical.

The objection is often made that since God is absolutely unknowable, names such as *Father* and *Son* can only express one's experience of God, not really anything about God himself. Thus, the first-order or noetic expressions of the New Testament are reinterpreted in the light of an a priori epistemology that puts experience not as its source of knowledge but as the ruling norm for knowledge. This contradicts the testimony of the New Testament, as well as the traditional understanding of revelation as an initiative on the part of God (see chapter 1). The experience of believers over the centuries is that they know themselves to be in contact with the Persons of the Trinity and that it is their love that moves them toward *Theos* even as their mind acknowledges its own inadequacy. When Celsus claimed that there can be no real knowledge of God since he is inaccessible by word *(logô ephiktos)*, Origen responded with a distinction: If it were a question of a *logos* in us, either interior or expressed, then it would certainly be true that God is inaccessible by word. When, however, we read that the *Logos* was near to God and is God, certainly then God is accessible to this Word, and he is understood *(katalambanomenos)* not only by this *Logos* himself but also by those to whom he reveals the Father.[16]

Once again, however, even in regard to the human language given to us by the Son and by the Holy Spirit through the New Testament tradition, we must apply what was said above about analogical predication. The terms *Father, Son,* and *Holy Spirit* apply to the Persons of the Trinity truly but imperfectly.[17] We understand to some degree the meaning *(ratio nominis)* of these terms, but how they apply and the manner in which they signify something of God is lost to us in the infinite abyss of God's mystery. Thus, the *economic* terms applied to the Trinity give us true but imperfect, analogous knowledge of the Persons of the Trinity.[18] Because this knowledge is personal, it varies in depth and intimacy according to the intensity with which the believer has appropriated the inner life of Christ.

---

ed. J. Coppens, Bibliotheca Ephemeridum Theologicarum Lovaniensium XLI (Gembloux, Leuven: Duculot, Leuven University Press, 1976), 331-35.

16. *Against Celsus* 6, 65 (*Sources Chrétiennes* 147, 342). For a fine study of the relationship between knowing and loving God in the thought of St. Ephrem, see Robert Murray, "St Ephrem's Dialogue of Reason and Love," *Sobornost/Eastern Churches Review* 2 (1980): 26-40.

17. Another triadic expression in the New Testament is that of *Pneuma, Kyrios,* and *Theos,* where *Theos* and *Kyrios* are names for Persons, but not necessarily personal names.

18. I will return to this in the following chapter.

FEMININE IMAGES OF GOD

One of the most profound and all-pervasive manifestations of the human mind's capacity to course through the whole universe, delighting in the manifold manifestations of being and in the surprising way in which individual realities reflect and illumine each other, is found precisely in the capacity to form images.[19] After some brief general considerations, this section will concentrate on feminine images for God in the Christian tradition. It is an eloquent testimony to the power of the crystallization mentioned in chapter 4 that not only has there been excessive suspicion of feminine images for God in the last two centuries, but it now requires extensive historical research to recover the fact of such imagery and disciplined theological reflection to understand it correctly.

An "Image," says Ezra Pound, "is that which presents an intellectual and emotional complex in an instant of time. . . . It is the presentation of such a 'complex' instantaneously which gives us the sense of sudden liberation; that sense of freedom from time limits and space limits; that sense of sudden growth, which we experience in the presence of the greatest works of art."[20] This same notion of *complex* is found in the descriptions of Gilbert Durand, who speaks of a "chain" or "constellation," a "swarm" or a "packet."[21]

Durand goes further and criticizes Sartre for not seeing in an image anything but a quasi-object, Eliade for classifying images according to objects (heaven, earth, stars, etc.), Bachelard for making the same error on the basis of elements (air, fire, water, etc.), and Freud for a mechanical treatment of images all motivated by the *Lustprinzip*.[22] All of these theoreticians insist too strongly on the *objectivizing* referent of symbols and fail to take account of how they are functioning in the consciousness of the symbol maker and receiver.[23] Durand correctly finds fault with such investigators who neglect the "non-linéarité" of images and who err "par un positivisme objectif qui tente a motiver les symbols uniquement l'aide de *données extrinsíques la conscience imaginante.*"[24] As it originates in

19. For a good introduction to this image-making faculty of a human being, see Gilbert Durand, *Les Structures Anthropologiques de L'Imaginaire,* 11th ed. (Paris: Dunod, 1992).

20. Ezra Pound, *Literary Essays of Ezra Pound,* ed. T. S. Eliot (London: Faber and Faber, 1960), 4.

21. *Les Structures,* introduction.

22. Ibid., 27-40.

23. This "objectification" is, however, considered within the confines of a representationalist epistemology. I will return to this.

24. Ibid., 35, emphasis mine.

the "imagining consciousness" of both the author and the recipient, the primary function of the image/symbol is to create an interior symbolic space that mediates (not represents) some facet of an object, an event, a person, an experience. One of the secrets of the power of imagery is that it draws energy from that mysterious inner point where body, psyche, cosmos, and society meet. The body supplies the basic sensible forms through its interaction with the cosmos, the psyche transposes and combines these into images while at the same time participating in the communicated image world of human intercourse. Durand is correct in maintaining that the experience of the body and its sensory and motor functions form the distillation point ("schème") for our images.[25]

Images can be classified according to the degree of their interiority. They cover a spectrum that runs all the way from those images that create a "mood" through which some reality is mediated to images that explicitly direct attention to some referent. Metaphors belong to this latter type. For an example of interiority, consider, for instance, these lines of John of the Cross:

> My beloved, the mountains,
> lonely wooded valleys,
> strange islands,
> sounding rivers,
> the whistling of breezes full of love.[26]

This complex gives us a sense of "sudden liberation and delight," and, to the degree that there is recognition, it touches us with both memory and desire. The space within us is filled with a presence that is at once ineffable and attractive. Although we are changed, we sense that we are changed by Someone, the Beloved — the impression created within us draws us out beyond itself to what it mediates. The image itself is a structure, an autonomous entity made up of a system of internal dependence. It is in movement

---

25. After relating what he calls "schème" to what others have called "symbole fonctionnel" (Piaget) or "symbole moteur" (Bachelard), Durand goes on to say of the schème: "Il fait la jonction, non plus comme le voulait Kant, entre l'image et le concept, mais *entre les gestes inconscients de la sensori-motoricité, entre les dominates réflexes et les représentations*. Ce sont ces schèmes qui forment le squelette dynamique, le canevas fonctionnel de l'imagination." *Les Structures*, 61; emphasis mine. This whole view can be seen to coalesce with that of Antoine Vergote's notion of the "psychic body" to be discussed in chapter 12. In that chapter I will also argue that the human body, female or male, both as subjective experience and as communicable symbol, expresses different aspects of causality.

26. *The Spiritual Canticle,* 13.

from intimacy to vast heights, protected and mysterious woodlands, far-away strangeness, exuberant movement and sound, back to an unelicited tenderness. The rhyme joins mountains to islands and manages to evoke seclusion, exuberance, and intimacy.

As an example of an image that seeks less to mediate by creating an interior space than by uncovering a hidden dimension, consider this famous line from Flaubert: "Human language is like a cracked kettle on which we beat out tunes for bears to dance to, when all the while we are longing to move the stars to pity." Cacophonous clanging, dancing bears, frustrated longing, unattainable heights, all of these provide a sense of "sudden growth" when the irony and pathos of our words are compassionately unmasked for us.

Although images can sometimes be cryptic analogies, this is not the case in the two examples given. Analogy asserts correspondence based on something shared; image, either interior or metaphorical, creates a climate for intuition and discloses something previously hidden. When what is intuited or disclosed is based on an objective correspondence, there can be that judgment of something shared which is the heart of analogy.

Feminine Imagery for God in the Bible

Because biblical speech is for the most part noetic rather than epistemic, we would expect it to abound in images and metaphors, and this is particularly true of the Old Testament.[27] We should note as well that the very extension of the semantic range of many Hebrew words makes the language a unique medium for the kind of evocative imagery we are discussing. This can be seen, for instance, in the manner in which anthropological terms are used symbolically.[28]

Old Testament imagery is found all along a spectrum, moving from images that create an interior climate to those which disclose. An example of the first type can be found in the foreboding picture of Judah's future in Jeremiah 4:19-26:

27. In addition to the work of Alonso Schökel already referred to, one can profitably consult Robert Alter, *The Art of Biblical Poetry* (New York: Basic Books, 1985); see the index under "imagery."

28. This will be touched upon briefly in chapter 11. For a more complete treatment see Hans Walter Wolff, *Anthropology of the Old Testament*, trans. Margaret Kohl (Philadelphia: Fortress, 1974), and especially Edouard Dhorme, *L'emploi métaphorique des noms de parties du corps en hébreux et en accadien* (Paris: Lecoffre, 1923).

My chest, my chest — the pain!
The house of my heart, inside my heart is surging
I cannot be still. . . .
I look at the earth, behold
waste and emptiness
at the heavens —
there is no light.
I look at the mountains, behold
they are shaking,
at the hills —
and they quake.
I look, behold
there is no one,
the birds of the heavens have flown away.
I look, behold
the garden is a desert,
all the cities are ravaged and charred
before Yhwh,
before his scowling flame.

Jeremiah the poet is using some of the same imagery as John of the Cross
(nature in general, the mountains in particular), but here the impression is one
of desolation, and the last line of the poem moves from the impressionistic
mode to that of direct predication, though still imaged ("scowling flame").

There are also many examples of images that disclose, as in these
lines from Hosea 11:1-4:

When Israel was a youth, I loved him;
Out of Egypt I called, "my son."
I call to them,
but they only walk away from me.
To the Baals they sacrifice,
to idols they burn their incense.
Yet it was I who helped Ephraim to walk,
I took him up in my arms;
and they did not know
that I cared for them.
With human ties I tugged at them,
with cords of love.
I was to them,
like one raising a suckling child
up close to his cheek.
I stooped to them and fed them.

The ruling image here, developed at some length, is that of a father. The text acts to disclose behind the events of the Exodus a tenderness and intimate care that have never changed. As the soliloquy continues, God thinks of destroying them; it is not Moses who steps in but God's own heart: "my own heart turns against me" (Hos 11:8).

Before approaching directly those instances where there are surely or possibly feminine images for God in the Old Testament, it is important to advert to those occasions when the imagery would be expected, given the milieu in which Israel lived, and is not found. First, obviously, is the fact that for Israel there is only one God, he has no consort, and his proper name is Yhwh, which is the masculine form of a verb.[29] Second, while the Hebrew verb system distinguishes between masculine and feminine subjects, there is not one verb in the Old Testament to be found in the feminine form when God is the subject. Given the imagery of language itself, to be discussed shortly, this is significant. Third, there is a near total absence of what is called "gender-matched synonymous parallelism" in speaking of God.[30] This poetic convention often dictates that a word of different gender be used in the parallel stich of a verse. It is very obvious in sentences such as: "A wise son makes a glad father, but a foolish son is a sorrow to his mother" (Prv 10:1).[31] On the basis of this convention we might expect to find in Jeremiah 3:18, "For I have been to Israel as a father, as a mother to Ephraim my first born son." In fact, we find: "For I have been to Israel as a father, while Ephraim is my first born son." Many other instances could be adduced to show that the absence of this type of gender parallelism in regard to God is significant.[32]

The scholar most often invoked by feminists in regard to feminine imagery for God is Phyllis Trible; and it is to her work that I now turn.[33]

---

29. Although it is difficult to establish, it may be a rare causative form. The possibility that the name is applied to a god of Samaria who has a consort, if this attribution is accepted, strengthens the position that the name is masculine. For a discussion of the name and a basic bibliography, see the article by Henry O. Thompson in *The Anchor Bible Dictionary* 6, 1011-12.

30. The term derives from the study of Wilfred G. E. Watson, "Gender-Matched Synonymous Parallelism in the Old Testament," *Journal of Biblical Literature* 99 (1980): 321-44.

31. Other examples of father-mother parallelism in Proverbs would be 4:3; 15:20; and 23:22.25.

32. I owe this observation to Mayer I. Gruber, "The Motherhood of God in Second Isaiah," *Revue Biblique* 90 (1983): 351-59. Gruber, however, does not consider these four texts in their function as images.

33. "God, Nature of, In the OT," in *The Interpreter's Dictionary of the Bible*, Supplementary Volume, ed. Keith Crim (Nashville: Abingdon, 1976), 368-69; *God and the Rhetoric of Sexuality*, Overtures to Biblical Theology (Philadelphia: Fortress, 1978).

If we look at the feminine images for God in the Old Testament,[34] we find
that the surest examples are to be found in four passages in the second part
of Isaiah.

> Yhwh like a warrior goes forth
> like a soldier he stirs up his fury,
> he shouts, yes he roars,
> over his foes he proves to be mighty.
> I have been silent for an age
> I have said nothing, holding myself in,
> like a woman in labor I groan
> I gasp and pant together.
>
> (42:13-14)

> Woe to him who contends with his Fashioner. . . .
> Woe to him who says to a father
> "What are you begetting?"
> and to a woman
> "What are you bringing to birth?"
>
> (45:9-10)

> Zion says:
> Yhwh has abandoned me
> my Lord has forgotten me.
> Does a woman forget her nursling
> or not pity the child of her womb?
> Even if they do forget
> I will not forget you.
>
> (49:14-15)

> As a man whose mother comforts him
> so I will comfort you
> and in Jerusalem you will be comforted.
>
> (66:13)

In the first of these texts, Yhwh's war cry is described as having been
pent up and is now bursting forth like the cries and groans, gasping and
panting, of a woman in labor. It is a striking image, but one that is glancing.
It creates an impression and leaves, neither allowing (or expecting) a

---

34. The only New Testament candidate is the image of the hen who gathers her chicks
under her wings (Mt 23:37; Lk 13:34). This is greatly exploited in patristic and medieval
spirituality. The image of a (mother) bird is also found in Dt 32:11 and Ex 19:4.

prolonged and linear referential movement of the mind. We have here a symbolic code that juxtaposes man of war/woman in labor as expressive of an inner compulsion to cry out.

There is little agreement as to the overall context for Isaiah 45:9-13, but the argument of the verses that concern us is clear.[35] A curse is pronounced against the one who would contend *(rāb)* with his Fashioner *(yōṣrô)*. The foolishness of such a thing is developed in three images: clay that says to its fashioner, "What are you doing?"; someone who says to a father (not *"his* father"), "What are you begetting?"; and someone who says to a woman (not "his mother"), "What are you bringing to birth?" Here we have three images thrown up for us to look at, which in turn compare God to a potter, to a father begetting, and to a woman giving birth. Again, there is no concentration upon the feminine image: it functions as one of three examples of the authority of the producer over the produced.

In Isaiah 49:14-15 we have the juxtaposition of the symbolic codes of bridegroom/bride and mother/child, applying the first in each case to Yhwh. Examples of the juxtaposition of images that in their objectifying dimension are simply incompatible abound in the Old Testament. For additional examples, one could consider the symbolic code of unfaithful women/spouse, child/father in Jeremiah 3:2-4, or son/father, unfaithful woman/spouse in Jeremiah 3:19-20; husband/unfaithful wife in Hosea 1-3, or father/son in Hosea 11.[36] In the text under consideration we have a disclosure image that reveals something of God — a love that is more tender and more loyal than even that of a mother for her child. This is significant in that it chooses not the tender love of a father as in Hosea 11 or Psalm 103:13 but that of a mother.

The last text is also significant in this regard. By making the comparison begin with the recipient ("As a man whose mother comforts him") the image is interiorized. A climate is produced that allows the audience to feel in anticipation the promised intimacy and trust in the act of being comforted by the Lord.

Of the four clear texts, two are disclosure images or symbols, they are a complex, they surely spring from and address the image-making juncture between body, psyche, cosmos, and society, and they reveal some-

35. See Claus Westermann, *Isaiah 40–66,* The Old Testament Library, trans. David M. G. Stalker (Philadephia: Westminster, 1969), 164-68; John Watts, *Isaiah 34–66,* Word Biblical Commentary 25 (Waco: Word Books, 1987), 157.

36. For Is 49:14-15 see Rémi Lack, *La Symbolique du Livre d'Isaie,* Analecta Biblica 59 (Rome: Pontifical Biblical Institute, 1973), 174. A complete list of the symbolic code pairs in Hosea can be found in Hans Walter Wolff, *Hosea,* Hermeneia, trans. Gary Stansell, ed. Paul D. Hanson (Philadelphia: Fortress Press, 1974), xxiv. Alonso Schökel considers incompatible images in his *Manual of Hebrew Poetics.*

thing about God. Repeated use of these images, something not done in the Scriptures, could make analogies of them. In any event, they mediate a new dimension of the tenderness and bondedness of God's love for his people. This is true revelation in that it manifests something about *God* and not merely something of someone's experience of the Transcendent.

To these certain uses of feminine imagery in regard to God, Phyllis Trible would like to add some particular uses of language. The first of these has to do with the use of the root *rhm*. She writes:

> Designating a place of protection and care, the womb *(rehem)* is a basic metaphor of divine compassion. The metaphor begins with a physical organ unique to the female and extends to psychic levels in the noun *rehamim* (mercies), in the adjective form *rahum* (merciful), and in the uses of the verb *raham* (to show mercy). It moves from the literal to the figurative, from the concrete to the abstract.[37]

There are two fallacies here. One has to do with usage and the other with derivation. In regard to usage, it is extremely difficult at this distance to judge whether our philological sensitivity, based on a tiny body of literature, in any way reflects the overtones of a word, regardless of its derivation, that might still be felt by an audience hearing the term in its original context. Few of us, for instance, would think of *womb* when hearing the word *hysterical,* though its derivation from the Greek word for womb *(hystera,* as in *hysterectomy)* is undoubted. Again, one of the clearest occurrences of the root *rhm* is in a text that explicitly ascribes this quality to a *father:* "As a father has compassion *(rahēm)* on his sons, so does Yhwh have compassion *(riham)* on those who fear him" (Ps 103:13).

In regard to derivation, namely the assertion that all the usages of the root *rhm* derive from and reflect the Hebrew word for womb, there are two difficulties. First, it is not at all clear that *rehem* is the source of the other words. The word for tender mercy *(rahûm)* could have been the source, or another root, now found in Arabic *(rahuma,* soft) could be the originating root.[38] From another aspect, Gruber argues that the Akkadian word *ra'āmu,* (love) is as likely a candidate for the derivation of the Hebrew term and usage as is the Akkadian *rēmu* (womb).[39] This may be confirmed by the fact that,

---

37. "God, Nature of," 368.
38. For a discussion of this and many other philological aspects see Paul Mankowski, "Old Testament Iconology and the Nature of God," in *The Politics of Prayer: Feminist Language and the Worship of God,* ed. Helen Hull Hitchcock (San Francisco: Ignatius, 1992), 151-76; especially pp. 161-62.
39. "The Motherhood of God," 352-53 and note 6.

in contradiction to Trible's statement that the use of *rahûm* is "distinctive to
the Mosaic faith,"[40] there are extant some fifty-two Akkadian names from
one period alone that refer to a god (all but five of whom are masculine) and
contain the word under discussion.[41] Either the word does not, as Trible
maintains, allude to an organ "unique to the female" (more male than female
gods in Akkadian have the quality) or the Hebrew word, especially as applied
to God, derives rather from the Akkadian word *ra'āmu*, (love).[42] In any case,
while tender compassion is certainly predicated of God, and is sometimes so
predicated using the root *rḥm*, Trible's use of this fact, in regard to both
philology and usage, is incorrect.

Another text studied by Trible is found in Deuteronomy 32:6, 8-9,
18:[43]

> Is he not your Father who created you,
> who made you and established you? . . .
> For Yhwh's portion is his people,
> Jacob his allotted inheritance.
> He found him in a desert land
> and in the howling waste of the wilderness. . . .
> You were unmindful of the Rock who begot you,
> and you forgot the God who gave you birth.

The dating of this text is notoriously difficult. Frank M. Cross considers
it to be very early, reflecting linguistic usage and imagery characteristic
of the beginning of the Iron Age.[44] Others consider the language to be
more archaizing than archaic.[45] The term translated above (RSV) as
"created you" *(qânekâ)* presents no problem: the root generally means
"to acquire" either by giving birth (Gen 4:1), or producing (Prv 8:22),
or the like.[46] The same can be said for the root *yld,* which underlies the

---

40. Ibid.

41. For example Irimanni-Marduk, "Marduk is compassionate toward me." See
Mankowski, "Old Testament Iconology," 163, and the literature referred to there.

42. Trible also maintains that the term *raûm* is "used only of the deity" (ibid.).
But this ignores the better reading, accepted by nearly all commentators, of Ps 112:4.

43. *God and the Rhetoric of Sexuality,* 62-64.

44. *Canaanite Myth and Hebrew Epic* (Cambridge, Mass.: Harvard University
Press, 1973), 68, 72.

45. For a brief discussion and bibliography see Peter C. Craigie, *The Book of
Deuteronomy,* The New International Commentary on the Old Testament (Grand
Rapids: Eerdmans, 1976), 373-76.

46. See the article *"qnh"* by W. H. Schmidt in *Theologisches Handwörterbuch
zum Alten Testament,* vol. 2, ed. Ernst Jenni and Claus Westermann (Munich: Kaiser,
1984), 650-59.

term *begot.* It is generally acknowledged that it applies to the action of either a male or a female. The term translated "gave you birth" by the RSV is a *masculine* participial form of the root *hyl,* which evokes the notion of pain in the loins that a woman experiences in labor, and in the manner already referred to, particularly in regard to Semitic language and use of imagery, can be extended to apply to other similar pains. Trible is simply wrong to state that the word describes "only a woman in labor pains."[47] Not only is there extrabiblical evidence that the root can also be applied figuratively to men and even to the land, but it often compares the spasmodic contractions caused by fear rather than the action itself of giving birth (e.g., Is 21:3), and once (Prv 25:23) it speaks of the wind giving birth to the rain.[48] Once again we are confronted with a misunderstanding of the role of images and metaphors in speech and the forcing of an image out of its allusive function. In the text of Deuteronomy we are meant only to see an allusion to God's begetting of Israel through his choice of them, and perhaps also to the struggle with the forces that opposed him. This text will be considered again in chapter 9.

Genesis 49:25 contains part of the blessing pronounced on Joseph:

> by the God of your father — may he help you
> and *'el šadday* — may he bless you
> the blessings of heaven above
> the blessings of the deep lying below
> the blessings of breasts *(šādayim)* and womb *(rāḥam).*

This part of the blessing is clearly linked to fertility; the blessings from heaven (rain) and the blessings of the deep (springs) both have to do with water. This leads to a consideration of human fertility described in terms of breasts and womb.[49] There is an undoubted word play intended by the use of the divine title *šadday* and the mention of breasts *(šādayim),* and this is particularly evocative since both terms are related. The title *'el šadday,* with or without *'el,* occurs forty-eight times in the Old Testament and refers to God as the "God of the mountains" or even "the exalted

---

47. "God, Nature of," 368.

48. See H. Eising, *"hyl,"* in *Theological Dictionary of the Old Testament,* vol. IV, ed. G. Johannes Botterweck and Helmer Ringgren, trans. David E. Green (Grand Rapids: Eerdmans, 1980), 344-55: "Much more common than direct reference to actual birth is the figurative use of the verb in situations of anxiety or fear, which outwardly recall the manifestations of labor" (p. 345).

49. See the curse in Hos 9:14, "miscarrying womb and dry breasts," cited by Trible, *God and the Rhetoric,* 61.

God" or "the exalted One."[50] Trible would interpret the play on words to imply that the notion of "breasts" has been recovered in this instance and thus that "[t]he God of the breasts gives the blessings of the breasts."[51] Although the words are etymologically related, it would be incorrect (or distorting) to translate the phrase in a way other than according to its primary meaning. The rich overtones (in which the language abounds) are meant to be background associations and not to replace the primary cognate. Trible's interpretation is another instance of the "linéarité" criticized by Durand.

Perhaps an example from modern Arabic will help. *Nuhad* is a woman's name. According to the colloquial use of the word, it refers to an elevated or honored position; applied to a person it means one in an eminent position with overtones of generosity.[52] According to the dictionary, however, the word is linked etymologically to the root *nhd* which means "to become round and full, [of breasts] to swell." If a man were to exploit all this in a poem about his wife Nuhad, he would be able to portray an honored, prominent woman, generous and fruitful, whose abundant and full breasts are the symbol of her ability to care for and nourish those about her, especially the children she brings into the world. The average Arabic speaker would respond to all of this even though none of it had entered his or her mind beforehand. I suspect that if we had literature in any abundance from the biblical period we would see that the word *šadday* was equally exploitable.

My point in all of this is to indicate how important it is to understand images as *mediating* by evocation rather than representing by direct referential allusions. Although there are other positions adopted by Trible that are equally wooden, my object is not to find fault with the search for feminine imagery in regard to God, though by any account it is extremely rare in the Bible. I wish rather to distinguish a poetic use of these images from an interpretation that has them declare things about God when they are really doing something much deeper. They are creating within us a space that adapts our imagination to some aspect of God, or they are hinting

50. For the statistics and basic information see the article *"šaddaj"* by M. Weippert in *Theologisches Handwörterbuch zum Alten Testament,* vol. 2, 874-82, and the remarks by Frank M. Cross, *Canaanite Myth and Hebrew Epic,* 52-60, who sees the primitive meaning to be "breast," but considers the name as applied to God to mean "the mountain one."

51. "God, Nature of," 368

52. I owe this explanation and reference to a personal communication from my colleague Ihsan Handal. For the root meaning, see *El-Munjid* 841, col. 2 (Beirut: Dar el-Mashreq, 1975).

at and disclosing something about God himself, something that the male images of God, frequently as they occur, are not able to do.

Another fruitful source of feminine imagery for God is to be found in the manner in which Wisdom is described. A beginning has been made in reflecting on this material and more must be done.[53] Since, however, the development of the Christological implications of this imagery is found in the patristic period, I will treat it in the next section.

Feminine Imagery in the Postbiblical Tradition

It is simply a fact that very early in the Christian tradition feminine images were applied to God to a degree not known in the Old Testament or Judaism. It is as though once the identity of the Persons in the Trinity was secure, once the Father, the Son, and the Holy Spirit were intimately known, people felt free to speak of them, especially the Son and the Spirit, in feminine terms. This mode of speech was quite common in the language of both prayer and theology until the two began to drift apart (see chapter 2). Although this and most other forms of imagery seem to have been gradually exiled from theological circles, feminine images continued to be used in the contemplative milieu, reaching a high point in the *Showings* of the fourteenth century English mystic Julian of Norwich, and figuring in such works as Langland's *Piers the Ploughman,* Dante's *Convivio,* and the like.[54] As the loss of a biblical mentality set in, imagery seemed strange as applied to the Divine Persons, and with a return to Deism in the eighteenth century it was simply ignored. The Enlightenment mind-set of the founders of modern history writing found little of interest in the history of women and even less in feminine imagery for God. That obliges modern students of history to work at recovering this imagery in order to achieve a more balanced understanding of our past.

The difficulty, however, is that much of the recovery has been under-taken up to now by feminist scholars whose often unrecognized epistemology is representationalist. Thus, the images are taken to be culturally conditioned efforts to articulate individual experience rather than a socially shared means

---

53. See for instance Claudia V. Camp, *Wisdom and the Feminine in the Book of Proverbs* (Sheffield: JSOT Press, 1985). The study by Elizabeth Johnson, "Jesus, the Wisdom of God: A Biblical Basis for Non-Androcentric Christology," *Ephemerides Theologicae Lovanienses* 61 (1985): 261-94, is clumsy in its understanding of how imagery functions and too intent on berating Philo as a misogynist to do the material justice.

54. For information on the history of feminine imagery in Christan history one may consult Ritamary Bradley, "Patristic background of the motherhood similitude in Julian of Norwich," *Christian Scholars Review* 8 (1978): 101-13.

of mediating knowledge of God. The few paragraphs that follow are, obviously, not a treatise on the subject of Christian feminine imagery for the Trinity. That treatise remains to be written and will be of great service. I would only remark that, by its nature, such a work of historical theology will have to be done by those who have experience of what they are writing about. In terms of the potential whole of theology, there must be not only the essence but also much of the power of a lived faith seeking understanding.

Although feminine imagery is sometimes applied to the Father, it is more often applied to the Spirit, and most frequently, at least in the West, it is used in regard to Christ. I will begin with some examples of application to the Holy Spirit.[55] Two different dimensions of the biblical tradition contributed to this application. First, the fact that the term *spirit* was used in connection with Wisdom in the Old Testament, and second, the fact that in semitic languages, in this case particularly Syriac (the Christian dialect of Aramaic), the term for spirit is feminine *(ruḥā')*. This latter fact is joined in the Syriac tradition with the image of the eagle hovering over its young in Deuteronomy 32:11 (in Hebrew *yěraḥēp*, masculine), which is assimilated to the Spirit in Genesis 1:2, who hovered over the waters *(měraḥepet,* feminine). This assimilation is exploited because of the overtones of the Syriac root *rḥp,* which includes notions of "cherish, pity, take care of." An example of a text that exploits the grammatical gender of *ruḥā'* and utilizes this allusion is found in the *Demonstration* (6,14) of Aphrahat: "For by baptism we receive the Spirit of Christ, and at that moment when the priests invoke the Spirit, She opens the heavens and descends and hovers over the waters, and those who are baptized put her on. For the Spirit is far from all who are born of the body until they come to birth from water, and they receive the Holy Spirit."[56] Such examples could be

55. For background and further literature see Yves Congar, *I Believe in the Holy Spirit,* vol. 3, trans. David Smith (New York: Seabury, 1983), part III, chapter 3, "The Motherhood of God and the Feminity of the Holy Spirit," 15-64; Susan Ashbrook Harvey, "Feminine Imagery for the Divine: The Holy Spirit, the Odes of Solomon, and Early Syriac Tradition," *St. Vladimir's Theological Quarterly* 37 (1993): 111-40.

56. Translation by Harvey, "Feminine Imagery," 117. See also *Odes of Solomon* 28, 1-2. Harvey points out that the earlier ambiguity in the way in which *ruḥā'* took either feminine or masculine verbal and adjectival forms when applied to the Holy Spirit was resolved by the beginning of the fifth century in favor of masculine forms. No satisfactory explanation has been found for this (the Syriac term that translates *logos* is also feminine, yet did not give rise to feminine imagery). It may be best accounted for by the desire to conform Syriac theological expressions to those of the Greeks and Latins; consult Harvey 118-21. This need not indicate some misogynist reaction, but rather a reduction of the linguistic possibilities available to image the Persons of the Trinity, the first two of whom were certainly considered to be more *he* than *she.*

multiplied particularly from the *Odes of Solomon* and the writings of Ephrem, and it may be noted that feminine imagery is applied both to the Father and to the Son in this tradition.

I wish now to give some examples of how feminine imagery, particularly that of mother, is applied to Christ.[57] Such speech derives from four matrices: exploitation of the grammatical femininity of Wisdom (already begun in the Old Testament); the image of the hen in Matthew 23:37 and Luke 13:34; the pain and blood by which we were given new life on the cross;[58] and the nourishment, guidance, and formation given to us now. Most often the themes are found combined. I will give several examples from the patristic period.

Clement of Alexandria:

O wonderful mystery! The Father of the universe is one, the Logos of the universe is one, and the Holy Spirit one and the same everywhere. One as well is the virgin become mother which I love to call the church. This mother when alone had no milk because alone she had not become a woman. She is at one and the same time virgin and mother; uncontaminated as a virgin, full of love as a mother. She calls her little ones to herself and nurses them with a holy milk, that is, the Word for nurslings. She did not have milk because the milk was this fair and comely child, the body of Christ, and thus she nurses them with the Word, these young ones, whom the Lord himself brought forth in the birth pangs of flesh, and swathed in his precious blood. Amazing birth, holy swaddling bands! The Word is all to the child: father, mother, pedagogue and nurse. He said, "Eat my flesh and drink my blood." This is for us suitable nourishment which the Lord generously supplies. He offers his flesh and pours out his blood; nothing is lacking to the little ones so that they might grow.[59]

57. In addition to the article by Bradley already mentioned, see the pioneering study by André Cabassut, "Une dévotion médiévale peu connue. La dévotion à 'Jésus nôtre mère'," *Revue d'ascétique et de mystique* 25 (1949): 234-45; and Carolyn Walker Bynum, *Jesus as Mother: Studies in the Spirituality of the High Middle Ages* (Berkeley: University of California, 1982).

58. The notion that the church was born from the side of Christ on the cross is, in our own day, an instance of a "lexicalized" metaphor: one that ceases to evoke wonder and is rather a stock figure of speech.

59. *The Pedagogue* 1,6,42,1-3 (*Sources Chrétiennes* 70, 186-88). This whole section is replete with images of Christ nursing his little ones with his blood. Clement is basing himself on the notion that a woman's blood becomes, in her breasts, milk for her child. See sections 43,4; 45,1; 49,3. See as well *Who is the Rich Man Being Saved?* 38 (*Patrologia Graeca* 9, 642), where Clement says that God in his ineffability is Father, but in his mercy towards us is Mother.

Augustine:

This kind of animal [the hen] has great affection for her little ones to the extent that, moved by their weakness, she becomes weak and you will find [in her] what is rather difficult for other animals: protecting her little ones with her wings, she fights against the kite. So too, our mother the Wisdom of God, who became weak to some extent by taking on flesh . . . protects *(protegit)* our weakness and resists the devil lest he snatch us away.[60]

The psalmist makes himself small in regard to God. He makes God his father, and he makes God his mother. God is a father because he created, calls, commands, rules. God is a mother because he warms, nourishes, nurses, holds.[61]

John Chrysostom:

Have you seen how Christ unites himself to his bride? Have you seen with what food he nurtures us all? It is by the same food that we have been formed and fed. Just as a woman nurtures her offspring with her own blood and milk, so also Christ continually nurtures with his own blood those whom he has begotten.[62]

"For how often would I have gathered your children together, even as a hen gathers her chickens, but you were not willing." He says this to show that they were scattering themselves by their sins. He shows them his love by this similitude since the hen has such warm love for her brood. This same image of wings is found everywhere in the prophets and in the Song of Moses and in the Psalms.[63]

It would not be difficult to multiply examples of imagery of this type in other early writers.[64] The use and combination of the four matrix images mentioned above seems to have become a sort of theological topos that was utilized throughout Christian tradition. An example of feminine terms applied to the Father may be found in the declaration of the local Council of Toledo (675), which states: "The Son should be believed to have been

---

60. *Questions on the Gospels* 2,26 (*Patrologia Latina* 35,1330). This same imagery can be found in *Sermon* 105, 8,11 (*Patrologia Latina* 38,623).

61. *Discourses on the Psalms* 26,18 (*Corpus Christianorum Latinorum* 38,164).

62. *Baptismal Instructions* 3,19 (*Sources Chrétiennes* 50, 162). Translation is by Paul W. Harkins, *Ancient Christian Writers* 31,62. Both sources point to the same expressions in Chrysostom's *Homilies on Matthew* 82 (*Patrologia Graeca* 58, 744A-B).

63. *Homilies on Matthew* 74,3 (*Patrologia Graeca* 58,682).

64. See Bradley, "Patristic Background."

begotten or born, not from nothing nor from some extraneous substance but from the womb, that is the substance, of the Father *(de Patris utero id est de substantia eius).*[65] I have translated *uterus* as "womb" in order to allow the text its strongest allusive power. In fact, however, according to the testimony of Isidore, in later Latin usage, *uterus* was used of either sex.[66] In addition, the Council is probably reflecting a common understanding that the Vulgate's rendering of Psalm 109:3 referred to the Word's eternal birth: *"ex utero ante luciferum genui te."*

In the medieval period, it was particularly the third and fourth feminine traits that were applied to Christ: the pain by which he gave us birth, and the love and affection by which he instructs and nourishes us. In this period, as Carolyn Walker Bynum has pointed out, men tended to use more female imagery for Christ than did women.[67] Not only did they apply the imagery to Christ, but prelates and abbots were urged to have, in imitation of him, maternal tenderness in nourishing and guiding those entrusted to them. Bernard of Clairvaux wrote to an erring monk:

> And I have said this, my son . . . to help you as a loving father. . . . I begot you in religion by word and example. I nourished you with milk. . . . You too were torn from my breast, cut from my womb. My heart cannot forget you.[68]

In regard to Christ himself as mother, indeed as mother hen, we have this prayer of Anselm of Canterbury:

> Christ my mother, you gather your chickens under your wings; this dead chicken of yours puts himself under your wings. . . . Warm your chicken, give life to your dead man, justify your sinner. Let your terrified one be consoled by you. . . .[69]

---

65. Denziger-Schönmetzer, 23rd ed. no. 526.

66. Albert Blaise, *Dictionnaire Latin-Français des Auteurs Chrétiens* (Brepols: Turnhout, 1954), 862.

67. See for instance *Jesus as Mother: Studies in the Spirituality of the High Middle Ages* (Berkeley: University of California, 1982); *Fragmentation and Redemption: Essays on Gender and the Human Body in Medieval Religion* (New York: Zone Books, 1992).

68. As cited in Bynum, *Fragmentation,* 160. For a development of this theme see her, "Jesus as Mother and Abbot as Mother: Some Themes in Twelfth-Century Cistercian Writings," *Harvard Theological Review* 70 (1977): 257-84.

69. *The Prayers and Meditations of St. Anselm,* trans. and with an intro. by Sr. Benedicta Ward (Harmondsworth, Middlesex: Penguin, 1973), 155-56, cited by Eleanor McLaughlin, "Christ My Mother: Feminine Naming and Metaphors in Medieval Spirituality," *St. Luke's Journal of Theology* 18 (1975): 367-86, quote on p. 372.

The most outstanding, and in some ways the most theological, use of this imagery is found in the anchoress Julian of Norwich (1342–ca. 1423). Julian, who is described by Evelyn Underhill as "the most philosophic of our mystics," received a series of visions when she was "thirty and a half years old."[70] They impressed upon her a deep sense of the love that God has for the whole world. Seeing Christ on the cross and the blood he shed, she understood the greatness of his love and suffering, the power of his blood, and his great care for us. She wrote an account of these visions, and then twenty years later wrote a longer account that is the fruit of those years of prayer, reflection, and interaction with the Lord. It is in this longer account, particularly in chapters 52–64, that we have her teaching on the motherhood of the Father and of Christ. The first time the expression comes is in the opening lines of chapter 52: "And so I saw that God rejoices that he is our Father, and God rejoices that he is our Mother, and God rejoices that he is our true spouse, and that our soul is his beloved wife."[71] This is a reference to the Trinity, in which the Son is called our Mother. Very often when God is referred to as our Mother, Julian intends us to see this as the Second Person of the Trinity who created us, redeemed us, and cares for us:

> I understand three ways of contemplating motherhood in God. The first is the foundation of our nature's creation; the second is his taking of our nature, where the motherhood of grace begins; the third is the motherhood at work. (ch. 59, 297)

In the following chapter Julian states equivalently that she considers this type of predication to be analogous, and not simply metaphorical, because it applies first to God and secondarily to creatures:[72]

---

70. *The Mystics of the Church* (New York: Schocken Books, 1964), 128. Scholars debate whether there was any direct influence of Anselm upon Julian. The content of their teaching, though not its form, has clear similarities. See Joan M. Nuth, "Two Medieval Soteriologies: Anselm of Canterbury and Julian of Norwich," *Theological Studies* 53 (1992): 611-45.

71. Julian of Norwich, *Showings,* trans. Edmund Colledge and James Walsh, The Classics of Western Spirituality (New York: Paulist, 1978), 279. Numbers in parentheses in this section refer to this translation.

72. "Since every perfection is in God and no imperfection, any perfection found in a creature can be said of God with respect to the perfection as such, if every imperfection is removed. If a name, however, is based on something imperfect, as stone or lion, then it is said of God symbolically or metaphorically; but if it is based on something perfect, then it is said properly though in a more eminent fashion." Thomas Aquinas, *Scriptum super libros Sententiarum* 1.4.1.1, trans. by Rocca, *Analogy as Judgment,* 590.

This fair lovely word, "mother" is so sweet and so kind in itself that it cannot truly be said of anyone or to anyone except of him and to him who is the true Mother of life and of all things. To the property of motherhood belong nature, love, wisdom and knowledge and this is God. (ch. 60, 298–99)

Julian's very rich thought may be partially summed up as follows. The Second Person of the Trinity is our mother because he is the author of our very existence. The depth of love he had for us in creation is more fully revealed in and through his humanity, which is the means of initiating his motherhood of grace. He saved us, he forms us by instruction and chastisement, and he nourishes us. These motherly activities are possible because after the resurrection his human nature partakes of the causality of the divine.[73]

Three remarks might be made here in regard to tradition's use of the image of motherhood. First, in all of the above traditions, there is no embarrassment in speaking of Jesus' birthing and nourishing activity or even of his breasts. The impression evoked by this latter image in the minds of the audience was not that of eroticism but rather of nourishment. A brief history of the change in attitude toward the body will be traced in chapter 12. Here it suffices to point out that our modern individualistic and self-conscious awareness of the contrasting sexuality of the body is foreign to the earlier mentality that used these images. Describing this older mind-set, Eleanor McLaughlin says: "Significant numbers of women and men felt comfortable with a self-image which included both male and female modes; significant numbers of men and women experienced God intimately in ways that the society would call female as well as male."[74]

Second, we should distinguish the abundance of feminine imagery applied to God, which operates at various levels of interiority and referentiality, from analogy properly so called. The images have a mediating

---

73. See the study by Christine (Prudence) Allen, "Christ Our Mother in Julian of Norwich," *Sciences Religieuses/Studies in Religion* 10 (1981): 421-28, where the author also points out the importance for Julian of the distinction between the substance and sensuality of the human soul (see *Showings,* chapter 56).

74. " 'Christ My Mother'," 384-85. We read as well this remark of Caroline Walker Bynum: "Thus, *female* was not to women writers primarily paired with *male* as a contrasting image. The one woman theologian (Hildegard of Bingen) who did discuss the two genders directly, stressed complementarity. The woman writer's sense of herself as female was less a sense of herself as evil or as not-male than a sense of herself as physical. And women saw the humanity-physicality that linked them to Christ as in continuity with, rather than in contrast to, their own ordinary experience of physical and social vulnerability." *Fragmentation,* 172.

function, that is they mediate something about God, they are not merely representative of someone's experience. Nevertheless, they do not express a judgment that there is objective correspondence. The notion of the motherhood of Jesus, particularly as it achieved expression in chapters 52–64 of Julian's *Showings,* is on the other hand a genuine analogy. The divine tenderness, loyalty, willingness to suffer and to nourish revealed in the life and risen existence of Jesus Christ as he cares for his church belong properly to him and secondarily to human beings. Although it is a minor theme in the tradition, it is a stable and responsible one. It has been preserved by some of the great theologians of the church's history and is confirmed by the *sensus fidelium.* In Soskice's terms cited earlier, "from its inception it seems appropriate"; or to use O'Neil's notion also quoted earlier, it has to do with a knowledge of God already acquired whose linguistic expression indicates an objective shared correspondence that, while it expresses similitude, maintains that what is predicated of God and the creature is more unlike than like, but it is still true. Nonetheless, the expression *Jesus Mother* is a particular kind of analogy, based on the economy of salvation, as are analogies such as *Jesus Priest* or *Jesus Savior.* While these differ among themselves, they can be classified as functional or metaphorical analogies, depending upon the viewpoint.

The third point to be observed in regard to this imagery in tradition is that while feminine qualities are attributed to God and particularly to Christ and the Spirit, with some possible rare exceptions, the one so described is always a *he,* and not a *she.*[75] In the light of the abundance of this imagery, which was not contested and was used by both men and women, we must ask ourselves why this is so. This brings me to the last point to be discussed in this section, masculine and feminine language for God.

Language and Imagery

The question of how to speak about God, particularly in respect to liturgical language, biblical translation, and theological predication, has been raised anew by feminist thinkers. The question is vast and would require a study

---

75. "As veryly as God is our fader, as veryly God is our moder; and that shewid he in all, and namely in these swete words where he seith: 'I it am', that is to seyen: 'I it am: the myte and goodness of the faderhed. I it am, the wisdam of the moderhede. I it am: the lyte and the grace that is al blissid love." Julian, *Showings,* chapter 59. I use the original text to indicate the oscillation between "he" and "it," never "she." Text cited in Bradley, "Patristic Background," 101.

of its own.[76] These few lines are dedicated to but one aspect of the question, the manner in which biblical language for God creates background mediating images.

There are three different aspects to consider when discussing language about God: sex, gender, and image. Since no Christian holds that God has a body and is physically male, we may dispense with a discussion of the first aspect, namely, that type of language use which would employ lexical terms (nouns, adjectives, full verbs, adverbs) intending to speak of God as physically male. The second aspect contains two questions. First, there is the use of lexical terms to speak of God using a gendered image, metaphor, or analogy. Analogy and image have been discussed and metaphor will be discussed shortly. In regard to regular lexical usage, feminists propose that terms for God be simultaneously male and female (e.g., God/ess), alternately male and female (e.g., God, Goddess), or nongendered (e.g., Creator, Sustainer). The first of these is only possible in English and is misleading, and the second is not only misleading but directly contrary to biblical usage, which must be determinative for Christians.[77] The third is quite usual, but could never replace all personal and anthropomorphic terms in common speech without depersonalizing the personal God and eliminating most biblical predication.[78]

In this second consideration of gendered language use in regard to God we come to a consideration of nonlexical terms that form the category of function or structure words: pronouns, prepositions, determiners, conjunctions, and linking verbs.[79] This category of words is termed *closed* because additions are rarely made to it, in contrast with lexical terms to which new words are added easily and frequently.[80] A pronoun in an

76. From a linguistic standpoint the most competent study is that by Donald D. Hook and Alvin F. Kimel Jr., "The Pronouns of Deity: The Theolinguistic Critique of Feminist Proposals," *Scottish Journal of Theology* 46 (1993): 297-323. Among the proponents of change, one of the basic articles is that by Gail Ramshaw-Schmidt, "De Divinis Nominibus: The Gender of God," *Worship* 56 (1982): 117-31. Two recent collaborative works have discussed the issue from several aspects and refer to most of the recent literature: *Speaking the Christian God: The Holy Trinity and the Challenge of Feminism*, ed. Alvin F. Kimel, Jr. (Grand Rapids: Eerdmans, 1992); *The Politics of Prayer: Feminist Language and the Worship of God*, ed. Helen Hull Hitchcock (San Francisco: Ignatius, 1992).

77. This point is well made by the post-Christian Daphne Hampson, *Theology and Feminism* (Oxford, Cambridge, Mass.: Blackwell, 1990).

78. For a development of this line of thought see Roland M. Frye, "Language for God and Feminist Language," in *Speaking the Christian God*, 17-43.

79. In this section I am particularly indebted to the study of Hook and Kimel, "The Pronouns of Deity."

80. There has been no new pronoun added to the English language in a thousand years.

analytic language like English[81] receives its total identity from its context, from what it refers to — for this reason theoreticians describe it as *anaphoric*. We should advert as well to the fact that in English, as in any analytical language, the pronoun *he* possesses what grammarians call "notional gender." Notional gender, in contrast to an arbitrary grammatical gender, is classified according to semantic or meaning-related distinctions, particularly sexual distinctions. The feminists argue that the use of the third person singular "he" makes God exclusively masculine, but this is to ignore the fact that, since recognition of intent is required for an understanding of pronouns, it is quite possible to use this pronoun in a way that is sexually neutral.[82] This is because anaphoric pronouns do not possess meaning in and of themselves; they take their meaning from what they refer to. In a wider context, the linguist Arey Faltz maintains: "[T]he default-masculinity of English usage makes it easier to apply a masculine word like Father to God, *without* transferring male characteristics than it is to apply Mother without transferring feminine characteristics."[83]

Given the world that surrounded Israel with its pervasive portrayal of gods and goddesses, and given the linguistic capacities of Hebrew to insinuate gender by such things as verb forms,[84] the consistent adoption of masculine verb forms, adjectives, pronouns, and the like represents a counter-cultural choice. This use of language is not the unconscious expression of a male-dominated culture; language and social mores move at different levels. As Levi-Strauss expresses it: "Social attitudes do not belong to the same level as linguistic structures, but to a different, more superficial level."[85] Although English linguistic patterns are different from those of Hebrew, Aramaic, and Greek, the final result manages to convey just about the same impression as the originals. As Hook and Kimel express it: "The claim that the notional gender of modern English 'masculinizes'

---

81. "Analytic languges are characterized by the regular use of function words, auxiliarly verbs, and changes in word order to indicate syntatic relationships and distinctions. It is a normal requirement of English that the subject of a sentence be explicitly stated." Hook-Kimel, "Prounouns of Deity," 320.

82. See Jane Duran, "Gender-Neutral Terms," in *Sexist Language: A Modern Philosophical Analysis,* ed. Mary Vetterling-Baggin (Totowa, N.J.: Rowman and Littlefield, 1981), 147-54.

83. Unpublished study cited in Hook-Kimel, "The Pronouns of Deity," 309-10.

84. There is no way in English to mediate, for instance, the delicate overtones of Yhwh's words of comfort and promise addressed to Jerusalem in Is 60. Every expression of direct address in verb and pronoun is in a feminine form.

85. Claude Lévi-Strauss, *Anthropologie Structurale* (Paris: 1958), 82. Cited by George H. Tavard, "Sexist Language in Theology?" *Theological Studies* 36 (1975): 700-724.

the deity beyond that of the original biblical languages is unsupported by the linguistic realities."[86]

Feminist objections to the masculine language for God used in the Scriptures are directed, then, not to the translations, but to the text itself. Many scholars are aware of this, but for them language is ideology. This would imply that the most dominating societies would have the most masculinized languages, but this is simply not the case. Neither Turkish nor Hungarian, for instance, have grammatically gendered nouns, verbs, or pronouns, yet they are hardly models of liberated societies.[87]

In the Hebrew Bible the use of masculine forms for God reflects the unique teaching of Israel concerning God as creator. This linguistic procedure is necessary in order to mediate consistently the otherness of God, not because of language itself, but because of the image mediated in and through the language. It is a transcultural fact that as natural images, *male* mediates transcendence and otherness and *female* mediates immanence and closeness. This has been established in regard to cosmic religion by Mircea Eliade,[88] in regard to images in general by Gilbert Durand,[89] and has been discussed from the aspect of sociobiology by Walter Ong.[90] The *values* attached to this symbolization differ from culture to culture, but the interior and mediating impression created by the imagery is constant. By ignoring the mediating function of images and replacing it with a form of representationalism, feminists are trying to introduce feminist imagery into Christian and other linguistic expressions for God. This is an error on two counts. First, it projects onto the biblical tradition the distortion of masculinity and femininity experienced in our culture. Rather than try to change the revelation of God mediated in this tradition, we would do better to change the misinterpretation of that tradition by serious intellectual effort to recover

86. "The Pronouns of Deity," 308.

87. Actually, the equation of language with ideology constituted the predominant Marxist view until 1950, when it was abandoned because it was unsupported by the linguistic facts; see Tavard, "Sexist Language," 704-5.

88. *The Sacred and the Profane,* trans. Willard R. Trask (New York: Harper and Bros., 1961), especially chapter 3, "The Sacredness of Nature and Cosmic Religion;" also, *Patterns in Comparative Religion,* trans. Rosemary Sheed (New York: World Publishing Co, 1963 repr.), especially chapter 2, "The Sky and Sky Gods," and chapter 7, "The Earth, Woman and Fertility." See also Manfred Hauke, *Women in the Priesthood? A Systematic Analysis in the Light of the Order of Creation and Redemption,* trans. David Kipp (San Francisco: Ignatius, 1988), chapter 7, "Sexuality and the Image of God: Inquiries Based on the Study of Religion."

89. *Structures Anthropologiques,* 256-68 and passim.

90. *Fighting For Life* (Amherst: University of Massachussetts Press, 1981), especially 167-83.

its true meaning. Also, and perhaps more profoundly, through the symbolic mediation of our own historical and physical activity, we should manifest the true nature of God's *agapē* as revealed in Christ.

The second error derives from the first. Feminists seem intent on trying to obfuscate the otherness, the causality, and the authority of God because these are perceived as domination rather than the foundation for the generous activity of God by which he shares his being with us and calls us to an eternal and personal fruition of that sharing. As feminist thought progresses, there is a decreased sense expressed of the absolute uniqueness of God, not as the opaqueness of an impassive Transcendent, but as the inexpressible wonder of a Creator who loves us. When the very linguistic mediation of God's otherness is attacked and eliminated, the result is not a more balanced view of the deity, effected by our own representations, but a distinct tendency to pantheism and a loss of the sense of the absolute freedom of God's creative and redemptive action. It is significant that the recent works of three important feminists are concerned with ecology, a theme that deserves attention precisely because of what we have done to our earth through the notion that our causality is an expression of domination. A careful reading of these works, however, shows them to be further imbued with a blurred understanding of how we know God, his freedom, and transcendent personal reality.[91]

METAPHORICAL THEOLOGY

The term *metaphorical theology,* as it is currently used, refers to a very specific understanding of metaphor and the way metaphors are used when speaking about God. Its two most salient characteristics are (1) our metaphors name our experience of the Transcendent, but cannot say anything about the Transcendent itself except relationally, and (2) these metaphors are the culturally conditioned representations forged by the mind as it imposes intelligibility upon experience. The feminist author most frequently associated with metaphorical theology, and the one who has most systematically developed it, is Sallie McFague. Most other feminist theologians are content to invoke her work, though not always with her nuances. Before discussing McFague's work directly, however, we need to

---

91. See Sallie McFague, *The Body of God: An Ecological Theology* (Minneapolis: Fortress Press, 1993); Rosemary Radford Ruether, *Gaia and God: An Ecofeminist Theology of Earth Healing* (San Francisco: Harper, 1992); Elizabeth A. Johnson, *Women, Earth, and Creator Spirit,* 1993 Madaleva Lecture in Spirituality (New York: Paulist, 1993).

consider one aspect of Paul Ricoeur's thinking on the subject of metaphor where he suffers from an excessively Kantian tendency, which then serves to strengthen a bias in McFague's presentation.

Paul Ricoeur

Paul Ricoeur is clearly the philosopher who has most influenced McFague's thinking about metaphor. Two of the dominant and recurring notions in her treatment of metaphor are "is and is not" and "redescription," both of which, as she often says herself, she owes to Ricoeur. Unfortunately, these two expressions embody the weakest aspect of Ricoeur's most valuable study of metaphor. This terminology is found with some frequency in Ricoeur; the most developed theoretical exposition is in Study 7, "Metaphor and Reference," of his principal work on metaphor.[92]

In this section of his book, Ricoeur is grappling with two extreme views of metaphor. For logical positivism metaphor as language must either be descriptive, giving facts, or emotional, describing states. For other theoreticians, metaphor is understood in a naive and uncritical manner or taken to be a pretense, or an imaginative description "as if." Ricoeur's aim is to define metaphor between these extremes. He seems to have borrowed the notion that metaphor presents both "what is and what is not" from Roman Jacobson, while for the use of the term *redescription* he expresses a debt to Mary Hesse.[93] Both of these expressions are intended to indicate that metaphor, as discourse, makes an assertion that cannot be taken literally ("time is a beggar"), and yet invents and creates a vision of what hitherto had been a possible but unsuspected dimension of being. As Ricoeur himself describes it: "metaphor is the rhetorical process by which discourse unleashes the power that certain fictions have to redescribe reality."[94]

The notion of redescription comes close to considering metaphor as a type of comparison. Some existing reality receives a new predication that gives it a new description. It is probably in order to avoid this consequence that Ricouer speaks of the suppression or suspension of the ostensive reference, and correspondingly, the building of metaphor upon "the ruins"

92. *The Rule of Metaphor: Multi-disciplinary Studies of the Creation of Meaning in Language,* trans. Robert Czerny, Kathleen McLaughlin, John Costello (Toronto: University of Toronto Press, 1977).

93. The reference to Jackobson is in *The Rule of Metaphor,* 224 and passim; the reference to Hesse is on p. 240.

94. *The Rule of Metaphor,* 7.

of the literal sense and reference.[95] In the overall context of his treatment of metaphor, and subsequently of narrative, this view of how metaphors are forged is provided with complementary correctives, but it is a deficiency that has come under criticism. Notable among these critics is Janet Martin Soskice, who finds fault with the duality of reference involved in Ricoeur's use of "is and is not" and "redescription."

> [R]edescription, however radical, is always re-description. The interesting thing about metaphor, or at least about some metaphors, is that they are used not to redescribe but to disclose for the first time.[96]

Soskice herself, relying partially on I. A. Richards, describes metaphor as an "interanimation" that makes a unity of the "tenor" (the underlying subject of the metaphor) and the "vehicle" that presents it. This means that there is not a redescription but a unity of subject matter formed by the interanimation of two or more sets of associations. From this comes the mediation of a discovery — a dimension of being that has been disclosed.[97]

In a similar vein, Kevin Vanhoozer maintains that, though Ricoeur's philosophical rehabilitation of metaphor is brilliant, he does not provide any criterion by which one can judge between good and bad metaphors. This indicates a weakness in speaking about the referent of a metaphor. Vanhoozer goes on to observe:

> The question remains whether Ricoeur's view of metaphor does not in the end slide down the "slippery slope" towards the "as if," into the arms not of Bultmann but Vaihinger. H. Vaihinger's The Philosophy of "As If," a study of religious fictions inspired by Kant, suggests that the referent of poetic discourse is ideal, by which he means unreal (or better, not actual). However, though they are only mental constructs, religious fictions are practically necessary.

There then follows a quotation from Vaihinger in which he says that the goal of the world of ideas is to provide us with "an instrument for feeling our way about more easily in the world."[98]

95. Ibid., 221.

96. Janet Martin Soskice, Metaphor and Religious Language (Oxford: Clarendon Press, 1985), 89.

97. For a description of this process see Metaphor and Religious Language, 49.

98. Kevin J. Vanhoozer, Biblical Narrative in the Philosophy of Paul Ricoeur: A Study in Hermeneutics and Theology (Cambridge: Cambridge University Press, 1990), 76. The reference to H. Vaihinger is to The Philosophy of "As If": A System of the Theoretical, Practical and Religious Fictions of Mankind, trans. C. K. Ogden (New York: Barnes and Noble, 1935).

The mention of Kant in Vanhoozer's quotation is suggestive. It is undoubtedly true that Ricoeur owes much of his epistemological thinking to Kant, particularly his notion of the productive or creative imagination. Although this is not the place to enter into an extended discussion of the relation between Kant's thinking in the first and third *Critiques* and aspects of Ricoeur's theory of metaphor that are tributary to it, this much should be said: Ricoeur sees both metaphor and narrative as being instances of productive reference,[99] and at the same time considers that the configuration by which action is emplotted in narrative is a work of "judgment" in the sense in which the word is used in the third *Critique*.[100]

I would suggest that there is a tendency in Ricoeur to view the work of the productive imagination as the operation by which we are able to surmount the Kantian restrictions placed on access to the intelligible. Metaphor and narrative both create a vision of the possible and transcend what is. Unless I am mistaken, however, the *is* in the phrase *what is* denotes for Ricoeur not the *what is* for a critical realist but the *what is* that results from the mediating role played by the imagination in a theoretical judgment. In this activity there is an adapting of the experience of the sensible to the universal categories, especially that of time.[101]

Having become trapped in a Kantian dichotomy between the sensible and the intelligible, Ricoeur must now find a way of accounting for the mind's ability to grasp the potential abundance of what is presented to it. He does this, as he says himself, by having recourse to the notion of the productive imagination as Kant develops it in the third *Critique, The Critique of Judgment*. Imagination, therefore, must do what mind cannot do, that is, it must move ecstatically in an act that, rather than assimilate

99. "It is this synthesis of the heterogenous that brings narrative close to metaphor. In both cases, the new thing — the as yet unsaid, the unwritten — springs up in language." Paul Ricoeur, *Time and Narrative*, vol. 1, trans. Kathleen McLaughlin and David Pellauer (Chicago: University of Chicago Press, 1984), ix.

100. "I cannot overemphasize the kinship between this 'grasping together,' proper to the configurational act, and what Kant has to say about the operation of judging." *Time and Narrative*, vol. 1, 66. See also "Narrative and Hermeneutics," in *Essays on Aesthetics: Perspectives on the Work of Monroe C. Beardsley*, ed. John Fisher (Philadelphia: Temple University Press, 1983), 149-60, esp. 155. In an earlier study, I expressed reserve concerning this aspect of Ricoeur's thought, particularly his reliance on Louis O. Mink; see my article "Literary Theory, Philosophy of History and Exegesis," *The Thomist* 52 (1988): 575-604; esp. 601.

101. "The task of the imagination is to mediate between the conceptual universality of the categories and the empirical particularity of sensible intuition. It does so by applying the categories to the most universal condition of sense, namely the form of time." Rudolf A. Makkreel, *Imagination and Interpretation in Kant* (Chicago: University of Chicago Press, 1990), 30.

the particular to the universality of the categories (as in a determinant judgment), finds a universal for a given particular. The redescription or configuration proposed by Ricoeur is a move through the play of images from something determined by the structure of the subject to something discovered by the creative ordering of the productive imagination.[102]

We must bear in mind, however, that redescription is only necessary because the *description* is something predetermined by the limits of the subject's access to the real. Thus, the manifold abundance of the concrete does not, through generosity, as described in the previous chapter, impart its intelligibility to the thinking subject. It is rather a passive, subjectively interpreted thing that can only receive the potential discovered in it by contributing to the further actualization of the subject.[103]

This observation, which seeks to find the basis for the critiques of Soskice and Vanhoozer, needs elaboration, but that must be given in another context.[104] What I have said here is sufficient for my purpose, which is to point to a subjectivist tendency in Ricoeur which creates a bias in McFague.

Metaphorical Predication

According to McFague, most religious language today appears to be either irrelevant or idolatrous. Irrelevant, because it moves within and expresses a world that is foreign to modern experience; idolatrous, because it is taken literally according to the norms of scientific positivism by people who do not think symbolically. Because former ages shared in the symbolic world of the Scriptures, and because at least some people practiced prayer and

---

102. ". . . the ideas of beginning, middle and end are not taken from experience. They are not features of some real action but the effects of the ordering of the poem." *Time and Narrative,* vol. 1, 39. For a perceptive critique of this notion in Ricoeur, see David Carr, "Review Article: *Temps et Récit.* Tome I, by Paul Ricoeur," *History and Theory* 23 (1984): 357-70.

103. For a good analysis of the work of the imagination in Kant's attempt to recover something of what was lost in the first *Critique,* see John Sallis, "Immateriality and the Play of the Imagination," *Proceedings of the American Catholic Philosophical Association* 52 (1978): 61-76.

104. It would have to be completed by a more positive analysis, one that would owe something to Kant's third *Critique,* but not the first. It would be an epistemological and phenomenological analysis of the role the imagination actually does play in providing, on the level of image, a necessary accompanying counterpart to the mind's receptivity of being's role in the act of knowledge. A very useful beginning has been made by Jacques Maritain, *Creative Intuition in Art and Poetry,* The A. W. Mellon Lectures in the Fine Arts (New York: Meridian Books, 1955).

contemplation, they were able to see that things stood for other things. We have lost that capacity, according to McFague. Our only access to knowledge about God is through metaphorical thinking and speech. This is exemplified in the parabolic preaching of Jesus, especially about the kingdom of God, and in Jesus himself, who is the parable of God. Earlier ages also spoke of analogy, but such a mental function requires a "symbolical sensibility" that depends upon the belief that "everything is connected, that the beings of this world are analogously related to God."

> In our time, however, when there is skepticism concerning the unity of all that is, symbols tend either to be literalized (as in fundamentalism or the doctrine of transubstantiation) or spiritualized (as in Feuerbach and Protestant liberalism).

There is, however, one form of speech that is open to us. It is metaphor.

> Thinking metaphorically means spotting a thread of similarity between two dissimilar objects, events or whatever, one of which is better known than the other, and using the better-known one as a way of speaking about the lesser known.[105]

This type of thinking characterizes not only poetry but also theoretical science and theology. In these latter two instances, when a metaphor is able to serve as a matrix for further predication about the object that has been "metaphored" we may speak of a "model." Thus, in science, the notion that *the brain is a computer* can be developed to include such notions as *processing, feedback,* and the like. In theology, notions such as *the church is a herald* or *the church is a servant* can give rise to a whole series of developments that can serve to complement each other.[106]

These general lines of McFague's thought are quite helpful and serve

---

105. McFague, *Metaphorical Theology,* 6, 15. See also *Models of God in Religious Language* (Philadelphia: Fortress, 1982). I find it difficult to combine this assertion, that our inability to understand the connectedness of things cannot change, with McFague's thesis in her subsequent book that "To feel in the depths of our being that we are part and parcel of the evolutionary ecosystem of our cosmos is a prerequisite of contemporary Christian theology." *Models of God: Theology for an Ecological, Nuclear Age* (Philadelphia: Fortress, 1987), 9. Would not such a prerequisite invite a reconsideration of analogy?

106. These examples are taken from Avery Dulles, *Models of the Church* (New York: Doubleday, 1978). This is one of the pioneering works in the use of models in theology.

to show the possibilities of a reflective use of metaphors and models in theology and the fact that theologians and scientists can learn from each other in the use of this approach. In fact, many of the authors invoked by McFague are those who have sought to find a way of bridging the gap between science and religion.[107]

There are some difficulties, however, with her position. These difficulties tend to strengthen what may be called a bias in her presentation. I would express it in these terms: Although there are statements in *Metaphorical Theology* and her other works that could temper the bias, it is clear that for McFague metaphorical predication about God is not about God but about relationships with God that are redescribed principally through the use of models. Her reason for this is twofold: first, although this is not directly said, no knowledge of God is possible for us, and therefore our language must be inferential and indirect; second, and this follows from the first, all literal predication about God is idolatrous.

On this basis, she constructs the following line of argument. Models, which are developed metaphors, redescribe relationships in the act of applying them to God. While it is true that some thinkers consider that models are either instrumental or at least expendable, a more correct view accords them a permanent place in thought and a genuine reference. Thus, the model of interacting billiard balls to explain the behavior of molecules in gases is in some sense explanatory (reference) and continues to be useful (permanent). In the same way, we can use such models as "Father," "Mother," "Friend," "Liberator" to speak of our relationship to God.

This line of argument contains several fallacies. One might almost speak of a "sleight of hand." Scientific models do often portray relationships: "as billiard balls are to each other in collision, so gas molecules are to each other as they interact as a result of heat." This is a paramorphic model that, to use Soskice's phrase, is "reality depicting." It is not principally saying something about the relation of gas molecules to billiard balls, it is saying something about *gas molecules*. In other words, gas molecules are spoken of *relationally* by saying that they are billiard balls colliding. This depicts something of the reality of the gas molecules and not merely

107. Among the more well known scholars who have studied this topic we find Frederick Ferré, *Language, Logic and God* (London: Eyre and Spottiswoode, 1970); Frederick Ferré, "Metaphor in Religious Discourse," in *Dictionary of the History of Ideas* (1973); Mary B. Hesse, *Models and Analogies in Science* (Notre Dame, Ind.: Notre Dame University Press, 1966); Mary B. Hesse, *The Structure of Scientific Inference* (London: MacMillan, 1974); Ian T. Ramsey, *Models for Divine Activity* (London: SCM Press, 1973); Ian T. Ramsey, "Facts and Disclosures," in *Christian Empiricism*, ed. Jerry H. Gill (London: Sheldon Press, 1974), 159-76.

the relation. The same could be said of other metaphors used in science: *the brain is a computer, electricity is a current,* and so on.

McFague slides from a relational depiction to a depiction of relation and then extends this to say that, in the same way, religious metaphors are about our relationship with God. They are not reality depicting, they are redescriptions of relations that we have among ourselves. But this is a false understanding of metaphor. If I say God is Father, I am saying something, rightly or wrongly, about *God*.[108] God is the tenor, father is the vehicle; or God is the source and father is the subject.[109] The vehicle or subject is a relational term, but, in keeping with the theory of metaphor, I am speaking of God *relationally* and not merely of the relation.

The *leit-motiv* of McFague's study is that we cannot literally describe God and therefore we must invent metaphors that mediate something of the relationship we experience with God.

> The images which tumble from the mouths of those experiencing the liberating love of God are not meant to *describe* God so much as to *suggest the new quality of relationship* being offered to them. Hence, religious metaphors and the models that emerge from them are not pictures of God but images of a relationship.[110]

Janet Martin Sockice, basically finding fault with Frederick Ferré and David Tracy (authors whose position precisely on the reference of religious metaphors McFague cites approvingly) concludes her discussion by saying:

> The conclusion that theistic models are descriptive and representational, but that what they describe and represent is the human condition, is not only disappointing when it comes at the end of a comparison of models in science and religion, but makes the whole comparison a nonsense.[111]

It strikes me that McFague is in a straitjacket of her own making. Having presupposed that no literal statements about God are possible, she

---

108. See the earlier discussion concerning the term *Father* as applied to God.

109. The terminology is that of R. Harré. See Soskice, *Metaphor and Religious Language,* 102.

110. McFague, *Metaphorical Theology,* 166 (emphasis in original).

111. Ibid., 106. Daphne Hampson, in discussing the move in feminist theology toward speaking no longer of God but rather of women's experience, has this to say about what I have called the bias in McFague's work: "Sallie McFague does consider what metaphor we should use for God. But when all is said and done it is unclear to me whether in fact she is speaking of God, or rather of an attitude to life." Daphne Hampson, *Theology and Feminism* (Oxford: Blackwell, 1990), 170.

augments the problem by invoking just those aspects of Ricoeur in which
he has restricted himself through a Kantian "limit" on the ability of the
mind to attain to being. For Kant at least, this results in concluding that
we cannot be sure if God is anything more than a "thinkable Object."[112]
McFague tries to rescue religious language from irrelevancy by searching
for metaphors that refer to a relation to God without really designating
God.

God as Friend

I would like to consider more at length one of the relational metaphors
employed by McFague, one that has a long history in the Christian tradition,
namely the notion of *God as Friend*. Taken in the usual sense of the words,
this is a metaphor that says something of God relationally, and not merely
of a relation or of an experience metaphorized as a relation. In concluding
the section, however, she reverts to her bias and speaks of motifs that model
"certain aspects of the parabolic understanding of life with God."[113]

Professor McFague's use of the term *friend* in relation to God provides
a good occasion to institute a comparison between herself as a representative
of feminist thinking and the larger Christian tradition. As just mentioned, the
metaphor *friend* is a common one in Christian tradition. When, for instance,
Thomas Aquinas asks whether the love relationship between God and the
believer can be called "friendship," he answers in the affirmative. He bases
his position on John 15:9 and 1 Corinthians 1:9 (where the Vulgate translated
koinōnia as *societas*) and uses an analogy based partly on Aristotle's notions
in book VIII of the *Ethics* that for friendship there must be the mutual love
of benevolence founded on what Aquinas calls *communicatio*.[114] The comparison between Aquinas and McFague is instructive. The authority for
Aquinas to assert that *caritas* is friendship comes from the personal relationship between Jesus and the disciples spoken of in John 15:9 and from the
action of God "who calls you into communion with his Son," in 1 Corinthians 1:9. McFague's authority, on the other hand, is the significance of the
image for our time. The difference is deeper, however. *God* for McFague is
the God of the theists: *God* for Aquinas is the Father of Jesus Christ. The

112. I am referring to the famous remark: "Gott is kein Apprehensibler sondern
nur ein denkbarer Gegenstand." ("God is not something apprehensible but merely a
thinkable object.") *Opus Postumum, Gessamelte Schriften* (Berlin: Preussiche Akademie der Wissenschaften, 1902ff.), XXI, 151.

113. McFague, *Metaphorical Theology*, 190.

114. *Summa Theologiae* 2-2,23,1.

aptitude of the term *friend* is determined by McFague according to the resonances it strikes in relating to the Transcendent. Its aptitude for Aquinas derives from the fact that an analysis of friendship can supply, analogically, some content for the New Testament authoritative assertions. For Aquinas, analogy is a way of articulating how he knows what he already knows. For McFague, metaphor is a way of expressing to herself and others what her mind imposes upon experience. The first mediates reality, even if imperfectly, the second represents it according to structures and norms established a priori.

I would like to reflect on these differences briefly. Most of McFague's study has to do with names for some sort of religious experience that is spoken of in terms of meaningful relations. The *God* who is metaphorized is, as I have said, the God of the theists. This is not the mode of Christian discourse and it results in some confusion, a confusion shared by many modern theologians who undertake to discuss *God* while ignoring the characteristic New Testament use of *Theos* to refer to the Father.

An example of this confusion is to be found in the study by Anne Carr already mentioned.[115] In a chapter entitled "Feminist Reflections on God," Carr, after carefully distinguishing between a symbol for God and its possible misunderstanding and abuse, goes on to suggest that male symbols for God have become "idolatrous": a common feminist adaptation of a modern theologoumenon. These symbols must be offset and modified by other symbols for God that take their origin from, or at least foster, women's experience.

> Christian feminist theology has rightly insisted on the urgent necessity of re-imaging and re-conceptualizing the symbol or doctrine of God if the gospel themes of inclusivity, mutuality, equality, and freedom are to be realized in society and in the church today.[116]

The equation between the symbol and doctrine of God in the above quotation is a common one in Carr. Examples of the process she envisages are given as: "The liberating God," "The incarnational God,"[117] "The relational God," "The suffering God," "The God who is future," "The

---

115. *Transforming Grace.*
116. Ibid., 144.
117. "The richly symbolic idea of God's incarnation in Christ . . . indicates that God and creation or the world are not in competition but are irrevocably united. . . . The symbol of God's embodiment also suggests that there is no fundamental matter/spirit, body/mind, female/male dichotomy in which one member of each pair is inferior to the other." Ibid., 149.

unknown, hidden God." In connection with this last, Carr mentions the
"symbol of the Trinity" (the only mention of Trinity in the book) and
seems to oscillate between considering this a helpful symbol, fostering as
it does mutuality, and a "mystery" that "God is somehow a society, a
community, a *perichoresis* of persons." This one ambiguous mention of
the Trinity does not save Carr's presentation from being basically a consideration of symbols that somehow mediate acceptable impressions of the
deity. If the idolatrous use of symbols is characterized by the way they are
used to enhance the power aspirations of some in the society, what is to
prevent these deistic symbols from being idolatrous? The only guarantee
against such a possibility lies in attending to what is mediated in the symbol
in terms of truth rather than subjective compatibility, and this requires a
radically different epistemology as I have already pointed out. The whole
of the biblical tradition, the source of the most profound teaching against
the idolatry of trying to capture God in symbol or image, witnesses to the
fact that idolatry is rectified not by the invention of competing symbols
but by a genuine knowledge of the living God.

The critique I have just offered of Anne Carr's books would apply
equally well to other works such as that by Eleanor Rae and Bernice
Marie-Daly[118] and most of the authors invoked there. If Daphne Hampson's
allegation, cited previously, is true that Rosemary Radford Ruether speaks
not of God but only of the idea of God (an allegation that seems justified
by my own reading of Ruether) then the critique applies in an even more
apposite manner.

Elizabeth Johnson, on the other hand, in her study *She Who Is,* speaks
frequently of the Trinity, but the influence of McFague's work on metaphor
is clearly perceptible in her work. Thus, despite the multiple references to
such authors as Aquinas, Kasper, and Rahner, it is impossible to decide
whether, for Johnson, speech about God has any truth content or is rather
to be judged for its subjective suitability. Johnson's position is simply not
clear. While continually approving of McFague's views on religious language, and after indicting Thomas Aquinas as a model of androcentric
thought, she goes on to cite him approvingly both in his teaching on the
incomprehensibility of God and on analogy, only to conclude her discussion
by stating that she "appreciates" the position of Frederick Ferré, ",who
holds that even though analogy may not be any longer metaphysically
credible, it still remains linguistically useful for speech about God." This
is to make religious language instrumentalist and to presume that the

118. *Created In Her Image: Models of the Feminine Divine* (New York:
Crossroad, 1990).

theologians cited by Johnson share her equation that "incomprehensible" always means completely unknowable: something that contradicts the constant witness of believers whether they are theologians or not. Johnson's use, then, of the notion of God's incomprehensibility is like that of Lindbeck's Crusader who proclaims *Christus est Dominus!* while splitting an infidel's skull — the phrase is correct, but its actual use falsifies it.[119] There are, then, several valuable insights in Johnson's work, but the agnostic context in which they are developed means that they must be rethought in the light of a better understanding of faith as a way of knowing.

In all of this the irony is that feminism, which considers any form of passivity to be the same as inertia, treats God as the totally passive object of our intellectual and moral strivings. God does nothing, he is merely sought or interpreted. This is not far from Irenaeus's description of the Gnostics, who thought they had found a "super-god."

> Above the true God, they imagine a god who actually does not exist, so they think they have found the "Great God" whom no one can know, who has no communication with the human race, who does not administer the affairs of this world; it is obvious that they have found the god of Epicurus, a god who does nothing profitable, either for himself or others, a god without a providence.[120]

In the Christian tradition, knowledge and speech about God are not merely a function of the mind. The mind appreciates the utter mystery of God's being and incomprehensibility, but love seeks to find ways of praising God and declaring his wonders to others. Love seeks for language because the beloved is known in his actions. We may understand Paul's statement that love believes all things (1 Cor 13:7) to refer to that interior activity by which the believer yields ever more and more to what is perceived in mystery and presented to faith. This is the rhythm of Christian speech about God. Where there is no living and personal contact with God who has revealed himself in the history of Jesus Christ, there is no desire to speak the mystery of God, and our temptation is to frame our language in terms that express and promote our own experiences. It is because of love that we lay hold of the words that God has provided himself and seek to penetrate their veil in order to reach the Triune God who has deigned to make himself known even as he is veiled in the revelation. To quote Irenaeus once again:

119. The example is found in George Lindbeck, *The Nature of Doctrine: Religion and Theology in a Postliberal Age* (Philadelphia: Westminster, 1984), 64. The example occurs in a discussion of "intrasystematic" truth.

120. *Against the Heresies,* 3,24,2 (*Sources Chrétiennes* 211,476-78).

As regards his grandeur, we cannot know God, for it is impossible to measure the Father. But as regards his love (for that is what leads us through the Word to God), those who obey him are evermore learning that there is a God who is so great and it is he, through himself, who has created and made and ordered all things.[121]

The next chapter will reflect somewhat on how we come to know the Father, "through the Word to God," in a process that, borrowing a phrase from Michael Polanyi, we may call "indwelling" the tradition.

---

121. *Against the Heresies* 4,20,5 (*Sources Chrétiennes* 100,625).

9

The God and Father
of Our Lord Jesus Christ

In the two preceding chapters, I have considered the fact that Christian revelation is often considered from without, and is judged by epistemic criteria that are foreign to it. I endeavored to show that the results achieved by a representationalist epistemology are so contrary to the faith of the Christian community of the last two millennia that any Christian theologian must conclude that there is clearly something wrong with its presuppositions. Such a mode of procedure is *apologetic* in the ancient sense of the term. It demonstrated that the manner in which feminism proposes to name God and interpret the texts of the tradition, particularly the Scriptural texts, deviates from the norm of faith. An apologetic function of this type belongs to what was called in chapter 1 the potential whole of theology. Because there is thinking with assent, the essence of theology is present. However, because faith in this instance is operating more as a negative norm (showing that the positions discussed are not in keeping with the tradition), the full power of theology is not in evidence. That full power is present to the degree that the light of faith is a conscious principle presiding over and guiding the thought processes of the believer, resulting in a personally appropriated understanding of the divine truth.

In this chapter I would like to indicate how a theological reflection that is subject to the active influence of faith might proceed. The procedure can aptly be termed "indwelling the tradition," an expression I owe to Michael Polanyi and the theologians who have studied him.[1] I will first

1. See especially his *Personal Knowledge: Towards a Post-Critical Philosophy* (Chicago: University of Chicago Press, 1958); *Knowing and Being,* ed. Marjorie Grene (Chicago: University of Chicago Press, 1969). For studies applying Polanyi's thinking

trace rapidly the operations that are involved in this reflective process, then sketch how one might try to "indwell" the biblical designation of God as Father. My purpose is to shed light on what is being communicated by this term in the tradition and what has consequently been understood by those believers who have entered into the rhythm of revelation.

In a previous chapter, I distinguished two views of causality. One, which is seen by Heidegger as the predominant mode of Western thought, is that all causality is a form of coercion, an imposition of the stronger upon the weaker. The other, a biblical view, is that both divine causality and the created causality that imitates it flow from generosity. In the first view, the only activity that merits consideration is that of transformative action, the imposition upon nature and upon the less enlightened and resourceful the unquestioned and enlightened vision of the more powerful. This notion is found already in one of the founding documents of the modern era, Francis Bacon's *New Atlantis*.[2] What the term *Father* as applied to the Deity then means is that as the most powerful and the most enlightened he has an unlimited sway over all reality. This view, as I mentioned earlier, has been unjustifiably projected back onto pre-Enlightenment Christian thinking about "God, the Father Almighty, Creator of heaven and earth." Furthermore, since the sphere of conflict and transformative action is that of public life, a domain that became almost exclusively male and increasingly isolated from that of private life, it was not a long step to the conclusion that "power is male and male is power."[3]

It is undeniable that, in such a world, *God* became the unknowable, frightening, powerful Deity whose name *Father,* in an utter travesty of what the term means in either Old or New Testament, became synonymous with nameless and coercive might. Much Christian theological thought succumbed to this attitude and, without a life of worship sustained by the great liturgical texts of antiquity, much popular devotion imbibed the same outlook, with the result in this latter case that true experience of God could only find expression in sentimental forms. It is against this equivalence of *Father* and *power,* what I called in the previous chapter the distortion of

---

to theology see Avery Dulles, "Faith, Church, and God: Insights from Michael Polanyi," *Theological Studies* 45 (1984): 537-50; Andrew Louth, *Discerning the Mystery: An Essay on the Nature of Theology* (Oxford: Oxford University Press, 1983).

2. "Bacon not only taught modernity to stand up to the ancient scourges of humanity; he also identified the New World discovered by Columbus as an adversary that had to be brought to its knees." Albert Borgmann, *Crossing the Postmodern Divide* (Chicago: University of Chicago Press, 1992), 23.

3. For a very insightful study of this process and its antecedents see Elshtain, *Public Man, Private Woman.*

masculinity, that feminism is correctly reacting. The objections range from the damaging effect such language can have on those who have suffered from their human fathers to the assertion that the term "Father" legitimates a patriarchal ordering of Christian life. It is asserted that such language derives from a culturally conditioned expression of Christianity and must be reinterpreted for our own age.

The problem is that while it seeks to offset androcentric names for the unknown Deity by the imposition of gynocentric and suitable names, it perpetuates the same twofold distortion. *God* is still an utterly unknown correlate to my feeling of dependence, and perhaps confidence, who is named from a position that equates knowledge and power and who must be considered a stranger: "When to know means to dominate, then of course God remains that which is definitively indomitable, and thus unknowable."[4] I wish now to return to an explicit consideration of a non-dominating mode of knowledge, namely indwelling.

The process of indwelling is part of a larger faith activity by which the believer participates in the life of the Christian community. Therefore, it is founded on a confidence in what is called "the rule of faith." The rule of faith must be lived by participation in the church's life of worship, in its care for those in need, in its preaching the gospel and bringing others to faith, in its generosity in forgiving, in its clear struggle against the tendencies and habit patterns of sin, and in its understanding of what has been passed on through the centuries by the action of the Holy Spirit. This basic confidence in the truth of what is being lived deepens to the degree that it is experienced as true by sharing, through *agapē,* in the mystery of Christ, a dying to sin and a living to God.

The ancient formula "believe that you may understand" called for an indwelling of what was being preached by the Holy Spirit through the words and actions of the believing community. Only by such an assent of the whole personality can there be *gnōsis,* a living knowledge of the mystery. This in no way implies a violent act of the will forcing submission to an abstract formulation of belief. Such coercion, whether imposed from without or from within, is merely the result of human resources; it is not faith. The truth of the gospel is established by the Holy Spirit, who commends the living reality of Christ to the conscience in such a way that every act of yielding is at once a real possibility and a preparation for a further step. This is why Paul can say

---

4. Hans Urs von Balthasar, *The Glory of the Lord. A Theological Aesthetics,* vol. V, ed. Brian McNeil and John Riches, trans. Oliver Davies, *et al.* (San Francisco: Ignatius, 1991), *The Realm of Metaphysics in the Modern Age,* 495. At this point von Balthasar is discussing the *via negativa* of Kant, which ultimately becomes "unadulterated formalism."

to the Romans, "you gave obedience from the heart to the pattern of teaching *to which you were entrusted"* (Rom 6:17).

The process of indwelling comprises two activities, both grounded in this sense of being entrusted to an objective pattern of teaching as the result of a free decision on the part of the believer. The first of these activities is that of acquiring familiarity with what the tradition actually does teach. It is a sympathetic and disciplined attempt to understand what is being mediated by the biblical text and the community life it sustains and illuminates. Just as in the sciences someone who has dwelt with the subject matter a long time has certain perceptive instincts and intuitions beyond the "book knowledge" of the novice, so in theology someone who has allowed the life of the community to "work on" him or her, and who has sought familiarity through disciplined study, has an inner instinct for the right way to understand what is being passed on. Generally, God's people recognize this by a certain discernment of spirits.

The second activity of indwelling produces knowledge by connaturality. Although, of course, the activity just described is also a knowledge through a sort of likeness to the subject matter, the connaturality referred to here is really what the New Testament calls conformity:

> My one desire is to know Christ and the power of his resurrection, and to share his sufferings in growing conformity with his death, in hope of somehow attaining the resurrection from the dead. (Phil 3:10-11, Revised English Bible)[5]

This is the *gnōsis* spoken of elsewhere in the New Testament and developed by the early theologians. The role of the sacred text in this process is that of being the instrument of an effective revelation.

THE TERM *Father* IN THE OLD TESTAMENT

The term *father ('ab)* is applied to God in the Old Testament rather infrequently, in all about twenty-two times. The majority of these texts refer to God as Father because he acquired a people who are the object of his special care.[6] Another smaller group of texts, echoing the oracle of Nathan,

---

5. For other similar notions see Rom 8:29; Col 3:10-11; for an echo of the above text see Phil 3:21.
6. Dt 32:5-6; Jer 3:4, 19; Is 63:15-16; Mal 1:6; 2:10; Ps 68:6; Tob 13:4; Wis 18:13. We should also add here: Ex 4:22; Jer 31:9, 20; Hos 11:1-4; Ps 103:13. Sometimes the Israelites are called "sons of God" but this applies to them individually only

refer to God as Father of the king.[7] In the later literature we sometimes find God addressed as Father by an individual.[8] In addition, there are about forty Israelite names compounded with the term *'ab* in which *'ab* stands for or is connected with the God of Israel. For instance *'ăbî'ēl* ([my] Father is God, 1 Sm 9:1). One may consult as well: *'ammî'ēl* ([my] Uncle is God, Num 13:12), *'ăḥîyâ* ([my] brother is Yhwh, 1 Kgs 4:3).[9]

I will treat of this latter category, the theophoric names, first. In all the cultures contiguous to Israel, but especially in Assyrian-Babylonian culture, there is an abundance of names compounded with the names or titles of deities.[10] These names may be of men (predominantly) or women, they may refer to the same god as *father* or *mother* (or *uncle* or *brother*), and the same person may refer to himself as the *son* of more than one god, though generally the title *Father* is reserved for the high god or father god of each respective pantheon. This same general pattern is found in Israel as well, another witness to the antiquity of the custom. There are, however, some notable exceptions. First, there is no Israelite name in which God is called *mother,* whether the bearer of the name be male or female.[11] Second, no believing Israelite would bear the name of any but the true God; thus, there is no multiplicity of patrons.[12] We should remark in the third place

---

as members of the people: Dt 14:1; Is 30:1, 9; Jer 3:14; 30:2. Angels are sometimes called "sons of God" to indicate that they have a certain "divine," that is, superhuman, quality. This is a completely different strain of thought, as is the notion that Wisdom is a child of God. For these latter aspects see Marie-Joseph Lagrange, "La Paternité de Dieu," *Revue Biblique* 5 (1908): 481-99, esp. 491-99.

7. 2 Sam 7:14; 1 Chr 17:13; 22:10; 28:6; Ps 89:27; see also Ps 2:7.

8. Sir 23:1, 4; 51:10; Wis 2:16-18; 5:5; 14:3. It may be that Prv 3:12 belongs here as well.

9. See Ernst Jenni, "'āb," in *Theologisches Handwörterbuch zum Alten Testament,* I, ed. Ernst Jenni and Claus Westermann (Munich: Kaiser, 1971), 1-17, esp. p. 8.

10. For a more complete treatment of this topic see W. Marchel, *Abba, Père. La Prière du Christ et des Chrétiens,* Analecta Biblica 19A (Rome: Pontifical Biblical Institute, 1971), and the literature given there. I should also like to express my indebtedness to the unpublished study by Paul Mankowski, *The Fatherhood of God in the Religion of Israel* (Weston School of Theology, 1988).

11. These texts tend to confirm the thesis that, with careful eliminations (such as never using *'ēm* [mother]), the Israelites used the same name forms as their neighbors, and that they were intended to describe, or invoke, a relationship of tutelage to Yhwh as God.

12. The rather infrequent use of *ba'al* in Israelite names dates back to a time when the term signified "lord" and its connection with the Canaanite fertility god was not so powerful. Because of these later connotations the term *ba'al* is frequently replaced by *bōšet* (shame) in the Hebrew Bible: see 2 Sam 4:4; 9:3-13; 21:8-9. For a discussion of this see *Harper's Bible Dictionary,* ed. Paul Achtemeier (San Francisco: Harper and Row, 1985), 626-27.

that these names, which never lost their capacity to evoke some resonance of their religious origin,[13] often served as a means of proclaiming faith in Yhwh or as a polemic against foreign worship.

It seems then that in Israel as elsewhere, theophoric names were a means of expressing the desire for a special relationship of tutelage or protection. The context within Israelite faith determined the significance of the epithet, just as, for instance, the figure of someone drawing a man out of the underworld is, in a pagan context, Hercules drawing Cerberus out of Hades, and in a Christian context, Christ drawing Adam out of Hell.[14]

The conclusion we may draw from all this is twofold: (1) the theophoric names in Israel reflect a transposition of the general piety of that period in the Middle East, to express faith in the protection of the God of Israel; and (2) although the custom of using the epithet *father* in some Israelite names did not derive from the same source as that of actually calling God *Father,* the two usages are not, in practice, completely distinct. In order to compare them we will look now at the manner in which *Father* was applied to God.

God as Father in Israel

Israel was not unique in considering God to be the Father of a people. The book of Numbers quotes a taunt song against the Moabites and their god Chemosh, berating him because "he let his sons become fugitives and his daughters be taken captive" (Num 21:29).[15] Once again then, it is not the common vocabulary but the context that must be attended to. In this regard there are two considerations: Israel described God in a way very different from that found in the mythology of the surrounding people, and Israel's God is unique in that he became Father of a people by an historical act in which he chose them and cared for them.

13. See Jeffrey Tigay, *You Shall Have No Other Gods: Israelite Religion in the Light of Hebrew Inscriptions,* Harvard Semitic Studies 31 (Atlanta: Schwartz, 1986), 159.

14. This example is used by Erwin Panofsky in his *Studies in Iconology: Humanistic Themes in the Art of the Renaissance* (New York: Harper Torchbooks, 1962), 19.

15. In the famous Moabite inscription from the 9th century B.C., the king Mesah calls himself "the son of Chemosh." *Ancient Near Eastern Texts,* ed. James Pritchard (Princeton: Princeton University Press, 1969), 320. For a notion of how the term *father* was interpreted we may turn to the inscription (9th-8th century B.C.) from Karatepe in which king Azitawadda, after describing himself as "father and mother" to his people, says: "Yea, every king considered me his father because of my righteousness and my wisdom and the kindness of my heart" (ibid., 654).

As already noted, the term *'ab,* while it can be applied to any god by way of securing his protection, is most often restricted to that god who is considered the high god, the father (and sometimes mother) of the other gods. Now the most remarkable thing about this god in the mythologies contiguous to Israel is that he is far from the patriarchal figure he is sometimes depicted as being. As John Miller has pointed out, the father god is characteristically brutish, incompetent, ineffective, and generally inert.[16] The effective activity of the gods is performed by the son(s) or daughter(s) or wife or consort(s) of this god. This is in striking contrast to the God of Israel, who is first and foremost unique, alone (without a consort or helpers), and is the only agent in the creation of the universe and in the forming of Israel. It is highly unlikely that Israel could have borrowed its notion of God as Father from the patriarchal image of the surrounding father gods.

The source of Israel's belief in God as the Father of his people was their theological reflection on the mystery of God's choice of Israel, expressed in his action by which they were rescued from slavery and given a land.

> Has it ever been known before that any god took action himself to bring one nation out of another one, by ordeals, signs, wonders, war with mighty hand and outstretched arm, by fearsome terrors — all of which things Yhwh our God has done for you before your eyes in Egypt? (Dt 4:34)

This reflection probably takes its origin in the prophetic transposition of a theme known in semitic culture but changed in its new context, where it mediated God's creation of a people and his choice to care for them. Thus, in the text from Hosea we have already considered for its imagery:

> When Israel was a youth, I loved him;
> Out of Egypt I called, my son.
> I call to them,
> but they only walk away from me.
> To the Baals they sacrifice,
> to idols they burn their incense.
> Yet it was I who helped Ephraim to walk,
> I took him up in my arms;
> and they did not know
> that I cared for them.

16. See John W. Miller, *Biblical Faith and Fathering: Why We Call God "Father"* (New York: Paulist Press, 1989), esp. chapter 4.

With human ties I tugged at them,
with cords of love.
I was to them,
like one raising a suckling child
up close to his cheek.
I stooped to them and fed them.

                                        (Hos 11:1-4)[17]

The image here is of a youngster, unable to walk, who is given identity, vigor, nourishment, and protection by Yhwh's free choice of him. This is not far from Ezekiel's image of Yhwh finding a girl child weltering in her own blood who is claimed by him and made his daughter (Ez 16:1-63). In both cases Yhwh's "begetting" of Israel consists in his choice of a nondescript group who become his people. He "created" a people in much the same way as a king "creates" an earl: through a benevolent act of choice, or as it is expressed in theology, through an election. It is to this that another early text, already considered in chapter 8, alludes by developing the image of *Father* to include the notion of begetting:

Is he not your Father who created you,
who made you and established you? . . .
For Yhwh's portion is his people,
Jacob his allotted inheritance.
He found him in a desert land
and in the howling waste of the wilderness. . . .
You were unmindful of the Rock who begot you,
and you forgot the God who gave you birth.

                                        (Dt 32:6, 8-9, 18)

17. Hosea may have played the same role in regard to the image of God as Father as he did with that of God as husband. In either case the notion may have pre-existed him, but he forged it into a powerful symbol. Evidence for antecedent use of "Father" outside Israel is available, as we have seen, and biblical texts such as Dt 32:6, Ex 4:22-33 may antedate Hosea. Evidence for a precedent for calling God "spouse" hinges on a difficult text in a Hittite covenant treaty in which the vassal promises not to "commit adultery," that is, not be unfaithful to the covenant. For the text and this interpretation, recently challenged, see E. Weidner, *Politische Dokumente aus Kleinasien. Die Staatsverträge in akkadischer Sprache aus dem Archiv vom Boghazkoi,* Boghazkoi Studien, 8-9 (Leipzig, 1923), 104, lines 58-59. In regard to either image it is important to attend to exactly what is being compared by way of analogy or metaphor: "As in the marriage metaphor, where the legal rather than the sexual aspects are important, . . . here the concept of Yahweh's care and nurture rather than that of procreation is significant." Hans Walter Wolff, *Hosea: A Commentary on the Book of the Prophet Hosea,* trans. Gary Stansell (Philadelphia: Fortress, 1974), 198-99, n. 44.

A rapid glance at other Old Testament texts that use the rather rare appellation *Father* in regard to God in his relation to the people would confirm what we have seen so far. Thus, Jeremiah 3:2-5, 19-20 employs a concatenation of images of disobedient child/faithless wife to accuse Israel of infidelity to the covenant of Yhwh, while Isaiah 63:15-16 and 64:7-8 appeals to God's choice of Israel using the notions of Father, near relative (*gōʾēl*), and potter to mediate the fact that Israel owes its existence to God and to remind the Lord of the care he has promised to them. The same thinking is expressed in Malachi 1:6 and 2:10.

The oracle of Nathan (2 Sm 7:14) and the texts that repeat it (1 Chr 17:13; 22:10; 28:6) as well as those that build on it (Pss 89:27; 2:7) speak of Yhwh as the Father of an individual, the king. While these texts echo extrabiblical precedent, they have been taken up into Israel's faith where the king is "created" son of God at his coronation (Ps 2:7) in an extension of the manner in which Israel was created God's firstborn son (Ex 4:22-24). The accent in both cases is on the fact that God will exercise the care and the right to discipline that characterize a father. These two notions linked with the term *father* are applied to the individual believer by Proverbs 3:11-12. Other examples, drawn mostly from Hellenistic piety, will be considered shortly (Sir 23:1, 4; 51:10; Wis 2:16-18; 5:5; 14:3; also Tob 13:4).[18]

Thus, Israel's speaking of God as Father was not a projection of the patriarchal pantheon of its neighbors. It was a true case of faith seeking understanding and producing something never seen before — an understanding of God as solitary, powerful, active, and generous, who became a father by creating a people and acting toward them as his children: "After all, you are our Father. If Abraham will not own us, if Israel will not acknowledge us, you, Yahweh are our Father, 'Our Redeemer' is your name from of old" (Is 63:16, The New Jerusalem Bible). Before expanding this consideration to include the discovery of the fatherhood of God within himself as this is revealed by Jesus, I would like briefly to point out how Israel's understanding of God produced a new kind of human fatherhood.

A great deal can be learned about a people by studying what they considered important in the formation of the young.[19] There is practically

---

18. It should be pointed out that even here only the texts in Sir 23 and Wis 14:3 are a direct address to God by an individual calling God "Father." The Sirach text is disputed, since we have this passage only in Greek and a later Hebrew paraphrase does not use the direct address. See Joachim Jeremias, *The Prayers of Jesus*, Studies in Biblical Theology, Second Series, 6 (London: SCM, 1967), 27-29. Another issue here is whether or not the texts that do seem to use *Father* in direct address to God are personal invocations or the conferring of a title.

19. In this section I am indebted to the work of John Miller referred to previously, *Biblical Faith and Fathering*, esp. chapter 6.

no mention in the Scriptures of the training of young men in the art of war, or even of schools where the basic skills of writing, arithmetic, and the like, were taught, though indications in the text, especially in the Wisdom literature, enable us to presume the existence of these latter.[20] This same literature is also the source from which we learn how deeply respect for the teaching authority of both father and mother was inculcated in children, especially sons (e.g., Prv 1:8; 6:20; 23:22; 31:26; Sir 3:1-16), thus providing a concept of co-educators unique in the world of that time.[21] We can also see how urgently fathers in particular were exhorted to care for and educate their children. Although the accent is often placed on the need for discipline (e.g., Sir 30:1-13; Prv 29:15-17), the purpose of the exhortation was to show that those who cared for their children loved them enough to undertake the sometimes onerous task of correcting them (e.g., Prv 13:24). In fact, in a text that, as we have seen, presupposes that God acts directly in the life of the believer, Yhwh's corrective action is described in terms of a father's love: "The discipline *(mūsar)* of Yhwh do not despise, my child *(běnî)*, do not resent his reproof; for Yhwh reproves those he loves as a father the child whom he loves" (Prv 3:11-12).

The main object of the father's training was the passing on of the sacred tradition of Israel (e.g., Dt 4:9; 6:6-7; Pss 78:3-8; 22:30-31; Ex 10:2; 12:26; 13:8). This was done in an informal way, "When your son asks you what does this mean?" (e.g., Ex 13:14) and in the context of ritual, for instance, at the celebration of Passover (Ex 12:26). The mention of ritual reminds us of the key role played by the father in the liturgical life of the people, since so much of the ritual centered around the home. This is true of course of the central commemorative ritual, the Passover, at which the father was expected to teach all his children, in the context of this re-enacted meal, the great act by which God had proved his fidelity to the patriarchs and saved his people. There were two other rites that served in a particular way to bind fathers and sons together: the redemption of the firstborn and circumcision. In the first of these, a father had to redeem his son and thus accept him as his own and choose his life (Ex 13:11-16). It was again normally the father himself who, in the company of other significant males of the clan or the village, performed the circumcision rite that enabled the infant to share in the covenant of Abraham (Gen 17:1-14) and prepared

20. See the discussion in Roland E. Murphy, *Wisdom Literature: Job, Proverbs, Ruth, Canticles, Ecclesiastes, Esther,* The Forms of Old Testament Literature, XIII (Grand Rapids: Eerdmans, 1981), 6-9; and de Vaux, *Ancient Israel,* 49.

21. In this connection Miller cites an article of Lothar Perlitt, "Das Bild des Vaters im Alten Testament," in *Das Vaterbild in Mythos und Geschichte,* ed. H. Tellenback (Stuttgart: Kohlhammer, 1976), 50-101; see esp. p. 61.

him, as the modern ritual states, to be "introduced to the study of the Torah, to the marriage canopy, and to good deeds."[22]

When the role of the father of the family is looked at from this perspective we can see the deficiencies of concentrating principally upon the legal texts when trying to understand what the term *father* meant in ancient Israel and how this relates to the use of the expression *patriarchal,* as feminist scholars propose to understand the notion.[23] No one could claim that every human father lived up to this ideal or that dimensions of God's authority were never misunderstood or misapplied. What is clear, however, is that the word *father* was not forged as a legitimation of coercive power. Such a notion is an anachronistic retrojection of the post-Enlightenment understanding that authority is necessarily coercive because heteronomous.

THE USE OF *Father* IN THE SECOND TEMPLE PERIOD

In striking contrast to the twenty-two times the word *Father* is applied to God in the whole of the Old Testament are the one hundred and seventy times in the gospel tradition where Jesus is recorded as speaking of God as "Father" (Mt, 42; Mk, 4; Lk, 15; Jn, 109). We must bear in mind, of course, that this figure includes the repetitions found in parallel passages as well as the marked tendency to introduce the title *Father* into sayings of Jesus as the gospel tradition develops.[24] Nevertheless, it is an impressive witness to a significant turn in the biblical tradition.[25] In order to understand the significance of this turn we must attend to the evidence in the literature

22. Cited by Miller, *Biblical Faith and Fathering,* 76.

23. A study that, though it is basically accurate in what it says, illustrates this deficiency is that by Phyllis Bird, "Images of Women in the Old Testament," in *Religion and Sexism: Images of Woman in the Jewish and Christian Traditions,* ed. Rosemary Radford Ruether (New York: Simon and Schuster, 1974), 41-88.

24. In addition to the eleven instances held in common in one way or another by the Synoptic Gospels, Matthew has thirty-one instances that are unique to him and there are another one hundred found only in the fourth Gospel.

25. The most extensive analysis of the data is that by Joachim Jeremias, *The Prayers of Jesus,* 29-35. In addition to the studies to be considered in a moment, it should be observed that Jeremias's work has been criticized by E. P. Sanders, "Jesus and the Kingdom: The Restoration of Israel and the New People of God," in *Jesus, The Gospels, and the Church: Essays in Honor of William R. Farmer,* ed. E. P. Sanders (Macon, Ga.: Mercer University Press, 1987), 225-39. It has been defended by Ben F. Meyer, "A Caricature of Joachim Jeremias and His Scholarly Work," *Journal of Biblical Literature* 110 (1991): 451-62 (with a reply by Sanders).

more closely preceding and contemporaneous with the gospel tradition for the use of the term *father* in statements about God and in addresses to him.

In the Second Temple period (roughly 500 B.C. to A.D. 70), writings can be found, particularly among Hellenistic Jews, which speak of God as Father. Some of these are expressions of individual piety while others address God as the Father of the nation. Again, some texts invoke God and others make statements to the effect that he is Father. It should be noted that the amount of prayer and related material available from the Second Temple period, while, of course, not exhaustive, does provide a good representation of the language use of the time. In this material there are extant about twenty-two texts that use father-type language in regard to God.[26] Of these, six state explicitly or equivalently that God is the Father of the nation,[27] and another six include this same notion in an address to God.[28] There are two texts that speak of God as the Father of an individual,[29] and nine that, in their present form, are a personal address to God as Father.[30] We have to note, however, that of the last-named nine texts, two (Sir 23:1, 4) are personal invocations to God as Father only in the Greek text, while it may be reasonably supposed that the Hebrew original (not extant) addressed God not as "Lord, Father and Master/God of my life" but rather as "God of my Father and Lord of my Life" as can now be found in a late Hebrew liturgical paraphrase of the Sirach text.[31] This conjecture is confirmed by comparing the Hebrew text of 1 Chronicles

26. These are: 1 Chr 29:10 (LXX); Sir 23:1.4; 51:10; Tob 13:4; Wis 2:16; 11:10; 14:3; 3 Mc 2:21; 5:7; 6:3.8; 7:6; Jub 1:25.28; 19:29; 1QH 9:35-36; 4Q372 1.16; 4Q460 5.6; Apoc Ez frg. 2; Joseph and Aseneth 12:8-15; Josephus, *Antiquities* 2,6,8 (152). I omit from the discussion two instances in the *Testaments of the Twelve Patriarchs* (T.Levi 18:6; T.Jud 24:2) and three occurrences in the *Testament of Job* (33:3.9; 40:3) because these are most probably Christian interpolations. There are also three other possibilities in the Qumran material, but Eileen Schuller says of them that the context is too fragmentary to establish them with certainty or the reading itself is doubtful. See "The Psalm of 4Q372 1 Within the Context of Second Temple Prayer," *Catholic Biblical Quarterly* 54 (1992): 67-79; especially nos. 32, 33.

27. Tob 13:4; 3Mc 2:21; 5:7; 7:6; Jub 1:25.28;

28. 1 Chr 29:10 (LXX; see discussion below); Tob 13:4; Wis 11:10; 1QH 9:35; *Antiquities* 2,6,8; Apocryphon of Ezekiel, fragment 2 (see *The Old Testament Pseudoepigrapha*, vol. 1, ed. James H. Charlesworth [New York: Doubleday, 1983], 494).

29. Wis 2:16; Jub 19:29 (both corporate and individual).

30. Sir 23:1.4; 51:10; 3 Mc 6:3.8; Wis 14:3; 4Q372 1.16; 4Q460 5.6; Joseph and Aseneth 12:8-15 (this is equivalently an invocation).

31. For a discussion of this text see Jeremias, *The Prayers of Jesus*, 28-29 and nos. 69-71; also Joseph Fitzmyer, "Abba and Jesus' Relation to God," in *A Cause de l'Evangile. Mélanges Offertes à Dom Jacques Dupont* (Paris: Cerf, 1985), 15-38; esp. 25.

29:10, "Blessed are you, Yhwh, God of Israel our father," with its Greek translation in the Septuagint, "Blessed are you, Lord, God of our fathers." In this latter text God is described as the Father of the nation while in the former Israel is so described.

Of the remaining seven references, five are in Greek and two are in Hebrew. Among the Greek texts, Sirach 51:10 and *Joseph and Aseneth* 12:8-15, while they are found in prayers to God, actually employ the term *Father* more as a title than an invocation.[32] This leaves us with 3 Maccabees 6:3, 8 and Wisdom 14:3 in Greek and the two fragments from Qumran Cave 4 in Hebrew, in all of which there is a direct personal invocation of God as Father.

> [The priest Eleazar is praying] King, great in power, Most High . . . look upon the seed of Abraham . . . perishing unjustly in a foreign land, O Father! . . . When Jonah was pining away . . . you, Father, restored him. . . . (3 Mc 6:3, 8)[33]

> [In a prayer about sea travel] But your providence, O Father, guides it [the boat]. . . . (Wis 14:3)

> [The prayer of Joseph when delivered up to strangers] My Father, my God, do not abandon me into the hands of the nations. (4Q372 116)[34]

> [This fragment is unpublished; it is reported by Schuller to contain the phrase "My Father and my Lord"]. (4Q460 5 6)[35]

32. Sir 51:10 reads; "I called out, Yhwh *(yyy)*, you are my Father, you are my champion and my savior." *Joseph and Aseneth* 12:8-15 is part of a prayer in which Aseneth is beseeching the God of Israel to help her: "For (just) as a little child who is afraid flees to his father, and the father . . . snatches him off the ground . . . and he rests at his father's breast, the father, however, smiles . . . likewise you too, Lord, stretch out your hands upon me as a child-loving father. [There then follows a passage in which the devil is described as the father of the gods of the Egyptians as well as the father of those who worship them. This is followed by] . . . you are the father of the orphan . . . you, Lord are a sweet and good and gentle father. What father is as sweet as you Lord . . . ?" (trans. by C. Burchard, *The Old Testament Pseudoepigrapha*, vol. 2, 221-22). It should be noted that Sir 51:1 is also a candidate for consideration as a text invoking God as Father, but it should be read, "I praise you, O God of my salvation; I shall thank you O God of my father." Compare Sir 23:1.4 and 1 Chr 29:10. For a discussion of Sir 51:1 see Fitzmyer, "Abba," 26, n. 50.

33. Translation basically that of H. Anderson, *Old Testament Pseudoepigrapha*, vol. 2, 526, though the first *pater* is not translated in this text.

34. Translation by Eileen M. Schuller, "4Q372 1: A Text about Joseph," *Revue de Qumran* 14 (1990): 355.

35. "The Psalm of 4Q372 1," 78, n. 44.

This representative material indicates that God was spoken of as Father and addressed as such in both Greek- and Hebrew-speaking Jewish milieu. The paucity of occurrences, however, also indicates that while such language use was intelligible and acceptable, it was quite rare. There are authors who seek to extend this usage by retrojecting later rabbinic expressions back into the earlier period. While this has some plausibility, it is impossible to be sure of what expressions were already in use by the end of the first century. This judgment may apply as well to the famous *'ābînû šĕbāššamāyim* (Our Father, who art in heaven) whose earliest firm attestation is precisely Matthew 6:9.[36]

'abbā' (Father)

It should be noted that in all the examples just cited, the word *'abbā'* does not occur. As a matter of fact, up until the second century A.D. this Aramaic word occurs only sporadically as a proper name or a patronym *(bar Abba'/h)* on two ossuaries and one ostracon, and it is never used of God.[37] Philologically, the term can represent three different grammatical possibilities: vocative (O father), possessive (my father), Aramaic emphatic (the father). When it does begin to occur, as in the Mishnah (redacted ca. A.D. 200) or the targums (whose dating is difficult), it is often as a replacement for the Hebrew *'ābî* (my father), as an honorific title (certain rabbis were called Abba), or as an expression of affection and respect employed by adults of their parents, teachers, etc. Although the term may have originated in the address of small children to their own parents, Jeremias, as he himself recognized, exaggerated this point.[38] Jeremias was not wrong however, in maintaining that no one was ever cited as applying the term *'abbā'* to God before Jesus did so.[39]

36. Regarding synagogal prayers, Geza Vermes has written that "it is not possible to prove that even the earliest form extant represents anything actually current during the age of Jesus." (*Jesus and the World of Judaism* [London: SCM, 1983], 40, cited by Schuller, "The Psalm of 4Q372," 77.) For examples of rabbinic usage that make it plausible, but not provable, that there was some speech about God as Father, see Asher Finkel, "The Prayer of Jesus in Matthew," in *Standing Before God,* ed. Asher Finkel and Lawrence Frizzel (New York: Ktav, 1981), 131-69, and in the same collection, Dieter Zeller, "God As Father in the Proclamation and Prayer of Jesus," 117-30.

37. For a complete account of the history of the term see Fitzmyer, "Abba and Jesus' Relation to God," 20-24.

38. For a critique of Jeremias on this point see James Barr, "Abba Isn't 'Daddy,'" *Journal of Theological Studies* 39 ns (1988): 28-47.

39. "There is no evidence in the literature of pre-Christian or first-century Palestinian Judaism that *'abbā'* was used in any sense as a personal address for God by an individual — and for Jesus to address God as *'abbā'* or 'Father' is therefore something new." Fitzmyer, "Abba and Jesus' Relation to God," 28. To look elsewhere

In order to understand the significance of this fact, we must place it in the context of Jesus' overall speech about God as Father, and more specifically as his Father. There are two issues to be considered here. There is first, the historical issue: how many of the one hundred and seventy occurrences of the word *Father* can be traced back to Jesus himself? Second, there is the theological issue: what is the significance of the growing tendency in the New Testament tradition to attribute this speech to Jesus? In regard to the historical issue, we may accept Jeremias's very cautious acceptance of four texts as deriving from stage I of the tradition, that is, from Jesus himself.[40] Three of these texts are:

Concerning that day or the hour no one knows, not the angels in heaven (not the Son), only the Father. (Mk 13:32)[41]

Blessed are you, Simon, son of Jonah, flesh and blood did not make this revelation to you, rather my Father who is in heaven. (Mt 16:17)

And I confer upon you, as my Father conferred upon my, a kingdom. (Lk 22:29)

The fourth text is the so-called Johannine logion, found in Matthew 11:25-27 and Luke 10:21-22. The text is very similar in both Gospels. I will present the text of Matthew, indicating in parentheses the significant differences in Luke:[42]

At that time Jesus responded (At that hour he rejoiced in the Spirit) and said: I praise you Father, Lord of heaven and earth, because you hid these things from the wise and intelligent and revealed them to little

---

for the origin of this expression, for example among the "ecstatics" of the early community, is to trivialize the manner in which the term was and is used and understood by the believing community, already in New Testament times. For an example of this tendency see Mary Rose D'Angelo, "Theology in Mark and Q: *Abba* and "Father" in Context," *Harvard Theological Review* 85 (1992): 149-74.

40. *The Prayers of Jesus*, 45-54. I refer the reader to these pages in order not to unduly prolong this part of the study. For a discussion of the three stages of the transmission of the gospel tradition see chapter 3.

41. The words in parentheses, despite some manuscript hesitation, are part of the canonical text. They are, however, most likely an addition at stage II. The Matthean text (Mt 24:36) is identical except for the addition of the word *alone* after *Father*.

42. Although the authenticity of this text is challenged by many, it continues to be maintained as deriving from stage I by many scholars. My argument for so maintaining it is not based solely on the presence of *Father* but also looks to the originality of what is said about the Father and the Son.

ones. Yes, Father, for thus it has been pleasing in your sight. All things have been handed over to me by my Father; and no one knows the Son (who the Son is) but the Father, and no one knows the Father (who the Father is) but the Son and the one to whom the Son wishes to make revelation.

We should first note that "Lord of heaven and earth" is a rather common Jewish manner of referring to God, and may have been known to Jesus from the liturgical prayers of his day.[43] What is unique is the direct address to God using "Father." The motive for Jesus' praise is that the Father has hidden "these things" from those who would be considered most apt for understanding and has revealed them to those who are righteous and eager to be taught.[44] Most probably, as Jesus originally uttered the saying, "these things" referred to the realities of the Kingdom (see Mt 13:11). This first section closes with another address to God as "Father," this time highlighting, in a very semitic phrase, the complete gratuity of God's initiative in revealing what only he knows (compare 1 Cor 1:21).

In the second saying[45] Jesus asserts that there is a unique and intimate relation of mutual knowledge between himself, "the Son," and God, "the Father." We should note the expressions, *the Father* and *the Son*. There is a tendency to treat these terms as a sort of anticipation of Johannine theology effected perhaps at the second stage of the gospel transmission.[46] There is, however, the very real possibility that this manner of speaking derives from Jesus himself. It is easier to understand how such terminology entered the gospel tradition on the basis of Jesus' authority than to suppose the authority of a later preacher or prophet. The same is to be said of the claim connected with the verb to *reveal (apokalypsai)*. Not only does Jesus attribute to himself the authority to make such a revelation of the Father,

43. See Joachim Jeremias, *New Testament Theology: The Proclamation of Jesus,* trans. John Bowden (New York: Charles Scribner and Sons, 1971), 187-88.

44. For this understanding of *nēpioi* see Davies and Allison, *Saint Matthew,* 275 and the literature given there: "The 'babes' are those who, in the eyes of the world, are weak and simple, but before God they are the elect."

45. This second saying may or may not have been uttered in the context of the first. For our purposes we need not determine that here. In their actual situation the texts of Matthew and Luke are completed by still a third saying. In Matthew this is the invitation of Jesus as Wisdom to those who labor and are burdened; in Luke we have Jesus' declaration that the eyes and ears of the disciples are blessed — words that Matthew places in the parable discourse (Mt 13:16-17).

46. These terms form the backbone of the Johannine development of the earlier tradition. See the treatment in Rudolf Schnackenburg, *The Gospel According to John,* vol. 2 (New York: Seabury Press, 1980), excursus 9, " 'The Son' as Jesus' Self-Designation in the Gospel of John," 172-86.

but he also claims that he can confer a share in the knowledge he himself has of the Father.

We may now consider Jesus' use of the term *'abbā'*. As we have seen there is the philological possibility that *'abbā'* underlies both the expression *the Father (o patēr)* of Mark 13:32 (Mt 24:36), and the expression *my Father (o patēr mou)* of Matthew 16:17 and Luke 22:29. The possibility is strengthened when we consider the one place in which the word *'abbā'* actually occurs in the gospel tradition, namely Mark 14:36. Mark's *abba o patēr* is rendered by a vocative in Luke 22:42 (Father! *pater*) and by a vocative and possessive in Matthew 26:39 (my Father! *pater mou*). While philologically possible, this observation is in no way necessary to establish Jesus' use of words related to the stem *'ab* when speaking about or to God. This much, however, is practically certain. No one would have begun to use the word *'abbā'* in regard to God if Jesus had not set the precedent. There is little enough evidence for the use of the word at all in first-century Palestine, and no evidence that it was ever applied to God. This may be considered a characteristic of Jesus' speech. He drew upon a recognizable but rare manner of referring to God as Father *('ab)* and made it peculiarly his own, investing it with his own meaning and calling attention to this by his original, though perhaps not unvarying, use of *'abbā'*. I say that this was not unvarying because he probably availed himself of other forms as well in connection with his Father: *'ab, 'ăbî,* and so on. However *'abbā'* was common enough on his lips to be considered a characteristic of his way of speaking to and about God. It was this whole complex of forms of address that provided the basis for the theological expansion of Father terminology in reporting the words of Jesus. Without such a basis, this expansion and the theological manner in which it is used to mediate something of the relation between the Father and the Son remains unexplained and unintelligible.[47]

This brings us to a theological consideration of this mode of address. In regard to the term *'abbā'* itself, we should note that it occurs in three prayer contexts. There is first of all the prayer of Jesus in Mark 14:36 in a pericope that shows many signs of liturgical influence, and particularly the influence of the "Our Father."[48] Jesus is portrayed as the ideal Son,

---

47. Mary Rose D'Angelo seems to appreciate the force of this argument when she seeks for another explanation and finds it in a New Testament polemic against calling the emperor "father." The instances of the use of such a title are rare, and the existence of such a polemic is extremely doubtful. As she herself recognizes, the corroborative rabbinic material she invokes, which is subject to another interpretation, postdates the Gospels by nearly 200 years. "*Abba* and "Father": Imperial Theology and the Jesus Traditions," *Journal of Biblical Literature* 111 (1992): 611-30.

48. See Francis Martin, "Literary Theory, Philosophy of History and Exegesis," *The Thomist* 52 (1988): 575-604, and the literature given there.

submitting in trust to the Father and addressing him in the words used by the community in imitation of his own prayer, though now modified by the addition of the Greek equivalent: *abba o patēr*. Mark is purposely using this form of address to help his readers enter into Jesus' prayer of love, trust and submission. It is common for the Gospels to employ the prayer language of the community when describing events in the life of Jesus.[49] The other two examples of the phrase *abba o patēr* are found in Galatians 4:6 and Romans 8:15. In both of these texts Paul is exploiting an expression well known in the community to draw out conclusions regarding the fact that, by the action of the Holy Spirit, Christians now know a share in the relation that Jesus had and has with the Father. In the letter to the Galatians, he uses this fact to insist on the freedom Christians have in regard to the Law. In the letter to the Romans he points to the same freedom, this time as a freedom from sin and its hold on the flesh. In fact, the antipode of life in the flesh is precisely this divinely conferred affection for and confidence in the Father.

To sum up: Jesus frequently spoke of and to God as "Father," thereby drawing out a latent theme in first-century Jewish thought and conferring on it his own unique understanding of God. In this prophetic witness to the true reality of God he employed the term *'abbā'*, most probably pressing into service for the first time an expression that had the capacity to evoke respect and affection and was still free enough from other associations to mediate his unique witness. After the Resurrection, this aspect of his teaching was cherished because of its prophetic truth and because Christians came to experience the reality of his witness in their own lives, coming into a relationship with the Father that they recognized as being a share in that which Jesus had spoken about and possessed in a unique manner. This led the later tradition to continue to speak of and to God as Father and also to use the expression *'abbā* in imitation of Jesus, in obedience to his instructions (see Lk 11:2).[50] It was undoubtedly this combination of lived experience and remembered teaching that provided the impetus in the

---

49. For some examples and further literature see Francis Martin, "Critique historique et enseignement du Nouveau Testament sur l'imitation du Christ," *Revue Thomiste* 93 (1993): 234-62; especially 240-41.

50. For a discussion of the authenticity of the Lukan address in the "Our Father" as opposed to the liturgically influenced rendering of Matthew, one may consult Joseph Fitzmyer, *The Gospel According to Luke (X–XXIV)*, Anchor Bible 28A (New York: Doubleday, 1985), 902-3, as well as commentaries on Matthew such as Ulrich Luz, *Matthew 1–7: A Commentary*, trans. Wilhelm C. Linss (Minneapolis: Augsburg, 1989), 375-76; W. D. Davies and Dale C. Allison, *The Gospel According to Saint Matthew*, International Critical Commentary, vol. I (Edinburgh: T. & T. Clark, 1988), 600-602.

earliest communities to include a mention of the Father in the tradition of Jesus' words, even in cases where the expression had not been handed down as part of the previous heritage. It was this same combination that provided the basis for the theological elaborations of Paul and John, who, each in his own way, developed a deep spiritual teaching concerning the transcendent fatherhood of *Theos* and the unique relationship that existed between himself and Jesus, his Son. *Abba* became the vehicle for that teaching and the experience that illuminated it.

THEOS (GOD)

Although there was as yet no attempt to define the relationship in precise terms, it is clear that for the New Testament the term *God (Theos)* meant the God and Father of our Lord Jesus Christ. As Raymond Brown observes: "It is quite obvious that in the New Testament the term 'God' is applied with overwhelming frequency to God the Father, i.e., to the God revealed in the Old Testament to whom Jesus prayed."[51] In fact, the three certain and five very probable instances where *Theos* is extended to include Jesus[52] are examples of the whole New Testament strategy of bringing terms (such as *Kyrios*), gestures (such as worship), and statements (such as "I and the Father are one" [Jn 10:30]) into relation with Jesus to mediate what the later tradition would appositely call his divinity.

It was from such predication that the triadic formulas of the New Testament developed, speaking of "Father, Son, and Spirit" or "Spirit, Lord, and God" where "God" *(Theos)* is obviously the same as *Patēr*.[53] In early Christian speech, when God was described as wise, omnipotent, forgiving, etc., it was presumed that the Son and the Spirit shared in these attributes because they are one with him. When later theological speculation defined that oneness by speaking of *homoousios* (one in substance), it

51. "Does the New Testament Call Jesus God?" *Theological Studies* 26 (1965): 545-73; citation is from p. 548.

52. The three certain are Jn 1:1; 20:28; Heb 1:8-9. The five very probable, with varying degrees of probability, are 2 Thess 1:12; Tit 2:13; 1 Jn 5:20; Rom 9:5; 2 Pet 1:1.

53. For a brief treatment of the triadic formulae in the New Testament and a bibliography, see Francis Martin, "Pauline Trinitarian Formulas and Christian Unity," *Catholic Biblical Quarterly* 30 (1968): 199-219. There are thirteen places in the New Testament where the congruence of *Theos and Patēr* occurs in a way that shows the identity of the referent of these two terms: Jn 6:27; 8:42. 54; 1 Cor 8:6; 2 Cor 1:3; 11:31; Gal 4:6; Eph 1:3.17; 4:6; 1 Thess 1:7; 2 Thess 2:16; 1 Pet 1:3.

became possible to think of the divine nature as being the "place" of the attributes shared in by the Divine Persons. So long as such a viewpoint was still within the magnetic field of a vital biblical and experiential faith, there was a instinctive oscillation between *God* as the divinely shared nature and *God* properly so called, the Father of Jesus Christ.[54] Since the Enlightenment, however, the inherent weakness of this position has caused it to fall apart (witness the manual treatises *De Deo Uno*) with the result bemoaned by Karl Rahner: "One might almost dare to affirm that if the doctrine of the Trinity were to be erased as false, most religious literature could be preserved almost unchanged through the process."[55]

CAN WE KNOW GOD AS FATHER?

Rahner himself was one of those who has helped to restore an awareness of the New Testament manner of speaking of God. I wish to refer to one aspect of that restoration that relates to the methods of reconstruction and recovery being used here. There is no doubt that the New Testament tradition, basing itself on the teaching of Jesus and the experience of his resurrection, called God "Father" and called Jesus his "Son" (nowhere in this tradition is Jesus ever called *Patēr*, though we have seen he is called *Theos*). The question that confronts us here is the nature of that predication, or perhaps one might say its referent. Do these terms refer to the inner life of God, what is called the "immanent Trinity," or are they merely adaptations of the unknowable and ineffable mystery of God's own reality to our weak human mode of understanding? The question, of course, relates

54. In itself, there would be no intrinsic objection to referring in private worship to the divine nature metaphorically as "mother" as it is sometimes referred to as "father," as designating the source of all existence. Such, however, is never the biblical mode of speaking about God, either in the Old or New Testament: the personal God of the Old Testament is revealed in the New to be Father "within himself," so to speak. For a discussion of this point see Joseph Augustine DiNoia, "Knowing and Naming the Triune God: The Grammar of Trinitarian Confession," in *Speaking the Christian God: The Holy Trinity and the Challenge of Feminism,* ed. Alvin F. Kimel, Jr. (Grand Rapids: Eerdmans, 1992), 162-87.

55. Karl Rahner, "Remarks on the Dogmatic Treatise 'De Trinitate,'" in *Theological Investigations,* IV, trans. Kevin Smyth (London: Darton, Longman and Todd, 1966), 77-102; citation is from p. 79. Whatever the great scholastics intended by discussing the wisdom, justice, and other attributes of God without specifying that this is a discussion of *Theos,* the later Catholic manuals certainly generated a "unitarian" mindset that is still with us. For a discussion of this see Walter Kasper, *The God of Jesus Christ,* trans. Matthew J. O'Connell (New York: Crossroad, 1984), esp. 133-57.

to the whole manner in which we speak about God, especially the Triune God.

There are, it seems, three possible ways that we may understand the terms *Father, Son,* and *Holy Spirit.* I will associate each of the positions with the name of a theologian. There is first of all the position of Karl Rahner, for whom "the Trinity of the economy of salvation *is* the immanent Trinity and vice versa."[56] Yves Congar rightly points to the truth of the first part of the statement, remarking that the New Testament, the early creeds, and the ante-Nicene Fathers all spoke of the Trinity as it is manifested in the work of salvation, and yet the Trinity they spoke of *is* the One Triune God.[57] Congar faults Rahner, however, for the "vice versa" of the last part of the phrase. The immanent Trinity is not completely revealed in the economy of salvation. The mystery of the Father, Son, and Holy Spirit as they exist in themselves remains unattainable to any created intellect, even in the light of glory.

At the other extreme is the position of Catherine Mowry LaCugna, who, on the basis of the "economic" language used of the Trinity before the Council of Nicea (325), concludes that the assertion of the Council that the Son is "of the same substance" *(homoousios)* as the Father initiated speculation on the very nature of the immanent Trinity with disastrous results.[58] It ought to be pointed out, first, that not all the language of the New Testament is "economic." To mention but two clear examples: the opening verses of John's Gospel describe the relation between the *Logos* and *Theos* in a way that prepares for but does not necessitate the economy of salvation (Jn 1:1-2), and the same can be said of the timeless present participle in Heb 1:3a that describes the Son as *"being* the radiance of his glory and the imprint of his substance."

Although LaCugna's book has much to commend it, her thesis that in actual fact we can know nothing of the internal relations of the Trinity but only their economic or enacted relations only serves to obscure the New Testament teaching that we are called to a true communion with the Father and the Son in the Holy Spirit (e.g., 1 Jn 1:3; Eph 2:18). The communion or shared life must exist independently of the work of salva-

---

56. "Remarks on the Dogmatic Treatise 'De Trinitate,' " 87. A similar remark can be found in the translation of Rahner's contribution as part of *Mysterium Salutis: The Trinity,* trans. Joseph Donceel (New York: Herder & Herder, 1970), 22: "The 'economic' Trinity is the 'immanent' Trinity and the 'immanent' Trinity is the 'economic' Trinity."

57. Yves Congar, *I Believe in the Holy Spirit,* vol. 3, trans. David Smith (New York: Seabury, 1983), 11-18.

58. *God For Us: The Trinity and Christian Life* (San Francisco: Harper, 1991).

tion; it is something into which we are called by a free decision of the Trinity itself.

The Council of Nicea correctly perceived that if the teaching of Arius were allowed to stand, if it were admitted that the Son was not equal to the Father, then we would be forced to admit that the communion of life that constitutes the very heart of the Christian message is not really with the divine Persons. In this case, the witness of the New Testament and the experience of believers would have been proven false. We could not say that when the completion of the time came, "God [*Theos*] sent his Son, born of a woman, born under the law, that he might redeem those under the law, that we might receive adoptive sonship." Nor that this same *Theos* "sent the Spirit of his Son into our hearts crying Abba, Father" (Gal 4:4-6). We could not be sure that we were speaking of the relations between Theos and his Son and the Spirit. We would know only the historical activity of God and really have no basis for being sure that the prayer the Holy Spirit brings about in us relates us to the Father who is really different from the Son.

The reasons that lead LaCugna to consider that the Nicene expression and its development by later theologians, especially the Cappadocians, brought about the "defeat" of the doctrine of the Trinity, are basically two. First, she considers that the need to maintain the impassibility of the *Logos,* once he was considered equal to *Theos,* forbade any realistic acceptance of the fact that the Son of God really suffered for us. But this can be derived from the sayings of Athanasius and others only by judging them by the vocabulary of later ages, a practice that LaCugna frequently, and correctly, eschews in other circumstances.[59]

The second reason, which is really a development of the first, is that the Nicene language precludes taking seriously the "economic subordinationism" of the New Testament and the early Christian writers. Economic subordinationism refers to the manner in which the Son and the Spirit are portrayed as subordinated to the Father in the work of salvation. They are said to be "sent," Jesus is described as "obedient," Jesus says "the Father is greater than I" (Jn 14:28), the Spirit prays to the Father in us, and so on. LaCugna seems to be convinced that if one maintains the *homoousios*

---

59. This thesis is clearly articulated on p. 35 of *God For Us.* It suffices to read the texts of Cyril of Jerusalem and others to see that the post-Nicene Fathers not only spoke of Christ's sufferings but expressly used *Theos,* in the extended manner mentioned earlier, as the subject of the verb "suffer." For a good presentation of the patristic thinking on this, as interpreted by Hans Urs von Balthasar, the reader may consult John Saward, *The Mysteries of March: Hans Urs von Balthasar on the Incarnation and Easter* (London: Collins, 1990).

of Nicea then one is obliged to so separate the economic from the immanent (or "theological") Trinity that, in fact, the force of these expressions is reduced to meaninglessness. It is better, she maintains, to insist that we know only the economic Trinity and to acknowledge that we have no idea whether, within the ineffable mystery of the Godhead, there are really three Persons or not.[60] Such a position can be called agnostic, or more graciously, "apophatic," as Congar does when describing the theses of Piet Schoonenberg.[61]

Let it be granted that there has been excessive and even unwarranted theological speculation about God's inaccessible trinitarian life. Let it further be granted that our knowledge of God comes through the historical activity of God, most especially and uniquely in the life, death, and resurrection of Jesus Christ. It does not follow that the triune life revealed to us and into which we are invited can only be asserted of the enacted or exteriorized relations of the Persons of the Trinity. We cannot with Rahner establish complete identity between what salvation history reveals and the inner triune life of God. But neither may we with LaCugna accept such a division between what is revealed and what is still hidden that we must reduce the clear statements of the New Testament and the subsequent tradition (including Nicea and Constantinople) to speech only about God's activity. There is a third way, that of understanding these statements as both correct and inadequate analogical assertions about the Father, the Son, and the Holy Spirit. It is this way that I wish to consider now. It is the way of the mainline tradition, and I will take as its representative Hans Urs von

---

60. "Because the essence of God is permanently unknowable as it is in itself, every attempt to describe the immanent Trinity pertains to the face of God turned toward us. . . . Theories about what God is apart from God's self-communication in salvation history remain unverifiable and ultimately untheological, since *theologia* is given only through *oikonomia*." *God For Us*, 230-31. "Unverifiable" is not the same as completely unknowable. It is precisely the role of faith to give us unverifiable knowledge that we know is true because of the light of the Holy Spirit and the truthfulness of God. For a review of LaCugna's book that expresses the same problems as those enunciated here see Thomas Weinandy, "The Immanent and Economic Trinity," *The Thomist* 57 (1993): 655-66.

61. *I Believe in the Holy Spirit*, 14. LaCugna does not divorce herself from this position of Schoonenberg and apparently makes it her own: "This naturally raises the question about whether God would be triune apart from creation, that is, could the one self-communication of God have been only eternal, God to God? P. Schoonenberg writes: 'That God is also trinitarian apart from his self-communication in salvation history may neither be denied nor presupposed as obvious'. . . . We have no vantage point from which we might determine whether or not God would be triune apart from creation; we stand already within the *fact* of creation." *God For Us*, 236, n. 21.

Balthasar because he has attempted to articulate this understanding within the context of modern thinking on the problem.

The theme that the self-emptying life of Jesus Christ reveals something of the eternal relation of the Father and the Son is a leitmotiv in the writings of von Balthasar.[62] While there is something new in the moment of the Incarnation, something that was not before ("Though being Son, he learned obedience from what he suffered . . ." [Heb 5:8]), this cannot be so unlike what has been for all eternity that there is no connection between them. There is an infinite abyss between the divine nature of the Son of God and the human nature that he assumed. Yet, it is the same Person acting, and the human nature which he personalizes and within which he acts, though it is more unlike than like the divine nature, is still "the image of the invisible God" (Col 1:15). This means that what is exteriorized in the historical deeds and words of Jesus must realize in a human way something that exists ineffably within God. Otherwise, the very prayers of Jesus and his obedience, his submission of will on the human level, represent nothing real within God, and his address to God as Father is meaningless. As von Balthasar expresses it:

> Jesus reveals God at the behest, not of the Trinity, but of the Father. Moreover, he, the only Son, who alone fully knows the Father as he is (Mt 11:25), desires to proclaim him, declare him (Jn 1:18).[63]

The obedience, the *kenosis* of Jesus reflects imperfectly but really the mystery of the ineffable equality and *kenosis* of love that transpires within the Trinity. "The exteriorization of God (in the Incarnation) has its ontic condition of possibility in the *eternal* exteriorization of God — that is, his tri-personal self-gift."[64] This understanding, as yet inchoate, lies at the root of the ease with which the New Testament and the pre-Nicene tradition can speak of the economic subordination of the Son and the Spirit and at the same time speak of the *name* of the Father, the Son, and the Holy Spirit (Mt 28:19), can describe the Lamb, different from the One on

---

62. Some of the places where von Balthasar develops his thought are *Theodrama: Theological Dramatic Theory,* vol. III, *Dramatis Personae: Persons in Christ,* trans. Graham Harrison (San Francisco: Ignatius, 1992), 220-28; *Mysterium Paschale,* trans. Aidan Nichols (Edinburgh: T. & T. Clark, 1990), esp. chapters 1 and 2. See also *Theodramatik,* vol. 4, *Das Endspiel* (Einseideln: Johannes Verlag, 1983), 74-80. Much of von Balthasar's teaching on this topic has been gathered by John Saward in *The Mysteries of March,* esp. chapters 2 and 3.

63. *Theodrama* III, 225.

64. *Mysterium Paschale,* 28, emphasis added.

the throne and yet the object of worship (Rev 5:9-13), can assert a pre-temporal relation of equality between the Father and the Son (Jn 1:1-2; Heb 1:3; Phil 2:6), and in so many other ways can consider the Triad as divine. The intellectual tool that enables us to understand this twofold manner of speaking, the *oikonomia* and the *theologia* as tradition designated it, is, as we have seen, the principle of analogy. Our language is inadequate, but it is not arbitrary.

So far we have considered the teaching of the tradition regarding the God and Father of Our Lord Jesus Christ through familiarity, reconstructing the environment in which the term *Father* is used of God, and recovering a sense of how the word is actually used, particularly in the Bible. This process of familiarization allows us to assert that, in a true but ineffable way, *Father* refers to the Unoriginate Source of the very triune life of God. It is the name given to him by Jesus and revealed in the life and speech and especially the death and resurrection of Jesus Christ. We know, therefore, that this name is that by which we say something true about the God and Father of Our Lord Jesus Christ. In order to complete this knowledge by familiarly appropriating it in a personal and lived manner, there is as well a knowledge through connaturality, a knowledge worked in us by the Holy Spirit not only through the tradition but within the sanctuary of our own consciousness. I would like now to briefly consider this form of knowledge.

KNOWLEDGE BY CONNATURALITY: KNOWING GOD AS FATHER

In this section I wish to apply descriptively the notion of *gnōsis,* that is, a knowledge born of love and desire, a personal knowledge that is brought about in the believer by the action of the Holy Spirit who both leads her or him to repentance and actively conforms the drives of the personality to the divine truth being made known. The soul of this action, at least as I would like to describe it here, lies in a reading of the sacred text with a desire to learn from Jesus. Learning, in this sense, however, also implies an active obedience to the commands of Jesus to love each other, to care for the poor, and to receive the kingdom as a child. The pondering of the sacred text with this desire to learn is what tradition called *lectio divina.*[65]

---

65. This practice is beautifully presented as it was practiced by Origen in Bernard McGinn, *The Presence of God: A History of Western Christian Mysticism,* vol. 1, *The Foundations of Mysticism: Origins to the Fifth Century* (New York: Crossroad, 1992), 108-33.

The Scriptures are the body, or the flesh, of the Word;[66] in them we can realize once again in our own lives the presence of the Word among us.

The Scriptures are the means by which the Holy Spirit reveals divine mysteries in such a way that the truths of God become an effective principle, a source of spiritual energy, empowering the believer to die to sin and live to God. The revelation is at once enticing and convicting, and if individuals will obey what they are shown, they will discover that they have power to live in a way which was not possible formerly. The action of the Holy Spirit brings the truth alive, and in that vision it is possible to distinguish between flesh and spirit, to call the drives of our personality by their right name, and to yield ever more profoundly to the desire of the Father that we be conformed to Christ. The life that Jesus lived in his time among us was a human realization, even amid the limitations of the likeness of sinful flesh, of his unique Sonship. It was a splendid revelation of the Father because it was lived in obedience to the Father. Now that he is risen from the dead, that life can be shared by those who yield to the action of the Holy Spirit. We can know in ourselves the "surpassing greatness of his power for us who believe, in accord with the exercise of his great might which he worked in Christ, raising him from the dead . . ." (Eph 1:19-20).

As a Christian believer indwells the message passed on through the believing community, the objective process of describing what that message is saying and the appropriative process of understanding what it is talking about begin to coalesce, each strengthening the other. In this rhythm two things happen. The believer is brought to understand what the text is really referring to, and this leads to an ability to take the words as they stand without bending them to a framework of our own making. As Martin Luther put it: "The one who does not understand the realities cannot get the meaning out of the words."[67] The Word who is present to the community is present to each believer who opens the door when he knocks. He gives to such a one the indescribable delight of knowing that he is truly the one who was dead, and behold he lives for ever! The intimacy and wonder of the life to which he invites us is one that is hidden with him in *Theos,* because it is through him that we have access in one Spirit to the Father. While this life, now hidden, will one day be revealed in glory when he appears, it is not so hidden that it is inaccessible to faith experience.

66. *Origen, Spirit and Fire: A Thematic Anthology of His Writings,* ed. Hans Urs von Balthasar, trans. Robert Daly (Washington: The Catholic University of America Press, 1984), 86-88.

67. "Qui non intelligit res non potest sensum ex verbis elicere." Quoted on the frontespiece of part two of Hans Georg Gadamer's *Truth and Method,* trans. Joel Weinsheimer and Donald Marshall (New York: Seabury, 1989).

Knowledge by connaturality in this sense is, as I mentioned before, knowledge through conformity. Saying "Abba" to God and knowing oneself to be his child means being led by the Holy Spirit. This is forcefully brought out by John Chrysostom, who remarks that Paul does not say that those who live by the Spirit or those who have received the Spirit, but only those who are *led* by the Spirit, are the children of God. He goes on to explain that being led by the Spirit means allowing him "such power over our life as a pilot has over a ship or a chariot driver has over a team of horses."[68] Such obedience means that we will not carry out the desires of the flesh. The usual means by which the Holy Spirit intimates to us how we are to be conformed to Jesus Christ is precisely the word of God.

The real obstacle to experiencing the reality mediated by the text is our sin, our preference of ourselves over God and over the truth of redemption. This is especially true of our deep and often overlooked habit patterns of sin. The Word of God challenges these and uses our desire to know as a goad, moving us to repent and to call upon the power of the cross of Christ to render the body of sin impotent (see Rom 6:6). A surprising dimension of this purifying role of the Word is the manner in which the misconceptions, false presuppositions, and darkness of our own age, all of which inhabit our mind, are brought to light and obliged to give way to the truth that is being revealed. In addition, we are led to see how profoundly our emotional life, particularly our memory, affects what we would have considered our objective reasoning, and we begin to appreciate the intimate connection between genuine spiritual insight and the repentance and *apatheia* spoken of by Clement and the subsequent tradition.[69] Without authority over one's own life, over the impulsive, half-hidden drives that affect us and prejudice our thinking, there can be no mature theology. None of this process is automatic — it can be resisted — nor is it the fruit of purely human resources. It is brought about by the activity of the Holy Spirit, who moves us to yield to the effective light of divine reality.

John of the Cross refers to a mature realization of the interior dimension of this obedience to the Spirit when he writes:

> Although it is true that a person will hardly be found whose union with God is so continuous that his faculties, without any form, are always divinely moved, nevertheless there are those who are very habitually

68. *On Romans,* Homily 14 (*Patrologia Graeca* 60,525).

69. For a good account of the spiritual battle and its relation to baptism according to Clement see Walther Völker, *Der Wahre Gnostiker nach Clemens Alexandrinus,* Texte und Untersuchungen aur Geschichte der Altchristlichen Literatur, vol. 57 (Berlin: Akademie Verlar, 1952), 147-89.

moved by God and not by themselves in their operations, as St. Paul says: the children of God (those who are transformed in God and united to him) are moved by the Spirit of God (that is, moved to divine works in their faculties) (Rom 8:14). It is no marvel that the operations are divine, since the union of the soul with God is divine.[70]

Paul's statement about those who are led by the Spirit of God, then, refers to a gradated reality, and this applies to the next statement as well:

For you did not receive a spirit of slavery for fear again; but you received a Spirit of sonship in which we cry Abba, Father! The Spirit himself bears witness to our spirit that we are children of God. If children, then heirs as well: heirs of God and coheirs of Christ, if indeed we are "co-suffering" so that we will also be "co-glorified." (Rom 8:15-17)

Surely it is not merely the recitation of the word *Abba* that Paul is referring to here. The ability to pray this way is part of the whole process by which the Spirit conforms us to Jesus in his death to sin so that we may live to *Theos*. There are moments when this conformity extends to our awareness of the Father, and we know ourselves to be loved by him who is the infinite Source of life within the Trinity itself. We are so overwhelmed by such mercy and tenderness that the very center of our gravity shifts from self-protection and self-glorification, from memories and fears, from shame and isolation, to a return of love to him who is the Father of our Lord Jesus Christ. There is born in us a divine affection for the Father and we understand at once the irreplaceable fittingness and unbridgeable inadequacy of the name bearing us along. We cry "Abba" and receive the witness of the Spirit that we are, in a way that defies definition, a child of *Theos*. This knowledge of awesome majesty, authority, and creative power all present in him who is beyond words, but present to us in love through the crucified humanity of Jesus, will stand as the criterion by which every other name and every other pretension to power will be judged. He who is Father, at once willingly and necessarily, within the divine life, is also Father, in a pure act of generosity, willingly but not necessarily, to those who share Jesus' humanity and give way to his Spirit. Such is the living knowledge, the treasure held in the earthen vessel of a weak and sinful church, "that the surpassing power be of God and not from us" (2 Cor 4:7).

70. *The Ascent of Mt. Carmel* 3,2,16, in *The Collected Works of John of the Cross*, trans. Kieran Kavanaugh and Otilio Rodriguez (Washington: Institute of Carmelite Studies, 1979), 219.

10

Human Rights and Ecclesial Communion

The most profound consequence of the fact that the believer is brought into a personal relationship with God the Father, in Christ and through the activity of the Holy Spirit, is that the limits of human life are expanded beyond both cosmological and political existence. This significantly affects how we think about human dignity and human rights. Respect for human dignity can be an effective negative norm. It discerns where rights are being violated and eliminates obstacles to the exercise of these rights. This has been the contribution of all the movements promoting human rights, particularly in the last two hundred years. The results, however, have been dubious. Viewed precisely in the light of the enhanced appreciation of human dignity, there has been, under many aspects, a significant loss rather than a gain in the actual capacity to exercise basic human rights. As the Pastoral Constitution *The Church in the Modern World* expresses it:

> In no other age has mankind enjoyed such an abundance of wealth, resources, and economic well being; and yet a huge proportion of the world is plagued by hunger and extreme need while countless numbers are totally illiterate. At no time have people had such a keen sense of freedom, only to be faced by new forms of slavery in living and thinking.[1]

Throughout the history of feminism there has been an intimate connection between human rights thinking and the effort to secure for women their rightful place in society and the church. This means that the successes and

---

1. §4. Translation, slightly adapted, is from *Vatican Council II: The Conciliar and Post Conciliar Documents,* ed. Austin Flannery (Northport, N.Y.: Costello Publishing Co., 1975), 906.

293

failures of the human rights movements characterize feminism as well. The most besetting problem in any discussion of rights is that of individualism, the third of the characteristics of modernity to have been taken over by feminism.

Individualism, as I am using the term, considers human beings to be constituted and endowed with rights *prior* to any relationship. Society is made up of those who, for the sake of a greater good, have surrendered a portion of their rights. What foundationalism is to epistemology, individualism is to social theory — both begin with the subject and make the subject the norm of what is true and right. In addition, individualism tends to see the person as a point of consciousness whose physical dimension is secondary to his or her existence. Relationalism, a term I will use for the alternate view, tends to consider the whole body person as a unique and unrepeatable act of being, constituted by a unique relationship to God and a web of human relationships that are also unique.

Rights, in an individualistic schema, are looked upon as entitlements to things necessary for existence, genuine human life, and self-actualization. In the Kantian outlook, the only limitation on self-actualization is provided by the norm "Act only according to that maxim by which you can at the same time will that it should become a universal law."[2] In several other systems, as we shall see, restraint on the subject's right to untrammeled self-actualization practically comes down to the coercive power of the state or the dynamic of economic or social laws.[3]

Individualistic thinking generally limits itself to the political and social arena, and only secondarily turns its attention to more philosophical concerns such as the basis within the person for the attribution of rights, what constitutes a person, and so forth. This has proven to be a weakness. Basically, the notion of human rights is derived in one way or another from the Christian understanding of person, which is itself based on the dignity of the human being as called into a relationship with God. It is as though the tree of the integral Christian view of human personality has been transplanted into successively different soils where it has continued to grow, but in a reduced and sometimes twisted form.[4]

2. Immanuel Kant, *Foundations of the Metaphysics of Morals,* trans. Lewis White Beck, Library of Liberal Arts (New York: MacMillan, 1959), 39.

3. There is no realistic way of dealing with sin in such a schema pushed to its extremes. One way of understanding the traditional notion of original sin is to see it as the drive to realize every potential in the subject without considering the will of God or the good of others. See in this regard Stephen J. Duffy, "Our Hearts of Darkness: Original Sin Revisited," *Theological Studies* 49 (1988): 597-622.

4. This has been discussed frequently. See, for instance, Charles Taylor, *Sources of the Self: The Making of Modern Identity* (Cambridge, Mass.: Harvard University

In this chapter I will first discuss the notion of person as it was forged by the early Christian thinkers. I will then consider the notion of rights as it developed both within the Christian tradition and outside of it. The third step will be a critique of modern thinking about the rights and dignity of the human person. Finally, I will consider the biblical notion of communion as the way of preserving the enhanced understanding of human rights that has arisen in recent centuries while freeing it from its individualistic bias. In this last step I will attempt to describe a genuinely Christian realization of the rights and dignity of women.

PERSONHOOD AND REVELATION

It is well known in modern scholarship that the notion of personhood resulted from the confluence of the biblical and Greek worlds of thought. The biblical thought world contributed the foundational understanding that the universe exists because of an act of freedom on the part of God, who is completely transcendent and distinct from his creation. It also provided a witness to the way God and human beings interact. God's activity had historical and not merely cosmic dimensions, and was thus personal. An understanding of personal identity grew as it was understood that each human being had the dignity and covenant responsibility of relating to God in worship, trust, gratitude, and obedience. Finally, in Jesus Christ this personality of God was revealed to be the one whom Jesus called "Father," thus creating an identity of his own as "Son." When Jesus was raised from the dead by the Father, it was revealed that the Son was in fact to be honored and worshipped along with God, who sent his Spirit to reveal in power the reality and majesty of the risen Christ.

The Greek world contributed a philosophical turn of mind that was able to formulate an understanding of how the Father shares himself with the Son and the Spirit. This occurred, however, only as philosophy was purified from the monism that saw the divine as part of the world. The steps along that way, which took nearly three centuries, are important to note since they will provide criteria by which to assess our modern understanding of personhood. I will trace some of those steps and indicate their abiding significance.

Press, 1989); John Milbank, *Theology and Social Theory: Beyond Secular Reason* (Oxford: Basil Blackwell, 1990).

The Biblical Manner of Speaking

The Bible does not use the term *person* in referring to either God or human beings. Nevertheless, the God of biblical revelation may rightly be designated as personal. According to Walter Kasper, this can be established in two ways. First, "in the biblical revelation God indisputably speaks as an 'I'; and it is equally indisputable that he permits himself to be addressed as a 'Thou.' "[5] Second, even though *person* is not found, the notion of a *name* by which God is addressed serves as an equivalent. Because of this, one cannot reduce the God of the Bible to the status of an *it* or an impersonal being.

Besides this concept of a name, there is yet another biblical idea that closely corresponds to the notion of person — the Hebrew term *pānîm* (face). "[T]he face identifies the person and reflects the sentiments and attitudes of the person . . . it is frequently used as a substitute for the self and the feelings and desires of the self."[6] As a means of expressing the person, *pānîm* can be used for the countenance both of God (Num 6:5; Ps 4:7; Jer 3:12) and of human beings (Dt 28:50; Job 29:24; Ps 34:6).

The Septuagint generally translates *pānîm* with *prosōpon,* and this usage is carried into the New Testament. *Prosōpon* in its original Greek usage designated the mask worn by an actor, and the meaning was gradually expanded to include the role that an actor assumed, and then an actor on "the stage of life": an individual.[7] Thus Paul uses *prosōpon* to depict the intimate personal encounter of Christians with the glory of God revealed in Christ (2 Cor 3:12-18). Elsewhere he uses it quite clearly in designating an individual (2 Cor 1:11). There are still other intimations of personhood on both the divine and human levels in biblical thought. In this regard one might note the personification of the Word, Wisdom, and Spirit in the Old Testament.[8]

The Latin term used to translate *prosōpon* is *persona,* the derivation of which is debated, but whose meaning eventually became linked with that of its Greek counterpart.[9]

5. "Revelation and Mystery: The Christian Understanding of God," in *Theology and Church,* trans. Margaret Kohl (New York: Crossroad, 1989), 19-31, esp. 26.

6. John L. McKenzie, "Face," in *Dictionary of the Bible* (New York: Macmillan Publishing Co., 1965), 266-67.

7. L. W. Geddes and W. A. Wallace, "Person (In Philosophy)," *New Catholic Encyclopedia,* 1967 ed.

8. Cf. Lawrence B. Porter, "On Keeping 'Persons' in the Trinity: A Linguistic Approach to Trinitarian Thought," *Theological Studies* 41 (1980): 530-48, esp. 541.

9. In the past it was commonly believed that *persona* was derived from the verb *personare* (to sound through), which suggested the mask worn by an actor through which the voice was projected out into the theater. Modern studies have determined that it is much more likely that the word derives from the Etruscan *phersu,* which

From Persona *to* Person

The earliest patristic development of the notion of person was carried on in scriptural exegesis through what is often described as a *prosopological* analysis.[10] This method was not unique to the first Christian writers, but rather was a development of an approach already used by classical writers such as the Stoics, who identified various literary characters with unique viewpoints and individuality in the text of Homer.[11] The technique was applied to the Old Testament by Philo, who distinguished between passages where God spoke through the person of Moses and those where revelation occurs through a dialogue between them.[12]

Early Christian writers employed a similar approach to the Old Testament, but from a distinctively Christian perspective. Justin in his first *Apology* explains his method in this way:

But when you listen to the words of the prophets spoken "as from a person" *(hos apo prosōpou),* do not suppose that they are said by the inspired people themselves, but by the divine Logos which is moving them. For sometimes by way of prognostication it says what things will happen, sometimes it speaks as from the person of God the Ruler and Father of all things, sometimes as from the person of the Christ, some-

---

described the masks worn in the worship of the goddess Persephone. In any case it is clear that from its original Latin meaning of "mask," *persona* evolved to include the meanings of a dramatic character, grammatical person, and concrete individuality by the time of Cicero. See Aloys Grillmeier, *Christ in Christian Tradition,* trans. John Bowden, vol. 1, *From the Apostolic Age to Chalcedon* (London: Mowbrays, 1965), 125-26; see also William Hill, *The Three-Personed God* (Washington: The Catholic University Press, 1982).

10. The seminal work in this area was that of Carl Andresen, "Zur Entstehung und Geschichte des trinitarischen Personbegriffs," *Zeitschrift für die neutestamentliche Wissenschaft* 52 (1961): 1-39. This work has recently been supplemented by an extensive study of patristic interpretation of the Psalms by Marie-Josèph Rondeau, *Les Travaux des Pères grecs et latins sur le Psautier. Recherches et bilan,* vol. I of *Les commentateurs patristiques de Psautier (IIIe-Ve siècles)* (Rome: Oriental Institute, 1982) and *Exégèse prosopologique et théologie,* vol. II of *Les commentateurs patristiques de Psautier (IIIe-Ve siècles)* (Rome: Oriental Institute, 1985). It has also been supplemented (and in some respects surpassed) by the excellent study by Michael Slussler, "The Exegetical Roots of Trinitarian Theology," *Theological Studies* 49 (1988): 461-76.

11. Cf. Andresen, "Zur Entstehung," 14-17. These and other techniques employed by the Alexandrian Jewish theologian provide an important antecedent to patristic writings.

12. Ibid., 12.

times as from the person of the people to the Lord or to his Father —
just as even in your writings it is to be noticed that while there is one
who writes everything, there are distinct persons speaking.[13]

A similar method can be found in the writings of Irenaeus, Tertullian,
Athanasius, and Origen.[14]

This method, as Ratzinger points out, underwent a transformation in
the hands of the Christian authors who used it. For the "roles" of which
they speak are not merely literary devices but realities. Commenting on
the text of Justin cited above, Ratzinger notes that

> the "role" truly exists; it is the *prosopon,* the face, the person of the Logos
> who truly speaks here and *joins* in dialogue with the prophet. It is quite clear
> how the data of Christian faith transforms and renews a pre-given ancient
> schema used in interpreting texts. The literary artistic device of letting roles
> appear to enliven the narrative with their dialogue reveals to the theologians
> *the one* who plays the true role here, the *Logos,* the *prosopon,* the person of
> the Word which is no longer merely role, but person.[15]

It is this tradition of prosopological exegesis that underlies the later use of
person in both the Trinitarian and Christological discussions in the following centuries.

Thus Tertullian employed the term *persona* when he sought to express
the plurality in God against the modalistic monarchianism of Praxeas. The
divine Persons are three, though united in their common possession of the
divine *natura* or *substantia.*[16] The same terms also appear in his Christology, *persona* designating that which is single in Christ and *natura* what
is twofold (divinity and humanity).[17] While it is true that Tertullian's

13. *First Apology* 36, 1-2 as translated in Slussler, "Exegetical Roots of Trinitarian Theology," 464.

14. Cf. Slussler, "Exegetical Roots of Trinitarian Theology," 463-66. For
Origen's use of the method see Rondeau, *Exégèse prosopologique,* 39-40.

15. "Concerning the Notion of Person in Theology," trans. Michael Waldstein,
Communio 17 (1990): 439-54; citation is from p. 442. Emphasis in original. Ratzinger
may be guilty of a certain amount of overstatement regarding the impact of Christianity,
insofar as this process was already begun in Philo's biblical reflection, but his point is
basically sound.

16. Porter rightly points out that the precise formula *una substantia in tribus
personis* cannot be found in Tertullian's thought even though it is often associated with
him. The closest approximation of it can be found in chapter 12 of *Adversus Praxean,*
where he speaks of *"teneo unam substantiam in tribus cohaerentibus."* See Porter,
"Persons in the Trinity," 545.

17. Thus he will state that in Christ "we see a twofold state, not confused but

understanding of such terms was not marked by profound theological speculation and was somewhat limited by Stoic concepts, the terminology he used was an important antecedent to the later definition of the Council of Chalcedon.[18]

Eastern theology, even though enjoying a far greater speculative depth than its Western counterpart, did not have the same conceptual and linguistic clarity. Here authors had to contend with at least four different terms — *prosōpon, physis, hypostasis,* and *ousia* — all of which could designate person and the last three of which could also indicate nature.[19] In such a situation conflict was inevitable. Even after the definitions of the ecumenical councils of Nicea (325) and Constantinople (381) had declared Christ to be one substance *(homoousios)* with the Father from all eternity, questions about the relationship of Christ's divinity and humanity remained unanswered.

A foundation for the resolution of these disputes had already been laid in the theology of the Cappadocian Fathers. In their Trinitarian theology these thinkers emphasized that the one Godhead *(ousia)* exists simultaneously in three hypostases *(prosōpon* or *hypostasis).*[20] Each of the divine hypostases is the essence of the Godhead, distinguished only by their

---

united in a single person, Jesus God and man." See *Adversus Praxean,* 27, 11, cited in Jean Galot, *Who Is Christ?: A Theology of the Incarnation,* trans. M. Angeline Bouchard (Chicago: Franciscan Herald Press, 1981), 224.

18. For a concise exposition of the meaning of these terms in Tertullian's thought and the impact of Stoic ideas on them see J. N. D. Kelly, *Early Christian Doctrines* (New York: Harper and Brothers Publishers, 1959), 111-15. For a more extensive examination of the same, see the treatment in Grillmeier, *Apostolic Age to Chalcedon,* 118-31. See also Galot, who differs from Grillmeier in *Who is Christ?* 225-26. It is clear that the term *person* was used in a Trinitarian context prior to Tertullian by Hippolytus and after him by Novatian. But Tertullian's specifically Christological application of the term — the *una persona* — seems to have lain dormant until the time of Jerome and especially Augustine, who discovered and used it on his own.

19. For a good exposition of these terms and especially *hypostasis* see the classic study by Marcel Richard, "L'introduction du mot 'hypostase' dans la théologie de l'incarnation," *Mélanges de Science Religeuse* 2 (1945): 243-70. Cf. A. de Halleux "Hypostase et Personne dans la formation de dogma trinitaire (ca. 375-381)," *Revue d'Histoire Ecclesiastique* 79 (1984): 313-69; 625-70. Halleux treats the use of these terms in the thought of Basil, Gregory of Nazianzus, Paulinus, and the confessors. T. E. Pollard in his study *Johannine Christology and the Early Church* (London: Cambridge University Press, 1990) observes that while Eastern Christology concerned itself with theologizing about the divine *Logos,* Western Christology focused on the divine Son, thus avoiding many of the middle-Platonic pitfalls found in the former.

20. A good examination of the Cappadocian doctrine of the Trinity is provided by Kelly, *Early Christian Doctrines,* 263-69.

particularizing characteristics, such as paternity or ingenerateness (for the Father), sonship or generateness (for the Son), and sanctifying power or mission (for the Holy Spirit).[21] Thus the distinction of the divine Persons is grounded in their respective origins and their mutual relations.[22]

It is important to note a subtle but profound difference in the approach of Eastern theology that has profound repercussions for an understanding of person.[23] While Western thought tended to consider one divine substance shared in by three *personae,* as we have seen, Greek thought began with *Theos* as the Father. Having established that the universe existed as a result of freedom, these thinkers, notably Athanasius and Basil, posited the Father as the possessor of this freedom. Since the Son exists in virtue of a freedom that is intrinsic to the Father, he is not created. In order to express this, the notion of *hypostasis,* which often had signified the same as *ousia* or substance, was shifted to mean *prosōpon* or person. Thus,

> the unity of God, the one God, and the ontological "principle" or "cause" of the being and life of God does not consist in the substance of God but in the *hypostasis,* that is *the person of the Father.* . . . If God exists, he exists because the Father exists, that is, He who out of love freely begets the Son and brings forth the Spirit. . . . What therefore is important in trinitarian theology is that God "exists" on account of a person, the Father, and not on account of a substance.[24]

The significance of understanding God in this way is that communion is established on the basis of a Person and not on the basis of a subsequent act of the will (which would make the Son a creature) that brings out a difference between the East and West. In thus grasping the reality of the Father, the Cappadocians made relation into an ontological category — relation does not follow upon substance or existence, it *is* the existence of the substance. God exists as Father and therefore as Son and Spirit. Their identity as Persons is their relationship.

As applied to the Incarnation this understanding unveiled a dimension of human existence hitherto only hinted at in the Old Testament's manner

---

21. Cf. Basil, *Epistulae* 214, 4; 236, 6. Gregory Nazianzen, *Orationes* 25,16; 26,19; 29,2.

22. Kelly, *Early Christian Doctrines,* 265.

23. The most succinct and helpful analysis of this difference is to be found in the study by John D. Zizioulas, *Being As Communion,* Contemporary Greek Theologians 4 (Crestwood, N.Y.: St. Vladimir's Seminary Press, 1985), esp. chapters 1 and 2.

24. Ibid., 40-42.

of speaking. In Greek thought the *prosōpon* or *persona* of a human being came about in a reciprocal movement between expectations and performance, between the role accorded by the family, the society, and the state, and that forged by the individual.[25] It was closer to our modern notion of a societal *role*. There was no enduring existence to the *prosōpon;* it was one of the ephemeral individual substances produced by nature that come into being and disappear as a result of biological laws.

The assertion that Jesus is the Son of *Theos* shattered the Greek category of *prosōpon*. This one, who was named by God and who named God his Father, bore that name in the fibers of his being. Theologians had to rethink their categories and began to understand that the *prosōpon* or *persona* of Jesus was precisely his Sonship. Being more than a biological *persona,* he revealed at his resurrection the full implications of the fact that his person and his substance were the same. The glory of his new life makes evident who he always has been.

As the reality and majesty of Jesus Christ was expressed in terms of person and substance, there was a momentous discovery. Not only is Jesus constituted by that personal relation to the Father, but all human beings have been enabled to share in that relation. Risen from the dead and existing in a transformed humanity, he is the Firstborn of many brothers and sisters who have been foreordained to be conformed to his image (Rom 8:29). Those who yield to that act of God in them by which they accept the true reality and mission of Jesus are joined to him and have a share in his divine and immortal life; they receive their being from the Father and they breathe the Holy Spirit.

Thus, in Christ, the full meaning of human existence is made manifest. The understanding of a unique responsibility to a unique God that grounded Israelite faith found its fulfillment in the revelation that each human being is indestructibly unique because he or she has been placed in a relationship to the Son of God, who himself has uniquely personalized human existence. The impact of this understanding on the thought and societal practice of the day was enormous, as both friends and opponents of Christianity, ancient and modern, have attested. In an interesting passage

---

25. This type of thinking underlay all the ancient notion of virtue and of honor and shame. For a discussion of the former aspect see Alasdair MacIntyre, *After Virtue* (Notre Dame, Ind.: University of Notre Dame Press, 1984), chapters 9-12. For a description of the power of honor and shame in ancient society one may consult *Honor and Shame and the Unity of the Mediterranean,* ed. David D. Gilmore, American Anthropological Association, special publication 22 (Washington: American Anthropological Association, 1987).

Jean Bethke Elshtain mentions Hannah Arendt's perception of the change wrought in social ordering. It is worth presenting here:

> Arendt hits the crux of what most disturbs her when she argues that Christianity accords each "individual life . . . [a position] once held by the life of the body politic. . . ." One might recast Arendt's indictment thus: Christianity redeemed and sanctified both *each individual life* as well as *everyday life,* especially the life of society's victims, and granted each a new found dignity . . . previously reserved only to the highborn, the rich or the powerful.[26]

A similar point is made by Erich Auerbach, who traces the increasing prominence given to "unimportant" people in Christian literature whereas in classical literature only the great and noble could be portrayed as worthy of consideration. Other characters were introduced for comic relief or some similar motive; their lives, because they did not embody the image and fate of the body politic, were not considered significant.[27]

HUMAN WORTH AND HUMAN RIGHTS

Besides developing the notion of person, biblical and Greco-Roman thought prepared for what later turned out to be the grounding of human rights in human worth. The biblical notions turned on the fact of God's interest in each individual, while the Greco-Roman world was concentrated more on securing the proper legal system. I will treat of these preparations rapidly and then pass to an explicit consideration of early Christian thinking about human rights.

Biblical Thought

Those who look to the teaching of Scripture for antecedents to the notion of human rights generally look to a number of primary moments in the sweep of biblical revelation — creation, the life of God's covenant people, and salvation in Christ. Attention is often drawn to the statement in the Priestly creation account that humanity was created in the "image and

26. Jean Bethke Elshtain, *Public Man, Private Woman: Women in Social and Political Thought* (Princeton: Princeton University Press, 1981), 58. Emphasis in the original.

27. Erich Auerbach, *Mimesis: The Representation of Reality in Western Literature,* trans. Willard Trask (New York: Doubleday Anchor, 1953).

likeness of God" (Gen 1:26-27). Among the unique features of this statement is its inherent *democratization* of the idea of personal dignity, since the statement is made in regard to every human person "irrespective of his/her belonging to a race, a people, a sex or a culture."[28] This stands in marked contrast to the view of other cultures of the time, which reserved the notion of imaging the divine (or its equivalent) for the king. Equally striking is the way this imaging is integrally related to the worship of God on the seventh day or Sabbath (Gen 2:1-3). Created on the sixth day with the beasts, humanity is created for, and images God most fully in, the Sabbath worship of the seventh day. Whenever humankind fails to acknowledge and worship God as its Creator and Lord, this image is obscured and it becomes in truth bestial.[29]

This notion of the dignity of humanity as created in the divine image is presupposed in later Jewish tradition concerning the value of human life. While other ancient Near Eastern legal codes had prohibitions against the taking of human life, the penalties associated with violation of these laws were often calculated in terms of the property the murderer must forfeit in order to make restitution. This practice contrasts sharply with the Old Testament insistence on the incommensurability of human life: "You shall not accept indemnity in place of the life of a murderer . . . he must be put to death" (Num 35:31).[30] The rationale for this legal principle is provided by Genesis 9:6: "If anyone sheds the blood of man, by man shall his blood be shed; for in the image of God has man been made."[31] Such principles gave rise to a sizable body of rabbinic writings that attempted to uphold the inviolability of human life even in the most difficult of cases.[32]

Human relations are governed by what the Hebrew Bible calls *ṣedeq* (righteousness), which Gerhard von Rad describes as "the highest value

---

28. Walter Kasper, "The Theological Foundation of Human Rights," in *The Church and Human Rights: Historical and Theological Reflections* (Vatican City: Pontifical Council for Justice and Peace, 1990), 55. Also, Francis Martin, "Male and Female He Created Them. Reflections on the Genesis Texts and Their Subsequent Development," *Communio* 20 (1993): 240-65.

29. This notion it would seem is behind the story of Nebuchanezzar's being deprived of his senses and spending seven years among the beasts after his self-adulation in Dan 4. It may also figure in the description of the boastful beast of Dan 7 and the blasphemous beasts of the book of Revelation (see esp. Rev 13:1-18).

30. On this point see the excellent study by Michael Fishbane, "The Image of the Human and the Rights of the Individual in Jewish Tradition," in *Human Rights and the World's Religions,* ed. Leroy S. Rouner (Notre Dame, Ind.: University of Notre Dame Press, 1988), 17-31, esp. 17-18.

31. Cf. Fishbane, 18-19.

32. See Fishbane, 19-25.

in life" for an Israelite.[33] It is that quality by which one honors in word and deed the truth of a relationship. A particular dimension of this respect for human dignity may be traced in the constant concern of the biblical authors with the powerless among God's covenant people — especially the poor, widows, orphans, and strangers (e.g., Ex 22:21-22).[34] While this theme can be traced throughout the Old Testament, it is a particularly prominent theme in prophetic teaching. Failure to care for the powerless and to "do justice" on their behalf is a constant prophetic indictment against the people of Israel and their leaders (e.g., Is 1:17, 23; 3:14-15; 10:2; Amos 5:7, 10-12). Such repeated failure helped to shape the expectation of the Messianic king who would meet the demands of justice for the powerless (Is 11: 4-5; Ps 72).

This concern for those who have little or no political or economic means is an important antecedent to the modern notion that certain fundamental privileges are owed to the person simply on the basis of his or her inviolable dignity, and are not bestowed through the largesse of the government. In the ancient pagan world, it is man who cries to the gods for justice. In Israel, it is God himself who, through the prophets, appeals for justice, especially for the poor.

The New Testament radicalizes the sense of human worth, as we have seen, by bringing all human beings into relation with Christ and conferring upon them the possibility of an eternal share in the very life of the Son of God. The prophetic injunction regarding the care for the poor is also radicalized, since Christ himself is identified with those in need.[35]

Jesus is the one in whom the Old Testament promises of Messianic liberation are fulfilled (cf. Lk 4:18-19).[36] In announcing the presence of God's kingdom, Jesus also declares the blessedness of the powerless who are most able to accept it (Mt 5:3-12; Lk 6:20-23). But the liberation that Jesus brings is not simply a partial one, but one that aims at the total salvation of the person. It is for this reason that the various New Testament

33. Gerhard von Rad, *Old Testament Theology,* trans. D. M. G. Stalker, vol. 1, *The Theology of Israel's Historical Traditions* (New York: Harper and Brothers, 1962), 370.

34. See James Limburg, "Human Rights in the Old Testament," *Concilium* 124/4 (1979): 20-26.

35. For an extended discussion of Mt 25:31-46 and a history of the interpretation of the "least of my brothers," one may consult Sherman Gray, *The Least of My Brothers: Matthew 25:31-46, A History of Interpretation,* SBL Dissertation Series, 114 (Atlanta: Scholars Press, 1989).

36. See Josef Blank, "The Justice of God as the Humanisation of Man — the Problem of Human Rights in the New Testament," *Concilium* 124/4 (1979): 31-33.

traditions see the liberation from sin won by Jesus on the cross as the ultimate revelation of the Father's love, and hence of the preciousness of humanity even as fallen (Jn 3:16, Rom 5:6-10; 1 Jn 2:2; 4:10). The fact that in Jesus God embraced the curse that rested upon human sin (Gal 3:3; cf. Dt 21:22) enabled him to "condemn sin in the flesh" (Rom 8:3) and demonstrated the wisdom and power of God and his plan (1 Cor 1:18–2:9).[37] The Christian concept of human dignity is thus inextricably interwoven with the mystery of salvation. It is therefore not surprising to see patristic anthropology rooted within Christology and soteriology.

Greco-Roman Thought

Parallel to the appreciation of human dignity found in the Old and New Testaments there are as well classical antecedents to human rights. These emerged from Greek philosophical reflection on human individuality, particularly in the realms of law, politics, and the nature of reason. It is the distinctive achievement of sixth century B.C. Athenian civilization to have broken with the determinism of Homeric and pre-Homeric societies, in which individuality and freedom were swallowed by the forces of fate.[38] With the advent of a kind of critical consciousness, there was a new awareness of personal identity and of the autonomy of reason. The notion of individuality in turn made possible a particular political arrangement known as democracy, in which citizens of a certain social standing had a voice in the organization and governance of their community — the *polis*.[39] In other words, freeborn male citizens had certain rights simply by being born into a particular community. It is important to note that this notion of rights cannot easily be equated with universal or human rights because they were usually not applied to those outside of one's own *polis,* nor to all those within it. Nevertheless, the idea of rights as a political power of participation has its roots in the Greek city states.

37. Cf. Xavier Léon-Dufour and Jean Audusseau, "Cross," in *The Dictionary of Biblical Theology,* ed. Xavier Léon-Dufour, 2nd ed. (New York: Seabury, 1973), 102-4.

38. See the discussion of the emergence of autonomous reason in Paul Tillich, *Systematic Theology,* vol. 1 (Chicago: University of Chicago Press, 1951), 83-86; also Joseph Joblin, S.J., "The Church and Human Rights: Historical Overview and Future Outlook," in *Human Rights and the Church,* 11-46, esp. 19-21.

39. On the rise of democracy in the Greek *polis* see David Held, *Models of Democracy* (Stanford, Calif.: Stanford University Press, 1987), 13-35; Cynthia Farrar, *The Origins of Democratic Thinking: The Invention of Politics in Classical Greece* (Cambridge: Cambridge University Press, 1988); Donald Kagan, *Pericles of Athens and the Birth of Democracy* (New York: Free Press, 1991).

The other stimulus for reflection on the place of the individual in the larger scheme of things can be found in the concept of natural law. Greek thinkers usually understood natural law in terms of some kind of conformity to the cosmic order. Aristotle demonstrates this outlook to some degree, using natural law to designate the universal order in which the individual takes his or her place as an artisan, warrior, or slave. This order is distinct from the various civic laws that concretize the moral demands of this order.[40] The notion of natural law received much greater attention in Stoic thought, with a strong emphasis on conformity. Reason discerns the natural law in the rhythms and processes of nature, and the human task is to achieve conformity with nature.[41]

Most Roman thinkers had a markedly different understanding of natural law, placing greater emphasis on human rationality and freedom. Cicero (d. 43 B.C.) exemplifies this view when he speaks of "true law which is right reason in accord with nature."[42] It was this optimism concerning the power of human reason that enabled the Romans to codify into a body of jurisprudence the order that many of their Greek counterparts had been content to abandon to the cycles of nature. Law for the Romans "was a technique, an art which the magistrate practiced in order to guarantee equitable harmony in the society."[43] It served the harmonious functioning of society by ensuring that everyone properly occupied and exercised their social role. Unlike the biblical understanding, however, it did not supply any notion of transcendent dignity that could serve as the basis for a claim of the individual against the power of the state. The individual's *persona* was enhanced by the philosophical and legal thinking of the Greeks and the Romans, but it remained something largely conferred by the political power.

The Christian Synthesis

The early Christian thinkers, though they were imbued with this remarkable sense of the abiding dignity of the human person, do not seem to have

40. Joblin, 21. Cf. M. Villey, *Le droit et les droits de l'homme* (Paris: Puf, 1983), 42.

41. For a good introduction to Stoic cosmology and ethics see Frederick Copleston, *A History of Philosophy,* vol. 1, *Greece and Rome* (New York: Image, 1962), part II, 132-44. For a more detailed study of Stoic cosmology, politics, and ethics see Malcolm Schofield, *The Stoic Idea of the City* (Cambridge: Cambridge University Press, 1991).

42. *De Republica,* lib. iii, c. xxii: *"Est quidem vera lex recta ratio, naturæ congruens."* The citation is from M. Tullii, ed. (Rome, 1852), 405-6.

43. Joblin, 22.

applied it directly to questions of human relationships. Instead, they continued to draw from the biblical teaching on *ṣedeq* and *agapē*. Their notion of the role of the state, while it included a clear understanding of the restricted area of its competence, seems mostly to have repeated the Greco-Roman view that the state was a realization of something *natural* to humanity.[44]

The most significant synthesis of Greco-Roman notions of natural law with a Christian theological vision of the universe as God's creation was effected by Thomas Aquinas. The synthesis consisted in uniting a view of nature's integrity, or autonomy, with the biblical notion of creation. This is a synthesis that characterized Aquinas's work in general.[45] Among its many novel features was the fact that it located the biblical notion of human dignity within human nature: "man is naturally free and existing for his own sake."[46] Thus human nature enjoys a certain freedom and creaturely autonomy in its pursuit of the goods toward which it is naturally inclined.[47] While there can be several precepts of natural law and several kinds of human inclinations, all of them are known and unified through the exercise of reason.[48]

Human beings share with all created things an inclination to self-preservation. With the animals, human beings share an inclination to reproduce and to raise and educate offspring. Finally, insofar as people are rational, they have a peculiarly human inclination to live together in society and to know the truth about God. These inclinations are designated by Aquinas as "good," and are all unified in the exercise of human reason.[49] Hence all of these various human needs must be respected, even though

---

44. For differing but complementary views of the patristic thinking on this issue, see Peter C. Phan, *Social Thought,* Message of the Fathers of the Church 20 (Wilmington, Del.: Glazier, 1984), and D. J. Herlihy, "Social Thought, Catholic. Patristic and Medieval," in *The New Catholic Encyclopedia* (1967): 346-49.

45. Most aspects of this discussion can be found in Cornelio Fabro, *Participation et Causalité selon S. Thomas d'Aquin* (Louvain: Publications Universitaires de Louvain, 1961).

46. *Summa Theologiae* II-II, 64,2 ad3. Actually the question concerns whether or not it is licit to kill those who disturb the good of the community by harming it. Aquinas answers in the affirmative because such people have ceased to act according to the reason in which their dignity consists and have become (recalling the first creation account) like the beasts.

47. In the prologue to the second part of the *Summa,* St. Thomas speaks of human beings as being "the principle of their own acts, and having a sort of free choice (quasi liberum arbitrium) and power over their own acts." See the discussion in Joblin, 27.

48. Cf. *Summa* I-II, 94,2.

49. Cf. *Summa* I-II, 94, A. 2, ad2.

not all are equally basic or excellent. While we do not have here a full-blown modern notion of rights, there is nevertheless a fundamental respect for the person and those human needs toward which he or she is naturally inclined. Despite this, it must be acknowledged that Aquinas shares with his predecessors, and most of his successors both within and without the Christian tradition, the notion that rights are grounded in human *nature* rather than in the *person*. I will return to this in the last part of the chapter.

The Modern Articulation of Human Rights

With the breakup of the social world that had formed the framework for Aquinas's synthesis, two streams of thought began, based ultimately on two different notions of *nature*. Within the Christian, basically Catholic, tradition, theologians such as Bartolomé de las Casas, Francisco Vitoria, and Francisco Suarez tried to locate human rights in a framework of nature and universal law.[50] The other stream, by far the more significant in creating the modern Western mind, was the political thinking preceding and within the Enlightenment. It is important to understand the direction of that stream in order to grasp what is right and what is aberrant in its movement.

Early Movements to Secure Human Rights

One manner of studying the history of human rights is to consider the watershed moments in the history of freedom in Western civilization. In the early stage, it was a question of *passive* rights, that is, activities and capabilities conceded by others. Such rights found a correspondence in law. Thus, historians usually point to the *Magna Charta Libertatum* granted by King John of England in 1215 as a paradigm of later documents expressing the rights of the citizens of a given territory. The paradigmatic character of the charter is indicated by the fact that it (1) was forced upon King John by his nobles, who were discontent with his arbitrary exercise of power, (2) curbed the authority of the ruler, especially his power to tax or imprison subjects at will, (3) was contractual in form, and (4) set forth certain liberties, thus implying rights.[51] Although the document said nothing about the rights of the

50. Valuable information and literature regarding these theologians can be found in Bernard V. Brady, "An Analysis of the Use of Rights Language in Pre-Modern Thought," *The Thomist* 57 (1993): 97-122. For a discussion of Protestant thinking and its relation to Enlightenment philosophy see Huber, "Human Rights — A Concept and Its History," *The Church and the Rights of Man, Concilium* 124/4 (1979).

51. See E. John, "Magna Charta," in *The New Catholic Encyclopedia* (1967).

common man, it was a symbolic beginning. The influence of the *Magna Charta* can be witnessed in the fact that it was periodically reissued in Britain and widely imitated throughout the rest of Europe, showing it to be representative of a larger impulse toward self-protection from the arbitrary powers of rulers.[52] The protections that it extended were expanded in later English law. The Habeas Corpus Act of 1679 protected individuals from arbitrary detention. This was followed ten years later by the Bill of Rights, which further limited the powers of the King in relation to Parliament, guaranteed the rights of Protestant subjects to bear arms, and attempted to ensure fair treatment of the accused by prohibiting such practices as excessive bail or cruel and unusual punishment.[53] The same year saw the passage of the Toleration Act, which granted Trinitarian Protestant dissenters freedom of worship, provided they fulfilled certain conditions.[54]

The *Magna Charta* is a thoroughly medieval document, granting protections only to those in positions of power in feudal society. Nevertheless it marks the beginning of a trajectory that would gradually expand such protections to all people, while at the same time identifying these protections with emancipation from coercive authority, whether political or religious. Eventually the idea of *natural rights* emerged, which asserted certain protections and privileges of the individual regardless of social standing and apart from any correlation to *duties* owed to others.[55] These are called "active" rights.

For Aquinas, as we have seen, the autonomy of nature was part of its createdness. For later thinkers, these two notions became separated — the autonomy of nature was no longer rooted in its dependence on God. This became especially true when the Creator himself was considered, at

---

52. See Joblin, 29. Some historians downplay the influence of the *Magna Charta* in its own day, arguing that its influence largely stems from its invocation in 17th century disputes between British monarchs with absolutist ambitions and members of Parliament determined to curtail them. See J. Bartlet Brebner, "Magna Charta," in *Great Expressions of Human Rights,* ed. R. M. MacIver (New York: Harper and Brothers, 1950), 61-68.

53. See the excerpts from this document in *Human Rights: National and International Documents* (Brussels: International Federation of Catholic Universities Center for Coordination of Research, 1989), 1-3.

54. This act, however, did not remove civil disabilities for religious dissent. See "Toleration Act (England)," in *The Westminster Dictionary of Church History,* ed. Jerald C. Baeur (Philadelphia: The Westminster Press, 1971), 825.

55. See W. Ernst, "Ursprung und Entwicklung der Menschenrechte in Geschichte und Gegenwart," *Gregorianum* 65 (1984): 231-70, esp. 238; Kenneth Minogue, "The History of the Idea of Human Rights," in *The Human Rights Reader,* ed. Walter Laquer and Barry Rubin (Philadelphia: Temple University Press, 1979), 3-17, esp. 4-5.

least in practice, to be an anonymous force (deism), or nonexistent (atheism). Thus, the movement symbolically initiated by the *Magna Charta* became more and more divorced from any relation to God. This became increasingly apparent when the unified medieval world order collapsed politically, religiously, and intellectually during the fourteenth through sixteenth centuries. The collapse of this order, however, did not bring about freedom but a vacuum for competing tyrannies. As Walter Kasper has expressed it: "Modern human rights are thus the expression both of release from the orders that hitherto reigned in the world and of protest against new, enslaving and degrading relationships."[56]

Enlightenment and Pre-Enlightenment Thinking on Human Rights

It was the achievement of the Enlightenment to complete the trajectory already begun by severing the notion of emancipation and hence rights from its religious and communal foundations and reconstituting it on a more secular and individualistic basis. The foundation for this shift is laid in the thought of Hobbes, Locke, and Kant.

For Hobbes, men are born free in what is known as the "state of nature." In this state each individual enjoys unlimited autonomy and hence unlimited rights — "even to one another's body." Therefore the natural state of humanity is one of constant warfare and struggle as individuals attempt to impose their will (i.e., their rights) on one another.[57] Because of this intolerable situation people authorize a sovereign to declare and enforce the rules by which they must live.[58] While Hobbes is thus one of the first to rest the authority of government on the consent of the governed (rather than some divinely imparted authority or God himself), paradoxically the subjects of government in his view have no recourse to any "rights" that would shield them from the coercive authority of the state.[59] The one duty of the subjects is obedience to the sovereign and whatever laws he may make. This is the demand of justice. The state is also the sole source or determinant of morality — there can be no appeal to individual conscience.[60] The choice Hobbes offers his contemporaries is thus a stark one — the jungle or the cage. Hobbes's notion of natural rights paves the way for modern totalitarianism in its various forms.

56. "The Theological Foundation of Human Rights," 51.
57. *Leviathan,* 1, 13.
58. Ibid., 2, 17.
59. Cf. Minogue, 7.
60. Hobbes describes such an appeal as a disease of a commonwealth. See *Leviathan* 2, 19.

John Locke, by his two Treatises of Civil Government (1689) also sought to establish a natural basis for human rights. Like Hobbes, he endeavored to base the authority of government on the consent of those governed, but he went beyond Hobbes in seeking to make this government responsive to the wishes of its subjects.[61] Hence Locke's account of the state of nature differed from Hobbes's vision of anarchy. The state of nature may be one of freedom, but not necessarily one of constant warfare. Rather it is governed by the law of nature that enjoins respect for the life, health, liberty, and possessions of others.[62] Such obligations also hold for those responsible for government. Indeed, for Locke, one of the primary reasons that human beings form associations known as governments is for the preservation of these very rights of life, liberty, and the pursuit of property.[63] Thus the authority of the state is not absolute, but rather holds only when exercised for the common good.

For Locke, these natural rights may be described as *self-evident.*[64] In what sense is this the case? Given Locke's thoroughly empiricist epistemology it is not surprising that his notion of natural law is attended by some ambiguity. Since there are no innate ideas, the mind can entertain ideas only by its powers of sensation and of reflecting on the impressions conveyed to it by the senses.[65] Yet Locke's basic affirmation is that Scripture and common sense testify that reason informed by experience provides us with sufficient knowledge of the moral law.[66] Natural rights, because of their self-evident character, enjoy a greater degree of certitude than religious ideas, the truth of which is never certain and must be submitted to the judgment of reason.[67] Faith is therefore removed from the realm of reasoned public discourse and relegated to the sphere of private opinion.[68]

A similar observation can be made in regard to the idea of autonomy.

---

61. Cf. Minogue, 8.

62. Cf. Locke's *Second Treatise of Civil Government,* 2, 6.

63. Cf. *Second Treatise,* 9, 123.

64. On the self-evident character of Lockean rights see Max L. Stackhouse, *Creeds, Society, and Human Rights: A Study in Three Cultures* (Grand Rapids: Eerdmans, 1984), 67-69.

65. See Locke's *An Essay Concerning Human Understanding,* 2.1.2.

66. Cf. *Essay* 1.1.5; 2.23.12. On the sources of moral knowledge in Locke see the extensive discussion in John Colman, *John Locke's Moral Philosophy* (Edinburgh: Edinburgh University Press, 1983), 29-50, 177-205. See also John C. Biddle, "Locke's Critique of Innate Ideas and Toland's Deism," *Journal of the History of Ideas* 37 (1976): 414-15; Grenville Wall, "Locke's Attack on Innate Knowledge," in *Locke on Human Understanding,* ed. I. C. Tipton (Oxford: Oxford University Press, 1977), 24.

67. See Locke's discussion in *Essay,* 4.18.5, 8.

68. Cf. David Synder, "Faith and Reason in Locke's *Essay,*" *Journal of the History of Ideas* 47 (1986): 213.

Here, Locke differs from Hobbes and prefigures Kant. In his attempt to be faithful to the mechanistic science of his day, Hobbes sought to eliminate notions such as moral freedom from his account of human behavior, reducing human choice and deliberation to the movement of various passions within the person.[69] Thus the natural world is the alien source that determines the human will. According to Locke, however, through their reasoned choices human beings shape the contingencies of the natural world, thus achieving a form of autonomy.[70]

This notion of self-determination is made by Kant into one of the cornerstones of his moral system.[71] For Kant, the will must be absolutely autonomous in order to make authentically good moral choices. That is, it must be free of influences such as interest or desire, or coercion or promise of reward. Each individual becomes the autonomous legislator of universal moral laws.[72] Within this vision of moral autonomy, however, Kant had an insight into human dignity, insisting that other persons must always be regarded as ends rather than means.[73] This latter idea has been interpreted in increasingly individualistic fashion in subsequent thought, often being reduced to personal freedom without Kant's correlation to duty and respect for the dignity of others.[74]

The preceding survey indicates something of the ambiguity of the Enlightenment's contribution to thinking about rights.[75] Through philosophers

69. See the discussion in *Leviathan,* 1, 6.

70. See the lengthy discussion in Andrzej Rapaczynski, *Nature and Politics: Liberalism in the Philosophies of Hobbes, Locke, and Rousseau* (Ithaca, N.Y.: Cornell University Press, 1987), 123-76.

71. This is not to suggest that Locke was the sole or even the primary influence on Kant in this regard, although there can be little doubt that Kant was influenced by Locke's empirical psychology, especially as mediated by Hume. For a comparison and contrast of Locke and Kant in regard to their notions of morality and agency, see Rapaczynski, 165-71.

72. See Kant's discussion in the *Groundwork of the Metaphysic of Morals,* in *Gesemmelte Schriften,* vol. 4 (Berlin: Prussian Academy of Sciences), 431-34.

73. *Groundwork,* 429.

74. Among the best studies that trace the subsequent influence of Kant's notion of freedom are Francis O'Farrell, "Kant's Concept of Freedom," *Gregorianum* 55 (1974): 425-69; Heinz W. Cassirer, *Grace and Law: St. Paul, Kant, and the Hebrew Prophets* (Grand Rapids: Eerdmans, 1988); Colin Gunton, *Enlightenment and Alienation: An Essay Toward a Trinitarian Theology* (Grand Rapids: Eerdmans, 1985). On Kant's political philosophy see Leslie A. Mulholland, *Kant's System of Rights* (New York: Columbia University Press, 1990).

75. Strictly speaking, Hobbes and Locke predate the Enlightenment. Their influence upon Enlightenment thinkers is, however, widely acknowledged. Kant is also something of a transitional figure, marking the end of the Enlightenment (at least in Germany) and the transition to idealism.

such as Hobbes, Locke, and Kant, rights came to be understood in a more general way than was done previously (in that, at least in principle, they did not pertain simply to members of a particular social class). Kant in particular captures something essential to an understanding of human dignity in his description of the person as an end in himself. At the same time, however, there was a growing secularism as rights were increasingly removed from the sphere of biblical revelation and founded on particular concepts of experience or simply upon reason.[76] Furthermore, there is a clear individualism that runs throughout all of these formulations.[77] This is at its most radical form in the atomic individualism of Hobbes, but it is also clearly present in Locke's empiricist psychology and Kant's notion of moral autonomy.

Of the thinkers just considered, it was Locke who was to have the greatest immediate impact on the developing notion of rights. Locke's modest political doctrine, crafted as a Whig limitation on the claims of divine right monarchy, took on increasingly revolutionary and secular overtones in the age of the Enlightenment.[78] It was his notion of natural rights to which disgruntled colonists and subjects appealed in overturning what they saw as oppressive governments in the American and, to some degree, the French revolutions.

Locke's influence is especially clear in the American declarations. Historians seem to be agreed that the first formulation of human rights, in the modern sense of the term, was in the Virginia Bill of Rights of 1776. This bill named as inalienable rights: "the enjoyment of life and liberty, the means for the obtaining and possession of property, and the pursuit and achievement of happiness and security."[79] The United States' Declaration of Independence is even more overtly Lockean in its formulation: "We hold these truths to be self-evident, that all men are created equal and are endowed by their Creator with certain inalienable rights; that among these are life, liberty, and the pursuit of happiness. That, to secure these rights, governments are instituted among men; that deriving their just powers from the consent of the governed. . . ."[80]

76. In this sense one may understand the observation of Wolfgang Huber: "In order to do justice to this historical development it is essential to recognize the human rights movement for what it is — a worldly secular phenomenon." In "Human Rights — A Concept and Its History," *The Church and the Rights of Man,* ed. A. Miller and N. Greinacher, *Concilium* 124/4 (New York: Seabury, 1979), 4-5.

77. For cogent critiques of the impact of Enlightenment upon modern thought and culture, see MacIntyre, *After Virtue;* Taylor, *Sources of the Self;* Milbank, *Theology and Social Theory.*

78. Cf. Minogue, 8-9.

79. Huber, 5.

80. The citation is from *The Human Rights Reader,* 107.

In similar fashion the French Declaration of the Rights of Man and of the Citizen declared the purpose of all political associations to be "preservation of the natural and inalienable rights of man; these rights are liberty, property, security, and resistance to oppression."[81] The same document also upheld freedom of speech and religion.

These formulations show a number of common features. Rather than guaranteeing the fulfillment of these rights, these documents curtail the power of the state to impede them. Furthermore, the rights secured are not for a particular group, but, in principle, for everyone. In fact, however, "everyone" meant white, male, landed gentry — this has provided the grist for the civil rights and women's rights movements ever since. Finally, the thinking behind the American and especially the French declarations was deist, reflecting the increasing secularism of the Enlightenment era that produced them.[82] This is not to say that these formulations have nothing in common with Christian ideas. One can note, for example, the following similarities: the understanding of reason as a universal possession and lawgiver, the Protestant notion of the inviolability of conscience, and the Christian notion that man is the image of God, implying that the law should not only *permit* the exercise of freedom, but *protect* the inalienable dignity of every human person (though this was not so expressed in the three landmarks we have just considered).[83] Nevertheless, the American and especially the French declarations and their subsequent interpretations betray something of the Enlightenment's own progression from rationalist Christianity and deism to more overt forms of atheism.[84]

The notion of rights has continued to evolve since the Enlightenment. Thus *natural* rights have gradually become *human* rights, inasmuch as they are no longer based on a notion of natural reason, but on particular con-

81. Ibid., 118.

82. Hence the U.S. Declaration of Independence appeals to the "laws of nature and nature's God" and to "the Creator" as the source of inalienable human rights; the 1789 French Declaration merely declares the National Assembly to be under the auspices of "the Supreme Being." See *The Human Rights Reader,* 106-7, 118.

83. Cf. Huber, 4-5.

84. Peter Gay's assessment of the Enlightenment as a revivified and self-consciously modern paganism is correct in many respects. See his *The Enlightenment: An Interpretation,* 2 vols. (New York: Alfred A. Knopf, 1967, 1969), which is still the standard work on the subject. Nevertheless, a number of scholars have challenged Gay's picture of a tidy, unified Enlightenment characterized by the militant secularism of the French philosophes. While this may have been the case in France, it was not so elsewhere. See, for example, the excellent study of Henry May, *The Enlightenment in America* (New York: Oxford University Press, 1976).

ceptions of what it means to be human.[85] Ideas of human rights have generally moved in two primary directions. The first is toward a description of the claims or rights of particular groups, communities, and people. This idea crystallized around the notion of a *right to self-determination* on the part of these communities. As such it has served to counteract some of the inherent individualism and rationalism of the Enlightenment. The second current has been to extend claims of equal rights to those groups not traditionally included in the definition of *man,* such as minorities and women.[86] This has led to an increasing attention to not simply political rights but various social, economic, and even cultural rights. Especially as these claims have been influenced by socialist and Marxist theory, they serve to advance a strongly egalitarian notion of the person. The role of government in this view is often not merely to protect rights but to actively foster and grant them as entitlements to help individuals achieve personal autonomy and self-expression.[87] It is in this egalitarian and activist strain of human rights that most feminist theory finds its home.[88]

PROBLEMS WITH THE MODERN THEORIES OF RIGHTS

In spite of its long history and general political success, the idea of human rights is not without its critics. This study will consider a few of their criticisms primarily from a philosophical and theological perspective.

One of the earliest critics was Karl Marx, who saw the liberal doctrine

85. Huber, 14.

86. Cf. Minogue, 15. See, for example, the 1965 UN "International Convention on the Elimination of All Forms of Racial Discrimination," and the 1979 UN "Convention on the Elimination of All Forms of Discrimination against Women." To this list could be added the 1959 UN "Declaration of the Rights of the Child." These statements can be found in *The Human Rights Reader,* 91-102, 203-14, and 61-64 respectively.

87. For critiques of this view see Harvey C. Mansfield, "The Old Rights and the New: Responsibility vs. Self-Expression," in *Old Rights and New* (Washington: American Enterprise Institute, forthcoming). On the anthropological presuppositions of the "new rights," see Milbank, 14ff. See also Taylor's description of the "expressivist self" in *Sources of the Self,* 368-90.

88. Some feminists such as Rosemary Radford Ruether acknowledge debts to both liberalism and Marxism; others such as Susan Okin have self-consciously attempted to appropriate exclusively liberal concepts of justice as the basis for feminist theory. See Rosemary Radford Ruether's *Sexism and God-Talk: Toward a Feminist Theology* (Boston: Beacon, 1983), 33ff; and Susan Moller Okin's *Justice, Gender and the Family* (San Francisco: Harper Collins, 1989).

of rights as nothing but a bourgeois defense of the status quo and the property rights of the privileged and powerful.[89] Through his own emphasis on social and economic rights, Marx gave new direction to the radical egalitarianism and millenialism of the French Enlightenment and revolution.[90]

A more recent criticism is that the notion of rights is strictly a modern innovation or aberration, having no foundation in biblical or genuine medieval theology. This argument has been made forcefully by Michel Villey. In this view, individual claims of rights represent not an authentic grasp of the dignity of the person but the reductionistic effect of nominalism.[91] A similar argument has been advanced on a philological level by Alasdair MacIntyre, who points out that

> there is no expression in any ancient or medieval language correctly translated by our expression "a right" until near the close of the middle ages: the concept lacks any means of expression in Hebrew, Greek, Latin, or Arabic, classical or medieval, before about 1400, let alone in Old English, or in Japanese even as late as the mid-nineteenth century.[92]

Hence whatever advantages, real or imagined, rights may offer, they are patently modern — a fact in conflict with the claim for their *universal* or *self-evident* status. We must add to this that even the United Nations' Declaration on Human Rights is not interpreted in the same way in Islamic or Marxist societies as in those that embrace Western liberalism.

Another criticism, also championed by MacIntyre, is that there can be no universal rights because there is no abstract or universal human to whom they pertain. All human beings exist within history, within the context of definite interpersonal relationships, and within definite intellectual traditions from which they cannot be extracted in Kantian fashion. Hence, universal rights are nothing more than fictions.[93] It is interesting to note that ultimately such a claim rests on the historicism that has flourished since the Enlightenment. Thus MacIntyre appears to be attempting to use the very weapons of the Enlightenment in his critique of Enlightenment thought. He does not,

---

89. Cf. the excerpts of the writings of Lenin and other Marxist thinkers in *The Human Rights Reader,* 179-192. For a thoughtful attempt to harmonize liberal and Marxist notions of rights see Mihailo Markovic, "Political Rights versus Social Rights," in *Human Rights and the World's Religions,* 46-60.

90. Minogue, 11-14.

91. Among many studies see, for example, his *Le droit et les droits de l'homme,* mentioned above.

92. *After Virtue,* 69.

93. "There are no such rights, and belief in them is at one with belief in witches and unicorns." *After Virtue,* 69.

however, explain his principle of selectivity. Nor does he consider the fact that this historicism is ultimately self-defeating, in that when taken to their logical conclusion historicist claims always undermine themselves.[94]

Other problems with the notion of rights have been touched upon in the preceding historical summary. There is in particular the inherent individualism in various formulations of rights. As noted above, this is most apparent in Hobbes, but it is more subtly present in Locke's politically influential version of natural rights.[95] A similar if more rationalist individualism is present in Kant's version of moral autonomy. Some feminist authors have identified individualistic thinking as a serious weakness in feminism itself.[96] In addition, Catherine Mowry LaCugna, following the work of Patricia Wilson-Kastner and others, has proposed a model of communion from a feminist perspective that includes some aspects of relationalism.[97] I will return to this later.

We have also noted the powerful secularism that the concept of rights imbibed from the Enlightenment, coupled with an increasingly radical egalitarianism inherited from the French revolution and subsequent socialist and Marxist critiques. It was these last two influences upon the developing notion of rights that serves to explain much of the Catholic Church's initial opposition to the movement.[98]

Finally, one might note that the very ambiguity of the concept of rights in its multitude of sources and divergent meanings makes it difficult to render the concept intelligible. The story is told that one of the members of the drafting commission for the United Nations' Universal Declaration

94. The point is aptly made in a study, which predates MacIntyre's work, by Leo Strauss, "Natural Right and the Historical Approach," *Review of Politics* 12 (1950): 422-42.

95. For an insightful consideration of the individualistic character of Locke's notion of rights and its impact on American culture and religion, see Robert N. Bellah's address to the U.S. bishops, "Leadership Viewed from the Vantage Point of American Culture," *Origins* 20 (1990): 217, 219-23. Cf. Felicien Rousseau, who sees the impact of nominalist philosophy in the individualism inherent in Lockian natural rights. *Les croissance solidaire des droits de l'homme: un rétour aux sources de l'éthique* (Montreal: Desclée et Cie, 1982), 163.

96. The most concerted use of this critique is in the work by Elizabeth Fox-Genovese, *Feminism Without Illusions: A Critique of Individualism* (Chapel Hill: University of North Carolina Press, 1991).

97. Catherine Mowry LaCugna, *God For Us: The Trinity and Christian Life* (San Francisco: Harper, 1991).

98. See Joblin, 33-38; Kasper, "The Theological Foundation of Human Rights," 53; and Bernard Plongeron, "Anathema or Dialogue? Christian Reaction to Declarations of the Rights of Man in the United States and Europe in the Eighteenth Century," *Concilium* 124/4 (1979): 39-47.

on Human Rights declared, "We are unanimous about these rights on condition that no one asks us why."[99] This weakness was obvious in the most recent United Nations World Conference on Human Rights (Vienna, June 14-25, 1993), where several nations objected that the notion of a universally applicable concept of human rights is part of Western colonialism.[100] Two examples may serve to illustrate the problem here. In the first place many who oppose an activist concept of rights as entitlements that the government has an obligation to foster appeal to the older Lockean view of natural rights as more viable both philosophically and politically. In this view, rights are grounded on the fixed character of human nature.[101] However, such an appeal overlooks the fact that the inherent nominalism of Locke's epistemology renders human nature unknowable. If rights, whether political or social, are to be grounded in human nature a more adequate account of this nature is necessary.

Second, arguing for the *equal rights* of various groups (such as women) requires some foundation to give content to such claims. Efforts to do so on a purely rational or empirical basis are notably deficient in their ability to account for obvious differences between human beings (whether these be of sex, or race, or various kinds of abilities).[102] Which, if any, of these are significant? It is the inability to ground such claims coherently that raises charges of ideology against the language of rights.[103] Indeed, historians have corroborated the reflection of *Gaudium et Spes* quoted earlier that even in our own century, for all of its rhetoric about rights, many of the greatest and most flagrant abuses of human rights have been committed in the name of adherence to abstract notions such as equality or other political ideals.[104]

99. Quoted by Walter Kasper in "The Theological Foundation of Human Rights," 48.

100. See the special report on the Conference in *Freedom Review* 24/5 (October, 1993).

101. Cf. Mansfield.

102. See, for example, the cogent critique made by Louis P. Pojman, "Are Human Rights Based on Equal Human Worth?" *Philosophy and Phenomenological Research* 52 (1992): 205-22. Pojman argues that, on strictly empirical grounds, there is a good deal of evidence for unequal human worth because of the vast difference in human intellectual and moral qualities. Feminism's own problems in recognizing all the rights of all its adherents was dramatically portrayed at the recent Women Church meeting held in Albuquerque. See Peter Steinfels, "Beliefs," *The New York Times,* May 1, 1993, A10:5.

103. See James V. Schall, "Human Rights as Ideological Project," *The American Journal of Jurisprudence* 32 (1987): 47-61.

104. Speaking of our own century, Paul Johnson notes that "by the 1980's, state

A Return to the Notion of Person

Given this apparent lack of foundation and consensus in the notion of rights, can it be reconciled with Christian revelation? Or can revealed truth provide the basis for an understanding of human dignity?

The Catholic tradition particularly has had to try to maintain and deepen an understanding of *nature* that insisted on nature's legitimate autonomy in the nature-grace debate with Protestantism. At the same time, it has had to try to develop an understanding of nature's dependence upon God as Creator and the need for healing grace in the debate with deism and atheism. Both of these debates have produced fruitful insights, but there is as yet no definitive expression of how to conceive of *nature* in relation to either of the above problems. There has been a valuable beginning in this regard, however, precisely in a way that will help in considering the feminist question: namely, the understanding that what must be considered is not merely nature but human nature, and this involves a consideration of the human person.

This focus on the person is evident in recent church teaching from *Gaudium et Spes* to John Paul III. It is perhaps no accident that roughly the same period witnessed a marked shift in the church's relation to the language of human rights, emerging most clearly in John XXIII[105] and culminating in the teaching of the present pope, who has made the defense of human rights integral to his own pontificate and to the church's work of evangelization.[106] As noted above, for John Paul II the church's grasp of God's great love for each and every person as created by God and redeemed by Christ is the ultimate basis for this defense of human rights.[107] Christ is also the full revelation of what it means to be human.[108] As the

---

action had been responsible for the violent or unnatural deaths of over 100 million people, more perhaps than it had hitherto succeeded in destroying during the whole of human history up to 1900." *Modern Times* (New York: Harper Colophon, 1985), 729.

105. On the role of John XXIII in this shift and his relationship to previous formulations in the church's developing social tradition, see Joblin, 35-40.

106. See John Paul II's discussion of human rights in *Redemptor Hominis,* no. 17. On the relationship of the church's prophetic role in condemning injustice and speaking out in defense of human rights to the work of evangelization, see *Solicitudo rei Socialis* (1987), no. 41. Much of this flows from his earlier philosophical work such as *The Acting Person,* trans. Andrzej Potocki and Anna-Teresa Tymieniecka, Analecta Husserliana 10 (Dodrecht/Boston: Reidel, 1979).

107. *Redemptor Hominis,* no. 10.

108. Cf. Vatican II's Pastoral Constitution on the Church in the Modern World, *Gaudium et Spes,* no. 22; *Redemptor Hominis,* no. 8.

possessor of this revelation, the church is an "expert in humanity" and is qualified to speak as such.[109]

Substantial Personhood

I would like at this point to return to some of the notions of person that were elaborated in the early Christian thinking about the Trinity and the Incarnation and apply them to the question of human dignity and human rights. In terms of rights, this means a return to the primacy of the person over nature, or in other words, an appreciation of relation, in the realm of spirit, as an ontological category.

Since the *discovery* of person, there has been a concerted effort, as we have just seen, to discuss personhood in terms of the endowments that make human nature what it is and give it its unique dignity. This is as true for the Thomistic tradition developed by las Casas, Vitoria, Suarez, and their modern counterparts as it is for Hobbes, Locke, Kant, and their successors. Although the premises of these two groups differ greatly, there has been a consensus reached that because human beings are endowed with reason and will they are autonomous, that is, they have mastery of their actions, and they cannot be treated by others as a means but only as an end.[110] In this regard one can point to a number of generally positive developments: that rights are now usually conceived of as universal, that rights have advanced the notion of the equal dignity of individuals and peoples, and that they have achieved legal and political expression in certain ways that are appropriate to the modern situation.

Difficulties arise when one attempts to push the consensus further.[111] The conclusion is then reached that human rights ultimately require a theological foundation.[112] It is from this point that modern Christian

109. The phrase was first used by Paul VI in his "Message to the United Nations General Assembly" (October 4, 1965), *Acta Apostolicae Sedis* 57 (1965), 878. It has been echoed by John Paul II in *Solicitudo rei Socialis,* no. 41.

110. This consensus is fragile and still quite modern. Consider the models of how Catholic theology dealt with autonomy traced by Kasper in "Theonomy and Autonomy," 45-53.

111. There is a parallel here with Taylor's notion of "moral sources." In his view there are only three: the traditional Judeo-Christian view of God; the notion of a free rational self; and the understanding of the natural world as the realm for human benevolence. These latter two grew out of the first but have since become detached from it and as such are integral to the modern identity.

112. See Claude Geffré, *The Risk of Interpretation: On Being Faithful to the Christian Tradition in a non-Christian Age,* trans. David Smith (Mahwah, N.J.: Paulist Press, 1987), 224-26; Charles Wackenheim, "The Theological Meaning of the Rights

thought has sought to return to an understanding of the person as the bearer of a unique set of relationships, or even as constituted by these relationships.[113] Illustrative of this development is the work of such theologians as Hans Urs von Balthasar, Walter Kasper, Wolfhart Pannenberg, Jean Galot, Joseph Ratzinger, Heribert Mühlen, and from another perspective, Karol Wojtyla.[114]

Individualism seeks to establish the person's rights in the abstract, prior to any actually existing situation; relationalism begins with an understanding of the created person's constitutive relation to God and others, and moves on to consider the actualization of this relation in the mutual

---

of Man," *Concilium* 124/4 (1979): 49-56. More incisive still is the discussion in Kasper, "The Theological Foundation of Human Rights," 47-71. This is also broadly the conclusion reached by Max L. Stackhouse in his cross-cultural study, *Creeds, Society, and Human Rights*. After a comparison of the fusion of Puritan and Liberal Christian elements in America, the civic religion of communist East Germany, and Indian society as informed by Hinduism, Stackhouse argues that it is only the Christian vision of the first of these which can sustain a notion of universal human rights. Even more broadly one might note the convergence of this insistence with the argument of Milbank's sweeping historical survey in *Theology and Social Theory*.

113. One of the philosophical predecessors of this move was John MacMurray, who challenged the indivualisitic presuppositions of most modern thinking about the person: *The Self as Agent* (New York: Harper and Brothers, 1957); *Persons in Relation* (New York: Harper and Brothers, 1961). Some of the most creative thought in this regard has come from Orthodox theologians. In addition to Zizioulas's *Being as Communion,* one could consult Christos Yannaras, *The Freedom of Morality* (Crestwood, N.Y.: St. Vladimir's Seminary Press, 1984). This latter work is highly dependent upon Heidegger and comes under some criticism by Zizioulas.

114. A summary of von Balthasar's thinking can be found in "On the Concept of Person," *Communio* 13 (1986): 18-26. The studies by Kasper in *Theology and Church* already referred to are representative of his thought; for Galot, see *Who Is Christ?;* much of Pannenberg's thinking on person is now found in *Anthropology in Theological Perspective,* trans. Matthew J. O'Connell (Philadelphia: Westminster, 1985); Ratzinger's work can be found in the article already referred to, "Concerning the Notion of Person in Theology"; Mühlen has considered this aspect of person in *Una Persona Mystica* (Munich: Schöningh, 1964), and *Der heilige Geist als Person* (Münster: Aschendorff, 1966); for Wojtyla see the study by Kenneth Schmitz, *At the Center of the Human Drama: The Anthropology of Karol Wojtyla/Pope John Paul II* (Washington: Catholic University of America Press, 1993). To this list should also be added, from a philosophical perspective, the recent article by W. Norris Clarke, "Person, Being, and St. Thomas," *Communio* 19 (1992): 601-18. An excellent account of the move "toward the person" in Catholic thought is found in Czeslaw Bartnik, "The 'Person' in the Holy Trinity," trans. Norbert Karava, *Collectanea Theologica* 53 (1983): 17-30, while a pioneering work in this direction is that by Dietrich Bonhoeffer, *The Communion of Saints: A Dogmatic Inquiry into the Sociology of the Church* (New York: Harper and Row, 1963).

interchange of justice and love. The different approaches have been summed up recently in this fashion:

> The liberal tradition starts with the individual; here is the significance of the observation that liberalism is the political equivalent of Unitarianism. In contrast, a trinitarian vision sees the individual and community as co-existent. There is no being apart from relatedness. . . . A political theory shaped by the Christian tradition can only understand the person as an individual in community. The most fundamental human right is the right to exercise the power of self-giving, the opportunity for entrance into relationship, for deeper participation in the life of the human community.[115]

Expressed another way, we may say that an appreciation of human dignity can be an operative principle, but it will founder unless it is also an ontological principle. An acceptance of subjectivity can establish a certain dignity, but it functions only as a negative norm — we can clearly see when rights are violated. Without an ontological basis, personhood is quickly reduced to *persona,* a role existing by common consensus and the laws of the state. There is really no way to move further without recourse to what we may call revealed relationalism, and this for two reasons. Only relation can ontologically ground uniqueness, and only eternal life can give substance to personhood.[116]

Person as Relation

Building upon the convergence of recent thought mentioned above, I would like to discuss person and relation in the human being and then go on to discuss the substantiality given to personhood through the grace of Christ.

There are two approaches in the effort to base personhood in relation. The first, which may be called "Western," tends to locate relation as a second act of being and link it to the activity of the person who moves out from a center of interiority in a rhythm of both giving and receiving. This general position is clearly articulated in the recent article by W. Norris Clarke just mentioned.[117] The difficulty with this approach is that, in

115. Michael J. Himes and Kenneth R. Himes, "Rights, Economics and the Trinity," *Commonweal* 113 (1986): 137-41; citation is from p. 139.

116. By the terms *substance* and *substantiate* used in connection with personhood, I mean to indicate that quality by which person continues to exist after death. It has a "substantial" existence.

117. "Person, Being, and St. Thomas."

distinguishing between existing *(esse)* and acting *(agere),* and placing person in the second of these moments, person is not really grounded in relation but rather is the result of an activity (giving or receiving) that follows upon and perfects existence. This leaves unclear the ontological basis for person and seems to place it in a self-constituting act. While there is certainly a way in which person is constituted by act, by exercising dominion over acts, by "becoming what one is not" through free choices, this cannot be the moment of constituting personhood and it leaves unexplained what the person is prior to act. Clarke himself recognizes this in a further article in dialogue with David Schindler.[118]

The second approach, which may be called "Eastern," is well represented in the work of John Zizioulas.[119] Zizioulas correctly, in my opinion, points to the fact that personhood is precisely the act of existing as a unique and unrepeatable entity. He lacks, however, a clear development of how the Persons of the Trinity differ from creatures in their manner of being free of necessity.

I think there is a manner of understanding personhood that includes what is valid in both these approaches but that avoids their shortcomings. The person is constituted in "first act," or in a primary way, by the very act by which he or she is created.[120] Other creatures also have a relation to the Creator based on the creative act, but this act does not constitute them as unique and unrepeatable in the same way. Only a being endowed with spiritual interiority has this kind of uniqueness and finds itself placed in a network of relationships that cannot be actualized without an act of freedom.[121]

In the very reception of existence, the person is the hypostasis, the unique act of existing, and this is constituted by a unique relation to God and then with all of created reality, particularly the human race. It is a relationship of indebtedness, which surrounds, as it were, the dignity that is the basis for rights. This relation of indebtedness, however, in order to

---

118. Ibid.

119. *Being as Communion;* also, "Human Capacity and Human Incapacity: A Theological Exploration of Personhood," *Scottish Journal of Theology* 28 (1975): 401-48. This latter work is an extremely subtle and helpful study. I am considering only one aspect of it.

120. The fact that personhood is constituted by the unique relation established by God to each person undercuts the notion that a child in the womb is not a person until the mother accepts and recognizes him or her, or that a comatose patient is not a person because he or she cannot enter into a conscious relation with others.

121. For a discussion of personal interiority and consciousness, see my remarks in chapter 6, and the literature given there.

be fully personal, or personal in *second act,* requires an act of freedom by which the radical receptivity of existing as a creature is appropriated and returned to God in an act of love.

But we must go further. Individualism is overcome by relationalism, first, because the constitution of the person derives its very uniqueness from relating to God and to the other persons with whom he or she comes in contact. The relationship to God, as we have just seen, is the foundational relationship and in its first act it is purely receptive. In this, the creature imitates in the created order the Son within the Trinity. The person exists as relationship, but this must be ratified and appropriated in an act of freedom that includes other human persons. This is the meaning of the Christian notion of *agapē.*

Having been created through the Word (Jn 1:2-4), the human being can only fully realize personhood by willing, in faith, to be in, that is related to, Christ. Jesus Christ shows forth in an historical, that is bodily, manner the eternal receptivity and return of love to the Father. Having been raised from the dead after having manifested this love to the world (Jn 14:31), he is "the source of eternal salvation for all who obey him" (Heb 5:9). Faith is that act by which we ratify our existence in Christ and thus enter into a life that is of a divine order and is unending. Both of these characteristics are implied in the New Testament notion of eternal life. That life is precisely relational — we participate in the eternal act of love of the Son, now made available by the Holy Spirit through the transformed humanity of Christ. This is what it means to say "Abba."

To posit a graced relation to the Father in the Son through the Holy Spirit as the only full actualization of the person is to change the perspective on the traditional nature-grace problem by shifting it to a person-grace context. This, I believe, preserves the legitimate integrity of nature and of person while acknowledging the biblical teaching that all creation can only find fulfillment in Christ. For our purposes here it suffices to accept the full consequences of this truth and conclude that personhood is only fully substantial when it is related in Christ to the Father, *Theos* is *agapē.*[122] Without this relation and its eternal consequences the person remains inchoate, the dignity of personhood remains insubstantial, and despite the quasi infinity of its spiritual nature which is *capax Dei,* the human person

---

122. It should be recognized that the Johannine statement that *Theos* is *agapē* (see 1 Jn 4:8, 16) is a statement about the *Father* who is constituted by his free gift of himself to the Son and the Holy Spirit, and who continues that activity in regard to human beings by creating them each in a unique relationship to himself that is perfected by becoming a sharer in the life of the Son.

can find no other existential ground for the recognition of its dignity. This is the challenge presented by Heidegger's notion that human being is "being toward death." In addition, the person, despite his or her metaphysical autonomy, is affronted by the actual reality of being constituted by the laws of the state and by societal acquiescence: the person becomes, existentially, a *persona*. This is the story of every totalitarian state and it also explains the outrage stirred up in us at the sight of people being treated as means rather than as an end.

Rights, as we understand them, are rooted in the person's unique relation to the Trinity and in the capacity for interiority and intimacy in actualizing this relation in itself and in regard to others. The *agapē* that we return to God is the same as that by which we are constituted in our gift to each other. This is the meaning of the biblical notion of communion. In the last section of this chapter, I wish to consider briefly the challenge which this offers to us Christians, a challenge made more insistent by the realization that very often the rights of some members of the church have not been respected within the church itself.

COMMUNION AS THE MODE OF CHRISTIAN EXISTENCE

I have said enough, I think, about the myth of total oppression perpetuated in some feminist theology. In the feminist advocacy stance problems arise when the evidence is presented in too selective a manner and when presuppositions are not subjected to a more stringent critique. Such a critique, in the instance we are considering, does not obliterate the claim that rights are violated, but it does serve to place it in a context which safeguards other realities revealed by God.

The presupposition most often underlying the discussion of rights is, as I have said, individualism. We have seen, however, that it is impossible to consider the person as being constituted independently of relation and to consider its dignity and rights prior to relationship.

In the theological tradition, *communio* or *koinōnia* refers first of all to the communion among local churches,[123] and second to the church as made up of persons who have an *agapē* relation to the Father in Christ through the Holy Spirit, and relate to each other with the same *agapē*. It is in this extended sense that I will be using the term in a discussion of rights.

123. See Yves Congar, "De la Communion des Eglises à une ecclésiologie de l'Eglise universelle," in *L'Episcopat et l'Eglise Universelle*, ed. Yves Congar and Bernard Dupuy, Unam Sanctam 39 (Paris: Cerf, 1962), 229-60.

The actual communion that is the nature of the church is, in the present state of things, only partially realized. The Old Covenant, which according to Hebrews 10:1 contained a "shadow" or "sketch" of the good things to come, has been replaced by the present dispensation, which is an "icon [image] of the realities themselves." We have the realities — our relation to God and to each other gives substantial and abiding existence to our personhood — yet we possess this reality in a mode of existence that is not proper to it; we possess its icon. The most profound realization of this iconic existence is found in a Eucharistic assembly where Christ, the risen Lord, presides over his people gathered to worship the Father in the Spirit and to be brought into communion with him. This assembly is authentic to the degree that it is grounded in a genuine communion between the community so gathered and all other communities. We are not talking about a ceremony but a sacrament.

The icon is genuine as well to the degree that there is an authentic participation of each member in the life of Christ, that is in his Trinitarian relations, and there is the sharing of that life, on all levels of human existence, between the members of the assembly. The Eucharistic act of the whole Christ distills and intensifies the actual daily life of communion of those who assemble. Communion, in this sense, implies the sharing of material goods. This is clear from the New Testament itself and from the practice of the Eucharist as it is described by Justin Martyr.[124] It also implies a respect for the dignity of each person regardless of social standing. This is insisted upon by the letter of James (Js 2:1-7), and is grounded in the fact that the *persona* accorded by this world has been superseded by the personhood conferred by faith and baptism: Galatians 3:28; 1 Corinthians 12:13; Colossians 3:11.

The question of rights is seen from a different perspective when it is considered within the communion of the church. From a strictly individualistic point of view, each person is restricted in the exercise of his or her rights by the coercion of the state, the laws of economic or social dynamics, or other forms of what Milbank calls "violence."[125] In such a viewpoint, there really is no person, but only an unmitigated drive for self-actualization, usually including the acquisition of property, modified and defined

---

124. 1 Jn 3:16-18. See also Francis Martin, "Monastic Community and the Summary Statements in Acts," in *Contemplative Community: An Interdisciplinary Symposium,* ed. Basil Pennington (Washington: Cistercian Publications 21, 1972) 13-46. Justin's remarks are found in *The First Apology* 67,6 (Ruiz Bueno, 258).

125. Milbank describes a new anthroplogy that "begins with human persons as individuals and yet defines their individuality essentialistically, as 'will' or 'capacity' or 'impulse to self preservation.' " *Theology and Social Theory,* 14.

by society. A Christian understanding of rights is founded on the dignity of the person, and while it includes such things as subjectivity, consciousness, self-realization, and autonomy, it sees these as constituted in the actually existing person through relationality. Such a view puts the understanding of rights in context and sees both their exercise and their deprivation in terms of something intrinsic to the person and not essentially definable by the state.

Feminist theologians have not sufficiently attended to two important dimensions in their consideration of rights. First, they have not understood the difference between the contexts of individualism and relationalism, and second, they have not been realistic about the reality of sin and the need of the power of the Cross to bring about the changes in personality and in community that must take place if there is to be a Christian communion worthy of the name.

This is not to say that all feminist theologians have restricted themselves to an individualistic foundation in considering *communio,* though most have, as can be verified by considering the works of Sandra Schneiders, Elizabeth Johnson, Anne Carr, and those whom they cite. As I mentioned previously, several thinkers have sought to develop the implications of a relational understanding of person in connection with the position of women in the church or even in regard to a feminine aspect of the Trinity. A useful summary of their views can be found in the work by Catherine Mowry LaCugna.[126] What is summarized there has genuine potential for forming the kind of dialogue needed in this area of Christian life. My basic question to this approach, as I already indicated in regard to Zizioulas, concerns the difference between divine personhood and human personhood. In God, the *what* of divinity exists only as Father, Son, and Holy Spirit, who exist with concomitant freedom. In a human being, the unique and relational act of existence, the person, is the act of existence of a human nature. In scholastic terms, there is a difference between the *what* that exists *(quid est)* and the *act* of existing *(esse).* There is also, as I mentioned before, a difference between the fact of being relational and the free appropriation of relationality, the conscious acceptance and ecstatic movement of love in Christian *agapē,* which gives personhood an immortal and substantial existence.[127] This threefold division in human persons, which is not in divine persons, finds expression in bodiliness. It is for that reason that I will postpone a longer conversation with the proposals of LaCugna until the following chapter.

126. *God For Us,* chapter 8, "Persons in Communion."
127. This is a particular realization of the distinction between "being" and "acting" used by W. Norris Clarke.

A relationalist understanding of rights has two sides. Negatively, a grasp of the dignity of each human being, based on his or her unique realization of interiority and autonomy, acts as a norm indicating where rights are violated. Positively, only a vision of such a person as receiving his or her substantial, immortal personhood in union with the risen Christ enables us actually to move from the *persona* created by the blood family, the society, and the state, to the *person*. It is in this sense that Paul says there is no longer slave or free, Greek or Barbarian, and so on, and inserts into Galatians 3:28 that there is "no male and female." When male and female are considered as *personae,* that is, when the norms of this world are taken to be definitive, and we do not live out, and help others live out, a genuine personhood in Christ, then we are false to the gospel. I believe that trying to understand what man and woman means in Christ is better served by contrasting *persona* and person than by arguing about gender and sex. The question, then, as to whether sexuality enters into personhood depends upon the way we understand the body, a discussion to which we shall shortly return.

The first letter of John describes communion as the goal of receiving and transmitting revelation from God: "What we have seen and hear we proclaim as well to you so that you may have communion with us, and our communion is with the Father and his Son Jesus Christ. And we write these things to you so that our joy may be complete" (1 Jn 1:3-4). Although Vatican II gave voice to the desire for a genuine people of God, a *communio,* we have not seen it develop to any notable degree. It is here, perhaps more than anywhere else, that we see our powerlessness in the face of sin, our own and that of others, and thus experience that isolation and alienation that, as Genesis 3 already pointed out, result from sin. This is the aspect of rights that feminism, and indeed all theology, must attend to.

It is relatively easy to understand how foundationalism and representationalism must be overcome in order to reestablish a context in which feminism's legitimate questions may be respected and responded to. Understanding *communio* is a more difficult task: a thing is only intelligible to the degree that it is in *act*. This means that we will achieve an understanding of how men and women are to live and relate in the body of Christ only through an actual obedience to the Holy Spirit, who will move us to die to the skewed self-affirming and self-promoting drive within us that is sin.[128] As Dietrich Bonhoeffer expresses it:

---

128. Here, it is important to grasp the error in the assertion of some feminists that such a description of sin is too "masculine." First and foremost, aggression is not the only form of self-affirmation and self-promotion; compliance is inspired by the same pride. Second, there can be little doubt that much of feminism is aggressive, and

Therefore sin in the community is not the newly-added individual will to self-preservation — which in fact makes community possible — but the sin is the will to affirm in principle oneself and not the other as a value, and to acknowledge the other only in relation to oneself.[129]

A turn to the subject that does not end up as the absolutizing of the self is only possible where there is the "ecstasy" (going outside of oneself) of love. But such a love is the *agapē* revealed to us in Christ, for no other love is genuinely a going out of self, and this love is not achieved by human resources. It is a commonplace of New Testament teaching that *agapē* never originates in a human being — its origin is always God.[130]

> In this God's love has appeared among us: God has sent his Son, his Only Begotten, into the world that we might live through him. In this is the love: not that we have loved God, but that he loved us and sent his Son, an expiatory offering for our sins. Beloved, if God loved us so, then we ought to love each other. (1 Jn 4:9-11)

Within the church, as in any society, the violation of rights can be discerned on the basis of the negative principle of the dignity of the human subject. Whereas in other societies the only curb on such violations is coercion through influencing the authority in the society, within the Christian community there is another power, that of *agapē*. It suffices to look at the dynamic qualities of that *agapē* as Paul lists them in 1 Corinthians 13 to see how they fulfill, that is, meet by transcending, the rights flowing from human dignity. The problem is that the power of sin and the weight of judgments that derive from the *persona* imposed by the world hinder us from according each other the dignity that is created and discerned only by faith. There have been injustices committed against women as well as against the poor, immigrants, and the young of both sexes. We cannot solve these inequities by having recourse to the same kind of power that has created them. This will serve to rearrange the power available but it will not set anyone, powerful or

---

this on an individualistic presupposition that insists on sharing the power-centered ethos of so much church life, an ethos rightly condemned by anyone who understands how far this is from a gospel understanding of person and church.

129. *The Communion of Saints,* 82.

130. "*Agapē* is not a love originating in the human heart and reaching out to possess noble goods needed for perfection; it is a spontaneous, unmerited, creative love flowing from God to the Christian and from the Christian to a fellow Christian." Raymond Brown, *The Epistles of John,* Anchor Bible, 30 (New York: Doubleday, 1982), 254-55.

powerless, free. Only a power in the service of love will realize the justice of God.

The constant teaching of the Christian tradition is that we love God and each other with the same love, *agapē*. In terms of communion, this means that our personhood, which is grounded in the fact that we receive our uniqueness from a creative act of God, can only be realized by giving to and receiving from each other. If we are to make present at all the icon of our eschatological reality as persons, we must strive to conceive of our rights in terms of our intrinsic relationality. If we succeed in the power of the Holy Spirit in actually giving existence to the communion initiated by Christ, we will be able to articulate how God intends us to live our personhood as women and men. In this instance a development of doctrine on the level of faith understanding can only take place after it has existed in practice.

II

The Body Person in
the New Testament and
Early Christian Thought

In stating that the act of being of each man or woman is uniquely relational, we also acknowledge that personhood exists, before any consciousness or act on the part of the person, in his or her relation to *Theos,* the Creator, and also in the relations that form the network of each person's life. Through grace the redemptive work of Jesus Christ has enabled us to appropriate on the level of a conscious and free decision that relationship to the Father *(Abba)* that is a share in the Son's relationship and to ratify the other relationships in our lives by a movement of other-centered *agapē.*

Faith is the name we give to that fundamental acceptance of the redemptive work of Christ. It is brought about in us by an act of God to which we agree. Faith is completed by the re-creative act of Christ in and through his body in the act of baptism so that "by one Spirit we are all baptized into one body" (1 Cor 12:13). Thus joined with Christ, the inchoate relationality brought about by creation is given a substantial and eternal existence in the church, the body of Christ.

It is important to realize that human personhood is the unique act of being of a *physical reality.* The constitutive relationality that is personhood is that of a self-conscious body, a body person. The freedom by which I am able to enter into and ratify those relations already constituting me on the level of being is a freedom exercised in and through my physicality. By freely and successively yielding, in faith and love, to the redemptive work of God in Christ transmitted to me by the Holy Spirit and the church, I give full graced existence to the relationships by which I am constituted. This is only possible because I am present to, and a part of, history.

My corporeal dimension is the reason why I have and make a history. Neither angels, who have no body, nor stones, which have no conscious interiority, have history. The work of salvation is intrinsically historical, and thus, in the famous phrase of Tertullian, "the flesh is the hinge of salvation," *caro salutis est cardo.*[1]

Within this horizon, the feminist question can be seen to be fundamentally anthropological. It may be expressed in the following terms: how is physicality constitutive of a human being? This leads to a further question: to what degree does male or female physicality enter into the constitution of the person? Phrased another way: persona, or the result of the interaction between societal expectations and performance, has often been linked to male or female physicality in ways that we now understand to have been over-determinative. Are we to conclude from this that person, as opposed to persona, is sexless? Most people would answer in the negative. Since personhood is the relational act of existence of a being who is intrinsically physical, and thus intrinsically male or female, we must pursue a line of thought that studies both physicality and relationality if we are to understand the question posed to us in our day.

Certain currents of feminism have acted as a corrective, not only bringing about the recognition of the rights and dignity of women but also effecting a distinction between what I am calling here the feminine persona and the feminine person. Now, since personhood only receives a lasting reality — one that transcends death — in Christ, it is especially incumbent upon Christians, who first introduced the concept into human thought in the first place, to show forth the real meaning of female and male as this dimension relates to person. This, as I have already said, will require a greater fidelity to the demands of the gospel — relationships are only intelligible as they actually exist.

In addition to giving this reality an historical existence we must attempt to give it conceptual and verbal expression. Such a conceptualization has its own role to play in an increased understanding of how the personae of male and female, that is, the roles that humanity without Christ has elaborated, have been done away with while feminine and masculine personhood is transposed or sublated in Christ.[2] Such an understanding

---

1. *On the Resurrection of the Dead,* 8,2 *Corpus Christianorum,* Series Latina, II,931.

2. What I mean by sublation is best described in this text of Bernard Lonergan, who says he is following Karl Rahner rather than Hegel: "[W]hat sublates [in our case the life of Christ imparted to the believer] goes beyond what is sublated, [the ungraced personhood] introduces something new and distinct, puts everything on a new basis, yet so far from interfering with the sublated or destroying it, on the contrary needs it,

and articulation is the work of theology operating according to the whole of its essence and the fullness of its power. In order for this to take place, the ascesis I have already described is essential, and this includes an ascesis of dialogue that is nonviolent and nonmanipulative. The result, I believe, will be a genuine development of doctrine.

I wish to contribute to that dialogue in this and the next chapter. The method followed in this chapter will be that already found in many of the preceding chapters. I will first offer a brief trajectory of the history of thought on the human body. This will begin with the Old Testament and continue into the revolution effected by the New Testament teaching on the Incarnation and the church as the body of Christ. The philosophical elaboration of this teaching effected by the early Christian thinkers will be considered in the next chapter, and this will be followed by the story of how this philosophical insight acted as a leaven upon Christian thought until the "dough" of the Enlightenment thinking finally overcame the leaven. I will then look at some efforts to return to the original biblical teaching made recently in order to overcome the various exaggerations and errors in modernity's understanding of the body person.

A history of thinking about the body is in reality a history of anthropology. It goes without saying that I am not going to attempt such a thing here. I wish merely to indicate some basic biblical teachings about the physical nature of the human person. I will then trace the vicissitudes of that teaching in the succeeding centuries in an attempt to apply a modern appropriation of that teaching to the question feminism poses within Christianity.

THE OLD TESTAMENT

As we have seen several times, the faith of Israel expressed itself through the medium of a culture that, while held in common with many of its neighbors, also manifests the transformation effected within it by the revelation Israel received from God. In what follows I will not attempt to point out what is common cultural heritage and what is unique to Israel. I will merely give some highlights of the teaching of the biblical tradition. Because of our Cartesian heritage, we must consciously put aside a set of concepts and images according to which the human body is considered to be an isolated mechanistic system only accidentally related to, and ob-

---

includes it, preserves all its proper features and properties, and carries them forward to a fuller realization within a richer context." *Method in Theology* (New York: Herder and Herder, 1972), 241.

jectified by, the thinking *ego*. Such an instinctive outlook makes it difficult
to effect a sufficient meshing of categories that would make the anthropological teaching of the Old Testament intelligible to ourselves.

We will concentrate most of our attention on the two terms *flesh
(bāśār)* and *soul (nepeš)*. Anticipating our results, we may say that the
flesh makes commonality possible, both for good and evil, while the *nepeš*
makes individuality possible precisely as a particular realization and
manifestation of relationships.

The biblical term that most nearly expresses all that the Hebrew mind
had to say about human beings is the word *nepeš*. Under the influence of
the Septuagint, *nepeš* is most often translated "soul." It occurs some 754
times as a noun and 3 times as a verb.[3] Its basic constellation of meaning
may be mediated by such terms as *throat, appetite,* and probably *breath*.
It is typical of the sliding effect of images that the physical organ by which
the appetite is satisfied, the throat,[4] can easily become the interior appetite
that is revived by food.[5] From here the image can slide to include the
interior of a person, what we might call their "consciousness" or inner
life.[6] Finally, the term can mean life, almost what we mean by *soul*.[7]

Very often *nepeš* can also designate the concrete living being manifesting itself in its physical presence, its breathing and its desire to be.[8] Thus

3. See the article by Claus Westermann, "Seele," in *Theologisches Handwörterbuch zum Alten Testament,* II, ed. Ernst Jenni and Claus Westermann (München: Kaiser,
1984), 71-95.

4. See such texts as "The underworld wrenches wide its *nepeš*, and opens its mouth
without measure" (Is 5:14); "He [the rapacious man] opens his *nepeš* wide as the underworld and is like death and never has enough" (Hab 2:5). A good example of the exploitation
of the ambiguity of the term can be seen in the question asked by the witch of Endor: "Why
do you want to lay a noose for my *nepeš* (neck/throat/breath/life), to bring about my death?"
(1 Sam 28:9). The examples given here and translations are for the most part taken from
Hans Walter Wolff, *Anthropology of the Old Testament,* trans. Margaret Kohl (Philadelphia:
Fortress, 1974), chapter 2.

5. Thus we read in Ps 107:5-9 of the "hungry and thirsty whose *nepeš* fainted
within them," being revived by Yhwh, "For he satisfies the thirsty *nepeš* and the hungry
nepeš he fills with good things."

6. As in Ps 103:1, "Bless the Lord O my *nepeš*, and all that is within me (bless)
his holy name." In Ex 23:9 the Israelites are warned about oppressing a stranger, "For
you know the *nepeš* of a stranger, you were strangers in the land of Egypt." There can
be the nuance of volition as when Yehu says to the citizens of Ramot-gilead, "If it be
your soul (will/desire), then let none go forth nor flee from the city . . ." (2 Kgs 9:15).

7. "He who kills the *nepeš* of a man shall be put to death. He who kills the *nepeš*
of a beast shall make it good" (Lev 24:17).

8. This occurs in texts where we could translate *nepeš* as "person": e.g., Gen
12:5; 14:21; 46:27; Ex 12:1; Lev 7:20.

Genesis 2:7 reads: "And Yhwh God molded the *'ādām,* dust from the earth, and breathed into his nostrils the breath *(nišmat)* of life and the *'ādām* became a living *nepeš*."[9] This one individual became the living totality of "adamhood," in the same way as the individual Moabite becomes the manifestation of "Moabite-hood," or the individual cow is a representation of "cow-hood." As J. Pedersen says, "That which the Israelite understands by soul is, first and foremost, a totality with a particular stamp."[10] The *nepeš* in this sense is at once visible and invisible.

The visible dimension of *nepeš* is *bāśār,* which we usually translate as "flesh."[11] The term applies equally to humans and animals and in fact occurs most often in the book of Leviticus in connection with the sacrificial system. While life is manifested and contained in "breath" *(nešāmâ* or *ruaḥ),* the link between *nepeš* and *bāśār* is provided by still another dimension of bodily existence, the blood *(dām).* Consider the following three texts.

Genesis 9:4 (this follows the statement that the animals were to be food for humans): "Only flesh *(bāśār)* endowed with its *nepeš,* its blood, you shall not eat." Here the word *blood* is an appositional explanation precising that to eat the flesh along with its "soul" or "vitality" means to eat flesh that still has blood. The text goes on to speak of the vengeance God will exact from any beast or human who spills human blood.

Leviticus 17:11 and 14 (verse 10 contains a prohibition against eating blood): "For the *nepeš* of the flesh is its blood, and I have given it to you upon the altar, to make atonement *(lĕkappēr)* for your lives (plural of *nepeš*) because it is the blood which makes atonement by/because of the *nepeš.* . . . Because the *nepeš* of all flesh (is) its blood; it is its *nepeš.* And I say to the children of Israel: the blood of all flesh you shall not eat, because the *nepeš* of all flesh is its blood; any who eat it will be cut off."[12]

---

9. Being a *nepeš ḥayyâ,* a living soul, is not what distinguishes *'ādām* from the rest of creation: the same is said in Gen 2:19 of all the animals named by the man, and is used in Gen 9:9; 1:20, 21, 24 of various living things. What makes *'ādām* unique is that he has been given life-breath directly by God; there is something of God in him.

10. Johs. Pedersen, *Israel: Its Life and Culture I-II* (London: Oxford University Press, 1926), 100. I also owe the illustration of "Moabite-hood" to Pedersen.

11. See N. P. Bratsiotis, "Basar," in *Theological Dictionary of the Old Testament II,* ed. G. J. Botterweck and Helmer Ringgren, trans. John T. Willis (Grand Rapids: Eerdmans, 1975), 317-32.

12. For a good study of these verses and their theological relevance to the biblical teaching on atonement, see Stanislaus Lyonnet and Léopold Sabourin, *Sin, Redemption, and Sacrifice: A Biblical and Patristic Study,* Analecta Biblica 48 (Rome: Pontifical Biblical Institute, 1970), chapter 7, "The Sacrificial Function of Blood."

Deuteronomy 12:23: "But you must strictly refrain from eating the blood, because the blood is the *nepeš,* and you shall not eat the *nepeš* with the flesh."

I have given all these examples because they serve to illustrate the intimate connection that exists between *soul,* or perhaps better, *vitality,* and *flesh.* These two concepts interpenetrate, particularly when considered from the aspect of blood as the vitality of the flesh: even so, they are far from identical. *Flesh* always designates the external, the obvious, dimension of a human being; *soul* as we have seen can also mean the interior aspect. In this regard it is not uncommon to find the terms *nepeš* and *bāśār* used either in parallelism as designations of human beings, or in a merism to indicate the whole of a human being by mentioning the two extremes.[13]

Another difference between *nepeš* and *bāśār,* is that the former evokes the notion of an individual, while *flesh* suggests something held in common.[14] From the point of view of this study, there are two significant and related aspects to this commonality of *bāśār.* First, there is the use of the term to evoke the ephemeral and sinful dimensions of human existence. In this sense it is often used to contrast humans and God: "In God I hope, I shall not fear, what can flesh do to me?" (Ps 56:4).[15] The expression *all flesh* usually evokes the same notion of the weakness and sinfulness of human beings: "All flesh is grass, and its beauty like the flower of the field. The grass withers and the flower fades when the breath of Yhwh blows on it" (Is 40:6); or again: "God looked upon the earth, and behold it was corrupted because all flesh had corrupted its way upon the earth" (Gen 6:12).[16] Yet all flesh is subject to God (Jer 32:27; Num 26:17), and

13. An example of parallelism is Gen 9:15-16; examples of naming the extremes for the whole are Is 10:18; Ps 63:2; 84:3; Job 13:14; 14:22; Prv 4:20.

14. There is as well in Hebrew a word that approximates our notion of *body* but its occurrences are mostly late and infrequent (28 times by a generous count), and it does not serve to individualize the person in the way that *sōma* will do in the New Testament, especially in Paul. For a study of *gěwiyyâ* and its cognates see the article by H.-J. Fabry in *Theological Dictionary of the Old Testament* II, 433-38.

15. For some other examples, see Ps 65:2, "To you all flesh shall come [for mercy], because of wicked deeds." Jer 17:5, "Cursed is the one who trusts in humankind and makes flesh his arm. . . ." "He remembered that they are flesh, a passing wind *(ruaḥ)* that does not return." (Cf. Ps 103:14; Eccl 12:7; other examples, 2 Chr 32:8; Job 34:14.)

16. It is difficult to know whether the accent was on fragility or evil when God says a few verses earlier, "My spirit will not remain in the *'ādām* forever, because indeed he is flesh; and his days shall be one hundred and twenty years" (Gen 6:3). For other examples, see Jer 25:31; 45:5; 12:12; Is 66:16. There are Qumran texts that accent the sinful dimension of *flesh* and serve as a bridge to the Pauline development. Thus, at the final moment, God will "purify the works of a man by his truth, and make pure

will praise God (Ps 145:21; Is 66:23 [here "all flesh" probably means all Israel]). Indeed at the decisive moment in the future, God will take from his people their hearts of stone and give them a heart of flesh, a heart that is human according to his will (Ez 36:26; 11:19), or again he will pour out his Spirit on all flesh (Jl 3:1).[17] These texts promise a union of what is most often contrasted in the Old Testament, namely flesh and S/spirit.

Second, in addition to the general notion of commonality evoked by *bāśǎr*, there is a particular use of the term that is signficant for our purposes. People share the same flesh in a successively intimate manner in so far as they belong to the same people, clan, or family. This understanding underlies the formula "bone of my bone and flesh of my flesh." The most famous occurrence of this phrase comes in Gen 2:23, in the poem of wonder and gratitude placed on the lips of the *'ādām,* when Yhwh God, like "the friend of the bridegroom *(sôsbîn),"* conducts her to him.[18]

Walter Brueggeman, relying on 2 Samuel 5:1 and 19:13-14, has proposed that the expression is covenant terminology, implying fidelity in both weakness and strength.[19] After considering all the instances in the Old Testament where we find this formula, either in its long form, as here, or in a shorter "from my flesh," Maurice Gilbert makes the following observations.[20] First, the formula expresses an interpersonal relation. Second, in every other instance this relation is between men. Third, the possessive pronoun is always attributed to the principal party in the relationship. Thus, when the tribes of Israel go to David in Hebron to ask him to be king they describe themselves as *"your* bone and *your* flesh," whereas David, offering peace after the rebellion of Absalom, says to the elders in Jerusalem, "You are my brothers, you are *my* bone and *my* flesh" (2 Samuel 5:1; 19:13). Fourth, the phrase always serves as an introduction establishing the interpersonal basis for a pact or agreement. The overtones are covenantal.

---

for himself the frame of a man destroying all spirit of perversity from the fabric of his flesh and purifying him by a holy Spirit from all wicked deeds" (1QS 4:20-21; see also the mention of "guilty flesh" in 1QM 12:12, and "the flesh of wickedness" in 1QS 11:9). For a study of this point, one may consult Karl Georg Kuhn, "New Light On Temptation, Sin, and Flesh in the New Testament," in *The Scrolls and the New Testament,* ed. Krister Stendahl (New York: Harper and Brothers, 1957), 94-113.

17. Also, all flesh will see his salvation (Is 40:5).

18. Commenting on this verse, Rabbi Abin said: "Happy the citizen for whom the king is the 'best man' (or bridegroom's friend)." *Genesis Rabbah,* 18,4.

19. "Of the Same Flesh and Bone (Gen 2:23a)," *Catholic Biblical Quarterly* 32 (1970): 532-42. We will return to consider other aspects of this phrase later.

20. " 'Une Seule Chair' (Gen 2,24)," *Nouvelle Revue Théologique* 100 (1978): 66-89, especially 67-71.

Finally, none of these texts have any resonances of marriage, even less of any sexual relationship. Gilbert also notes that the two other instances of the phrase in Genesis (Gen 29:41; 37:21) are the only occasions where the interlocutors are of the same family. The present text, however, is the only instance of a conjugal relationship.

In this light we can see the meaning of the phrase in the verse that follows (Gen 2:24): "For this reason a man *('îš)* leaves his father and his mother and cleaves to his wife, and they become one flesh."[21]

If we try to sum up the cumulative effect of the overtones of this poem and its sequel, we may say that it is first of all an exclamation of wonder and joy in the recognition that "this one" (feminine) is "at last" someone who belongs to the same family as the man. She is truly his counterpart.

Sharing bone and flesh forms a totally human basis for an interpersonal and covenantal relationship which owes its possibility to an action of God. The relationship precedes and includes the conjugal union and its ultimate fruitfulness in the children who are to play a part in God's plan for the formation of Israel. In the act of recognition it is the man who speaks and who describes the woman as "my bone" and "my flesh." He is thus the initiator and, in some sense, the more prominent member of the relationship. But in another sense, the woman, who is not a replica of the man but a realization of divine aid and his counterpart,[22] removes the man from his solitude, from a situation that is "not good." She is taken from him and given to him so that, together, they may be what they cannot be alone.

In brief, the relational community within the human race is realized in a particular and typological manner in the relationship between woman and man, between husband and wife.

No attempt is being made here to present the complete anthropological teaching of the Old Testament. That would entail a thorough study of such

21. The vocabulary in Gen 2:24, while describing an inner change of attachment, certainly does not describe what took place on the societal level. The terms *leave* and *cleave* (*'āzab* and *dābaq*) are, in a high percentage of their instances, theological expressions evoking the image of leaving idols to cling to the Lord. (For the statistics and examples see Jacques Bernard, "Genèse 1 à 3: Lecture et Traditions de Lecture," *Mélanges de Science Religieuse* 41 [1984]: 109-27, particularly 121; 43 [1986]: 58-78.) Such commingling of marriage and covenant terminology is typical of the sapiential tradition that viewed marital infidelity as symbolic and conducive of covenant infidelity. (See texts such as Prv 2:16-19; 23:26-28; Mal 2:14-17).

22. Nineteen of the twenty-one instances of the noun *'ēzer* (aid) refer to divine help. See Jean-Louis Ska, " 'Je vais lui faire un allié qui soit son homologue' (Gen 2,18). A propos du terme 'ezer-aide," *Biblica* 65 (1984): 233-38. Marie de Merode, " ''Une aide qui lui corresponde.' L'exégèse de Gen 2,18-24 dans les récits de l'Ancien Testament, du judaïsme et du Nouveau Testament," *Revue Théologique de Louvain* 8 (1977): 329-52.

terms as *heart,* the center of the person where memories, ideas, plans, and decisions are formed, and *spirit,* the divinely related dimension of a special force or power. It would also involve a deeper understanding of the manner in which human physicality is seen as symbolic of human interiority.[23]

The rapid look at the two terms *nepeš* and *bāśār* provides a basis for understanding the often repeated statement that the Hebrew mind saw the human being as a multifaceted unity rather than as a dichotomy. The interior individuating dimension is present only in and through the physical dimension which bound the person into the totality of the human race, the tribe, clan, and family.

Since for the Israelites the fundamental unity was that of the people, who were one in virtue of the covenant that God had initiated, the biological substratum has already been redefined in terms of a relationship to God. The sign of this relationship was incised into the very flesh of the sons of Abraham (Gen 17:13). Thus, because of his membership in the people, every Israelite was an embodiment of "Israelite-hood," to repeat the expression of J. Pedersen.[24]

THE GOSPELS AND OTHER NON-PAULINE WRITINGS[25]

For the whole of the New Testament there are three factors that intensify and immeasurably deepen the prevalent anthropology inherited from the Old Testament and the intertestamental period. These are the Incarnation

---

23. One of the best studies is still that by Edouard Dhorme, *L'emploi métaphorique des noms de parties du corps en hébreux et en accadien* (Paris: V. Lecoffre,1923).

24. This insight of Pedersen concerning the Hebrew understanding of *nepeš*, which is another way of speaking of the Hebrew "totality concept," is remarkably close to Zizioulas's speculation on the "catholic" character of each human person. See "Human Capacity and Human Incapacity," 408, where Zizioulas makes the same observation. This same type of thinking lies behind the priestly theology's teaching that male and female image God. Each individual realization of the reality of image contains all that there is of image, yet differently and only in relationship. See Martin, "Male and Female He Created Them."

25. I will restrict this rapid survey only to the basic information necessary in order to understand what the New Testament teaches about the body person. Because of the importance of the notion of *body* in Paul and the Pauline writings this will form a special section after a consideration of the rest of the New Testament. Valuable material for this section on the New Testament can be found in the articles *"sarx"* and *"sōma,"* *Theological Dictionary of the New Testament,* trans. Geoffrey W. Bromiley, vol. VII (Grand Rapids: Eerdmans, 1971).

of the Son of God, the universal significance and causality of his death, and the fact of his resurrection.

It is explicitly stated that the physical existence of Jesus began because of an action of the Holy Spirit (Mt 1:20; Lk 1:25), and this may be implicit in other texts as well.[26] The earlier gospel tradition is completed by the statement in the fourth Gospel that the *Logos* became flesh. That is, he became part of the human reality with roots and relations that serve to define him as part of the race as it now exists. The reality of this flesh dimension is insisted upon in the letters of John, particularly the first, which defends the teaching that is now found in the fourth Gospel.[27]

The fact that the New Testament is unanimous in attributing a universal effect to the passion of Christ meant that human, and therefore historical, activity was invested with a much more profound significance. This appreciation could be summed up in the teaching of Maximus the Confessor, which may be paraphrased by saying that we are saved by the human decision of a divine Person.[28]

The New Testament insistence on the importance of this one contingent event was indebted to the whole of the Israelite tradition that saw God's activity as personal, in the way described previously. Such personal activity must be responded to with human activity that is also personal. This insight grounded a unique understanding of sin and reconciliation, making both personal and locating the arena for their existence within the confines of historical activity. In this frame of reference, the passion of Christ served to manifest the interiority of human activity, its relationship to God, what Jean Lacroix calls the "vertical dimension" of history.[29]

The importance of human bodily existence and the consequent historical nature of human acts is dramatically brought out by the letter to the Hebrews when it states that the whole sacrificial system of Israel has been replaced by the offering of the body of Christ, through which the will and plan *(thelēma)* of God was given historical existence. Exploiting the wording of the Septuagint text of Psalm 40:7-9, the author argues in the following manner:

26. See, for instance, Albert VanHoye, "La Mère de Fils de Dieu selon Gal 4,4," *Marianum* 40 (1978): 237-47.

27. It seems clear that 1 John is defending the teaching that is in the Gospel of John. This need not mean that the Gospel as we know it was already composed and in circulation.

28. For a study of this phrase see F. M. Léthel, *Théologie de l'agonie de Christ: la liberté humaine du Fils de Dieu et son interprétation sotériologique mise en lumière par Saint Maxime le Confesseur,* Théologie Historique, 52 (Paris: Beauchesne, 1979).

29. Jean Lacroix, *Histoire et Mystère* (Tournai: Castermann, 1962), 7.

Sacrifice and offering you did not want; rather you fitted a body for me. . . . After saying above, "Sacrifices and offerings and holocausts and sin sacrifices you did not want nor take pleasure in" . . . he then said, "Behold I come to do your will." . . . In this will/plan we have been sanctified through the offering of the body of Jesus Christ once for all. (Heb 10:5-10)

Finally, the resurrection of Jesus Christ conferred upon human physicality a dignity and eternal signficance that gave to human personhood what I called in the last chapter its "substantiality." The reality of the resurrection is never very absent from any statement in the New Testament. The abiding signficance of the act of love in which Jesus died is etched into the transformed physical existence he possesses now. Through faith, it is possible to come into living contact with Jesus in this existence: the power that went out from him when he was in "the days of his flesh" (Heb 5:7) is even more available now. This is the significance for the community of the stories of healings at a distance,[30] and in some ways of all the healing stories.

These three dimensions of a christologically reinterpreted understanding of human physicality are already operative in the Synoptic presentation of the Eucharistic tradition. The body destined for death in prophecy is now transformed in glory: by doing what he commanded in memory of him, that body becomes once again his presence in history. We will proclaim his death in such a memorial until he comes.[31] The Johannine insistence on using the term *flesh* in this regard (Jn 6:51-65) is, as we have seen, part of the fourth Gospel's theological exploitation of the Old Testament notion in order to accentuate the fact that the Word of God is one among us. Jesus is the manna/Wisdom of God, and it is by feeding on him in faith and sacrament that we enter into that relationship that gives a divine stability to our personhood: "Just as the living Father sent me and I live because of the Father, so the one who feeds on me will live because of me" (Jn 6:57).

The basic outlook on human physicality just discussed forms, along with the new experience and understanding of God's Spirit, the context into which the Old Testament terminology is transposed. Thus, expressions

30. The two incidents of healing at a distance now found in the written gospel tradition are the healing of the daughter of the Canaanite-Syro-Phoenician woman (Mt 15:21-28; Mk 7:24-30), and the healing of the son of the Centurion-Royal Official (Mt 8:5-13; Lk 7:1-10; Jn 4:46-54).

31. There is, of course, no way that I can do more than merely touch on the significance of the Eucharist for Christian anthropology. Much basic material can be found in Xavier Léon-Dufour, *Sharing the Eucharistic Bread: The Witness of the New Testament,* trans. Matthew J. O'Connell (New York: Paulist, 1982).

such as *flesh and blood,* continue to mean humanity in contrast with God, while the antithesis *flesh* and *S/spirit* (Mt 26:41 par.; Jn 6:63; 1 Tim 3:16; 1 Pet 3:18) takes on a whole new significance, contrasting now the dubious resources of human nature and the transforming power of the Spirit conferred upon believers by which they demonstrate a new understanding of existence and a new power to live it.

The Incarnation, the universally saving death, and the present transformed physical existence of Jesus Christ reveal the true dignity and significance of the human body person. While this is present throughout all of New Testament teaching, it receives a special emphasis in Pauline theology. I would like to turn now to the Pauline teaching regarding human physicality to consider briefly some of its aspects in order to more deeply appreciate the importance of historical, corporal existence as the sphere of action for the relationally constituted person.

PAULINE TEACHING ON THE BODY PERSON

Ever since the work of Rudolf Bultmann, there has been an appreciation of the importance of Pauline anthropology for an understanding of Pauline theology. Despite the efforts expended over the past decades, however, there is no real consensus on many aspects of Pauline anthropology.[32] I will take an approach that maximizes the overlap in the current opinions, and restricts the investigation to what is necessary for an understanding of Pauline teaching on the body person.

The current slogan "A human being does not have a body, but rather is a body" is not completely true. The mystery of human existence lies in the fact that my physicality both is identical with myself and is the object of reflective consciousness. Not only the Old Testament use of the term *nepeš* to indicate the interior dimension of human existence, but the very fact that one can speak of "my hand," "my head," and so on, indicates that the *I* has two dimensions.[33] These two dimensions of being and having

32. Bultmann's work can be found principally in his *Theology of the New Testament,* vol. 1 (London: SCM, 1952), 185-353. For two studies that take different approaches from each other and from Bultmann and contain ample bibliography, see Robert Jewett, *Paul's Anthropological Terms: A Study of Their Use in Conflict Settings,* Arbeiten zur Geschichte des antiken Judentums und des Urchristentums, 10 (Leiden: Brill, 1971); Robert H. Gundry, *Soma in Biblical Theology: With Emphasis on Pauline Anthropology* (Grand Rapids: Zondervan, repr. 1987).

33. This question is well treated by Antoine Vergote, "The Body as Understood in Contemporary Thought and Biblical Categories," *Philosophy Today* 35 (1991):

a body are respected in the Pauline use of the term *sōma*. *Sōma* indicates the person's presence to, and participation in, history, though the exact perspective or accent is different from text to text.

Robert Gundry is quite correct to insist that the term *sōma* in Paul always includes physicality, but it must be added that since the body is never conceived of as an object, the physicality intended by Paul is to be found along a spectrum that runs all the way from a consideration of the human body as an individuated and objective reality[34] to a transformed mode of physical existence described as a "spiritual body" (*sōma pneumatikon*, 1 Cor 15:44). A complete understanding of *sōma* in the Pauline writings involves a consideration of other anthropological and theological terms such as *spirit, flesh, soul, inner* and *outer man*, and *heart*. That, of course, will not be undertaken here. It will suffice to look at some of the points of the spectrum constituted by Paul's understanding of body.

The most common use of the word *sōma* in Paul is to designate the individual mode of physicality. It is the means of being present to the human situation both as dominated by sin and as open to the action of God. By *sin* I mean that concatenation of societal, economic, political, cultural, emotional, mental, volitional, and demonic forces that rule "this present evil age" (Gal 1:4). It is in this sense that Christ died to sin (Rom 6:10). Human beings personalize and interiorize this reigning force through their own sin and experience the power of that disordered energy that separates from God, the source of life, and brings about death. It is for this reason that Paul sometimes simply speaks of the power of sin in terms of its consequence — Death.[35]

The many facets of the term *sōma* respond to the ambiguity of human historical existence in a world deeply influenced by sin. Because Christ's total victory over sin and death is still awaited (1 Cor 15:23-28), each person has and is a "death-destined" *(thnēton)* body.[36] Sometimes the mention of death evokes the nuance of the sin-force bringing about death through our partici-

---

93-105. Vergote quotes Gabriel Marcel, "Of this body I can neither say that it is I, nor that it is not I, nor that it is *for* me (object)." *Being and Having: An Existentialist Diary,* trans. Katherine Farrer (New York: Harper and Row, 1965), 12.

34. In such texts as ". . . considering his nearly dead body" (Rom 4:19), or the whole description of the body given in 1 Cor 12:14-25.

35. This is strikingly illustrated if, in keeping with Joseph Fitzmyer's proposal, we read the latter part of Rom 5:12 as consecutive rather than explanatory: "Therefore, just as sin came into the world through one man, and through sin, death, so death spread out to all human beings, *with the result that all have sinned.*" See Joseph Fitzmyer, "The Consecutive Meaning of ἐφῷ in Romans 5.12," *New Testament Studies* 39 (1993): 321-39.

36. "Do not let sin reign in your death-destined body so as to obey its cravings" (Rom 6:12). Other texts relating sin and body are Rom 6:12 and 1 Cor 10:16.

pation in history.[37] Yet, this same physicality has an eternal destiny for those who are joined to Christ by faith and the Holy Spirit.[38] Again, in the counter-cultural statement regarding the mutual rights of husband and wife over each other's bodies, we must understand that to be of much wider extent then merely sexual relations.[39] There are times when *sōma* means for Paul the person viewed as the physical focal point of historical activity within which Christ is manifested and glorified,[40] and times when it signifies this existence as contrasted with the heavenly existence of the body person.[41]

When the term *body* is used of Christ, it has three very intimately connected applications. It can refer to the physical body of Christ offered on the cross for us, to the Eucharist, and to the church. In the first category we have only Romans 7:4, "and you have died to the law through the body of Christ, so that you might belong to another who has been raised from the dead, in order that we might produce fruit for God." The body of Christ was the necessary dimension of his existence so that the freedom he won

37. "I am a miserable man. Who will rescue me from this death-dominated body? [lit. the body of this death]" (Rom 7:24); "If Christ is in you, the body indeed is dead because of sin, the spirit, however, is alive because of righteousness" (Rom 8:10).

38. "If the Spirit of him who raised Jesus from the dead dwells in you, then he who raised Christ from the dead will give life to your death-destined bodies because of his indwelling Spirit in you" (Rom 8:11). This is the burden of much of 1 Cor 15, in which Paul describes this body as "spiritual" (1 Cor 15:44). In Phil 3:21 we are told that our bodies will be changed to be conformed to Christ's body of glory.

39. 1 Cor 7:4.

40. ". . . that I shall be put to shame by nothing, but rather in complete confidence, as always so now, may Christ be glorified in my body, either through life or through death" (Phil 1:20; for a similar line of thought see 1 Cor 6:19-20). "For the rest, let no one give me trouble. I bear in my body the brand marks of Jesus" (Gal 6:17). This probably refers to the scars on his body from beating and stoning: they are the historical embodiment and manifestation of his communion in the sufferings of Christ (Phil 3:10). "Always bearing about the death of Jesus in the body, so that the life of Jesus may be manifest in our body" (2 Cor 4:10). Besides referring to the same reality as Phil 3:10, this text includes the notion of the *weakness* involved in being an apostle (2 Cor 12:6-15): poverty, persecution, fatigue, loneliness, physical suffering. Thus Paul can urge all Christians to offer their bodies as a living sacrifice, holy and pleasing to God, and mean by this their whole life of faith on this earth to be a consciously willed dedication to God (Rom 12:1). In contrast, Paul must carefully distinguish for the Corinthians between food, "for the belly," and sexual activity that involves the whole body person and affects that person for eternity since, on the cross and even now, "the body is not for sexual immorality but for the Lord, *and the Lord is for the body*" (1 Cor 6:13); for a similar use of *sōma* in connection with sexual activity and its effect on the whole personality, see Rom 1:24.

41. ". . . we are groaning within ourselves awaiting our adoption as sons, the redemption of our body" (Rom 8:23). See as well 2 Cor 5:6-10.

for us might have genuinely historical existence. The thought is not far from Hebrews 10:5-10, which we considered earlier. The risen and transformed physicality of Christ, however, is also present in this notion as can be seen by the fact that our death to the law results in belonging to Christ in such a way that, as a wife, we may be rendered fruitful.

The notion that we are somehow so joined to Christ that we form part of his flesh-body is related to Hebraic thinking[42] about marriage in at least two other contexts. In 1 Corinthians 6:12-20, intercourse with a prostitute makes a man "one flesh" with her, and thus makes the members of Christ joined to her members, since he who is joined to a prostitute is one body with her as Genesis 2:24 already states,[43] while someone joined to the Lord is one spirit with him. This line of reasoning presupposes that faith and baptism, which is "into one body" (1 Cor 12:13), so join the believers with Christ that they make one reality that in some way is physical. The other text that utilizes Genesis 2:24 and compares marriage and the relation between Christ and the church in terms of *one flesh* and *one body* is, of course, Ephesians 5:21-33. I will discuss this text briefly later in this chapter.[44]

Although Paul's use of semitic thinking about marriage provides some understanding of his teaching on the church as the body of Christ, other aspects must be taken into account as well. In stating outright to the Corinthians, "Now you are Christ's body, and individually parts of it" (1 Cor 12:27), Paul clearly indicated that the metaphorical notion of the "body politic," which he had been applying to the Corinthian community, has its roots in something unique that far transcends the rhetorical and philosophical use of the image in Greco-Roman culture.[45] We have seen already that the historical existence of an individual can localize and manifest the reality of the risen Christ. In the same way, all those who believe in Christ and are joined to him are, because of their

---

42. The notion that a wife is the *flesh* of her husband is found in the first-century *Life of Adam and Eve*, 3. In response to Eve's plea that Adam kill her in order to placate God, Adam says, "How is it possible that I should let loose my hand against my flesh?" *The Old Testament Pseudoepigrapha*, vol. 2, ed. James H. Charlesworth (New York: Doubleday, 1985), 258.

43. Paul, in this context, focuses on the manner in which intercourse makes a man and woman one flesh.

44. The description of the Corinthian community as a bride of Christ in 2 Cor 11:2 does not enter into the line of our discussion.

45. Lucien Cerfaux elaborates three differences between Paul's use of the notion of *sōma* and that of Greco-Roman thinking about the state: (1) the *sōma* is identified with Christ, (2) a specific group is called by the name Christ (1 Cor 12:27; Rom 12:5), (3) the unity of the body does not result from *nature* but from the presence and activity of the Spirit. *The Church in the Theology of St. Paul*, trans. Geoffrey Webb and Adrian Walker (New York: Herder and Herder, 1959), 276-82.

union with him and one another in the Holy Spirit, the historical presence of Christ, they are his body. It is in this sense that the church is called a sacrament, a sign and instrument of salvation, since the church is the historicizing medium of the activity of the risen Christ, revealing him in mystery.[46] The analogy is operative for Paul on the basis of his concept of the human *sōma* — the body is the historical, and therefore symbolic, expression and instrument of the person. We should consider the person under the aspect of physicality, not, however, omitting the dimension of consciousness, which makes personhood and not just individuality possible. The person transcends the body through reflection, though it can only act through its bodily existence.

Since, however, in the present mode of historical existence sin holds sway even in some way in the lives of those who are joined to Christ, it is a better thing to set out and be with Christ (Phil 1:23). That is why Paul would rather leave the present mode of physical existence, though he knows that that does not mean being *bodiless* altogether since he, along with other believers, is still joined to the transformed body of Christ, forming "an eternal dwelling not made by hands."[47] A thorough study of this problem would have to distinguish between human corporeity, the physicality essential to human existence, and human corporality, the mode of being *sōma* within this sin-dominated history. The first is given substantial existence in the heavenly mode of being in the body of Christ, the second is what we experience now.

When Paul tells the Corinthians that the reason so many among them are sick and dying is because they are eating and drinking judgment on themselves in that they do not "discern the body" (1 Cor 27–32), he is referring, as he says himself, to the body and blood of the Lord, the Eucharist. Yet, the sins that he lists are all sins against the community: factions, self-indulgent neglect of others, despising the poor (1 Cor 11:17-22). This has lead commentators, both ancient and modern, to understand correctly that the *body* that is not discerned is as well the body of Christ formed by the community. The intimate reciprocity between these two modes of being present in history are both symbolic because they are both

---

46. "Cum autem Ecclesia sit in Christo veluti sacramentum seu signum et instrumentum intimae cum Deo unionis totiusque generis humani unitatis. . . ." *Lumen Gentium* §1. (Because the church is, in Christ, a sort of sacrament or sign and instrument of intimate union with God the unity of the whole human race. . . .)

47. This is probably the best way to interpret the notoriously difficult 2 Cor 5:1-10. For two opinions that, in my view, can be reconciled by understanding *sōma* as I have just described it, see André Feuillet, "La demeure céleste et la destinée des Chrétiens," *Recherches de Science Religieuse* 44 (1956): 360-402; Norbert Baumert, *Täglich Sterben und Auferstehen. Der Literalsinn von 2 Kor 4,12–5,10*, Studien zum alten und neuen Testament, 34 (Munich: Kösel Verlag, 1973).

bodily. Sharing in one means sharing in the other. The one loaf is the body of the risen Christ made present once again in space and time (see 1 Cor 10:16-17). Our sharing *(koinōnia)* in this life is through a faith appropriated eating of the loaf that makes of all who share in it one body, the one bride of Christ, his flesh, and the one physical reality that gives expression to the unity established by our union with him.

Pauline Teaching on the Body Person, Male and Female

I wish in this section to look at a certain series of texts, some Pauline, others probably deutero-Pauline, which provide some principles for understanding how to respond to the feminist question. Some of these texts are "difficult to understand" (2 Pet 3:16). I will treat of them only briefly, under the one aspect that affects the present study.

There is a fundamental statement repeated in the Pauline writings that must be considered in regard to the issue of women in the church. I refer to the baptismal formulae that declare former divisions to be eliminated in light of the unity we have in Christ. That union, which is strengthened and actualized by the Eucharist as we have seen, is created by baptism: "In one Spirit we were all baptized into one body, whether Jews or Greeks, slaves or free, and we were all given to drink of one Spirit" (1 Cor 12:13).

This theme, that the personae contructed by the societal and legal dynamics of this present age, along with the divisions they effect between human beings, have been done away with in Christ, is repeated once again in Colossians 3:11 and Galatians 3:28 (see also Eph 2:13-18). The differences between slave and free, Greek and barbarian are purely of human devising; for example, the division between the latter is the result of a divine election being lived out according to the limitations and sinfulness of "the flesh." This distinction is now eliminated by the divine call to all human beings ratified in the blood of Christ and actualized by the indwelling of the Holy Spirit. There is, however, another division, that between male and female, mentioned in Galatians 3:28, that is also declared to be no longer operative. The text reads:

> For you are all children *(huioi)* of God through faith in Christ Jesus. For all of you who were baptized into Christ have put on Christ. There is neither Jew nor Greek, there is neither slave nor free, there is not male and female, for you are all one in Christ Jesus. (Gal 3:27-28)

We should note first of all that the contrast between male and female is not expressed as "neither . . . nor" as in the case of the other two but rather as a denial: "there is not male and female." The interruption of the rhythm of the phrase and the explicit citation of Genesis 1:27 indicates that somehow a Jewish understanding of this Scriptural expression is being set aside. It is impossible to think that Paul is saying that from now on there are no men and women. It is precisely on the basis of this distinction that he appeals to the same Genesis texts when speaking of the relation between husband and wife and conduct in the community. The immediate context of the passage is a consideration of the effects of faith and baptism into Christ — all believers are one "person" (*eis* is masculine, not neuter) in Christ. The wider context is the whole debate of the letter to the Galatians concerning the true children of Abraham. In this context the denial of "male and female" is a denial of the manner in which this biblical phrase operated in the law and the current interpretation of the law. In this view "male and female" refers primarily to marriage and fruitfulness. This is not the basic orientation of the Genesis text.[48] Moreover, it may be that the order of naming, that is, first male and then female, was understood by some to indicate dignity.[49] The most fundamental significance of the phrase, however, is that it was considered to express the manner in which males were considered full members of the people, while women were not so considered.[50]

By alluding to the Genesis text, Paul is declaring that the female persona created by Judaism, by which a woman found her dignity in marriage and childbearing and was a member of the people in a derivative manner, has now been set aside. Women as well as men enter God's new people through baptism and not through circumcision and have the same responsibilities and privileges. Moreover, the decision to remain unmarried and dedicated directly to Christ is an option available to women. Their dignity, as was already implied in the Genesis text, does not derive from fruitfulness but from their being an image of God.[51]

---

48. See Francis Martin, "Male and Female He Created Them," 240-65, and the literature given there.

49. In the Mishna (*Keritot* 6,9) the statement is made that "father" is always (*bkl mqwm*) mentioned before "mother," but this is challenged by citing Lev 19:3, which inverts the order. Although the Mishna was redacted in A.D. 200, much of the material of which it is composed antedates that period. A saying in material considered as additional to the Mishnah recommends three prayers in which a man thanks God that he was not made a Gentile, a woman, or a boor (*t.* Berakot 7:18).

50. For a collection of some of the material see R. Loewe, *The Position of Women in Judaism* (London: S.P.C.K., 1966).

51. For this last point see Martin, "Male and Female." For two interpretations of Gal 3:27-28 that are largely in agreement with the one I propose here see Ben

As is well known, there is a series of texts, some Pauline and some deutero-Pauline, that consider the question of the behavior of women in the community, usually in the light of Genesis 1–3. These texts also contribute something to our understanding of how to understand the New Testament, specifically the Pauline, teaching on the body person. Setting aside the abuses that these texts have been invoked to justify, I wish here to outline some principles that ought to govern our interpretation.[52] First, these texts are coherent with the positive orientation already seen in 1 Corinthians 7, Galatians 3:28, and other texts that express Paul's relation to women, such as Romans 16:1-16 and Philippians 4:2-3.[53] Thus, they are not instances in which Paul lapses into a former pharisaic mind-set, as Paul Jewett mantains,[54] nor are they non-Pauline interpolations as has been frequently asserted. They are part of his teaching on the implications for the Christian life of the fact that human physicality has an eternal significance even as we live in history: "For we must all appear before the judgment seat of Christ, so that each one may receive recompense, according to what he or she did in the body, whether good or evil" (2 Cor 5:10).

The texts in which Paul draws practical consequences for family and community life from his understanding of woman and man as body persons are found in 1 Corinthians 11:2-16 and 14:33b-36. The first of these texts is echoed in Ephesians 5:21-33, and the second in 1 Timothy 2:9-15. These texts have been the object of innumerable studies, especially in recent years. It is not my intention here to enter into a full discussion but merely to glean

---

Witherington III, *Women in the Earliest Churches,* SNTS Monograph Series 59 (Cambridge: Cambridge University Press, 1988), chapter 3; Elisabeth Schüssler Fiorenza, *In Memory of Her: A Feminist Theological Reconstruction of Christian Origins* (New York: Crossroad, 1987), chapter 6. It is hard to imagine the revolution introduced into society by the Christian attitude that left women free to choose an unmarried state dedicated to Christ. For a treatment of some aspects of this, see Peter Brown, *The Body and Society: Men, Women, and Sexual Renunciation in Early Christianity* (New York: Columbia University Press, 1988), along with the modifications proposed by Charles Kannengiesser, "Early Christian Bodies: Some Afterthoughts on Peter Brown's *The Body and Society,*" *Religious Studies Review* 19 (1993): 126-29.

52. Many feminist authors have collected abusive interpretations of these texts. For a balanced presentation of the material and a remarkable illustration of the need for some communal and traditional context for biblical interpretation, see the work by William M. Swartley, *Slavery, Sabbath, War, and Women: Case Issues in Biblical Interpretation* (Scottdale, Pa.: Herald Press, 1983).

53. Other examples can be adduced from Acts. For some examples, see Witherington, *Women in the Earliest Churches,* 143-57.

54. *Man as Male and Female* (Grand Rapids: Eerdmans, 1975), 111-19.

some indications of New Testament teaching on male and female as body persons.

The issue being discussed in 1 Corinthians 11:2-16 has to do with the comportment of women and men in the assembly gathered for worship. Since Paul praises the Corinthians for holding fast to the traditions he passed on to them, the discussion has to do with correcting an erroneous understanding of what he taught them. Most probably this had to do with his teaching on man and woman in Christ based on an interpretation of Genesis 1-3.[55] Paul begins with a principle: "But I want you to understand that Christ is the head of every man, man is the head of a woman,[56] and God is the head of Christ." The difficulty in understanding this principle lies in the translation of *kephalē* (head.) Paul may have chosen the word because the heart of his discussion has to do with how people do or do not cover their heads. *Kephalē*, as a metaphorical expression, can signify, among other things, *source* or *ruler.*[57] Paul's argument requires that the term indicate a certain priority that is due to the fact that the *head* is the source of what is *headed.* Although it is not said explicitly, it is clear that *head* as applied to the three relationships mentioned can only be applied analogically. There is a certain resemblance, but the relationships are more unlike than like.

The principle is then applied to the way men and women should pray

---

55. For a good development of this aspect of the question, see L. Ann Jervis, "'But I want you to know . . .': Paul's Midrashic Intertextual Response to the Corinthian Worshippers (1 Cor 11:2-16)," *Journal of Biblical Literature* 112 (1993): 211-30. There are some who maintain that Paul's praise here is nothing but a *captatio benevolentiae,* but a glance at his explicit statement in the following section (1 Cor 11:17), introducing another aspect of community worship, should dispel that notion. He says quite clearly he does *not* praise them.

56. Although the discussion in this passage is about "man" and "woman" in a general sense, Paul seems to be thinking principally about husbands and wives even when he is referring to Genesis texts or discussing the usual course of nature in which "man is of woman." I do not agree with Antoinette Clark Wire, who, amid some valuable remarks, maintains that Paul has in mind the celibate women he has discussed previously: *The Corinthian Women Prophets: A Reconstruction Through Paul's Rhetoric* (Minneapolis: Fortress, 1990).

57. There has been an effort to deny that *kephalē* ever means "ruler" in literature contiguous to Paul. See for instance Jerome Murphy-O'Connor, "Sex and Logic in 1 Corinthians 11:2-16," *Catholic Biblical Quarterly* 42 (1980): 482-500, and the literature given there. But this has been shown to be inadequate. For instance: Wayne Grudem, "Does *kephalē* ('Head') Mean 'Source' or 'Authority' in Greek Literature? A Survey of 2336 Examples," *Trinity Journal* 6 (1985): 38-59; Joseph Fitzmyer, "Another Look at KEPHALE in 1 Corinthians 11.3," *New Testament Studies* 35 (1989): 503-11; and again, "*Kephalē* in I Corinthians 11:3," *Interpretation* 47 (1993): 52-59.

or prophesy in the community; the perspective is honor and shame.[58] Despite the difficulty posed by the terms usually translated "covered/uncovered" it seems that the question is that of men praying and prophesying with uncovered head and women doing the same with some covering or veil on their head.[59] To do the opposite is to shame one's head (in the literal and figurative sense of the term).

The next step in the discussion (vv. 7-12) develops the background for the line of thinking in verses 3-6, and makes more explicit reference to Genesis 1 and 2. There are two steps in the discussion. Verses 7-10 provide another argument that leads to the conclusion that a woman should "have authority upon her head," adding "because of the angels." The argument is based on understanding Genesis 1, regarding the image, in the light of Genesis 2, the creation of man and then woman. Under this very specific perspective, since the man was created first, he is the image and glory of God. The woman is also the image of God, though this is not said, but she is the glory of man because she was created to rectify his aloneness and to be a counterpart, making community possible. She somehow "reflects" the man (again, as with *kephalē,* the term *doxa* is applied analogically to two different relationships). The next two verses (8-9) repeat the same line of thought by saying that the first man is not from the woman, but vice versa, and that the man was not made on account of the woman, but rather the woman on account of the man. The conclusion is that a woman should have her head covered in the assembly as a sign of her authority over her own life and actions, her ability to live out her vocation.[60] The mention of the angels refers to their participation in the community's worship.[61]

Having established his point about the fittingness of a woman cover-

58. Recall what was said earlier about the power of these realities in the ancient world: *Honor and Shame and the Unity of the Mediterranean,* ed. David D. Gilmore, American Anthropological Association, special publication 22 (Washington: American Anthropological Association, 1987).

59. For an argument in favor of the more usual translation, see Joël Delobel, "1 Cor 11,2-16: Towards a Coherent Interpretation," in *L'Apôtre Paul. Personnalité, Style et Conception du Ministère,* ed. Albert VanHoye, Bibliotheca Ephemeridum Theologicarum Lovaniensium, 73 (Leuven: Leuven University Press, 1986), 369-89.

60. I owe this notion of "having authority" to J. Delobel: "Of course, v. 10 has to do with the wearing of the head covering, because according to v. 5 this covering is the concrete way in which the woman behaves correctly as far as her head is concerned, the actual way in which she exercises control over her head" (ibid., 387).

61. See Joseph Fitzmyer, "A Feature of Qumran Angelology and the Angels of 1 Cor 11:10," in *Essays on the Semitic Background of the New Testament* (Missoula, Mont.: Scholars Press, 1974), 187-204.

ing her head, Paul returns to the Genesis text and to the actual nature of things to assert: "Nevertheless *(plēn)* there is not woman without man, there is not man without woman in the Lord.[62] For just as the woman is from the man, so too the man is through the woman. The whole is from God" (vv. 11-12). These verses form a diptych with verses 8-9 and intend to modify them. "In the Lord," the woman's original dependence upon the man for existence is now counterbalanced by taking into account the man's need for a woman to give birth to him. This whole arrangement *(ta panta)* is from God. To put it another way: the creation of woman and the birth of a man are part of the order created by God that can now be seen to have been all along a prophecy of how the relation of equality between men and women is realized "in the Lord." In more theological but also more restrictive terms: the order of creation only yields its full intelligibility as a moment in, and a prophecy of, the order of grace.

In the final four verses of the section (vv. 13-16), Paul returns to argue from "nature" and from the practice of the "churches of God." The term *nature (physis)* evokes nothing of our post-Cartesian concept of an alienated and mechanistic universe. It refers rather to the common perception of organic existence as modified by commonsense practice. Our bodily comportment, transpiring as it does within a humanly interpreted environment, cannot but be symbolic. Within Paul's environment, a man having long hair or a woman exercising a public function in the communal gathering without her head covered "says something." In the latter case, something more than equality is being expressed by this practice at Corinth, which is not the practice elsewhere.[63] There is a subversion of good order and of a certain priority given to men by God in the order of creation. This priority, while emptied of its power-laden significance and abusive practice in both Jewish and Greek environments by the fact of being in Christ, still has some significance, most especially in the family. There is no other way of honestly interpreting Paul's use of such phrases as woman's being the "glory" of man or being created "on account of" man and the fact that the word *kephalē* is never used of her, while at the same time he insists that there is not man without woman nor woman without man in the Lord.

<hr>

62. Fiorenza, following Joseph Kürzinger, translates *chōris* in this verse as "different from" (*In Memory of Her,* 229-30). Besides being philologically less plausible, this proposal does not enhance the meaning supplied by the following explanatory verse, which states that as woman came from man, so man comes through woman.

63. This is the third time in this letter (see 4:17; 7:17) that Paul has appealed to a more general observance of what he teaches in all the churches, and there will be another in 14:33b.

When the original equality at creation is restored by baptism into Christ and interpreted through the Christian understanding of Genesis 2, the result is that there is "not male and female." What then is left of the priority suggested by Genesis 2, and why does Paul retain these phrases? I suggest that this can best be understood not in terms of superior and inferior, or empowered and subject to power, but rather in a *mode of relating*. If a person is constituted by relationship, then while the persona of male and female has been done away with in Christ, the body person of male and female remains. I will return to this later in the chapter.

In the light of Paul's presumption that women will pray and prophesy in the community gatherings, his words in 14:33b-36 are difficult to understand, so difficult in fact that many treat them as an intrusive addition.[64] In fact, however, the passage is but one more in a series of Pauline injunctions in this part of chapter 14 involving the use of the terms *be subordinate (hupotassesthai*, v. 32) and *be silent (sigan*, vv. 28 and 30), by which Paul is trying to prescribe order and peace in the meetings of the Corinthian church. The passage runs:

> "As in all the churches *(ekklēsiais)*, let the women be silent in the meetings of the community *(ekklēsiais)*. It is not permitted them to speak, rather let them be subordinate, as the law itself says. If they wish to learn about something, let them ask their own husbands at home, for it is shameful for a woman to speak at the meeting of the community *(ekklēsia)*. Or has the word of God gone out from you? Or has it reached you alone?

The opening and closing lines indicate that, at the gatherings of the Corinthian community for worship, the women are doing something that is not done in all the churches, that it is against the law and shameful. It is the last instance treated in this chapter of an idiosyncratic manner of acting which creates the impression that the Corinthians think they are free to give practical expression of the gospel message in any way that suits them. What are these women doing? Obviously, it cannot be the simple fact of speaking, since they are presumed to be prophesying and praying in the community assemblies. Somehow, rather, their speaking is disruptive of the gathering and they are told to be silent as are those who have a message in tongues but no interpreter (v. 28), or who are prophesying when

---

64. For an enumeration of the arguments in favor of considering this passage as an interpolation and a response, see Ben Witherington III, *Women in the Earliest Churches,* SNTS Monograph Series 59 (Cambridge: Cambridge University Press, 1988), 90-104.

a prophetic word comes to someone else (v. 30). The injunction to "subordination" (v. 34) may reflect a lack of order in regard to their husbands, or it may echo a previous injunction that the spirit of the prophets is "subordinate" to the prophets. That is, no one moved by the Spirit of God is under such compulsion that they cannot either stop themselves or submit to the judgment of other spiritual persons in the community.

Obviously, every word in this passage has been subjected to minute scrutiny, particularly in these last decades. This is not the occasion to discuss all the opinions. I wish only to indicate what I consider to be the most satisfactory manner of understanding the text as part of this study into the New Testament teaching on body person. The secret of success in deciphering texts such as this one is much like that in trying to interpret a complex musical score that is missing its clef — that interpretation is the best which supplies a clef producing a satisfactory melody with the fewest additions of sharps and flats. I will give here the summary of Ben Witherington III, which strikes me as having achieved that result in the most satisfactory manner so far:

> Thus, the scenario we envision is as follows. During the time of the weighing of the prophet's utterances, some of the wives, who themselves may have been prophetesses and entitled to weigh verbally what was said, were asking questions that were disrupting the worship service. The questions themselves may have been disrespectful or they may have been asked in a disrespectful manner. The result was chaos. Paul's ruling is that questions should not be asked in worship. The wives should ask their husbands at home. Worship was not to be turned into a question and answer session.[65]

In both the texts we have seen thus far, Paul is striving to maintain his teaching, based on his experience in Christ, of the abolition of those female and male personae that derive from society, culture, or even the law as understood without the Spirit. At the same time he is reacting against exaggerations, perhaps stimulated by his own teaching, that have created confusion at Corinth. Paul wishes, on the one hand, to protect the traditions already common in the New Testament community, and developed by himself in particular, concerning the equal dignity and responsibility of women and men in Christ. On the other hand, he wishes to avoid a superficial understanding of body person that easily creates new personae which derive from the same world as the former and lead to the same perverted value systems. In order to do this, he has recourse to a Christian

65. Ibid., 103.

reinterpretation of Genesis 1–3. Before attempting to sketch out a line of investigation that could help in understanding Paul's teaching, we must look at two other New Testament texts that depend upon and develop this teaching. These texts obviously derive from the background and explicit material present in 1 Corinthians 11 and 14.

The first text to be considered is Ephesians 5:21-33. It is generally agreed that Ephesians draws from earlier Pauline material, especially Colossians, Romans, 1 Corinthians, and Galatians.[66] Although there is a resemblance between the Ephesians passage and other New Testament texts, particularly Colossians 3:18–4:1, only here do we find an extended use of Genesis 1–3 in connection with the relation between husband and wife.[67] In addition to this similarity with 1 Corinthians 11:2-16, there is also the notion that the husband is the *kephalē* of his wife, though here as in all the New Testament texts the word *obey* is not used for the husband-wife relationship[68] (though it is used in connection with children and slaves), but rather the term *be subordinate,* which is used of "the Son" in 1 Corinthians 15:28.

We should note first of all that the *genre* of this text, as that of all New Testament texts which treat household relationships, is one of exhortation, rather than one of abstract speculation as in the extrabiblical parallels. It is a second-person address to equals in Christ, not a third-person description of

66. The question of the authorship of Ephesians does not enter into our argument, though it does seem more likely that the letter is the work of a disciple who utilizes the previous material to advance the thought of the master, particularly in regard to ecclesiology.

67. It has become a commonplace to point to those places in the New Testament and early Christian literature that treat of life in a Christian household and to try to subsume them under one heading. As I mentioned in chapter 3, the texts usually invoked are Col 3:18–4:1; Eph 5:21–6:9; 1 Pet 2:17–3:9; 1 Tim 2:8-15; 6:1-10; Didache 4:9-11; Epistle of Barnabas 19:5-7; 1 Clement 21:6-9; and the Epistle of Polycarp to the Philippians 4:2–6:3. The first two in this list bear a real resemblance, the others have in common only the subject matter, not any real literary form or structure. This leads me to doubt that line of argument which seeks to reduce them, and other Hellenistic and Jewish texts, to a common *topos*. The *topos* was then supposedly invoked by Christians who, as I mentioned previously, are presumed to have suffered a loss of nerve and capitulated to the pressure of their pagan neighbors in order to avoid persecution because of the liberty given to women in a Christian context. For some recent work on *topos* see John C. Brunt, "More on the *Topos* as a Literary Form," *Journal of Biblical Literature* 104 (1985): 495-500; Edward P. J. Corbett, "The *Topoi* Revisited," in *Rhetoric and Praxis* (Washington: Catholic University Press, 1986), 43-57. Some work has been done to rectify the thinking based on the notion of *topos* and Christian capitulation by Ben Witherington III in *Women in the Earliest Churches*.

68. With the possible exception of 1 Pet 3:6, by implication.

what ought to be. This presupposes then that the wife's response to her husband is that of a free and responsible agent who answers her husband's love for her. Second, as a corollary to this, we may remark that almost seventy percent of the text is addressed to the husbands, outlining for them what *agapē* means in their imitation of Christ, laying down their lives for their spouses as Christ did for the church (5:25).[69] Third, although the wife is urged to be subordinate to her own husband, the context is that of mutual subordination in the fear of Christ (v. 21). This means that there are two forms of subordination being described. The man's subordination to his wife is expressed in terms of love and of laying down his life. The woman's relation is described by repeating the two terms from verse 21 describing the mutual relationship — subordination and fear.[70] Finally, we may note that the terms *body* and *flesh* are used to describe both the church in relation to Christ and the wife in relation to her husband. This advances the Pauline understanding of Genesis 1–2, combining earlier reflection on the *Adamic* character of Christ with that of the relation between Christ and the church, and applying it analogously to the relation between husband and wife.

In this application, neither wife nor husband is considered to be more "Christ" than the other. What is being accented is the sacramental (bodily/historical) manifestation of the *relationship* between Christ and the church effected in marriage. The author says that Genesis 2:24 is a great *mysterion*. That is, correctly understood, this text uncovers the marriage relationship inscribed in the very order of human existence as being a prophecy of the relationship between Christ and the church. The transposition of marriage from one level to the other is effected by *agapē*. It is *agapē* that transforms the *relationship* without abolishing it, and it is *agapē* that gives substantiality to the persons who are being constituted by their relation to

---

69. The theme for this whole section is set by Eph 5:1-3, which is addressed to all believers: "Be then, imitators of God as beloved children and walk in love just as Christ loved us and gave himself over for us [see Gal 2:20], an offering and sacrifice to God for a fragrant odor." As Fiorenza puts it, "Patriarchal domination is thus radically questioned with reference to the paradigmatic love relationship of Christ to the Church" (*In Memory of Her,* 269-70). It may also be noted that, in the household texts, the primary duty of the husband is that of love for his wife (Eph 5:25; Col 3,19; equivalently, 1 Pet 3:7; Tit 2:6).

70. The most adequate treatment of the meaning of *phobos* in this context is to be found in Markus Barth, "Ephesians 4-6," in *Anchor Bible 34A* (New York: Doubleday, 1974), 608, 648-50, 662-68. To employ terms I will use in the next chapter, there is both a *male* and a *female* way of being subordinate to the other. We can read in *Mulieris Dignitatem,* §24, "All the reasons in favor of the subjection of woman to man in marriage must be understood in the sense of a mutual subjection of both out of a reverence for Christ."

each other and to Christ. There is still an order in marriage, but it has been transformed to be centered now on the well-being of the wife, just as Christ's care is for the church, his body. Because of Christ (the new Adam) and his bride (the church), every Christian man and wife are enabled to recover God's plan for Adam and Eve. This is well summed up by Stephen Miletic:

> The wife's role in the New Creation also reverses the role of the first Eve by doing battle with the forces of darkness (Eph. 6.1-20), forces which until the eschatological age had the power to deceive her. . . . According to Eph. 5.22-25, subordination is not simply obedience to a despot, nor is it something the wife does by coercion, at the behest of cultural traditions in step with social stereotypes. . . . By redefining subordination and headship in terms of New Creation theology, the author of Ephesians has dislodged androcentric marriage from its power-base of domination and relocated it in the sphere of discipleship which participates in and makes a contribution to the New Creation.[71]

1 Timothy 2:9-15

The so-called Pastoral Epistles probably stand in relation to the previous Pauline material in much the same way as the letter to the Ephesians does.[72] The passage under consideration shows dependence upon 1 Corinthians 14:33b-36, but tends to accentuate conservatively one aspect of that teaching more than others, probably because of the situation to which it was addressed. Once more, we are faced with a musical score with no clef, and attempts to supply the clef are made the more difficult because we cannot be sure of the exact climate of thought and activity being addressed. We may accept the information in 1 Timothy 1:3, that the letter was being addressed to Timothy at Ephesus, as being at least paradigmatically correct. If Ephesus is not the actual destination, the situation is not vastly different.

The exhortation begins in verse 8 with an injuction that men pray, "lifting up holy hands without anger or argument," which implies that this was not always the case. Then the author continues by directing his attention to women: "Similarly," women are to adorn themselves with modesty and

71. Stephen Francis Miletic, *"One Flesh": Eph. 5.22-24, 5.31, Marriage and the New Creation,* Analecta Biblica 115 (Rome: Pontifical Biblical Institute, 1988), 117.

72. For a balanced assessment of this problem, see Jerome Quinn, "Timothy and Titus, Epistles to," in *Anchor Bible Dictionary* 6, ed. David Noel Freedman (New York: Doubleday, 1992), 560-71.

self-control, and not with elaborate hair styles made up with pearls and gold,[73] but rather with good deeds as befits women who profess reverence for God. Again, we are entitled to presume that what is proscribed was actually taking place and that there was something immodest and disruptive in the conduct of some of the women. It is in this context, then, that the injunction continues:

> Let a woman learn in quietness and in complete subordination. I do not permit a woman to teach or have authority over a man, but rather to be quiet. For Adam was formed first, then Eve; and Adam was not deceived, but the woman, deceived, came into transgression. She will be saved through childbearing, provided they persevere in faith and love and holiness with self control.

The most plausible scenario underlying this text is as follows. Some women were acting in a way that was *seductive* in many senses of the term. Their conduct and mode of dress was immodest and they were teaching false doctrines, which probably had to do with "myths and genealogies" (1 Tim 1:3-5), the forbidding of marriage and the need for an ascetic diet (1 Tim 4:3), and, in general, things that did not agree with "the sound words of Our Lord Jesus Christ" (1 Tim 6:3-5). When it is recalled that teaching was always considered to be a function endowed with a certain authority, and that, contrary to our academic approach, was always geared to some practical conduct, it can be seen that this way of acting could involve, and probably did in this case, a domineering over men in general or perhaps more particularly the woman's own husband. The ministry of teaching was being abused and treated as though it were the office of teaching. The teaching, moreover, was probably of a gnostic character.[74]

The injunction, then, to learn in quietness and complete subordination is calling for a more modest, peaceful, and teachable conduct that respects the good order both of the community gathering and of marriage. The allusion to Adam's having been formed first reflects the same teaching in 1 Corinthians 11:8-9 and probably depends upon it and the doctrine behind it. The remark that Eve was deceived, reflecting as it does one strand of Jewish thinking obliquely referred to by Paul only once (2 Cor 11:3),[75] is

---

73. For an idea of the type of hair styles envisaged, see Witherington, *Women in the Earliest Churches,* 119, and the literature given there.

74. Simone Pétrement, *A Separate God: The Christian Origins of Gnosticism,* trans. Carol Harrison (San Francisco: Harper, 1990), part 1, chapter 4, "The Signs of Gnosticizing Heresies at Ephesus."

75. For examples from early Jewish literature that accent Eve's responsibility

probably invoked here in order to accent the notion that the women in question have been deceived; a theme present elsewhere.[76] The statement that women will be saved through childbearing is a rebuttal of the doctrine that forbade marriage, and envisages not only the conception and birth of children but the whole Christian activity of raising children referred to in 1 Timothy 5:10. Once again, the importance of the *body* person is being stressed.

Since women are described as having some ministry that involved "training" (*sōphronizein,* Tit 2:3) the younger women, as well as having some functions parallel to those of deacons (1 Tim 3:11) and performing various good works (1 Tim 5:9-10), it is not a question of total silence (*hēsuchia* implies more tranquillity than silence) but of a return to both marital and community order on the part of some women who are taking functions to themselves and disrupting the group. Once again, we see that there is an assertion, though here in a very conservative context, of the equal dignity and responsibility of both sexes. Yet, the mention of Adam and the use of the term *subordination* implies a certain priority of the man, most probably the husband. An understanding of this twofold assertion, so difficult for our modern rights-oriented society and power-oriented sense of worth to grasp, must lie in the direction already pointed out by Ephesians 5:21-33. We will return to this after considering the history of Christian thinking about the body person.

PATRISTIC THINKING ABOUT THE BODY PERSON

The latter part of the first century and the early years of the second provide evidence of how the New Testament teaching regarding the role of the body in enabling human beings to share the life of God was perpetuated. This can be seen in the stress placed on three areas of the Christian message: the reality of Christ's body, the meaning of martyrdom, and the importance of how one lives the physical dimension of life. In all three of these areas there was a profound appreciation of the real significance of historical activity. Change, human historical activity, the most prominent dimension of human physical existence and the aspect most neglected and misunder-

---

and those that place the blame on Adam, see Susanne Heine, *Women and Early Christianity: A Reappraisal,* trans. John Bowden (Minneapolis: Augsburg, 1988), 14-19.

76. A description of this process of deception may be provided by 2 Tim 3:6-9. See also 2 Pet 2:1-3, 10b-18; Rev 2:20-23, Irenaeus, *Against the Heresies* 1,13,1-4.

stood by the Greek mind, is now revealed to be the central arena where
God reveals himself, imparting himself and a knowledege of his plan of
salvation.

The insistence on the authenticity of Christ's physical and thus historical existence is already to be found in the New Testament, especially
in John: "Every spirit confessing that Jesus Christ has come in the flesh
is of God . . ." (1 Jn 4:2).[77] The insistence reflects the fact that the physicality of the Son of God had already become a problem for some.

Ignatius of Antioch is a witness to the thinking of this early period in
regard to the three aspects mentioned above.[78] His letters were composed
within a milieu quite similar to that of the Johannine letters. Although the
opponents they faced were not identical, we find Ignatius continually ac-
centing the real historical nature of Jesus' activity in his life, death, and
resurrection. These human acts are the revelation of God and the means by
which humanity, joined to Christ in the act by which he embraced his
transcendental relationship to every human being, is reconciled to God. If
Christ's body is illusory, that is, if it is not physical and historical, then there
is no relational unity with the rest of the human race and there is no salvation.

> Under Pontius Pilate and the Tetrarch Herod, he was really (alēthōs)
> nailed to the cross in the flesh for our sake. As the fruit of this, and of
> his divinely blessed suffering, we exist. . . .[79]

> Jesus Christ, of David's race, of Mary, who was really (alēthōs) born,
> who ate and drank, who was really persecuted under Pontius Pilate, who
> was really crucified and died while heaven and earth and the underworld
> looked on, who was also really raised from the dead, since his Father
> raised him, the Father who in likeness to him will raise us up who believe
> in him, he will raise us up in Jesus Christ without whom we have no

77. See also 2 Jn 7. For a balanced discussion of the heresy opposed by the
letters of John, see Rudolf Schnackenburg, *The Johannine Epistles: A Commentary,*
trans. Reginald and Ilse Fuller (New York: Crossroad, 1992), 17-24.

78. For a more complete treatment of the manner in which early Christian thinkers
spoke about the body, see Frank Bottomley, *Attitudes to the Body in Western Christendom* (London: Lepus, 1979); Cipriano Vagaggini, *The Flesh Instrument of Salvation:
A Theology of the Human Body,* trans. Charles Underhill Quinn (New York: Alba House,
1968).

79. *To the Smyrneans* 1,2 (*Sources Chrétiennes* 10, 132). In the same letter (5,2)
Ignatius calls it "blasphemy" to deny that Christ was *sarkophoros.* For an excellent
résumé of Ignatius's teaching on the reality and importance of Christ's flesh, see the
introduction by P. Th. Camelot in the volume of *Sources Chrétiennes* already referred
to.

real life. But if as some atheists, that is unbelievers, say his suffering was but a make-believe — when in reality they themselves are make-believes — then why am I in chains? Why do I even pray that I may fight wild beasts? In vain, then, do I die![80]

The latter of the two texts just cited introduces the theme of the relation between the death and resurrection of Christ and that of the believer, most particularly the martyr. On the basis, once again, of bodily existence this is carried still further. Writing to the Smyrneans, Ignatius challenges those who would consider Christ's death a "make-believe" by evoking his own desire for martyrdom, which he describes as "suffering with" *(sympathein)* Christ.[81] This would make no sense if Ignatius' bodily action and passion did not somehow bring him into union with the risen Christ whose body still bears the wounds, now glorious, of his own passion.

The theme of the union between Christ and the martyr, based on this vision of the Christian life, is one of the most constant motifs of early Christian thinking.[82] It finds its origin, as we have seen, in the Pauline notion of the body as the sphere which manifests the power of Christ: "To know him, and the power of his resurrection, and a share in his sufferings being conformed to his death, if somehow I might arrive at the resurrection from the dead" (Phil 3:10; also Gal 6:17). This is the most perfect imitation of and participation in the life of Christ. All the texts available to us insist that in this act of self-donation Christ is present in power, sacramentally showing forth his life in the bodies of women as well as of men.[83]

There is another dimension of this bodily union between Christ and the martyr, and that is its Eucharistic character. A passage in Ignatius's *Letter to the Romans* is justly famous for setting forth this doctrine. Ignatius describes himself as the "wheat of God" who will be rendered the "pure bread of Christ" by the teeth of the beasts who effect his act of dying for Christ. He

---

80. *To the Trallians,* 9-10 *(Sources Chrétiennes* 10, 100-102).

81. *To the Smyrneans,* 4,2 *(Sources Chrétiennes* 10, 136).

82. See Louis Bouyer, *The Spirituality of the New Testament and the Fathers,* trans. Mary P. Ryan, History of Christian Spirituality (New York: Desclée Company, 1963), chapter 8; also Everett Ferguson, "Martyr, Martyrdom," in *Encyclopedia of Early Christianity,* ed. Everett Ferguson (New York: Garland Publishing Co., 1990), 575-79.

83. Consider this famous reply of Felicity when her jailer asked her if, now, in giving birth to a child in jail she cried out so loud, how would she respond when thrown to the beasts. She answered, "Now it is I who suffer; then there will be another in me who will suffer for me, because it is for him that I will then be suffering." *Passio Felicitatis et Perpetuae,* cited by L. Bouyer, *The Spirituality of the New Testament and the Fathers,* 205.

goes on to describe his own longing for the flesh and blood of Christ.[84] In a similar way, when Polycarp is burned to death, the bystanders are said to perceive his body, "Not as flesh burning, but as bread baking. . . ."[85]

The final aspect of Christian bodily existence to consider is that of moral activity. Although there are very practical moral directives given in every document of the New Testament, the most explicit linking of historical existence and union with Christ is found in Paul, whose teaching can be summed up in the injunction "Glorify God in [by] your body" (1 Cor 6:20).[86] This same earnestness in regard to bodily conduct can be found in *First Clement,* the Apologists, and other early writers. One Christian moralist of this early period expresses himself in this manner:

> Guard this flesh of yours, pure and undefiled, that the Spirit which dwells in it may bear it witness and your flesh may be justified. See to it, lest the idea enter your heart that this flesh of yours is mortal and you abuse it in some defilement. For if you defile your flesh, you defile also the Holy Spirit, and if you defile the Spirit you will not live.[87]

Although none of the early Christian writers we have considered can equal the depth and subtlety of those we will now briefly consult, they do share in the revolutionary New Testament understanding of the uniqueness and eternal vocation of every body person. They reinforce the New Testament intuition and advance it. This is especially true of their understanding of martyrdom and the Eucharist. Although they did not explicitly consider the question of how the physical sexual dimension of bodily and historical existence would affect thinking about person, as opposed to persona, they did manage to avoid a Platonic understanding of the issue, a feat not always repeated in their more brilliant successors.[88]

84. *To the Romans,* 4,1; 7,3 (*Sources Chrétiennes* 10,110;114).

85. *Martyrdom of Polycarp,* 15,2 (*Sources Chrétiennes* 10, 228).

86. This advice concludes a section in which Paul is opposing a notion that "all things are legitimate" for a Christian; just as the belly is for food and food for the belly, so sexual activity is equally insignificant. Paul counters, not by speaking of the sexual organs, which would be the parallel to "the belly," but rather of *the body,* which is for the Lord as the Lord is for the body (1 Cor 6:13).

87. *The Shepherd of Hermas,* Similitudes 5,7,1-2 (*Sources Chrétiennes* 53, 240). The translation is basically that of Frank Bottomley, *Attitudes to the Body in Western Christendom* (London: Lepus, 1979), 50. This study should be consulted by anyone who wants a more developed consideration of what I am presenting here.

88. A complete study, especially of the role of the body in Christian moral life would have to include the profound teaching of Clement of Alexandria. For a good brief treatment see Peter Brown, *The Body and Society: Men, Women, and Sexual Renunciation in Early Christianity,* chapter 6.

My purpose in considering some of the figures of the succeeding generations is to establish as firmly as possible what the biblical tradition, as enhanced and developed by these thinkers, has to say about the importance of human physicality and its correlate, human history.

From Irenaeus to the Cappadocians

Irenaeus, perhaps more than any other Christian thinker, understood clearly that the Gnostic interpretation of reality struck at the very heart of the Christian revelation. Its particular brand of spiritualism and elitism, while concocted of Christian elements, denied any significance, except negative, to the world of change and matter, the world, that is, in which human decisions achieve a genuinely historical existence. They denied any reality to the physical appearance of the Logos and ignored the human world of material existence.

> All the solemn declarations of the heretics come down to this: blasphemy against the Creator, denial of salvation to God's handiwork, which is what the flesh is.[89]

Although Irenaeus does not have much to say on the nature of woman, two points should be noted in regard to his teaching on this issue. First, he is very faithful to the Genesis text and considers the creation of man and woman to be described in *both* creation accounts. In this he differs from the Cappadocians, as we will see. The same unified understanding is to be found in the manner in which he sees responsibility for sin in the garden. Second, in his contrast between Eve and Mary, he presupposes a determinative causality to have been exercised by these two woman. In Irenaeus, this contrast is not merely symbolic, it is genuine and historical.[90]

The famous phrase about the flesh being the "hinge of salvation" is not unique in Tertullian, who has a keen sense of the role of human physicality in God's plan of salvation. The most salient passages for our purpose are to be found in his treatise *On the Resurrection of the Dead,* the same treatise in which the *cardo salutis* phrase is found. Tertullian

---

89. *Against the Heresies*, 4, preface. The translation is from *The Scandal of the Incarnation. Selected and Introduced by Hans Urs von Balthasar,* ed. Hans Urs von Balthasar, trans. John Saward (San Francisco: Ignatius, 1990), 14. This book is a collection of Irenean texts touching on the question of human physical existence.

90. For a study of this issue see Domingo Ramos-Lissón, "Le rôle de la femme dans la théologie de saint Irenée," *Studia Patristica* 21 (1987): 163-74.

insists that whatever was expressed in the "clay" at creation reveals God's thoughts about Christ the future man. "Thus, that clay, already putting on the image, in the flesh, of the future Christ, was not only God's handiwork, but also his promise."[91] This means that Christ, even in his risen state, is the point of contact between the action of God and the body of the believer. This is dramatically realized in the sacraments.

> When the soul is enlisted by God, it is the flesh which brings it about that the soul can be enlisted by God. For the flesh is washed that the soul might be purified, the flesh is anointed that the soul might be consecrated, the flesh is signed that the soul might be fortified, the flesh is overshadowed by the imposition of hands that the soul might be enlightened by the Spirit, the flesh is fed by the body and blood of Christ that the soul might be nourished by God. These two which are united in service cannot be separated in reward.[92]

The text goes on to speak of virginity, widowhood, fasting, and mortification as important expressions of what Ignatius had earlier called "honoring the flesh of the Lord."[93]

We do not find in Tertullian any explicit consideration of male and female physicality, but we do find statements of such divergence in regard to women that it is hard to reduce them to one single vision. Tertullian's ambiguity in this regard has been treated by Suzanne Heine,[94] while a generally positive assessment has been offerred by Elizabeth Carnelley.[95]

The thinking of the Cappadocians in regard to human physicality and salvation was influenced by both Origen and Athanasius. From Athanasius, they received a vigorous understanding of the role of the body in transmitting divine life: "If the divine works of the Word had not been accomplished by means of the body, human beings would not have been divinized."[96] From Origen they received, among many things, an interpretation of Genesis 1–3 that considered sexuality to belong to the "second creation."[97]

---

91. *On the Resurrection of the Dead,* 6, 3-5 (*Corpus Christianorum,* Series Latina, II,928).
92. Ibid., 8,2-3 (*Corpus Christianorum,* II,931).
93. *Letter to Polycarp,* 5,1 (*Sources Chrétiennes* 10, 150).
94. *Women and Early Christianity,* 27-32.
95. "Tertullian and Feminism," *Theology* 92 (1989): 31-35.
96. *Against the Arians,* 3,33 (*Patrologia Graeca* 26,393).
97. Origen seems to be dependent here upon a notion found in Philo, highly influenced by Platonic examplarism, according to which the first human, the idea, whose creation is described in Gen 1, is incorruptible, neither male nor female, while the second, found in Gen 2–3, is the object of sense perception, consisting of body and

For the sake of brevity, I will accent the second point, profiting by some recent studies on Cappadocian anthropology.[98] In regard to the first point, the importance of the body in salvation, it will suffice to cite the thinking of Gregory of Nyssa. Gregory develops his notion of the "mystery of the Lord's flesh"[99] in an important passage in the *Catechetical Oration* indicating the power of the causality exercised by the "body that had received God," which now, through the Eucharist, "blends with the bodies of the believers so that human beings, through union with the Immortal, might partake of incorruptibility."[100]

Earlier, I touched upon the influence women thinkers and ascetics exercised upon the Cappadocians. This led them, as Verna Harrison has pointed out, to a very particular appreciation of the New Testament teaching about male and female. The example of the women martyrs and ascetics provided proof of the fact that, "The nature *(physis)* being one, their activities *(energeiai)* are also the same; and the work *(ergon)* being equal, their reward also is the same."[101] The Cappadocians, particularly Gregory Nazianzen, were among the very first to speculate directly upon the consequences of a Christian understanding of bodily existence for the question of male and female relationships and roles in the church. Nazianzen's thinking is quite balanced and reflects many of the New Testament intuitions we have already considered. It is, however, in his attempt to find a theoretical justification for the equality of women and men that the platonic influence of Origen becomes apparent. By the grace of Christ, women have proven themselves to be equal and at times superior to men in virtue,

---

soul, and male or female. *On the Creation,* 134. See Henri Crouzel, *Origen: The Life and Thought of the First Great Theologian,* trans. A. S. Worrall (San Francisco: Harper and Row, 1989), 94. On the difficulty of grasping Origen's thought in this regard see Jacques Dupuis, *"L'Esprit de l'Homme." Étude sur l'anthropologie religieuse d'Origene,* Museum Lessiansum, section théologique, n. 62 (Desclée de Brouwer, 1967).

98. Among the relevant studies, one may consult Robin Darling Young, "On Gregory of Nyssa's Use of Theology and Science in Constructing Theological Anthropology," *Pro Ecclesia* 2 (1993): 345-63; Verna E. F. Harrison, "Male and Female in Cappadocian Theology," *Journal of Theological Studies* 41 (1990): 441-71; Lawrence R. Hennessey, "Gregory of Nyssa's Doctrine of the Resurrected Body," in *Studia Patristica,* XXII, ed. Elizabeth A. Livingstone (Leuven: Peeters Press, 1989), 28-34.

99. *". . . to kata tēn sarka tou Kyriou mysterion. . . ." Against Eunomius,* 5 *(Patrologia Graeca* 45,700).

100. Chapter 37 *(Patrologia Graeca* 45, 93C-97B).

101. Basil, *Homily on Psalm 1 (Patrologia Graeca* 29, 216D-217A), trans. Harrison, "Male and Female in Cappadocian Theology," 448-49.

heroism, and understanding. This is because these qualities belong to the soul, which is neither male nor female.[102] Already in this life, these women are approaching that eschatological state in which there will be no gender, because in the future life of the resurrection each soul will receive a body commensurate with its virtue and resemblance to Christ. This will be a return, this time with a physical dimension, to the state of the first creation.

> This is the great mystery planned for us by God, who for us was made human and became poor, to resurrect the flesh and recover his image and refashion the human, that we might all become one in Christ, who became perfectly in all of us all that he himself is, that we might no longer be male and female, barbarian, Scythian, slave or free (which are identifying marks of the flesh), but might bear in ourselves only the form of God, by whom and for whom we came to be, and be shaped and imprinted by him to such an extent that we are recognized by this alone.[103]

This text illustrates both the strength and the weakness of the Cappadocian position. The strength of the position lies in the fact that it takes seriously the New Testament teaching about the equality of man and woman and understands that there is a way in which "male and female" belong to the realm of "the flesh," even while there is a way in which God takes the physical dimension of human beings seriously enough to make it eternal. The weakness, however, lies in a platonic understanding of human physicality that underplays the obvious biblical insistence that it is as male and female that human beings image God. For this tradition, the "flesh," which is to be transcended by the practice of Christian virtue and finally by the eschatological state of human beings, also includes those physical characteristics that specify someone as male or female. The soul becomes deiform and will be joined, ultimately, to a genderless body that is part once again of the "first creation."

A theological expression of the meaning of male and female that is as faithful to the biblical teaching as the strength of the Cappadocian position must be joined to an understanding of human physicality that moves beyond its platonism to a better perspective on the body person. Modern thinking about the body person can be of great help in recovering and advancing the biblical teaching. Some of the elements of such a

---

102. In *Theological Oration* 8,14 (PG 35, 805B; *Sources Chrétiennes*) we read, "the distinction between male and female is one of body not of soul."

103. *Theological Oration* 7,23 (*Patrologia Graeca* 35,785C). Translation is basically that of Harrison, "Male and Female in Cappadocian Theology," 459.

perspective have been elaborated recently, and they can contribute to a developed understanding of Christian anthroplogy. After a brief look at the trajectory of thought that has prepared for these elements, we will consider them directly.[104]

104. More could be said regarding the patristic understanding of physicality and historical activity, and this should include the negative remarks of some of the Fathers, such as Ambrose, regarding women, but this will suffice for our purposes. For a more developed account see Vagaggini, *The Flesh,* and Bottomley, *Attitudes to the Body.*

12

The Body Person in More Recent Thought

THE MEDIEVAL PERIOD:
HILDEGARD OF BINGEN AND THOMAS AQUINAS

The most reflective consideration published in the medieval period concerning male and female human physicality is undoubtedly that of Hildegard of Bingen (1098-1179).[1] Although she utilizes the Aristotelian cosmological notion of the four basic elements, she does not follow Aristotle in assigning the two higher and more mobile elements (air and fire) to man and the two lower and heavier elements (earth and water) to woman. Rather, she attributes the highest and the lowest to man and the middle two to woman (air and water). Thus, neither sex has a physical superiority to the other. She carries this through in regard to generation, contradicting the Aristotelian notion that the seed of the male required only a place in a female body in order to grow. For Hildegard, the male seed is cold and requires the heat provided by the female if there is to be generation: once again male and female are equal in their roles, though these roles are different. Although her framework remains basically Aristotelian, Hilde-

---

1. For a detailed summary of her thinking see Prudence Allen, *The Concept of Woman: The Aristotelian Revolution 750 BC–AD 1250* (Montréal: Eden Press, 1985), 292-314. These ideas are developed in further studies that are referred to in her article, "Sex and Gender Differentiation in Hildegard of Bingen and Edith Stein," *Communio* 20 (1993): 389-414; particularly relevant for our purposes is her "Hildegard of Bingen's Philosophy of Sex Identity," *Thought* 64 (1989): 231-41. In general much work remains to be done in investigating, through the works of women who wrote, what their own self-understanding was. Often it was not what men of their period (or ours) thought it to be.

368

gard's observations consist mostly in a very insightful understanding into what we would call the psychosomatic typology of men and women. In this she is almost a phenomenologist before her time. She concludes that in the resurrection all will rise in the integrity of their bodies and their sex.

The medieval attitude toward the body was perhaps given its most complete theological expression in the thought of Thomas Aquinas, and I will use him as an illustration of this outlook. Aquinas's notion of the human person as a microcosm of the rest of the created universe captures the heart of the medieval affirmation of the fundamental order and goodness of the universe as God's creation and the certainty of humanity's place within it.[2]

In this instance, his Aristotelianism, with all its deficiencies, gave Aquinas a greater proximity to the biblical notion of physicality than that of some of his contemporaries. Most important for our purposes is his understanding of the soul as the substantial form of the body. This is closer to the biblical notion we considered in the previous chapter, and it provided a way to overcome the residual Platonic dualism of much Augustinian anthropology.[3] Thus he rejects the idea that the soul is created before the body: "It is inconsistent with the perfection of the first production of things, that God should have made either the body without the soul, or the soul without the body, since each is a part of human nature."[4] Seriously considered, this understanding of the human person is only possible in a Christian context. Body and soul as matter and form are only a unity until death. Once the concept of person, however, with its dimensions of interiority and relationality, is added to this, then it is clear that only eternal life gives genuine perdurance to the body person. In the same line of thought, Aquinas recognized the centrality of the body for all human knowing since knowledge is not innate, but rather acquired through the senses.[5]

2. Cf. *Summa Theologiae* 1,91,1.

3. See Benedict Ashley, *Theologies of the Body: Humanist and Christian* (Braintree, Mass.: Pope John Center, 1985), 154. Ashley rightly argues that Aquinas's anthropology represents a genuine synthesis of Aristotelian categories with the Platonic thought of the Augustinian tradition; see 152-53. For a good overview of Aquinas's account of the relationship between body and soul, see Frederick Coppleston, S.J., *Medieval Philosophy: Albert the Great to Duns Scotus*, vol. 2, part II, of *A History of Philosophy* (New York: Image, 1962), 94-107. Particularly valuable in this regard is the study by Anton Pegis, "Some Reflections on *Summa Contra Gentiles* II,56," in *An Étienne Gilson Tribute*, ed. C. J. O'Neil (Milwaukee: Marquette University Press, 1959), 169-88.

4. *Summa Theologiae* 1,91,4,ad3.

5. "Now it is natural for man to acquire knowledge through the senses . . . and for this reason the soul is united to the body, that it needs it for its proper operation; and this would not be so if the soul were endowed at birth with knowledge not acquired

Unlike Hildegard, Aquinas does not challenge the Aristotelian notion that, since the female does not have an active role in producing her own kind, woman is deficient. This results in a notion that woman is inferior according to nature, but equal in the order of grace: "The image of God, in its principle signification, namely the intellectual nature, is found both in man and in woman."[6] This same theme is sounded in his understanding that the eschatological state of human beings includes their sexuality, though he also insists that there is no hierarchy based on nature since the "perfect man" of Ephesians 4:13 refers to "virtue of soul," not male sexuality.[7]

Like his patristic predecessors, Aquinas insisted on the soteriological significance of Christ's body. But this is true not just of his Passion, which is the preeminent source of our salvation, but of every one of his earthly (and hence bodily) acts.[8] Jesus' body is the instrumental cause of our salvation in his earthly life and in his ongoing sacramental presence in the church. This is seen most clearly in the Eucharist, but is also true by way of extension of the other sacraments as well.[9]

---

through the sensitive powers." *Summa Theologiae* 1,101,1. Cf. 1,55,2; 84,6. For a more complete discussion of Aquinas's account of knowledge, see Coppleston, 108-17; and Sheldon H. Cohen, "St. Thomas Aquinas on the Immaterial Reception of Sensible Forms," *The Philosophical Review* 91 (1982): 193-209.

6. *Summa Theologiae* 1,93,5,ad1. Thomas goes on to qualify this statement by adding that in a secondary sense it is only man that is the divine image — attempting thus to harmonize the teaching of Genesis 1:27 with the understanding of 1 Cor 11:7-8 current in his time. On woman as a "misbegotten male" see 1,92,1.

7. *Summa Theologiae, Supplement 81,3,ad1*. This article, composed of material from Aquinas's *Commentary* on the Lombard's *Sentences,* explicitly bases itself on the Genesis account and on the principle that the resurrection will return humanity to its "first condition," which included woman as well as man. As the *Sed contra* of the article indicates, this is Augustine's position as well (*City of God* 22,17). See also in the Supplement 79,1; 80,1. It may be, however, that Aquinas maintains a certain inferiority of woman on the level of nature, though not on that of grace, even in the resurrection: see *Summa Contra Gentiles* 4,83,5; 88,3. This would be contrary to Augustine's opinion.

8. For Aquinas's account of Jesus' passion and the role of his body in attaining our salvation see *Summa Theologiae* 3,46. Elsewhere Aquinas will assert that Christ merited grace (for himself and us) from the first moment of his conception (3,9,4; 34,3) and states that his resurrection and ascension may be deemed efficient causes of our salvation (3,57,6,ad1); see the study by J. Lécuyer, "La causalité efficiente des mystères du Christ selon saint Thomas," *Doctor Communis* 6 (1953): 91-120.

9. On the reality of Christ's corporeal presence in the Eucharist see *Summa Theologiae* 3,75,1. Elsewhere Aquinas argues that the Eucharist is the greatest of the sacraments because Christ himself is substantially present within it while the other sacraments are merely instruments of his power and because all of the other sacraments are in some sense ordered to the Eucharist; see *Summa Theologiae* 3,65,3. It is inter-

Two points are to be made in regard to medieval thinking about the body. First, we find very little appreciation of that dimension of human body person that I have described as historicality, a dimension that is still present in the earlier thinkers because of their consciousness of the way in which it challenges non-biblical, particularly gnostic, thought. One of the reasons for the decline in theological appreciation of human embodiment lies precisely in this lack of understanding the nature of historical activity. Second, as already discussed in chapter 8, medieval people looked upon themselves and upon bodily existence in ways very different from ourselves. In our highly individualistic mentality, *male* and *female* denote isolated concatenations of factors that are clustered around irreducible individuals. For them, there was a much less differentiated understanding of what was male or female.

THE LATE MIDDLE AGES AND THE RENAISSANCE

In this section, I will consider various attitudes to the body as they are evidenced in art, social conventions, and literary attitudes. There was some direct reflection on male and female characteristics on the part of such authors as Bocaccio and Petrarch, but this dimension of the thought of the period needs further research. The purpose of this survey is to provide a place to stand in offering a critique of the feminist notion of the body and the conclusions derived from it.

Even before the rise of the Renaissance the intellectual and social order reflected in the medieval understanding of the body were dealt staggering blows in the outbreak of the Black Death and the rise of nominalism. The virulent outbreaks of bubonic plague that first reached Europe in 1347 and eventually killed up to half of its population were to create a preoccupation with death that poisoned the generally positive outlook of the body as a microcosm of the universe characteristic of the Middle Ages.[10]

---

esting that Aquinas's rational for the church having seven sacraments in its possession is because there is a kind of analogy between bodily and spiritual life and each of these sacraments corresponds to a moment of this process — baptism as birth, confirmation as growth, the Eucharist as nourishment, penance and extreme unction as forms of healing, orders as the power to govern community, and matrimony as the power to reproduce it; see *Summa Theologiae* 3,65,1.

10. Speaking of the impact of the Black Death on the medieval "near synthesis" regarding the body, Bottomley remarks: "If this disaster did not kill the Middle Ages, it rendered it too weak to survive the further crises that were to arrive in the following centuries" (p. 127).

The reemergence of nominalism in fourteenth century thought reflects something of this destabilization on an intellectual level, demonstrating a fundamental skepticism about the intelligibility (and goodness) of the universe and about the ability of the material singular (including the body) to reflect it.[11] The resulting shift in focus from the ontological structure of things to more juridical categories led to an increasingly atomized and utilitarian view of the body.[12]

This fragmentation was ultimately carried forward by the Renaissance despite the fact that initially this movement was something of a cultural revival after the tumult of the fourteenth century and maintained a good deal of continuity with medieval thought throughout.[13] Hence the humanism of the Renaissance is not necessarily always an atheistic celebration of the greatness of humanity apart from God, but in some cases an affirmation of the biblical idea strongly developed in Eastern theology of the creation of humanity in God's image and likeness.[14] Building on the realism and sacramental thought of the Middle Ages, the Renaissance made its own contribution to the development of reflection concerning the body. As Bottomley observes:

11. Although certainly other factors besides the Black Death contributed to the rise of nominalism, such as disillusionment with previous epistemological disputes and a political shift toward absolute monarchy. Nevertheless there can be no contesting the instability of the intellectual climate. David Knowles has rightly described the fourteenth century as a period in which all intellectual positions were pushed to extreme formulations. See "A Characteristic of the Mental Climate of the Fourteenth Century," in *Mélanges offerts à Étienne Gilson* (Toronto: Pontifical Institute of Medieval Studies, 1959), 315-25. Cf. Gordon Leff, *The Dissolution of the Medieval Outlook* (New York: Harper and Row, 1976).

12. For an incisive discussion of the effect of nominalism on the understanding of the body, see Ashley, 160-64.

13. Jakob Burkhart championed the view that the Renaissance was an essentially pagan reaction against Christianity. See his *The Civilization of the Renaissance in Italy* (New York: Harper, 1958), 2 vols. More recent scholarship, however, has criticized this position and emphasized the Christian background and convictions of many Renaissance figures; see Henri Busson, *Le pensée religieuse de Charron à Pascal* (Paris: J. Vrin, 1933); M. I. Bush, *Renaissance, Reformation, and the Outer World* (New York: Humanities Press, 1967), 148ff.; Don Cameron Allen, *Doubt's Boundless Sea: Skepticism and Faith in the Renaissance* (Baltimore: John Hopkins, 1964). In regard to the body, Bottomley argues that even the Renaissance in many ways carried forward the medieval and Christian view of the body though its form of expression proved to be fundamentally unstable; see viii, 129-42.

14. Cf. Paul Oskar Kristeller, *The Philosophy of Marsilino Ficino* (Gloucester, Mass.: Peter Smith, 1953); and Charles Trinkhaus, *In Our Image and Likeness: Humanity and Divinity in Italian Humanist Thought* (London: Constable, 1970), 2 vols.

The human body, particularly as portrayed in art, becomes a symbol or quasi-sacrament of divine truths and, consonant with this traditional respect for an essential element of human nature, we find more emphasis being given in education on its care and importance.[15]

But it was this very exaltation of the body that provided the seeds of further dissolution. In the influx of classical ideas that accompanied Renaissance scholarship, one that proved particularly influential was the Platonic conception of beauty.[16] There is therefore a marked shift in the representation of the human body in the art of this period. While the preceding Gothic period was not unaccustomed to the presentation of the human body, the Gothic nude tended to be realistic and did not emphasize nudity for its own sake.[17]

The Renaissance nude, however, seeking to enflesh the Platonic ideal, used predetermined proportions to give the body godlike attributes so as to foster an appreciation of spiritual beauty through the medium of the flesh.[18] For all of its appeal, this Platonic view of the body proved unstable and was increasingly undercut by the influx of the pagan ideas of classical antiquity and the growing cult of the individual, which abstracted the person from his or her social and ontological framework.[19] Hence, by the time of the late Renaissance, this contemplation of the body had begun to be reduced to the anti-feminine voyeurism that is the precursor of modern pornography.[20] A growing sensuality and eroticism for its own sake was

15. Bottomley, 137.

16. On the Platonic character of much Renaissance thought and art see the discussion in Ashley, 165-69. Cf. Bottomley, 138-39.

17. Bottomley identifies four different meanings of nudity in medieval thought: *nuditas naturalis* (a sign of humility and of man's natural state before God as a creature); *nuditas temporalis* (a sign of poverty either willingly chosen for the sake of Christ, such as St. Francis's famous divestiture before his father, or involuntary); *nuditas virtualis* (a sign of innocence and of the soul cleansed of guilt, often related to the sacrament of penance); and *nuditas criminalis* (a sign of vanity, lust, and the lack of virtue). See n. 31, p. 219.

18. The classic study of the contrasts between the Gothic and the Renaissance nudes is that of Kenneth M. Clark, *The Nude: A Study in Ideal Form* (New York: Pantheon, 1956), see esp. 3-29 and 308-47. On other contrasts between medieval and Renaissance art see W. M. Ivins, *Art and Geometry* (London, 1964), 61ff.

19. Cf. Bottomley, 135-38, 162-64.

20. Around the year 1524 an artist by the name of Giulio Romano published a number of crudely graphic engravings of various positions for intercourse that inspired one Aretino to compose sonnets to accompany each. Bottomley sees this event and the attitudes that it reveals as the beginning of pornography as we know it; see 223, n. 50. Others place this beginning somewhat later: "The rise of commercialized pornography

characteristic of the Rococo style that was the last universal style of Europe and flourished among the aristocracy in the early eighteenth century.[21]

The Christian understanding of the body was further strained by the controversies that divided the church during the Reformation period. The Reformers' mistrust of reason, their subordination of sacraments to preaching and the Word, and their suspicion in regard to art served to undermine the sacral and sacramental character of the body as a revelation of the spiritual.[22] The Catholic Counter-Reformation with its inherent legalism, its voluntaristic conception of God retained from medieval nominalism, and its involvement in controversies concerning grace and moral systems, was largely ineffective in countering this development.[23] While the body was still presented positively in dramatic and often grandiose art of the Baroque period, this presentation suffered from the conflicting pressures of a growing sensuality on the one hand (which was to culminate in the final mutation of the Baroque to the Rococo), and an increasingly puritanical fear of the body on the other.[24]

The seventeenth century wars of religion, which erupted from the embers of the religious conflicts smoldering within a divided Christendom, had the effect of exhausting and discrediting Christian thought and culture and leaving it vulnerable to the secularism of the Enlightenment. Because of its weakened state Christian theology, both Catholic and Protestant, spent much of the next few centuries attempting to cope with (and in some cases to accommodate itself to) the rationalism and mechanism of the Enlight-

---

as we know it today began in the seventeenth century and emerged in recognizable form in the eighteenth. In the nineteenth and twentieth centuries it developed with great rapidity and would appear now to be at flood stage in Europe and America, were it not for the fact that it continues to rise." M. Peckham, *Art and Pornography* (New York: 1969), 289.

21. Bottomley describes this style as "the last glitter from the shattered [medieval] synthesis" (150).

22. This is the argument of Ashley, 172-80, 186. Ashley's presentation on the impact of the Reformation on the theology of the body is far more balanced than that of Bottomley (p. 153), who cites with approval the dictum of Erasmus "*ubicumque regnat Lutherismus, ibi literarum est interitus* (wherever Lutheranism reigns culture is destroyed)" as descriptive of the disintegration of the medieval "near synthesis" in the period of the Reformation.

23. See the overview of the Counter-Reformation provided by Ashley, 180-85.

24. On the art of the Baroque period see Heinrich Wölfflin, *Renaissance and Baroque* (Ithaca, N.Y.: Cornell University Press, 1964). Concerning the evolution of Baroque to Rococo see A. C. Sweter, *Baroque and Rococo* (New York: Harcourt, Brace Jovanovich, 1972). On the banal eroticism of the Rococo see Hauser, vol. 3, 31ff. For an analysis of the "Catholic puritanism" that followed the Council of Trent, see Bottomley, 151-53.

enment. Hence, there is little real development concerning the theology of the body in this period.

While a mechanistic view of the universe and the body has antecedents in ancient thought and in the thought of some late Renaissance figures such as Leonardo Da Vinci, this outlook came into its own with the rise of Cartesian and Newtonian physics in the Enlightenment. The efforts of Descartes to find within human subjectivity a sure basis on which to base his mechanistic philosophy produced, as we have seen, a sharp dichotomy between the knowing subject and the objects of his or her knowledge — a dichotomy that was compounded by his rather crude opposition of soul and body, mind and matter.[25] This mechanistic view of the universe and the dichotomy between subject and object were intensified in the physics of Isaac Newton, under whose influence the universe came to be seen as a stable mechanical system, governed by unchanging natural laws.[26]

While men such as Descartes and Newton were possessed of fervent,

25. For some of the beneficial effects for women of the Cartesian insistence on the dichotomy of mind and body see Prudence Allen, "Descartes, The Concept of Woman and the French Revolution," in *Revolution, Violence, and Equality*, ed. Yeager Hudson and Creighton Peden (New York: Edwin Mellen Press, 1990), 61-78. For a brief overview of the thought of Descartes, see Ashley, 207-10. Ashley rightly observes that Descartes wrote as a Christian influenced by the Augustinian tradition. He exaggerates the continuity between the two, regarding the Cartesian *cogito, ergo sum,* "I think, therefore I am," however, as a valid epistemological extension of Augustine's maxim *si fallor sum,* "If I am mistaken, I exist." For a more adequate treatment of the differences between these two sayings and the role that they played in the thought of their authors see Coppleston, *Modern Philosophy: Descartes to Leibniz,* vol. 4 of *A History of Philosophy* (New York: Image, 1960), 100-107. For a good overview of Descartes's mechanistic understanding of bodies and their relation to mind see the same work by Coppleston, 125-46. See also René Dugas, *Mechanics in the Seventeenth Century,* trans. Freda Jacquot (Neuchatel, Switzerland: Éditions du Griffon, 1958), 174-99.

26. This is the case even though Newtonianism and Cartesianism represented differing conceptions of science, the latter being deductive and mathematical while the former integrated this mathematical approach within a inductive and empirical view. On Newton's synthesis of these two kinds of science see Edwin Arthur Burtt, *The Metaphysical Foundations of Modern Science* (Garden City, N.Y.: Doubleday, 1932), 213-14; and *Towards a Mechanistic Philosophy* (Milton Keynes, The Open University Press, 1974), 85-87. A discussion of the competition between the Cartesian and Newtonian conceptions of science especially in France can be found in Henry Guerlac, *Newton on the Continent* (Ithaca, N.Y.: Cornell University Press, 1981). Yet in spite of the methodological and other differences between Descartes and himself, Newton retained aspects of Cartesian epistemology and actually served to further them through his own influence. ◄

if not altogether orthodox, Christian convictions, their thought was quickly harnessed by scientists (e.g., LaPlace), and philosophers (Voltaire and Hume) eager to use their insights to champion the scientific rationalism of the Enlightenment at the expense of Christian faith.[27]

The mechanism of the Enlightenment was in its own way a sort of crystallization of neo-pagan thinking about the body. It managed to obliterate most if not all of the Christian view in regard to both dignity and role of the body in the plan of salvation and consequently its significance for an understanding of history. The notion of history that has arisen since, with its many positive contributions, does not have much of a notion of the interiority of events and tends to treat historical subjects more like objects.

In the same way, in the Enlightenment approach the body, and the person as a whole, is reduced to a series of mechanical processes — matter in motion.[28] Such a philosophy underlies much modern science, such as the determinism of behavioristic psychology and some extreme forms of sociobiology, the view that has dominated much Western medicine of the body as a machine to be kept running efficiently with the aid of drugs and surgical intervention, or technological applications of such a model in the field of cybernetics.[29]

27. Concerning the influences on Descartes and his religious views, see Coppleston, *Modern Philosophy,* 74-83; also see the very accessible treatment of his background and ideas by Hans Küng, *Does God Exist?* trans. Edward Quinn (Garden City, N.Y.: Doubleday, 1980), 3-80. For a good overview of Newton's religious beliefs and theological writings see Gale E. Christianson, *In the Presence of the Creator* (London: Collier Macmillan Publishers, 1984), 247-65, 566-67; for a more in-depth study see Frank E. Manuel, *The Religion of Isaac Newton* (Oxford: Clarendon Press, 1974). On the growing estrangement of Newtonian theism and his scientific views in the work of subsequent scientists see the excellent article by Herbert H. Odom, "The Estrangement of Celestial Mechanics and Religion," *Journal of the History of Ideas* 28 (1966): 533-48. For an overview of Newton's influence upon and utilization by the European intelligentsia during the Enlightenment see Peter Gay, *The Science of Freedom,* vol. 2 of *The Enlightenment: An Interpretation* (New York: Alfred A. Knopf, 1969), 128-62; and also Michael Buckley, "The Newtonian Settlement and the Origins of Atheism," in *Physics, Philosophy, and Theology: A Common Quest for Understanding,* ed. W. Stoeger, R. Russell, G. Coyne (Vatican City State: Vatican Observatory, 1988), 81-102.

28. Ashley, 213.

29. See Ashley, 23-28, 79; and Bottomley, 171-73. Some branches of modern science, including phenomenology, psychoanalysis, holistic medicine, and anthropology, however, are currently rediscovering the notion of the person as an integral unity of body and soul; see for example the discussion in Antoine Vergote, "The Body as Understood in Contemporary Thought and Biblical Categories," *Philosophy Today* 35 (1991): 93-105.

Given the rediscovery of a largely pagan view of the body in the eighteenth century, it is not surprising that this same period witnesses a profound depersonalization of women and a marked resurgence of the ancient antipathy between the sexes. Here the process begun in the late Renaissance of presenting the body, and particularly the female body, as an object of enjoyment (for a male audience) rather than the expression and representation of the person who is also a subject reaches new heights.[30] The mechanism and materialism of Enlightenment thought could find no more lofty rationale for the body than to be an object of study, manipulation, or pleasure. It is no small irony that an age which glorified human subjectivity managed to reduce human persons, and especially women, to the status of objects.[31]

Current philosophy and theology are witnessing a rebirth of interest in the body as an important category for an understanding of humanity. This can be traced to a number of factors: a reaction against the mechanism and rationalism of much Enlightenment thought (already underway in Romanticism and Idealism), the rise of phenomenology and its utilization by theologians, a growing interest in theological anthropology as a prime category for theological reflection, and an increased interest in the theological significance of human sexuality and sexual differentiation. This last point is in large part due to the impact of feminist thought and questions.

CONTEMPORARY REFLECTIONS

This section will look at two strains of current thought regarding the body person. The first of these still owes a great deal to the subjectivity and individualism that were considered in chapter 10; it is ambivalent about the body. I will restrict my remarks principally to its presence in feminist thinking. The second line of thought is searching for a way of expressing the fundamental unity of the body person, and usually speaks of the body as the symbolic expression of the person. Some of these efforts are directly concerned with the body as sexually differentiated; more time will be spent with this aspect to prepare for the discussion in the following section on the body person and relationality.

30. Cf. Bottomley, 154, 162-66.
31. Subsequent art has deepened this objectification although it shuns the expression of it in realistic terms. Hence while the body continues to figure in the various impulses within modern art — impressionism, symbolism, expressionism, surrealism, cubism — it is primarily as a means of expressing the subjectivity and *angst* of the individual artist, at times in very grotesque fashion. Cf. Bottomley, 165-67; Ashley, 79-80.

Feminist Ambivalence Toward the Body

Given that feminist thought is in part responsible for the renewed interest in the body and especially the body as sexually differentiated, it is curious that many feminists thinkers demonstrate what can only be described as a fundamental ambivalence toward the body. This can be seen in certain important features of feminist method, in attempts to "recover" the history of the female body, and in efforts to grapple with the significance of the body for their own thought. According to most feminists it is unclear where biologically based sexual traits end and culturally imposed ones begin. In order to distinguish between these two kinds of traits many feminists distinguish between *sex,* as indicating the biological realities of maleness and femaleness, and *gender,* as referring to "the social, cultural, psychological, or religious meanings that are attributed to sex."[32] This notion of gender approximates what I have been calling persona. Presupposing such a distinction, Rosemary Radford Ruether asserts rather baldly that

> maleness and femaleness exist as reproductive role specialization. There is no necessary (biological) connection between reproductive complementarity in either psychological or social role differentiation. These are the works of culture and socialization, not of 'nature.'[33]

In the theological realm this distinction is often used by feminists to argue against what they see as the exaggerated importance given to sexual characteristics and to the nuptial symbolism of Scripture, and of traditional ecclesiology and sacramental theology.[34] It is also used to critique Catholic

---

32. Anne Carr, *Transforming Grace: Christian Tradition and Women's Experience* (San Francisco: Harper and Row, 1988), 76. For a more in depth presentation of this distinction and related issues in feminist scholarship see Judith Van Herik, *Freud on Femininity and Faith* (Berkeley: University of California Press, 1982), 112-19; Ann Oakley, *Sex, Gender, and Society* (New York: Harper and Row, 1972); and John Archer and Barbara Lloyd, *Sex and Gender* (Cambridge: Cambridge University Press, 1985).

33. *Sexism and God-Talk: Toward a Feminist Theology* (Boston: Beacon, 1983), 111.

34. Arguments such as these are often employed to advocate the ordination of women. See, among many, Pauline Turner and Bernard Cooke, "Women Can Have a Natural Resemblance to Christ," in *Women Priests: A Catholic Commentary on the Vatican Declaration,* ed. Leonard and Arlene Swindler (New York: Paulist, 1977), 258-59; Sonya A. Quitslund, "In the Image of Christ," in *Women Priests,* 260-70; and Sidney Callahan, "Misunderstanding of Sexuality and Resistance to Women Priests," in *Women Priests,* 291-94.

church teaching on women and sexuality as stereotypical reinforcements of traditional gender roles designed to "keep women in their places."[35]

According to many feminist thinkers, another important aspect of feminist methodology is the recovery of women's history that has been lost or suppressed due to the oversights or biases of patriarchal culture and scholarship.[36] I have discussed the role of a method of recovery earlier when discussing its utility in historical exegesis of the biblical text, as well as the need to understand the first and second order heuristic structures that preside over its application.

Utilizing the fundamental distinction between sex and gender, feminists arrive at a very different picture of attitudes toward the body and especially the female body in Christian history. Thus Ruether finds a growing patriarchal ideology used to subordinate women beginning before but proceeding through the Christian era.[37] In the patristic period, for example, Ruether finds praise of women as virgins and a growing veneration of Mary coexisting in "schizophrenic" fashion with a hatred of women and sex.[38] This is not the opinion of scholars such as Harrison, Heine, and

---

35. See, for example, Christine E. Gudorf, "Encountering the Other: The Modern Papacy on Women," *Social Compass* 36 (1989): 295-310; and Susan A. Ross, "The Bride of Christ and the Body Politic: Body and Gender in Pre-Vatican II Marriage Theology," *The Journal of Religion* 71 (1991): 345-61. For a sweeping polemic that attempts to find this oppression throughout the history of the church, see Uta Ranke-Heinemann, *Eunuchs for the Kingdom of Heaven: Women, Sexuality and the Catholic Church,* trans. Peter Heinegg (New York: Doubleday, 1990). For an initial catalogue of the numerous errors in both thinking and citation to be found in Ranke-Heinemann's work see the reviews by Jean Porter (*America,* March 30, 1991, 350), and Ralph McInerny (*Fellowship of Catholic Scholars Newsletter* 14/3 [June, 1991]: 25-28). For a defense of the natural symbolism that grounds the Catholic position, see Mary Douglas, "The Debate on Women Priests," in *Risk and Blame: Essays in Cultural Theory* (London: Routledge, 1992), 271-94.

36. Writing from a theological perspective, Joann Wolski Conn describes a threefold process in the recovery of past women's history: first, an investigation of the ways in which both Judaism and Christianity both contributed to and helped combat misogynism within their histories; second, recovering the history of how women did act as agents in a male-dominated world; third, a revisioning of history as a whole through the eyes of women. See "A Discipleship of equals: Past, Present and Future," *Horizons* 14 (1987): 233-44.

37. See her *New Women/New Earth: Sexist Ideologies and Human Liberation* (New York: Seabury, 1975), 6-28; and *Womanguides: Readings Toward a Feminist Theology* (Boston: Beacon, 1985), 37-44.

38. See "Misogynism and Virginal Feminism in the Fathers of the Church" in *Religion and Sexism,* 150-83. Ruether believes that Christianity inherited this dualistic outlook through a syncretistic assimilation of ideas from Jewish apocalypticism, Hellenistic thought, and Oriental religion. See 150-51.

Young, quoted in the previous chapter. Furthermore, for Ruether the idea that Christianity elevated the status of women is false: "it actually lowered the position of women compared to the more enlightened legislation in the later Roman society as far as the *married* woman was concerned, and elevated woman only in her new 'unnatural' and antifemale role as 'virgin.'"[39] This approach is part of the myth of total oppression already considered.

Other scholars have accented that aspect of medieval times which provides evidence of the attempt to control women through ecclesiastical legislation. We have discussed this evidence in a broader context earlier. Still others endeavor to read the reduction of woman to an object in the art of the late Renaissance and Enlightenment periods into the whole history of Western Christian thought and art.[40] This position as well must be modified in the light of what we have just considered. Feminists are certainly justified in protesting against the depersonalization of women and their reduction to the status of objects. Their attempt to locate the impetus for this degradation within Christianity, however, is one more example of a selective reading of history, based on the myth of total oppression, and filtered through the crystallization process of the Enlightenment. Only an unsparingly unsympathetic reading, determined to avoid all evidence to the contrary, could project upon Christianity itself the fundamentally pagan antipathy toward the body and sexuality that reemerged in the thought of the late Renaissance and Enlightenment.[41] It is surprising that more feminist scholars do not see that

39. "Misogynism and Virginal Feminism," 165. Emphasis in original. It should be pointed out that such a judgement, for which little evidence is offered, seems to overlook the condition and treatment of the vast number of women in the Roman empire who were not married citizens with legal rights but prostitutes, slaves, and concubines. See Rousselle, "Personal Status and Sexual Practice," 301-33.

40. This is the argument of Margaret R. Miles, *Carnal Knowing: Female Nakedness and Religious Meaning in the Christian West* (Boston: Beacon, 1989). To the Kantian notion that there is no genuinely "objective" notion of beauty or meaning (it is rather constituted by the knowing subject), she weds the feminist idea of the social construction of gender (see 6-18). Using these tools of analysis, she argues that while the naked male body is most often a sign of spiritual discipline or religious commitment, its female counterpart is most often presented by male artists as a "cipher for sex, sin, and death" (see xii, 12, 144). She maintains that authentic female subjectivity can only be adequately presented by (feminist) women artists (see 169-85).

41. Ruether betrays something of this sort of critical attitude in her attempt to encompass patristic and medieval thought in a no-win situation: where patristic and medieval theologians express negative views of women and sexuality they are condemned as misogynists, where they praise women as examples of holiness or virtue they are guilty of a proto-Romantic glorification of women which is actually an even deeper denigration. It should also be noted that the labeling of patristic or medieval

the myopia and selectivity they criticize in history writing was born, not of a Christian view of reality, but from the crystallized view of the Enlightenment, which was also the matrix of the modern science of history.

Recent feminist studies that attempt to grapple directly with the significance of the body reflect the same ambivalent attitudes as those just mentioned. Thus Susan A. Ross in a recent study criticizes Catholic sacramental theology and current theologies of the body as "dualist." After noting the ambivalence of much feminist theology, she attempts to solve the "dichotomy" between male and female bodies by reducing human nature to history and opting for the rather vague affirmation that the body can lead to an appreciation of the interconnectedness of reality and of the "spiritual dimension of the physical."[42]

More incisive and less given to ontological vagaries is Elizabeth V. Spellman, who, even more than Ross, is critical of the legacy of "somatophobia" within feminism.[43] Spellman catalogues the way in which (especially Platonic) mind-body dualism has been used to oppress women, the feminist experience of "alienation" from one's body, and the need to formulate a distinctively feminist (as opposed to patriarchal) view of what female embodiment means.[44] She gives some concrete intimation of such a feminist notion of embodiment when she speaks of the need for physicality to be experienced as a resource for women under their own control — rather than as their destiny.[45] Everything hinges here on the relation between physicality and autonomy. Despite her opposition to Platonic thought, Spellman tends toward a Cartesian understanding of the body as an "object" to be used instrumentally rather than as a dimension of the personality which must be included in both self-knowledge and self-direction.

A similar minimizing of the significance of the sexual characteristics of the body can be found in the writings of other contemporary theologians. Among these might be included Hans Küng and Edward Schillebeeckx, who

---

praise of women as "Romantic" is rather dubious because it flows not from a glorification of woman as woman but an appreciation of woman as Christian.

42. See " 'Then Honor God in Your Body' (1 Cor. 6:20): Feminist and Sacramental Theology of the Body," *Horizons* 16 (1989): 7-27.

43. See "Woman as Body: Ancient and Contemporary Views," *Journal of Feminist Studies* 8 (1982): 109-31, esp. 119ff. Spellman points in particular to secular feminist thinkers such as Simone de Beauvoir, Betty Friedan, and Shulamith Firestone.

44. Spellman derives this notion ("alienation") from the analysis of a woman's experience in childbirth provided by Adrienne Rich, *Of Woman Born* (New York: Norton, 1976).

45. Spellman, 126-27. Cf. Rich, 39.

wish to forestall a theological objection to the ordination of women.[46] Even
more clear in this regard is the thought of George Tavard, who advocates an
androgynous conception of the person based on the separation of the biological underpinnings of sexual differences (which he believes to be minimal)
from the varying cultural interpretations of them, thus closely approximating
the feminist distinction between sex and gender.[47] Another example of this
trend can be found in the later thought of Karl Rahner.[48] Rahner will assert
"that in Scripture, strictly speaking, nothing is revealed *per se* with regard to
the two sexes, their difference and the diversity of their function required by
human nature which goes beyond biological paternity and maternity."[49] The
gratuity of such a statement should be obvious from even the rapid consideration given to biblical thought in the preceding chapter. The reflections of these
theologians show a basic agreement with feminist approaches in their attempt
to subordinate the body and its inherent sexuality to an autonomous subjectivity freed of biological and material constraints.

Positive Evaluations of the Body

There is a strong current of modern philosophical and theological thought
that has attempted to understand the biblical and patristic position outlined in
the preceding chapter and to give it expression in a way that appropriates all
that has been learned about the body in the intervening centuries. I will
consider this current in two steps. There is first a more general approach that
looks upon the body as the symbolic expression of the person: two examples

46. See Hans Küng, *Truthfulness in the Future of the Church,* trans. Edward
Quinn (New York: Sheed and Ward, 1968), 175; and Edward Schillebeeckx, *Ministry:
Leadership in the Community of Jesus Christ,* trans. John Bowden (New York:
Crossroad, 1981), 96-97.

47. See his *Woman in Christian Tradition* (Notre Dame, Ind.: University of Notre
Dame, 1973), 198-206.

48. The positions that Rahner advocated concerning the significance of sexuality
in his later writings seem to stand in marked contrast to some of his earlier views. See,
for example, his early essay "Men in the Church," in *Theology for Renewal: Bishops,
Priests, Laity,* trans. Cecily Hastings (New York: Sheed and Ward, 1964), 57-84.

49. See Rahner's letter of December 19, 1975 to a member of the Pontifical
Study Commission on Women in the Church and Society published in *Pro Mundi Vita
Bulletin* 108 (1987): 21. Cf. his remarks to the German journalist Anita Röper in their
published conversation *Ist Gott ein Mann? Ein Gesprach mit Karl Rahner* (Düsseldorf:
Patmos-Verlag, 1979): 50-54, 60. Also in this regard see Rahner's essay "The Position
of Women in the New Situation in Which the Church finds Herself," in *Theological
Investigations,* vol. 7, trans. David Bourke (New York: Herder and Herder, 1971), 75-93.

of this approach are Rahner and Wojtyla. Second, there are those who explicitly consider the symbolic role of the body as sexually differentiated. Most of these thinkers then seek to express the other-oriented dimension of the body person in terms either of complementarity or nuptiality.

One of the first and most important contemporary theologians to reflect at length on the significance of the body was Karl Rahner himself. Like the Fathers, Rahner insists upon the importance and centrality of the body in the economy of salvation. This truth can be demonstrated by reflection on some of the basic points of Christian faith: the creation of the body by God, its being the self-utterance of God to humanity in the Incarnation, its centrality in our salvation through Jesus' bodily death and the administration of the sacraments, its future resurrection, and the ongoing mediation of Jesus' human body in the beatific vision.[50] Rahner also wants to stress the unity of body and soul, and spirit and matter, within the human composite. In his later writings he eschews the term *soul* as having dualistic connotations and opts to speak of *spirit* in its place. In this sense the body may be described as the visible manifestation of spirit within space and time: "What I see the spirit of man in space and time to be is, in an ambiguous sense, precisely what I call body."[51] Related to this notion in Rahner's thought is his treatment of the symbolic character of the body.

For Rahner all beings are in a certain sense symbolic "because they 'express' themselves to attain their own nature."[52] In this light the body may be said to be the material expression of the interior element of the person — the soul or spirit.[53] If one speaks of the soul as the form of the body, it must

---

50. Cf. "The Body in the Order of Salvation," in *Theological Investigations,* vol. 17, trans. Margaret Kohl (New York: Crossroad, 1981), 71-80. In spite of such affirmations some have rightly noted that Rahner maintains a certain idealist ambivalence toward materiality in much of his thought. See Tina Allik, "Karl Rahner on Human Materiality and Knowledge," *The Thomist* 49 (1985): 367-86.

51. "The Body in the Order of Salvation," 84. Elsewhere Rahner argues that spirit and matter themselves are not totally dichotomous. See "The Unity of Spirit and Matter in the Christian Understanding of the Faith," in *Theological Investigations,* vol. 6, trans. Karl H. Kruger (Crossroad: New York, 1966), 153-77; and *Hominisation: The Evolutionary Origin of Man as a Theological Problem,* trans. W. T. O'Hara, Quaestiones Disputate, vol. 13 (New York: Herder and Herder, 1965), 46-61. Rahner's critics have been quick to point out the Hegelian and pantheistic overtones of some of these statements. See Thomas Pearl, "Dialectical Pantheism: On the Hegelian Character of Karl Rahner's Key Christological Writings," *Irish Theological Quarterly* 42, no. 1 (1975): 119-37; and Allik, "Rahner on Materiality and Human Knowing," 386.

52. "The Theology of the Symbol," in *Theological Investigations,* vol. 4, trans. Kevin Smyth (Baltimore: Helicon Press, 1966), 224.

53. See "The Theology of the Symbol," 246-47.

be understood that the whole person is present in every human expression and bodily part. Hence each part of the body is more or less symbolic of the whole, especially those which are of "irreplaceable value for the survival and perfection of the whole."[54] Thus for Rahner the body is the outward expression of the interior spiritual uniqueness of the person. It is the "symbol" of the person, in an ontological rather than figurative sense.

Given these insights it is somewhat surprising that Rahner never applied this theology and ontology of the symbol to the sexual qualities of the body, instead preferring in his later writings to minimize the theological significance of sexual difference as seen above. It would seem that if the body expresses and enfleshes the interior spiritual uniqueness of the person and the whole person is represented in each bodily part and activity, this should indicate *interior* or *spiritual* differences between male and female persons.

A similar understanding of the body as the expression or revelation of the person emerges from the phenomenological and existential reflections of the Lublin Thomists, most notably Karol Wojtyla.[55] In Wojtyla's work *The Acting Person,* written originally as a doctoral dissertation at the University of Lublin/Cracow, he sought to combine the phenomenological method of Edmund Husserl and Max Scheler with a Thomistic metaphysics of the person so as to lay the foundation for an effective contemporary moral philosophy.[56] Concerning the body, Wojtyla argues that while the

54. Ibid., 248-49.
55. Among the best known figures in this school are Mieczylaw A. Krapiec, O.P. and, of course, Wojtyla. For a good overview of the thought of this school and its relationship to other current philosophical and theological movements see Roger Duncan, "Lublin Thomism," *The Thomist* 51 (1987): 307-24. For an incisive examination of some of the foundations of this form of personalism see Prudence Allen, "Analogy and Human Community in Lublin Existential Personalism," *Toronto Journal of Theology* 5 (1989): 236-46.
56. Karol Wojtyla, *The Acting Person,* trans. Andrzej Potocki and Anna-Teresa Tymieniecka, Analecta Husserliana 10 (Dodrecht/Boston: Reidel, 1979). For a helpful exposition of the background and some of the key ideas of this work see P. Gilbert, S.J., "Personne et Acte," *Nouvelle Revue Théologique* 106 (1984): 731-37. A less sophisticated but more thorough summary is provided by Peter Hebblethwaite, "Pope John Paul II as Philosopher and Poet," *The Heythrop Journal* 21 (1980): 123-36. It is testimony to the novelty of the synthesis Wojtyla achieved that his work has set off a sharp controversy among commentators as to whether his work may be better classified as phenomenologist or Thomist. For some of the literature see Ronald Modras, "The Moral Philosophy of Pope John Paul II," *Theological Studies* 41 (1980): 684-85; Ronald Lawler, *The Christian Personalism of Pope John Paul II* (Chicago: Franciscan Herald, 1982), 45-46; Peter Hebblethwaite, "Husserl, Scheler, and Wojtyla: A Tale of Three Philosophers," *The Heythrop Journal* 27 (1986): 441-45; and Jerzy W. Galkowski, "The Place of Thomism in the Anthropology of K. Wojtyla," *Angelicum* 65 (1988): 181-84.

human body is not to be reductionistically identified with the whole of the person and indeed has its own autonomous dynamism, nevertheless bodily experience serves to ground human subjectivity and the body is the indispensable means of the person's expression, especially in conscious human action.[57] When one acts, one both *is* one's body and simultaneously *uses* this body.[58] Hence the body and bodily action and communication serves to reveal the person as a whole. As will be seen below, these basic phenomenological insights underlie the theology of the body that Wojtyla has developed in his biblical reflections as Pope John Paul II.

While Rahner failed to extend his reflections on the symbolic nature of the body to the question of sexual differences, others have done so. In an essay that wrestles with the theological status of sexuality, Walter Kasper asserts that the doctrine of creation warrants neither a materialistic nor an idealistic understanding of the person.[59] Rather, Christian realism sees the body as the "real symbol" or "excarnation" of the human spirit and is thus opposed to any gnostic denigration of the body or sexuality. Unlike Rahner, whose ideas and language his treatment recalls, Kasper applies this insight to the sexual qualities of the body.

> If the body is the real symbol of the human spirit, then bodily, sexually specific differences cannot be irrelevant to the constitution of the person. So we cannot say that there is just a minor biological difference between man and woman with admittedly great social consequences; the sexual is not a specialized zone or sector but a determination of the human being which affects the whole person, all that is human.[60]

Since the body expresses and enfleshes the person, it follows that bodily sexual differences are revelatory of deeper differences within the person. But how ought these differences to be understood and expressed?

One means of attempting to describe the theological significance of the body as sexually differentiated is through the language of "complementarity" employed by a number of theologians and in some recent church teaching.[61] The basic idea here is that the bodily differences between men

---

57. See *The Acting Person,* 203-15.
58. Ibid., 205-6.
59. "The Position of Women as a Problem of Theological Anthropology," trans. John Saward, in *The Church and Women: A Compendium,* ed. Helmut Moll (San Francisco: Ignatius, 1988), 58.
60. "The Position of Women," 58-59.
61. A partial list of contemporary theologians and philosophers who utilize some version of the language of complementarity includes Hans Urs von Balthasar, Louis

and women indicate equally different gifts and capabilities in other aspects of their personalities (e.g., mental and emotional qualities, familial or social roles, spiritual gifts and so forth). While these differences are strongly underscored, emphasis is also placed on the idea that the contributions of both are equally valuable and necessary for the proper functioning of family, society, and church. Given this approach, it is not surprising that the prime example for this paradigm is procreative sexual intercourse, in which both husband and wife have indispensable yet very distinct roles and contributions.[62]

In spite of such basic similarities, there are also clear differences between some of the theological expressions of the complementarity of the sexes. Some current theologians such as Ashley and Hauke express what they see as the basic ontological polarity between the sexes in the Aristotelian and Thomistic categories of form and matter, or act and potency.[63] Others such as Bouyer and von Balthasar, representing a more Augustinian approach to theology, utilize biblical and traditional nuptial symbolism to express this polarity. In such a view Mary and the church are seen as archetypes or "real symbols" of femininity, while Christ and the Father

---

Bouyer, Barbara Albrecht, Jutta Burggraf, Joyce Little, Benedict Ashley, Manfred Hauke, Germain Grisez, William E. May, Paul Quay, and Prudence Allen. For examples of this usage or its equivalent in Church teaching see Pius XII, address to Italian women, 21 October 1945, *Acta Apostolicae Sedis (AAS)* 37 (1945): 291-92; "Convenuti a Roma," *AAS* 53 (1961): 611; Pastoral Constitution of the Church in the Modern World, *Gaudium et Spes,* no. 52; Paul VI, "Soyez les bienvenues," 18 April 1975; *The Pope Speaks* 20, 37; "Après Plus," *The Pope Speaks* 21, 165; John Paul II, "Parati semper," 31 March 1985; *The Pope Speaks* 30, 210; Apostolic Letter, *Mulieris Dignitatem,* no. 21, *The Pope Speaks* 34, 36.

62. See, for example, Hans Urs von Balthasar, "Ephesians 5:21-33 and *Humanae Vitae:* A Meditation," in *Christian Married Love,* ed. Raymond Dennehy (San Francisco: Ignatius, 1981), 55-73; Louis Bouyer, "The Ethics of Marriage: Beyond Casuistry," in *Christian Married Love,* 33-53; Paul M. Quay, S.J., *The Christian Meaning of Human Sexuality* (San Francisco: Ignatius, 1985), esp. 24-39. For an application of the idea of sexual complementarity in procreation to the relationship between Christ and the Church see Hans Urs von Balthasar, *Truth is Symphonic: Aspects of Christian Pluralism,* trans. Graham Harrison (San Francisco: Ignatius, 1987), 92-95. The fact of women's greater role and contribution in human procreation leads some of these theologians to argue for a certain superiority of woman both in her maternal role and in her very being. Thus Bouyer will speak of the father's involvement in the family as "episodic, and in the best of case, always more or less amateur," his contribution in procreation as fragmentary and fleeting, and the "being" of the male as "fundamentally unstable" and only completed in its humanity by a woman. See *Woman in the Church,* trans. Marilyn Teichert (San Francisco: Ignatius, 1979), 34-35, 56-58, 111.

63. Cf. Ashley, 544-46; Hauke, 111-20.

serve to reveal the ultimate meaning of masculinity. These masculine and feminine exemplars also point to the marital covenant between God and his people.[64] Yet other theologians such as Joyce Little endeavor to transpose Aristotelian polarities into a more Augustinian framework in order to maintain both the equality and the difference of the sexes.[65] Finally, Prudence Allen has sought to overcome one of the obvious handicaps of complementarity language by arguing that it ought not to be understood as indicating a lack of wholeness on the part of individual men and women ("fractional sex complementarity") but rather differing forms of a common wholeness ("integral sex complementarity").[66]

In the light of such a diversity of ideas and presentations it is difficult to fully evaluate the adequacy of complementarity language as a means of describing the sexual character of the body; however, a few comments are in order. One of the chief dangers in such an approach is that it can so strongly assert the polarity and difference between the sexes that it undermines the fundamental unity and equality between them. Hence, both

---

64. In addition to the references cited above see Bouyer, *The Seat of Wisdom: An Essay on the Place of the Virgin Mary in Christian Theology*, trans. A. V. Littledale (New York: Pantheon, 1960); Hans Urs von Balthasar, *Love Alone*, trans. Alexander Dru (New York: Herder and Herder, 1969), 96-111; *A Theological Anthropology*, trans. Benziger Verlag (New York: Sheed and Ward, 1967), 306-14; "Epilogue," in *Woman in the Church*, 113-21; *The Christian State of Life*, trans. Mary Frances McCarthy (San Francisco: Ignatius, 1983), 224-49; *Theology: The New Covenant*, trans. Brian McNeil, C. R. V., ed. John Riches, vol. VII of *The Glory of the Lord: A Theological Aesthetics* (Edinburgh: T. & T. Clark, 1989), 470-84. It should be noted that this does not mean that Thomistic scholars see Mariology or Christology as anthropologically unimportant. See, for example, Frederick Jelly, O.P., "Towards a Theology of the Body through Mariology: Reflections on a Workshop," *Marian Studies* 34 (1983): 66-84; and Benedict Ashley, O.P., "Moral Theology and Mariology," *Anthropotes* 7 (1991): 137-53.

65. See her "Sexual Equality in the Church: A Theological Resolution to an Anthropological Dilemma," *The Heythrop Journal* 27 (1987): 165-78. Arguing that Aquinas's transformation of Aristotelian essentialism in his *esse*/essence distinction changes the act/potency structure of Aristotelian metaphysics to an act/act structure, Little asserts that feminine receptivity can be understood as simultaneously active. This enables her to employ a series of complementary dichotomies such as *esse*/essence, Christ/Mary, and Christ/church in order to shed light on the male/female relationship. The ultimate unity of these pairs is not organic but marital or nuptial. Little's transposition of Thomist categories and understanding of the covenant as marital owes much to the work of Donald Keefe, S.J. See his *Thomism and the Ontological Theology of Paul Tillich* (Leiden: NL, 1971); and *Covenantal Theology: The Eucharistic Order of History*, 2 vols. (Lanham, Md.: University Press of America, 1991).

66. "Integral Sex Complementarity and the Theology of Communion," *Communio* 17 (1990): 523-44; and "Fuller's *Synergetics* and Sex Complementarity," *International Philosophical Quarterly* 32 (1992): 3-16.

feminist and other theologians object that behind the rather romantic glorification of the "eternal woman" can lie a denigration of actual women.[67] The validity of such an objection can be seen in considering the difficulty involved in presenting form and matter or Christ and the church as *equal* in an ontological sense.[68] Furthermore when sexual differences are seen to be rooted in human nature itself, the fundamental unity of humanity as created and redeemed seems to be jeopardized.[69] In light of difficulties such as these it would seem that the language of complementarity needs to be supplemented in order to adequately express the revelatory character of the body as sexual.

A promising candidate for augmenting the language of complementarity is found in recently emerging discussions of the body as nuptial or sacramental. This idea has its roots in the sacramental theology and art of the Middle Ages and Renaissance.[70] The body, having been created fundamentally good, can be the bearer and expression of spiritual truth, goodness, and beauty.[71] In more scholastic language, the body can be an outward sign of an inward reality or grace. In considering the sexual character of the body, the language of the sacramentality of the body is more sharply focused when one speaks of its *nuptial* character. It has been pointed out that in a century that has witnessed enormous scientific advances in physics and medicine and at the same time has witnessed killing, atrocities, and systematic oppression on a scale never before

67. See, for example, the remarks of Karl Lehmann, "The Place of Women as a Problem in Theological Anthropology," in *The Church and Women*, 18. Cf. Ruether's "Misogynism and Virginal Feminism," 150-83.

68. Ashley attempts to blunt such an objection by pointing to the analogous character of terminology such as form and matter in describing the sexes and to their mutual interdependence (i.e., form cannot exist without matter). See *Theologies of the Body*, 545. However, this seems to overlook the obvious hierarchy of form over matter in Aristotelian/Thomist metaphysics. The same question might be asked of Little. As much as it is true that the church and its members may actively cooperate with Christ in their reception of his grace, this active cooperation cannot compare with Christ's activity nor can the church in any sense be said to be Christ's equal.

69. This criticism is made by feminist thinkers in regard to what they describe as a "dual nature" model of anthropology. See Anne Carr, *Transforming Grace*, 52, 112; and Rosemary Radford Ruether, "Can a Male Savior Save Women?" in *To Change the World: Christology and Cultural Criticism* (London: SCM, 1981), 45-56.

70. As Paul Elmen has demonstrated, this idea is not foreign to the Anglican tradition and liturgy. See "On Worshipping the Bride," *Anglican Theological Review* 68 (1986): 241-49.

71. The use of the conditional in this formulation is not accidental. It is evident that the body and its sexual qualities can also be misused, which radically diminishes its sacramental quality.

imagined, such a nuptial understanding of the body has enormous implications.[72]

One of the first contemporary theologians to utilize this formulation has been Donald Keefe. Keefe has developed an understanding of the sacramental significance of embodied sexuality that insists on the masculine-feminine bipolarity both as an expression of the goodness of creation and as a key to the sacramental worship of the church.[73] He seeks to uphold the fundamental equality of the sexes, even while vigorously maintaining their difference and irreducibility to one another.[74] Like von Balthasar, Keefe underscores the significance of the designation of marriage as a symbol of the covenantal relationship between God and his people in both the Old and the New Testaments.[75] But this marital relationship is more than a mere symbol; it also expresses the very reality of God's Trinitarian presence made historically concrete in the relationship of Christ and Mary in the Incarnation and in the ongoing Eucharistic presence of Christ in the worship of the bridal church.[76] In such a view the bipolarity of the sexes is the foundation for the church's sacramental ministry and the worship of

72. Mary Timothy Prokes in her article "The Nuptial Meaning of Body in the Light of Mary's Assumption," *Communio* 11 (1984): 157-76, develops some of these implications of John Paul II's description of the body as nuptial, especially in the light of the doctrine of the Assumption and the impact of contemporary physics. She points out that the definition of Mary's bodily assumption by Pius XII in *Munificentissimus Deus* (November 4, 1950) followed soon after the exposé of World War II's horrors — pogroms, concentration camps, death by radiation. The dogma constituted an affirmation of the goodness and eternal destiny of the human body in the face of these attempts at genocide and the degradation of millions of bodies. Furthermore, she argues that the splitting of the atom itself has far-reaching consequences for our understanding of the person because of its demonstration of the fluid interplay of matter and energy on the level of subatomic particles. This calls into question the strict separation of body and soul and of matter and spirit found in most Christian thought and suggests the need for a new and more dynamic understanding of the human person.

73. In addition to the works already cited see "Biblical Symbolism and the Morality of *in vitro* Fertilization," *Theology Digest* 22 (1974): 308-23; "A Methodological Critique of Hans Urs von Balthasar's Theological Aesthetics," *Communio* 5 (1978): 40-43; "Sacramental Sexuality and the Ordination of Women," *Communio* 5 (1978): 228-51; "Mary as Created Wisdom: The Splendor of the New Creation," *The Thomist* 47 (1983): 395-420; "The Sacrament of the Good Creation," *Faith and Reason* (1983): 128-41.

74. "Sacramental Sexuality," 249.

75. Cf. "Biblical Symbolism and Morality," 314-15. However, Keefe and von Balthasar also have sharp disagreements about the systematic nature of theology and the precise relationship of Christ to creation; see "A Methodological Critique," 23-43, and von Balthasar's reply in "Response to My Critics," *Communio* 5 (1978): 70-72.

76. "Sacramental Sexuality," 250-51. Cf. "Mary as Created Wisdom," 407-8.

its members.[77] Masculinity is fundamentally disclosed in the sacrificial love of Christ, while femininity is revealed through the mediation and activity of Mary and the church.[78] Both of these realities are approached and appropriated, not so much intellectually, but in the liturgical worship of the church.

Perhaps the best known presentation of the nuptial character of the body is that developed in the teaching of Pope John Paul II. The majority of this teaching was given by the pope in his weekly general audiences between September of 1979 and January of 1983.[79]

The pope derives much of this teaching from his phenomenological analysis of the opening chapters of the book of Genesis. His justification for this he finds in Jesus' appeal to "the beginning" in the debate about divorce (Mt 19:3-9; Mk 10:2-12). In the words of Daryl Glick, "creation is the pope's preferred prism for developing a Christian anthropology."[80]

Through this form of biblical analysis, the pope locates and develops three original experiences of humanity in the Garden of Eden: original solitude, original unity, and original nakedness. By becoming aware of himself as a person, the man became aware of himself as the "subject of

---

77. "Sacramental Sexuality," 249. As noted in the previous chapter, Keefe criticizes von Balthasar for his suppression of the meaning of masculinity in relation to God. See "A Methodological Critique," 41-42.

78. "Sacramental Sexuality," 250. Cf. "Biblical Symbolism and Morality," 318.

79. Much of this teaching can be found in the following collections published by the Daughters of St. Paul: John Paul II, *The Original Unity of Man and Woman: Catechesis on the Book of Genesis,* trans. *L'Osservatore Romano,* English ed. (Boston: Daughters of St. Paul, 1981); John Paul II, *Blessed are the Pure in Heart: Catechesis on the Sermon on the Mount,* trans. *L'Osservatore Romano,* English ed. (Boston: Daughters of St. Paul, 1983); John Paul II, *The Theology of Marriage and Celibacy: Catechesis on Marriage and Celibacy in the Light of the Resurrection of the Body,* trans. *L'Osservatore Romano,* English ed. (Boston: Daughters of St. Paul, 1986). Some of these addresses may also be found in John Paul II, *Sacred in All its Forms,* trans. *L'Osservatore Romano,* English ed., ed. James V. Schall (Boston: Daughters of St. Paul, 1984). A brief but adequate introduction to the pope's understanding of the theology of the body and its moral implications may be found in the study by Daryl Glick, "Recovering Morality: Personalism and Theology of the Body of John Paul II," *Faith and Reason* 12 (1986): 7-25. A more extensive summary and analysis can be found in Andrew N. Woznicki, S.Ch., *The Dignity of Man as a Person: Essays on the Christian Humanism of His Holiness John Paul II* (San Francisco: Society of Christ, 1987), 1-46.

80. Glick, "Recovering Morality," 11. This is also observed by Georges Kalinowski in his study "La Pensée de Jean-Paul II sur L'Homme et la Famille," *Divinitas* 26 (1982): 3-18. Kalinowski remarks that the first four chapters of Genesis "contiennent les éléments fondamentaux de l'anthropologie théologique qualifée par Jean Paul II d'adéquate" (p. 8).

a covenant" or as the "partner of the Absolute."[81] That is, he became aware of the gift character of his own existence and of his freedom to enter into a covenant relationship with God by giving himself as a gift to God in gratitude and submission. It was also through this awareness of his own uniqueness among created things that the man experienced a profound solitude and longing for another who was like himself.

Because he or she is made in the image of the Triune God, the human person is fulfilled only in community, only in unity or solidarity with others. The individual is thus called to form a "communion of persons" with others.[82] God therefore knowing that "it is not good for the man to be alone" created them male and female (Gen 2:18; cf. 1:27). The fact of the creation of two sexes indicates "that the knowledge of man passes through masculinity and femininity, which are, as it were, two 'incarnations' of the same metaphysical solitude, before God and the world — two ways, as it were, of 'being a body' and at the same time a man."[83] Hence there are two utterly distinct and original ways of being a human person. This very bisexuality bespeaks the necessity to live as mutual gift to each other. The brief words of the first man at the sight of the woman in Genesis 2:23, "This at last is bone of my bones and flesh of my flesh," are laden with meaning. According to the pope, the man exults because at last he has encountered "a body which expresses the 'person.'" He explains:

> The body, which expresses femininity, manifests the reciprocity and communion of persons. It expresses it by means of the gift as the fundamental characteristic of personal existence. This is the body: a witness to creation as a fundamental gift, and so a witness to Love as the source from which this same giving springs. Masculinity-femininity — namely sex — is the original sign of a creative donation and of an awareness on the part of man, male-female, of a gift lived so to speak in an original way.[84]

This complete self-donation of one to the other in love is what is meant by the experience of original unity.[85]

---

81. See the general audience of October 24, 1979, in *Original Unity*, 50-54.

82. Cf. the pope's general address of November 14, 1979, found in *Original Unity*, 70-77. For an exposition of the notions of participation and community in Wojtyla's prepapal writings, see Elzbieta Wolicka, "Participation in Community: Wojtyla's Social Anthropology," *Communio* 8 (1981): 108-18; and Alfred Wilder, O.P., "Community of Persons in the Thought of Karol Wojtyla," *Angelicum* 56 (1979): 211-44.

83. See the general audience of November 21, 1979, in *Original Unity*, 79.

84. General audience of January 9, 1980, in *Original Unity*, 106-12.

85. Hogan and Levoir point out that this self-donation which is love must be

Because human persons are no longer integrated within themselves (their bodies do not express their reality as persons) and are no longer able to relate to others in the way that God intended, their very humanity is threatened. It is only through the redemption won by Christ that these effects of sin can be overcome and that individuals can realize their own humanity. This is the sense of the pope's words in his first encyclical when he quoted *Gaudium et Spes:* "Christ, the new Adam, in the very revelation of the mystery of the Father and his love, fully reveals man to himself and brings to light his most high calling."[86] Explaining this text he states:

> The man who wishes to understand himself thoroughly — and not just in accordance with immediate, partial, often superficial, and even illusory standards and measures of his being — he must . . . draw near to Christ. He must, so to speak, enter into Him with all his own self, he must "appropriate" and assimilate the whole of the reality of the Incarnation and the Redemption in order to find himself.[87]

This idea has implications for the theology of the body. In this sense the pope speaks often of "the redemption of the body." By this he refers to the effect of the grace of Christ in enabling the human body to express the person once again. This grace of Christ, while it does not erase humanity's history as a fallen being or restore men and women to a state of original innocence, makes it possible for them to live as body persons as God intended "from the beginning."

---

distinguished from both sentiment and sensuality. Because the first man and woman were integrated, sentiment and sensuality played a role in their love for one another but did not dominate them. This love rather was "a mutual self-donation of their persons made through an informed choice of their wills (efficacy and freedom)." See *Covenant of Love,* 16-18. Cf. John Paul II's own thoughts on the distinction between love as "an ambition to ensure the true good of another person, and consequently as the antithesis of egoism" versus mere sentiment or sensual attraction in his prepapal work *Love and Responsibility,* trans. H. T. Willets (New York: Farrar, Strauss, and Giroux, 1981), 40-44. After the fall when this integration was lost, sentiment or sensuality often became the prime motivation in human relationships, with the result that "the other" and his or her body is seen simply as an object or a means of gratification instead of the manifestation of a person with transcendent dignity.

86. *Gaudium et Spes,* no. 22, cited in *Redemptor Hominis,* no. 8.
87. *Redemptor Hominis,* no. 10.

THE BODY PERSON AND RELATIONALITY

If the body may properly be described as the revelation of the totality of the person and thus a sacrament, and if the body as sexually differentiated may be called nuptial, insofar as masculinity and femininity pertain to the interior uniqueness and originality of the person, it follows that sexuality is intrinsic or essential to the human person. This conclusion emerges from the theology of the body of John Paul II outlined above. It also, however, finds confirmation in recent proposals made by Walter Kasper and Karl Lehmann. For Lehmann sexual differences are related "to the essence of the person," and hence men and women are persons in different, yet equal, modes.[88] Kasper likewise observes that there are no persons in the abstract: "the human person exists only in the 'dual version' of man and woman."[89]

It pertains, however, to human nature also to have not only a soul and spirit, but also a body with its inherent sexual qualities, and thus the question arises as to the exact relationship between human sexuality and nature. It has already been observed that an association which makes nature the primary locus of sexual difference seems to threaten the fundamental unity of humanity. Hence Kasper is again correct in characterizing the personal diversity of the sexes as "two equally valuable but different expressions of the one human nature."[90]

It is important to note that the body and its sexual character are integral to the creation of man and woman in the image of God (Gen 1:27) and to the marital communion of persons to which they are called (both sacramentally and in the New Covenant itself). Hence the ultimate referent of the nuptial character of the body, that to which it ultimately points, if only dimly and by analogy, is to the Trinitarian *communio*.

This point emerges with even greater clarity when human personhood is conceived in relational rather than substantialist terms. In such a view, as we have seen, human personhood is to be conceived in a manner analogous to the subsistent relations of the Trinity.[91] As Walter Kasper

88. Lehmann, "The Place of Women," 29.
89. Kasper, "The Position of Women," 58.
90. "The Position of Women," 59. A similar conclusion emerges from a consideration of the thought of Karol Wojtyla insofar as in *The Acting Person* he describes nature as a dynamic foundation for personal subjectivity and originality (and therefore sexuality). See 76-86.
91. Joseph Ratzinger in his overview of the notion of *person* points out the novelty of the category of subsistent relation that Augustine used to defend the doctrine of the Trinity against Arian critics and his failure to apply this to the human person, utilizing instead his psychological analogies, which bequeathed a legacy of growing

points out, God must be regarded as personal in a way that is infinitely higher and more profound than human personhood, which can only be regarded as a simile or image of its divine counterpart.[92] Furthermore because God is the highest and all-determining reality, it may be asserted that *"being as a whole* is personally defined."[93] This idea is at the heart of the more relational and personal metaphysics that Kasper advocates. Because God is not only personal, however, but tri-personal, it follows that *"love is the all-determining reality* and the meaning of being."[94] These considerations strengthen what was said before concerning the relationality of human personhood and its capacity to image the Triune God.[95]

I would like to try to advance the discussion concerning body personhood and man-woman relations. If persons are constituted by relationality, in first act at the moment of creation and in second act as a movement of *agapē,* and if physicality enters into the reality of person in an essential way, then an understanding of the ramifications of physicality will shed some light on the modality of relationships lived by women and men respectively. I will proceed in two steps. I will first try to establish the pervasive modification present in the human personality by the fact of male and female physicality. That is, I will maintain that the physical dimension of the person makes male and female different *modes* of humanity, to use the term already employed by Karl Lehman. In the second step, I will apply this notion to a description of modes of relatedness while acknowledging that, given the uniqueness of each human person, these modes are generalities.

Female and Male Modes of Humanity

In chapter 11, I pointed to the fact that the human personhood is constituted by a relationship of indebtedness to God and to all of creation that is

---

individualism to subsequent Western thought. See "Concerning the Notion of Person in Theology," 443-54.

92. See "Revelation and Mystery: The Christian Understanding of God," 28. Cf. *The God of Jesus Christ,* trans. Matthew J. O'Connell (New York: Crossroad, 1986), 155.

93. "Revelation and Mystery," 29-30. Emphasis in original.

94. Ibid. Emphasis in original.

95. A complete presentation of such a relational ontology and its implications has yet to be made. Besides the work of Ratzinger, Kasper, Clarke, and Zizioulas cited above, some indications of it can be found in the Christology of Jean Galot, S.J., *Who is Christ? A Theology of the Incarnation,* trans. M. Angeline Bouchard (Chicago: Franciscan Herald Press, 1981). See also the reflections of Czeslaw Bartnik, " 'The Person' in the Holy Trinity," trans. Norbert Kavara, O.F.M. Cap., *Collectanea Theologica* 53 (1983): 17-30, who attempts to utilize a personalist understanding of the Trinity to shed light on human personhood.

actualized by a return of love to God and to all persons and even beyond in some sense. In this second act, one that is an act of freedom, the person participates in the movement of self-definition by assuming his or her existence and directing it according to the uniquely human demands of love. I wish now to look more closely at personhood as an incommunicable act of existence that, in relationship, is also the vital unifying act of a complex being which is at once physical and spiritual. My purpose is to attempt an articulation of personhood that takes the physical, and therefore the masculine and feminine, dimensions of human existence into account.

Following the lead of Maurice Merleau-Ponty, Antoine Vergote suggests a return to the biblical notion of *flesh* in order to describe more accurately that central reality in a human being that mediates between physicality as such, the intricate union of organic systems, and mind, the source and receiver of cultural language.[96] A closer study of biblical anthropological terms would reveal, I think, that the term *nepeš*, as described in the preceding chapter, would more closely approximate the important insight of these thinkers.

For Vergote, as well as for Merleau-Ponty before him, it is important to establish *the flesh* as that dimension of a human being that is a primordial unity before any subject-object or ego-world opposition.

One can infer from the junction between the organic body and a symbol system that a primordial reality renders this unity possible and that the differentiated realities form themselves beginning with an originary being.[97]

There is thus an organic body, a "psychic body," and a mind. The unity of man, however, is not just a system of systems as in other organisms. "In man, the meeting of both the organic and energetic systems with a symbolic system produces a tensional unity."[98] The degree and manner of interaction between these systems and their mutual effect on each other is still a vast uncharted area for interdisciplinary investigation.

In a way what Vergote is proposing is a serious acceptance of the position that the soul is the substantial form of the body. This means that

---

96. Antoine Vergote, "The Body as Understood in Contemporary Thought and Biblical Categories," *Philosophy Today* 35 (1991): 93-105. For the thought of Merleau-Ponty see especially *Signs*, trans. Richard C. McCleary, Northwestern University Studies in Phenomenology and Existential Philosophy (Chicago: Northwestern University Press, 1964), chapter 6, "The Philosopher and His Shadow."

97. Vergote, "The Body as Understood," 103.

98. Ibid., 104.

consciousness is not something added to body but rather something that permeates body, giving it a unique multi-layered unity while being itself dependent upon the physical reality of the body in all its complex interaction of somato-vegetative dynamisms, which in turn affect and are affected by the conscious and unconscious psycho-emotive dynamisms. A human being is a mysterious unity of energies that derive from the physical universe, and from the spiritual world mediated in and through language as communication in all its forms. The meeting place where these energies reciprocally intersect is what Vergote calls the "psychic body" or "the flesh."

It should be obvious, then, that since the human being is a continuum stretching all the way from matter to spirit, it is impossible in this instance to divorce physicality from personhood. Feminists who seek to ignore this and to describe the difference between men and women as a question of "body parts" external to their essential manner of existing are returning to a severe form of Platonic anthropology. We must seek, rather, to find a way of understanding how male and female physicality, realized on successive levels of integration along the one continuum, expresses two ways of being human.

The problem in trying to grasp the human reality as male and female, and as masculine and feminine, is helped by saying that male and female correspond to Vergote's "organic body," while the designations *feminine* and *masculine* extend to include the *psychic body,* Merleau-Ponty's "the flesh." The organic body forms the base, as it were, and it is successively sublated[99] into the multiple dimensions of psychic existence. The integration of the human being is effected in the power of the vital and dynamic point of consciousness or interiority that as actually existing is the ground of the relationality that is personhood. Only in human beings does the relation of indebtedness mentioned before enshrine a dignity that integrates the being in its act of existence and orients it to the second act of self-giving love.

The foundational reality, the organic body of the person, is either male or female.[100] The psychic body is the corporal existence as it is assumed into consciousness, which in its turn is affected by the entire gamut of cultural language available to the person. It is because of the profundity of the interaction at this level that there is so much debate concerning sex

---

99. I refer the reader to the definition of *sublation* given in the previous chapter.

100. This holds true even if there are anomalies in the physical constitution. See James A. Monteleone, "The Physiological Aspects of Sex," in *Human Sexuality and Personhood* (St. Louis: Pope John Center, 1981), 71-85.

and gender. Every human being has qualities that can be identified as masculine and feminine, but it cannot be denied that these are sublated within the personality on the basis of the fundamentally male or female organic body. Thus there is a male way of being masculine and feminine, and a female way of being masculine and feminine.[101] Male and female are therefore the two modes in which humanity exists, but the actually existing man and woman have qualities that are both feminine and masculine.

As a matter of fact, however, this actually existing man or woman is first constituted in existence by an act of being that is of its nature relational in the way described. Existence does not come to an already formed being but is rather the very act by which it comes to be and is. Thus personhood is the act of the individual human being while at the same time it is refracted through the organic and psychic bodies, through physicality and culturally formed interaction in and by language and affection. It is in this sense that philosophers and theologians have spoken of the body as being the symbolic expression of the *person*. Thus, while every person exists in the mode of either male or female, their actual existence is a unique and irrepeatable realization of human physicality and therefore of historicality in and through which they define themselves in freedom by their manner of relating.

Person and Persona Once Again

There are, in my opinion, two aspects of anthropology that have been developed in an effort to penetrate more deeply into the biblical teaching on the relation between man and woman that will contribute to genuine development of doctrine. They are the notions, first, that receptivity is a category of actuation in no way inferior to activity,[102] and second, that

---

101. I am indebted here to the work of Prudence Allen mentioned previously and especially to her "Fuller's *Synergetics* and Sex Complementarity," *International Philosophical Quarterly* 32 (1992): 3-16. Allen uses the model of a tetrahedron, borrowed from Buckminster Fuller, to portray the complementary structures of male and female as individuals. She continues this line of thought, establishing more clearly the basis for male and female in what I am calling the organic body in "Sex and Gender Differentiation in Hildegard of Bingen and Edith Stein," *Communio* 20 (1993): 389-414.

102. For a development of this notion, in addition to the material already cited, see David Schindler, "Catholic Theology, Gender, and the Future of Western Civilization," *Communio* 20 (1993): 200-239; also Joyce Little, "Sexual Equality in the Church: A Theological Resolution to an Anthropological Dilemma," *The Heythrop Journal* 27 (1987): 165-78.

human personhood is the dynamic, integrating relational act of being which sublates the physical, psychic, and interior into one unique human being. Both of these achievements of modern thought owe something to the urgency with which the feminist question has been posed in this century. Assuming the first of these acquisitions and the rectification it can bring into our Western fascination with power as the active capacity to effect change, I wish to dwell for a moment, by way of conclusion, on this second aspect.

We have seen how the crystallization process initiated by the Enlightenment so distorted masculinity and thus femininity that it produced a culture of the practical intellect with its concomitant prioritizing of what can produce change through "domination" (Heidegger). In this period, the diminution of the public role of women reached its fullest development. It was followed by a rebellion against this situation that attempted to claim for women not only equality with men but also, with a few insignificant physical differences, identity. Such a position is untenable and has been followed by an attentive study of how women live, act, and judge differently than men. A worthwhile study in this regard is that by Carol Gilligan.[103] Her findings, however, tend rather to support the position I have developed here rather than her own position, which is that feminine perspectives on reality have little to do with the organic body but are the result of profound cultural influences, most notably the fact that the primary parent in early years is of the same sex as the female child. A study that has more respect for the physical basis of male and female differences is that of Walter Ong.[104]

As women move into positions in society that Enlightenment thought had considered to be exclusively male domains, we are not merely returning to a situation in which women exercised these functions in society in the past. What is being sought is a more adequate theoretical understanding of human beings that can form a basis for this new role of women. Vergote's notion of a psychic body and Allen's use of the model of a tetrahedron are both ways of distinguishing male ways of possessing masculine and feminine traits from female ways of possessing the same traits. In this line of thought we can see that there can be a female manner of being a professor, a personnel manager, a prime minister, as well as a male manner. This is a different perspective on women's and men's aptitudes, and it avoids arguments, offered on both sides

103. *In a Different Voice* (Cambridge, Mass.: Harvard University Press, 1982). Despite its many good insights, the work by Gilligan is vitiated, particularly in the second part, by its consistent pro abortion stand.

104. *Fighting For Life: Contest, Sexuality, and Consciousness* (Amherst: University of Massachussetts Press, reprint, 1989).

of the debate, as to whether women or men are intrinsically better suited to perform certain roles. If, along with Jean Bethke Elshtain, we define a role as "a socially constituted and sanctioned activity with a relatively fixed range of operation,"[105] we can then see that our question is really about the relation between person and persona.

Posed in this way, certain realities are not roles, they belong to the person and flow from the mode of relating. Such non-role or non-persona relationships are those of motherhood and fatherhood. These affect all the persons involved in the relationship and are not interchangeable. They far exceed those "socially constituted and sanctioned" functions formed by societal expectations. In these examples we have a concrete illustration of how the organic body of a person forms the basis of the mode of relating and affects that whole person on every level of their being.[106] There is not a female way of being a father, nor a male way of being a mother, though there may be very different cultural expressions of these relationships.[107]

I would propose that this irreducible fact is the basis for the New Testament language about the man (husband) being the "head" of the woman (wife). The predominant consideration is not that of the friendship between husband and wife, but of the manner of relating within a *household* with children. Headship is an active, caring relationship, an expression of the self-giving *agapē* that husbands are consistently told to have in regard to their wives. As an expression of the mutual subordination called for "in the fear of Christ" (Eph 5:21), it is not a power base, but a particular way of being a disciple, and the husband's way of being subordinate to the wife. This love, by which he lays down his life for his partner, is part of his contribution to the vocation of the Christian husband and wife by which they share in and bring about the new creation.

Allowing, then, for all the positive culturally changed realities of our day, and taking into account all the errors and injustices that have been perpetrated in the name of headship, there is still, for Christians, a particular way in which the husband has responsibility to care for his wife and their

105. *Public Man, Private Woman*, 243.
106. In this I agree with Virginia Held, *Feminist Morality: Transforming Culture, Society, and Politics* (Chicago: University of Chicago Press, 1993), 126, who challenges Simone de Beauvoir's notion that childbirth is primarily a biological event restricting women to the repetitive rather than the transcendent realm.
107. For an initial discussion of this obvious fact see the cover story in *Time* magazine, June 28, 1993, "Bringing Up Father." For some cross-cultural comparisons see Margaret Mead, *Sex and Temperament in Three Primitive Societies* (New York: Dell Publications, 1969); also *Male and Female: A Study of the Sexes in a Changing World* (New York: Dell Publications, 1968).

household. This has nothing to do with power or domination and requires the actual living out of the unique relation of two unique persons. We must bear in mind as well that, since sin is a factor in all relationships, it is only by the transforming power of the grace of Christ that the domination and connivance in domination (which can be either capitulation or rejection) described in Genesis 3:16 will be overcome. Yet, in the lives of those modern Christians who have been able to learn from the Holy Spirit how to implement this New Testament teaching, something is beginning to emerge that commends itself by its authenticity and fruit. Once again, it is only the lived reality that can provide a basis for further theological reflection, and as *Mulieris Dignitatem* implies, contribute to a genuine development of doctrine.[108]

A far more difficult question, and one that is posed particularly in the Catholic and Orthodox Churches, is this: "Is there a female manner of being a bishop or a priest?"[109] The answer to this question must be based as well on an understanding of the body person, but it does not yield as obvious an answer as the answer to the question as to whether there is a female manner of being a father. The first step in responding to the question is to show that priesthood is not a role, it is a relationship. There are many ministries, and these can be "constituted and sanctioned" by the church and assigned to men and women as roles, but the priesthood, while it includes in its notion many ministerial dimensions, is more than a ministry — it shares in the reality of office as I have described this in chapter 3.

Once again, there have been many errors and injustices committed under the title of preserving the special character of the priesthood. The result has been an excessive concentration of influence reserved to the clerical state. This should be rectified, and in many cases is being so rectified. Neither clerics nor lay people, however, can arrive at the solution desired by Christ, who is Head of the church, if we do not free ourselves of the understanding, already described at length in these pages, that the ultimate value in human affairs is power. In such a point of view, relationships are to be regulated in "free market" competition for the ability to influence others by subtle and overt forms of domination. This is the sinful situation typified in man-woman relationships by Genesis 3:16, and expressly condemned by Jesus in saying "It is not like that among you" (Mk 10:43; Mt 20:26; Lk 22:26).

---

108. *Mulieris Dignitatem,* 24.

109. I do not intend to enter into the discussion concerning the difference between bishop and priest in regard to office. Neither will I discuss whether deacon is an office, though I do not think so. These issues do not affect what I am saying about office and male and female.

Office and Relationship

The fact that the function of office pertains to the *otherness* dimension of the church by which Christ, in and through certain members of his body, maintains continuity with the original apostolic message confided at the beginning has already been discussed. Biblically, such a function is one of *remembering*, that is, keeping the reality transmitted by the preaching present to God's people in such a way that it can be appropriated and lived.[110]

It is not my intention here to enter into a discussion of the historical forms by which the authority of office has been conferred and the cultural factors that have influenced the manner in which it has been exercised. Part of this discussion can be found in the earlier chapters of the book, and the literature given there can lead the reader into an appreciation of how the reality of office, which pertains to the *genetic code* of the church, has existed and been deformed and reformed throughout the centuries. My purpose here is to understand how the general principle regarding body person as constituted by relationship can shed some light on the practice of the Orthodox and Catholic Churches in restricting the ministry of office to males.

It is certainly fair to refer to this tradition as a constant practice, though I do not deny that some evidence of women being ordained to office may be recovered from the past. The amount of energy expended in finding such examples and the paucity of the acknowledged results show that, if they are attested at all, they are extremely rare and isolated instances of a departure from a universal practice. This is all the more striking when one considers the number of examples of women exercising real causality, though in diminishing proportions, in the secular and ecclesiastical worlds during the periods preceding the Enlightenment.

In the church, charism, ministry, and office exist only in *persons*. Ministry, particularly ordained ministry, and office, since they are stable personal functions in the church, cannot be restricted simply to their role aspect; they pertain to person rather than persona. The reason for this is that such endowments are part of the personal call of Christ, who alone can confer such gifts, to the believer: they are not primarily functions within

110. I refer the reader to my remarks in this regard in chapter 3 and to the article mentioned there by Karl Kertlege, "Der Ort des Amtes in der Ekklesiologie des Paulus," in *L'Apôtre Paul. Personalité, style an conception du ministère*, ed. Albert Vanhoye, Bibliotheca Ephemeridum Theologicarum Lovaniensium 73 (Leuven: Leuven University Press, 1986), 184-202.

an institution. The authority of office, moreover, is different from the authority of charism or ministry. These latter influence the church when they are recognized as the work of the Spirit. In this sense their authority derives from popular and official recognition. Office also derives its authority from the truth of the gospel, but it requires in addition that it be conferred by Christ through an act on the part of others who have office. Its authority is not derived principally from the consent of the governed, and it is this quality which enables it to show forth the otherness of Christ.

The call to office forms part of a personal call to discipleship.[111] In fact, the primary manner in which an office holder keeps alive the mystery in the church is by being a "witness to the sufferings of Christ and a sharer in the glory that is going to be revealed." The memory of Christ is kept alive because the office holder himself is a "*typos* for the flock" (see 1 Pet 5:1-4).[112] He accomplishes this by bearing in his own body the death of Jesus in order that the life of Jesus may also be made manifest in his body, that is, in his whole historical existence (see 2 Cor 4:10). Since the call to office is to be actualized as part of the call to discipleship, the one who is called should represent Christ by his actual participation in the reality of Christ, and the more he does so, the more he actualizes the mission to which he is called. Obviously, no one is equal to this, yet it is precisely in the weakness of the disciple that the power of Christ is made manifest (2 Cor 12:8-10). In this sense, the New Testament, and most especially the Pauline, descriptions of office present a "figure" of office in a way similar to the way in which the various sublated New Testament accounts present a figure of Peter.

To be a "witness of the sufferings of Christ" means not only to behold them but also to portray them. To the degree that this is operative in a disciple called to office, the other dimensions of this same witnessing — in preaching, in leading the community in its sacramental remembrance and proclamation of the death of the Lord until he comes (1 Cor 1), in reprimanding and encouraging through all patience and teaching (2 Tim 4:2) — more fully sacramentalize the presence and authority of Christ. One grows in the fullness of office as the form (or image) of Christ is received

111. In this part of my presentation, I am indebted to two studies of Hans Urs von Balthasar, *The Office of Peter and the Structure of the Church*, trans. Andrée Emery (San Francisco: Ignatius, 1986); and "Office in the Church," trans. A. V. Littledale and Alexander Dru, in *Explorations in Theology*, Sponsa Verbi 2 (San Francisco: Ignatius, 1991), 81-142.

112. David Power notes that this theme is sounded in nearly every ordination rite known to us: *The Christian Priest: Elder and Prophet* (New York: Sheed and Ward, 1973), 7.

into one's life. That way of imitating Christ which is particular to office is found in representing him, that is, in keeping his truth and power alive in the memory of the community. This is especially done by manifesting his power in weakness and setting forth his truth despite fear and opposition.

I was among you in weakness and fear and much trembling, and my message and my preaching were not with persuasive words of wisdom, but with a demonstration of Spirit and power, so that your faith might rest not on human wisdom but on the power of God. (1 Cor 2:3-5)

Such thinking lies behind the ancient formula that a bishop/priest is an *alter Christus*.[113] Unless the governing, teaching, and sacramental dimensions of office are rooted in a discipleship that is actively receptive to the conforming action of the Holy Spirit, office itself runs the risk of becoming a minimal provision of institutional structure. Antiquity was no less aware that we run the possibility of failure in regard to office. And while it never denied the "character" imprinted by the act of Christ upon the office holder,[114] and knew that there was always some minimum presence of Christ in an unworthy bearer of office, it also proclaimed this to be a deformity and even worse. " 'For to be a true priest, a man must be clothed, not with the sacrament alone, but with righteousness,' and even though the official acts of a bad priest are valid, 'not only is he not a true priest, he is no priest at all.' "[115]

I wish now to approach the problem of office as belonging exclusively to males by applying to the ideal of office, as I have just stated it, what I said previously about person being the dynamic and relational integrating point of all the levels of physical, psychic, and interior existence.

113. For some development of this theme one may consult an earlier work of Edward Schillebeeckx, *Christ the Sacrament of the Encounter with God* (New York: Sheed and Ward, 1963), 171, where he states: "priestly acts are the personal acts of Christ himself made visible in sacramental form. . . . On the plane of ecclesial manifestation of the heavenly mystery of Christ as the Way to the Father, the priest is the 'sacramental Christ,' *alter Christus,* here present for the faithful." Although Schillebeeckx is here thinking primarily of the sacramental reality of the bishop or priest in terms of liturgical celebration, the notion of sacramentality is much broader.

114. For some examples see J.-M. Garrigues, M.-J. Guillou, and A. Riou, "Le caractère sacerdotal dans la tradition des pères grecs," *Nouvelle Revue Théologique* 93 (1971): 801-92; H. Crouzel, "La doctrine du caractère sacerdotal, est-elle en contradiction avec la tradition occidentale d'avant le XIIᵉ siècle et avec la tradition orientale?" *Bulletin de Littérature Ecclésiastique* 74 (1973): 241-62.

115. Augustine, *Against the Letters of Petilianus,* 2,30,69 (*Patrologia Latina* 43). The text is quoted in von Balthasar, *The Office of Peter,* 178.

Office is a personal, and therefore a relational, reality. It is not a role but rather involves the whole of the person who is personally called by Christ to be a disciple in this way. It is also a sacramental reality in that the person so endowed represents Christ as *other* in relation to the church. In stating that the male person is uniquely apt for office, tradition is not stating that only males have authority, but rather that only males have this particular realization of Christ's authority. This should be clear from all that was said in chapter 3 especially. The two deficiencies already mentioned, that office tended to absorb charism and ministry and that there was misogyny in the church's life, have served to obscure the precise nature of what is being maintained by the church in regard to office. This is compounded by an individualistic understanding of personhood and a post-Enlightenment concentration on authority as the power of domination: both of these characterize feminist thought as I have demonstrated.

If we put aside these obfuscating factors and try to articulate the intuition that has animated the church's practice, we may express it this way.[116] In a male person the personal act of existence is a relational mode of being that sublates and integrates the bodily and psychic levels in a unique individual realization of humanity. Maleness and femaleness, therefore, while grounded in bodily existence, are modes of being that are realized at every level in the person, which is why the body is the sacramental expression of the whole person. Since this is so, there is a personal and relational aptitude in female and male body persons to sacramentalize aspects of Christ and of the Christian mystery. Office is a personal, and therefore relational, endowment by which the disciple represents Christ as other, as over against the church. In and through such a person Christ sacramentalizes his governing, teaching, and sanctifying activity in serving his body, the church. Only male body persons are apt for this kind of sacramentalizing, because they embody that aspect of causality that is termed *active*. Females show forth the receptivity of Christ, a reality that characterizes him within the Trinity and is historicized in the Incarnation and continued in the church. It is in this way that male and female are made in the image of God who is Christ; who is at one

---

116. In speaking of "church" in this section, I am aware of the fact that not all Christians who make up the church have the same view of office as that which I am propounding. I am basing myself, however, not only on the Catholic and Orthodox traditions but on the many ecumenical statements that have been issued in recent years. These were referred to in chapter 3 and many of them are collected in *Growth in Agreement. Reports and Agreed Statements of Ecumenical Conversations on a World Level,* ed. Harding Meyer and Lukas Vischeer, Ecumenical Documents, II, Faith and Order Paper, no. 108 (New York, Geneva: Paulist, World Council of Churches, 1984).

and the same time *other* and actively active as well as immanent and actively receptive.

It must be borne in mind that there are a male and a female way of being masculine and feminine. There is, therefore, a female way of embodying *active action* just as there is a male way of embodying *passive action*. What I am maintaining here is that only the male way of being masculine and feminine is apt for the sacramentalizing of the active action of Christ in and through office. Surely the male disciple to whom the gift of office has been confided shows forth the feminine dimension of Christ who, in the Trinity, is infinite receptivity. He does this in the manner in which he receives the imprint of the death and resurrection of Christ in his life, and in the fact that whatever he gives to the church he has received from Christ. On the other hand, such a disciple sacramentalizes the masculine dimension of Christ in and through his personal existence and activity of office in which Christ preserves the church in the living truth of the gospel. Thus, it pertains to office to judge whether a teaching is in conformity with the apostolic rule of faith, and to preside at the Eucharist, which is the most intense form of the community's remembering. Neither of these functions can be done in isolation from the community and the gifts with which it is endowed, including others who have office, yet neither can the community continue long in the truth of the gospel without that prophetic gift that protects all other prophecy, namely office.

What I have said here is an attempt to locate the basic intuition that has governed the church's practice beyond the various and deficient cultural understandings of men's and women's *roles* that have been proposed heretofore. While my position derives in part from sociobiology, it is really a theological attempt, based on recent philosophical understanding of the body person, to understand the reality of man and woman in the light of faith. We are heirs to a prophetic teaching on who man and woman are in Christ. Our task is to indwell this tradition and understand it in relation to the increase of both the understanding and the ambiguity that our age has acquired.

The two aspects of modern thought on the subject of the participation of women in the life of the church that are most pertinent to the discussion are (1) the sacramental and nuptial nature of the body, and the reality of this as sublated into personal existence; and (2) the specificity of the gift of office in the whole panoply of what the Spirit has conferred upon the church as being that which sacramentalizes the otherness of Christ. Both of these offset an individualistic understanding of woman and man with one which is more correctly relational. In addition, by locating office as one of the intrinsic components of the church, the paradigm or narrative heuristic structure that sees it as part of an overall patriarchal decline is challenged.

We are merely at the threshold of an understanding that will provide a genuine development of doctrine in regard to what it means to be human in Christ. For this understanding to deepen and yield its full harvest for the church and for the world, we must all practice the ascesis of striving to understand the tradition and each other. This will involve not only a more authentic yielding to the light of faith but also a radical change in the way charism, ministry, and office actually function in the church. For nearly thirty years I have had the privilege of living as a priest in lay communities under lay leadership, including that of women. We are learning that the authority of ministry and of office never function in the abstract but only in a network of personal relationships. The goal of any endowment of the Spirit is to empower the community to respond, personally and communally, to that work of the Cross that brings about death to sin, an understanding of the divinizing intent of God's plan, and committed evangelization. The Holy Spirit enables all the gifts to contribute to this goal harmoniously to the degree that we are willing to die to ego and live by *agapē*.

Epilogue

This book began with the observation that there are two ways in which we can understand the phrase *the feminist question*. First, the expression could be understood to refer to the existence of a feminist movement in the Christian church which has become an intense and wide-ranging issue. Second, the feminist question can be understood to refer to the question posed by feminism to the Christian tradition. In this sense it is an insight into humanity that must be taken into account in the life of faith. It gives rise to a correlative process in which the tradition is confronted by the question and in turn questions it. The result is a deeper question that has taken on the dimensions of faith seeking understanding. This first step in the development of doctrine is the one to which I have attempted to contribute in this book.

A second step in the process of the development of doctrine consists in a reappropriation of the modified question which has emerged from interaction with the light of revelation. The new articulation can then act as a guide in a further theological effort to render explicit what up to now had been a tacit and partially unassimilated dimension of revelation. In this procedure, undertaken in faith, there is a deeper penetration into the reality of Christ always present to the church, leading it to the goal set by the Father.

In these few pages I wish to glance back over the interactive process between the feminist question and Christian tradition. At that point I will re-form the original question and make a proposal for how the next step toward a development of doctrine might proceed.

From all that I have said and quoted in this study it is now possible to express in a few words the question feminism is posing to the church. It could be framed this way:

> How must we form a new understanding of what a woman is, one that is articulated by women themselves in keeping with their experience and

407

raised consciousness? As a consequence, how must we seek to re-express the nature of God? Finally, how must the institutions, attitudes, and Scriptures of the church be changed in view of this new awareness and the consequent cognizance of the pervasive and long-standing androcentric and patriarchal bias of these realities, which merely reflect the bias of the surrounding culture?

I wish now to trace the manner in which I have attempted to critique that question. My critique has been based upon what I understand to be the tradition, that is, the prophetic interpretation of reality conferred upon the church through the revelatory act of God, culminating in Jesus Christ.

First then, the question: At the root of this question lies a valid and manifold insight. It is witnessed to by the documents, both civil and ecclesiastical, mentioned in the introduction and again in chapter 10 that express an increased sensitivity to human rights. Again, the question points to the fact that most people, in the church and outside it, recognize the existence of a worldwide intuition that something is stirring, that there is a need to grow in practical understanding of the role of woman in humanity. Negatively, the question calls attention to the manner in which a post-Enlightenment disparagement of the feminine aspect of humanity has also come into the church. This can be seen, among other ways, in the increase of clericalization that not only shares in the distortion of masculinity characteristic of our age, but that also contradicts the ideals set forth for the People of God at Vatican II. Christian feminism is bearing witness to these three aspects of modern life, and rightly so.

I have endeavored in this study to allow the light of revelation to question this question in order to disengage its truth from what is erroneous and even harmful. I will concentrate on what I consider to be wrong in the question as I have posed it, taking for granted that the reader will remember the many ways in which these criticisms were nuanced by a positive evaluation of other aspects of feminism.

THREE PROBLEMS WITH THE FEMINIST QUESTION

The Question as Framed Is Not Theological

As framed, the question reflects the increased insistence that feminist thought, even in a Christian milieu, must take as its starting point and norm feminist consciousness. It does this even when it enlists the concepts and terminology of theology. A theological question, on the other hand, has as its basis the teaching of revelation and expects to be modified by it. My principal purpose in the first two chapters was to show that this is indeed the nature of theology: it is always *from* revelation and not merely *about* revelation. Revelation is an act of God deriving from his initiative and leading us to a share in his divine life. As received in the believer through faith, revelation is a way of *knowing* in which the divine realities themselves, most particularly the act of love of Jesus Christ on the cross, become a living source of interior and exterior activity. The place of revelation is the church, in its life, worship, and privileged means of transmitting the message, particularly the Scriptures.

While theological reflection admits of degrees of intensity and depth (the potential whole), its essence is always a thinking with assent, a yielding to the action of God, who moves us to believe and to appropriate what he is communicating. Increase in theological knowledge takes place through the action of the Holy Spirit, who leads the believer to grasp all things in the light of God, and so to appreciate what is true in what humanity as a whole is learning. It grows, therefore, by indwelling the tradition. Theology is mature when it contributes to that inner life by which the community worships God and attains to him, and when it builds that outer life by which the community cares for its own, especially the young and those in need, and preaches the Good News in word and effective action in the world.

Christian feminist thought is faulty from a methodological point of view insofar as it is not *from* revelation. It is deficient in its content insofar as it does not have a biblical view of God, and this, I believe, is the area of its greatest weakness, a weakness it shares with most modern Western thought. Scripture witnesses to a Creator who, in a movement of infinite and loving generosity, brings all things into being, cares for them, and leads human beings into a share in his own infinite life and bliss. God is not the passive object of our thinking, he is the active and loving initiator of our existence, who freely gave us an ability to share in his intimate life, and, in an act of unfathomable mercy, repaired that ability when it was lost through sin. This witness of Scripture has been repeated in the lives and testimony of believers for nearly two millennia.

Much feminist thought reflects the rationalist Enlightenment understanding of causality as a form of dominating self-imposition (see chapter 6). It cannot accept God as Other since that would lead to the intolerable situation in which an Other, with infinite power, could impose itself upon us at will (see Ockham in chapter 2). God must remain the Transcendent, unknown and unknowable, who can only be named by human beings through the labeling of their experiences in keeping with the structure of their minds.

Other forms of feminist thought acknowledge the biblical view of

God as the generous initiator of our being and our future, but cannot allow that we know anything of God's own inner life. We cannot, they maintain, except in a metaphorical sense, name the Personal inner life of God, we cannot know what we name when we say "Father, Son, and Holy Spirit." While part of this difficulty lies in a misunderstanding of analogical speech, its roots lie deeper, since here too the language we use for God is considered to be of purely human fashioning. This seems to deny that there is any divine guidance in the articulation and understanding of the terms of Scripture, and does not take seriously the reality of the Son of God among us and his own mode of speaking about and relating to the Father (see chapter 9).

A feminist reading of the Scriptures usually judges them from the standpoint of a foundationalist hermeneutics that treats the text as an inert object to be rendered intelligible by the activity of the thinking subject. This is an extension of the feminist foundationalism that takes women's experience or consciousness as the matrix of thought (chapter 6) and applies it to the act of interpretation. Such a position misconstrues our experience and understanding of any text, and the traditional experience and understanding of the Sacred Text, by failing to see a text as an instance of *communication* (chapter 7). Consonant with this position is the standpoint that considers all language about God to be metaphorical in the sense that theological metaphor is the projection onto the Transcendent of an experience articulated according to the structure of the thinking subject. The fittingness of the metaphor is evaluated on the basis of its ability to contribute to human well-being, judged according to standards predetermined by feminist thought.

Thinking about God and language for God are thus considered to be purely human enterprises undertaken according to norms established a priori by a more general philosophy of being and knowledge. In opposition to this form of a priori theorizing is the unchanged witness of the biblical tradition that God is known primarily in and through his action in the world. He is known in his effects, and these extend to that action by which he touches the soul and produces a created likeness to his Word in which his Wisdom is known. Reflection on the ways by which God is known is, in the biblical tradition, genuine *reflection*. That is, it is an attempt to articulate how the knowledge already possessed can be described in terms that are in accord with the dynamics of human knowing. Human knowing can legitimately express itself in isotopic language, and, more frequently in theology, in image, metaphor, or analogy (chapter 8).

Although feminist thought most often lacks the essence of theology, its critique of much other thought that passes for theology is frequently quite apposite. The rationalism that treated language for God as practically univocal is rightly criticized by feminism for not respecting the poverty of our concepts in attempting to say something about the infinite majesty of God. In addition, when feminism joins its voice to that of liberation theology in order to point to our need to repent for not taking the gospel seriously in regard to those who have no voice, it is expressing the will of God. No genuinely Christian thought about God and the mystery of redemption is complete until it changes hearts and leads to effective action to make the church's life and witness more consistent with the gospel, which is directed to the poor. Feminist theory also makes a contribution in calling everyone in the church to abandon those attitudes and practices in regard to women that are false to the gospel.

The Question Presupposes an Anthropology at Odds with Revelation

Feminism reflects the dilemma of most modern thought in that it has inherited an Enlightenment understanding of the dignity of the human person that ignores the relational foundation of personality. Biblical thought has always based the dignity of the person on the fact that a human being can have a relationship with God. In fact the notion itself of person was forged in reflection upon the mystery of Jesus Christ and his relation to the Father. For the most part feminist thought is individualistic. It begins with a consideration of the person as an isolated entity endowed with rights, the exercise of which is limited by the competition of others, by the state, and by the larger forces of society, such as economics. Based on this notion feminism appeals to a "raised consciousness" that enables women to see the extent of the oppression they suffer. The problem here is that not every raised consciousness is a true consciousness. To call a second state of consciousness an improvement over a first state, there must be some norms by which this is judged. On the level of the exercise of rights these norms are largely agreed upon. When, however, one seeks to ground these rights in the very nature of the person, difficulties arise. There is no universally accepted vision of human existence and its future that can act as the framework for the discussion. Unless this is achieved by understanding how the human person is constituted by relation, particularly relation to God, one of the most precious insights of our age will be submerged in a neo-pagan exercise of power by the state (see introduction). When speaking of relation it is important to distinguish this from *relationship*, which is the result of freely appropriating relatedness. When relatedness is not appropriated, we have a fierce competition for power as the only means of achieving full expansion of one's potential. Then the norm is not God's will for us; it arises rather from a referred striving for self-actualization.

This is not biblical but rather post-Enlightenment anthropology. It understands autonomy as an absolute rather than as the foundation for appropriating relation and raising it to the level of conscious relationship in a deep surrender of love in freedom. This view of the person cannot grasp, ultimately, the eternal dignity and destiny of the human person that lasts through death and is preserved in a continued existence in Christ (chapter 10).

Although feminism is one of the factors that have stimulated an effort to penetrate more deeply into an understanding of physicality, it tends to misunderstand the role of the body, both as part of the mode by which a person is able to relate and as the essential constituent of historical activity (chapters 11 and 12). The true dimensions of physical existence, and thus the human body, are a Christian discovery that has deepened the original revelation within Israel. By ignoring the role of Christ's body in bringing about redemption, feminism tends to view salvation mostly in terms of knowledge and enhanced power rather than as a liberation from the cosmic, societal, and spiritual forces that have perverted history. Sin, in a feminist viewpoint, risks being defined as compliant ignorance in one's state of oppression rather than a human act, at once spiritual and physical, which is unfaithful to the covenant established by God with us. The liberating power of that covenant is found not primarily in enlightenment (raised consciousness) but rather in the completely human, bodily act of the Son of God, who died and rose and is fixed in that act of love forever: "The flesh is the hinge of salvation."

Much modern thought, including feminism, conceives of the body person in two contradictory ways. First, the body, particularly in its sexuality, is individualized and becomes part of an adversative definition of the person. This results in a false self-consciousness that cannot understand an undifferentiated attribution of male and female characteristics to someone without affecting their basic sex and gender (Jesus as Mother) or allow that a term can refer to a male precisely as male in one context and be gender neutral in another (masculine pronouns for God).

In a contrary manner, when arguing for an homogenization of human beings in regard to persona, modern thought tries to ignore the fact that physicality, and thus sexuality, enters into the constitution of the person so that the body is the symbol, the sacrament, of the person. Feminism echoes this contradiction when raising the question of woman's place in the church. What should be discussed in terms of living out male and female characteristics as integral body persons is treated rather as a difference of *body parts*. This neglects the biblical understanding of man and woman as both the image of God, needing each other to sacramentalize his reality in the universe, and their consequent differing capacities to show forth different aspects of Christ (chapter 12). Thus, it succumbs to the Enlightenment notion that receptivity is inferiority (chapters 4 and 11). This has repercussions in the failure to distinguish between autonomy and independence, and between knowing as active and knowing as determinative (chapter 6).

Once again, it is important to bear in mind that the anthropological questions raised by feminism are valuable in that they move the whole Christian community to return to a deeper consideration of what the tradition contains regarding this issue and to turn from attitudes and practices that are often little more than reflections of the culture surrounding us.

The Question Shows Little Understanding of the Nature of the Church

One of the most enduring characteristics of the New Testament witness, taken up by each succeeding age, is a love for the church as the continuing historical, human presence of God's plan, the body of Christ. Feminist thought has borrowed from the modern study of religions its antipathy to anything that claims to be unique, that claims to exceed the categories established for it by a philosophy of human existence. Armed with this conviction feminism attacks the church as the very embodiment of all that is wrong with our modern situation, insisting that the church conform itself to norms derived from an outlook that explicitly rejected the church in the first place.

The church is always in need of reform. One has only to read the outrage of Paul at the sin that disfigures the church, the admonitions in the Gospel redactions concerning laxity in the community, the threats in the letters to the churches in the book of Revelation, to understand that the prophetic word of God is always addressed to a church that is *simul justus et peccator*. These words come from a love that originates in God, a love which cannot abide the mediocrity and darkness, the evil and self-seeking, that hold men and women from the fullness of what God has planned for them and Christ has won for them. It is this love that authenticates the prophetic words, just as it is hope in the efficacious desire of God that motivates the call to repentance. When this is lacking, there is only a movement to dismantle and to refashion according to the blurred and often angry vision of human beings who are frequently penetrating and accurate in their criticism, but harsh and destructive in their project.

The church is the work of God; it is not a human work to be classified exclusively according to criteria borrowed from the human sciences, even though, of course, as a fully human reality, it presents itself to the world as amenable to such study. A historical study of the church based on a model of ineluctable decline due to compromise with foreign elements does not take seriously the promise of Jesus to be always with his own. A better model is that of a zygote or a musical score that plays out according to its own intrinsic code but that is modified, for better or worse, by the elements it takes up in its realization (chapter 3). An unbiased reading of the history of Europe can reveal to us both the leaven of the gospel as it affected the life of women and a general recalcitrance to embrace fully the implications of the gospel. It is wrong, however, to read history as a story of the unmitigated oppression of women. Such a position can only be established by a selectivity in regard to the data and a reading of the past as though the ambiguity held in solution during all those centuries had already achieved the crystallization effected by the Enlightenment (chapter 4).

The Scriptures belong to the church, and they are submitted to by the church. The writings proposed by the church as capable of mediating the rule of faith cannot be treated merely as historical data that, as reconstructed according to the norms of modern history writing, are no more valuable than any other witness and may even be more suspect. They are, because they form part of the church's preaching of the mystery of Christ, a privileged instrument of the Holy Spirit in making Christ present to every generation. While they must be interpreted, they must be respected and cannot be trimmed to serve a present preoccupation (chapter 7).

As the body of Christ, the church is made of diversified and complementary elements, but the final dignity of those in whom these elements are invested lies not in what is done but in the depth and maturity of love with which it is accomplished (1 Cor 13). Each gift of the Spirit and each ministry conferred by the Spirit bears within it its own authority, and these gifts and ministries are given to both men and women. There is another dimension of Christ's authority in the church, however, one that has to do with the faithful transmission of the apostolic heritage which represents the otherness of Christ in regard to the church. Here, feminist thinking is bifurcated. On the one hand, there is a rejection of this form of authority: both the canon of Scripture and the office of leader elicit only responses that first filter out whatever is opposed to feminist consciousness. On the other hand, feminists insist that office is not an exclusively male position in the church, and that women should be ordained to this position of authority and power. In both instances, the notion of authority bears with it the Enlightenment equation that authority equals causality equals domination. This is directly opposed to the notion of authority taught by Jesus (Mk 10:43) (chapter 3).

Many feminists advocate the forming of an *ekklēsia* of women. As a sociological term, borrowed from the meeting of the Greek city state, such a proposal might have some sense. As a theological term, however, the expression is a contradiction. There is only one *ekklēsia* — the church willed by the Father and assembled by the Spirit in Christ is an *ekklēsia* neither of men nor of women, but of all people who are called to be one "for the praise of the glory of his grace" (Eph 1:6). Such an *ekklēsia* is formed by those who share in God's life and who work for the restoration of all human beings. An *ekklēsia* of women seeks to unite, not on the foundation of God's work in Christ, but on the basis of a concern to realize a social and political agenda.

A PROPOSAL

In the review just completed, I tried to show how a biblical understanding of revelation both as a source of knowledge and as a body of knowledge listens to the question being posed by feminist thought in the church and advances that question by freeing it from what is incompatible with revealed truth. This was accomplished by confronting it with the teaching of tradition and by looking at the philosophical presuppositions governing the way the question is posed. At this point, the question might be rephrased as follows:

> What is God's plan for humanity? What is he teaching us by the light he sheds on what he has revealed to the church as well as on the truth stirring within humanity today? How is our increased awareness of the dignity and rights of all human beings to be confirmed and integrated within our lives as the Christian community? More specifically, how can we live in a way that corresponds more perfectly to God's will for the place of women in the church? Finally, how can we articulate in words and deeds this deeper understanding in a way that will help all humanity advance toward the goal set for it by the Trinity?

The program for an answer is to be found in this line in the letter to the Ephesians:

> Having made known to us the mystery of his will,
> in keeping with his good pleasure,
> which he set forth in him [Christ]

for the administering of the fullness of the times
to recapitulate everything in Christ,
things in heaven and on earth.

(Eph 1:9-10)

The first thing we may notice about this text is the fact that it is
describing an act of revelation. God the Father has made known to us the
mystery of his will. This is in keeping with the author's prayer in which
he asks that "the God of Our Lord Jesus Christ, the Father of glory, give
to you the Spirit of wisdom and revelation in knowledge of him," so that
his audience (including ourselves) may be able to know "what is the hope
of his calling, what are the riches of the glory of his inheritance among the
saints, and what is the surpassing greatness of his power for us, the believers, in keeping with the operation of the might of his strength which he
effected in Christ, raising him from the dead . . ." (Eph 1:17-20).

Knowledge of God's plan, an understanding of what he has done and
where he is leading history, is initiated by an act of God by which he
manifests and communicates himself and confers this knowledge. The
object of that knowledge is described as "the mystery of his will," referring
to God's hidden purposes as they are made known to his people. We have
an expression of God's ultimate purpose earlier in the hymn: "He chose
us in him [Christ] before the foundation of the world, to be holy and
blameless in his sight in love." This plan is worked out because we
are graced in the Beloved "In whom we have redemption in his blood, the
remission of transgressions, in keeping with the riches of his grace
which he has made abound in our regard in all wisdom and understanding"
(Eph 1:4-8).

In the verses we are considering the author reiterates this theme by
speaking of the spontaneous freedom of the Father (his "good pleasure"),
by which he has proposed this plan in Christ through whom he has been
governing all the succession of ages to arrive at the fullness of time. Jesus
Christ was predestined from all eternity to be the Lord and Head of the
whole universe, and this plan included that work of restoration by which
humanity was not only to be returned to the state it had lost, but was to be
saved and healed through the outpoured lifeblood of Christ. The process
is described in a verb, *anakephalaiōsasthai,* which might be rendered in
English as "bring to a head" in the sense of summing up a line of thought
and action as well as providing a dynamic gathering point which brings
what is gathered forward.

As applied to God's activity in Christ, there are four aspects to be
noticed within the context of the letter to the Ephesians. First, what is

accomplished is *in Christ,* that is, it cannot be a mere summing up or regathering of all things since their point of unity is the absolutely new historical entry of Christ into the universe. What is accomplished is therefore new; what is gathered is brought to a point that transcends its former reality even while this is respected: restoration is not a return but an advance, *"ana-storation."* Second, the verb is used in a past (aorist) tense. This means that the eschatological goal of all creation already exists and is drawing all to himself (Jn 12:32). Third, this process of reunification is typified by the joining together of Jew and Gentile, which takes place precisely "in one Body, to God, through the cross" (Eph 2:16). Finally, the headship of Christ over the universe is not in itself the goal: " [God] established him Head over all *for the Church* which is his Body" (Eph 1:22). It is through the church that the manifold wisdom of God is made known to the principalities and powers in the heavenly realm (Eph 3:10). According to what is probably the better translation of Ephesians 1:23, Christ is "the Fullness of that which is being filled in every way [the Church]," and this filling is only possible because of the historical activity of Christ: "the one who descended is also the one who went up, above all the heavens, that he might fill all things" (Eph 4:10).

The theologian who most profoundly understood this teaching of the Letter to the Ephesians was undoubtedly Irenaeus of Lyons. Before applying the notion of *anakephalaiōsis* to the question posed at the beginning of this section, it will be helpful to consult some of Irenaeus's texts.

With regard to the first point, that what is brought about in Christ is new and brings former things to a "fresh start," a higher level of existence and meaning:

> When He became incarnate and was made man, He recapitulated in Himself the long history of mankind and, in that summing up, procured for us the salvation we lost in Adam. (110)[1]

> How could we be partakers of adoption as God's sons without receiving from Him, through the Son, the gift of communion with him? . . . This is why He passed through all the ages of human life, restoring to all men communion with God. (113)

The second point, namely that the recapitulation has been initiated already by God in Christ:

---

1. All citations are taken from *The Scandal of the Incarnation. Selected and Introduced by Hans Urs von Balthasar,* ed. Hans Urs von Balthasar, trans. John Saward, (San Francisco: Ignatius, 1990), and the numbers in parentheses refer to that work.

For just as the bread which comes from the earth, having received the invocation of God, is no longer ordinary bread, but the Eucharist, consisting of two realities, earthly and heavenly, so our bodies, having received the Eucharist, are no longer corruptible, because they have the hope of the resurrection. (158)

The Church is the sign and the place of the unity God wishes to bring about in the universe:

He fulfilled all things by his coming, and still, in the Church, to the final consummation, He fulfills the covenant foretold by the Law. (142)

There is one God the Father . . . and one Jesus Christ our Lord, who came by means of this whole dispensation, recapitulating all things in Himself. Now this "all" includes man, the handiwork of God, and so He recapitulated man in Himself, the invisible becoming visible, the incomprehensible becoming comprehensible, the impassible becoming passible, the Word becoming man. He recapitulates all things in himself, so that, as the Word of God rules over the supercelestial, spiritual, and invisible, so He has primacy over the visible and corporeal. Appropriating the primacy and appointing Himself Head of the Church, he draws all things to himself at the proper time. (119)

This recapitulation took place in the historical activity of Christ and is being worked out within the midst of the humanity that brought about and suffers the disaster:

The first formed man, Adam, received his substance from the untilled and still virgin earth . . . and was fashioned by the Hand of God, that is the Word of God. . . . Similarly, the Word, recapitulating Adam in Himself, very fittingly received from Mary, who was still a virgin, the birth that made recapitulation possible. . . . Why did God not take dust again? Why did he make the formation come from Mary? Precisely so that there was not some different formation, that it was not some different handiwork which was saved, that it was the very same one which was recapitulated, the likeness being preserved. (114)

These things took place in actual reality, not in mere imagination. If He had appeared as man without actually being man, He would not have remained what in truth He was, the spiritual reality that is God, for the spiritual is invisible. Nor would the truth have been in Him, because he would not have been what he seemed to be. (107)

Nor would the Lord have recapitulated all this in Himself if He had not been made flesh and blood in conformity to the original handiwork. In the end he saved in Himself what in the beginning had perished in Adam. (118)

Recapitulation, as taught in Ephesians and developed by Irenaeus, is an important element in discovering how to respond to the question asked by feminism. Thus, when we seek to understand God's plan for humanity, we must begin with its goal: the union of all human beings in Christ, sharing God's life forever. According to this principle, the church, which is the place in and for which the primacy of Christ is exercised, realizes itself amid the limitations of this life to the degree that the life of heaven is actualized within it. Each person must appropriate the communal reality to which we are called. In this way, we will begin to live out the answer to this question, and a development of doctrine can be brought about by reflecting on the work of God as it is taking place in our midst.

Part of that appropriation is the search to understand who men and women are in Christ. How has this dimension of our existence received a fresh start which heals and transposes the former situation? Having understood the true dimensions of what is being asked of tradition we must seek the light of faith in two directions at once: toward the deeper dimensions of revealed reality, and toward the aspirations of humanity for a life that is worthy of human dignity. That is, we must look to what the New Testament teaches us about our life in Christ, and we must listen to what we have discerned as the truth being spoken by women and men all over the world. We must expect to advance our understanding of what has been confided to the church and thus enable the heritage to develop. Here the problem is complicated by the fact that the church, which is meant to reflect divine truth for all to see, is itself a fragmented mirror which distorts the image portrayed upon it. Nevertheless, this image can be made out, even if only dimly, if we seek to come together and to obey the movement of the Holy Spirit.

We should try now to apply the four aspects of *anakephalaiōsis* to the feminist question. First, men and women in Christ recapitulate Adam and Eve: they fulfill and bring to a new level the original relationship. The relationship between Adam and Eve as it is described in Genesis 1 and 2 is acknowledged in Genesis 3 to have been disfigured. But now, because of the redemption brought about by Christ, the relationship is not only restored but raised to higher level. The cross of Christ has given us the power to take from our personalities the sin, the domination, and the connivance in domination described in Genesis 3:16, which is the type of every corrupted relationship between us: "your longing shall be for your husband, and he will lord it over you." When the light of the cross is shed on this description it unmasks our own participation in the system of the world that can only conceive of relationships in terms of power. All of us dominate, and, through the drive for self-preservation and self-promotion, we also connive in others' domination. The new work of Christ not only repairs this structure of sin but becomes an icon of the fulfilled plan of the Father.

To manifest this new work and to image the eternal life to which we are being moved requires that we consent to the action of the Holy Spirit, who wishes to put sin to death within us and make us able to call others into the same mystery of life. One of the primary places where the *fresh start* conferred upon humanity in Christ is meant to be actualized is in marriage. It is there that Christ can show forth the splendor of his work amid the very real experiences of travail. A home where this new relationship between man and woman actually exists and is shared with children is an indisputable proof of the seriousness and truth of God's redeeming power in Christ. Such a place not only educates in the meaning of *agapē,* it gives the world hope that there can be shared life where repentance and forgiveness are the realistic response to sin.

Many feminists can see something of the system of domination that reaches into the very sinews of human relating. They are correct in describing it in terms of man and woman as Genesis 3:16 has already done. They are wrong, however, in not understanding the profundity of the typological description given there and in imagining that some human effort can repair the ravages of sin. What is described in Genesis 3:16 applies to *all* human relating, and this situation can only be repaired by the cross of Christ, the act of love in which Jesus Christ died and in which, in his transformed humanity, he lives. When Paul tells us that those who belong to Christ Jesus have, in virtue of that act of surrender and allegiance which is faith, crucified the flesh with its passions and desires (Gal 5:24), he is describing a *change* brought about by an action of the Holy Spirit. The flesh is precisely that drive toward self-preservation, self-glorification, and self-gratification that corrupts every relationship. The hope of the Gospel bases itself on the fact that this drive can be rendered powerless and we can recover God's original intention in forming one human family.

But there is more. The recapitulating work of Christ is not only restorative; it is fulfilling, it brings wine to our desire for water. Our love for each other, once again typified by the love between man and woman, particularly husband and wife, shares in the love God has for us and for his whole people. This insight lies at the root of the claim of Ephesians

5:30-32 that the relation of husband and wife in Christ shows forth the love Christ has for his church, thus making the description of God's plan for nature in Genesis 2:24 a prophecy of grace. This same insight governs the constant tradition that, out of love, the Word of God espoused the whole of humanity in Jesus Christ. An adequate response to the question feminism brings to the church involves a contemplative pondering of these truths, an honest embracing of the power of the cross, and a *metanoia* in the way we think of each other.

The second aspect of recapitulation is that it has begun in Christ and is continuing because of his action in and through the church. It is particularly in this regard that our faith is challenged to be active. Once again, the critique of exegetes and theologians for being fascinated by history but short on praxis proves justified. The intention of the Father is to have Christ the Head of all creation for the sake of the church. We cannot, however, conceive of the risen Christ as some impassive magnet drawing all things into some cosmic unity. Recapitulation is a *personal* work in the sense that Christ, in his risen reality, personally chooses to call people to himself, change and purify them, and make them able to announce and effect the unity he desires.

From the side of the believer as well, recapitulation is personal; it is based on the fact that the deeper the truth, the deeper the level of personal commitment required in order to lay hold of it. The physical sciences can present "compelling evidence," but moral truth, and even more deeply, revealed truth, is neither coercive nor subject to coercion — it requires personal risk. The truth that God's injunction to Adam has been and is yet to be recapitulated in Christ and the Church is acquired only at the price of an act of trust in God's plan: "Now, however, we do not yet see all things made subject to him, but we do see him who for a little while was made less than the angels: Jesus, because of the suffering of death crowned with glory and honor in order that, by the grace of God, he might taste death for all" (Heb 2:8-9).

The third and fourth notes of recapitulation imply that even now the church is meant to be the "light of the nations" because Christ, having ascended on high, is filling his body with the energy it needs to build itself up in love. The world has the right to see in this community of believers the solution to the dilemmas posed by our new awareness of human dignity and our incapacity to understand its basis or live out its demands. When feminists point to objective injustice in the church they must be listened to. The challenge, however, lies in forming a vision of the human person as relational, bodily, and eternal. To ignore any one of these notes, or even to try to restore them fully without the work of the Spirit is simply not possible, and it is even less possible to bring them to their new level of existence in Christ.

The attractive humanity of some of the saints consists precisely in the fact that they embody in themselves and clearly illustrate for the rest of us those inchoate desires and images we have of what it means to be human. We can admire them and can sense that their restored humanity is due to something greater than they are, a presence of Christ that, like a perfume, can be discerned but never analyzed. The church must be that for the world. In the humanity being caught up in God's recapitulating action there is "not male and female" (Gal 3:28) and yet there is man and woman. To give both sides of this truth actual human existence, one that will show forth the true goal of humanity imperfectly but in promise, is one of the great tasks of the church today. In order to achieve this we must all of us, by the mercies of God, offer our bodies (our histories, our physicality, our mode of relating) to God as a living sacrifice and be transformed by the renewal of our minds to discern what is the will of God, what is good and pleasing and perfect (see Rom 12:1-2). We cannot achieve, for ourselves or for the world, the development in theoretical and practical understanding which will liberate us and them unless we are willing to seek the face of God, expect him to make an active answer, and refuse to divide the Body of Christ any further.

The process of historicizing the recapitulating action of Christ begins with a turning toward him and a turning away from sin. Recapitulation is not a mental acquisition but a work of God that changes those who desire it. Unless the reality of what he has done for us is a living experience, we have no common basis for desiring and seeking his will and we have little personal foundation for expecting that he will act to instruct and change us. Perhaps those on either side of the issue for whom this issue of feminism is a point of division should meet together and pray for each other, not as a strategy to gain a more acceptable position, but as a means of honestly dying to egotism, self-righteous anger, infidelity to the truth, and fear. The answers to this question are more likely to be found by those who know personally the unity that the Holy Spirit earnestly desires to bring about in the church.

Bibliography

Abbott, Walter M., ed. *The Documents of Vatican II*. Piscataway, N.J.: New Century Publishers, 1966.

Achtemeier, Paul. *"Omne verbum sonat:* The New Testament and the Oral Environment of Late Western Antiquity." *Journal of Biblical Literature* 109 (1990): 3-27.

Alexandre, Monique. "Early Christian Women." In *A History of Women in the West*, ed. Pauline Schmitt Pantel, vol. 1, *From Ancient Goddesses to Christian Saints*, 409-43. Cambridge: The Belknapp Press of Harvard University Press, 1992.

Allen, Christine (Prudence). "Christ Our Mother in Julian of Norwich." *Sciences Religieuses/Studies in Religion* 10 (1981): 421-28.

Allen, Don Cameron. *Doubt's Boundless Sea: Skepticism and Faith in the Renaissance*. Baltimore: John Hopkins, 1964.

Allen, Prudence. *The Concept of Woman: The Aristotelian Revolution 750 BC–AD 1250*. Montréal: Eden Press, 1985.

———. "Descartes, The Concept of Woman and the French Revolution." In *Revolution, Violence, and Equality,* ed. Yeager Hudson and Creighton Peden, 61-78. New York: Edwin Mellen Press, 1990.

———. "Fuller's Synergetics and Sex Complementarity." *International Philosophical Quarterly* 32 (1992): 3-16.

———. "Hildegard of Bingen's Philosophy of Sex Identity." *Thought* 64 (1989): 231-41.

———. "Integral Sex Complementarity and the Theology of Communion." *Communio* 17 (1990): 523-44.

———. "Sex and Gender Differentiation in Hildegard of Bingen and Edith Stein." *Communio* 20 (1993): 389-414.

Allik, Tina. "Karl Rahner on Human Materiality and Knowledge." *The Thomist* 49 (1985): 367-86.

Andresen, Carl. "Zur Entstehung und Geschichte des trinitarischen Personbegriffs." *Zeitschrift für die neutestamentliche Wissenschaft* 52 (1961): 1-39.

423

Ankersmit, F. R. *Narrative Logic: A Semantic Analysis of the Historian's Language,* vol. 7. Marinus Nijhoff Philosophy Library, The Hague, Boston, London: Nijhoff, 1983.

Aquinas, St. Thomas. "In Boet. De Trin." In *Faith, Reason and Theology: Questions I-IV of his Commentary on the De Trinitate of Boethius.* Toronto: Pontifical Institute of Medieval Studies, 1987.

————. *Super Epistulas S. Pauli Lectura.* Rome: Marietti, 1953.

————. *Super Evangelium S. Joannis Lectura.* Rome: Marietti, 1952.

Aristotle. *The Basic Works of Aristotle.* Trans. W. Rhys Roberts. Ed. Richard McKeon. New York: Random House, 1941.

Ashley, Benedict. "Gender and the Priesthood of Christ." *The Thomist* 57 (1993): 343-79.

————. "Moral Theology and Mariology." *Anthropotes* 7 (1991): 137-53.

————. *Theologies of the Body: Humanist and Christian.* Braintree, Mass.: Pope John Center, 1985.

Auerbach, Eric. "Figura." In *Scenes from the Drama of European Literature,* 11-76. Gloucester, Mass.: Peter Smith, 1973.

————. *Mimesis: The Representation of Reality in Western Literature.* Trans. William Trask. New York: Doubleday Anchor Books, 1953.

Babock, William S. Review of *In Memory of Her. Second Century* 4 (1984): 177-84.

Baeur, Jerald C., ed. *The Westminster Dictionary of Church History.* Philadelphia: Westminster Press, 1971.

Banks, Olive. *Faces of Feminism: A Study of Feminism as a Social Movement.* Oxford: Basil Blackwell, 1981.

Barbour, Ian G. *Myths, Models and Paradigms: A Comparative Study in Science and Religion.* New York: Harper and Row, 1974.

Barth, Markus. "Ephesians 4–6." In *Anchor Bible 34A,* 641-47. New York: Doubleday, 1974.

Bartnik, Czeslaw. "The 'Person' in the Holy Trinity." *Collectanea Theologica* 53 (1983): 17-30.

Baumert, Norbert. "Charisma und Amt bei Paulus." In *L'Apôtre Paul. Personalité, style et conception du ministère,* ed. Albert Vanhoye, 203-28. Leuven: Leuven University Press, 1986.

————. *Täglich Sterben und Auferstehen. Der Literalsinn von 2 Kor 4,12–5,10.* Studien zum alten und neuen Testament, vol. 34. Munich: Kosel Verlag, 1973.

Beckworth, R. *The Old Testament Canon of the New Testament.* Grand Rapids: Eerdmans, 1985.

Behr, John. "Shifting Sands: Foucault, Brown and the Framework of Christian Asceticism." *Heythrop Journal* 34 (1993): 1-21.

Bell, Susan Groag. "Medieval Women Book Owners: Arbiters of Lay Piety and Ambassadors of Culture." In *Women and Power in the Middle Ages,* ed. Mary Erler and Maryanne Kowaleski, 149-87. Athens, Ga.: University of Georgia Press, 1988.

Bellah, Robert N. "Leadership Viewed from the Vantage Point of American Culture." *Origins* 20 (1990): 217-23.

Bennett, Judith M. "Public Power and Authority in the Medieval English Countryside." In *Women and Power in the Middle Ages,* ed. Mary Erler and Maryanne Kowaleski, 18-36. Athens, Ga.: University of Georgia Press, 1988.

Berger, Peter. *The Sacred Canopy: Elements of a Sociological Theory of Religion.* New York: Doubleday Anchor, 1969.

Berger, Peter, and Thomas Luckman. *The Social Construction of Reality: A Treatise in the Sociology of Knowledge.* New York: Doubleday Anchor, 1967.

Berkof, Hendrikus. *Two Hundred Years of Theology: Report of a Personal Journey.* Grand Rapids: Eerdmans, 1989.

Bernstein, Richard. *Beyond Objectivism and Relativism: Science, Hermeneutics, and Praxis.* Philadelphia: University of Pennsylvania Press, 1985.

Biancho, M. G. "Deaconess." In *Encyclopedia of the Early Church,* vol. 1, ed. Angelo de Berardino, 221. Cambridge: James Clark and Co., 1992.

Biddle, John C. "Locke's Critique of Innate Ideas and Toland's Deism." *Journal of the History of Ideas* 37 (1976): 411-22.

Bird, Phyllis. "Images of Women in the Old Testament." In *Religion and Sexism: Images of Woman in the Jewish and Christian Traditions,* ed. Rosemary Radford Ruether, 41-88. New York: Simon and Schuster, 1974.

Blank, Josef. "The Justice of God as the Humanisation of Man — the Problem of Human Rights in the New Testament." *Concilium* 124/4 (1979): 31-33.

Boismard, M.-E. "La connaissance dans l'Alliance Nouvelle d'après la Première Lettre de Saint Jean." *Revue Biblique* 56 (1949): 366-91.

Bolton, Brenda. "Mulieres Sanctae." In *Women in Medieval Society,* ed. Susan Mosher Stuard, 141-58. Philadelphia: University of Pennsylvania Press, 1976.

Bonhoeffer, Dietrich. *The Communion of Saints: A Dogmatic Inquiry into the Sociology of the Church.* New York: Harper and Row, 1963.

Bordo, Susan. "The Cartesian Masculinization of Thought." *Signs* 11 (1986): 439-57.

Borgmann, Albert. *Crossing the Postmodern Divide.* Chicago: University of Chicago Press, 1992.

Bottomley, Frank. *Attitudes to the Body in Western Christendom.* London: Lepus, 1979.

Boughton, Lynne C. "From Pious Legend to Feminist Fantasy: Distinguishing Hagiographical License from Apostolic Practice in the Acts of Paul/Acts of Thecla." *Journal of Religion* 71 (1991): 362-83.

Bouyer, Louis. *Gnosis. La connaissance de Dieu dans l'Écriture.* Paris: Cerf, 1988.

———. *The Seat of Wisdom: An Essay on the Place of the Virgin Mary in Christian Theology.* Trans. A. V. Littledale. New York: Pantheon, 1960.

———. *The Spirituality of the New Testament and the Fathers.* Trans. Mary P. Ryan. New York: Desclée Company, 1963.

———. *Woman in the Church.* Trans. Marilyn Teichert. San Francisco: Ignatius, 1979.

Bradley, Ritamary. "Patristic Background of the Motherhood Similitude in Julian of Norwich." *Christian Scholars Review* 8 (1978): 101-13.

Brady, Bernard V. "An Analysis of the Use of Rights Language in Pre-Modern Thought." *The Thomist* 57 (1993): 97-122.

Branca, Patricia. *Women in Europe Since 1750.* New York: St. Martin's Press, 1987.

Bratsiotis, N. P. "בשׂר." In *Theological Dictionary of the Old Testament II,* ed. G. J. Botterweck and Helmer Ringgren, 317-32. Grand Rapids: Eerdmans, 1975.

Brebner, J. Bartlet. "Magna Charta." In *Great Expressions of Human Rights,* ed. R. M. MacIver, 61-68. New York: Harper and Brothers, 1950.

Brennan, Irene. "Women in the Gospels." *New Blackfriars* 52 (1971): 291-99.

Brock, Sebastian. *The Luminous Eye: The Spiritual World Vision of St. Ephrem.* Rome: C.I.I.S., 1985.

Brooten, Bernadette J. *Women Leaders in the Ancient Synagogue: Inscriptional Evidence and Background Issues.* Brown Judaic Studies, 36. Chico, Calif.: Scholars Press, 1982.

Brown, Peter. *Augustine of Hippo.* Berkeley: University of California Press, 1967.

———. *The Body and Society: Men, Women and Sexual Renunciation in Early Christianity.* New York: Columbia University Press, 1988.

Brown, Raymond. "Does the New Testament Call Jesus God?" *Theological Studies* 26 (1965): 545-73.

———. "The Gospel of Peter and Canonical Gospel Priority." *New Testament Studies* 33 (1987): 321-43.

———. "The Roles of Women in the Fourth Gospel." *Theological Studies* 36 (1975): 688-99.

———. "The Semitic Background of the New Testament Mysterion." *Biblica* 39 (1958): 426-48.

Brown, Raymond E., Karl P. Donfried, and John Reumann, eds. *Peter in the New Testament: A Collaborative Assessment by Protestant and Roman Catholic Scholars.* Minneapolis, New York: Augsburg, Paulist, 1973.

Brueggemann, Walter. *Israel's Praise: Doxology Against Idolatry and Ideology.* Philadelphia: Fortress, 1988.

———. "Of the Same Flesh and Bone (Gen 2,23a)." *Catholic Biblical Quarterly* 32 (1970): 532-42.

Brun, Rudolf B. "Principles of Morphogenesis in Embryonic Development, Music, and Evolution." *Communio* 20 (1993): 528-43.

Brundage, James A. "Sexual Equality in Medieval Canon Law." In *Women and the Sources of Medieval History,* ed. Joel T. Rosenthal, 66-79. Athens, Ga.: University of Georgia Press, 1990.

Brunt, John C. "More on the Topos as a Literary Form." *Journal of Biblical Literature* 104 (1985): 495-500.

Buckley, Michael. *At the Origins of Modern Atheism.* New Haven: Yale University Press, 1988.

———. "The Newtonian Settlement and the Origins of Atheism." In *Physics, Philos-*

ophy, and Theology: A Common Quest for Understanding, ed. W. Stoeger, R. Russell, G. Coyne, 81-102. Vatican City State: Vatican Observatory, 1988.

————. "Religion and Science: Paul Davies and John Paul II." *Theological Studies* 51 (1990): 310-24.

Bühner, J.-A. *"Apostolos."* In *Exegetical Dictionary of the New Testament,* vol. 1, ed. Horst Balz and Gerhard Schneider, 142-46. Grand Rapids: Eerdmans, 1990.

Bultmann, Rudolph. *Theology of the New Testament,* vol. 1. London: SCM Press LTD, 1952.

Burgraff, Jutta. "The Mother of the Church and the Women in the Church: A Correction of Feminist Theology Gone Astray." In *The Church and Women: A Compendium.* San Francisco: Ignatius, 1988.

Burkhart, Jakob. *The Civilization of the Renaissance in Italy.* New York: Harper, 1958.

Burrell, David. *Analogy and Philosophical Language.* New Haven: Yale University Press, 1973.

Bush, M. I. *Renaissance, Reformation and the Outer World.* New York: Humanities Press, 1967.

Busson, Henri. *Le pensée religieuse de Charron à Pascal.* Paris: J. Vrin, 1933.

Butler, Cuthbert. *Western Mysticism. The Teaching of SS Augustine, Gregory and Bernard on Contemplation and the Contemplative Life.* New York: Dutton, 1923.

Butterfield, Herbert. *The Origins of Modern Science,* rev. ed. New York: The Free Press, 1957.

Bynum, Carolyn Walker. *Fragmentation and Redemption: Essays on Gender and the Human Body in Medieval Religion.* New York: Zone Books, 1992.

————. *Holy Feast and Holy Fast.* Berkeley: University of California, 1987.

————. *Jesus as Mother: Studies in the Spirituality of the High Middle Ages.* Berkeley: University of California, 1982.

————. "Jesus as Mother and Abbot as Mother: Some Themes in Twelfth-Century Cistercian Writings." *Harvard Theological Review* 70 (1977): 257-84.

Cabassut, André. "Une dévotion médiévale peu connue. La dévotion à 'Jésus nôtre mère'." *Revue d'ascétique et de mystique* 25 (1949): 234-45.

Camelot, Th. *Foi et Gnose. Introduction à l'Étude de la Connaissance Mystique chez Clément d'Alexandrie.* Études de Théologie et d'Histoire de la Spiritualité, 3. Paris: Vrin, 1945.

Carr, Anne. *Transforming Grace: Christian Tradition and Women's Experience.* San Francisco: Harper and Row, 1988.

Carr, David. "Review Article: *Temps et Récit.* Tome I, by Paul Ricoeur." *History and Theory* 23 (1984): 357-70.

Carroll, Berenice A. "Mary Beard's *Women As a Force in History:* A Critique." In *Liberating Women's History: Theoretical and Critical Essays,* ed. Berenice A. Carroll, 26-41. Chicago: University of Illinois Press, 1976.

Cerfaux, Lucien. *The Church in the Theology of St. Paul.* Trans. Geoffrey Webb and Adrian Walker. New York: Herder and Herder, 1959.

Chafetz, Janet Saltzman, and Anthony Gary Dworkin. *Female Revolt: Women's Movements in World and Historical Perspective.* Totowa, N.J.: Rowman & Allanheld, 1986.

Charlesworth, James H., ed. *The Old Testament Pseudoepigrapha.* New York: Doubleday, 1985.

Chenu, M.-D. *La Théologie comme Science au XIIIe Siècle.* 3rd ed. Paris: Vrin, 1957.

Childs, Brevard. *The Book of Exodus: A Critical, Theological Commentary.* Philadelphia: Westminster, 1974.

Clark, Elizabeth. "Ascetic Piety and Women's Faith: Essays on Late Ancient Christianity." In *Ascetic Piety and Women's Faith: Essays on Late Ancient Christianity,* 175-208. Lewiston: The Edwin Mellen Press, 1986.

————. "Devil's Gateway and Bride of Christ: Women in the Early Christian World." In *Ascetic Piety and Women's Faith: Essays on Late Ancient Christianity,* 23-60. Lewiston: The Edwin Mellen Press, 1986.

————. *Women in the Early Church.* Message of the Fathers of the Church, 13. Wilmington, Del.: Glazier, 1983.

Clarke, W. Norris. "Analogy and the Meaningfulness of Language About God: A Reply to Kai Nielsen." *The Thomist* (1976): 61-95.

————. "Person, Being, and St. Thomas." *Communio* 19 (1992): 601-18.

————. *The Philosophical Approach to God. A Neo-Thomist Perspective.* The Fourth James Montgomery Hester Seminar. Winston-Salem: Wake Forest University, 1979.

Clayton, John P. *The Concept of Correlation: Paul Tillich and the Possibility of a Mediating Theology.* Berlin: de Gruyter, 1980.

Cohen, Sheldon H. "St. Thomas Aquinas on the Immaterial Reception of Sensible Forms." *The Philosophical Review* 91 (1982): 193-209.

Collins, John N. *Diakonia: Re-interpreting the Ancient Sources.* New York: Oxford University Press, 1990.

Collins, Raymond. *Divorce in the New Testament.* Collegeville, Minn.: The Liturgical Press, 1992.

Colman, John. *John Locke's Moral Philosophy.* Edinburgh: Edinburgh University Press, 1983.

Colson, Jean. *Ministre de Jésus-Christ ou le Sacerdoce de l'Évangile.* Théologie Historique, 4. Paris: Beauchesne, 1966.

Congar, Yves. "De la Communion des Eglises à une ecclésiologie de l'Eglise universelle." In *L'Episcopat et l'Eglise Universelle,* ed. Yves Congar and Bernard Dupuy, 229-60. Paris: Cerf, 1962.

————. "Dum Visibiliter Deum Cognoscimus: A Theological Meditation." In *The Revelation of God,* 67-96. New York: Herder and Herder, 1968.

————. *A History of Theology.* Trans. and ed. Hunter Guthrie. New York: Doubleday, 1968.

————. *I Believe in the Holy Spirit.* Trans. David Smith. New York: Seabury, 1983.

————. *The Word and the Spirit.* Trans. David Smith. San Francisco: Harper and Row, 1986.

Conn, Joann Wolski. "A Discipleship of Equals: Past, Present and Future." *Horizons* 14 (1987): 23-44.

Conzelmann, H. "1 Corinthians." In *Hermeneia*. Philadelphia: Fortress Press, 1975.

Cooke, Bernard. *Ministry to Word and Sacraments*. Philadelphia: Fortress, 1976.

Coolidge, Olivia. *Women's Rights: The Suffrage Movement in America 1848-1920*. New York: E. P. Dutton, 1966.

Copleston, Frederick. *A History of Medieval Philosophy*. Notre Dame, Ind.: University of Notre Dame Press, 1990.

————. *A History of Philosophy*. 8 vols. New York: Doubleday Image, 1962-1967.

Coppens, J. "Dieu le Père dans la théologie paulinienne. Note sur *Theos patèr.*" In *La Notion Biblique de Dieu. Le Dieu de la Bible et le Dieu des Philosophes*, ed. J. Coppens, 331-35. Gembloux, Leuven: Duculot, Leuven University Press, 1976.

Corbett, Edward P. J. "The Topoi Revisited." In *Rhetoric and Praxis*. Washington: Catholic University Press, 1986.

Corley, Katherine E. *Private Women, Public Meals: Social Conflict in the Synoptic Tradition*. Peabody: Hendrickson, 1993.

Corrigan, Kevin. "Syncletica and Macrina: Two Early Lives of Woman Saints." *Vox Benedictina* 6 (1989): 32-47.

Coste, J. "Notion grecque and notion biblique de la 'souffrance educatrice' (A propos d'Hébreux, v,8)." *Recherches de science religieuse* 43 (1955): 481-523.

Cross, Frank M. *Canaanite Myth and Hebrew Epic*. Cambridge, Mass.: Harvard University Press, 1973.

Crossan, John Dominic. *The Cross that Spoke: The Origins of the Passion Narrative*. San Francisco: Harper and Row, 1988.

————. *Four Other Gospels: Shadows on the Contour of Canon*. Minneapolis: Winston, 1985.

————. *The Historical Jesus: The Life of a Mediterranean Jewish Peasant*. New York: Harper Collins, 1991.

Crouzel, Henri. *Origen: The Life and Thought of the First Great Theologian*. Trans. A. S. Worall. San Francisco: Harper and Row, 1989.

Curtius, Ernst Robert. *European Literature and the Latin Middle Ages*. Trans. Willard Trask. New York: Harper and Row, 1953.

Cyril of Jerusalem. *The Works of Saint Cyril of Jerusalem*, vol. 2. Trans. Leo P. McCauley and Anthony Stephenson. The Fathers of the Church, 64. Washington, D.C.: Catholic University of America Press, 1970.

D'Angelo, Mary Rose. "Theology in Mark and Q: *Abba* and 'Father' in Context." *Harvard Theological Review* 85 (1992): 149-74.

Dalferth, Ingolf U. *Theology and Philosophy*. Signposts in Theology. Oxford, New York: Blackwell, 1988.

Daly, Mary. *Beyond God the Father: Toward a Philosophy of Women's Liberation*. Boston: Beacon, 1973.

————. *Gyn/Ecology: The Metaethics of Radical Feminism*. Boston: Beacon, 1978.

Danielou, Jean. *The Ministry of Women in the Early Church*. Trans. Glyn Simon. Leighton Buzzard: The Faith Press, 1974.

de Beauvoir, Simone. *Le deuxième sexe*. Paris: Gallimard, 1949.

de Halleux, A. "Hypostase et Personne dans la formation de dogma trinitaire (ca. 375-381)." *Revue d'Histoire Ecclesiastique* 79 (1984): 313-69; 625-70.

de la Potterie, Ignace. *La Vérité dans Saint Jean*. Analecta Biblica, 73/74. Rome: Pontifical Biblical Institute, 1977.

————. "L'impeccabilité du Chrétien d'après I Joh. 3,6-9." In *L'Évangile de Jean. Études et Problèmes*, 161-78. Desclée de Brouwer, 1958.

de Lange, Nicholas. *Origen and the Jews: Studies in Jewish-Christian Relations in Third Century Palestine*. University of Cambridge Oriental Publications, 25. Cambridge: Cambridge University Press, 1976.

de Lubac, Henri. *The Drama of Atheist Humanism*. Trans. Edith M. Riley. New York: Sheed and Ward, 1950.

————. *Exégèse Médiévale. Les Quatre Sens de l'Écriture, I and II*. Théologie, 41-42. Paris: Aubier, 1959/60.

————. *Mémoire sur l'occasion de mes écrits*. Namur: Culture et Vérité, 1989.

————. "Mysticism and Mystery." In *Theological Fragments*, 53-55. San Francisco: Ignatius, 1989.

————. *The Splendor of the Church*, reprint ed. Trans. Michael Mason. San Francisco: Ignatius, 1986.

de Pisan, Christine. *The Book of the City of Ladies*. Trans. Earl Jeffrey Richards. New York: Persea Books, 1982.

de Vaux, Roland. *Ancient Israel*. Vol. 1, *Social Institutions*. New York: McGraw Hill, 1965.

Delobel, Joël. "1 Cor 11,2-16: Towards a Coherent Interpretation." In *L'Apotre Paul: Personnalité, Style et Conception du Ministère*, ed. Albert VanHoye, vol. 73, 369-89. Leuven: Leuven University Press, 1986.

Deman, Th. "La Prudence." In *St. Thomas D'Aquin, Somme Théologique*, Appendice 11. 2me ed. Paris: Desclée, 1949.

Dennehy, Raymond. "The Ontological Basis of Human Rights." *The Thomist* 42 (1978): 434-63.

Descartes, René. *The Philosophical Writings of Descartes*, vols. I and II. Trans. John Cottingham, Robert Stoothoff, and Dugald Murdoch. Cambridge: Cambridge University Press, 1985.

Dhorme, Edouard. *L'emploi métaphorique des noms de parties du corps en hébreux et en accadien*. Paris: Lecoffre, 1923.

DiNoia, Joseph Augustine. "Knowing and Naming the Triune God: The Grammar of Trinitarian Confession." In *Speaking the Christian God: The Holy Trinity and the Challenge of Feminism*, ed. Alvin F. Kimel Jr., 162-87. Grand Rapids: Eerdmans, 1992.

Dock, Terry Smiley. *Women in the Encyclopédie: A Compendium*. Potomac, Md.: Studia Humanitatis, 1983.

Dodds, E. R. *Pagan and Christian in an Age of Anxiety.* Cambridge: Cambridge University Press, 1965.

Dörrie. *Leid und Erfahrung: Die Wort und Sinn-Verbindung μαθεῖν — παθεῖν im griechieschen Denken.* Wiesbaden: Steiner, 1956.

Duffy, Stephen J. "Our Hearts of Darkness: Original Sin Revisited." *Theological Studies* 49 (1988): 597-622.

Dulles, Avery. *The Craft of Theology.* New York: Crossroad, 1992.

————. "Faith, Church, and God: Insights from Michael Polanyi." *Theological Studies* 45 (1984): 537-50.

————. *Models of the Church.* Image Books ed. New York: Doubleday, 1978.

Duncan, Roger. "Lublin Thomism." *The Thomist* 51 (1987): 307-24.

Dunn, Patrick J. *Priesthood: A Re-examination of the Roman Catholic Theology of the Presbyterate.* New York: Alba House, 1990.

Dupré, Louis. "Experience and Interpretation: A Philosophical Reflection on Schillebeeckx' *Jesus* and *Christ.*" *Theological Studies* 43 (1982): 30-51.

————. "Notes on the Idea of Religious Truth in the Christian Tradition." *Thomist* 52 (1988): 499-512.

Duran, Jane. "Gender-Neutral Terms." In *Sexist Language: A Modern Philosophical Analysis,* ed. Mary Vetterling-Baggin, 147-54. Totowa, N.J.: Rowman and Littlefield, 1981.

Durand, Gilbert. *Les Structures Anthropologiques de L'Imaginaire.* 11th ed. Paris: Dunod, 1992.

Durkin, Mary G. *Feast of Love: Pope John Paul II on Human Intimacy.* Chicago: Loyola University Press, 1983.

Egan, Harvey. " 'The Devout Christian of the Future Will . . . Be a "Mystic." ' Mysticism and Karl Rahner's Theology." In *Theology and Discovery: Essays in Honor of Karl Rahner,* ed. William Kelly, 139-58. Milwaukee: Marquette University Press, 1980.

Eising, H. "חיל." In *Theological Dictionary of the Old Testament,* vol. 4, ed. G. Johannes Botterweck and Helmer Ringgren, 344-55. Grand Rapids: Eerdmans, 1980.

Elman, Paul. "On Worshipping the Bride." *Anglican Theological Review* 68 (1986): 241-49.

Elshtain, Jean Bethke. *Public Man, Private Woman: Women in Social and Political Thought.* Princeton: Princeton University Press, 1981.

Ernst, W. "Ursprung und Entwicklung der Menschenrechte in Geschichte und Gegenwart." *Gregorianum* 65 (1984): 231-70.

Fabro, Cornelio. "The Intensive Hermeneutics of Thomistic Philosophy; the Nature of Participation." *Review of Metaphysics* 38 (1984): 17-32.

————. *Participation et Causalité selon S. Thomas d'Aquin.* Louvain: Publications Universitaires de Louvain, 1961.

Farrar, Cynthia. *The Origins of Democratic Thinking: The Invention of Politics in Classical Greece.* Cambridge: Cambridge University Press, 1988.

Ferguson, Everett. "Martyr, Martyrdom." In *Encyclopedia of Early Christianity,* ed. Everett Ferguson. New York: Garland Publishing Company, 1990.

Ferré, Frederick. *Language, Logic and God.* London: Eyre and Spottiswoode, 1970.

———. "Metaphor in Religious Discourse." In *Dictionary of the History of Ideas,* 3rd ed. New York: Scribner, 1973.

Feuillet, André. "Jésus et la Sagesse Divine d'après les Evangiles Synoptiques." *Revue Biblique* 62 (1955): 161-96.

———. "La Demeure céleste et la destinée des Chrétiens." *Recherches de Science Religieuse* 44 (1956): 360-402.

Finke, Laurie. "Mystical Bodies and the Dialogics of Vision." *Philological Quarterly* 67 (1988): 439-50.

Finkel, Asher. "The Prayer of Jesus in Matthew." In *Standing Before God,* ed. Asher Finkel and Lawrence Frizzel, 131-69. New York: KTAV, 1981.

Finnis, John. *Natural Law and Natural Rights.* Oxford: Oxford University Press, 1980.

Fiorenza, Elisabeth Schüssler. *Bread Not Stone: The Challenge of Feminist Biblical Interpretation.* Boston: Beacon Press, 1984.

———. *But She Said: Feminist Practices of Biblical Interpretation.* Boston: Beacon Press, 1992.

———. *Discipleship of Equals: A Critical Feminist Ekklesia-logy of Liberation.* New York: Crossroad, 1993.

———. "Feminist Hermeneutics." In *Anchor Dictionary of the Bible,* vol. 2, ed. David Noel Freedman, 783-91. New York: Doubleday, 1992.

———. *In Memory of Her: A Feminist Theological Reconstruction of Christian Origins.* New York: Crossroad, 1987.

———. "Justified by All Her Children: Struggle, Memory, and Vision." In *On the Threshold of the Third Millennium,* ed. The Foundation, 19-38. Philadelphia: Trinity Press, 1990.

———. "The Politics of Otherness: Biblical Interpretation as a Critical Praxis for Liberation." In *The Future of Liberation Theology: Essays in Honor of Gustavo Gutiérrez,* ed. Marc H. Ellis and Otto Maduro, 311-25. Maryknoll: Orbis Books, 1989.

———. "Remembering the Past in Creating the Future: Historical-Critical Scholarship and Feminist Biblical Interpretation." In *Feminist Perspectives on Biblical Scholarship,* ed. Adela Y. Collins, 43-64. Chico, Calif.: Scholars Press, 1985.

———. "Toward a Feminist Biblical Hermeneutics: Biblical Interpretation and Liberation Theology." In *The Challenge of Liberation Theology,* ed. L. Dale Richesin and Brian Mahan, 91-112. Maryknoll: Orbis Books, 1981.

———. "The Will to Choose or Reject: Continuing Our Critical Work." In *Feminist Interpretation of the Bible,* ed. Letty M. Russel, 125-36. Philadelphia: Westminster, 1985.

———. "Word, Spirit and Power: Women in Early Christian Communities." In *Women of Spirit: Female Leadership in the Jewish and Christian Traditions,* ed. Rosemary Radford Ruether and Eleanor McLaughlin, 29-70. New York: Simon and Schuster, 1979.

Fiorenza, Francis Schüssler. *Foundational Theology: Jesus and the Church.* New York: Crossroad, 1984.

———. *Systematic Theology: Roman Catholic Perspectives.* Philadelphia: Fortress, 1991.

Firestone, Shulamith. *The Dialectic of Sex: The Case for a Feminist Revolution.* London: Jonathan Cape, 1971.

Fishbane, Michael. "The Image of the Human and the Rights of the Individual in Jewish Tradition." In *Human Rights and the World's Religions,* ed. Leroy S. Rouner, 17-31. Notre Dame, Ind.: University of Notre Dame Press, 1988.

Fitzmyer, Joseph. "Abba and Jesus' Relation to God." In *A Cause de l'Evangile. Mélanges Offertes à Dom Jacques Dupont,* 15-38. Paris: Cerf, 1985.

———. "Another Look at *KEPHALE* in 1 Corinthians 11.3." *New Testament Studies* 35 (1989): 503-11.

———. "The Consecutive Meaning of ἐφ' ᾧ in Romans 5.12." *New Testament Studies* 39 (1993): 321-39.

———. "A Feature of Qumran Angelology and the Angels of 1 Cor 11:10." In *Essays on the Semitic Background of the New Testament,* 187-204. Missoula, Mont.: Scholars Press, 1974.

———. "*Kephalē* in I Corinthians 11:3." *Interpretation* 47 (1993): 52-59.

———. "The Semitic Background of the New Testament *Kyrios*-Title." In *A Wandering Aramean,* 115-42. Missoula: Scholars Press, 1979.

Flannery, Austin, ed. *Vatican Council II: The Conciliar and Post Conciliar Documents.* Northport, N.Y.: Costello Publishing Company, 1975.

Ford, David, ed. *The Modern Theologians: An Introduction to Christian Theology in the Twentieth Century.* Cambridge, Mass.: Blackwell, 1989.

Fox-Genovese, Elizabeth. *Feminism Without Illusions: A Critique of Individualism.* Chapel Hill: University of North Carolina Press, 1991.

Freeman, Jo. "Women's Movements." In *Colliers Encyclopedia,* vol. 23, 562. 1986.

Frei, Hans. *The Eclipse of Biblical Narrative: A Study in Eighteenth and Nineteenth Century Hermeneutics.* New Haven: Yale University Press, 1974.

———. *The Identity of Jesus Christ: The Hermeneutical Basis of Dogmatic Theology.* Philadelphia: Fortress, 1975.

Friedan, Betty. *The Feminine Mystique.* New York: Norton, 1963.

Gadamer, Hans George. *Truth and Method.* Trans. Joel Weinsheimer and Donald Marshall. New York: Seabury, 1989.

Galot, Jean. *Who Is Christ? A Theology of the Incarnation.* Trans. M. Angeline Bouchard. Chicago: Franciscan Herald Press, 1981.

Gamble, H. Y. "The Canon of the New Testament." In *The New Testament and Its Modern Interpreters,* ed. Eldon Jay Epp and George W. McCrae, 201-43. Atlanta: Scholars Press, 1989.

Gay, Peter. *The Enlightenment: An Interpretation.* Vol. 2, *The Science of Freedom.* New York: Norton, 1969.

Geddes, L. W., and W. A. Wallace. "Person (In Philosophy)." In *New Catholic Encyclopedia*. New York: McGraw-Hill, 1967.

Geffré, Claude. *The Risk of Interpretation: On Being Faithful to the Christian Tradition in a Non-Christian Age*. Trans. David Smith. New York: Paulist Press, 1987.

Gies, Frances, and Joseph Gies. *Life in a Medieval City*. New York: Harper Colophon Books, 1969.

————. *Women in the Middle Ages*. New York: Thomas Crowell, 1978.

Gilbert, P., S.J. "Personne et Acte." *Nouvelle Revue Théologique* 106 (1984): 731-37.

Gill, Jerry. *Mediated Transcendence: A Postmodern Reflection*. Macon, Ga.: Mercer University Press, 1989.

Gilligan, Carol. *In a Different Voice*. Cambridge, Mass.: Harvard University Press, 1982.

Gilmore, David D., ed. *Honor and Shame and the Unity of the Mediterranean*. American Anthropological Association, special publication 22. Washington: American Anthropological Association, 1987.

Gilson, Étienne. *Reason and Revelation in the Middle Ages*. New York: Scribner's, 1938.

Glick, Daryl. "Recovering Morality: Personalism and Theology of the Body of Pope John Paul II." *Faith and Reason* 12 (1986): 7-25.

Gold, Penny Schine. "Male/Female Cooperation: The Example of Fontevrault." In *Medieval Religious Women*, ed. John A. Nichols and Lillian Thomas Shank, vol. 1, *Distant Echoes*, 151-68. Kalamazoo, Mich.: Cistercian Publications, 1984.

Goldstein, Valerie Saiving. "The Human Situation: A Feminine View." *Journal of Religion* 40 (1960): 100-112.

Grant, Robert M. "Review of *In Memory of Her*." *Journal of Religion* 65 (1985): 83-88.

Green, Garrett. "The Gender of God and the Theology of Metaphor." In *Speaking the Christian God: The Holy Trinity and the Challenge of Feminism*, ed. Alvin F. Kimel, 44-64. Grand Rapids: Eerdmans, 1992.

Greeven, H. "Propheten, Lehrer, Vorstehr bei Paulus." *Zeitschrift für die neutestamentliche Wissenschaft* 44 (1952/53): 1-43.

Grelot, Pierre. *Église et ministères. Pour un dialogue critique avec Edward Schillebeeckx*. Paris: Cerf, 1983.

————. "Une mention inaperçue de "ABBA" dans le Testament araméen de Lévi." *Semitica* 33 (1983): 101-8.

Grillmeier, Aloys. *Christ in Christian Tradition*. Vol. 1, *From the Apostolic Age to Chalcedon*, trans. John Bowden. London: Mowbrays, 1965.

Gruber, Mayer I. "The Motherhood of God in Second Isaiah." *Revue Biblique* 90 (1983): 351-59.

Grudem, Wayne. "Does *kephalē* ('Head') Mean 'Source' or 'Authority' in Greek Literature? A Survey of 2336 Examples." *Trinity Journal* 6 (1985): 38-59.

Gudorf, Christine E. "Encountering the Other: The Modern Papacy on Women." *Social Compass* 36 (1989): 295-310.

Guerriere, Daniel, ed. *Phenomenology of the Truth Proper to Religion.* Albany: State University of New York Press, 1990.

Gundry, Robert H. *Soma in Biblical Theology: With Emphasis on Pauline Theology.* Grand Rapids: Zondervan, 1987.

Gunton, Colin. *Enlightenment and Alienation.* Grand Rapids: Eerdmans, 1985.

Hadewijch. *The Complete Works.* Trans. Mother Columbia Hart. The Classics of Western Spirituality. New York: Paulist, 1980.

Hampson, Daphne. *Theology and Feminism.* Oxford, Cambridge, Mass.: Blackwell, 1990.

Haren, Michael. *Medieval Thought.* New York: St. Martin's Press, 1985.

Harrison, Peter. *'Religion' and the Religions in the English Enlightenment.* New York: Cambridge University Press, 1990.

Harrison, Verna E. F. "Male and Female in Cappadocian Theology." *Journal of Theological Studies* 41 (1990): 441-71.

Hartmann, Heidi. "Capitalism, Patriarchy, and Job Segregation by Sex." In *The Signs Reader: Women, Gender, and the Scholarship,* ed. Elizabeth and Emily K. Abel, 193-225. Chicago: University of Chicago Press, 1983.

Harvey, Susan Ashbrook. "Feminine Imagery for the Divine: The Holy Spirit, the Odes of Solomon, and Early Syriac Tradition." *St. Vladimir's Theological Quarterly* 37 (1993): 111-40.

Hauke, Manfred. *Women in the Priesthood? A Systematic Analysis in the Light of the Order of Creation and Redemption.* Trans. David Kipp. San Francisco: Ignatius, 1988.

Haulotte, E. "Formation du Corpus du Nouveau Testament. Recherche d'un 'Module' Generatif Intratextuel." In *Les Canons des Ecritures. Etudes Historiques, Exegetiques, et Systematiques,* ed. C. Theobald, 255-440. Paris: Cerf, 1990.

Hausherr, Irenée. *Leçons d'un contemplatif. La Traité de l'Oraison d'Evagre le Pontique.* Paris: Beauchesne, 1960.

Hazard, Paul. *European Thought in the Eighteenth Century: From Montesquieu to Lessing.* Trans. L. May. Gloucester, Mass.: Peter Smith, 1973.

Hebblethwaite, Peter. "Husserl, Scheler, and Wojtyla: A Tale of Three Philosophers." *The Heythrop Journal* 27 (1986): 441-45.

———. "Pope John Paul II as Philosopher and Poet." *The Heythrop Journal* 21 (1980): 123-36.

Heine, Susanne. *Women and Early Christianity: A Reappraisal.* Minneapolis: Augsburg Publishing House, 1987.

Held, David. *Models of Democracy.* Stanford, Calif.: University of Stanford Press, 1987.

Held, Virginia. *Feminist Morality: Transforming Culture, Society, and Politics.* Chicago: University of Chicago Press, 1993.

Hellwig, Monika. *Whose Experience Counts in Theological Reflection?* The 1982 Pere Marquette Theology Lecture. Milwaukee: Marquette University Press, 1982.

Henderson, Katherine Usher, and Barbara F. McManus. *Half Humankind: Contexts and Texts of the Controversy about Women in England, 1540-1640.* Chicago: University of Illinois Press, 1985.

Hennessey, Lawrence R. "Gregory of Nyssa's Doctrine of the Resurrected Body." In *Studia Patristica,* ed. Elizabeth A. Livingstone, 28-34. Leuven: Peeters Press, 1989.

Herlihy, David. "Did Women Have a Renaissance? A Reconsideration." In *Medievalia et Humanistica: Studies in Medieval and Renaissance Culture,* ed. Paul Maurice Clogan. Totowa, N.J.: Rowman and Allanheld, 1985.

———. "Land, Family and Women in Continental Europe, 701-1200." *Traditio* 18 (1962): 89-119.

———. "Social Thought: Catholic, Patristic and Medieval." In *The New Catholic Encyclopedia,* 346-49. New York: McGraw-Hill, 1967.

Hesse, Mary B. *Models and Analogies in Science.* Notre Dame, Ind.: Notre Dame University Press, 1966.

———. *The Structure of Scientific Inference.* London: MacMillan, 1974.

Hickey, Anne Ewing. *Women of the Roman Aristocracy as Christian Monastics.* Ann Arbor: University Microfilms, 1983.

Hildegard of Bingen. *Scivias.* Trans. Mother Columbia Hart and Jane Bishop. The Classics of Western Spirituality. New York: Paulist, 1990.

Hill, William. *Proper Relations to the Indwelling Divine Persons.* Washington: The Thomist Press, nd.

———. *The Three-Personed God.* Washington: The Catholic University Press, 1982.

Himes, Michael J., and Kenneth R. Himes. "Rights, Economics and the Trinity." *Commonweal* 113 (1986): 137-41.

Hitchcock, Helen Hull, ed. *The Politics of Prayer: Feminist Language and the Worship of God.* San Francisco: Ignatius, 1992.

Hoffman, T. "Inspiration, Normativeness, Canonicity, and the Unique Sacred Character of the Bible." *Catholic Biblical Quarterly* 44 (1982): 447-69.

Hogan, Richard M., and John M. LeVoir. *Covenant of Love: Pope John Paul II on Sexuality, Marriage, and Family in the Modern World.* Garden City: Doubleday and Company, 1985.

Hook, Donald D., and Alvin F. Kimel Jr. "The Pronouns of Deity: The Theolinguistic Critique of Feminist Proposals." *Scottish Journal of Theology* 46 (1993): 297-323.

Hopko, Thomas. "Apophatic Theology and the Naming of God in Eastern Orthodox Tradition." In *Speaking the Christian God,* ed. Alvin F. Kimel Jr., 144-61. Grand Rapids: Eerdmans, 1992.

Huber, Wolfgang. "Human Rights — A Concept and Its History." In *The Church and the Rights of Man,* ed. A. Miller and N. Greinacher, 4-5. *Concilium* 124/4. New York: Seabury, 1979.

Jackson, Pamela. "Cyril of Jerusalem's Use of Scripture in Catechesis." *Theological Studies* 52 (1991): 431-50.

Jaggar, Alison M. "Sexual Difference and Sexual Equality." In *Theoretical Per-*

spectives on Sexual Difference, 239-54. New Haven: Yale University Press, 1990.

Janeway, E. Man's World, Women's Place. New York: Delta Books, 1971.

Jeanrond, Werner. Text and Interpretation as Categories of Theological Thinking. Trans. Thomas Wilson. New York: Crossroad, 1988.

Jelly, Frederick, O.P. "Towards a Theology of the Body through Mariology: Reflections on a Workshop." Marian Studies 34 (1983).

Jenni, Ernst. "אב." In Theologisches Handwörterbuch zum Alten Testament, vol. 1, ed. Ernst Jenni and Claus Westermann, 1-17. Munich: Kaiser, 1971.

Jeremias, Joachim. New Testament Theology: The Proclamation of Jesus. Trans. John Bowden. New York: Charles Scribner's Sons, 1971.

————. The Prayers of Jesus. Studies in Biblical Theology, Second Series, 6. London: SCM, 1967.

Jervis, L. Ann. " 'But I want you to know . . .': Paul's Midrashic Intertextual Response to the Corinthian Worshippers." Journal of Biblical Literature 112 (1993): 211-30.

Jewett, Paul. Man as Male and Female. Grand Rapids: Eerdmans, 1975.

Jewett, Robert. Paul's Anthropological Terms: A Study of Their Use in Conflict Settings, vol. 10. Arbeiten zur Geschichte des antiken Judentums und des Urchristentums. Leiden: E. J. Brill, 1971.

Joblin, Joseph, S.J. "The Church and Human Rights: Historical Overview and Future Outlook." In The Church and Human Rights: Historical and Theological Reflections, 19-21. Vatican City: Pontifical Council for Justice and Peace, 1990.

John, E. "Magna Charta." In The New Catholic Encyclopedia. New York: McGraw-Hill, 1967.

John of the Cross. The Collected Works of John of the Cross. Trans. Kieran Kavanaugh and Otilio Rodriguez. Washington: Institute of Carmelite Studies, 1979.

Johnson, Elizabeth. She Who Is: The Mystery of God in Feminist Theological Discourse. New York: Crossroad, 1992.

————. Women, Earth, and Creator Spirit. 1993 Madaleva Lecture in Spirituality. New York: Paulist, 1993.

Johnson, Paul. Modern Times. New York: Harper Colophon, 1985.

Julian of Norwich. Showings. Trans. Edmund Colledge and James Walsh. The Classics of Western Spirituality. New York: Paulist, 1978.

Kagan, Donald. Pericles of Athens and the Birth of Democracy. New York: Free Press, 1991.

Kalinowski, Georges. "La Pensée de Jean-Paul II sur L'Homme et la Famile." Divinitas 26 (1982): 3-18.

Kannengiesser, Charles. "Early Christian Bodies: Some Afterthoughts on Peter Brown's The Body and Society." Religious Studies Review 19 (1993): 126-29.

Kant, Immanuel. Critique of Judgment. Trans. J. H. Bernard. Indianapolis: Hackett, 1987.

————. *Critique of Pure Reason.* Trans. Norman Kemp Smith. New York: St. Martin's Press, 1929.

————. *Foundations of the Metaphysics of Moral.* Trans. Lewis White Beck. Library of Liberal Arts. New York: MacMillan, 1959.

————. *What is Enlightenment?* Trans. Lewis White Beck. The Library of Liberal Arts. New York: Macmillan, 1959.

Kasper, Walter. *The God of Jesus Christ.* Trans. Matthew J. O'Connell. New York: Crossroad, 1984.

————. "The Position of Women as a Problem of Theological Anthropology." In *The Church and Women: A Compendium,* ed. Helmut Moll, 51-64. San Francisco: Ignatius, 1988.

————. "The Theological Foundation of Human Rights." In *The Church and Human Rights: Historical and Theological Reflections,* 47-70. Vatican City: Pontifical Council for Justice and Peace, 1990.

————. *Theology and Church.* Trans. Margaret Kohl. New York: Crossroad, 1989.

Kaufman, Michael. "Spare Ribs: The Conception of Woman in the Middle Ages and the Renaissance." *Soundings* 16 (1973): 139-63.

Keefe, Donald, S.J. *Covenantal Theology: The Eucharistic Order of History.* Lanham, Md.: University Press of America, 1991.

————. "Mary as Created Wisdom: The Splendor of New Creation." *The Thomist* 47 (1983): 395-420.

————. "The Sacrament of the Good Creation." *Faith and Reason* (1983): 128-41.

————. "Sacramental Sexuality and the Ordination of Women." *Communio* 5 (1978): 228-51.

Kelly, J. N. D. *Early Christian Creeds.* 3rd ed. London: Longman, 1972.

————. *Early Christian Doctrines.* New York: Harper and Brothers Publishers, 1959.

————. *Jerome: His Life, Writings, and Controversies.* London: Gerald Duckworth and Company, 1975.

Kelly, Joan. "Early Feminist Theory and the Querelle des Femmes, 1400-1789." In *Women, History, and Theory: The Essays of Joan Kelly,* 65-109. Chicago: University of Chicago Press, 1984.

Kelly-Gadol, Joan. "Did Women Have a Renaissance?" In *Becoming Visible: Women in European History,* ed. Renate Bridenthal and Claudia Koontz, 138-64. Boston: Houghton Mifflin, 1977.

Kelsey, David. "Method, Theological." In *The Westminster Dictionary of Christian Theology,* ed. Alan Richardson and John Bowden, 363-68. Philadelphia: Westminster, 1983.

Kertlege, Karl. "Der Ort des Amtes in der Ekklesiologie des Paulus." In *L'Apôtre Paul. Personalité, style et conception du ministère,* ed. Albert Vanhoye, 184-202. Leuven: Leuven University Press, 1986.

Kimel, Alvin F., Jr., ed. *Speaking the Christian God: The Holy Trinity and the Challenge of Feminism.* Grand Rapids: Eerdmans, 1992.

Klubertanz, George. *St. Thomas and Analogy.* Chicago: Loyola University, 1960.

Knowles, David. "A Characteristic Mental Climate of the Fourteenth Century." In *Mélange offerts à Étienne Gilson*, 315-25. Toronto: Pontifical Institute of Medieval Studies, 1959.

Kraemer, Ross S. "Review of *In Memory of Her.*" *Journal of Biblical Literature* 104 (1985): 722-25.

Kung, Hans. *The Church*. Trans. Ray and Rosaleen Ockenden. New York: Sheed and Ward, 1967.

————. *Truthfulness in the Future of the Church*. Trans. Edward Quinn. New York: Sheed and Ward, 1968.

Lacroix, Jean. *Histoire et Mystère*. Tournai: Castermann, 1962.

LaCugna, Catherine Mowry. *God For Us: The Trinity and Christian Life*. San Francisco: Harper, 1991.

————, ed. *Freeing Theology: The Essentials of Theology in Feminist Perspective*. San Francisco: Harper, 1993.

Ladner, Gerhart. *The Idea of Reform: Its Impact on Christian Thought and Action in the Age of the Fathers*. Cambridge, Mass.: Harvard University Press, 1959.

Laffey, Alice L. *An Introduction to the Old Testament: A Feminist Perspective*. Philadelphia: Fortress Press, 1988.

Lagrange, Marie Joseph. "La Paternité de Dieu dans l'Ancien Testament." *Revue Biblique* 5 (1908): 481-99.

Laquer, Walter, and Barry Rubin, eds. *The Human Rights Reader*. Philadelphia: Temple University Press, 1979.

Lash, Nicholas. "When Did the Theologians Lose Interest in Theology?" In *Theology and Dialogue*, ed. Bruce Marshall, 131-47. Notre Dame, Ind.: University of Notre Dame Press, 1990.

Lawler, Ronald. *The Christian Personalism of Pope John Paul II*. Chicago: Franciscan Herald, 1982.

Leclercq, Jean. *The Love of Learning and the Desire for God: A Study of Monastic Culture*. Trans. Catharine Misrahi. New York: Fordham University Press, 1974.

Lécuyer, J. "La Causalité efficiente des mystères du Christ selon saint Thomas." *Doctor Communis* 6 (1953): 91-120.

Leff, Gordon. *The Dissolution of the Medieval Outlook*. New York: Harper and Row, 1976.

Lehmann, Karl. "The Place of Women as a Problem in Theological Anthropology." In *The Church and Women*, ed. Helmut J. Moll, 11-33. San Francisco: Ignatius Press, 1988.

Lemaire, André. *Ministry in the Church*. Trans. C. W. Danes. London: SPCK, 1977.

Lenoble, R. *Histoire de l'idée de nature*. Paris: Albin Michel, 1969.

Léon-Dufour, Xavier. *Sharing the Eucharistic Bread: The Witness of the New Testament*. Trans. Matthew J. O'Connell. New York: Paulist, 1982.

Léon-Dufour, Xavier, and Jean Audusseau. "Cross." In *The Dictionary of Biblical Theology*, ed. Xavier Léon-Dufour, 102-4. New York: Seabury, 1973.

Lerner, Gerda. *The Grimké Sisters from South Carolina: Rebels against Slavery.* Boston: Houghton Mifflin, 1967.

Limburg, James. "Human Rights in the Old Testament." *Concilium* 124/4 (1979): 20-26.

Lindbeck, George. *The Nature of Doctrine.* Philadelphia: Westminster, 1984.

Little, Joyce. "Sexual Equality in the Church: A Theological Resolution to an Anthropological Dilemma." *The Heythrop Journal* 27 (1987): 165-78.

Loades, Ann. "Feminist Theology." In *The Modern Theologians: An Introduction to Christian Theology in the Twentieth Century,* ed. David F. Ford, vol. 2, 235-52. New York: Blackwell, 1989.

Locke, John. *An Essay Concerning Human Understanding.* London: Routledge, nd.

———. *Two Treatises of Government.* Ed. Peter Laslett. Cambridge, 1963; New York: New American Library, 1965.

———. *The Works of John Locke.* London: Robinson et al., 1801.

Loewe, Robert. *The Position of Women in Judaism.* London: S.P.C.K., 1966.

Lonergan, Bernard. *Insight: A Study of Human Understanding.* London: Longmans, Green, 1958.

———. *Method in Theology.* New York: Herder and Herder, 1972.

Louth, Andrew. *Discerning the Mystery: An Essay on the Nature of Theology.* Oxford: Oxford University Press, 1983.

———. *The Origins of the Christian Mystical Tradition: From Plato to Denys.* Oxford: Oxford University Press, 1981.

Lynch, John J. "Prosopon in Gregory of Nyssa: A Theological Word in Transition." *Theological Studies* 40 (1979): 728-38.

MacIntyre, Alasdair. *After Virtue: A Study in Moral Theory.* 2nd ed. Notre Dame, Ind.: University of Notre Dame Press, 1984.

———. *Whose Justice? Which Rationality?* Notre Dame, Ind.: University of Notre Dame Press, 1988.

MacMurray, John. *Persons in Relation.* New York: Harper and Brothers, 1961.

———. *The Self as Agent.* New York: Harper and Brothers, 1957.

Makkreel, Rudolf A. *Imagination and Interpretation in Kant: The Hermeneutical Import of the Critique of Judgement.* Chicago: University of Chicago Press, 1990.

Mancini, Italo. *Kant e la teologia.* Assisi: Cittadella, nd.

Mankowski, Paul. "Old Testament Iconology and the Nature of God." In *The Politics of Prayer: Feminist Language and the Worship of God,* ed. Helen Hull Hitchcock, 151-76. San Francisco: Ignatius, 1992.

Marchel, W. *Abba, Père. La Prière du Christ et des Chrétiens.* 2nd ed. Analecta Biblica 19A. Rome: Pontifical Biblical Institute, 1971.

Maritain, Jacques. *Creative Intuition in Art and Poetry.* The A. W. Mellon Lectures in the Fine Arts. New York: Meridian Books, 1955.

———. *Existence and the Existent.* New York: Doubleday, 1957.

———. *Man and the State.* Chicago: University of Chicago Press, 1951.

Markovic, Mihailo. "Political Rights versus Social Rights." In *Human Rights and the World's Religions,* ed. Leroy S. Rouner, 46-60. Notre Dame, Ind.: University of Notre Dame Press, 1988.

Marks, Elaine, and Isabelle de Courtivron, eds. *New French Feminisms: An Anthology.* Amherst: University of Massachusetts Press, 1980.

Markus, R. A. *Saeculum: History and Society in the Theology of St. Augustine.* New York: Cambridge University Press, paperback, 1988.

Marshall, Bruce. "Aquinas as a Postliberal Theologian." *Thomist* 53 (1989): 353-402.

Martimort, Aimé Georges. *Deaconesses: An Historical Study.* Trans. K. D. Whitehead. San Francisco: Ignatius Press, 1986.

Martin, Francis. "The Biblical Canon and Church Life." In *Recovering the Sacred: Catholic Faith, Worship and Practice, Proceedings of the Twelfth Convention of the Fellowship of Catholic Scholars,* ed. Paul Williams, 117-36. Pittston, Pa.: Northeast Books, 1990.

―――. "Critique historique et enseignement du Nouveau Testament sur l'imitation du Christ." *Revue Thomiste* 93 (1993): 234-62.

―――. "Feminist Hermeneutics: An Overview." *Communio* 18 (1991): 144-63; 398-424.

―――. "Feminist Theology: A Proposal." *Communio* 20 (1993): 334-76.

―――. "Healing, Gift of." In *Dictionary of Pentecostal and Charismatic Movements,* ed. Stanley M. Burgess and Gary B. McGee, 350-53. Grand Rapids: Zondervan, 1988.

―――. "Literary Theory, Philosophy of History and Exegesis." *The Thomist* 52 (1988): 575-604.

―――. "Male and Female He Created Them: Reflections on the Genesis Texts and Their Subsequent Development." *Communio* 20 (1993).

―――. "Monastic Community and the Summary Statements in Acts." In *Contemplative Community: An Interdisciplinary Symposium,* ed. Basil Pennington, 13-46. Washington, D.C.: Cistercian Publications, 1972.

―――. *Narrative Parallels to the New Testament.* SBL Resources for Biblical Study 22. Atlanta: Scholars Press, 1988.

―――. "Pauline Trinitarian Formulas and Christian Unity." *Catholic Biblical Quarterly* 30 (1968): 199-219.

Matter, E. Ann. *The Voice of My Beloved: The Song of Songs in Western Medieval Christianity.* Philadelphia: University of Pennsylvania Press, 1990.

May, Henry. *The Enlightenment in America.* New York: Oxford University Press, 1976.

McCarthy, Vincent A. *Quest for a Philosophical Jesus: Christianity and Philosophy in Rousseau, Kant, Hegel, and Schelling.* Macon, Ga.: Mercer, 1986.

McCool, Gerald, ed. *Catholic Theology in the Nineteenth Century: The Quest for a Unitary Method.* New York: Seabury, 1977.

―――. *From Unity to Pluralism: The Internal Evolution of Thomist.* New York: Fordham University Press, 1989.

―――. *The Universe as Journey: Conversations with W. Norris Clarke, S.J.* New York: Fordham University Press, 1988.

McFague, Sallie. *The Body of God: An Ecological Theology.* Minneapolis: Fortress Press, 1993.

———. *Metaphorical Theology: Models of God in Religious Language.* Philadelphia: Fortress, 1982.

———. *Models of God: Theology for an Ecological, Nuclear Age.* Philadelphia: Fortress, 1987.

McGill, Arthur. *Suffering: A Test of Theological Method.* 1968; Philadelphia: Westminster, 1982.

McGinn, Bernard. *The Presence of God: A History of Western Christian Mysticism.* Vol. 1, *The Foundations of Mysticism: Origins to the Fifth Century.* New York: Crossroad, 1992.

McInerny, Ralph. "Natural Law and Human Rights." *The American Journal of Jurisprudence* 36 (1991): 1-14.

McKenzie, John L. "Face." In *Dictionary of the Bible,* 266-67. New York: Macmillan, 1965.

McLaughlin, Eleanor. " 'Christ My Mother': Feminine Naming and Metaphors in Medieval Spirituality." *St. Luke's Journal of Theology* 18 (1975): 366-86.

———. "The Christian Past: Does It Hold a Future for Women?" *Anglican Theological Review* 57 (1975): 36-56.

McNamara, Jo Ann. "Living Sermons: Consecrated Women and the Conversion of Gaul." In *Peaceweavers,* ed. Lilian Thomas Shank and John A. Nichols, 19-37. Kalamazoo, Mich.: Cistercian Publications, 1987.

———. "Muffled Voices: The Lives of Consecrated Women in the Fourth Century." In *Medieval Religious Women,* ed. John A. Nichols and Lillian Thomas Shanks, vol. 1, *Distant Echoes,* 11-29. Kalamazoo, Mich.: Cistercian Publications, 1984.

McNamara, Jo Ann, and Suzanne Wemple. "The Power of Woman through the Family in Medieval Europe, 500-1100." In *Women and Power in the Middle Ages,* ed. Mary Erler and Maryanne Kowaleski, 83-101. Athens, Ga.: University of Georgia Press, 1988.

———. "Sanctity and Power: The Dual Pursuit of Medieval Women." In *Becoming Visible: Women in European History,* ed. Renate Bridenthal and Claudia Koontz, 90-118. Boston: Houghton Mifflin, 1977.

Meier, John. *A Marginal Jew: Rethinking the Historical Jesus.* New York: Doubleday, 1991.

Metzger, Bruce. *The Canon of the New Testament: Its Origin, Development and Significance.* Repr. Oxford: Clarendon Press, 1988.

Meyer, Ben F. "A Caricature of Joachim Jeremias and His Scholarly Work." *Journal of Biblical Literature* 110 (1991): 451-62.

Milbank, John. *Theology and Social Theory: Beyond Secular Reason.* Oxford: Basil Blackwell, 1990.

Miles, Margaret R. *Carnal Knowing: Female Nakedness and the Religious Meaning in the Christian West.* Boston: Beacon, 1989.

Miletic, Stephen F. *"One Flesh": Eph. 5.22-24, 5.31; Marriage and the New*

Creation. Analecta Biblica, vol. 115. Rome: Pontifical Biblical Institute, 1988.

Mill, John Stuart. *On the Subjection of Women.* Greenwich, Conn.: Fawcett Publications, 1970.

Miller, John W. *Biblical Faith and Fathering: Why We Call God "Father."* New York: Paulist Press, 1989.

Millet, Kate. *Sexual Politics.* New York: Doubleday, 1970.

Mink, Louis O. "The Autonomy of Historical Understanding." *History and Theory* 5 (1966): 24-47.

————. "History and Fiction as Modes of Comprehension." *New Literary History* 1 (1970): 541-58.

Minogue, Kenneth. "The History of the Idea of Human Rights." In *The Human Rights Reader,* ed. Walter Laquer and Barry Rubin, 3-17. Philadelphia: Temple University Press, 1979.

Modras, Ronald. "The Moral Philosophy of Pope John Paul II." *Theological Studies* 41 (1980): 684-85.

Molnar, Paul. "Can We Know God Directly? Rahner's Solution From Experience." *Theological Studies* 46 (1985): 228-61.

Montagnes, Bernard. *La Doctrine de L'Analogie de L'être d'après Saint Thomas d'Aquin.* Philosophes Médiévaux 6. Louvain, Paris: Publications Universitaires, Béatrice-Nauwelaerts, 1963.

Mouroux, Jean. *The Christian Experience: An Introduction to a Theology.* Trans. George Lamb. New York: Sheed and Ward, 1954.

Mühlen, Heribert. *Der heilige Geist als Person.* 2nd ed. Münster: Aschendorff, 1966.

————. *Una Persona Mystica.* Munich: Schöningh, 1964.

Mulholland, Leslie. *Kant's System of Rights.* New York: Columbia University Press, 1990.

Muniz, Francisco. "De Diversis Muneribus S. Theologiae Secundum Doctrinam D. Thomae." *Angelicum* 24 (1947): 93-123.

Murphey, Nancy, and James Wm. McClendon Jr. "Distinguishing Modern and Postmodern Theologies." *Theology Today* 5 (1989): 191-214.

Murphy, Roland E. *Wisdom Literature: Job, Proverbs, Ruth, Canticles, Ecclesiastes, Esther.* The Forms of Old Testament Literature XIII. Grand Rapids: Eerdmans, 1981.

Murphy-O'Connor, Jerome. "Sex and Logic in 1 Corinthians 11:2-16." *Catholic Biblical Quarterly* 42 (1980): 482-500.

Myers, Carol. "Procreation, Production, and Protection: Male-Female Balance in Early Israel." *Journal of the American Academy of Religion* 51 (1983): 569-93.

Nardoni, Enrique. "Charism in the Early Church since Sohm: An Ecumenical Challenge." *Theological Studies* 53 (1992): 646-62.

Nelson, Janet L. "Women and the Word in the Earlier Middle Ages." In *Women in the Church: Papers Read at the 1990 Winter Meeting of the Ecclesiastical*

History Society, ed. W. J. Sheils and Diana Wood, 53-78. Oxford: Basil Blackwell, 1990.

Nichols, Aidan. *From Newman to Congar: The Idea of Doctrinal Development from the Victorians to the Second Vatican Council.* Edinburgh: T&T Clark, 1990.

Noonan, John T., Jr. "Development in Moral Doctrine." *Theological Studies* (1993): 662-77.

Nuth, Joan M. "Two Medieval Soteriologies: Anselm of Canterbury and Julian of Norwich." *Theological Studies* 53 (1992): 611-45.

O'Farrell, Francis. "Kant's Concept of Freedom." *Gregorianum* 55 (1974): 425-69.

O'Neil, Colman. "Analogy, Dialectic, and Inter-Confessional Theology." *The Thomist* 47 (1983): 43-65.

O'Neil, J. C. "Biblical Criticism." In *The Anchor Bible Dictionary,* ed. David Noel Freedman, 725-30. New York: Doubleday, 1992.

O'Neill, Kathleen. "Seminar on Women's Spirituality in the Cistercian Tradition. New Melleray/12-20 May 1987." *Cistercian Studies* 23 (1988): 86-94.

O'Neill, William. "The Origins of American Feminism." In *The Other Half: Roads to Women's Equality,* ed. Cynthia Fuchs Epstein and William J. Goode, 159-64. Englewood Cliffs, N.J.: Prentice-Hall, 1971.

Oddie, William. *What Will Happen to God? Feminism and the Reconstruction of Christian Belief.* San Francisco: Ignatius Press, 1988.

Offen, Karen. "Defining Feminism: A Comparative Historical Approach." *Signs* 14 (1988): 119-57.

Okin, Susan Moller. *Justice, Gender and the Family.* San Francisco: Harper Collins, 1989.

Ong, Walter. *Fighting For Life.* Amherst: University of Massachussetts Press, 1981.

Osborne, Kenan B. *Priesthood: A History of the Ordained Ministry in the Roman Catholic Church.* New York: Paulist, 1988.

Osiek, Carolyn. "The Feminist and the Bible: Hermeneutical Alternatives." In *Feminist Perspectives on Biblical Scholarship,* ed. Adela Y. Collins, 93-106. Chico, Calif.: Scholars Press, 1985.

Pannenberg, Wolfhart. *Anthropology in Theological Perspective.* Trans. Matthew J. O'Connell. Philadelphia: Westminster, 1985.

Panofsky, Erwin. *Studies in Iconology: Humanistic Themes in the Art of the Renaissance.* New York: Harper Torchbooks, 1962.

Parke-Taylor, G. H. *Yahweh: The Divine Name in the Bible.* Waterloo, Ontario: Wilfrid Laurier University Press, 1975.

Paul VI. "Message to the United Nations General Assembly." *Acta Apostolicae Sedis* 57 (1965).

Pearl, Thomas. "Dialectic Pantheism: On the Hegelian Character of Karl Rahner's Key Christological Writings." *Irish Theological Quarterly* 42 (1975): 119-37.

Pedersen, Johs. *Israel: Its Life and Culture.* 2 vols. London: Oxford University Press, 1926.

Pegis, Anton. "Some Reflections on Summa Contra Gentiles II, 56." In *An Étienne*

Gilson Tribute, ed. C. J. O'Neill, 169-88. Milwaukee: Marquette University Press, 1959.

Pelikan, Jaroslav. *The Christian Tradition: A History of the Development of Doctrine.* 5 vols. Chicago: University of Chicago Press, 1978-1989.

Pellauer, Mary D. *Towards a Tradition of Feminist Theology: The Religious Social Thought of Elizabeth Cady Stanton, Susan B. Anthony, and Anna Howard Shaw.* Chicago Studies in the History of American Religion. Brooklyn: Carlson, 1991.

Perkins, Pheme. "Theological Implications of New Testament Pluralism." *Catholic Biblical Quarterly* 50 (1988): 5-23.

Perlitt, Lothar. "Das Bild des Vaters im Alten Testament." In *Das Vaterbild in Mythos und Geschichte,* ed. H. Tellenback, 50-101. Stuttgart: Kohlhammer, 1976.

Pernaud, Régine. *Pour en finir avec le Moyen Age.* Paris: Éditions du Seuil, 1977.

Petersen, Alvyn. "Perpetua — Prisoner of Conscience." *Vigilae Christianae* 41 (1987): 139-53.

Petrement, Simone. *A Separate God: The Christian Origins of Gnosticism.* Trans. Carol Harrison. San Francisco: Harper, 1990.

Phan, Peter C. *Social Thought.* Message of the Fathers of the Church 20. Wilmington, Del.: Glazier, 1984.

Plaskow, Judith. *Sex, Sin and Grace: Women's Experience in the Theologies of Reinhold Niebuhr and Paul Tillich.* Washington: University Press, 1981.

Plongeron, Bernard. "Anathema or Dialogue? Christian Reaction to Declarations of the Rights of Man in the United States and Europe in the Eighteenth Century." *Concilium* 124/4 (1979): 39-47.

Pojman, Louis P. "Are Human Rights Based on Equal Human Worth?" *Philosophy and Phenomenological Research* 52 (1992): 205-22.

Polanyi, Michael. *Knowing and Being.* Chicago: University of Chicago Press, 1969.

———. *Personal Knowledge: Towards a Post-Critical Philosophy.* Chicago: University of Chicago Press, 1958.

Porter, Jean. *Recovery of Virtue.* Louisville: Westminster, 1990.

Porter, Lawrence B. "On Keeping 'Persons' in the Trinity: A Linguistic Approach to Trinitarian Thought." *Theological Studies* 41 (1980): 530-48.

Pound, Ezra. *Literary Essays of Ezra Pound.* London: Faber and Faber, 1960.

Power, Eileen. *Medieval Women.* Cambridge: Cambridge University Press, 1975.

———. "The Position of Women." In *The Legacy of the Middle Ages,* ed. C. G. Crump and E. F. Jacob, 401-33. Oxford: Clarendon, 1926.

Price, J. R. "The Objectivity of Mystical Truth Claims." *The Thomist* 49 (1985): 81-98.

Prokes, Mary Timothy. "The Nuptial Meaning of Body in the Light of Mary's Assumption." *Communio* 11 (1984): 157-76.

Purvis, Sally B. "Christian Feminist Spirituality." In *Christian Spirituality: Post-Reformation and Modern,* ed. Louis Dupré and Don E. Sallers, 500-519. New York: Crossroad, 1989.

Quay, Paul M., S.J. *The Christian Meaning of Human Sexuality.* San Francisco: Ignatius, 1985.

Rabkin, Peggy A. *Fathers to Daughters: The Legal Foundations of Female Emancipation.* Westport, Conn.: Greenwood Press, 1980.

Rae, Eleanor, and Bernice Marie-Daly. *Created In Her Image: Models of the Feminine Divine.* New York: Crossroad, 1990.

Rahner, Karl. "The Body in the Order of Salvation." In *Theological Investigations,* vol. 17, 71-89. New York: Crossroad, 1981.

———. "Courage for an Ecclesial Christianity." In *Theological Investigations,* vol. 20, 3-12. New York: Crossroad, 1981.

———. "The Doctrine of the 'Spiritual Senses' in the Middle Ages." In *Theological Investigations,* vol. 16, 104-34. London: Darton, Longman and Todd, 1979.

———. "Experience of Self and Experience of God." In *Theological Investigations,* vol. 13, 122-32. London: Darton, Longman and Todd, 1975.

———. *Hominisation: The Evolutionary Origin of Man as a Theological Problem.* Trans. W. T. O'Hara. Quaestiones Disputatae 13. New York: Herder and Herder, 1965.

———. "The Logic of Concrete Individual Knowledge in Ignatius Loyola." In *The Dynamic Element in the Church,* 84-170. New York: Herder and Herder, 1964.

———. "Men in the Church." In *Theology for Renewal: Bishops, Priests, Laity.* New York: Sheed and Ward, 1964.

———. "The Position of Woman in the New Situation in Which the Church Finds Herself." In *Theological Investigations,* vol. 8, 75-93. New York: Herder and Herder, 1971.

———. "Reflections on the Experience of Grace." In *Theological Investigations,* vol. 3, 86-90. Baltimore: Helicon, 1967.

———. "Religious Enthusiasm and the Experience of Grace." In *Theological Investigations,* vol. 16, 35-47. New York: Seabury, 1979.

———. "Remarks on the Dogmatic Treatise 'De Trinitate'." In *Theological Investigations,* vol. 4, 77-102. London: Darton, Longman and Todd, 1966.

———. "The 'Spiritual Senses' According to Origen." In *Theological Investigations,* vol. 16, 81-103. London: Darton, Longman and Todd, 1979.

———. "Theology of the Symbol." In *Theological Investigations,* vol. 4, 221-52. Baltimore: Helicon Press, 1966.

———. *The Trinity.* Trans. Joseph Donceel. New York: Herder & Herder, 1970.

———. "The Unity of Spirit and Matter in Christian Understanding of the Faith." In *Theological Investigations,* vol. 3, 153-77. New York: Crossroad, 1966.

———. "Women and the Priesthood." In *Theological Investigations,* vol. 20, 35-50. New York: Crossroad, 1981.

Ramos-Lisson, Domingo. "Le role de la femme dans la théologie de saint Irenée." *Studia Patristica* 21 (1987): 163-74.

Ramsey, Ian T. *Christian Discourse: Some Logical Explorations.* Oxford: Oxford University Press, 1965.

―――. "Facts and Disclosures." In *Christian Empiricism*, ed. Jerry H. Gill, 159-76. London: Sheldon Press, 1974.

―――. *Models for Divine Activity*. London: SCM Press, 1973.

Ramshaw-Schmidt, Gail. "De Divinis Nominibus: The Gender of God." *Worship* 56 (1982): 117-31.

Ranke-Heinemann, Uta. *Eunuchs for the Kingdom of Heaven: Women, Sexuality and the Catholic Church*. Trans. Pater Heinegg. New York: Doubleday, 1990.

Rapaczynski, Andrzej. *Nature and Politics: Liberalism in the Philosophies of Hobbes, Locke, and Rousseau*. Ithaca, N.Y.: Cornell University Press, 1987.

Rashdall, Hastings. *The Universities of Europe in the Middle Ages*. Oxford: Clarendon, 1936.

Ratzinger, Josef. "Concerning the Notion of Person in Theology." *Communio* 17 (1990).

Reid, Daniel G., et al., eds. *Dictionary of Christianity in America*. Downers Grove, Ill.: InterVarsity Press, 1990.

Reventlow, Henning Graf. *The Authority of the Bible and the Rise of the Modern World*. Philadelphia: Fortress, 1985.

Rezak, Brigitte Bedos. "Women, Seals and Power in Medieval France, 1150-1350." In *Women and Power in the Middle Ages*, ed. Mary Erler and Maryanne Kowaleski, 61-82. Athens, Ga.: University of Georgia Press, 1988.

Rich, Adrienne. *Of Woman Born*. New York: Norton, 1976.

Richard, Marcel. "L'introduction du mot 'hypostase' dans la théologie de l'incarnation." *Mélanges de Science Religeuse* 2 (1945): 243-70.

Ricoeur, Paul. *Conflict of Interpretations: Essays in Hermeneutics*. Northwestern University Studies in Phenomenology and Existential Philosophy. Evanston: Northwestern University Press, 1974.

―――. "Explanation and Understanding: On Some Remarkable Connections Among the Theory of the Text, Theory of Action, and Theory of History." In *The Philosophy of Paul Ricoeur: An Anthology of His Work*, ed. Charles E. Reagan and David Stewart, 149-66. Boston: Beacon Press, 1978.

―――. *From Text to Action: Essays in Hermeneutics, II*. Trans. Kathleen Blamey and John B. Thompson. Evanston, Ill.: Northwestern University Press, 1991.

―――. "The Hermeneutics of Testimony." In *Essays on Biblical Interpretation*, ed. Lewis S. Mudge. Philadelphia: Fortress, 1980.

―――. *History and Truth*. Trans. Charles A. Kelbley. Northwestern University Studies in Phenomenology and Existential Philosophy. Evanston: Northwestern University Press, 1965.

―――. "Narrative and Hermeneutics." In *Essays on Aesthetics: Perspectives on the Work of Monroe C. Beardsley*, ed. John Fisher, 149-60. Philadelphia: Temple University Press, 1983.

―――. *The Rule of Metaphor: Multi-disciplinary Studies of the Creation of Meaning in Language*. Trans. Robert Czerny, Kathleen McLaughlin, John Costello. Toronto: University of Toronto Press, 1977.

————. *Time and Narrative.* 3 vols. Trans. Kathleen McLaughlin and David Pellauer. Chicago: University of Chicago Press, 1984-1988.

Riley, Maria. *Transforming Feminism.* Kansas City: Sheed and Ward, 1989.

Rocca, Gregory. *Analogy as Judgment and Faith in God's Incomprehensibility: A Study in the Epistemology of Thomas Aquinas.* Ph.D. diss., Catholic University of America. Ann Arbor: University Microfilms International, 1989.

————. "Aquinas on God Talk: Hovering Over the Abyss." *Theological Studies* 54 (1993): 641-61.

————. "*Res Significata* and *Modus Significandi* in Aquinas." *Thomist* 55 (1991): 173-98.

Rondeau, Marie-Josèph. *Exégèse prosopologique et théologie,* vol. II. Les commentateurs patristiques de Psautier (IIIe-Ve siècles). Rome: Oriental Institute, 1985.

————. *Les Travaux des Pères grecs et latins sur le Psautier. Recherches et bilan,* vol. I. Les commentateurs patristiques de Psautier (IIIe-Ve siècles). Rome: Oriental Institute, 1982.

Rose, Phyllis. *Parallel Lives: Five Victorian Marriages.* New York: Alfred A. Knopf, 1983.

Ross, Susan A. "The Bride of Christ and the Body Politic: Body and Gender in Pre–Vatican II Marriage Theology." *Journal of Religion* 71 (1991): 345-61.

————. " 'Then Honor God in Your Body' (1 Cor. 6:20): Feminist and Sacramental Theology of the Body." *Horizons* 16 (1989): 7-27.

Rousseau, Felicien. *Les croissance solidaire des droits de l'homme: un rétour aux sources de l'éthique.* Montreal: Desclée et Cie, 1982.

Rousselot, Pierre. *The Eyes of Faith.* Trans. Joseph Donceel. New York: Fordham University Press, 1990.

Roy, L. "Wainwright, Maritain, and Aquinas on Transcendant Experiences." *Thomist* 54 (1990): 655-72.

Ruether, Rosemary Radford. "Can a Male Savior Save Women?" In *To Change the World: Christology and Cultural Criticism,* 45-56. London: SCM, 1981.

————. "The Development of My Theology." *Religious Studies Review* 15/1 (January 1989).

————. "Is Feminism the End of Christianity? A Critique of Daphne Hampson's *Theology and Feminism.*" *Scottish Journal of Theology* 43 (1990): 390-400.

————. "Feminist Interpretation: A Method of Correlation." In *Feminist Interpretation of the Bible,* ed. Letty M. Russel, 111-24. Philadelphia: Westminster, 1985.

————. "Feminist Theology." In *The New Dictionary of Theology,* ed. J. Komonchak and M. Collins, 391-96. Wilmington, Del.: Glazier, 1987.

————. *Gaia and God: An Eco-feminist Theology of Earth Healing.* San Francisco: Harper, 1992.

————. *New Women/New Earth: Sexist Ideologies and Human Liberation.* New York: The Seabury Press, 1975.

————. *Sexism and God-Talk.* Boston: Beacon Press, 1983.

————. *Womanguides: Readings Toward a Feminist Theology.* Boston: Beacon, 1985.

————. *Women-Church.* San Francisco: Harper and Row, 1985.

Ruether, Rosemary Radford, and Daphne Hampson. "Is There a Place for Feminists in a Christian Church?" *New Blackfriars* 68/801 (1987): 7-24.

Sakenfeld, Katherine Doob. "Feminist Perspectives on Bible and Theology: An Introduction to Selected Issues and Literature." *Interpretation* 42 (1988): 5-18.

Sallis, John. "Immateriality and the Play of the Imagination." *Proceedings of the American Catholic Philosophical Association* 52 (1978): 61-76.

Schall, James V. "Human Rights as Ideological Project." *The American Journal of Jurisprudence* 32 (1987): 47-61.

Schelbert, Georges. "Abba, Vater! Stand der Frage." *Freiburger Zeitschrift für Philosophie und Theologie* 40 (1993): 259-81.

Schillebeeckx, Edward. *Christ the Sacrament of the Encounter with God.* New York: Sheed and Ward, 1963.

————. *The Church with a Human Face: A New and Expanded Theology of Ministry.* Trans. John Bowden. New York: Crossroad, 1985.

————. *Ministry: Leadership in the Community of Jesus Christ.* Trans. John Bowden. New York: Crossroad, 1981.

Schillebeeckx, Edward, and Bas van Iersel, eds. *Revelation and Experience.* Concilium 113. New York: Seabury, 1979.

Schleiermacher, Friedrich. *The Christian Faith.* New York: Harper and Row, 1963.

Schmidt, W. H. *"qnh."* In *Theologisches Handwörterbuch zum Alten Testament,* ed. Ernst Jenni and Claus Westermann, vol. 2, 650-59. Munich: Kaiser, 1984.

Schmitz, Kenneth. *At the Center of the Human Drama: The Anthropology of Karol Wojtyla/Pope John Paul II.* Washington: Catholic University of America Press, 1994.

————. "Neither With Nor Without Foundations." *Review of Metaphysics* 42 (1988): 3-25.

Schnackenburg, Rudolf. "Apostles Before and During Paul's Time." In *Apostolic History and the Gospel: Biblical and Historical Essays Presented to F. F. Bruce on His 60th Birthday,* ed. W. Gasque and R. Martin, 287-303. Grand Rapids: Eerdmans, 1970.

————. *Die Johannesbriefe.* 7th ed. Herders theologischer Kommentar zum Neuen Testament XIII/3. Freiburg: Herder, 1984.

Schneiders, Sandra M. *Beyond Patching.* Mahwah, N.J.: Paulist, 1989.

————. "Feminist Spirituality." In *The New Dictionary of Catholic Spirituality,* ed. Michael Downey, 394-406. Collegeville, Minn.: Liturgical Press, 1993.

————. *The Revelatory Text: Interpreting the New Testament as Scripture.* San Francisco: Harpers, 1991.

Schner, George. "The Appeal to Experience." *Theological Studies* 53 (1992): 40-59.

Schofield, Malcom. *The Stoic Idea of the City.* Cambridge: Cambridge University Press, 1991.

Schökel, Luis Alonso. *A Manual of Hebrew Poetics.* Subsidia Biblica 11. Rome: Pontifical Biblical Institute, 1988.

Scholder, Klaus. *The Birth of Modern Critical Theology: Origins and Problems of Biblical Criticism in the Seventeenth Century.* Trans. John Bowden. London: SCM, 1990.

Schulenburg, Jane Tibbetts. "Strict Active Enclosure and Its Effects on the Female Monastic Experience (500-1100)." In *Medieval Religious Women,* ed. John A. Nichols and Lillian Thomas Shank, vol. 1, *Distant Echoes,* 51-86. Kalamazoo, Mich.: Cistercian Publications, 1984.

Schuller, Eileen. "4Q372 1: A Text about Joseph." *Revue de Qumran* 14 (1990): 349-76.

———. "The Psalm of 4Q372 1 Within the Context of Second Temple Prayer." *Catholic Biblical Quarterly* 54 (1992): 67-79.

Schürmann, Reiner. *Heidegger on Being and Acting: From Principles to Anarchy.* Trans. Christine-Marie Gros and Reiner Schürmann. Bloomington, Ind.: Indiana University Press, 1987.

Schwartz, E. *Acta conciliorum oecumenicorum.* Vol. 2. Berlin, 1927-1928.

Schwartz, Sanford. "Hermeneutics and the Productive Imagination." *Journal of Religion* 63 (1983): 290-300.

Segovia, A. *La iluminación bautismal en el antiguo cristianismo.* Granada: Camacho, 1958.

Shoof, Mark. *A Survey of Catholic Theology 1800-1970.* Trans. N. D. Smith. Paramus, N.J.: Paulist, 1970.

Silberstein, Laurence J. "Literary Theory and Modern Jewish Studies." *Religious Studies Review* 19 (1993): 25-31.

Slussler, Michael. "The Exegetical Roots of Trinitarian Theology." *Theological Studies* 49 (1988): 461-76.

Snyder, David. "Faith and Reason in Locke's Essay." *Journal of the History of Ideas* 47 (1986): 197-213.

Sokolowski, Robert. *The God of Faith and Reason: Foundations of Christian Theology.* Notre Dame, Ind.: University of Notre Dame Press, 1982.

———. *Husserlian Meditations.* Northwestern University Studies in Phenomenology and Existential Philosophy. Evanston: Northwestern University Press, 1974.

Soskice, Janet. "Knowledge and Experience in Science and Religion: Can We Be Realists?" In *Physics, Philosophy, and Theology: A Common Quest for Understanding,* ed. William R. Stoeger, Robert J. Russel, George V. Coyne, 173-84. Vatican City State: Vatican Observatory, 1988.

———. *Metaphor and Religious Language.* Oxford: Clarendon Press, 1985.

Southern, R. W. *Western Society and the Church in the Middle Ages.* Vol. 2. Pelican History of the Church. Baltimore: Penguin Books, 1970.

Spellman, Elizabeth V. "Woman as Body: Ancient and Contemporary Views." *Journal of Feminist Studies* 8 (1982): 109-31.

Spitzer, Leo. *Linguistics and Literary History.* Princeton: Princeton University Press, 1948.

Stackhouse, Max L. *Creeds, Society, and Human Rights: A Study in Three Cultures.* Grand Rapids: Eerdmans, 1984.

Stanley, David. "Become Imitators of Me: The Pauline Conception of Apostolic Tradition." *Biblica* 40 (1959): 859-77.

Stendahl, Krister. *The Bible and the Role of Women.* Philadelphia: Fortress Press, 1966.

Sternberg, Meir. *The Poetics of Biblical Narrative: Ideological Literature and the Drama of Reading.* Bloomington, Ind.: Indiana University Press, 1987.

Strauss, Leo. "Natural Right and the Historical Approach." *Review of Politics* 12 (1950): 422-42.

Stroup, George W. "Between Echo and Narcissus." *Interpretation* 42 (1988): 19-32.

Stuard, Susan. "The Dominion of Gender: Women's Fortunes in the High Middle Ages." In *Becoming Visible: Women in European History,* ed. Claudia Koontz, Renate Bridenthal, Susan Stuard. Boston: Houghton Mifflin, 1987.

Swartley, William M. *Slavery, Sabbath, War, and Women.* Scottsdale, Pa.: Herald Press, 1983.

Swidler, Leonard, and Arlene Swidler, eds. *Women Priests: A Catholic Commentary on the Vatican Declaration.* New York: Paulist, 1977.

Swinburne, Richard. *Revelation: From Metaphor to Analogy.* Oxford: Clarendon Press, 1992.

Tarnas, Richard. *The Passion of the Western Mind.* New York: Ballantine Books, 1991.

Tavard, George. "Sexist Language in Theology?" *Theological Studies* 36 (1975): 700-724.

————. *Women in Christian Tradition.* Notre Dame, Ind.: University of Notre Dame Press, 1973.

Taylor, Charles. *Sources of the Self: The Making of Modern Identity.* Cambridge, Mass.: Harvard University Press, 1989.

Terrien, Samuel. "Toward a Biblical Theology of Womanhood." *Religion in Life* 42 (1973): 322-33.

Thiselton, Anthony C. *New Horizons in Hermeneutics: The Theory and Practice of Transforming Biblical Reading.* Grand Rapids: Zondervan, 1992.

Tigay, Jeffrey. *You Shall Have No Other Gods: Israelite Religion in the Light of Hebrew Inscriptions.* Harvard Semitic Studies 31. Atlanta: Schwartz, 1986.

Tillich, Paul. *Systematic Theology.* Vol. 1. Chicago: University of Chicago Press, 1951.

Tolbert, Mary Ann. "Defining the Problem: The Bible and Feminist Hermeneutics." In *The Bible and Feminist Hermeneutics,* ed. Mary Ann Tolbert, 113-23. Chico, Calif.: Scholars Press, 1983.

Torjesen, Karen Jo. *When Women Were Priests.* San Francisco: Harper's, 1993.

Tracy, David. *Blessed Rage for Order.* New York: Seabury, 1975.

————. "Particular Questions within General Consensus." In *Consensus in Theology?* ed. Leonard Swidler, 34. Philadelphia: Westminster, 1980.

————. "The Uneasy Alliance Reconceived: Catholic Theological Method, Modernity, and Postmodernity." *Theological Studies* 50 (1989): 548-70.

Traets, C. *Voir Jésus et le Père en Lui selon l'Evangile de Saint Jean.* Analecta Gregoriana 159. Rome: Editrice Pontificia Università Gregoriana, 1967.

Trible, Phyllis. "Depatriarchalizing in Biblical Interpretation." *Journal of the American Academy of Religion* 41 (1973): 30-48.

————. *God and the Rhetoric of Sexuality.* Overtures to Biblical Theology. Philadelphia: Fortress, 1978.

————. "God, Nature of, in the OT." In *The Interpreter's Dictionary of the Bible: Supplementary Volume,* ed. Keith Crim, 368-69. Nashville: Abingdon, 1976.

Uitz, Erika. *The Legend of Good Women: Medieval Women in Towns and Cities.* Trans. Sheila Marnie. Mt. Kisco, N.Y.: Moyer Bell, 1988.

Ulpian. *Imperatoris Iustiniani Institutionum.* Oxford: Clarendon, 1923.

Vagaggini, Cipriano. *The Flesh the Instrument of Salvation: A Theology of the Human Body.* Trans. Charles Underhill Quinn. New York: Alba House, 1968.

Vaihinger, H. *The Philosophy of "As If": A System of the Theoretical, Practical and Religious Fictions of Mankind.* 2nd ed. Trans. C. K. Ogden. New York: Barnes and Noble, 1935.

Vallin, P. "La Bible, Object Culturel ou Livre Chrétien?" In *Le Canon des Écritures. Études Historiques, Exégétiques et Systématiques,* ed. C. Theobald, 551-58. Paris: Cerf, 1990.

van Beeck, Franz Jozef. "Divine Revelation: Intervention or Self-Communication?" *Theological Studies* 52 (1991): 199-226.

Vanhoozer, Kevin J. *Biblical Narrative in the Philosophy of Paul Ricoeur: A Study in Hermeneutics and Theology.* Cambridge: Cambridge University Press, 1990.

Vanhoye, Albert. "The Biblical Question of 'Charisms' After Vatican II." In *Vatican II: Assessment and Perspectives,* ed. René Latourelle, 439-68. New York: Paulist, 1988.

Vanhoye, Albert, and Henri Crouzel. "The Ministry in the Church: Reflections on a Recent Publication." *The Clergy Review* 5 (1983): 155-74.

Veach, Henry. *Human Rights: Fact or Fancy?* Baton Rouge: Louisiana State University Press, 1985.

Vergote, Antoine. "The Body as Understood in Contemporary Thought and Biblical Categories." *Philosophy Today* 35 (1991): 93-105.

Villey, M. *Le droit et les droits de l'homme.* Paris: Puf, 1983.

Vlahos, Olivia. "The Goddess That Failed." *First Things* 28 (1992): 12-19.

Völker, Walther. *Der Wahre Gnostiker nach Clemens Alexandrinus.* Vol. 57 of *Texte und Untersuchungen zur Geschichte der Altchristlichen Literatur,* ed. Walther Eltester and Erich Klostermann. Berlin: Akademie Verlag, 1952.

von Balthasar, Hans Urs. *The Christian State of Life.* Trans. Mary Frances McCarthy. San Francisco: Ignatius, 1983.

――――. "Ephesians 5:21-33 and Humanae Vitae: A Meditation." In *Christian Married Love*, ed. Raymond Dennehy, 55-73. San Francisco: Ignatius, 1981.

――――. *Explorations in Theology*. 2nd ed. Vol. 1, *The Word Made Flesh*. Trans. A. V. Littledale. San Francisco: Ignatius, 1989.

――――. *The Glory of the Lord: A Theological Aesthetics*. Vol. 2, *Studies in Theological Style: Clerical Styles*. Trans. A. Louth, Fr. McDonagh, B. McNeil. San Francisco: Ignatius, 1984.

――――. *The Glory of the Lord: A Theological Aesthetics*. Vol. 3, *Studies in Theological Style: Lay Styles*. Trans. A. Louth, J. Saward, M. Simon, R. Williams. San Francisco: Ignatius, 1986.

――――. *The Glory of the Lord: A Theological Aesthetics*. Vol. 5: *The Realm of Metaphysics in the Modern Age*. Trans. Oliver Davies, Andrew Louth, Brian McNeil, John Saward, Rowan Williams. San Francisco: Ignatius, 1991.

――――. *The Glory of the Lord: A Theological Aesthetics*. Vol. 7, *The New Covenant*. Trans. Brian McNeil, C.R.V. Edinburgh: T. & T. Clark, 1989.

――――. *Love Alone*. Trans. Alexander Dru. New York: Herder and Herder, 1969.

――――. *Mysterium Paschale*. Trans. Aidan Nichols. Edinburgh: T. & T. Clark, 1990.

――――. "Office in the Church." In *Explorations in Theology*, 81-142. Sponsa Verbi 2. San Francisco: Ignatius, 1991.

――――. *The Office of Peter and the Structure of the Church*. Trans. Andrée Emery. San Francisco: Ignatius, 1986.

――――. "On the Concept of Person." *Communio* 13 (1986): 18-26.

――――, ed. *Origen, Spirit and Fire: A Thematic Anthology of His Writings*. Washington: The Catholic University of America Press, 1984.

――――. "Patristik, Scholastik und wir." *Theologie der Zeit* 3 (1939): 65-109.

――――. "A Response to My Critics." *Communio* 5 (1978): 70-72.

――――, ed. *The Scandal of the Incarnation*. Selected and introduced by Hans Urs von Balthasar. San Francisco: Ignatius, 1990.

――――. *Theo-Drama: Theological Dramatic Theory*. Vol. 3, *Dramatis Personae: Persons in Christ*. Trans. Graham Harrison. San Francisco: Ignatius, 1992.

――――. *Theodramatik*. Vol. 4, *Das Endspiel*. Einseideln: Johannes Verlag, 1983.

――――. *A Theological Anthropology*. Trans. Benziger Verlag. New York: Sheed and Ward, 1967.

――――. *The Theology of Karl Barth*. Trans. Edward Oates. San Francisco: Ignatius, 1992.

――――. *Truth Is Symphonic: Aspects of Christian Pluralism*. Trans. Graham Harrison. San Francisco: Ignatius, 1987.

von Rad, Gerhard. *Genesis*. Trans. John H. Marks. Old Testament Library. Philadelphia: Westminister Press, 1961.

――――. *Old Testament Theology*. Vols. 1 and 2. Trans. D. M. G. Stalker. New York: Harper and Brothers, 1962-1965.

Vorgimler, Herbert. *Karl Rahner: His Life, Thought and Work*. Trans. Edward Quinn. Montreal: Palm, 1965.

Wackenheim, Charles. "The Theological Meaning of the Rights of Man." *Concilium* 124/4 (1979): 49-56.

Wall, Grenville. "Locke's Attack on Innate Knowledge." In *Locke on Human Understanding,* ed. I. C. Tipton. Oxford: Oxford University Press, 1977.

Walsh, W. H. *Philosophy of History: An Introduction.* New York: Harper, 1960.

Warner, Marina. *The Book of the City of Ladies.* Trans. Earl Jeffrey Richards. New York: Persea Books, 1982.

Weaver, Mary Jo. *New Catholic Women: A Contemporary Challenge to Traditional Religious Authority.* San Francisco: Harper, 1985.

Wellek, René, and Austin Warren. *Theory of Literature.* New York: Harcourt, Brace and Co., 1956.

Wemple, Suzanne. "Female Spirituality and Mysticism in Frankish Monasteries: Radegund, Bathild and Aldegund." In *Peaceweavers,* ed. Lillian Shank Thomas and John A. Nichols, vol. 2, 39-53. Kalamazoo, Mich.: Cistercian Publications, 1987.

———. "S. Salvatore/S. Giulia: A Case Study in the Endowment and Patronage of a Major Female Monastery in Northern Italy." In *Women of the Medieval World: Essays in Honor of John H. Mundy,* ed. Julius Kirshner and Suzanne F. Wemple, 85-102. Oxford: Basil Blackwell, 1985.

———. *Women in Frankish Society: Marriage and the Cloister 500 to 900.* Philadelphia: University of Pennsylvania Press, 1981.

Westermann, Claus. *Genesis 1–11.* Trans. John J. Scullion. Minneapolis: Augsburg, 1984.

———. "נפשׁ." In *Theologisches Handwörterbuch zum Alten Testament,* ed. Ernst Jenni and Claus Westermann, vol. 2, 71-95. Munich: Kaiser, 1984.

Whyte, Martin King. *The Status of Women in Preindustrial Societies.* Princeton, N.J.: Princeton University Press, 1978.

Wiethaus, Urike. "Sexuality, Gender, and the Body in Late Medieval Women's Spirituality: Cases from Germany and the Netherlands." *Journal of Feminist Studies in Religion* 7 (1991): 35-52.

Wilder, Alfred. "Community of Persons in the Thought of Karl Wojtyla." *Angelicum* 56 (1979): 211-44.

Wilson, Katharina M. "The Saxon Canoness: Hrotsvit of Gandersheim." In *Medieval Women Writers,* ed. Katharina M. Wilson, 30-63. Athens, Ga.: University of Georgia Press, 1984.

Wire, Antoinette Clark. *The Corinthian Women Prophets: A Reconstruction Through Paul's Rhetoric.* Minneapolis: Fortress, 1990.

Witherington, Ben, III. *Women in the Earliest Churches.* SNTS Monograph Series 59. Cambridge: Cambridge University Press, 1988.

———. *Women in the Ministry of Jesus: A Study of Jesus' Attitudes to Women and Their Roles as Reflected in His Earthly Life.* SNTS Monograph Series 51. Cambridge: Cambridge University Press, 1984.

Wojtyla, Karol. *The Acting Person.* Trans. Andrzej Potocki and Anna-Teresa Tymieniecka. Analecta Husserliana 10. Dodrecht/Boston: Reidel, 1979.

————. *Blessed Are the Pure in Heart: Catechisis of the Sermon on the Mount.* Trans. L'Osservatore Romano. Boston: Daughters of Saint Paul, 1983..

————. *The Original Unity of Man and Woman: Catechesis on the Book of Genesis.* Trans. L'Osservatore Romano. Boston: Daughters of Saint Paul, 1981.

————. "The Person: Subject and Community." *Review of Metaphysics* 33 (1979): 273-308.

————. *Redemptor Hominis.* Boston: Daughters of St. Paul, 1979.

————. *Sacred in All its Forms.* Trans. L'Osservatore Romano. Boston: Daughters of Saint Paul, 1984.

————. *Sign of Contradiction.* Trans. St. Paul Publications. New York: Seabury, 1979.

————. (John Paul II) *Solicitudo Rei Socialis.* Boston: Daughters of St. Paul, 1987.

————. *The Theology of Marriage and Celibacy: Catechesis on Marriage and Celibacy in the Light of the Resurrection of the Body.* Trans. L'Osservatore Romano. Boston: Daughters of Saint Paul, 1986.

Wolff, Hans Walter. *Anthropology of the Old Testament.* Trans. Margaret Kohl. Philadelphia: Fortress, 1974.

————. *Hosea: A Commentary on the Book of the Prophet Hosea.* Trans. Gary Stansell. Philadelphia: Fortress, 1974.

Wolicka, Elzaieta. "Participation in Community: Wojytla's Social Anthropology." *Communio* 8 (1981): 108-18.

Woznicki, Andrew N., S.Ch. *The Dignity of Man as a Person: Essays on the Christian Humanism of His Holiness John Paul II.* San Francisco: Society of Christ, 1987.

Yannaras, Christos. *The Freedom of Morality.* Crestwood, N.Y.: St. Vladimir's Seminary Press, 1984.

Yarbrough, Anne. "Christianization in the Fourth Century: The Example of Roman Women." *Church History* 45 (1976): 149-65.

Young, Robin Darling. "Recent Interpretations of Early Christian Asceticism." *Thomist* 54 (1990): 123-40.

Zeller, Dieter. "God as Father in the Proclamation and Prayer of Jesus." In *Standing Before God,* ed. Asher Finkel and Lawrence Frizzel, 117-30. New York: KTAV, 1981.

Zizioulas, John. *Being As Communion.* Contemporary Greek Theologians 4. Crestwood, N.Y.: St. Vladimir's Seminary Press, 1985.

————. "Human Capacity and Human Incapacity: A Theological Exploration of Personhood." *Scottish Journal of Theology* 28 (1975): 401-48.

Index